AS LEVEL PSYCHOLOGY

for AQA Specification B

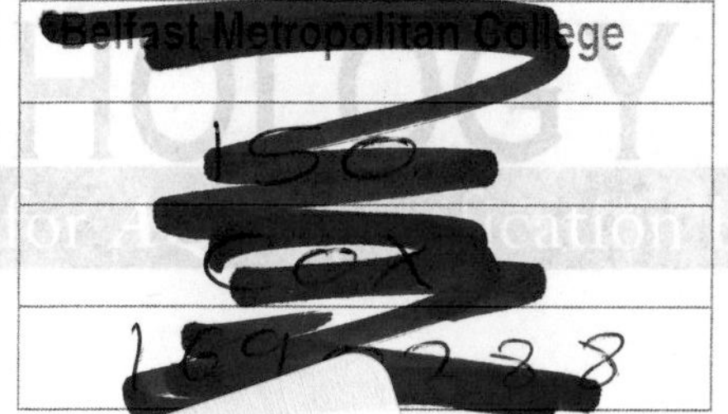

ERIKA COX

OXFORD

OXFORD
UNIVERSITY PRESS

Great Clarendon Street, Oxford OX2 6DP

Oxford University Press is a department of the University of Oxford. It furthers the University's objective of excellence in research, scholarship, and education by publishing worldwide in

Oxford New York

Auckland Bangkok Buenos Aires Cape Town Chennai Dar es Salaam Delhi Hong Kong Istanbul Karachi Kolkata Kuala Lumpur Madrid Melbourne Mexico City Mumbai Nairobi São Paulo Shanghai Taipei Tokyo Toronto

Oxford is a registered trade mark of Oxford University Press in the UK and in certain other countries

First published 2002

British Library Cataloguing in Publication Data

Data available

ISBN 0 19 913438 3

10 9 8 7 6 5 4 3

Typeset by TechSet, Gateshead, Tyne and Wear.
Printed in Italy by G. Canale and C.S.p.A.

The author and publishers would like to thank the following for permission to reproduce photographs:

Cover photo Science Photo Library; p32 Science Photo Library/Mark Thomas; p33 Science Photo Library/Dr Monty Buchsbaum, Peter Arnold Inc; p95 Wellcome Trust Photo Library; p97 Professor Albert Bandura, Stanford University; p139 Professor Phillip G. Zimbardo, Stanford University; p142 Moviestore Collection; p144 Popperfoto; p145 from the film 'Obedience' by Stanley Milgram; pp195/196 ©Exploratorium; p199 Ascending and Descending by M.C. Escher. ©Cordon Art, Baarn, Holland. All rights reserved; p206 ©Exploratorium; p216 Science Photo Library/Ed Young; p252 (top) BBC Natural History Unit/John Cancalosi, (centre) FLPA/Leonard Lee Rue 111, (bottom) BBC Natural History Unit/John Cancalosi; pp289/290 Tografox/Bob Battersby.

Illustrations by Bill Piggins, Robert Cox, Hardlines and TechSet. Special thanks to Bexhill Photographic for their assistance.

The author and publisher also acknowledge permission to reproduce statistical tables in Chapter 12.

Appendix 1: 'Critical values of *U* for (Mann-Whitney)' reprinted from R Runyon and A Haber: *Fundamentals of Behavioural Statistics* 3e (McGraw Hill, 1976), reprinted by permission of The McGraw Hill Companies. Appendix 2: 'Critical Values of *T* in the Wilcoxon Signed Ranks Test' adapted from R Meddis: *Statistical Handbook for Non-Statisticians* (McGraw Hill, London 1975). Appendix 3: 'Critical Value of Spearman's *r*' data reprinted from Table 1, Critical values of the Spearman Rank Correlation Coefficient r_{SI} for two-tailed and one-tailed probabilities, a(2) and a(1) respectively, p579 from J H Zhar: 'Significance testing of the Spearman Rank Correlation Coefficient' in *Journal of the American Statistical Association*, Vol. 67, No 399, September 1972, pp578-80, by permission of the American Statistical Association. Appendix 4: 'Level of significance for a one-tailed test' abridged from R A Fisher & F Yates: *Statistical Tables for Biological, Agricultural and Medical Research* 6e (Longman, 1974), copyright © R A Fisher and F Yates 1963, reprinted by permission of Pearson Education Ltd. Appendix 5: 'Critical Values in the Bionomial Sign Test' reprinted from F Clegg: *Simple Statistics* (Cambridge University Press, 1982), by permission of the publisher.

We have tried to trace and contact copyright holders before publication but this has not been possible in all cases. If notified, the publisher will be pleased to rectify any errors at the earliest opportunity.

Contents

Preface

This textbook is precisely targeted at AQA AS Level Psychology, Specification B. It will also be of interest to those who are new to psychology, and who want to get a flavour of the kinds of topics in which psychologists are interested.

It aims to be a user-friendly text which explains the material clearly and in simple language, while at the same time giving good coverage to the sometimes complex ideas psychologists have put forward. There are frequent summaries (marked by S symbols) throughout each chapter. These can be used to provide an overview of each topic and should also be useful when it comes to revision. References for the theories and research discussed, some of which will be needed for the practical investigation which makes up Module 3 of the AQA B specification, can be found on the OUP website (see the note on the next page).

The text contains a range of activities (questions, short tests, mini-practicals, and so on) to encourage you to engage with the material. Many of these activities are designed to help you remember the information being put across and check your understanding of it. The mini-practicals will help you get a feel for how psychologists go about their research, and experience for yourself some of their findings. They should also help you to prepare for carrying out your own practical investigation for Module 3.

I would like to thank Julie Harris for her useful contributions to chapters 1, 9 and 11. I would also like to thank Sue Cave for contributing sections on the localisation of cortical function and the genetic basis of intelligence, both in chapter 1. Nick Oliver has made many helpful suggestions, which I am sure have made the book much better than it would otherwise have been. I would also like to thank my editor Don Manley for his unflagging support and encouragement. Last but not least, my thanks to Robert for contributing some of the illustrations and cartoons, helping me to keep going and providing endless cups of tea.

Psychology is a fascinating subject. I hope you enjoy using this book as an introduction to what it can offer.

Erika Cox
Fakenham, April 2002

Note on References

For full details of bibliographical references, the reader is referred to the Oxford University Press website:

www.oup.com/uk/aqabaspsychology

A free printout is also available on request. Please write to:

AQA (B) AS Psychology References
Promotions Department
Education Division
Oxford University Press
Great Clarendon Street
OXFORD
OX2 6DP

Approaches in psychology

1.1 WHAT IS PSYCHOLOGY?

When I tell people I am a psychologist, I often get one of two responses. One is: 'I'll have to be careful what I say to you'. The other is: 'I hope you're not going to psychoanalyse me'.

The first response seems to imply that psychologists have developed skills which allow them to read people's minds and easily unearth their deepest secrets in a casual conversation. It is true that when you start to study psychology, you are likely to notice and think about behaviour, and perhaps what people say, and relate it to what you have learned, in the same way that someone starting to learn about geology might notice different rock formations. But psychology is not a basis for reading people's minds.

The second response assumes that psychology and psychoanalysis are the same thing. This is understandable in a way, since Sigmund Freud, the founder of psychoanalysis, is probably the best-known name in psychology. Many of his ideas (though perhaps in a distorted form, such as 'Freud is all about sex') are widely known, and some terms associated with psychoanalytic theory have filtered down into general use. You may perhaps have heard of the **Oedipus complex**, the **ego** or **repression**. But there is a vast amount of psychology beyond Freud.

The *Concise Oxford Dictionary* defines psychology as 'the scientific study of the human mind and its functions, especially those affecting behaviour in a given context'. This definition is not without its problems. There are very many different kinds of psychologist, and each of these concepts – 'scientific', 'mind' and 'behaviour' – can be considered to be either more or less important, depending on what kind of psychologist you are. As a working definition, though, this gives us some general idea of what psychology is about. But what exactly does this study entail?

As you have chosen to study psychology, you probably have an idea of some of the kinds of questions in which psychologists are interested.

Activity 1: topics in psychology

Which of these topics do you think psychologists might be interested in?

- why people help others (or don't)
- treatments for depression
- how children learn language
- the relationship between stress and illness
- the behaviour of animals
- astrological signs and personality
- why some people are more outgoing than others
- the causes of schizophrenia
- extra-sensory perception
- how people solve logical problems
- improving performance in sport

When you have finished, see the notes on page 52.

This activity should have given you some idea of the broad range of topics in psychology. Obviously not all psychologists are interested in all of them; just as in other disciplines, psychologists specialise.

There are six main topic areas with which most psychologists are concerned. **Cognitive** psychologists are interested in the ways in which we process information – for example, when we use our memory. **Developmental** psychologists are mainly interested in the ways in which children develop – for example, how their thought processes and personality develop. More recently, the developmental approach has also looked at changes across the rest of the lifespan. **Physiological** psychologists are interested in the way in which the body functions, and how these physiological processes can be linked to psychological experience and behaviour. Stress and the effects of brain damage are examples of the kinds of topic in which they are interested.

Social psychologists focus on the idea that people are essentially social creatures, and that therefore much of a person's behaviour is influenced by others. They are interested in topics such as relationships, helping behaviour and obedience. **Comparative** psychologists study animal behaviour, both as a subject that is interesting in its own right – for example, predator–prey behaviour – and because an understanding of animals may help to establish general principles which also apply to humans.

All these areas are interested in establishing general laws – the functioning of people in general – but psychologists are also interested in **individual differences** – for example, personality, intelligence and mental disorders.

All these areas may also have practical **applications**. Developmental psychology, for example, may provide insights which can help children with educational problems. Similarly, within cognitive psychology, studies of attention may provide a basis for improving the concentration of those engaged in competitive sport.

Psychologists vary in the methods they use in their investigations, although they all set about the task of understanding behaviour and experience in an organised and systematic way. This enables them to collect information or **data** which can provide evidence to support or challenge psychological ideas. The **experimental method,** the traditional method of scientific enquiry, has been the main method used by psychologists. **Watson** (1878–1958) argued that psychology was like any other science, and that its methods should be those of a science.

Activity 2: the experimental method

What procedures do scientists go through to collect information, and form and test theories?

You will need to think about the methods of investigation you are familiar with from your study of chemistry, physics or biology.

When you have finished, see the notes on page 52.

However, not all psychological research is experimental. Many psychologists feel that this approach is not always appropriate, given the subject matter of psychology. They argue that the experimental approach, with its focus on general principles of psychological functioning, cannot capture the richness of individual experience. Nor is it suitable for the study of rare psychological characteristics – for example, Luria's (1968) study of S, a man with a phenomenally good memory. Alternative techniques such as observation, case studies, correlational techniques, questionnaires and surveys are all widely used. We will look at these, together with the experimental method, in rather more detail in the next chapter.

- Psychology covers a wide range of topic areas. It can be generally defined as **the science of mind and behaviour**.
- The boundaries of the subject are not clear-cut. Some topics are seen as marginal by some psychologists.
- The **six main areas** of psychology in which psychologists are interested are **cognitive**, **developmental**, **physiological**, **social**, **comparative** and **individual differences**. Psychology can have practical **applications**.
- Different psychologists use different methods. Many take a broadly **experimental** approach, although alternative methods may sometimes be more appropriate.

Psychology and common sense

It may seem questionable whether psychology has much to tell us which is not just a matter of common sense. After all, we all observe what is going on around us and how people behave, and we draw conclusions about what people are like from what we observe. We seem to understand people quite well without the help of psychologists. So what does psychology have to offer?

One way of looking at this is to think of psychology as *organised* common sense. Psychology can give us a more detailed understanding of people, supported by evidence. This evidence has been reached in a systematic way, compared with the rather sporadic observations we may make of a very limited number of cases.

Common sense also has its problems. We may assume, for example, that what is true for us is also true for everybody else. Given the nature of Western society, for example, we could assume that people are 'naturally' competitive. Research in other cultures, which are based more on co-operation, suggests that this may not be the case. These assumptions, then, may have come about because we are particular individuals, who live in a particular community, in a particular culture, at a particular time. In a different setting, common sense could let us down. Psychology can take a wider view.

Some of the subject matter of psychology may not be within the experience of all of us. The physiological basis of behaviour is an obvious example, if we are not trained physiologists. For example, common sense can tell us little about the relationship between brain damage and behaviour.

Finally, common sense is sometimes wrong. For example, common sense tells many of us that if you punish someone for doing something, they will not do it again. (We know this in spite of prisons being full of people who have reoffended!) Psychological research, however, has shown that punishment is not the best way of stopping behaviour, and can also suggest more effective ways of changing behaviour.

Common sense can of course be useful. It may give us useful insights, which start us off on a more precise psychological investigation. At the same time, psychology can extend and organise our understanding.

- Psychology can be thought of as **organised common sense**. It can provide evidence for common sense theories, and can take a wider perspective than the individual.
- Sometimes the findings of psychologists may contradict common sense.

1.2 A BRIEF HISTORY OF PSYCHOLOGY

Psychology has its roots in philosophy, going back at least as far as the ancient Greeks. Plato argued, for instance, that we need to make a distinction between mind and body (this belief is known as **dualism**). He also believed that we have innate ideas and knowledge, so that learning is not so much a matter of experience, but rather a process by which we reveal to ourselves knowledge we already have. The motivation to do this is also innate. This general approach is known as **rationalism** or **nativism**.

In your study of psychology, you will come across many examples of modern psychological theories which have their roots in rationalist ideas. Later in this chapter, we will be looking in some detail at one of them, Freud's psychodynamic theory.

Aristotle was a pupil of Plato, but disagreed fundamentally with Plato's belief in innate ideas. He argued that all learning must come from experience, and that we learn by associating aspects of the world which commonly occur together. This approach is known as **associationism**. These general ideas were taken up by a group of seventeenth-century philosophers, in particular Locke, Hobbes and Hume. They argued that **experience** is the basis of all knowledge of the world. They are referred to as **empiricists**, from Greek words meaning 'from experience'. In other words, we find out about the world not because of innate knowledge, but through our experience of it. Again, you will come across many examples of modern psychological theories which have their roots in associationism, notably the learning theories of Pavlov and Skinner, which we will be discussing later.

A further tradition in psychology, bringing together rationalism and associationism, has its roots in the rather more recent ideas of the eighteenth-century philosopher, Immanuel Kant. In his *Critique of Pure Reason* (1991), written in 1781, he agreed with the associationist position that experience is important to learning. At the same time, he argued, something must already be present in the mind if we are to make any sense of reality. In brief, we have an innate rule-forming capacity which enables us to *construct* models of reality on the basis of this experience. For this reason, this point of view is known as **constructivism**. A major theorist whose work has its roots in this philosophical position was Jean Piaget (1896–1980), who was interested in the development of thinking in children.

Psychology, then, did not emerge from a vacuum; many of the beliefs that psychologists have and the ideas which they explore go back a long way. At the same time, producing philosophical arguments is far removed from modern psychology. In order to provide a framework for the kind of psychology you will find in this course, we now need to turn a period starting at the end of the nineteenth century and focus on some of the main theorists who made their mark.

The beginnings of modern psychology

Wilhelm Wundt (1832–1920)

Wundt opened the Institute for Experimental Psychology at the University of Leipzig in Germany in 1875. This was the first laboratory dedicated to psychology, and its opening is usually thought of as the beginning of modern psychology. While philosophy involves speculation about the mind, Wundt and his co-workers were attempting to analyse the workings of the mind in a rather more structured way, with the emphasis being on measurement and control.

Wundt's background was in physiology, and this was reflected in the topics with which the Institute was concerned, such as the study of reaction times and sensory processes. For example, participants would be exposed to a standard stimulus (e.g. a light or the sound of a metronome) and asked to report their sensations.

Asking people to report on their mental processes is known as **introspection**. This method has been criticised; in particular, for providing only subjective data. However, Wundt's participants underwent extensive training to give precise and consistent responses, and to the extent that Wundt's work was controlled and organised in this way, his approach could be said to represent a generally scientific approach.

Wundt's aim was to record thoughts and sensations, and to analyse them into their constituent elements, in much the same way as a chemist analyses chemical compounds, in order to get at the underlying structure. For this reason, the school of psychology founded by Wundt is known as **structuralism**.

On the basis of his work, and the influence it had on psychologists who were to follow him, Wundt can be regarded as the founder of experimental psychology, so securing his place in the history of psychology. At the same time, Wundt himself believed that the experimental approach was limited in scope, and that other methods would be necessary if all aspects of human psychology were to be investigated.

Charles Darwin (1809–1882)

The **theory of evolution** developed by Charles Darwin in his book *On the Origin of Species* (1859) has also been influential in psychology. Darwin's starting point was that as the result of genetic variation the characteristics of individuals belonging to a particular species will vary. Some characteristics will be more **adaptive** than others, i.e. more likely to contribute to survival in a particular environment. The ability to survive long enough to pass on genes to the next generation, and to raise viable offspring, is called **fitness.** A key concept here is the idea of **natural selection**: characteristics which produce patterns of behaviour which are adaptive in a particular environment will be selected and passed on through the genes to the next generation, while characteristics which are not adaptive are less likely to be passed on.

Darwin developed his ideas during a five-year voyage as a naturalist on HMS Beagle. In the Galapagos islands, he observed that there were 14 different kinds of finch. They differed in the shapes of their beaks and their feeding habits. Darwin believed that all these finches had ancestors in common, and that these variations in beak shape had come about in response to features of the environment. In this case, beak shape had changed over very many generations as an adaptation to the different kinds of food supply, e.g. seeds and insects, offered by the different islands.

Activity 3: explaining giraffes' long necks

How could Darwin's evolutionary theory explain the development of a long neck in giraffes?

When you have finished see the notes on page 52.

Another example is the peppered moth, before and after the Industrial Revolution. These moths were originally light in colour, but around 1850 a darker form appeared. As a result of industrial activity, surfaces in the moth's environment (e.g. tree trunks) had become blackened by soot, which meant that they provided better camouflage against predators for the darker moths than the lighter ones. By 1900, about 50 generations later, the numbers of the darker moths in industrial areas were far greater than the lighter ones, which had almost disappeared. As industrial areas were cleaned up, the darker moths became rarer and the lighter-coloured ones more common again.

The example of the peppered moth describes the processes of evolution in terms of physical changes. However, evolutionary psychologists have also drawn on the principles Darwin put forward to explain a vast range of human behaviours. Even behaviour which may on the surface seem to be maladaptive may nonetheless have some adaptive function, or may have been adaptive in our evolutionary past. For example, arachnophobia (an extreme fear of spiders) could be interpreted as adaptive in that it would have led to avoidance of spiders. This would have reduced the risk of an individual with this characteristic being killed by a poisonous spider, and thus failing to reach maturity and pass their genes on to the next generation.

Darwin's theory is of central importance in that it proposes that animal morphology and behaviour are the result of a long process of selection, resulting in a well-adapted animal. It therefore suggests that there should be *functional* explanations of behaviour, i.e. explanations in terms of the function that the behaviour has for the survival of the genes which code for it. As it highlights the continuity of species, it justifies looking at the characteristics and behaviour of animal species in order to discover something about the genetics and the evolution of human behaviour.

However, evolutionary explanations of human behaviour have been criticised on the grounds that these ideas are not directly testable. This does not of course mean that the explanations they offer are incorrect, but rather that we have no way of knowing whether or to what extent they provide an accurate account of human behaviour, so they remain little more than speculation. In their lack of emphasis on the role experience and culture play in shaping our behaviour, these ideas have also been criticised for being reductionist, i.e. limited in the kinds of factors which are seen to be important in shaping our behaviour.

Sigmund Freud (1856–1939)

Freud is another major name in the history of psychology. He started to develop his **psychodynamic theory** around 1900. Freud was interested in the relationship between childhood development and aspects of adult functioning. For him, the **unconscious mind** is central, and he believed that much of our behaviour is influenced by material deep in our unconscious. Freud developed the therapy of **psychoanalysis** along with his theory, and the information on which his theory was based was provided by patients who had come to him for therapy.

Freud's is what is known as a **grand theory**, in that it relates to a wide range of aspects of human experience and behaviour. He has something to say about personality, aggression, moral behaviour, mental disorders, memory – the list is virtually endless. Because it is so extensive and has been so influential, we will be looking at this theory in more in the section on the Psychodynamic perspective later in the chapter.

B.F. Skinner (1904–1990)

In complete contrast to Freud, Skinner adopted a much more traditionally scientific approach. Skinner worked within the framework of behaviourism, an approach which had its roots in the ideas of Watson. Watson argued that if psychology were to be carried on in a scientific way, and to gain wide acceptance as a science, it needed to be objective. It must use the same methods and collect objective data in the same way as other sciences. The contents of a person's consciousness were not objectively measurable and were therefore not valid data, but studying behaviour would provide observable, measurable events. He therefore saw behaviour as the only acceptable data, which led to this approach being known as **behaviourism**.

Within this general framework, Skinner proposed that new behaviours are learned by association, and in particular the association between a behaviour and its consequences. He was particularly interested in the ways in which these principles could bring about behaviour change. Skinner's theory is of huge importance in the context of the behaviourist school in psychology, so we shall be returning at it in more detail in the section on the Behaviourist perspective.

Carl Rogers (1902–1987)

Rogers represents yet another very different approach in psychology. He was a prime mover behind **humanistic psychology**. Humanistic psychology is sometimes known as the **third force**, since it arose as a result of Rogers' dissatisfaction with the ideas of Freud and Skinner, the two major names in psychology at the time. For Rogers, Freud's ideas about human nature were unduly pessimistic, with people being seen as at the mercy of unconscious forces over which they have no control, and with their developmental pathway laid down through their experiences of development through childhood. Skinner's belief that virtually all our behaviour is determined by environmental events also seemed both pessimistic and mechanistic to Rogers.

In contrast to these two theories, he suggested that people have the capacity to think about their lives, decide how they would like to develop, and are capable of making positive changes. Development arises from choices made by the individual. The focus of the psychologist should therefore be on the individual, and his or her personal experience. This school of thought has also been very influential, so will be covered in a little more detail in the section on the Humanistic perspective.

- Psychology has its roots in philosophy, starting with the ideas of **Plato** and **Aristotle**. Different philosophical positions about the nature of man – **rationalism**, **associationism** and **constructivism** – are reflected in the different beliefs of modern psychologists about the nature of man.
- The **structural** approach of **Wundt** marks the beginning of modern psychology.
- **Darwin's theory of evolution** has provided a framework within which some psychologists explore ways of explaining human behaviour.
- **Freud's theory** has explanatory power in many areas of psychology, and includes the therapy of **psychoanalysis**.

- **Skinner** has taken a scientific approach to the study of human behaviour which has many possible applications.
- **Rogers** exemplifies the **humanistic position**, with its emphasis on the individual, and their capacity for personal development.

1.3 Perspectives in psychology

Different approaches in modern psychology can be summarised under five major headings: psychodynamic; behaviourist; humanistic; cognitive; and biological. We will look here at the basic assumptions, characteristics and methods of the first four of these. The final section of this chapter will look in rather more detail at the biological approach.

The psychodynamic perspective

The psychodynamic approach is based on the work of **Sigmund Freud**. There are a number of fundamental ideas which formed the basis of his theory: the principle of psychological determinism, the role of the unconscious, and the importance of childhood in determining adult behaviour.

Psychological determinism is based on the idea that all behaviour is motivated, and the reasons we behave as we do are often unconscious. Unconscious motivation can be illustrated by Freudian slips or **parapraxes**, where a person says or does something which they had not consciously intended to say or do. Here is a parapraxis reported by Freud:

Activity 4: a parapraxis

Read through this description of the behaviour of one of Freud's patients:

A young man who was rather cautious about commitment finally proposed to his girlfriend and was accepted. When he had taken her home, he got on a tram to go home himself, and asked the conductress for two tickets.

Six months after his wedding, he was not entirely happy with married life. He missed his friends and did not get on with his parents-in-law. One evening he fetched his wife from her parents' house, got on a tram with her and asked for one ticket.

What unconscious reasons might the young man have had for the mistakes he made in asking for tram tickets?

When you have finished, see the notes on page 52.

The concept of the **unconscious** is one of the unique contributions Freud made to psychology. This was not in itself a new idea, but before Freud, the unconscious was seen as a dumping ground for experiences which were no longer of any importance, and so the unconscious itself had no particular status. Freud conceived of a **dynamic unconscious**, an active force, motivating much of our behaviour. He believed that a lot of material in the unconscious, far from being unimportant, is there because it is too painful or disturbing for us to acknowledge consciously, and that this kind of material can only be accessed using the special techniques of the therapy he developed called **psychoanalysis**. The unconscious can be contrasted with the preconscious, ideas of which we are not at the moment conscious but which we can recall if we want to – for example, a friend's telephone number. There is also the conscious, those ideas we are currently aware of.

The idea of **unconscious conflict** is central to Freud's theory – for example, conflict between our desires and the demands of our conscience. It can show itself as parapraxes, as disturbing emotional states, and can also be revealed in dreams, where conflict expresses itself through the use of symbols.

Freud believed that adult behaviour is shaped by our experiences in **childhood**. He saw instinctual needs such as hunger, thirst and sex as being very important sources of motivation; at the same time, however, he thought that the social environment, which constrains the gratification of these instincts, was crucial to a child's development. He placed particular emphasis on the conflict between instinctual needs and the demands of society as the basis of personality development and the development of mental disorders.

The experiences of the first five years of life and the conflicts which arise during this time are seen as particularly important to the development of an individual's personality, and we will be coming back to his ideas about children's development later in this section.

The structure of the mind

Freud proposed a theoretical (i.e. non-anatomical) account of the structure of the mind. He believed it consisted of three parts: the **id**, the **ego** and the **superego**.

Figure 1: the structure of the mind

id The id is present at birth. It is the seat of our instincts, and is unconscious. It operates on the **pleasure principle**, in that it tries to get immediate gratification and to avoid pain. It is the source of psychic energy, the **libido**.

ego This develops in childhood out of the id, as children learn that immediate gratification is not always possible and that pain cannot always be avoided. The ego works on the **reality principle**. It decides what actions are appropriate, and which id impulses will be satisfied, and how. The ego tries to balance the demands of the id, the realities of life, and the demands of the **superego**. Many ego processes are conscious, but some are preconscious and others, especially the **ego defences** we shall come to later, are unconscious.

superego This consists of the values and morals of the child, and develops around the age of five. It is the child's **conscience** and **ego-ideal**, a model of what the child would like to be.

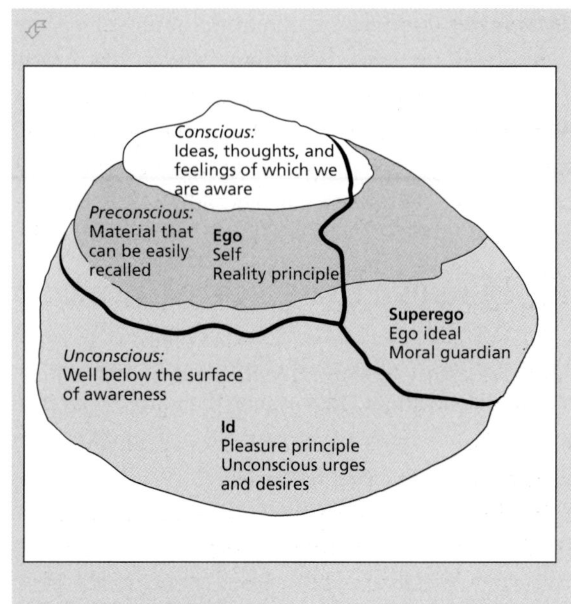

The forces of the superego and the id are often in opposition, with the superego curbing the primitive impulses of the id when they don't fit in with socially acceptable behaviour. For example, your superego would find it socially unacceptable if you decided to have sex on a crowded bus, no matter how frustrated your id was. So your ego would then decide that the action was inappropriate and must wait until later, or be expressed in some other more socially acceptable way. The dynamics of personality, according to Freud, are rooted in this conflict, originating in the id and fuelled by the libido. The way conflict is resolved is a crucial part of the way people develop.

- One major principle of Freud's theory is **psychological determinism**; all behaviour is seen to be motivated. This idea can explain **parapraxes**. Another central idea is the **dynamic unconscious**. **Childhood experience** is seen as being crucial to later development.
- The mind consists of the **conscious**, the **preconscious** and the **unconscious**.
- Freud suggested that personality is made up of the theoretical constructs of the **id**, the **ego** and the **superego**. **Unconscious conflict** between them is important to personality development.

Defence mechanisms

States of conflict may lead to the unpleasant sensation of anxiety developing, and people deal with this in different ways. One way is by the use of ego **defence mechanisms**, coping mechanisms which allow id impulses to be expressed in ways acceptable to the ego, and so reduce anxiety. They are quite effective, particularly in the short term.

Displacement is one defence mechanism: where feelings cannot be expressed towards their real targets, substitute objects on which feelings can be taken out are chosen. For example, if a child is angry with its mother, these unacceptable feelings may be expressed by being unkind to a younger sibling.

Sublimation is a type of displacement where a socially acceptable activity is found to express an unacceptable impulse. For example, you might play squash to re-channel either your aggressive impulses, or sexual energy which lacks a sexual outlet. This is the only defence mechanism which can be effective long-term.

There are several other defence mechanisms. In **denial**, a fact which is too painful to cope with – such as the knowledge that you have a life-threatening illness – is not consciously acknowledged. **Repression** is motivated forgetting when a person may unconsciously 'forget' something that is too distressing to remember, such as memories of being abused as a child, or the death of a relative. Repression is discussed in chapter 9 in 'Reasons for forgetting'. **Rationalisation** involves finding superficially acceptable reasons for a behaviour. You might, for example, blame your awful exam results on the fact that you had a cold on the day you sat the exam, to protect yourself from feelings of inadequacy. In **reaction formation**, a person consciously feels or thinks the opposite of their unconscious feelings or thoughts. For example, a person who is deeply prejudiced against a minority group could protect themselves from these unacceptable feelings by becoming actively involved in the Campaign for Racial Equality. **Regression** involves a symbolic return to an earlier stage of development, for example, sucking your thumb to comfort yourself.

Psychosexual development

As we saw earlier, the importance of childhood is central to Freud's theory, and he describes how children progress through a sequence of **psychosexual stages**. Everyone goes through these stages in the same order, and their experience of them is crucial not only to the child, but also to the adult. At each stage, interest is focused on the pleasurable sensations associated with different **erotogenic** (pleasure-giving) zones.

The **oral stage** lasts from birth to around one year. During this time, the source of pleasurable sensations is the mouth. You may have noticed that babies and very young children automatically put anything new into their mouths, and seem to derive pleasure from doing so. This stage is divided into two sub-stages. In the first few months, in the **incorporative** sub-stage, the baby is relatively passive; activity is largely focused on sucking and swallowing. This is followed by the **aggressive** sub-stage, when biting and chewing become important.

The **anal stage** lasts from around one to around three. Once weaned, the libido focuses on the anus and the muscles of the urinary system. Again, there are two sub-stages. In the **expulsion** sub-stage, the child gets great pleasure from defecating, while in the **retention** sub-stage, there is pleasure from holding in faeces. During this stage, the child comes up against external restrictions in terms of where and when defecation is acceptable, and will find that this aspect of behaviour has social implications in terms of pleasing parents, or not.

The **phallic stage** lasts from around three to around five. In this stage, pleasure centres on the genitals, and the stage is experienced differently by boys and by girls.

The young boy goes through a crisis which Freud called the **Oedipus complex**, during which he develops unconscious sexual feelings towards his mother. He is envious of his father, and jealous of the love and attention he gets from his mother. The boy's feelings for his mother and rivalry with his father lead to fantasies of getting rid of his father, and taking his place with the mother.

The hostile feelings he has for his father lead to anxiety that his father will retaliate by castrating his son, as a suitable punishment for the crime of desiring his mother. Freud believed that at this age, a boy realises that girls do not have a penis, and thinks that they have been castrated already.

To cope with this castration anxiety, the boy uses the ego defence mechanism of identification. He identifies with his father and introjects (or takes in) his father's attitudes and moral values. **Identification** and **introjection** are the source of the boy's superego.

Development is slightly different for girls as they experience the **Electra complex**. The young girl becomes aware that she does not have a penis and develops **penis envy**. She blames her mother for this lack, and so transfers her love from her mother to her father. She realises that she can not possess her father, and copes with this knowledge by identifying with the mother, introjecting the mother's attitudes and values. Freud called this process **anaclitic identification**.

In the **latency period**, from five to puberty, children turn aside from their sexuality, concentrating instead on developing socially and intellectually. This continues until the onset of adolescence. At adolescence, the child moves into the **genital stage**. In this stage, recognisably adult sexual feelings develop, and mature love becomes possible.

Freud suggested that the developmental stages which a child goes through help to form the personality of that child as an adult. The adult personality is determined not only by the interaction of id, ego and superego, together with the use of particular defence mechanisms, but also by **fixation**, an unconscious preoccupation with a particular psychosexual stage. This causes problems with adult personality if the child experiences frustration or overgratification while passing through a stage. If this happens, these early fixations are expressed symbolically in adult behaviour.

Activity 5: personality and psychosexual stages

Below are descriptions of personality characteristics which may develop in an adult if the child becomes fixated at a particular psychosexual stage.

Use the characteristics to match each person with the stage or substage at which they became fixated.

1 Jason has a preoccupation with orderliness and punctuality. He never likes his routine to be disrupted, and you could imagine him developing obsessive–compulsive behaviour.

2 Jamila loves food and tends to be greedy. She is a smoker. She is interested in foreign languages, and is good at them, and enjoys gossiping with her friends. She has been described as a 'compulsive talker'.

3 Sally can be sarcastic and scornful at times. She bites her nails

4 Jolyon is mean and miserly. He collects matchboxes and beer mats, and likes to save the string and wrapping paper from parcels.

5 Brian avoids close relationships with women, since he finds it impossible to become emotionally involved in sexual activity. He is happier reading.

6 Mark regularly loses money gambling.

7 Khalid is excessively generous. He gives a percentage of his salary to charity each month, and buys his family and friends presents that he can ill afford.

8 Faye shows excessive displays of femininity, and would never be seen in public without full make-up and immaculately dressed. She is extremely self-centred, and has great ambitions for herself; she is prepared to tread on anybody to get to the top.

When you have finished, see the notes on page 52.

- Unconscious conflict causes **anxiety**, which can be dealt with using ego **defence mechanisms**. Only the mechanism of **sublimation** is effective in the long term. People differ in the kinds of mechanisms they use, and the extent to which they use them.
- Children develop through **psychosexual stages: oral, anal, phallic, latency** and **genital**. **Fixation** in one of these stages has implications for adult personality characteristics.

Overview of the psychodynamic model

The basic model here is of behaviour being shaped by **unconscious** forces. The idea of **conflict** is also central, with problems being created as the result of conflict between different parts of the personality. These in turn are determined by the **psychosexual development** which takes place in childhood, considered to be an extremely important time within this perspective, since our experiences at this time can affect us throughout our lives. Freud's is a **nativist** theory, since psychosexual development is determined by the sex into which we are born. On the basis of our sex, we are shaped by early childhood experiences.

The aims of this approach are twofold. Firstly, Freud seeks to explain development and behaviour within this general framework. However, this is not only a theory, but also a therapy: **psychoanalysis**. The aims here are to uncover unconscious conflict and help the patient understand its causes. They can then come to terms with their problems.

In developing his theory, Freud used a clinical method known as the **case study**. Listening to patients and exploring their problems allowed him to understand the course of development which he claimed we all go through. Psychoanalysis is often referred to as the 'talking cure'. The methods here involve asking patients to talk about their concerns (**free association**) and to describe their dreams. This material allows the analyst to uncover unconscious conflict and start the process of curing the patient.

Freud's theory has been widely criticised, not least for its emphasis on childhood sexuality. His methods too mean that his data needed to be interpreted, which introduces the problem of researcher bias. While the case study method yields very rich, detailed data, it does not offer the kind of objectivity of the strictly scientific approach associated with traditional sciences like physics and chemistry. At the same time, the breadth of Freud's theory offers much that is of interest, some of which – like the idea of the unconscious and the importance of childhood – has intuitive appeal. Freud has also been extremely influential, with many theorists building on his basic ideas in interesting ways.

The behaviourist perspective

In proposing what a science of psychology should be, Watson suggested that behaviour should be the only acceptable, objective data in psychology. He was concerned with the connection between an event in the environment, a stimulus (e.g. touching something hot, or a voice saying your name) and the behaviour which follows, a response (e.g. taking your hand away quickly, or turning your head towards the sound of the voice). For this reason, the behaviourist approach to psychology is sometimes called **stimulus–response** (or S–R) psychology. Watson saw learning as the process of associating stimulus and response, and believed this would prove a fertile area for psychological research. These ideas were developed by others interested in the nature of learning, and their theories are grouped together as **learning theory**.

Classical conditioning

Watson's ideas tied in with research being carried out by Pavlov (1849–1936), a Russian physiologist interested in the digestive processes of dogs, in particular the salivation reflex. A **reflex** is a fixed and automatic response to a particular stimulus; the response cannot be controlled. Pavlov was interested in accurate measurement of the relationship between the **stimulus** of food in the mouth and the **response** of salivation. In the course of his research (which won him a Nobel prize), Pavlov developed a technique for collecting the saliva secreted by the dog as part of the digestive process, and this made accurate measurement of the strength of the salivary reflex possible.

Pavlov noticed that the dog would salivate not only when it could taste the food, but also when it could only see it. The experiments he carried out demonstrate a phenomenon known as **classical conditioning**, one of the two kinds of learning processes in the behaviourist tradition. The other is **operant conditioning**, which we shall come to later.

Box A: Pavlov (1927)

Procedure: A dog was held in a harness so that little movement was possible. A bell, which the dog had not heard before, was rung to check that the dog didn't have an automatic salivary response to this sound.

Pavlov called the bell a **neutral stimulus (NS),** because there was no automatic response to it. The experimenter then rang the bell and immediately afterwards presented food to the dog. The pairing of bell and food was repeated several times. Finally, the bell was rung on its own.

Results: The paired presentation of bell and food automatically produced the response of salivation on each presentation. Finally the bell alone also produced salivation.
Conclusion: The bell which had previously not produced salivation eventually did so because of its repeated pairings with food. This response came about as the result of an **association** being formed between bell and salivation.

We need now to look at a few technical terms. Pavlov referred to the food in this experiment as the **unconditional stimulus** (**UCS** or **US**) because it automatically or unconditionally causes salivation. Salivation in response to the food is referred to as the **unconditional response** (**UCR** or **UR**), for the same reason. The bell is originally referred to as a **neutral stimulus** (see box A). After its pairing with food, it becomes a **conditional stimulus** (**CS**), because it can only cause salivation *on condition* that it has been paired with food. The salivation caused by the bell on its own is the **conditional response** (**CR**), because it only occurs on condition that the bell–food pairings have taken place.

Activity 6: classical conditioning

Use the terms NS, UCS, UCR, CS and CR to complete this diagram:

bell (.....) ⟶ no salivation (before conditioning)
food (.....) ⟶ salivation (.....)
{bell (.....) / food (....)} ⟶ salivation (.....) (during conditioning)
bell (.....) ⟶ salivation (.....) (evidence of conditioning)

When you have finished, see the notes on page 52.

With the dog salivating to the sound of the bell, we have an objectively measurable change in behaviour, so the dog can be said to have *learned* to salivate to the sound of a bell.

It is possible to condition any reflex. Humans as well as animals have reflex responses – for example, the knee-jerk response. We also show the reflex response of blinking when air is blown into our eyes.

Activity 7: trying out classical conditioning

a See if you can use Pavlov's method to condition a response in someone else (if you can find a willing participant). You will find that blowing gently but briskly into someone's eye will make them blink. You will probably need to practise this a few times, to make sure you are the right distance away for air to reach the eye, and are not blowing so hard as to make this an unpleasant experience for your participant. Blowing down a straw or an empty biro tube helps to aim the puff of air. Tap with a pencil on the table for your NS/CS, the equivalent of Pavlov's bell.

b Prepare a diagram like the one in Activity 6. Fill in the terms 'puff', 'blink' and 'tap', as well as NS, UCS, UCR, CS and CR.

When you have finished, see the notes on page 52.

Pavlov found that after a few presentations of the bell on its own, the response became weaker, as measured by the amount of saliva the dog produced. Finally, after 20 or so trials, no saliva at all was produced by the sound of the bell. Pavlov referred to this procedure as **extinction**, and the CR is said to have been extinguished when it is no longer produced by the CS.

Watson was enthusiastic about Pavlov's work, since it was an example of the scientific study of behaviour he wanted to see in psychology. He used Pavlov's procedure for experiments into human learning. A classic study is shown in box B:

Box B: Watson and Rayner (1920)

Procedure: An eleven-month-old child known as Little Albert was the participant in this study. Two months earlier, his reactions to various stimuli had been tested: a white rat, a rabbit, various other animals, cotton wool and burning newspapers. He showed no fear of any of these, and seems to have been a rather unemotional child. However, hardly surprisingly, he did show a fear reaction to a loud noise behind him, a hammer hitting a steel bar. The experimenters made this noise several times, at the same time presenting him with a white rat.

Results: Albert developed a fear of the white rat. The fear response to the rat became less extreme over time, but was still evident a month later.

Conclusion: Classical conditioning is one way of explaining fear responses. This is an example of a **conditioned emotional response** (CER). It is possible that people develop phobias through forming this kind of association.

The case of Little Albert shows that Pavlov's findings do have some relevance to human learning. Psychologists have made use of this in various ways, most notably in **behaviour therapy**. If behaviour is learned, it can also be unlearned, and more appropriate behaviours learned instead. These ideas have been used to help people who suffer from disorders such as phobias.

- Watson wanted a scientific psychology, using objective methods. He saw behaviour as the only legitimate data for psychology.
- He was interested in the relationship between a **stimulus** to which an animal is exposed and its **response**. His ideas have been incorporated into **learning theory**.
- Pavlov's work on the salivary reflex in dogs led him to demonstrate what has come to be known as **classical conditioning**. His ideas can also be used to condition humans. The principles of classical conditioning are used in **therapy**.

Operant conditioning

The most famous name in operant conditioning is Skinner. The term 'operant' means an action: the animal **operates** on its environment. While sharing some general principles of classical conditioning – the emphasis on observable behaviour and explaining behaviour in terms of learning theory – operant conditioning is a move away from looking at associations between stimulus and response. In operant conditioning, what is important is the association between **behaviour** and the **consequences** of that behaviour. The basic principle behind Skinner's theory is that behaviour is shaped and maintained by its consequences.

While Pavlov's work relates to reflex behaviour, Skinner's theory applies to voluntary behaviour. He believed that behaviours which have positive consequences are strengthened, and are therefore more likely to be repeated than those which are not. He believed that any organism, human or animal, could be taught to produce any behaviour of which it was physically capable by the use of appropriate techniques.

Much of Skinner's work involved the use of animals, using a **Skinner box**. There was a bar to press if rats were being tested, or a key to peck for pigeons. Hungry animals learned to produce this behaviour if they were reinforced with food, delivered to a food tray:

Figure 2: Skinner box

Two key terms in Skinner's theory are shaping and reinforcement. **Shaping** is a way of gradually changing behaviour. **Reinforcement** refers to a positive consequence of a behaviour, which makes the behaviour likely to be repeated. To understand the theory, we will need to look at what he meant by these terms in a little more detail.

Shaping

If you wanted to train a pigeon to peck a disc in a Skinner box, you might have quite a long wait before the pigeon produced the desired behaviour spontaneously. To shorten this time, Skinner used **shaping**. To bring this behaviour about, you would reinforce a (hungry) pigeon with food when it moved in the direction of the disc. Once this behaviour was established, the pigeon would have to come a bit closer to what was required before being reinforced – for example, touching the disc. You would then require the pigeon to get even closer to disc-pecking – perhaps contact between beak and disc – to receive food, and then finally only reinforce when the pigeon produced a distinct disc peck. In this way, you would be reinforcing **successive approximations** to the behaviour you were aiming at. Skinner himself managed to train pigeons to play table tennis using these methods!

Reinforcement and punishment

Although most of his original work was carried out on rats and pigeons, Skinner also applied his ideas to humans, and his research into the effect on learning of both reinforcement and punishment is of considerable relevance to human behaviour. He distinguished between positive and negative reinforcement. **Positive reinforcement** is when something with pleasurable consequences, which is likely to encourage a particular behaviour, is introduced into a situation. An example could be food for a hungry animal. It could also be praise or attention; it doesn't have to be anything tangible, just something which is pleasurable for the animal (or human) who is being reinforced. **Negative reinforcement** is when something aversive is removed from a situation. An example could be a child sent to his room for misbehaviour being allowed to come downstairs when he apologises.

Both positive and negative reinforcement strengthen a particular behaviour. **Punishment**, on the other hand, weakens behaviour. It also differs from both positive and negative reinforcement, because it involves introducing something aversive into a situation, or taking something pleasurable away from it. These distinctions are summarised in figure 3.

Figure 3: reinforcement and punishment

term	what happens	effect	examples
positive reinforcement	something pleasurable is added to a situation	behaviour is strengthened	praise, food if hungry
negative reinforcement	something aversive is removed from a situation	behaviour is strengthened	pain stops
punishment	something aversive is added to a situation	behaviour is weakened	physical punishment
	something pleasurable is removed from a situation	behaviour is weakened	pocket money taken away

Activity 8: reinforcement and punishment

In each of these examples, identify the use of:

a positive reinforcement
b negative reinforcement
c punishment

1 John often misses the school bus because he gets up too late. His mother, who is normally pleasant and cheerful, shouts at him to get up, which he hates, and often carries on grumbling even when he has finally dragged himself downstairs. When he does get up early enough, he has time to enjoy his breakfast.

2 Peter is allowed to stay up late on Saturday and watch TV if he has helped his mother with the hoovering. He often helps his father wash the car after lunch on Sunday. It is Peter's job to wash up after the meal, but if his father wants help with the car, he may come in while Peter is still clearing the table and get Peter's brother to finish washing up. Peter enjoys cleaning the car, and can't stand washing up.

3 Jenny thinks her partner doesn't always pay her enough attention, as he often disappears behind the newspaper over breakfast, and likes to make straight for the sports pages when he gets in from work. He likes big band music like Glenn Miller and can't stand anything classical. Jenny puts on a Glenn Miller CD as background music in the morning when he talks to her. When he hides behind the newspaper, however, she puts on a Beethoven CD. Sometimes she is playing this music when he gets home, but turns it off if he starts to talk to her.

When you have finished, see the notes on page 52.

In discussing ways of changing behaviour, Skinner himself was strongly in favour of the use of positive reinforcement, and to a lesser extent negative reinforcement. Punishment may be necessary to put an immediate stop to dangerous behaviour, like stopping a child playing with a knife, but otherwise Skinner was very much against it.

One of the reasons for this is that it does not strengthen any alternative behavioural response and so indicate what appropriate behaviour might be. A further problem is that if you try to use punishment to change behaviour, initially it seems to work. What typically happens, however, is that this change is only temporary, and the undesired behaviour comes back, perhaps even more strongly than before. Although punishment may not be a good way of stopping a behaviour once and for all, it is very effective in temporarily suppressing unwanted behaviour. It could perhaps be useful, then, in stopping unwanted behaviour for long enough to allow desired behaviour to occur; this desired behaviour could then be shaped and reinforced, using positive reinforcement.

The implications of operant conditioning

Skinner and his followers believed that patterns of behaviour are learned. This is true both for animals and for humans. Our behaviour is shaped and maintained by its consequences. It therefore follows that, in theory, anyone can be taught to do anything which is physically possible.

Skinner considered that the principles of behaviour change which he had established could be very widely used well beyond the laboratory. His principles have been applied in many areas; for example, helping children with learning difficulties to acquire skills, and behaviour management in the classroom.

- **Operant conditioning** is the term used to refer to the work of Skinner and his followers. Skinner explained learning as the association between a behaviour and its consequences.
- He believed behaviour is learned through **shaping** and **reinforcement**.
- Behaviour is reinforced when the consequences are positive. Shaping allows behaviour to be developed which would not occur spontaneously.
- Skinner distinguished between **positive reinforcement**, **negative reinforcement** and **punishment**. He strongly advocated the use of positive reinforcement as the most effective way of changing behaviour.
- The principles of operant conditioning have been applied in a variety of contexts.

Overview of the behaviourist model

The behaviourist model claims that behaviour can be accounted for within the framework of **learning theory**, with S–R associations being learned within a classical conditioning framework, and behaviour which is reinforced being strengthened and therefore likely to recur within an operant conditioning framework.

Behaviourism emphasises the continuity between humans and other animals, since the same principles of learning are believed to apply in both cases. It assumes that very little is innate, and that therefore most of our behaviour needs to be learned. It is fundamentally an **associationist** approach.

Its aims are to establish by experimentation the rules which establish and change behaviour. This is often done by studying **animal behaviour** to establish basic principles. Animals are easier to control than humans, and because animal behaviour is less complex than human behaviour it is easier to isolate particular variables. These principles may then be helpful in understanding human behaviour. Human behaviour has also been studied directly using behavioural methods.

The behaviourist approach has been criticised for being somewhat mechanistic. Many people dislike the implication that we have little control over our own behaviour and are at the mercy of environmental contingencies. It has also been argued that by factoring out any internal processes, such as thinking or feeling, the behaviourist approach misses what many people believe to be essential in making sense of human behaviour. However, a behavioural approach has provided some useful therapies; since all behaviour is learned, it can be unlearned and more appropriate behaviour learned in its place. This principle forms the basis of behavioural attempts to help people with problems, for example those suffering from phobias, with considerable success.

The humanistic perspective

The humanistic approach grew out of dissatisfaction with the other perspectives we have described. Some psychologists, in particular Carl Rogers, were unhappy with the rather pessimistic view of the psychodynamic approach, which saw people as being at the mercy of unconscious forces, as well as the behaviourist approach, with its disregard for conscious experience. In response to the huge influence of behaviourism and psychodynamic psychology, humanistic psychology therefore emerged as a **third force**, concerned with people's conscious experience and their ability to direct their lives.

Humanistic psychologists also question the use of the scientific method as the most useful one for psychologists to follow. This method has been dominant in much of psycholoogy – for example, in research taking a behaviourist approach – and aims at objectivity. It is interested in the measurement of behaviour and exploring cause and effect relationships through rigorously controlled experiments.

In contrast, humanistic psychologists argue that what is important is the experience of being a person, and the methods used in the more traditional sciences are inappropriate for this kind of study. A rigorously scientific approach constrains our understanding of the individual. Like Freud, humanistic psychologists prefer to use a **case-study** method, and to make use of **introspective data**, which allow the psychologist to understand the individual in depth.

There are three basic principles of humanistic psychology. First, what is important is the **experience** of being human, with a focus on people's subjective awareness of their worlds, as opposed to others' views of them. This is known as a **phenomenological approach**. An important aspect of this is that we are aware of our own existence as distinct individuals, moving through life towards old age and death.

The second principle is that we should take a **holistic approach**, in other words look at the person as a whole. Instead of studying specific psychological processes in isolation, the focus should be on the whole person, the physical person with thoughts and feelings, within a particular social context.

The final principle is that we all have **personal agency**. In most situations, we are aware of having choices. There may well be social constraints on our choices, and we may not be fully aware of the alternatives open to us. We may even be afraid of the consequences of making particular choices. None the less, we do have the potential to choose. An extension of this principle is that we can play a part in the kind of person we become. Humanistic psychologists believe that people can be helped to change and develop by becoming as aware as possible of their feelings and motivations and the influences upon them. This process of change is referred to as **personal growth**.

The idea of personal growth is central to the theory of motivation proposed by **Maslow** (1954). He suggested that there is a range of human needs which form a hierarchy on seven different levels:

Figure 4: Maslow's hierarchy of needs

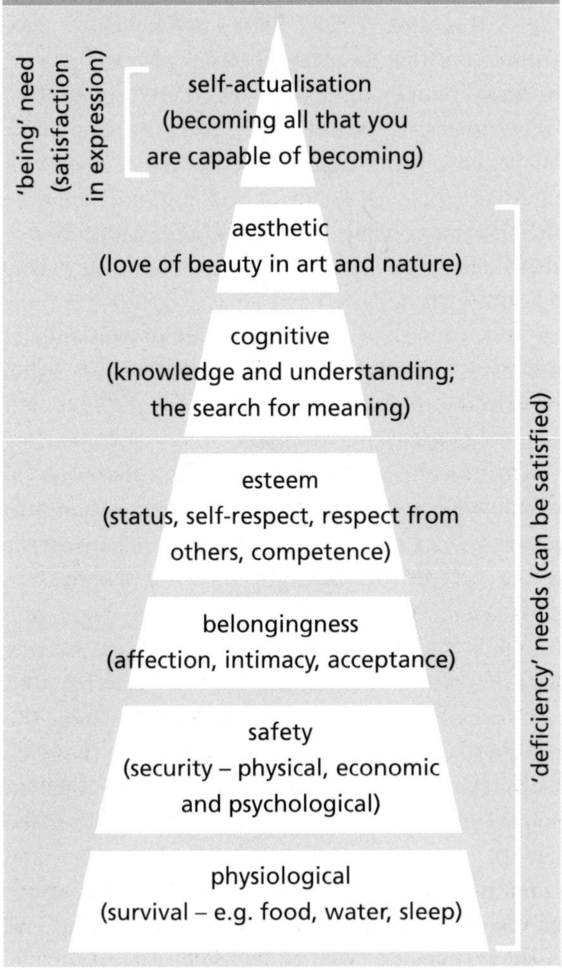

'being' need (satisfaction in expression)

self-actualisation
(becoming all that you are capable of becoming)

aesthetic
(love of beauty in art and nature)

cognitive
(knowledge and understanding; the search for meaning)

esteem
(status, self-respect, respect from others, competence)

belongingness
(affection, intimacy, acceptance)

safety
(security – physical, economic and psychological)

physiological
(survival – e.g. food, water, sleep)

'deficiency' needs (can be satisfied)

This model proposes that basic needs, those at the bottom of the hierarchy, need to be satisfied before we can move to a higher level. As the needs at lower levels are satisfied, we can move up through the levels of the hierarchy to meet the other 'deficiency' needs of safety – belongingness and so on.

At the highest level is **self-actualisation**, a 'being' need. This differs from the other levels in that it is a need which cannot be satisfied, but whose expression is an end in itself. Since it is to do with realising our own potential, how this need is expressed varies from person to person; it depends on how we would like to develop and what we would like to work towards. For a professional footballer, these needs could include training and practising skills, working towards playing an increasingly effective part in his team's performance. For a musician, they could include developing his creativity in writing and performing songs.

Maslow originally suggested that deficiency needs must be met before the process of self-actualisation can take place. At the same time, he does point out that the distinction between them is not necessarily clear-cut. A chef or a gourmet, for example, could satisfy the physiological need for food in a 'being' way, by finding satisfaction and pleasure in the way food is prepared and presented. It is also possible that what seems to be a process of self-actualisation could be pursued in a 'deficiency' way. This would be true, for example, if a professional footballer were developing his skills purely to achieve the respect of others, rather than as part of personal growth.

People can be helped in their personal growth by **client-centred therapy (CCT)**, developed by Rogers. This is a talking therapy, and is non-directive, in that the therapist does not suggest how the person might wish to change, but by listening and mirroring back what the client tells them, helps them to explore these possibilities for themselves, and decide what kinds of changes they would like to make.

While Rogers believed that people were fundamentally good, and had a generally optimistic view of human nature, he was aware that we all have the capacity for more negative behaviour – for example, becoming angry or treating others cruelly.

However, he believed that we can choose whether or not to behave in these ways. The decisions we make depend to some extent on social conditioning, but we also have voluntary choice.

The influence of social conditioning suggests that choices are not entirely free. Negative elements brought about by social conditioning cause people to become neurotic and what Rogers calls **incongruent**, in that the self which has developed and is shown in behaviour is not their true self. Rogers believed that this can come about in childhood, if children are offered only **conditional positive regard**, i.e. love is offered on condition that the child behaves in certain ways which fit in with the wishes and expectations of others. To become a healthy and fully functioning person, children need to be offered **unconditional positive regard**, so that personal growth is not distorted, and the true self and the actual self are congruent.

However, even where personal growth has become distorted, there is always the possibility of change. Particularly through therapy, we can choose to focus our personal growth on changing incongruent elements of the self, to become happier and more fulfilled. There are some constraints on the choices we make, but choices are always possible.

Humanistic psychology has been criticised for perhaps overemphasising the possibilities for change inherent in personal agency, and downplaying the personal, social and cultural constraints which affect our choices. It has also been argued that there has not been sufficiently rigorous evaluation of the ideas of this approach, and indeed that given its nature, such evaluation is not possible. At the same time, this aproach has been extremely influential, particularly in counselling, where many people claim to have found it beneficial.

- Humanistic psychology came about as a **third force** in response to dissatisfaction with the dominant perspectives of **psychodynamic** psychology and **behaviourism**. It proposes that what is important is the **experience** of the individual, that we should take a **holistic** approach and that we are capable of **personal growth**.
- The possibility of change is reflected in **Maslow's hierarchy of needs**.
- People are instrinsically motivated to work towards **self-actualisation**.
- Rogers' **CCT** is a humanistic therapy which helps people to explore the possibility of personal growth. To develop as a fully functioning person, children need to receive **unconditional positive regard**. However, distortions in personal development can be worked on in therapy.
- This approach has been criticised for overestimating personal agency and downplaying the social and cultural constraints which limit our choices. **Counselling** based on humanistic principles is nonetheless extremely popular.

The cognitive perspective

While behaviourism was a very popular approach in the 1940s and 1950s, some psychologists have pointed out that internal processes play a large part in many human functions, and therefore study of these processes should have a place in psychology. While behaviourists acknowledge the existence of internal processes such as thinking and emotion, they do not consider them an appropriate focus of study since they are not directly observable. Many psychologists believe, however, that to focus entirely on observable behaviour and ignore the mental processes which lead to the behaviour being produced provides an unnecessarily limited account of psychological functioning.

Cognitive psychology focuses on the ways in which we take in, process, store and respond to information. Cognitive psychologists are particularly interested in the mental processes involved in perception, attention, memory, language and thinking. Perception refers to taking in and making sense of information. Attention allows us to focus on one or more sources of information from the possible sources available to us. Memory is to do with taking in, storing and retrieving information about facts, events and skills. Language involves the use of symbols to manipulate information and communicate it to others. Thinking includes a range of mental activities such as decision-making and problem-solving.

Largely as a result of the development of computers, the cognitive approach took over from the behavioural approach as the dominant approach in psychology in the 1950s and 1960s. Computers were first of all influential in providing an analogy of human mental processes: information is taken in, processed in some way, and this processing in turn affects behaviour and experience. This is known as the **computer analogy**. The underlying model is of man as an **information processor**, and the aims are to establish the different forms and stages of processing which create our understanding of the world.

The influence of computers was taken further in the late 1960s in **computer simulation**, creating computer programs which could model simple cognitive processes. This developed into what became known as **artificial intelligence (AI)**, combining cognitive psychology with computer science. This has focused on the development of computer programs which can carry out the kinds of complex cognitive tasks typical of human functioning. The most recent theoretical framework taking this approach is **connectionism**, which has been influential in such areas as explaining how children develop language and why they make particular kinds of linguistic errors.

Groome *et al.* (1999) have suggested that cognitive psychology can be divided into three areas: experimental cognitive psychology, cognitive science and cognitive neuropsychology. **Experimental cognitive psychology** uses the experimental method to explore mental processing. While it is not possible to observe cognitive processes directly, they can be observed indirectly by looking at the *results* of processing information. For example, much research into memory asks people to carry out memory tasks in controlled conditions. Varying the conditions allows us to establish what factors facilitate or inhibit the cognitive processes involved in memory. **Cognitive science** is concerned with computer simulations of human cognitive processes. **Cognitive neuropsychology** looks at cognitive processes in the living brain, for example identifying cognitive deficits which occur as the result of brain damage. There are more examples of this approach in the later section of this chapter on the **localisation of cortical function**.

As well as providing insight into human cognitive functioning, the cognitive approach also has practical applications. One of these is the study of **eye-witness testimony (EWT)**. Juries seem to find EWT amongst the most convincing evidence of all. The Devlin Report (1976), which was concerned with EWT, found that in more than 300 cases, eye-witness identification was the *sole* evidence of guilt, yet the conviction rate was 74%. It is therefore essential, if justice is to be done and mistakes avoided, that EWT is as complete and as accurate as possible. Working with the police, cognitive psychologists have applied their understanding of how human memory works to develop a police interview technique called the **cognitive interview**. Fisher *et al.* (1987) found that this technique was significantly superior to standard police interview techniques in terms of the amount of information accurately recalled. It is now widely used by police forces in the UK and the USA.

The cognitive approach has also been influential in the development of **therapies**. The cognitive model of mental disorders suggests that psychological disorders are due to faulty thinking, and therapy should therefore aim to challenge inappropriate cognitions so that more adaptive ways of thinking can be developed. One example is **rational emotive therapy (RET)**, developed by **Ellis** (1955). Ellis developed the ABC model to show how irrational thinking can lead to maladaptive behaviour. An example is shown in figure 5 overleaf.

Activity 9: using Ellis' ABC model

Alex has just received a very disappointing grade for a psychology test. Use the ABC model to describe how he might deal with this, using the irrational pathway on the right of Fig. 5. How might he use the rational pathway on the left?

When you have finished, see the notes on page 53.

Ellis's therapy involves trying to change clients' illogical beliefs, using logical reasoning and argument. Treatment may include 'behavioural experiments', where the client is instructed to take

Figure 5: Ellis' ABC model

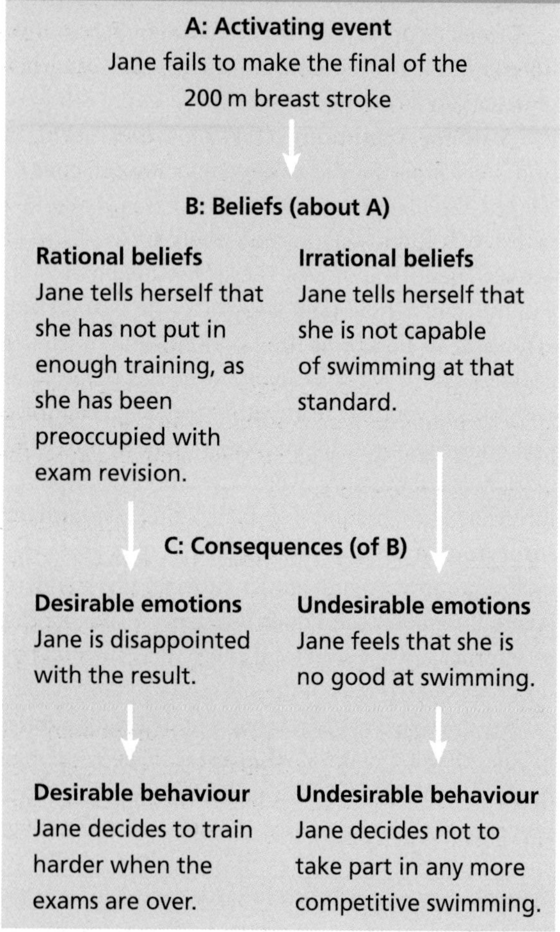

A: Activating event
Jane fails to make the final of the 200 m breast stroke

↓

B: Beliefs (about A)

Rational beliefs	**Irrational beliefs**
Jane tells herself that she has not put in enough training, as she has been preoccupied with exam revision.	Jane tells herself that she is not capable of swimming at that standard.

↓

C: Consequences (of B)

Desirable emotions	**Undesirable emotions**
Jane is disappointed with the result.	Jane feels that she is no good at swimming.
Desirable behaviour	**Undesirable behaviour**
Jane decides to train harder when the exams are over.	Jane decides not to take part in any more competitive swimming.

risks, carrying out behaviours which they would expect to lead to awful consequences, in order to test the reality of their beliefs.

One of the strengths of the cognitive approach is that it is scientific, in that it is based on carefully controlled research. In addition, it has succeeded in providing a lot of information about human mental processes, and there are useful practical applications. However, it can be seen as rather limited in its scope, in that it does not consider other psychological influences on behaviour, such as social and cultural factors.

- The cognitive approach focuses on internal mental processes. It uses a **computer analogy** to propose the model of the person as an **information processor**.
- It can be divided into **experimental cognitive psychology**, **cognitive science** and **cognitive neuropsychology**.
- The cognitive approach has **practical applications**, such as the development of the **cognitive interview** and **cognitive therapies**.

Activity 10: identifying perspectives

Try to match each of the following statements to one (or more) of the perspectives described above:

psychodynamic behaviourist humanistic cognitive

1 It is important to study what makes the individual unique.
2 Like any other science, psychology needs to use scientific methods.
3 Animal research can be useful in helping us to understand how people function.
4 The principles of psychology can be used in therapies.
5 It is important to focus on people's unconscious processes.
6 We have no direct access to internal psychological processes; we should therefore concentrate on what is observable.

When you have finished, see the notes on page 53.

Activity 11: summarising perspectives

Look back through this section and draw up a table to compare these aspects of the four perspectives:

a what their aims are
b their view of what people are like
c the extent to which they can be seen as scientific
d the extent to which they see people as having control over their lives (free will) or being at the mercy of forces beyond their control (determinism)
e the range of psychological phenomena they aim to explain
f possible applications
g strengths
h criticisms

1.4 The biological approach

All the wide range of behaviour and experience which adds up to being human must have a physiological basis. Some psychologists therefore believe that to understand human psychological functioning, we need to focus on the basic physiological processes which underlie it. We will look in this section at some of the main areas in which biopsychologists are interested, and how their research has contributed to psychological knowledge.

The nervous system

The **nervous system** is the network of all the **neurons** or nerve cells in the body. This system allows us to receive, process and transmit information from both within and outside the body. The nervous system has been classified into different divisions according to function. It consists of the **central nervous system (CNS)** and the **peripheral nervous system (PNS)**. The CNS consists of the brain and spinal cord. The function of the CNS is to analyse information arriving from the PNS and initiate appropriate responses, to be sent via the PNS to the muscles and organs of the body. The PNS consists of the **somatic nerves** ('somatic' means to do with the body) which run to and from the CNS. The PNS can be further divided into the two divisions of the **autonomic nervous system (ANS)** (figure 6).

We will be returning to these divisions and their functions later in the chapter, but overall they act together in an integrated way to ensure that the body acts and reacts appropriately in different situations.

The structure and function of neurons

In the human nervous system, there are between 10 and 12 billion neurons, 80% of which are found in the brain, and in particular the cerebral cortex, the outer layer of the brain.

A neuron can be of three types, with different functions. **Sensory** (or **afferent**) **neurons** carry information about external stimuli, e.g. light or touch, from sensory receptors to the CNS. **Motor** (or **efferent**) **neurons** carry information from the CNS to muscles and glands.

Interneurons (or **connector neurons**) are those which transmit information to other neurons but do not fall into the other two categories. They are only found in the CNS.

Figure 6: divisions of the nervous system

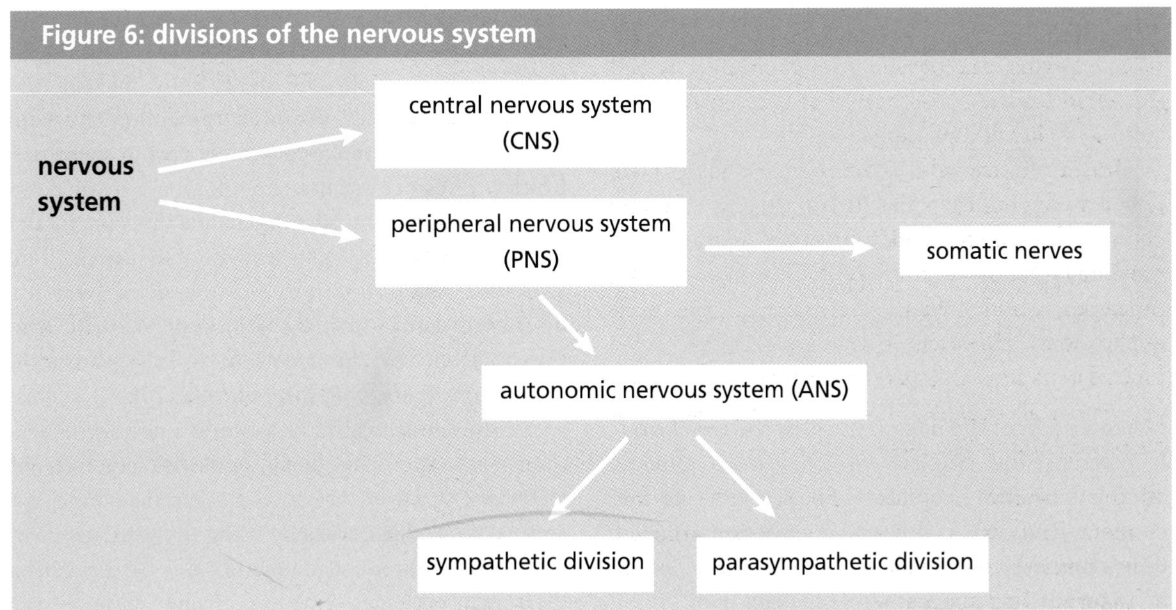

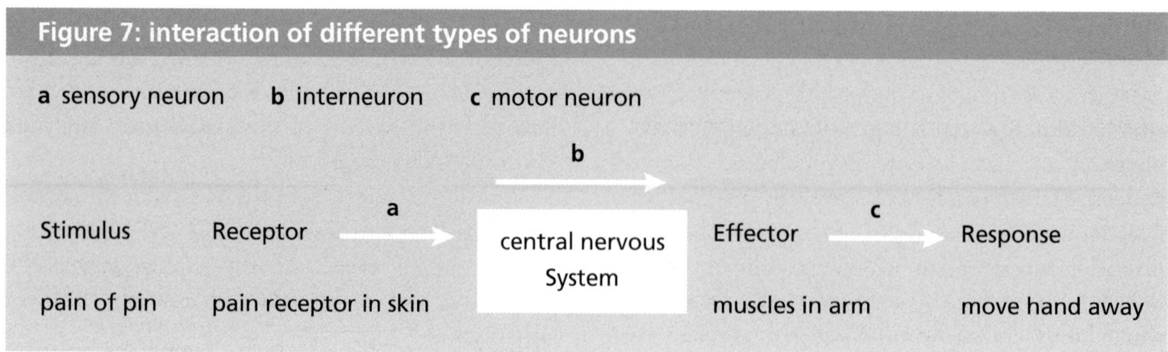

Figure 7: interaction of different types of neurons

This is best illustrated with a specific example. This is what happens when you put your hand on a drawing pin (figure 7).

No two neurons are identical. In addition, motor neurons, sensory neurons and interneurons also all have their own characteristics. To give you an indication of how neurons work, we will look in a little more detail at the stucture and function of a motor neuron. Figure 8 shows the typical structure of a motor neuron:

Figure 8: structure of a motor neuron

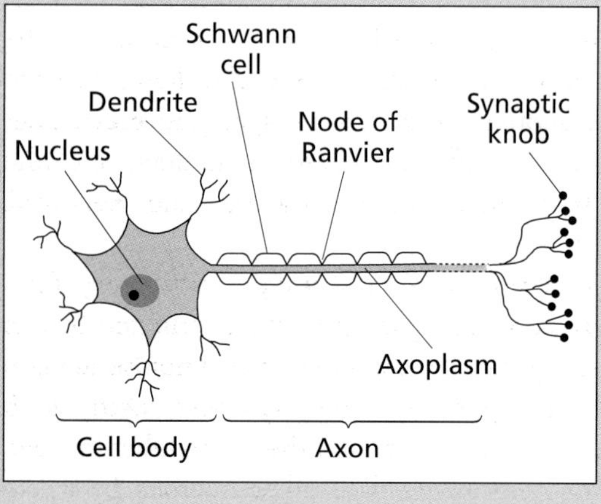

The main part of the neuron is called the **cell body**. It contains the **nucleus** which carries genetic information, and co-ordinates the activities of the neuron. The cell body has extensions called **dendrites** which receive information from other neurons and transmit it towards the cell body.

The **axon** is a structure which can be up to a metre long or less than one thousandth of a centimetre. It transmits infomation along its length. It is filled with a jelly-like substance called **axoplasm**, and wrapped in **Schwann cells**, which form a fatty **myelin sheath** around the axon. This myelin sheath has two functions. First, it insulates neurons from each other so that an electrical impulse travelling along one neuron will not affect neighbouring neurons. This is rather like the way the earth, neutral and live wires in an electrical cable are insulated from each other with sheaths of coloured plastic. The second function of the myelin sheath is to speed up information transmission by means of the Schwann cells.

The myelin sheath is not continuous; it has gaps called **nodes of Ranvier** along its length. The impulse being transmitted jumps from one node of Ranvier to the next, thus making the impulse travel much faster. At the end of the axon are a series of extensions which end in **synaptic knobs.** These are structures which are involved in transmitting an impulse from one neuron to the next, across a tiny gap called a **synapse**. The structure and functions of synapses will be discussed later, but we will look first at the transmission of information in the form of electrical impulses within neurons.

This process is difficult to study, since nerve cells themselves are very small, and the amounts of electricity involved are tiny. Researchers have got around these difficulties by using the giant axons of squid (up to 1 mm in diameter) and by measuring the small voltages involved using cathode ray oscilloscopes, machines which pick up electrical charges and display them on a screen.

The process of sending an impulse involves the transport of **sodium ions** and **potassium ions** into and out of the axoplasm. A sodium ion is a tiny particle of sodium which is electrically charged. When an axon is at rest, sodium ions are pumped out of the axon and potassium ions are pumped in. But when an impulse passes along the axon, the sodium ions rush in, and this causes an electrical signal called an **action potential** to pass along the axon. An action potential will only be produced if the stimulus to the neuron is strong enough, i.e. if the stimulus reaches the **threshold level**. Once this threshold level is reached, the action potential travels to the end of the axon. The action potential is the same no matter how large or small the stimulus. This is known as the **all-or-nothing law**; the same impulse will be sent whether the stimulus is huge or tiny.

So if action potentials are all the same size and all travel at the same speed, how can our brains detect the strength of a stimulus? The answer is by the frequency of impulses sent, as a very strong impulse will lead to lots of impulses being sent in quick succession. A very strong impulse will also lead to a larger number of neurons being stimulated.

- There are several subdivisions of the **nervous system** which work together in an integrated way.
- There are three types of nerve cell or neuron: **sensory neurons**, **interneurons** and **motor neurons**. The transmission of information within neurons is electrical. **Action potentials** are transmitted along **axons**, provided the stimulus is strong enough.

Transmission between neurons

Each neuron is separated from other neurons by a tiny gap called a **synapse**. Transmission of information across a synapse is chemical.

The gap between one neuron and the next is called the **synaptic cleft**. Floating in the cleft are many **calcium ions** and **sodium ions**, charged particles of calcium and sodium. The membrane that lies *before* the cleft is the pre-synaptic membrane and the one that lies *after* the cleft is the post-synaptic membrane. On the post-synaptic membrane are **receptor molecules**; these can open or close holes called **ion channels** in the membrane.

Figure 9: structure of a synapse

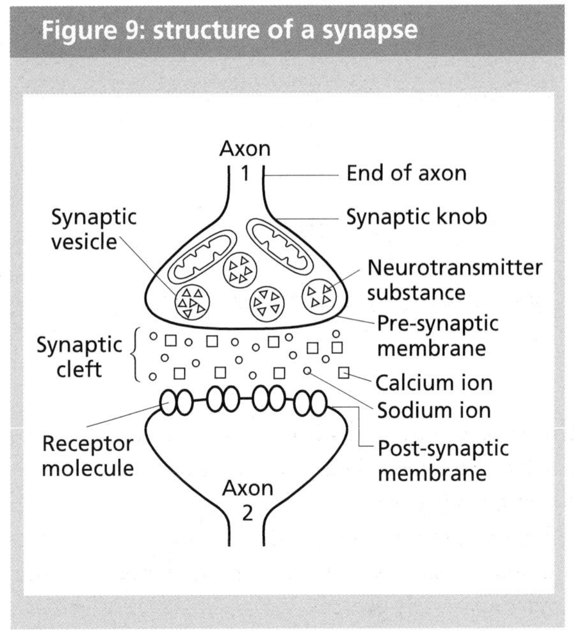

The synaptic knob contains **synaptic vesicles,** small bags filled with chemicals called **neurotransmitters**. These are the chemicals which pass information across the **synaptic cleft**. There are many different neurotransmitters, including **acetylcholine**, **noradrenaline** and **serotonin** (figure 10).

Synapses can be **excitatory** or **inhibitory**. Firing of excitatory synapses gives the instruction that the receiving neuron should send an impulse along its axon. Firing of inhibitory synapses instructs the neuron *not* to send an impulse. Remember that each neuron is connected to other neurons by a large number of synapses, so whether a neuron will send an impulse or not will depend on the combined effect of *all* these synapses; some cells in the brain may have up to 10 000 synapses. Inhibitory synapses are vital to ensure the spread of electrical impulses is kept channelled within the correct 'circuits' and not allowed to spread through all other neural networks.

Figure 10: how an impulse crosses the synaptic cleft

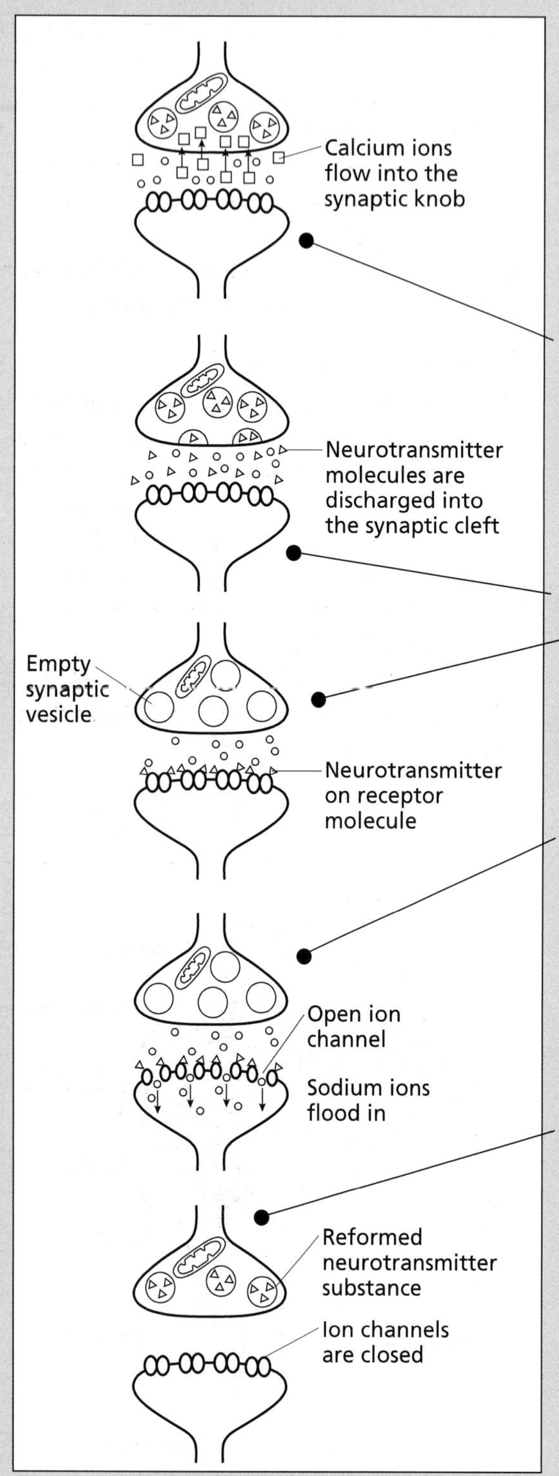

The impulse arrives at the synaptic knob, and makes the pre-synaptic membrane more permeable to calcium ions, i.e. it lets calcium ions flow through it more easily.

Because there is a high concentration of calcium ions in the cleft, these now flow into the synaptic knob.

The influx of calcium ions makes the synaptic vesicles fuse with the pre-synaptic membrane, and discharge their contents into the cleft.

The calcium ions have now served their purpose and are pumped out of the synaptic knob.

The neurotransmitter substances released from the synaptic vesicles diffuse across the cleft and attach to the receptor molecules on the post-synaptic membrane.

When the neurotransmitter attaches to the receptor sites, it makes them open their ion channels. This allows the sodium ions in the synaptic cleft to diffuse through the post-synaptic membrane.

The neuron that has received the sodium ions can now transmit the impulse along its axon *or* inhibit an impulse from occurring.

The neurotransmitter substance has now served its purpose and is broken down by chemicals called enzymes. Its constituent parts are reabsorbed by the pre-synaptic membrane and made back into neurotransmitter substance in the synaptic vesicles.

The synapse is now ready to receive another impulse.

Activity 12: describing synaptic activity.

Put this series of statements, describing how an impulse passes across a synapse, in the correct order. Fill in the gaps, using the words listed below, as you go:

a Now the job of the __________ is over, and they are pumped out.

b The receptor sites open their __________ and sodium ions flood in.

c The impulse arrives at the synaptic knob. This causes the __________ to let in more __________.

d Now the neurotransmitter substance's job is over; the neuron that has received the sodium ion is ready to __________

e The neurotransmitter substances attach to the __________ molecules on the __________ membrane.

f The __________ join to the presynaptic membrane and pass their contents into the __________.

calcium ions	**synaptic vesicles**
presynaptic membrane	**post-synaptic**
	receptor
synaptic cleft	**transmit an impulse**
calcium ions	**ion channels**

When you have finished, see the notes on page 53.

Because there are so many synapses, the sensitivity of the nervous system is increased; a motor neuron in the spinal cord will have over 1 000 dendrites, each joined to other neurons by synapses. Even a very weak stimulus can cause an impulse to be sent, by a process of **summation**. Summation is where stimuli are added together to achieve enough stimulation to trigger an impulse. The neurotransmitter from more than one dendrite can be accumulated in **spatial summation**, or the neurotransmitter from one dendrite over a period of time can build up and trigger an impulse; this is **temporal summation**.

Synapses also give **precision** to the nervous system – because receptor molecules are situated only on the post-synaptic membrane, the impulse can pass along a pathway in one direction only. This is known as **unidirectionality**.

- Neurons are linked by tiny gaps called **synapses.** Information crosses a synapse using chemical **neurotransmitters.**
- Firing of **excitatory** synapses gives the instruction for an impulse to be sent; firing of **inhibitory** synapses instruct a neuron *not* to send an impulse.
- Synapses give the nervous system **flexibility** and **precision**, and increase its **sensitivity**.

The central nervous system (CNS)

The CNS consists of the brain and spinal cord. It is the centre in which huge amounts of complex incoming information are processed to 'decide' what responses are appropriate in various situations. The brain and spinal cord are protected by three membranes called **meninges**, and the space between the inner two meninges is filled with **cerebrospinal fluid**.

An adult person's brain contains millions and millions of neurons and is without a doubt the most complex organ in the human body.

Figure 11: the human brain

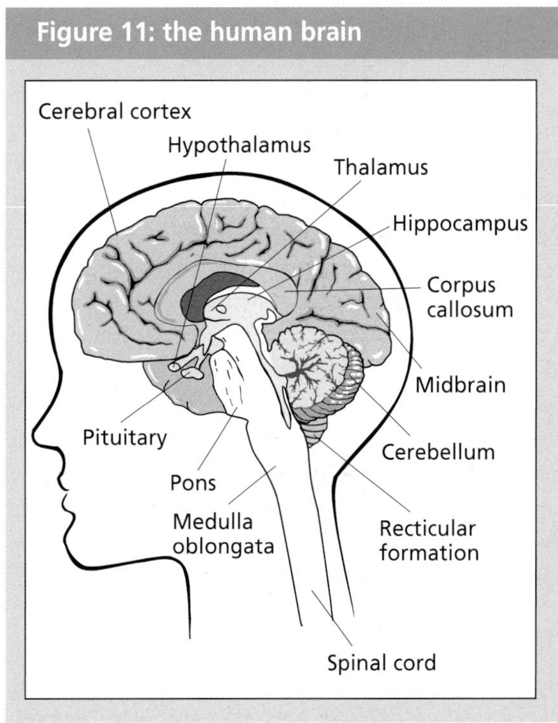

The **hindbrain** consists of the **medulla oblongata**, the **pons**, and the **cerebellum**. These structures contain many nerve fibres that connect the brain with the spinal cord and have functions relating to the control of heart rate and breathing system, as well as the reflex control of hiccupping and sneezing. Many of the 12 pairs of **cranial nerves** (which control many sensory and motor functions) also originate in the hindbrain.

The **midbrain** is involved (amongst other things) with **selective attention**, ensuring that you are not consciously aware of the huge number of environmental stimuli you are receiving at any one time. The **reticular formation** is part of the midbrain and is involved in arousal and sleep.

The **forebrain** is made up of the **cerebrum**, the **hypothalamus** and the **thalamus**. The outer **cortex** of the brain makes up some of the cerebrum, and this is where most cerebral activity (such as thinking and planning) occurs. The hypothalamus controls the ANS and the pituitary gland, as we will see when we look at the fight-or-flight response later in this chapter. It also has a role in regulating hunger and thirst, and is involved in aggression and rage. Together with part of the midbrain, it is also involved in the sleep/waking cycle. The thalamus acts as a relay station for sensory information.

The spinal cord makes up the other part of the CNS. Between the vertebrae, pairs of spinal nerves join the cord, one either side. These nerves contain neurons which transmit impulses to the spinal cord from receptors such as the sense organs, and neurons which transmit impulses from the brain to the muscles and organs of the body. The spinal cord is particularly important in terms of the **reflex pathways** which it controls; reflexes are very quick, automatic responses that protect the body, such as removing our hand quickly from a hot iron. The benefit of involving the spinal cord in these reflexes, and not involving the brain, is that the impulse has less distance to travel, and the message to 'move it!' therefore reaches the relevant organ more quickly.

The peripheral nervous system (PNS)

The PNS makes up the rest of the nervous system. It is further divided into the **somatic nerves**, bundles of neurons which form a communication network within the body, and the **autonomic nervous system (ANS)**, the system which controls activities such as sweating and breathing, which are generally involuntary, and over which we don't normally have conscious control.

People can, however, learn to control these metabolic processes. In 1970, for example, Ramanand Yogi survived for over five hours in a sealed box, using only half the amount of oxygen which is normally needed to stay alive. It is also worth noting that many bodily functions are controlled by both voluntary *and* involuntary nerves. You can consciously decide when to urinate, but if you fail to respond to signals that your bladder is full, involuntary impulses will eventually contract the bladder anyway!

The ANS can be divided into two parts, the **sympathetic division** and the **parasympathetic division**. Both of these systems contain unmyelinated motor neurons which connect the CNS to effector organs like internal organs and involuntary muscles. The two divisions have opposite effects; generally, stimulation by the sympathetic division prepares the body to mobilise energy resources, and stimulation by the parasympathetic division prepares the body for the storage of energy resources, due to the secretion of different neurotransmitters. The neurons of the sympathetic division use **noradrenaline** as their neurotransmitter, and generally serve to prepare the body for an emergency – widening the pupils, speeding up the heart rate, and tightening the anal and bladder sphincters. The neurons of the parasympathetic division use **acetylcholine** as their neurotransmitter substance, and have the opposite effects:

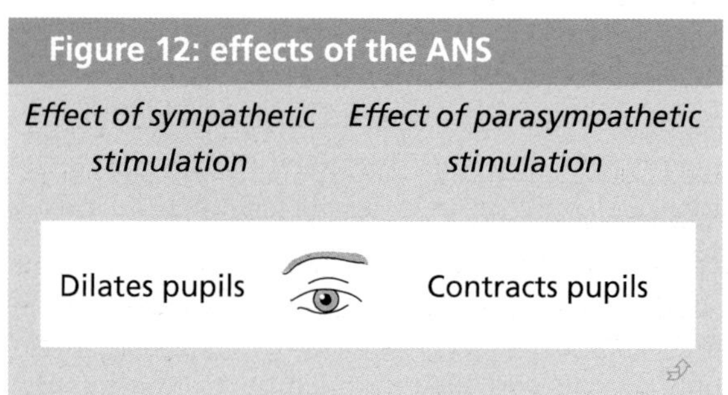

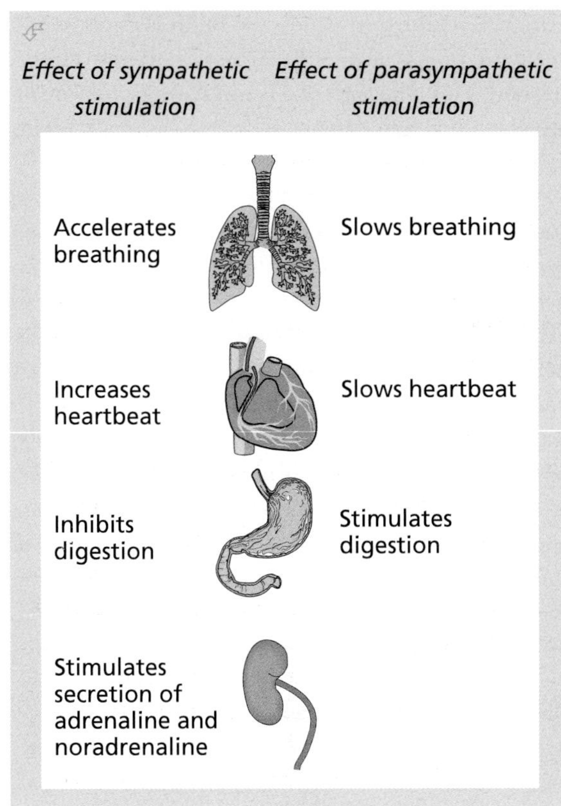

- The **central nervous system (CNS)** consists of the brain and spinal cord. The **peripheral nervous system (PNS)** consists of the network of nerves serving the body and the autonomic nervous system.
- The **autonomic nervous system** (ANS) has two divisions: the **sympathetic** division and the **parasympathetic** division. Neurons of the sympathetic division secrete **noradrenaline** across their synapses. Those of the parasympathetic division secrete **acetylcholine**.

The localisation of cortical function

In this section, we will be looking at an important area of debate related to the CNS. The issue here is whether (or to what extent) specific areas of the cerebral cortex are specialised for different functions, and to what extent the cortex works as a whole. First we look at the methods used in investigating this topic.

One of the earliest attempts at mapping cortical functions was the system of **phrenology**, introduced by Gall in the early part of the nineteenth century. This approach claimed to be able to associate bumps on the skull with the development of the underlying areas of the brain, and made links between specific abilities and specific parts of the skull. For instance, language was supposedly located in the area below the left eye socket. As more scientific techniques for investigating the structure and function of the brain have been developed, both of these claims are now known to be false.

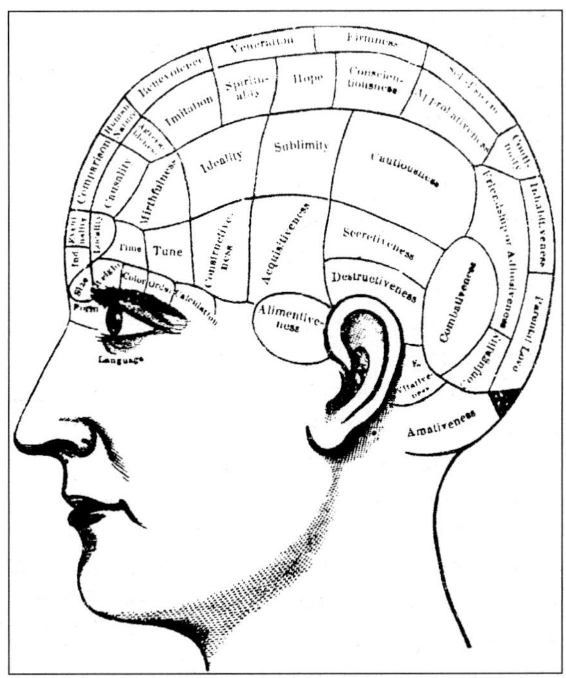

The system of phrenology

Current methods of investigating the brain can be broadly divided into **invasive** methods, where the brain is physically interfered with by the experimenter and the results are observed, and **non-invasive** methods, where the activity of the brain is recorded without such radical interference taking place. The more invasive techniques are used in animal research rather than in research using human participants; however, the effects of accidents or surgical procedures can also give us information about the effects of brain damage in humans.

Another useful distinction can be made between **classic techniques** used in earlier research, and the more recent **brain scanning techniques** which rely on computer-based analysis of recordings made of the brain.

Classic techniques

Anatomical techniques

Anatomical techniques are used on the dead brain, to investigate its structure. After it has been sliced into sections and mounted on slides, different types of tissue or even transmitter substances can be stained with dyes to make them show up more clearly. Alternatively, radioactive amino acids can be injected into the brain of a live animal, tracing the nerve tracts and the pathways being studied. The animal is then killed so that slides can be made to clarify where the nerves go.

There are two drawbacks with these anatomical techniques. Firstly, they can only tell us about structures, and can give no information about the function of different areas. Secondly, they can only be used with the dead brain.

Some research which would previously have been carried out by anatomical studies can now be carried out by scanning, which is described later in the chapter.

Investigating the effects of brain damage

Investigating how the damaged brain works can help researchers find out how the normal, undamaged brain functions. If damage to a particular area of the brain results in the loss of a particular ability, it is tempting to conclude that the damaged part of the brain controlled the ability that was lost. This may not necessarily be the case, though. It may be that the damage disrupted communication between other areas, or caused inflammation and biochemical change to adjoining areas, or that the damaged area contributed to the ability lost, but only in a very specific way.

Even so, studying the damaged brain has generated a great deal of knowledge about the workings of the normal brain. One method is that of **clinical studies**, in which the brain is damaged by accident or by necessary surgery, and the effects studied. The other method is **ablation** or **lesioning studies**, in which damage is done to animals' brains solely for the purpose of observing the effects.

A famous example of a clinical study arising from accidental damage is the case of Phineas Gage, an American railway worker, who in 1848 had an iron bar shot into the frontal part of the brain when an explosive charge went off prematurely. Surprisingly, he survived the experience with no obvious handicap. The main effect of this on his behaviour was that he became much less inhibited than previously, swearing, removing his clothes in public, and generally being more impulsive and less conscientious. This suggests that damage to parts of the brain can affect the personality, and that therefore the control of the personality must be located in some way in certain parts of the brain.

The case of Phineas Gage

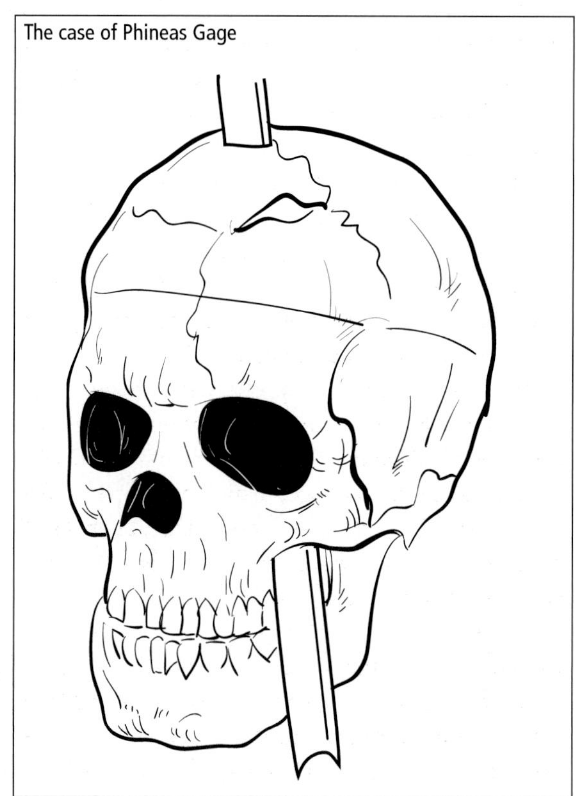

A tamping iron, over 1m long, and tapering from $1\frac{1}{4}$" in diameter, entered under the left cheekbone and came out through the top of the head.

Another useful source of information is the study of patients who have suffered strokes or cerebral haemorrhages. In both cases, the blood supply to the neurons of the brain is interrupted and the neurons are starved of oxygen. Because the two sides of the brain have separate blood supplies, it is often the case that only one side of the brain is affected. For example, stroke patients may be paralysed down one side only.

Sometimes surgery may be carried out with the specific intention of changing a patient's behaviour; this is known as **psychosurgery**. For example, this was used by Moniz (1937), who injected alcohol into the frontal lobes of schizophrenic patients, carrying out what has come to be known as a **frontal lobotomy**, on the assumption that destruction of the frontal lobes would cure them of their problems (it didn't!).

Another example is **split-brain** research. In order to prevent the spread of epileptic seizures from one hemisphere of the brain to the other, patients may undergo an operation called a **commisurotomy**. In these people, the corpus callosum, which connects the two hemispheres of the brain, has been severed, so they have what is known as a 'split brain'. Sperry (1961) carried out a series of studies to investigate the deficits shown by these patients, and was awarded the Nobel prize for his work. The effects of surgery for epilepsy on memory are discussed in chaper 11.

However, these approaches have their limitations. Some of these limitations result from the general difficulties researchers have had when looking at brain damage, which we have already discussed. In addition, assessing changes in behaviour after brain damage is far from straightforward, since an accurate record of behaviour before the damage may not be available. Moreover, the damage may also extend over several areas of the brain, making it impossible to reach any definite conclusions about the functions of any one area. Finally, it has not always been possible to determine the extent of the brain damage from the outside, though this can now be done using the brain scanning techniques discussed later.

Some of the problems associated with clinical studies can be overcome by the use of studies which involve deliberate but precisely controlled brain damage. There are different terms related to the amount of damage inflicted. In a **lobotomy**, an entire lobe of the brain (each side of the cortex contains four) is destroyed. Simply cutting the connections between a lobe and the rest of the brain is known as a **leucotomy**. Destruction of a large area of the cortex, but less than a lobe, is called an **ablation**, and destruction of a small area is a **lesion**. This technique was used by Lashley in the 1920s to study in rats the effects on memory of removing areas of the cortex.

One advantage of this approach is that the damage can be precisely located, particularly when it is produced using a **stereotaxic apparatus** in conjunction with a **stereotaxic map** of the brain:

Figure 13: a stereotaxic apparatus for performing brain surgery on rats

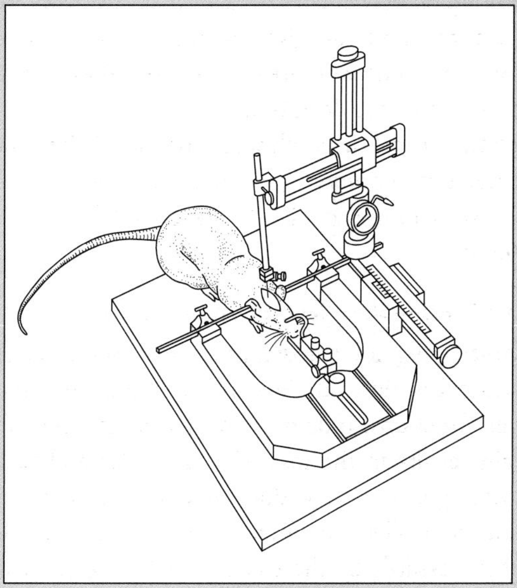

The stereotaxic map is a three-dimensional drawing of the brain on which the position of the various structures is marked. Measurements are given of their position relative to particular seams in the skull where bones have joined together during development.

The animal can be put into the apparatus, the skull exposed, and a needle inserted into the correct site in the brain with the use of the map, thus allowing a precise lesion to be carried out. This method has been used to identify the different areas of the brain involved in different behaviours. For example, different parts of the hypothalamus are involved in eating and drinking behaviour.

In humans, the method has been used surgically to eliminate some of the excessive trembling that occurs in Parkinson's disease. The area which is malfunctioning can be located, and then burnt out using lasers or radioactive rods. Another example is the commisurotomy, mentioned above.

Research using these techniques is useful in pin-pointing specific areas involved in various behaviours. However, the use of animals in many studies means that findings must be regarded with caution. There is also a problem with the interpretation of findings, in that areas being investigated may simply be part of the pathway that co-ordinates behaviour, rather than being the prime organiser. In fact it seems likely that brain areas are so interconnected and behaviour so complex that no one area can be considered to be responsible for any particular behaviour.

Electrical recording and stimulation studies

Another group of methods are those which rely on the electrical nature of communication in the nervous system. By recording or stimulating this communication, it is possible to explore the functions of different areas of the cortex.

Electrodes can be used in two different ways. One possibility is to present a stimulus, and record, amplify and display visually the activity of the nerve cells which respond to it. This method was used by Hubel and Wiesel (1962) who implanted microelectrodes in single cells in the visual cortex of an anaesthetised cat, and were able to show the existence of cortical cells which respond to patterns of light falling on the retina.

Alternatively, the electrodes can be used to stimulate the nerve cells in the brain by passing an electric current through them. This is known as **electrical stimulation of the brain** or **ESB**. The effects which this has on behaviour can then be observed. This approach was used by Olds and Milner (1954) in their study of the pleasure centres of the brain:

Box C: Olds and Milner (1954)

Procedure: Olds and Milner were investigating the effects of electrical stimulation of a region of the brain called the **reticular formation,** which is involved in arousal and sleep. They accidentally inserted the electrode into a different part of the brain, with the result that the animal kept returning to the area of the cage where it had received the stimulation, evidently looking for more. They then devised a system whereby the rats could administer the electric shocks themselves, known as **self-stimulation.**

Results: Rats would stimulate themselves in this way more than 700 times an hour. The area of the brain responsible for this behaviour is the **medial forebrain bundle,** a bundle of nerve fibres which passes through the lateral part of the **hypothalamus.**

Conclusion: ESB was a useful technique for identifying the function of this area of the brain, known as the pleasure centre.

As an extension of the electrical techniques already discussed, **electrical recordings** can be made of the electrical activity of the brain by means of electrodes attached with electrode jelly to the surface of the scalp. This technique was discovered by Caton in 1875 (Caton, 1977), who tried it out on animals. Berger applied it to humans and called it the **electroencephalogram** or **EEG**.

The electrodes can detect activity in the underlying brain cells, which is then amplified and either drawn on paper or displayed on a computer:

Figure 14: an EEG record

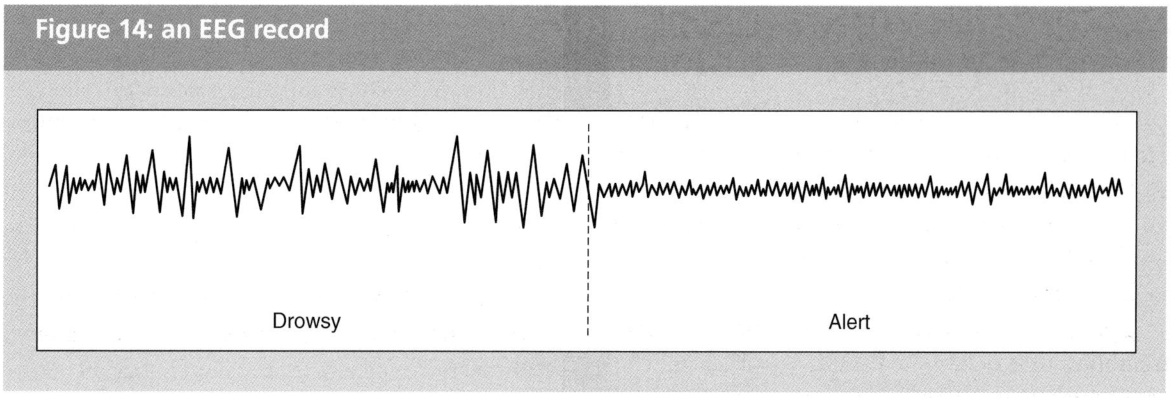

The resulting EEG pattern is termed **synchronised** when the individual is asleep, but not dreaming, or drowsy. In these circumstances, it is made up of waves of a particular **amplitude** (height) and **frequency** (measured in the number of waves per second). When people are awake, aroused, or asleep and dreaming, the EEG becomes **desynchronised**. It is irregular in activity and no clear wave form can be seen.

However, there are also some limitations to electrical techniques. For example, the use of microelectrode recording to map the responses of individual cells in the cortex is a very slow way to build up a picture of how the brain operates. Stimulation techniques are also limited in that they do not necessarily elicit the same behaviour when used on different occasions. Moreover, electrical stimulation cannot tell us that a particular part of the brain *initiates* a particular behaviour or experience. It can also give the impression that each behaviour is only determined by one area of the cortex, which as we shall see is not in fact the case.

Chemical techniques

As well as electrical activity, the brain communicates by chemical means, so it is possible either to record this information or to interfere with it, and then look for links with behaviour.

Stimulation techniques can involve the use of a **micropipette** which delivers drugs or other chemicals through a cannula, a thin glass tube inserted into the brain at the required site. Different drugs or neurotransmitters can be delivered through this, to see which chemicals the neurons in that particular area respond to, and observe the behavioural effects of the drugs. Radioactive chemicals can also be introduced, and their uptake by different areas of the brain measured after the animal has carried out a particular behaviour. For example, if glucose were introduced this technique would show which areas of the brain have used glucose and were therefore active during the behaviour. This is the principle on which the PET scanner works, described in the section on brain scanning techniques. Other methods of introducing chemicals are by mouth, or by injection into the bloodstream.

As well as stimulation by chemicals, it is possible to measure responses using chemical analyses. For example, cerebrospinal fluid can be analysed to detect the effect of drugs on neurotransmitter levels. The fluid collected is analysed by **high-precision liquid chromatography (HPLC)**, a very sensitive method of detecting the presence of transmitter substances. For example, this has shown that many addictive drugs, such as cocaine, cause the neurotransmitter dopamine to be released in certain parts of the brain known as **reward pathways**, which is why they are so pleasurable to take. Chemical techniques such as these are useful, but again can be criticised for being based on animal research.

Activity 13: cortical function: the classic techniques

Complete the gaps in this passage using one of the items given below. Each should be used only once:

dead	**neurotransmitters**
lesioning	**clinical**
chemical	**cerebrospinal fluid**
ablation	**stereotaxic**
macroelectrodes	**micropipette**
stimulate	**inflammation**

Anatomical techniques are based on the .... brain, which can be examined under the microscope.

.... studies look at the effects of brain damage which has been caused for non-experimental reasons. .... and .... studies, on the other hand, are carried out exclusively on animals, and involve deliberate destruction of parts of the brain, often using a .... apparatus.

Electrical techniques record electrical activity or .... the brain.

.... techniques either deliver drugs (sometimes via a ....) into the brain, or analyse extracts such as .... for the presence of ....

When you have finished, see the notes on page 53.

Brain scanning techniques

These techniques all rely on the enormous calculating power of modern computers, which can generate pictures of slices of the brain from radiation either passing through or coming from the brain. For this reason, they are known also as **computed tomographies**. The name 'tomography' comes from the Greek 'tomos', meaning 'slice', and 'graphein' meaning 'to draw'.

As well as being ethically more sound than some of the classic techniques, and therefore able to be carried out on human beings, brain scans have the advantage of allowing us to examine the function of different areas of the cortex much more directly than was previously possible.

The earliest technique was the **X-ray**, which relies on the principle that dense material such as bone absorbs the rays, and this makes bones show up on a photographic plate. The brain is not dense enough to do this unless a dye is injected into the bloodstream to make it more visible, a technique known as an **angiogram**. This has been used to show if the blood supply has been blocked or diverted to one side (for example, as the result of the growth of a tumour), but gives little other information.

Computerised axial tomography (CAT) scans

Figure 15: a computerised axial tomography (CAT) scanner

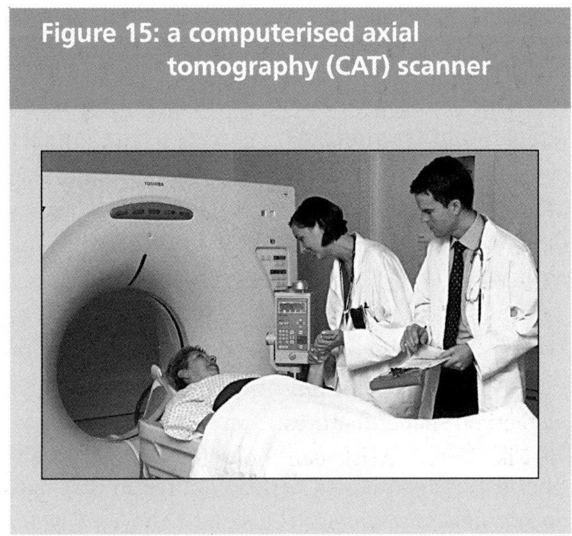

In the 1970s, **CAT scans** were introduced. As shown in figure 15, the person being tested lies with their head inside a device shaped like a doughnut. This contains an X-ray transmitter and detector on opposite sides of the head. X-rays are passed through the head from front to back. The ring is moved round so that the head can be scanned from all angles, and then up and down, so that different sections of the head can be taken. The major limitation of CAT scans is that they can only give structural information. A further limitation is that sections can only be taken in the horizontal plane, but these can be used to build up a three-dimensional picture and show where damage has occurred to structures.

Figure 16: how a CAT scanner works

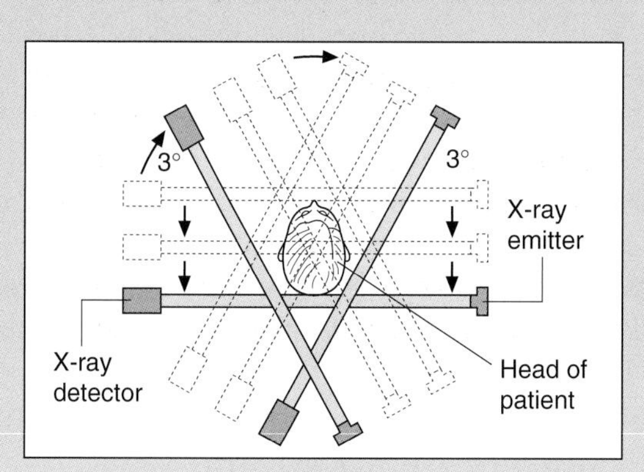

Magnetic resonance imaging (MRI) and functional magnetic resonance imaging (fMRI)

MRI uses a similar principle to CAT, but passes a magnetic field through the head instead of X-rays. This picks up the activity of hydrogen molecules, which are present in different brain tissues to different degrees. Again, it only shows structures, but it can take sections in planes other than the horizontal, and these sections can be used to build up a 3D image. It is more sensitive and gives much sharper pictures with more detail, so it is capable of detecting smaller features.

Like CAT, MRI can only tell us about the structure of the brain. However, **fMRI** can give details of brain activity by assessing changes in blood flow. It can locate the activity precisely within 1–2 mm, and updates itself second by second. Apart from the claustrophobia occasionally induced by having the whole body put inside an 11-ton magnet, the only disadvantage of fMRI is that there is a one-second delay in reporting activity in the cortex.

Positron emission tomography (PET) and Single positron emission computerised tomography (SPECT)

PET allows functioning to be monitored by assessing metabolic activity in different parts of the brain. Radioactive glucose is injected or radioactive oxygen is inhaled while the individual is in a scanner. Occasional exposure to these small amounts of radioactive chemicals is not considered to be harmful. They emit particles called **positrons**, which can be detected by the scanner, and the levels in different parts of the brain are shown on a computer image as differences in colour. Positrons are taken up most by the areas of the cortex which are metabolically the most active, and these areas will generally be displayed by the computer as being red or white:

Figure 17: PET scans of (top) a normal brain and (bottom) the brain of a schizophrenic

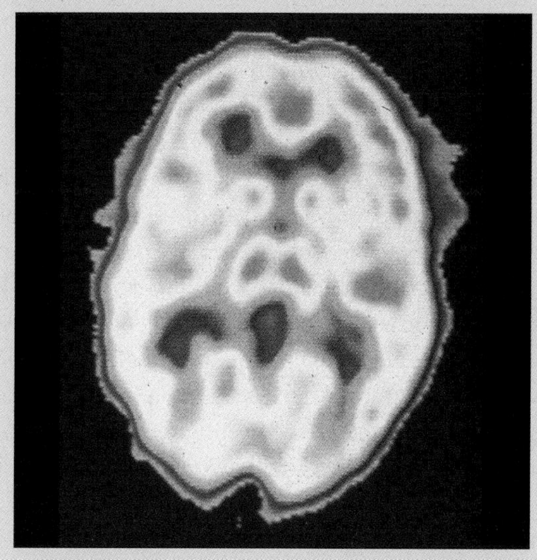

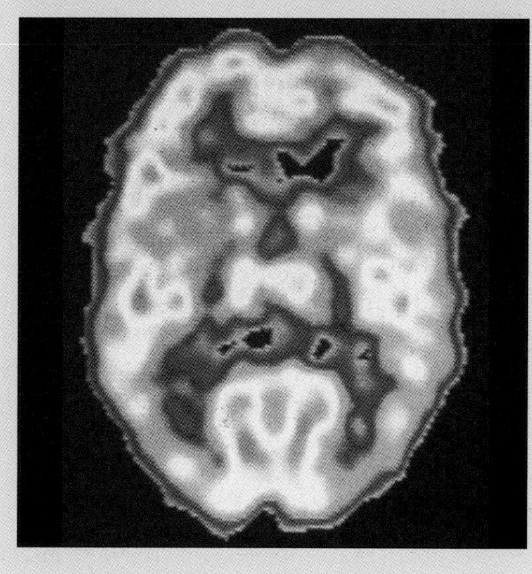

This technique permits the activity of different areas of the brain to be monitored while people are performing different tasks, such as speaking, or solving problems. Apart from the use of radioactive materials, one disadvantage of PET is that it is quite slow. Using radioactive oxygen, scans can be updated every 40 seconds, whilst glucose requires 40 minutes (Harding, 1993).

A more recent development is **SPECT**. Like PET, it is rather slow, and can only provide pictures of the working brain at intervals of 0.25–10 seconds.

Magnetoencephalogram (MEG)

MEG picks up the weak magnetic field that results from electrical activity in the brain. Both the strength and area of origin of the magnetic field can be measured. MEG scanners use helmets containing as many as 128 **SQUIDS (superconducting quantum interference devices)** to measure magnetic changes around and inside the head. In this way, an image of the functioning brain can be produced. MEG has to operate in a magnetically shielded room to reduce interference and is therefore not a very portable system. A further problem is that magnetic fields can be easily distorted. However, MEG is cheaper than PET or MRI, and is less invasive than PET since it does not require injection or inhalation of radioactive tracers. It also has the advantage of being very rapid, and showing the changes in the brain as they occur.

Activity 14: acronyms

Match each of these acronyms with a description saying what it does:

a ESB — 1. assesses metabolic activity in different parts of the brain
b HPLC — 2. shows patterns of brain waves
c EEG — 3. picks up the magnetic field produced by electrical activity in the brain
d MEG — 4. gives a clear and detailed picture of brain structures
e CAT — 5. detects the presence of neurotransmitter substances
f MRI — 6. shows horizontal sections of the brain
g PET — 7. stimulates the brain electrically

When you have finished, see the notes on page 53.

- The brain can be investigated using **classic** or **brain scanning** techniques.
- **Classic** techniques include **anatomical**, **clinical**, **ablation**, **lesioning**, **electrical** and **chemical** approaches.
- Brain scanning procedures include **CAT**, **MRI**, **fMRI**, **PET**, **SPECT** and **MEG**.
- Major differences in procedures include: the extent to which they are invasive; the amount of detail they show; and how quickly they update themselves.

Localisation of function in the cerebral cortex

The **cortex** is the outer layer of the brain, and it is the area which is most highly developed in humans compared with animals. In appearance it is deeply wrinkled. These wrinkles serve to increase the surface area and allow more active cells to be packed into the available space. The parts of the brain which lie beneath the cortex are known as the **subcortex**.

The cortex is divided from front to back into two symmetrical halves, known as the right and left **hemispheres**. Between the two hemispheres is the longitudinal fissure, but the two remain joined by a mass of nerve fibres known as the **corpus callosum**.

Each hemisphere can also be divided into four **lobes**: the **frontal** lobe (at the front), the **temporal** lobe (at the side); the **occipital** lobe (the lower part at the back) and the **parietal** lobe (the upper part at the back). They are marked off from one another by two deep fissures, the **central** and **lateral fissures**.

One important debate about the cortex centres on the issue of localisation of function. In the days of phrenology, mentioned at the start of this section, it was thought that specific areas of the brain, indicated externally by bumps on the skull, were associated with specific functions, such as language or emotional behaviour.

Figure 18: the four lobes of the left hemisphere

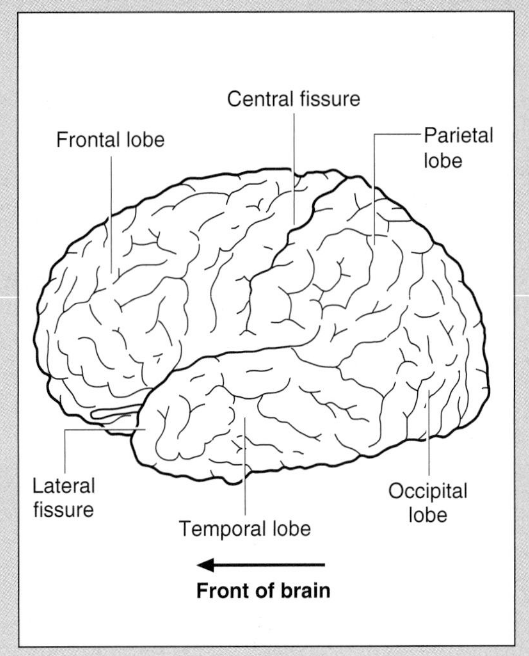

The modern version of this idea argues that distinct areas of the cortex are associated with specific behaviours, i.e. functions are localised. This is also referred to as the **modular** approach. Different parts of the brain are believed to be specialised for different mental capacities, such as memory and language. Each module has its own processes and will only deal with certain types of data. For example, it is argued by some (e.g. Marr, 1982) that the visual system consists of modules which process different aspects of visual information, such as colour or movement.

The alternative to this is the argument that there is very little localisation of function, and the cortex tends to work as a whole. The **law of mass action**, proposed by Lashley (1929), stated that the severity of the effects of cortical lesions depended on the size of the lesion and not its location. The **law of equipotentiality** suggested, in its extreme form, that all areas of the cortex were equally capable of carrying out all functions. However, Lashley himself probably had in mind a weaker form, which is that the cortex as a whole is equipotential for some processes, such as learning or problem-solving (Milner, 1970).

Another principle which is relevant here is the **principle of multiple control**, which suggests that a particular part of the brain may well be involved in many different types of behaviour. For example, the **hypothalamus** is involved in both eating and drinking *and* aggressive behaviour, while **Broca's area**, in the left frontal lobe, is involved in both word production and grammar. A particular behaviour may therefore be produced with the involvement of many different brain areas. This has been shown by PET scans carried out during speech.

Some early research on localisation of function was carried out by Lashley in the 1920s:

Box D: Lashley (1920s)

Procedure: Rats were trained to run through a maze. An area of the brain was then destroyed and they were tested again to see if they could still remember how to get through the maze. Lashley was searching for the **engram**, a memory trace thought to be laid down in the brain during learning.

Results: There did not seem to be any one area which appeared to contain the memory in the way he had expected. The most important determinant of whether the rats could remember the way or not was the amount of cortex destroyed.

Conclusion: These experiments supported the law of mass action. All areas of the cortex were equally involved in learning.

The modern version of the antilocalisation stance is the idea of **distributed functions** (or **connectionism**), which takes the holistic view that the brain functions as a whole. All areas are interconnected, and have multiple tasks to carry out. Information is distributed in networks made up of millions of neurons.

In the following sections, we will be looking at evidence for and against localisation of function by considering research on motor, sensory and association areas of the cortex, and looking at the organisation of memory and language skills in the brain.

Motor and sensory areas

Pioneering early work on the sensory and motor areas of the brain was carried out by Penfield in the 1950s. These areas are shown in figure 19, together with some other areas associated with specific functions:

Figure 19: localisation of function in the left cortex

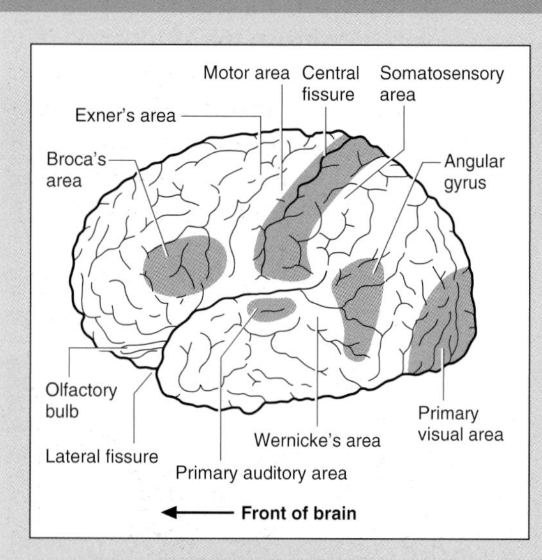

Figure 19 shows only the left cortex. The motor and sensory areas are found on both sides of the brain in all species (including humans) which have a well-developed cortex. They include motor, somatosensory (concerned with sensory input from the skin, i.e. temperature, touch, pain and movement), visual, auditory and olfactory areas. Other areas shown here are only found on one side of the brain. These include **Broca's area** and **Wernicke's area**, which are to do with producing and understanding language, and which we will be discussing later, together with the **angular gyrus**, which is involved in matching the visual form of a word with its sound. The right side of the brain, also has its own specialised functions, including some aspects of music perception and the analysis of complex visual scenes.

Penfield used patients who were waiting for brain surgery to explore the effects of delivering electrical stimulation to different cortical regions. He found that stimulation just in front of the central fissure produced bodily movements. For example, stimulation on the left side of the brain would cause a movement of the right leg. This suggests that each hemisphere controls the opposite side of the body, known as **contralateral representation**:

Figure 20: contralateral system

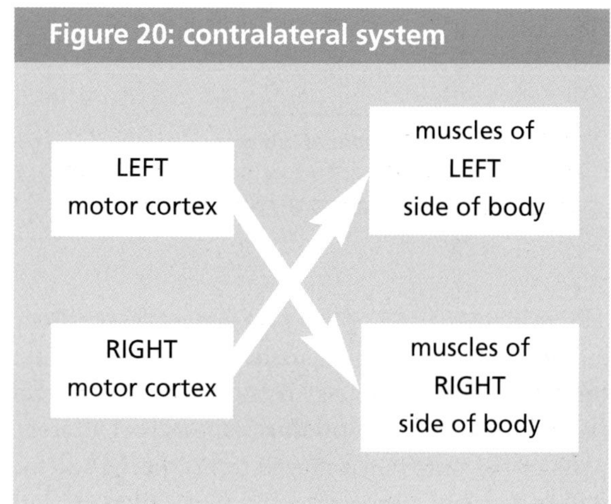

He also found that the body is represented upside down in the brain, so that stimulation near the top of the head produced movement of the lower body, and stimulation lower in this motor area led to movement of the upper body (see figure 21).

Another important finding was that some parts of the body had large areas of the brain devoted to them, while others only had small representations. These differences did not relate, as you might expect, to differences in the size of the body parts. They were instead found to depend on the amount of control, co-ordination and sensitivity needed. For example, the fingers and mouth have large cortical representations.

Figure 21: representation of different body parts in the motor cortex

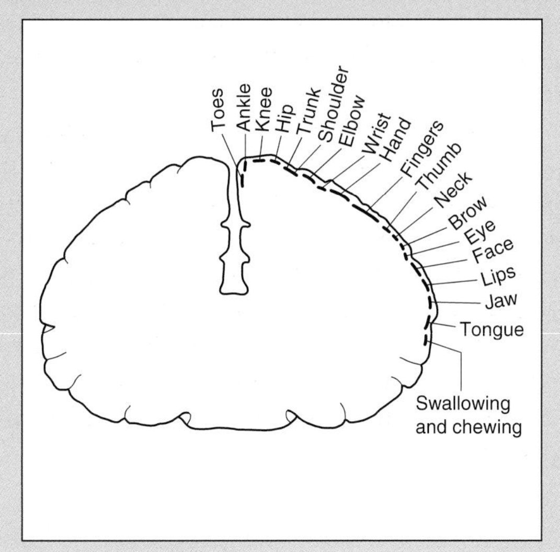

Although this **motor area** is not responsible for making the decision to move, it is responsible for carrying out commands and for ensuring smooth movement, so fine control will be lost if it is damaged.

The **primary sensory areas** of the cortex deal with incoming messages rather than outgoing ones. Several different areas have been identified, dealing with information from different senses.

The **somatosensory area**, shown in figure 22, is to the rear of the central fissure in the parietal lobe. It deals with information from the bodily senses and from the taste receptors. As in the motor areas, the information received comes from the opposite side of the body. The body is represented upside down, so the face is lower and the legs are higher in the cortex.

As figure 22 shows, the size of the area devoted to a particular bodily region again depends on sensitivity and use. For example, Robertson (1995) found that people who use Braille to read have larger cortical areas for some fingertips than normally sighted people. From this, it is possible to conclude that allocation of space within the somatosensory cortex is flexible; parts of the body which are used more for sensory activities will expand their cortical areas. This flexibility is known as **plasticity**.

Damage to the primary sensory areas of the cortex can lead to a variety of problems, such as the inability to tell the difference between different temperatures.

The **primary auditory area** is in the temporal lobe beside the lateral fissure. It receives input from the ear via the auditory nerve and a subcortical structure called the **thalamus**. When it is stimulated electrically, sounds will be reported, the nature of which will depend on the precise area stimulated. Damage to the left auditory cortex tends to result in problems in identifying and naming sounds, while damage to the right auditory cortex leads more to difficulties with the perception of pitch, rhythm and melody.

Hearing is a **partially-crossed system**. It is partly **contralateral**, i.e. each hemisphere receives input from the ear on the opposite side of the body, and partly **ipsilateral**, i.e. some information is dealt with by the hemisphere on the same side as the ear. Around 90% of auditory information is

Figure 22: representation of different body parts in the sensory cortex

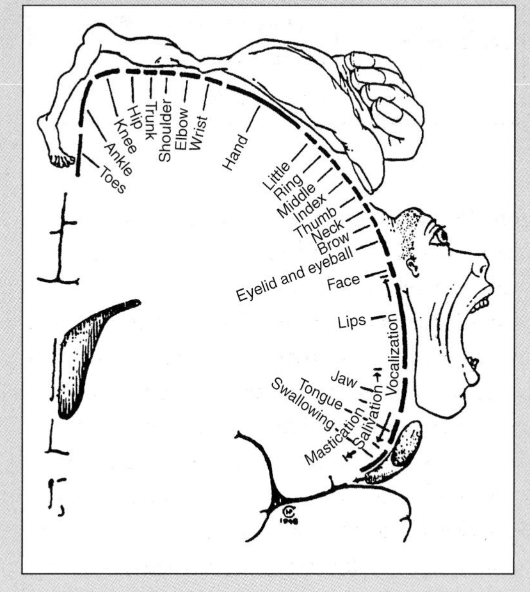

processed contralaterally, with the remaining 10% being processed ipsilaterally:

Figure 23: partially-crossed system

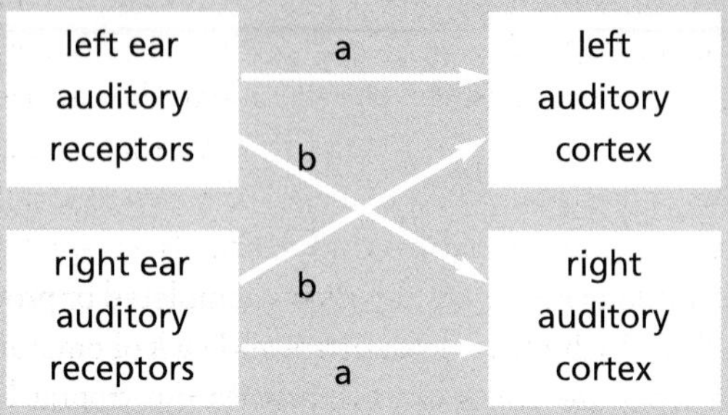

left ear auditory receptors — a → left auditory cortex
left ear auditory receptors — b → right auditory cortex
right ear auditory receptors — b → left auditory cortex
right ear auditory receptors — a → right auditory cortex

a = ipsilateral b = contralateral

The **primary visual area** is at the back of the occipital lobe, and receives input from the eyes via the optic nerve. Each hemisphere deals with information from the same side of each eye, e.g. information from the right side of each eye is passed to the right hemisphere. The visual system, then, shows the same partial crossing as the auditory system. This means that damage to the primary visual area can cause loss of sight on just one side of the visual field, or a hole in vision. Equally, loss of one eye means that vision can still be quite good, as information will go to both hemispheres.

Figure 24: partial crossing in the visual system

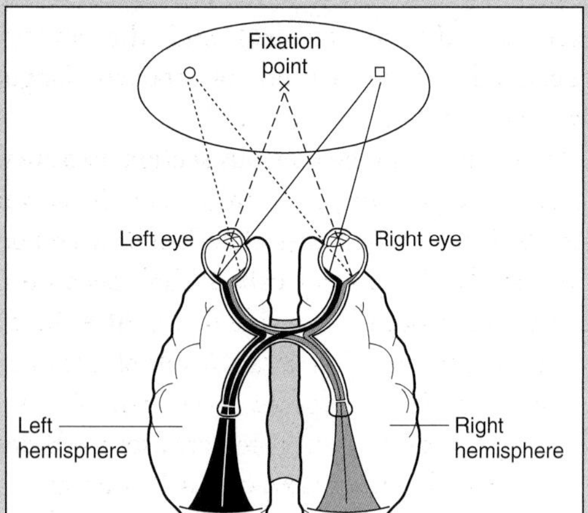

Fixation point
Left eye
Right eye
Left hemisphere
Right hemisphere

Association areas

Each of the sensory areas mentioned above has an association area next to it, to which it sends information. Motor association areas, by contrast, are areas adjacent to the motor area which send information to the motor area.

Motor association areas deal with planning and carrying out movements as a result of the information they receive. These orders are then dealt with by the primary motor area. For example, the left parietal lobe contains an area which helps us to follow the movements we make. Damage to this area results in severe difficulties in drawing.

The sensory association areas lie alongside the primary sensory areas. The **somatosensory association area** operates to provide awareness of the body through the skin. If it is damaged, a condition called **sensory neglect** results (Halligan, 1995), which leads the individual to ignore one side of the body. For example, when shaving only one side of the face will be shaved:

Box E: Halligan (1995)

Procedure: Patients with right hemisphere damage to the somatosensory association area were asked to produce drawings. They were also asked questions about pictures, and to imagine and report a view from a building when they were facing towards it and then facing away from it.

Results: Their drawings showed only the right side of what they were drawing, e.g. the right half of a flower with no corresponding left side. When they were shown a picture of a burning house, the flames were not reported if they were shown on only the left side of the house. However, patients reported a preference for living in a house that was identical, except that it was not on fire! When asked to imagine a building, they did not report details on the left of the building when they imagined they were facing it. However, when facing away from it, they reported

details from the left side, in spite of having left them out of their previous description.
Conclusion: Information from the left side reaches the brain, but cannot always be used. This may be because it cannot enter conscious awareness.

The **auditory association area** is in the posterior part of the occipital lobes and deals with encoding and decoding sound in order to make sense of it. Damage to this part of the left hemisphere can lead to an inability to understand and to produce spoken language, while damage to the right leads to an inability to recognise rhythms.

There are **visual association areas** in the temporal, parietal and occipital lobes. These carry out higher-level visual processes, such as the ability to recognise faces and objects, and distinguish an object from its background. Damage to these areas can cause a variety of difficulties associated with visual recognition, which are known as **visual agnosias**. The famous case reported by Oliver Sacks (1985) of the man who mistook his wife's head for a hat is an example of a visual agnosia. Other patients with damage to these areas find it difficult to integrate details into a whole object, as seen in drawings by patients with this kind of damage, and produce drawings which contain all the correct elements but in a disjointed form.

Other areas on the borders between the different association areas combine information from different sensory modalities, linking sight, sound, taste, smell etc. to give a complete representation of a scene.

Overall, then, different functions are carried out by different lobes of the brain. For example, motor responses are dealt with by the frontal lobes, and vision is dealt with by the occipital lobes. Hearing is dealt with by the temporal lobes, and somesthetic senses (i.e. somatosensory input) and movement are dealt with by the parietal lobes.

Obviously we carry out a great many other activities not yet mentioned, such as thinking and remembering. Where in the brain do these take place?

The frontal lobes appear to play an important part in planning, decision-making and creativity. When they are damaged, people become impulsive, with little thought for the future and an inability to delay rewards. You will remember that in the case of Phineas Gage, this was the area which was damaged, and his behaviour after the accident showed these kinds of changes. A phenomenon called **perseveration** has also been noted, when people will carry on with tasks or with methods of problem-solving long after they have been completed or proved useless. Inability to concentrate and lack of emotional reactivity are also seen. Damage to the frontal lobe was found by Broca (1861) to be associated with loss of the ability to produce language.

The temporal lobes are involved in memory and learning. Penfield (1969) found that stimulation in some areas led to reliving a past experience. Although it is difficult to verify such reports, other research has looked at the effects of removal of parts of the temporal lobes. This has been carried out in animals and humans, e.g. tumour and epilepsy patients. It has been found that this produces severe impairment of the ability to form new memories. This is now known to be due to the removal of the **hippocampus**, a structure embedded in the temporal lobes which seems to serve as a 'printing press' for new memories.

Other effects of damage to the temporal lobes include the impairment of emotional responses (also possibly due to damage to another subcortical area called the **limbic system**) and the ability to understand either written or spoken language (Wernicke, 1874).

As mentioned in the previous section, two areas of the cortex appear to play a major part in language skills. In 1861, French physician Paul Broca reported a case study of a patient called 'Tan', because that was the only word he was able to say. After he died, an autopsy revealed that as the result of a stroke, he had suffered damage to the lower part of the left frontal lobe. Observation of similar cases led Broca to propose that this area, now called Broca's area and shown in figure 19, was responsible for the *production* of spoken language; however, *understanding* of speech did not seem to be impaired.

The problem suffered by Tan was termed **expressive aphasia**. Aphasia refers to disorders in the comprehension or production of speech.

The role of Broca's area in language has been demonstrated in studies of patients who suffer damage to this part of the cortex. This kind of damage may lead to the patient suffering from **Broca's aphasia**, discussed in detail in the section on language disorders later in this chapter.

In 1874, Carl Wernicke reported his research on patients who appeared to be able to speak fluently – although their speech often made little sense – but were unable to understand the speech of others. This was termed **receptive aphasia**, and seemed to be associated with damage to the top of the left temporal lobe, now called **Wernicke's area** (see figure 19).

The key theory of language which links the activities of Broca's area and Wernicke's area is known as the **Wernicke–Geschwind theory**:

Box F: the Wernicke–Geschwind theory

The processes involved in language: Speech is heard and passed to the auditory cortex via the auditory nerve. It then goes to Wernicke's area, where the sounds are analysed, and the words identified and analysed for meaning. When speech is being produced, the motor plans for how to say words are activated in Broca's area. These are passed to the motor cortex, and converted to instructions to the speech muscles so that the words can be said.

Reading involves the visual system sending information to the **visual cortex**, and these visual patterns then have to be identified as particular words. The area responsible for this is the angular gyrus (see figure 19) which assembles visual word patterns. These are then transmitted to Wernicke's area nearby for comprehension.

Activity 15: terms in localisation of function

What is:

a contralateral representation
b ipsilateral representation
c sensory neglect
d perseveration
e Broca's area
f Wernicke's area?

Look back over the previous section to check your answers.

Activity 16: identifying areas of the cortex

On this diagram, label these areas:

Broca's area	**Wernicke's area**
angular gyrus	**motor area**
visual area	**somatosensory area**
occipital lobe	**parietal lobe**
temporal lobe	**frontal lobe**

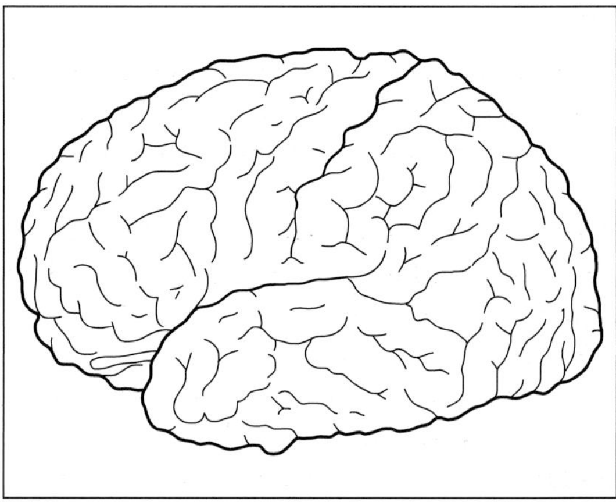

Check your work by looking back at through this section.

In conclusion, there is some evidence that particular areas of the cortex may have key roles in the organisation of some behaviours. However, other behaviours are more difficult to pinpoint, as shown by Lashley. Even where there is localisation, it is not very precise, and may involve relatively widespread areas.

One way of resolving this is by looking at the structure of the cortex more closely. The cortex consists of layers of cells which are arranged in columns (Hubel and Wiesel, 1962). According to Milner (1970), the lateral interconnections between columns are not very important in normal functioning. What is more relevant in connecting columns are axons which leave the cortex and pass through the underlying white matter before returning to another part of the cortex, creating a distributed network which links modules. This fits well with what is believed to be the most likely arrangement for visual processing.

Humphreys *et al.* (1992) pointed out that a system which combines partial information from different processing modules may well be the best way of dealing with the input received. Clearly, as shown by scanning studies, even the most simple activities involve a wide range of interconnected areas. A useful analogy offered by Ramachandran and Blakeslee (1999) is that of a television programme, which cannot be localised to any one part of the television.

- The **cortex** is divided into right and left cerebral **hemispheres**, each of which is divided into four **lobes**: **frontal**, **temporal**, **parietal** and **occipital**.
- There has been a major debate about whether functions are **localised** in different cortical areas (**modular**) or whether they are **distributed**.
- Primary **motor** and **sensory** areas have been located in different lobes, each of which has an **association area** linked with it.
- **Planning**, **decision-making** and some aspects of **language** are the responsibility of the **frontal lobes**. **Memory**, **emotionality** and other aspects of **language** are dealt with by the **temporal lobes**.
- The **Wernicke–Geschwind** model of language explains the production and comprehension of language with reference to **Broca's area**, **Wernicke's area** and the **angular gyrus**.
- Some areas of the cortex are specialised for paticular functions, but localisation is not very precise. Any one function may involve separate areas.

The fight-or-flight response

In this section we will be looking in a bit more detail at the functioning of the ANS, and in particular at its role in what Cannon (1927) has termed **fight or flight**, i.e. a behavioural response to stress. When we are exposed to a stressful situation, there are bodily changes involving the sympathetic division of the ANS which prepare us to respond to it, either by running away or by fighting back.

This response can be understood in evolutionary terms. Early in our evolutionary history, when a person was under stress (such as being faced by a predator, or having a stranger encroaching on his territory) only two choices were available: to fight off the attack or to run away. The physiological boost provided by activity of the sympathetic nervous system would facilitate either of these responses. We have the same autonomic response as our distant ancestors, even though this response is now often less useful (and can even be detrimental to health) since most of the stressful events and situations which we encounter cannot easily be resolved by the physical response of fight or flight, but need to be responded to in a more relevant way.

Selye (1956) proposed that there is a similar pattern of physiological response to stressors, irrespective of the nature of the particular stressor. He came to this conclusion on the basis of studies of rats. They were exposed to extreme cold, fatigue, electric shocks and surgical trauma, and in each case the physiological response was the same, which led him to believe that there was a non-specific reaction of the body to any kind of damage. He called this the **general adaptation syndrome (GAS)**. It is also known as the **pituitary–adrenal stress syndrome**, since the pituitary and adrenal glands are involved in the stress response. Selye described three stages of the stress response: the **alarm reaction**, the **resistance** stage and **exhaustion**.

The **alarm reaction** is concerned with the physiological changes associated with arousal. The first part of this reaction is the **shock phase**, an immediate reaction to a stressor. The person experiences tachycardia (an abnormally rapid heartbeat), and both temperature and blood pressure are lowered. This is followed by the **countershock phase**, as the body marshals defensive forces against the stressor. The mechanisms of the alarm reaction centre on the **ANS** and the **pituitary gland**.

As we saw earlier, the ANS regulates many aspects of our functioning over which we do not need to have conscious control, such as breathing and digestion. It controls a number of internal organs, for example, the heart muscle and the gut, and a number of glands, such as the salivary and adrenal glands. The sympathetic branch of the ANS is involved in the alarm reaction. In a situation of possible threat, your body needs to prepare itself for action, so high levels of sympathetic activity help to cope with the demands of the situation by increasing your heart rate and the blood supply to your muscles.

The main system involved in the stress response is called the **hypothalamic–pituitary–adrenal axis**, and it is highly sensitive to environmental change. We will look briefly at the elements which go to make up this system.

The **hypothalamus** plays a central role in the stress reaction. It is a small structure in the forebrain, just above the pituitary gland, to which it is connected by a structure called the **infundibulum**. Through this connection, it controls the secretion of all the hormones released by the pituitary gland. It controls ANS centres in the brainstem, which in turn control the ANS. It is particularly involved in states of arousal, and for this reason is important in the stress response.

We have two **adrenal glands**, two small glands above the kidneys, each of which is made up of the **adrenal medulla** and the **adrenal cortex**. The **pituitary gland**, a gland at the base of the brain, controls the adrenal cortex. When the adrenal cortex is stimulated by the pituitary hormone **ACTH (adrenocorticotrophic hormone)**, it secretes **corticosteroids** into the bloodstream. Even very mild stimuli, if they are unexpected, can trigger the release of ACTH, and set this process in motion. There are many different corticosteroids, but those relevant to stress are the **glucocorticoids**, e.g. cortisone and hydrocortisone. These substances facilitate the conversion of stored fat and protein into energy. They also suppress the body's **immune system**.

The ANS controls the **adrenal medulla**. When it is stimulated, the adrenal medulla releases two hormones into the bloodstream, **adrenaline** and **noradrenaline**. They increase heart rate, blood pressure and sweat gland activity. They also mobilise fat reserves, in preparation for energy expenditure, so they prolong the effects of SNS arousal.

Activity 17: the stress reaction

Use the words from this list to complete this diagram and show the processes involved in the stress response:

ACTH, adrenaline, blood pressure, cortex, corticosteroids, energy, heart rate, hypothalamus, immune, medulla, noradrenaline, pituitary, stressor, sweat gland activity, sympathetic

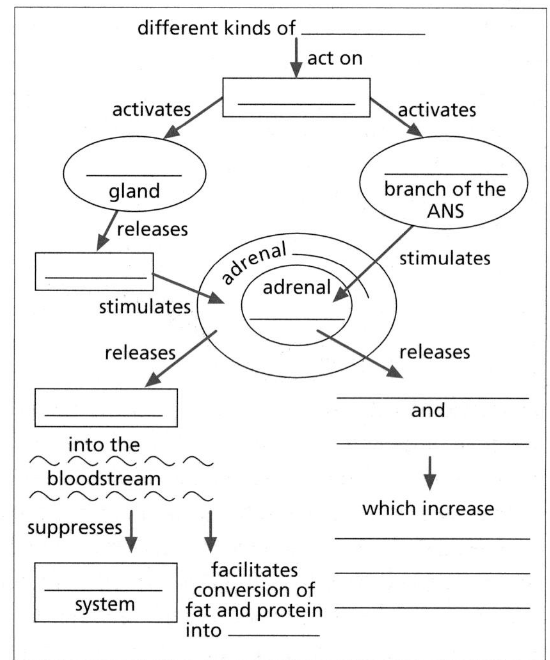

The overall effect of the alarm reaction is to make the body more alert and active.

The effects of the alarm reaction include **pupil dilation**, **deeper breathing**, a **faster heartbeat**, and **digestive changes** (where sugar metabolism is speeded up, but not the processing of foods like proteins and fats which take longer to work their way through the digestive system). The spleen releases stored red blood cells.

Activity 18: the alarm reaction and fight-or-flight

If you were exposed to physical threat, how would these elements of the alarm reaction help you to produce a fight-or-flight response?

a pupil dilation
b deeper breathing
c faster heartbeat
d conversion of stored fat and protein
e release of red blood cells

When you have finished, see the notes on page ??.

As well as these changes, additional **blood platelets** are produced. These help clotting, and so prepare the body to repair physical damage. The brain produces neurotransmitters called **endorphins**, which block out the immediate feelings of pain. **Sweating** helps to cool down the body. All these contribute to an effective fight-or-flight response. The physiological response to stress in the alarm reaction can be assessed by measuring the levels of corticosteroids and adrenaline in the urine.

The pattern of physiological activity in the fight-or-flight response cannot be maintained for long, and the body moves into the **resistance stage**. In this stage of the stress response, the body starts to recover from the alarm reaction. There is full adaptation to the stressor, during which symptoms improve or disappear altogether. There is a decrease in the activity of the sympathetic branch of the ANS, with a lower output of adrenaline and noradrenaline. However, there is still an increase in output from the adrenal cortex. Blood sugar levels, which have been raised during the alarm reaction, return to normal. If the stressor is removed, the body reverts to normal functioning, though increased hormone levels persist for some time. However, there is little likelihood of there being any permanent physiological damage.

If the stressor is not removed, the parasympathetic branch of the ANS acts to return the functioning of internal organs, such as the heart, to normal. However, while the body is attempting to defend itself against stressors, it is only partially successful. Cell repair is inhibited, and the immune system may be damaged, increasing the likelihood of infection and a lowered ability to cope with physical damage. If there is a second stressor, resistance is lower, and the final (exhaustion) stage is reached sooner (see figure 25).

Figure 25: the effects of a second stressor

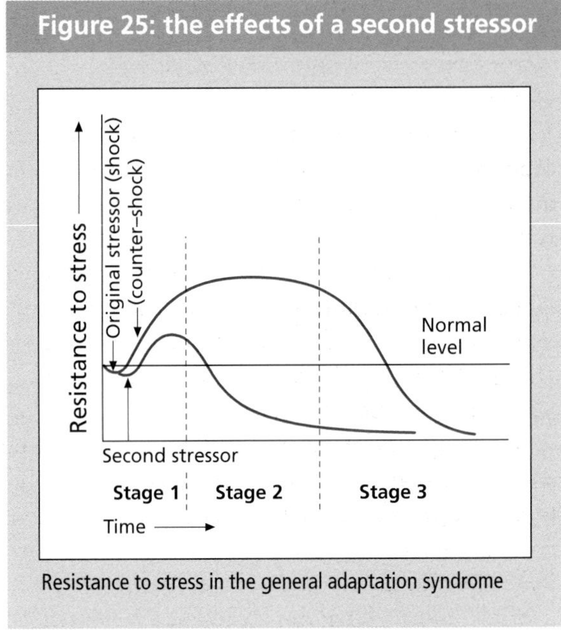

Resistance to stress in the general adaptation syndrome

If the stressor is severe, and experienced over a prolonged period of time, the final stage of **exhaustion** follows. Heart rate and blood pressure return to apparently normal levels, but the excessive levels of adrenaline and noradrenaline in the bloodstream cause the adrenal glands to stop functioning properly. Body tissue and internal organs are damaged. Even mild sources of additional stress cause an immediate and strong reaction. Symptoms reappear, and if stress continues, death may be the result.

Solomon (1969) found that at this stage resistance to illness is lowered. People have a tendency to fatigue, and feel generally weak and unwell. These effects are linked to the suppression of the immune system, discussed earlier. It is in this stage that what Selye called **diseases of adaptation** occur, such as ulcers and coronary heart disease (CHD). In the long term, the individual will suffer from **burnout**, where they are no longer capable of functioning adequately.

Figure 26: the stages of Selye's GAS

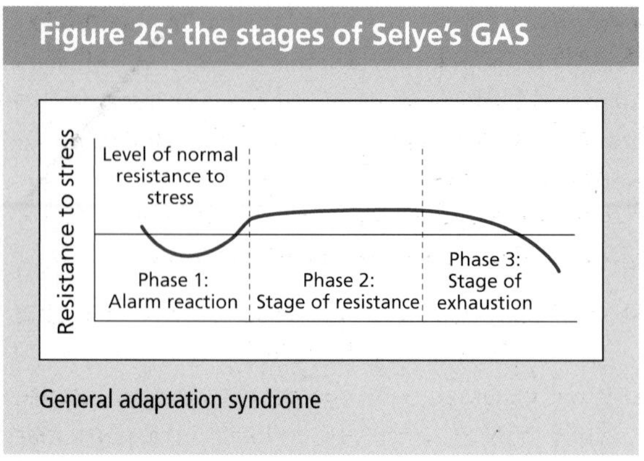

General adaptation syndrome

Selye's model is a useful guide to the physiological response to stressors. However, it was developed as the result of work with non-human animals, so it does not take into account psychological factors in the stress response. For example, people are likely to make a cognitive appraisal of a stressful situation – to what extent is this situation threatening? how able am I to cope? – which will affect their response.

- Selye proposed the **GAS** as a non-specific physiological response to stress of any kind. There are three stages: the **alarm reaction**, the **resistance stage** and the **exhaustion stage**.
- The **alarm reaction** involves the **hypothalamus**, the **pituitary gland** and the **adrenal glands**. It prepares the body for **fight-or-flight**.
- Long term exposure to a stressor leads to **physiological damage**, including a damaged **immune system**. This stage is associated with the development of **diseases of adaptation**. It can lead to **burnout**.

The genetic basis of behaviour

Genetics is another area of interest to biopsycholgists. Physical characteristics (such as eye colour) and some physical disorders (such as cystic fibrosis) can be passed on through the genes from parent to child. Biopsychologists have investigated the possibility that psychological characteristics (such as intelligence) and mental illnesses (such as schizophrenia) can be inherited in the same way. Before looking at this possibility, we will look briefly at the role of genes in development.

The set of genetic instructions which make up an organism is called its **genotype**. However, the genotype can express itself in different ways depending on the characteristics of the environment within which development takes place. The end result of a genotype's expression within a particular environment is called the **phenotype**. Different phenotypes can therefore develop from the same genotype if they develop within different environments. For example, if identical twins (two genetically identical organisms) were to be raised, one in an environment where food was plentiful and one in an environment where food was scarce, the phenotype (the body size which developed) could differ quite considerably.

While it is the genotype, then, which is passed on in reproduction, both genes and environment have a part to play in development. Psychologists have been interested in the relative influence of these factors on psychological development. We will look first at the methods used in their investigations, before turning to the specific topics of schizophrenia and intelligence.

Methods in investigating genetic influence on psychological characteristics

Long before genetics was established as a science, people manipulated the genotypical characteristics of domestic animals to produce animals with desirable characteristics, a process known as **selective breeding**. Various breeds of dog – for example hunting dogs, such as the spaniel and working dogs, such as sheepdogs – were selectively bred using individuals with particular physical and behavioural characteristics which would make them well adapted for the purposes for which they were required.

Activity 19: selective breeding

What kinds of characteristics would be desirable in:

a a racehorse and

b a horse for farmwork?

You will need to think of both physical and behavioural characteristics.

When you have finished, see the nots on page 53.

This is not a method which is available for studying human genetics, however, so rather more indirect methods have been adopted: family studies, adoption studies and twin studies.

Family studies look at the incidence of a particular characteristic within families. If it has a genetic basis, it would be expected that if one member of a family has the characteristic, other members are also more likely than unrelated people to have it, particularly if they are close relatives. This approach has been used in establishing the possible genetic basis of mental disorders, and usually relies on interviewing family members about the family, both current and past generations.

Activity 20: family studies

Can you think of any problems with this technique?

Why might we need to be be wary of drawing conclusions, using this method?

When you have finished, see the notes on page 53.

Adoption studies take a different approach. They compare the occurrence of a characteristic in children adopted early in life with its frequency in the biological children or the parents in their new family, and with their birth parents. A high concordance (i.e. agreement) between the occurrence of the characteristic in adopted children and their birth parents would suggest a genetic basis for the characteristic, whereas a high concordance with members of the adopting family would suggest that environmental factors are more important.

Twin studies are a final way in which a possible genetic influence can be investigated. Twins can be **fraternal** (**dizygotic/DZ**: they develop from different fertilised eggs) or **identical** (**monozygotic/MZ:** developing from only one fertilised egg). Fraternal twins share on average 50% of their genes, the same proportion as any brother or sister. Identical twins, as the name suggests, have 100% of their genes in common.

The reasoning behind twin studies is that if one identical twin has a particular characteristic, and the characteristic is genetic, then the other twin must also show it, since they have all their genes in common. In other words, there should be 100% concordance between identical twins. For fraternal twins, however, there should be a much lower concordance rate, approximately 50%, similar to that between brothers and sisters who are not twins. If the environment is important, a low concordance between MZ twins reared apart would be expected.

- Psychologists are interested in the possible **genetic** basis of psychological characteristics.
- What is passed on in the genes is the **genotype**, while how this expressses itself in a particular environment is the **phenotype**. Both genes and environment influence development.
- The **selective breeding** of animals has manipulated the genotype in animals. Research into human characteristics has used **family** studies, **adoption** studies and **twin studies**.

Genetic explanations of schizophrenia

Schizophrenia is a severely disabling mental disorder. It can often be managed by medication, but not cured. The term 'schizophrenia' means 'split mind', because there is a split between the world of the schizophrenic and reality. Symptoms may include thought disorders, for example the belief that thoughts are being put into your head by outside forces, such as aliens or the government; hallucinations, often taking the form of a voice in your head commenting on your behaviour or telling you what to do; and delusions, such as the belief that people are plotting against you.

There is a convincing amount of research that suggests that at least a predisposition to develop schizophrenia is passed on in the genes. The probability of someone developing schizophrenia is one in a hundred. If you have a schizophrenic parent, however, this may rise considerably. Kety *et al.* (1988) found that children with a schizophrenic birth parent were 10 times more likely than average to develop schizophrenia. In a study carried out by Kendler *et al.* (1983), this rose to 18 times more likely.

A longitudinal study looking at adopted children, carried out over a number of years, also supports the idea of a genetic basis for schizophrenia:

Box G: Tienari (1969 onwards)

Procedure: In this study, the **Finnish Adoption Study,** 112 adopted-away children of schizophrenic birth mothers were compared with a matched control group of 135 adopted-away children of non-schizophrenic birth mothers. The age range at the start of the study was five to seven, and all had been separated from their mothers before the age of four.

Results: In a follow-up study reported in 1987, 7% of the index children, compared with 1.5% of the control group, had been diagnosed as schizophrenic.

Conclusion: There is a genetic component to schizophrenia

Twin studies also support the idea of a strong genetic influence. The results of two studies comparing the concordance rates of MZ and DZ twins are shown in box H:

Box H: concordance rates for MZ and DZ twins

	concordance rate	
	MZ twins	*DZ twins*
Gottesman and Shields (1972)	42%	9%
Kendler (1983)	50%	15%

However, although both pieces of research found lower concordance rates between DZ twins than MZ twins, neither study comes close to the concordance rate of 100% for MZ twins which would be expected if the disorder were entirely genetic. Gottesman and Shields (1982) found a 58% concordance rate in monozygotic twins reared apart, which is also much lower than would be expected if the disorder were entirely genetic.

Alternative explanations have also been put forward. Some psychologists have tried to explain schizophrenia in terms of **dysfunctional families**. Bateson *et al.* (1956) suggested that some parents may predispose their children to schizophrenia by giving them conflicting messages. A mother might tell her child to give her a hug, for example, while at the same time telling him when he does so that he is too old to show affection in that way. Bateson argued that as a result of this kind of interaction, for which he used the term **double bind**, children may start to doubt their own understanding and lose their grip on reality.

Laing and Esterson (1964) put forward the **family interaction model**, which also suggests that family members communicating in pathological ways is the cause of the schizophrenia. In their book *Sanity, Madness and the Family*, they described case-studies of eleven families. In each family history, one member of the family was diagnosed as a schizophrenic, and Laing and Esterson suggest that the cause of their schizophrenia was the way in which their family relationships worked. More recently, Norton (1982) found that if parents were communicating poorly, this was a good predictor of the later onset of schizophrenia in their offspring.

However, there is a lack of evidence to support these ideas, and it seems rather harsh to blame families coping with a schizophrenic member when there is no clear-cut evidence that they are in fact responsible for it. There is also the problem of cause and effect when trying to establish a link between the ways in which families function and the development of schizophrenia. Klebanoff (1959), for example, argued that the kinds of behaviour that families show to an affected family member may well be a reasonable response to an unusual child.

Research has shown structural differences between the brains of schizophrenics and controls. MRI studies, e.g. Brown *et al.* (1986), have shown that many schizophrenics have lighter brains with enlarged ventricles, cavities which hold cerebrospinal fluid. It has been suggested that both these neurological abnormalities and schizophrenia are the result of infection by a virus during foetal development:

Box I: Mednick et al. (1988)

Procedure: In 1957, there was a five-week influenza epidemic in Helsinki. The incidence of schizophrenia in people who had been exposed to this virus during their mothers' pregnancy was investigated.

Results: Those exposed during the second trimester of pregnancy were significantly more likely to be schizophrenic than those exposed during the first or third trimesters, or controls.

Conclusion: The second trimester is a crucial time for cortical development. Exposure to the virus at this time could therefore have led to the neurological abnormalities associated with schizophrenia.

However, Seidman (1983) has estimated that only around a quarter of schizophrenics have any form of gross brain abnormality. It is also possible that where such abnormalities have been found, it may be the result of antipsychotic drugs or other as yet unidentified factors.

More recently, Frith (1987) has suggested that schizophrenia should be seen in information-processing terms. Alien control symptoms, for example, are due to faulty monitoring of intentions and plans by the schizophrenic, so that he does not recognise thoughts and behaviours as being self-generated.

As noted earlier in the discussion of genotype and phenotype, genetic and environmental factors both have a part to play in development. Within the field of mental disorders, the relationship between the two is expressed in the **diathesis–stress model**. Diathesis refers to vulnerability to a disorder. This vulnerability can be genetic, or may have come about as the result of earlier life experiences, for example bereavement or abuse. In a vulnerable person, stress may then trigger the disorder. Stress can take the form of a relatively unusual experience, such as being mugged, or a more common experience which involves change in our lives; for example, going away to college or starting work.

In the case of schizophrenia, a completely genetic explanation has not been supported, but it is clear that there is a strong genetic component. It therefore seems likely that people may be genetically predisposed to develop the disorder, but whether in fact they develop it will depend on the amount of stress in their lives.

- Findings from **adoption** and **twin studies** support the idea that the cause of schizophrenia is at least in part **genetic**. There is similar evidence from on-going **prospective studies**.
- Alternative explanations see schizophrenia as arising from **dysfunctional families**, the result of a **viral infection**, or as faulty **information processing**.
- The **diathesis–stress model** incorporates genetic vulnerability and stressors which may trigger the disorder in vulnerable people.

Genetic influences on intelligence

Investigations of intelligence are difficult because of problems in producing a precise definition of what this term means. However, most theorists would agree that it involves abstract reasoning ability, and the ability to cope with novel situations effectively. In psychology, the dominant approach to intelligence has been a **psychometric** one, which takes a quantitative approach, and is interested in the measurement of intelligence using standardised tests, so intelligence can perhaps best be thought of as what these tests measure. Many of them give a score known as a person's **intelligence quotient** or **IQ**, where the average score is 100.

There are differences between children in their performance on intelligence tests. The reasons underlying these differences, however, are in question. Some theorists believe that intelligence is innate, and differences in test performance are therefore the result of genetic variation. Others believe these differences are the result of environmental factors. This is an example of the **nature–nurture debate**. This issue in relation to intelligence raises a wide range of ethical and political issues, such as streaming in schools, and is therefore a key area for discussion.

At the same time, it is important to bear in mind that the question of whether nature or nurture is the more important influence is ultimately rather simplistic, since the two are interlinked. Genetic information, like a plant seed, requires the right environmental conditions to develop; but without the right 'formula' in the genes, the nutrients provided by the environment cannot be fully utilised. What is of interest here is the maximum range of measured intelligence which can be produced from the same genotype, and that different genotypes can produce within the same environment.

Studies have examined the relationship between IQ scores of different family members, to see if more closely related individuals are more similar in IQ. This work originates from Galton's study of 'Hereditary Genius' (1869), in which he investigated the family trees of 415 eminent people. He found that a large proportion of their relatives were also eminent; this was particularly true of closer relatives. From this he argued that genetic factors are important in intelligence.

However, Galton looked at a very narrow range of people who were not representative of the general population. More importantly, it is likely that the families of the eminent men he studied would have had good educational opportunities, and would have known people who could help them to advance in their chosen professions, and so environmental factors played a part in their eminence.

Adoption studies have also been carried out in which the IQs of adopted children are compared with those of their adopted and natural parents. This approach also started with Galton, who compared the progress in life of the adopted 'nephews' of Popes and other Roman Catholic priests with that of the natural sons of eminent men. When the nephews proved to be less successful, he argued that because both groups had similar environmental advantages, their lack of achievement must mean that they lacked the necessary genetic qualities. Therefore he saw intelligence as largely genetic.

There have also been some more recent and better controlled studies than Galton's. Some typical findings of adoption and fostering studies are shown in box J. These studies use a correlational technique, where a positive relationship between two sets of figures is expressed as a decimal between 0 (no relationship) and 1 (a perfect positive relationship). You can read more about correlation in chapter 2.

The obvious conclusion to be drawn from these studies is that because the correlation is always higher between the parent and the natural child, and the child and the natural parent, IQ must be largely genetically determined. At the same time, however, there have been a great many criticisms of these studies.

Firstly, not all studies have given the same results. Snygg (1938), for example, found a correlation of only 0.13 between the IQs of adopted children and their natural mothers. The correlation from the Horn *et al.* study in Box J also shows this correlation to be rather low, bearing in mind the proportion of genes they have in common.

The principle of **selective placement**, whereby adoption agencies have a policy of trying to match the birth mother with the adoptive mother, means that the environment provided by the natural and the adoptive parents would be similar. This would

Box J: IQ correlations from adoption and fostering studies

	parents/ natural child	*parents/ adopted child*
Burks (1928)	0.52	0.20
Leahy (1935)	0.60	0.18

In both these studies, data from two separate sets of families produced these correlations.

	child/ natural parent	*child/ adopted parent*
Skodak & Skeels (1949)	0.44	0.02
Horn *et al.* (1979)	0.28	0.15

IQ was not directly measured for the adopted parent in the Skodak and Skeels study, only the parent's educational level.

lead to an underestimation of the possible effects of the environment.

Another approach is that of Scarr and Weinberg (1977), who tested adopted children in families with a natural child of the same age.The correlations of both adopted and natural children's IQ scores with that of the mother of the family were similar, despite the fact that the adopted children were often from a disadvantaged background, and were black and living in a white adoptive family. Similarly, Schiff *et al.* (1978) found that adopted children from disadvantaged backgrounds, who were adopted by high-status parents, scored higher on IQ tests (average 111) than siblings who had remained with their natural parents (average 95).

The quality of the environment in the adoptive home has also been investigated. Freeman *et al.* (1928) rated foster homes on six factors, including material conditions, social activity, education of parents and their occupation. They found a reasonably strong correlation of 0.48 between these factors and the foster child's IQ, suggesting an environmental influence.

Overall, then, the problems of interpretation appear to be so great that firm conclusions are difficult to reach, but it does seem that the effect of genes is not as great as might be supposed; the environment may contribute more than was previously thought.

Studies have also compared twins reared together in the same environment with twins reared apart in different environments. Some typical results are given in box K:

The most important of the above studies is that of Bouchard and McGue (1981), who drew together the results of 111 studies of intelligence in related people. The overall conclusion they reached is that both genetic factors and environment are important, but genetics has the bigger role. But is this conclusion justified?

There are several ways in which these studies can be criticised, most of which were proposed by Kamin (1974). Firstly, many of the early studies were based on small samples, e.g. Shields (1962), who studied only 37 pairs of twins. Colman (1987) pointed out that the entire psychological literature on this topic is based on the study of 121 pairs of separated MZ twins.

Another problem is that many early studies used dubious techniques for assessing zygosity (i.e. whether twins were MZ or DZ). Newman *et al.* (1937), for example, simply based their assessment on how similar the twins looked, and did not include in their sample any who differed in appearance or behaviour.

Separated twins often go to similar environments, either because twins are brought up by relatives, or because of selective placement. This leads to an underestimation of the effects of the environment. Kamin (1974) reported that only 13 of the 37 pairs studied by Shields were raised in unrelated families; some lived in the same street, played together and sat together at school. In the study by Newman *et al.*, twins separated by long distances (e.g. one in Alaska and one in Canada) were excluded from the study on the grounds of cost!

Box K: IQ correlations in twin studies

	name of study			
	Newman et al. (1937)	*Shields (1962)*	*Burt (1966)*	*Bouchard and McGue (1981)*
MZ twins reared together	0.91	0.76	0.94	0.86
MZ twins reared apart	0.67	0.77	0.77	0.72
DZ twins reared together	0.64	0.51	0.55	0.60

It is also possible that MZ twins may be treated more similarly than DZ twins (they are more likely to be dressed the same, for example, or treated as if they are the same person in other ways) so their environment as well as their genes will be more similar.

Burt's study has caused a geat deal of controversy, since it almost certainly included faked data. The correlations obtained in different studies, for example, were identical to three decimal places. Non-existent research assistants and dubious techniques for measuring IQ have also increased suspicions that he manipulated the outcomes to support his genetic theories (Hearnshaw 1979). Burt's studies were not included in the review by Bouchard and McGue for this reason.

Both the Shields and Newman *et al*. studies involved IQ testing by the researcher who knew which twins were MZ and which DZ; this could have led to **experimenter bias**. Kamin found that the twins tested by Shields, for example, showed an IQ difference of 8.5 points (leading to a correlation of 0.84), whereas the five pairs tested by other researchers showed an average difference of 22.4 points (giving a correlation of 0.11). Kamin interpreted this difference in terms of researcher bias.

Overall, then, it seems that the heritability estimates obtained from these studies (which vary from 0.5 to 0.8) may not be reliable. Kamin (1974) argues further that neither the twins nor their environments were representative of the variation that exists more widely in genes or environmental conditions.

Some twin studies have not in fact been able to show differences between MZ and DZ twins; Scarr-Salapatek studied 779 twins and refused to publish non-significant results because she felt they would not be accepted. This is an example of a more general problem in psychology, i.e. the tendency to present for publication (and to accept for publication) only work in which a significant difference or correlation has been established. After all, significant findings allow conclusions to be drawn, which is not the case for non-significant results.

An interesting meta-analysis by Taylor (1980) aimed to re-analyse data from all of the published studies apart from those of Burt, after removing some of the confounding environmental factors. Taylor found only five pairs of twins who had dissimilar educational and socioeconomic environments, had not been re-united after separation, and lived with unrelated families. The correlation between their IQ scores was only 0.24. Again, though, as with many of the twin studies we have discussed, the very small sample size means that these findings must be treated with caution.

In attempting to make sense of all these findings, one idea which may be useful is that of the **norm of reaction**, introduced by Anastasi (1958), whereby genetic information imposes an upper and a lower limit on development. Within this range, the environment will be influential. According to Scarr-Salapatek (1971), this range is 20–25 IQ points.

- **Family studies** have found higher correlations for IQ between close relatives than between more distant ones. However, the environments in this case are also likely to be more similar.
- Most **adoption studies** have found higher correlations with the natural mother than with the adoptive mother, but other factors suggest that environment has a considerable influence.
- Some **twin studies** have claimed to show that intelligence is largely genetic. Most have been criticised on methodological grounds.
- There are **methodological problems** with all these approaches.

Overview

We have looked at some important topics investigated by psychologists who take a biological approach, so we should now consider what this approach has to offer and what its limitations might be.

The biological approach has given us a lot of information about how our physiology links to behaviour and experience – for example how different areas of the brain are responsible for language and vision, and what is happening to our body when we feel stressed. With the rapid development of technology, our knowledge in these areas is set to expand. The scientific nature of this approach, firmly rooted in the experimental method, can also be seen as a positive point. Neither should it be forgotten that this approach has produced many important applications, for example the use of drugs to alleviate the suffering of people with a mental disorder.

However, this approach can also be criticised for being somewhat simplistic, in that, as we saw in the discussion of localisation of function within the cortex, it can oversimplify the enormous complexity of physiological systems, and also overlook how such systems interact with environmental factors.

The biological approach has been criticised for being reductionist. **Reductionism** can be defined as the attempt to explain a complex phenomenon in terms of the units which make it up. It rests on the idea that we have the best chance of understanding something if we break it down into its simplest component parts, and in the case of the biological approach, this is expressed as the belief that all psychological phenomena can be explained by ever more detailed reference to physiological activity, and in particular brain function. The focus is purely on the physiological functioning of the individual, and so does not take into account the possible influence on psychological functioning of cognitive, social and cultural factors, nor how these factors interact with physiological factors. The explanations offered are therefore only partial.

One example would be explaining the causes of a mental disorder like depression in terms of low levels of the neurotransmitters serotonin and noradrenaline with which it is associated. However, whether or not we become depressed in a particular situation can be influenced by cognitive factors such as our assessment of the situation, and by social factors such as the amount of social support available to us.

Similarly, differences in intelligence might be explained only in terms of genetic variation. For a more complete picture, we would need also to take into account environmental factors, such as the quality of education a person receives, whether intellectual development is nurtured within the family, and so on.

This links to a further issue, the relationship between the mind (awareness) and body (physiological processes). This is known as the **mind–body problem**. Within the study of emotion, for example, the biological approach can identify systems within the brain involved in emotional response, and describe the neural activity involved when we experience fear or disgust. However, it can not tell us anything about consciousness, i.e. how such neural activity is translated into our subjective experience of these emotions. To try to reduce these states to a physiological account is not to explain, but to explain away.

- The biological approach has provided a lot of information about physiological functioning, and has important **applications**.
- However, it has been criticised for being at times **oversimplistic**, for being **reductionist**, and for its inability to explain how physiological events are translated into psychological experiences (the **mind–body problem**).

Notes on activities are on page 52.

Notes on activities

1 You would be right in thinking that psychologists are interested in nearly all these topics. There are some areas, though, which are controversial. An interest in animal behaviour is one example. Many psychologists believe that since animals and people are all living creatures, insight into the behaviour of rats and dogs may give us a head start in understanding human behaviour. Others argue that people are unique, and we therefore need to concentrate directly on the behaviour and experience of people.

The relationship between astrological signs and personality is not a topic in psychology, though perhaps psychologists could be interested in the relationship between personal characteristics and a *belief* in astrology. There are also some areas (e.g. extra-sensory perception) which many psychologists would not regard as psychology, or at best, as being on the fringes of psychology.

2 First of all, a precise area to be studied needs to be identified. This is followed by **observation** of a phenomenon, and from this observation, a general explanation or theory can be produced (although in practice, much new research is triggered off by an existing theory or research). This in turn will lead to a specific and testable **hypothesis:** a precise prediction of what the results of an experiment will be.

An **experiment** or test must then be set up, which isolates the factor in which you are interested, and controls other factors which are not relevant to your research. Information or **data** must be collected. This needs to be objective, so that someone else running a similar experiment could check their results against the results you have found. **Conclusions** can then be drawn on the basis of the findings.

3 Where there is a shortage of food, only those giraffes who had longer necks would be able to reach the leaves at the top of trees, and thus have a relatively plentiful food supply. They would thus be more likely to survive and breed, and so pass genes for longer necks to the next generation.

4 Freud believed that on the first occasion, the young man asked for two tickets because he wished his fiancée was with him. Asking for only one ticket on the second occasion expressed the unconscious wish for her <u>not</u> to be there, as he was dissatisfied with his marriage.

5 **1** anal-retentive **2** oral-incorporative **3** oral-aggressive **4** anal-retentive **5** latency **6** anal-expulsive **7** anal-expulsive **8** phallic. However, some of these behaviours could be explained in terms of a combination of fixation and reaction formation. In Mark's case, for example, he could be an anal-retentive personality, and reaction formation has led to his gambling.

6 The bell starts off as an NS. Before and during conditioning, food is a UCS which produces the UCR of salivation. Finally, when it produces the response of salivation on its own, the bell becomes a CS which produces the CR of salivation.

7 The tap starts off as an NS and becomes a CS in the course of conditioning. It is a CS when it elicits a blink on its own. The puff of air is the UCS; the blink is the UCR before and during the conditioning procedure, and a CR when it is a response to the tap on its own.

8 For John, his mother shouting is a punishment, since it is something he finds unpleasant, which should weaken the behaviour of staying in bed. On the other hand, getting up on time is positively reinforced by breakfast. If his mother continues to grumble when he has got up late, she is punishing getting out of bed, which could help to explain why this strategy might not be very effective.

For Peter, helping with the hoovering is positively reinforced by being allowed to watch TV. The pleasure experienced is a positive reinforcement for washing the car, and car washing is also negatively reinforced by not having to do the washing up.

Having Glenn Miller on in the background positively reinforces Jenny's partner talking to her. Reading the newspaper is punished by Jenny putting on the Beethoven CD. Talking to her is negatively reinforced by this music being turned off.

9 Alex might think, irrationally, that the poor result means that he is not going to do well in psychology. He therefore feels he is no good at it, and considers giving up the course. More rationally, he realises that he spent very little time on revision. Although he is disappointed, he decides to revise more thoroughly for the next test.

10 The first statement very much describes the humanistic approach. Scientific methods are a major feature of behaviourist and cognitive psychology. Animal research has been important in behaviourist psychology. All four perspectives can have therapeutic applications. You should have identified the emphasis on unconscious processes as being associated with psychodynamic psychology. The final statement typifies the behaviourist view, though it could also relate to some extent to cognitive psychology.

12 **c** presynaptic membrane; calcium ions. **f** synaptic vesicles; synaptic cleft. **a** calcium ions. **e** receptor; post-synaptic. **b** ion channels. **d** transmit an impulse.

13 dead; clinical; ablation; lesion; stereotaxic; stimulate; chemical; micropipette; cerebrospinal; neurotransmitters.

14 **a**7; **b**5; **c**2; **d**3; **e**6; **f**4; **g**1

18 Pupil **dilation** would allow more light to enter the eye so that you become more aware of external stimuli, and thus better able to respond to them. **Deeper breathing** takes more oxygen into the lungs; your muscles require oxygen if they are to work effectively. A **faster heartbeat** speeds up blood circulation, and so carries oxygen to the muscles more quickly. Glucose is also necessary for the production of energy, so the formation of glucose from glycogen in the liver, and from **fats** and **proteins** (stimulated by cortisol) provides the source of energy needed for increased muscular activity. Stored red blood cells from the spleen mean that the blood can carry more oxygen.

19 There are lots of possibilities here. For example, if a racehorse is to run fast, it needs to be thinner and lighter than a working horse. A horse for farmwork would need to be bred for strength and stamina. Being temperamental may not be a drawback in a racehorse, but this quality would be undesirable in a farm animal.

20 The technique asks ordinary people, untrained in diagnosing mental disorders, to draw conclusions about the mental health of members of their family. Information about past generations relies on the accuracy of the memory of the interviewee. These kinds of problems have been overcome to some extent by looking at the medical records of family members, but this can only be done when people have presented for treatment. Even if it is clear that family members do have similar disorders, we cannot assume that the disorder is therefore genetic; close family members are likely to share the same physical and psychological environment, and this could account for the similarity.

Research methods

2.1 Methods in psychological research

You will remember from chapter 1 that psychology goes beyond common sense in that it attempts to set about the task of understanding behaviour and experience in an organised and systematic way. It does not rely on casual observation to support its ideas because this approach is very limited and can be misleading. For these reasons, psychologists carry out studies to investigate their ideas in a structured way which will enable them to collect information or data which can provide objective evidence to support or challenge psychological ideas.

Not all psychologists give priority to research, however. As we saw in chapter 1, for humanistic psychologists, with their focus on the experience of the individual, research is of much less importance than for, say, cognitive psychologists. The work of most psychologists, however, is focused on research, and a wide range of methods has been used to try to understand how people function.

The experimental method, which is the traditional method of scientific enquiry, has been the main method used by psychologists. However, alternative ways of carrying out research also have their place, and may be more suitable for some research areas. We will look first at what the different methods used in psychological research involve.

The experimental method

There are two criteria which define a piece of research as an experiment. Firstly, an **independent variable (IV)** is manipulated by the experimenter, with all other variables being kept constant. Secondly, there is an element of **random selection** and/or **allocation** of participants to conditions. There are other methods which do not fully meet these criteria yet which may loosely be called experiments, but we will start by looking at each of these two criteria in turn.

A variable is anything which can vary, i.e. can have different values. The **IV** is the variable in which the experimenter is interested, in terms of its effect on the **dependent variable (DV)**, i.e. the performance of participants in an experiment.

In terms of manipulation of the independent variable, in an experiment the researcher creates two or more different conditions. The differences between the conditions constitute the **independent variable**, with all other variables being kept constant. The effect of these different conditions on the **dependent variable** is measured and compared.

To give a simple example, a researcher may be interested in how different instructions for carrying out the memory task of learning a word list affect the number of words remembered. One group of participants could be instructed to learn the words by reading through the list over and over again, repeating them in their heads, i.e. rehearsal. A different group of participants could be asked to use story linkage, making up a story in which all the words appear. Both groups would then be asked to write down as many of the words as they could remember. The independent variable here is the instructions given to the participants, since it is the difference between the groups. The dependent variable is the number of words remembered, since that is what is being measured.

Activity 1: identifying the IV and DV

For each of these studies, identify the IV and the DV:

a A researcher is interested in whether older or younger people are more helpful. Drivers are observed at a junction. The number of older people (apparently over 45) and younger people (apparently under 25) who give way to another vehicle (and who do not give way to another vehicle) are counted.

b Do people work more efficiently first thing in the morning or later in the day? The productivity of workers making soft toys in a factory is compared between 9–10am on the morning shift and 7–8pm on the evening shift on a given day.

c Participants are asked to remember word pairs, either by rehearsing the pairs of words to themselves or by forming a mental image linking the two items. They are tested by being given the first word of each pair and then asked to supply the word with which it was paired.

When you have finished, see the notes on page 84.

The experimenter would also need to control **confounding variables**. These are any variables which could affect the outcome of the study but are not the IV in which the researcher is interested. It is important to control or eliminate confounding variables in an experiment in order to be sure that any differences between conditions in the dependent variable can only be the result of the manipulation of the independent variable.

A confounding variable can take the form of a random error or a constant error. A **random error** is any uncontrolled or inadequately-controlled variable which could affect the results in an unpredictable way. For example, performance on a task could be affected for some participants by a disturbance outside the room in which they are being tested, or by not being motivated to perform the task they are asked to carry out. A **constant error** is something other than the IV which consistently affects the DV – for example, participants in one condition being given unclear instructions.

Confounding variables can also be classified as **subject variables**, i.e. differences in the participants in the two conditions, or **situation variables**, i.e. differences in the testing situation. For an example of a subject variable, let us go back to the memory experiment described above. If all the participants in one condition were male and all the participants in the other were female, gender could be a confounding variable: it is not the variable in which the researcher is interested but could be the reason for any differences in the test scores of the two groups.

Similarly, in the same experiment, time of day could be a situation variable. For example, if one group were tested early in the morning and the other group late at night, any differences found between the scores of the two groups could be explained in terms of the time they were tested (e.g. people may be more alert in the morning) rather than in terms of the instructions they were given.

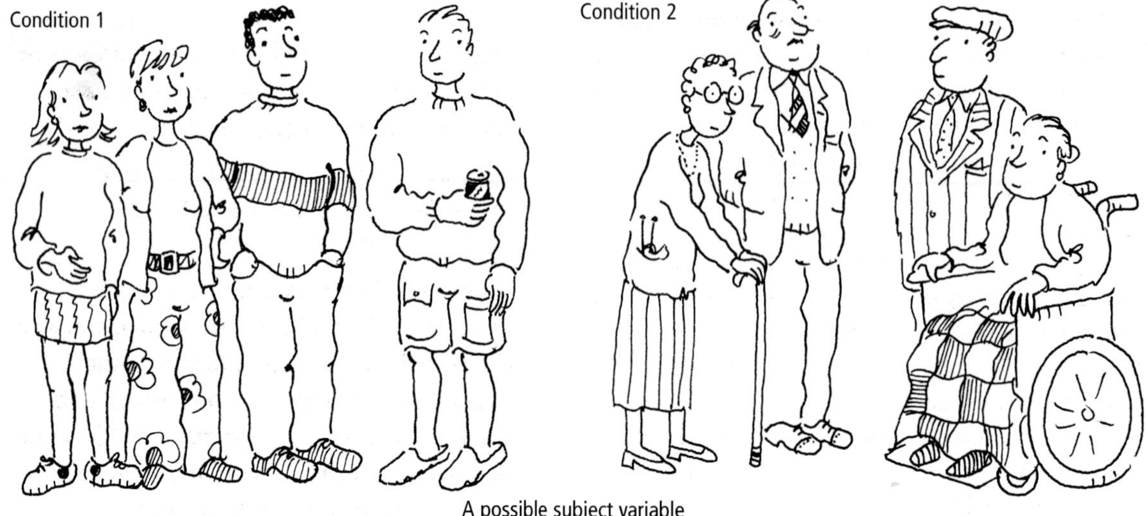

A possible subject variable

Activity 2: identifying confounding variables

Look back to the studies in activity 1. In each study, identify possible confounding variables. Say whether each is a subject or a situation variable. When you have finished, see the notes on page 84.

Laboratory experiments are carried out in many areas of psychology, because they give the researcher more control over the procedure. In this context, 'laboratory' refers to a place in which all aspects of the environment are controlled, as far as possible, and which is arranged specifically for a particular psychological study. Participants are usually aware that they are taking part in an experiment, although they may not be aware of the nature of the study. Laboratory conditions make it easier to control confounding variables and isolate the one variable in which the researcher is interested, i.e. the IV. If this is done successfully, the researcher can claim that there is a cause and effect relationship between the IV and the DV. The control the laboratory experiment offers makes it easy for other researchers to repeat or **replicate** the experiment to check the findings. It also means that researchers can set up the conditions they need, and do not have to wait for a suitable opportunity to present itself naturally. Another advantage of this kind of experiment is that it can easily be structured to provide **quantitative data**, i.e. results in a numerical form. These can be analysed using statistical tests which indicate how likely the results are to have come about by chance. A laboratory experiment also means that sophisticated technical equipment can be used, e.g. presenting a visual stimulus for a precisely measured fraction of a second.

Laboratory experiments also have their drawbacks, however. A major problem is **ecological validity**, i.e. the extent to which a laboratory study shares the characteristics of a real-life situation. For example, Ebbinghaus (1885) used nonsense syllables to investigate the nature of memory. However, this kind of material is very different from the kinds of things which we would normally try to learn.

A related problem is what Orne (1962) called **demand characteristics**. In a laboratory situation, participants are usually well aware that they are taking part in an experiment, and so may try to make sense of what they are being asked to do. They may pick up cues from what the researcher says and does, or from the layout of the laboratory. They could then change their behaviour in a way that they see as being helpful to the researcher, or possibly set out deliberately to go against what they perceive to be the experimenter's aims. If participants are responding to demand characteristics, clearly the ecological validity of the study is compromised.

Related problems are **evaluation apprehension**, where participants' performance may be affected by concern that their behaviour will be judged by the experimenter, and **social desirability** effects, where behaviour may be distorted in an attempt to give what the participant believes to be a good impression.

Experimenter effects are a further problem. These occur when the characteristics or behaviour of the experimenter may influence the behaviour of the participants. For example, experimenter characteristics could include gender, race, age or physical attractiveness, while experimenter behaviour which might affect participants' behaviour could include being very friendly or patronising.

A related problem is **experimenter bias**, when the experimenter shows unintentional bias when recording the data from an experiment. One way to overcome this kind of problem is to use a **double blind** technique. In most research, participants are unaware of what the experimenter is expecting the study to show (though of course demand characteristics may make this less true). Keeping participants unaware of the nature of the study is known as the **single blind** technique. In a double blind study, the collection of data is carried out by someone other than the experimenter, so that neither the participant nor the person running the study is aware of what the results are expected to be.

Not all experiments are carried out in a laboratory. Some experiments are **field experiments**. These are studies which take place in natural conditions, but where the criteria for an experiment are met. Field studies are carried out when it is thought to be important that what is being studied happens in the natural environment. An example is this study carried out into helping behaviour:

Box A: Piliavin *et al.* (1969)

Procedure: A scene was staged in the New York subway, in which a man appeared to collapse as the train pulled away from the station. In one condition, the man was carrying a cane; in the other condition he was carrying a bottle. The percentage of people offering help within 10 seconds was noted.

Results: In the 'cane' condition 95% of bystanders helped, compared to 50% in the 'bottle' condition.

Conclusion: Bystanders interpreted the 'cane' situation as illness, for which the person could not be held responsible, and the 'bottle' situation as arising from drunkenness, and therefore the person's own fault. Judgements about the reasons a person needs help can affect whether or not help is given.

The main advantages of field experiments are that they have high ecological validity and reduce the possibility of people responding to demand characteristics. However, control is more of a problem, with an increased likelihood of the study being influenced by confounding variables. This also makes replication more difficult. While high ecological validity may mean that the results of field experiments can be more readily generalised, i.e. the conclusions drawn from the experiment can be assumed to apply to similar situations, it may also be more difficult to apply general conclusions from a field study to other situations which differ from the situation in which the study was carried out. There are also ethical problems, which we shall come to later in this chapter. In particular, participants will not have given consent to having their behaviour observed if they are unaware that they are taking part in a study. Field experiments must also be done without complicated technical equipment.

A final kind of experiment is the **natural experiment**. This is a procedure which takes advantage of a naturally occurring IV. Study b in activity 1 is an example. Here the participants were not put into conditions by the experimenter, but constituted two groups, working different shifts, which were roughly equivalent, allowing the productivity of each (the DV) to be compared.

There are also **quasi-experiments**, which take a broadly experimental approach but where the criteria for an experiment are not completely met. Study a in activity 1 is an example of a quasi-experiment. Random allocation of participants to age groups would not be possible – participants would come to the study already allocated as over 45 or under 25!

- In the **experimental method**, researchers manipulate an **independent variable** to find its effect on the **dependent variable**, while controlling **confounding variables**.
- **Laboratory experiments** take place in controlled conditions, while **field experiments** take place in the natural environment. **Natural experiments** take advantage of a naturally occurring situation, while **quasi-experiments** do not completely meet the criteria for an experiment.
- All these kinds of experiment have both advantages and drawbacks.

Non-experimental methods

As well as experiments, psychologists have a range of other methods open to them. Because none of these methods involves manipulating the independent variable, they do not offer the control of an experiment, and so it is more difficult to establish cause and effect relationships. They do, however, enable researchers to carry out research into a wider range of variables, and they can be more suitable than the experimental method for some kinds of investigations.

Correlational analysis

Correlational analysis is a statistical technique which measures the relationship between two variables. An example of research using correlational analysis could be a study of the relationship between the number of everyday hassles experienced and the psychological symptoms of stress: is the more frequent experience of hassles associated with higher stress levels? A positive correlation occurs when as values for one variable increase, values for the other also tend to do so; in this case, people who experience more hassles could be expected to suffer more stress symptoms, while those who score low on a hassles scale could be expected also to score low for stress. A negative correlation occurs when as values for one variable increase, values for the other tend to decrease. There would probably be a negative correlation, for example, between the amount of alcohol people had drunk and how well they performed on a test of hand–eye co-ordination.

Statistical tests measuring correlation produce a value or **coefficient** between +1 (a perfect positive correlation) and –1 (a perfect negative correlation). A coefficient of 0 shows that an increase in one variable does not predict a consistent increase or decrease in the other variable. A correlation coefficient must always have a value between +1 and –1. In practice, coefficients are rarely as high as +1, and negative correlations are rarely as low as –1, but usually fall somewhere in between these extreme values. A correlation of 0.7, for example, would show a fairly strong positive relationship between two variables, while a correlation of –0.3 would show a fairly weak negative relationship.

Activity 3: correlation

For each of these pairs of variables, say whether you would expect to find a positive correlation, a negative correlation or no correlation. Estimate what value between +1 and –1 you would expect the coefficient to have:

a height and shoe size

b scores on a French test and scores on an English test

c how stressed a person feels and their state of health

d bodyweight and scores on a video game

When you have finished, see the notes on page 84.

This technique allows us to measure the strength and direction of relationships between two variables. It can also be used at the start of research to establish whether there is a phenomenon which could be investigated more thoroughly using the experimental method.

Its main drawback is that it cannot establish cause and effect. There is likely to be a strong positive relationship between the number of puddles that you see and the number of umbrellas, but there isn't a causal relationship between puddles and umbrellas, since both are caused by a further variable, i.e. rain.

Correlation also cannot show non-linear relationships. For example, the relationship between arousal and performance is initially a positive one, but when arousal becomes too great, and can be described as stress, performance drops off and the relationship becomes a negative one. These two trends would cancel each other out to give a correlation coefficient close to 0, masking the real relationship between these two variables. This kind of relationship is called a **curvilinear relationship**. Although a correlation coefficient cannot express this kind of relationship, a scattergraph – the most fequently used graphical method of representing a correlation – can do so. We will return to graphical representation later in the chapter.

❸ **Correlational analysis** shows the direction and strength of the relationship between two variables. A major drawback is that it cannot establish **cause and effect**, nor can it show **curvilinear relationships**.

Observational studies

This method makes no attempt to manipulate variables, but simply records aspects of behaviour in a particular situation as they occur. This technique can be used in a laboratory setting, but more often takes place in a more natural setting. It therefore has high ecological validity. If participants are unaware of being observed, demand characteristics are avoided. It allows researchers to collect a wide range of interesting data.

In **participant observation**, the researcher joins in with the group of people being studied. Hargreaves (1967), for example, investigated social relationships at a school by becoming a teacher at the school for a year. In **non-participant observation**, such as observations of children's play, the researcher remains apart from those being studied, who may or may not be aware that their behaviour is being watched.

It is often possible to record on video the behaviour which is being observed. This has the advantage of allowing the behaviour to be viewed as many times as is necessary for a full analysis to be carried out. Where this is not possible, the methods of time sampling and event sampling may be used to make the observation more manageable.

In **time sampling**, observations are made for only short periods of time during the observational period. For example, if a researcher was interested in the kinds of play shown by children in a playground, it would be impractical to observe the children's behaviour and at the same time make detailed notes. Time sampling could be used by watching the children for a two-minute period in every quarter of an hour, using the rest of the time before the next observation to make notes on what had been observed. If the observer was interested in the frequency of particular kinds of play, this method would be a manageable way of making comparisons across the period of the observation.

In **event sampling**, observations are made of a specific event each time it occurs. If the researcher observing children's play, for instance, was interested in whether boys show more aggression in their play than girls, each example of behaviour from both boys and girls which could be classified in this way would be noted.

Naturalistic observation is a useful technique when the researcher is interested in something which would be very hard to recreate in a laboratory – for example, the behaviour of drivers or the interaction of children at school. It can also be used in exploratory studies, to establish which phenomena could be explored in a more controlled way in a laboratory setting.

One practical problem of observational techniques is the **observer effect**, where observing a phenomenon may in itself affect what is being observed. A good example is the **Hawthorne effect**, which takes its name from the Hawthorne works of the Bell Telephone Company where it was first observed. It refers to the fact that in an industrial setting, productivity may improve simply as the result of changes being introduced, even if this was not the intention behind introducing the change. In psychological research, the Hawthorne effect is often referred to when a research participant's behaviour may have been affected by their awareness of being observed.

Observer bias is also possible; unless rigorously controlled measurement is taking place, observers may interpret what they see in line with the expectations and beliefs they bring to the study. One way of trying to overcome this problem is to have two people making observations of the same event(s), and to check that their observations are similar. This is known as **inter-observer reliability**.

A further problem of observational techniques is the difficulty of **replication**; it is very unlikely that all aspects of an observational study would remain the same if the study were to be repeated. For this reason, too, there are difficulties with **generalisation**, i.e. applying the conclusions drawn from a study of this kind more widely. For example, it might be unwise to draw general conclusions about the nature of children's play from observation of a particular playgroup, since there are likely to be a number of uncontrollable variables which could have affected the observations. For instance, the skills of the playgroup staff, the kinds of toys and materials available and the number of children attending the group could all have an effect on children's behaviour.

It is also more likely in this kind of study than in an experiment that relevant aspects of the behaviour being observed could be missed. For example, in an observation of children's play in a group situation there could be so much movement that it would be difficult to keep track of everything which took place. As noted already, this kind of difficulty can be minimised by making a filmed record, which can be replayed as often as is necessary for a complete record.

- **Naturalistic observation** focuses on naturally occurring behaviour. In **participant observation**, observers themselves take part.
- **Time sampling** and **event sampling** may be used.
- Observation is a useful technique when studying behaviour which could not easily be translated to a laboratory setting.
- There may be **observer effects**, and **replication** may be difficult. Carrying out this kind of study can present **practical problems**.

Case studies

Unlike the methods we have talked about so far, a case study is a detailed study of one individual or a small group of individuals. A range of methods can be used, including interviews, detailed observation, records such as a medical history, information from others about the person being studied, and so on. Quite often at least some of the data is **qualitative**, being largely descriptive, rather than **quantitative**, i.e. providing precise measures. A case study is an **idiographic** approach, since it is an in-depth study, focusing in detail on particular characteristics of the individual(s).

This method is widely used in clinical psychology; Freud's research, for example, consisted entirely of case studies of patients. It can be a very useful approach for increasing understanding of all relevant aspects of a person's experience and behaviour. It is also useful for investigating the characteristics of people who are unusual in some way, as shown, for example, by Luria's (1968) study of S, a man with a phenomenal memory.

One of the advantages of this method is that it can increase our knowledge within a certain topic area, when a more experimental technique would be unethical. One example is an investigation into the effects of social isolation:

Box B: Curtiss (1977)

Genie spent the first years of her life alone, tied to a potty chair and fed on baby food. She had lived her life in virtual silence, not being spoken to and being punished for making any sound herself.

She was found at the age of $13\frac{1}{2}$. She developed attachments to her foster carers, but after a settled period in their care, she was moved to a succession of short-term carers, some of whom mistreated her.

Her mother eventually refused to allow anyone access to her, and it is not known what happened to her later in life. During the years when her whereabouts were known, Genie acquired only limited language skills.

The case study method can be useful in the initial stages of researching a topic, to identify particular areas which might usefully be followed up using other methods. The detail it provides means that it can also be used as the basis for challenging an existing theory, if the results of the case study call the theory into question. It also gives detailed information about a real person or people, where techniques such as the experimental method are more interested in general trends, and so may lose valuable information about individual differences. Finally, since the numbers of participants are so small, it lends itself to a **longitudinal** approach, where people are studied over time.

However, there are also some drawbacks to this method. A major problem is **generalisability**; we cannot conclude that what is true of one person or a small group of people is also true of people more generally. **Researcher bias** is also a problem; for example, Freud's case studies have been criticised on the grounds of the high level of interpretation they involved. Finally, if a case study involves in-depth interviews, this relies heavily on the person being interviewed giving accurate answers. For instance, an adult asked about their childhood may not be able to remember relevant information or may inaccurately reconstruct their memories.

- **Case studies** are in-depth studies of one or a small number of people. They provide detailed, often **qualitative**, data.
- They are a useful way of studying unusual characteristics, particularly where a more experimental approach would raise ethical difficulties.
- The results are not necessarily **generalisable**. **Researcher bias** may also be a problem.

Interviews and surveys

Interviews and surveys cover a wide range of related techniques – **interviews**, **questionnaires**, **attitude surveys**, and the **clinical method** used in diagnosing psychological problems – but they all involve asking people for information about themselves. Interviews can be **structured**, where every respondent (the person being interviewed) is asked the same questions, or more **unstructured**, where there is room for flexibility in terms of what is asked.

Questionnaires and surveys may use open-ended or closed-ended questions. **Closed-ended questions** provide the respondent with answers from which they must choose, while **open-ended questions** allow them to answer in any way they feel is appropriate:

Activity 4: closed- and open-ended questions

A closed-ended question:

Why did you choose to take A-level Psychology? Was it because:

a it sounded more interesting than the other options?

b it was recommended by a friend?

c you like the teacher?

d you thought it might be easier than the other options?

An open-ended question:

Why did you choose to take A-level Psychology?

What are the advantages and disadvantages of each of these types of question?

When you have finished, see the notes on page 84.

One example of the use of surveys is to measure people's attitudes to various issues. Likert (1932) developed the principle of measuring attitudes by asking people to respond in a structured way to a series of statements relevant to the attitude being measured. A series of statements – perhaps 30 – is prepared, relevant to the particular attitude to be measured, with half the statements being favourable and half unfavourable. This balance is necessary in order to eliminate **response set**; if all the statements were favourable to the attitude being measured, participants might respond without reading each statement carefully, and so reduce the accuracy of the information being gathered. Statements are presented in random order and participants rate each statement on a five-point scale, to which numerical values are attached.

Examples of the sorts of items which might be used to measure attitudes to the royal family, together with the scoring system, are shown in figure 1. You will see that a high score shows a favourable attitude to the royal family, and a low score an unfavourable attitude. A person's attitude is the sum of their scores from all the items. The numbers would not appear on the questionnaire completed by participants; they are only there to show you how the system works.

In a different area, **Eysenck's Personality Inventory (EPI)** is a personality **questionnaire** using a similar approach. It is an example of a **psychometric test**, i.e. a test which aims to measure particular psychological characteristics. In this case the characteristics being measured are extroversion and neuroticism, the two dimensions which Eysenck believed are sufficient to describe an individual's personality. A typical extrovert is sociable, gregarious, impulsive and enjoys taking risks, while a typical neurotic is guilt-ridden and anxious. Sample questions relating to extroversion are shown in activity 5:

Activity 5: measuring extroversion

Here are some sample questions on extroversion. For each one, answer 'yes' or 'no'.
You can answer '?' if you really cannot decide, but try to avoid this if possible.
Don't spend too long thinking about how to respond – it is usually best to stay with your first reaction.

1	Are you inclined to be slow and deliberate in your actions?	Y ? N
2	Do you often buy things on impulse?	Y ? N
3	Do you often change your interests?	Y ? N
4	Are you rather cautious in novel situations?	Y ? N

Did any problems occur to you as you were answering these questions? Are there any ways you think this method of measuring personality could be criticised?
When you have finished, see the notes on page 84.

Given the kinds of problem often found with these kinds of questionnaires, Eysenck included a lie scale in the EPI. This uses questions such as: 'Have

Figure 1: sample of a Likert scale to measure attitudes

1. The royal family are good ambassadors for this country

strongly agree	agree somewhat	undecided	disagree somewhat	strongly disagree
5	4	3	2	1

2. It would be a good idea to have a president instead of the royal family

strongly agree	agree somewhat	undecided	disagree somewhat	strongly disagree
1	2	3	4	5

you ever been late for an appointment?', working on the principle that we have all at some time been late for something, even if only slightly late for something not very important. This is perhaps a little limited, but it is one way of alerting the tester to the possibility of a **social desirability** effect.

A structured approach has the advantage of focusing on specific questions which are of interest to the researcher, and is likely to produce quantitative data, i.e. in the form of scores, which are more easily analysed using statistical methods. This is particularly the case where the range of possible answers to questions is limited. In their written form, techniques such as attitude surveys and personality questionnaires allow a lot of information to be gathered relatively easily from large numbers of respondents. Given the constraints on what is asked using this kind of structured technique, interviewer bias is less likely than with a more unstructured approach.

An unstructured interview, on the other hand, while being more open to bias, allows the interviewer to follow up responses which are of particular interest, and thus to collect potentially richer data. It has the advantage of being very flexible and giving access to information which might not easily be gained using other methods.

In practice, a **semi-structured interview** technique is often used to tap into the advantages of both the structured and unstructured approaches. An example of a semi-structured technique is the **clinical interview**, used to assess a person with a mental disorder. Specific questions are asked, but there is also the possibility of following up responses in more detail if this is thought to be useful. This technique may be used not only to diagnose the particular disorder from which the person is suffering, and so form a basis for deciding which kinds of therapeutic intervention might be appropriate, but also to provide material for research purposes. Mental health professionals use this technique to collect information about the psychiatric, medical, personal and family history of the patient, their social circumstances, and their personality. In addition, they use a more structured approach to make a cognitive assessment, e.g. of memory and IQ, test the functioning of the central nervous system and make a physical examination.

One of the drawbacks to unstructured or semi-structured techniques, where the range of possible answers is open, is that they may be limited by how easily respondents can express themselves. This in turn may be affected in face-to-face interviews by the sensitivity and skill of the interviewer. The interviewer must also be aware of ethical considerations. Respondents should not feel coerced into giving replies, nor feel that judgements are being made about them on the basis of the information they give.

Sometimes postal interviews are carried out, usually anonymously, which go some way to addressing these concerns. With this method, though, flexibility is lost and the return rate is usually very low. More importantly, the kinds of people who choose to return completed postal interviews or questionnaires are a self-selected sample, and so may not be typical of the group of people in whom the researcher is interested. We shall be returning to sampling later in the chapter.

❺ **Interviews**, **questionnaires**, **attitude surveys** and **clinical interviews** are techniques which ask people directly for information. They can be **structured** or **unstructured**. A structured approach offers precision and ease of analysis, while an unstructured approach offers richness of data.

2.2 Quantitative and qualitative data

Many of the research methods used by psychologists are concerned with collecting **quantitative data**, i.e. numerical data which can be put in categories, or in rank order, or measured in units of measurement. This emphasis on quantitative data is the result of psychologists adopting a similar approach to research to that used in traditional sciences such as physics and chemistry. This approach is **positivist**, which means that it sees only measurable events as worthy of scientific study.

However, we have also looked at methods which do not have this focus, and are more interested in collecting much more loosely-structured **qualitative data**, which do not easily yield this kind of numerical information.

Activity 6: qualitative data in research

Look back through the different methods used in psychology outlined in this chapter. Which methods described provide qualitative data?

When you have finished, see the notes on page 85.

An interest in qualitative data came about as the result of the dissatisfaction of some psychologists with positivism. Since psychologists study people, the traditional approach to science is not seen as an appropriate way of carrying out research, as it fails to capture the totality of human experience and the essence of what it is to be human. Exploring the experience of participants is known as a **phenomenological** approach.

It is argued that to focus on isolated pieces of behaviour, as is most often the case in studies interested in collecting quantitative data, is rather superficial, and ignores the social context within which behaviour takes place. Given that psychological research is something which happens in a social context, the objectivity of the researcher, central to traditional methods, is seen as essentially false within psychology. As people studying people, researchers necessarily have attitudes and values which they bring to their research. It is therefore more honest that researchers' attitudes and values should be acknowledged, and form part of the context of research.

Experimental methods limit the possible ways in which a research participant can react to and express appropriate social behaviour. Findings are therefore likely to be context-bound and simply a reflection of the assumptions which the researcher brings to the investigation.

The traditional method of using research to confirm or falsify a particular theory, model or hypothesis is also seen as inappropriate. Rather, theories, models and hypotheses should emerge from the data, as a co-operative effort of researcher and participant. These ideas also link to the **deconstructionist** approach and the **feminist perspective**. According to many who work within this perspective, the traditional positivist approach is seen to be very male-oriented, with its emphasis on control, manipulation and objectivity, and as such is dehumanising.

Qualitative methods necessarily involve interpretation of data, which from a traditional viewpoint could be seen as a criticism. However, psychologists interested in a qualitative approach believe that objectivity is unattainable in psychological research, and given the nature of the subject matter, they consider that even to attempt to be objective is undesirable.

- Some psychologists have challenged the traditional emphasis on **quantitative data** using a scientific model in psychological research.
- They have argued that **qualitative methods** may be more appropriate, given the subject matter of psychology.

2.3 Variables, operationalisation, and hypotheses

In the section on the experimental method in psychology, we discussed how the aim of a piece of research is to find out whether an IV affects the DV. This is done by manipulating the IV between conditions, and controlling possible confounding variables. Correlational research, on the other hand, looks for a relationship between two variables.

The variables in a particular piece of research need to be **operationalised**, i.e. defined in terms of how they are to be used in a particular study. A study by Loftus and Palmer (1974), for example, was interested in whether the wording used in a question about an event (IV) affected memory of that event (DV). Participants watched a video showing a car crash, and were then asked a question about the speed of the cars involved: 'How fast were the two cars going when they hit each other?' For some participants, the word 'hit' was replaced by 'smashed', 'collided', 'bumped' or 'contacted'. The IV here was operationalised as the inclusion of the word 'hit', 'smashed', and so on. The DV was the answer a week later to the question: 'Did you see any broken glass?'.

Activity 7: operationalisation

Here are some research ideas. For each one, identify the IV and the DV and suggest ways in which each could be operationalised:

a Do people remember more about a topic they are interested in than about one in which they have little interest?

b Are there gender differences in the amount of aggression shown by children in play?

c Are neurotic people more likely to suffer from phobias?

When you have finished, see the notes on page 85.

Much psychological research aims to test a specific **hypothesis**. This is a precise prediction about the expected findings of a study, and includes the IV and DV in their operationalised form, or the two co-variables in the case of correlational analysis. A study uses two hypotheses, the **null hypothesis** and the **alternative hypothesis** which is also known as the **research** or (in an experiment) the **experimental hypothesis**.

The **null hypothesis** predicts that there will be no difference between the conditions, or no relationship between the co-variables, in the case of a correlational study. For example, in the Loftus and Palmer study the null hypothesis would predict that there would be no difference between the conditions they tested in the percentage of people claiming to have seen broken glass. Statistical tests tell us what the probability is that the results of a study have come about by chance. If this probability is relatively high, then the null hypothesis has to be retained. If it is relatively low, then the null hypothesis can be rejected, and the alternative hypothesis accepted.

In a study, the null hypothesis is what is being tested when data are analysed using statistical tests. The **alternative hypothesis** (i.e. the alternative to the null hypothesis) predicts that there will be a difference between conditions, e.g. in the Loftus and Palmer study that a higher percentage of participants in one group would report having seen broken glass. In a correlational study, the alternative hypothesis will be that there is a relationship, not necessarily causal, between the two variables.

Alternative hypotheses can be **one-tailed** (**directional**) or **two-tailed** (**non-directional**). In an experiment, a two-tailed hypothesis predicts that there will be a difference in the DV between the conditions of the study, e.g. that there will be a difference in the number of words remembered in a memory task by participants using rehearsal and those using story linkage. In the case of a correlational design, it predicts a relationship between the variables, e.g. that there will be a relationship between extroversion scores and preference for bright colours on a colour preference questionnaire. It does not, however, specify what the difference or relationship will be.

If the hypothesis is one-tailed, the direction of the difference or relationship is also predicted. In the above examples, one-tailed hypotheses would be: 'participants using story linkage will remember *more* words than those using rehearsal' and 'there will be a *positive* relationship between extroversion scores and preference for bright colours on a colour preference questionnaire'.

Activity 8: hypotheses

Read through these examples of alternative hypotheses, and identify whether each is one- or two-tailed:

a There will be a difference in scores on an intelligence test between people who eat fish and those who do not eat fish.

b There will be a relationship between extroversion and a preference for loud music.

c People will remember more words in a foreign language if the information is presented in picture form, rather than as words alone.

Now rewrite these hypotheses. For each one, if it is one-tailed, rewrite it as a two-tailed hypothesis. If it is two-tailed, rewrite it as a one-tailed hypothesis.

When you have finished, see the notes on page 85.

- Variables need to be **operationalised** in terms of how they are to be used in the context of a particular piece of research.
- The **alternative (research/experimental) hypothesis** proposes that there will be a difference or a relationship between two or more sets of data. The **null hypothesis** proposes that there will be no such difference or relationship.
- Experimental hypotheses can be **directional** (one-tailed) or **non-directional** (two-tailed).

2.4 Populations and samples

A target population is a group of people who share specific characteristics, and who the researcher is interested in testing. Populations can be small (e.g. female A-level Physics students in a particular sixth-form college) or large (e.g. people living in Britain). Populations are usually too large, however, for every individual to be tested, so only a subset of the population – a sample – is tested instead. Ideally this should be a **representative sample**, i.e. one in which all the characteristics of the parent population are represented. If the sample is representative, any conclusions drawn from the results of the study can be generalised to the population as a whole, since the sample will be accurate in terms of representing important aspects of the population.

A small population: left-handed trainspotters living in Norwich with their birthdays in May

Activity 9: representative samples

Imagine you are planning to use A-level students at your college as participants in an investigation into the relationship between study habits and exam success, and you intend to select a sample to test. Which characteristics would need to be included in your sample to make it representative of A-level students as a whole?

When you have finished, see the notes on page 85.

The larger the sample, the more likely it is to be representative of the population from which it is drawn. If the sample in activity 9, for example, consisted of only five students, it would be very unlikely that all the different characteristics which might be important to the research would be represented. If the sample is not representative of the population, it is said to be **biased**, i.e. some characteristics of the population are either over- or under-represented, so the sample does not reflect accurately the characteristics of the population.

The problem in deciding on an appropriate size for a sample is essentially a practical one. A very small sample is likely to be biased, but on the other hand a very large sample will take a long time to test, and could be expensive in terms of additional materials which may be necessary. Whatever the sample size, there is likely to be **sampling error**, i.e. inaccuracies in the sample in terms of its representativeness of the parent population. This is reduced (though not necessarily eliminated) by testing a larger sample.

Sampling methods

There are several ways of selecting a sample. In a **random sample**, every member of the parent population has an equal chance of being included in the sample. To select a random sample, a list of all the members of the population is necessary, e.g. in the study in activity 9, a list of all the students taking A-levels at your college.

There should be no bias in who is selected as part of the sample. This could be achieved by putting all the names into a hat, stirring them round, and then picking out names to make up the sample until the planned sample size is reached.

Alternatively, if the population is too large for this to be practicable, every member of the population could be given a number. A computer program which generates random numbers could then be used to select the sample, matching up the numbers given by the computer with the numbers given to the members of the population.

The strength of this method is that it avoids possible experimenter bias in selecting a sample. One drawback is that random sampling is only possible if each member of the parent population can be identified and listed. Another drawback is that a random sample may well not be representative of the population. For example, a random sample of A-level students could by chance consist entirely of males. However, this kind of bias becomes less likely as the size of the sample increases.

Another possibility is a **systematic sample**, where members of the population are picked on the basis of some system. A sample of voters, for example, could include every tenth person on the electoral roll. This is not strictly speaking a random sample, since only those who are in the relevant position on the roll can be selected, but it is likely to be relatively unbiased, and a faster process than random sampling. It is sometimes called a **quasi-random** sample.

An **opportunity sample** is frequently used. This means that the sample is selected on the basis of who is available at the time of testing and willing to take part. Since it is so straightforward, it is frequently used by students carrying out A-level Psychology coursework.

Activity 10: problems with opportunity sampling

Imagine you are planning to carry out the research into study habits and exam success described in activity 9, and you decide to test an opportunity sample. What kinds of factors might lead to this not being a representative sample?

When you have finished, see the notes on page 85.

In practice, the problems associated with opportunity sampling may often not be too serious. For example, in a study measuring physiological responses to stress, people forming this kind of sample would be unlikely to produce results which would differ radically from those of samples selected in other ways.

In a **self-selecting sample**, people volunteer either directly or indirectly to take part in a study. The problem here is that those who volunteer directly may not be typical of the target population, so the sample would be biased. This problem has already been mentioned in the discussion of postal interviews.

People may also volunteer indirectly. For example, if you were interested in possible gender differences in superstition you could set up a ladder and note how many males and how many females avoided walking underneath it. The people you were observing would be unaware that they were taking part in a study, but would indirectly be volunteering to take part by walking where the ladder was set up.

For **stratified sampling**, variables considered to be relevant to the sample are identified (as in activity 9), and the sample is made up of subgroups (strata) representing these variables.

Each subgroup must be represented in the sample in the proportion in which it appears in the parent population. For example, in activity 9, if the college population is made up of 200 males and 300 females, the sample would need to be made up of males and females in the ratio of 2:3. Within the strata, sampling should be random, e.g. each male should have an equal chance of being part of the sample of males.

This is rather a time-consuming method of sampling, and requires detailed knowledge of the relevant characteristics of the population, and their relative proportions. However, it is likely to produce a much more representative sample than the other sampling methods described.

Cluster sampling draws on established groups (or clusters) of people, for example children attending different schools or families living in different areas in a town. Participants are then randomly selected from each cluster to make up the sample. This sampling method is convenient and economical, for example in cutting down researcher travel time. However, each cluster may not be closely representative of the parent population.

Activity 11: identifying sampling techniques

In each of these studies, identify the sampling technique used, choosing from :

random **systematic** **opportunity**
cluster **stratified** **self-selecting**

a A student research group is interested in attitudes to the legalisation of cannabis among the student population of the college they attend. The sample they interview has the same proportions in terms of gender and choice of academic subjects as the whole college population.

b A psychologist is interested in comparing attitudes to learning a foreign language of city children and those living in the country. Samples are drawn from children attending an inner city high school and children at a rural high school.

c A Psychology student carrying out a study on the effects of stress on problem-solving puts up a notice on the college notice board asking people willing to take part in her study to sign up.

d Students in a Psychology class have been asked to carry out a memory test on one participant each. Some ask people in the library and the study area, some ask those in the canteen, while others go to find participants in the common room.

e Are there gender differences in the ability of male and female students to carry out verbal reasoning tests? The names of all the male students in a college are put into a hat, and the names of all the female students into another hat. Names are drawn from each hat until here are enough males and females to form the sample.

Identify the examples in which the sample might not be representative of the parent population, and say why not.

When you have finished, see the notes on page 86.

- A study tests a sample of the population in which the researcher is interested. If this is a **representative sample**, results can then be **generalised** to the population as a whole.
- In a **random sample**, every member of the population has an equal chance of being part of the sample. A **systematic sample** selects on the basis of some kind of system. An **opportunity sample** consists of members of the population who are available at the time of testing, and willing to take part. In a **self-selecting sample**, participants offer themselves, either directly or indirectly, as part of the sample. In a **stratified sample**, characteristics of the population are represented in the sample in the same proportion in which they occur in the population. A **cluster sample** takes a sample from established groups of people.
- Sampling methods can introduce **sampling error** which can lead to a **biased sample**.

2.5 Experimental design

Some of the factors which need to be taken into account when planning experimental research have already been discussed. The IV and the DV need to be operationalised, and possible confounding variables need to be eliminated as far as possible. The size of the sample to be tested and the sampling method need to be considered. Another decision which needs to be made is the design of the study, and we will be looking in this section at three possible designs.

One possibility is an **independent measures** design. You may also find this referred to as an **unrelated design** or a **between-groups** design. In this design, different participants are tested in each condition of the experiment, and participants are randomly allocated to conditions. To go back to the earlier example of a study comparing the effectiveness of rehearsal and story linkage on recall, one set of participants would take a memory test using rehearsal, while a different set of participants would be asked to use story linkage.

The experiment could consist of two or more conditions, where each condition receives a different experimental treatment (as in the memory test example), or one or more experimental conditions and a control condition. In a **control condition**, participants are given no particular treatment; in this example they would be asked to memorise a list of words with no strategy being suggested. The principle here is that the data from this group provides a baseline with which the experimental condition(s) can be compared.

Manipulation of the IV is one criterion for defining a study as an experiment. The second is random allocation of participants to conditions. Randomly allocating participants to conditions means that all participants should have an equal chance of taking part in either condition, or in any condition if there are more than two; in the memory experiment example, a third condition could be introduced where participants were asked to use a third method to help them remember the words, e.g. putting pairs of words into a meaningful sentence. The principle of random allocation is to prevent any kind of bias in selecting which participants will take part in which condition, and so avoid bias in the way in which the experiment is carried out.

To achieve random allocation the person conducting an experiment may 'take names out of a hat' or use random number tables. In natural or quasi-experiments, however, discussed in the section on methods in psychology, this is not possible.

In a **repeated measures design** (sometimes known as a **related design** or **within-groups design**), participants take part in both (or all) the conditions. Their performance in the different conditions is compared. Since participants take part in both (or all) conditions, random allocation does not apply in quite the same way. The order in which they carry out the conditions, however, should be randomised.

Evaluation of independent measures design

The main advantage of the independent measures design is that it eliminates the possible problem of **order effects**. If all participants take part in both or all conditions in the same order, there may be a **practice** effect. They may do better in the second condition in which they take part, not because of the nature of the condition itself, but because they may be helped through practice. Alternatively, **boredom** or **fatigue** as they work through the conditions could account for differences in performance. Taking part in only one condition eliminates this possibility.

Using this design also helps to reduce the effect of **demand characteristics**. If people take part in more than one condition, they are more likely to guess the aim of the experiment and perhaps adjust their performance than if they take part in only one condition. In some cases, fewer materials are needed, since the same materials (e.g. the list of words to be remembered) can be the same in both or all conditions, as each participant will be exposed to them only once.

The major drawback to an independent measures design is the possibility of the results being affected by **individual differences** between the participants in each condition. In the memory test example, any difference between the two conditions could come about as the result of participants in one group having in general better memories than those in the other, rather than the manipulation of the IV, i.e. the strategy they have been asked to use. Random allocation of participants helps to minimise this source of bias. This design also requires more participants (i.e. twice as many in a two-condition experiment) than a repeated measures design, in which each participant provides data in both or all conditions.

Evaluation of repeated measures design

The main advantage of a repeated measures design is that it eliminates the influence of **individual differences**, since each participant's performance in one condition is compared with that same person's performance on the other(s). As noted above, it also requires fewer participants.

The main drawback, however, is the possible influence of **order effects**, i.e. practice, boredom and fatigue. Sometimes it is possible to minimise these effects by **counterbalancing**, i.e. varying the order in which participants carry out conditions. In the memory test example, half the participants could start with the rehearsal condition, and then go on to use story linkage, while for the other participants, this order would be reversed.

Counterbalancing is not always a solution, however. For example, in the memory experiment, participants who started with the story linkage condition could find it so effective that they used it in the rehearsal condition as well in spite of the instructions they were given. Counterbalancing may not even be possible. For example, if the effectiveness of coaching for an intelligence test were to be investigated, intelligence test scores before and after coaching could be compared, and clearly the 'before' condition would need to be measured first.

With a repeated measures design, **demand characteristics** are likely to be more of a problem. It is also possible that additional materials would need to be prepared. For instance, in the memory test example, different word lists would need to be constructed for each condition; otherwise participants might remember more words on the second condition simply because they had already seen them once. The word lists would also need to be matched in terms of word length and how common the words are, which could be a time-consuming process. A word list in one condition with words like 'cat' and 'chair' matched with a word list in the other condition with words like 'chandelier' and 'antigropeloes' would clearly introduce an unwanted bias!

Matched pairs design

A final design possibility is a **matched pairs design**. This aims to pick up on the advantages of both independent measures and repeated measures designs, while avoiding some of the drawbacks of both. In this design, each participant is matched with another participant on characteristics which are considered relevant to the experiment. These characteristics could include age, sex, personality or intelligence. One participant from each pair is then allocated at random to each condition, and each participant takes part in only one condition. This method assumes that the matching process creates pairs which are so similar that for the purposes of the study they can be treated as if they were the same person.

To return to the memory experiment example, potential participants could be matched on the basis of their memory ability. They would be given an initial memory test requiring them to learn a list of nonsense syllables, for example, and would be put into pairs on the basis of having similar recall scores. One member of each pair would then be randomly allocated to each condition.

Activity 12: matched pairs design

Look back through the discussion of the advantages and drawbacks of the independent measures and repeated measures designs. Identify the strengths of each which are incorporated in a matched pairs design.

What are the drawbacks of this design?

When you have finished, see the notes on page 86.

Pilot studies

Whichever design is selected, a **pilot study** is normally carried out before starting the process of gathering data. A pilot study is a small-scale study carried out with a few participants to highlight any possible problems in the planned study. For example, the instructions given to participants may not be clear, or the statements used in an attitude questionnaire may be ambiguous. A pilot study also clarifies aspects of the research such as whether the method used to collect data in an observational study is workable, or how long the optimal time would be for a participant to be exposed to materials in a study on memory. If the time allowed is too long, there is likely to be a **ceiling effect**, where most of the participants remember virtually everything, and so the procedure fails to discriminate between the performance of different participants. Similarly, if it is too short, there may be a **floor effect**, where very little is remembered by anyone.

- An experiment has one or more **experimental conditions**, where participants receive particular treatments. For the purposes of comparison, it may also have a **control condition**, where there is no experimental intervention.
- In an **independent measures** design, different participants take part in each condition of a study.

In a **repeated measures design**, each participant provides data in both or all the conditions.

- Each design has both strengths and weaknesses in terms of **order effects**, **demand characteristics** and the influence of **individual differences**.
- A **matched pairs** design attempts to combine the strengths of independent measures and repeated measures designs. It is, however, an unwieldy and time-consuming method.
- A **pilot study** is usually carried out before starting full-scale research in order to identify any possible problems with the design of the study.

2.6 Descriptive statistics

The term 'descriptive statistics' refers to ways in which sets of data can be summarised. Two important ways in which this can be done are by using measures of central tendency and measures of dispersion. We will look first at these, before moving on to look at a further kind of descriptive statistics, the use of tables, charts and graphs.

Levels of measurement

In order to discuss measures of central tendency and of dispersion, we need first to look at levels of measurement. When carrying out research, psychologists collect data. While sometimes the data are qualitative, many of the techniques described produce quantitative data, and it is this kind of data which will be discussed here. The information collected varies in how precise it is, and the term 'levels of measurement' refers to these differences in precision. It is important to assess the level of measurement of a particular set of data because this will determine how it can be analysed statistically. The different levels can be illustrated by the example shown in figure 2.

At its simplest, measurement is at **nominal level**. This is sometimes also referred to as category data, because it means that each piece of data is put into a category. Measurement at this level is basically a head count. It gives us very little information. For example, in figure 2, someone classified as 'helping' could be someone who barely helped at all or someone who was overwhelmingly helpful.

Figure 2: levels of measurement

example: study of possible gender differences in helping behaviour, where the behaviour of potential helpers is observed.

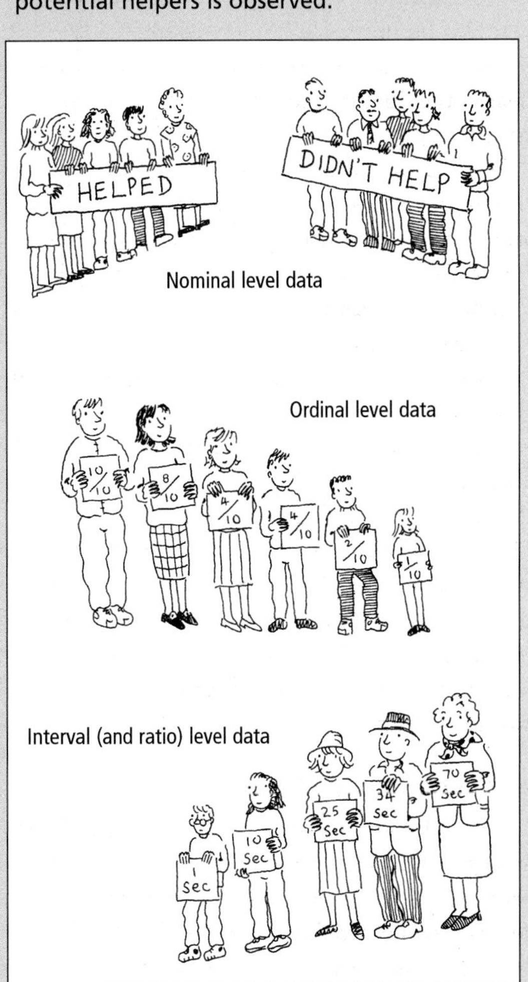

nominal level: Each person is classified as either 'helping' or 'not helping'.
ordinal level: Each person is rated on a helpfulness scale of 1–10, where 1 = 'request for help ignored' to 10 = 'overwhelmingly helpful'.
interval level: The amount of time spent helping is measured. This would also be a measurement at ratio level, since the baseline measurement of time spent helping is zero.

The next level of measurement is **ordinal level**. This goes beyond the simple categorisation of nominal data in that each piece of data is in the form of a score, and so the data can be put in order. However, the measurement is still not very precise. In figure 2, for example, we cannot assume that someone rated 8 for helpfulness is exactly twice as helpful as someone rated 4; all that can safely be said is that someone rated 8 is more helpful than someone rated 4. Since the measuring scale is so imprecise, the data are reduced to rank-ordered scores, i.e. the researcher will focus on the order of the scores rather than the scores themselves.

Interval level measurement is more precise, since it refers to measures which, in contrast to ordinal level measurement, have equal intervals between the points on the scale being used; there is exactly the same distance between 2 cm and 3 cm, for example, as between 14 cm and 15 cm. The most common examples of interval level measurement are measures of temperature, length and time.

Length and time are also examples of **ratio level** data. This is the same as interval data, but additionally the scale has a genuine zero or starting point; it is not possible, for example, to measure something as being –3 cm. Measures of temperature provide interval level data, but not ratio level: 0°C or 0°F are not a baseline measure since temperatures such as –13° are possible.

Data do not come ready labelled with a particular level of measurement; the level to be used must be decided by the researcher. If we go back to the example from figure 2, the amount of time spent helping is interval (and indeed ratio) level data. We could, however, choose to ignore the actual number of seconds spent helping, and focus instead on the order of the scores, i.e. reduce the data to ordinal level. It would also be possible to assign participants to categories, e.g. 'helped for less than 10 seconds', 'helped for 10–30 seconds' and 'helped for more than 30 seconds', thereby treating the data as nominal.

❺ Data can be described in terms of different **levels of measurement**. The level of measurement determines appropriate statistical analysis.

❺ **Nominal level**, where data are put into categories, is the least precise level. **Ordinal level** gives more information since it uses scores. It focuses on the order of the scores rather than the scores themselves. More precise still, **interval level** refers to data where there are equal intervals between the points on the measuring scale. Where there is a genuine zero, this is also **ratio level** data.

Measures of central tendency

These measures are ways of reducing a set of numerical data to one value which represents the whole set. Look back to sample study (e) in activity 11. If you had carried out this study with 40 participants in each condition, it would be quite hard work to see from the sets of scores which method produced higher recall. A good way of summarising these data to provide an easy comparison of how many words were remembered in each condition would be to work out the average, or **mean**; all the scores would be added together and the total divided by the number of scores.

The **median** is another measure of central tendency. If a set of scores is put in numerical order, the middle score of the sequence is the median. If there are two middle scores (i.e. an even number of scores in the set), the average of these two scores is the median.

The final measure of central tendency is the **mode**. This is the most frequently occurring score in a set of scores. Sometimes there may be two equally frequent scores, in which case there are two modes, known as **bimodal** values, or even more, giving **multimodal** values.

Activity 13: mean, median and mode

a These are the scores on a Psychology test for a class of students. Work out the mean, the median and the mode:

7 7 8 10 11 11 11 13 13 15 15

b The mean number of children in the average British family is 2.4. Why might this not be the best way of expressing this kind of information? Which measure of central tendency do you think might be better, and why?

c These are people's scores on a general knowledge test. Which measure of central tendency do you think would be the best way of summarising the data? Give your reasons:

5 6 12 17 18 18 25 29 31 31 36 37 64

When you have finished, see the notes on page 86.

The three measures of central tendency all have their uses and are appropriate in different circumstances. If you are collecting very precise data, i.e. interval data, like reaction time in seconds, it makes sense to use the mean to summarise the data, as it is the most precise of the three measures.

It would make less sense to use the mean where the data itself is ordinal and so is less precise, as in the use of rating scales. In general, the median is used to summarise this kind of data.

The mode is in practice rarely used except with nominal data. It would, however, make sense to use it to summarise data which fall into a limited number of categories. For example, if people were being rated on a three-point helpfulness scale (1 = didn't help; 2 = quite helpful; 3 = very helpful), identifying the category which was used most would seem to be the most effective way of summarising the data.

To highlight the usefulness and limitations of each of the measures of central tendency, work through activity 14:

Activity 14: mean, median and mode: advantages and drawbacks

For each measure of central tendency, answer the following questions:

a is this measure always an actual score?
b does it use all the scores?
c does it use the values of all the scores?
d is it distorted by an extreme value?

Decide whether your answer to each question is an advantage or a drawback of this measure, and enter each answer in this table:

measure of central tendency	advantage	disadvantage
mean	1 ______ 2 ______	1 ______ 2 ______
median	1 ______ 2 ______	1 ______ 2 ______
mode	1 ______ 2 ______	1 ______ 2 ______

When you have finished, see the notes on page 86.

Measures of dispersion

A measure of dispersion is another way of summarising data. This measure gives an indication of the spread of scores, i.e. the extent to which scores deviate from the measure of central tendency. In these sets of scores:

13 14 15 16 17 and 5 10 15 20 25

the mean for each sample is 15, but the second set of scores shows a much greater spread than the first. A measure of dispersion is therefore a further way of summarising data and gives more useful information than a measure of central tendency alone.

A simple way of expressing this spread of scores is to use the **range**. This is simply the smallest score subtracted from the largest score. In the above example, the range for the first set of scores is therefore 4, and for the second set 20. For technical reasons, if there is an even number of scores, 1 is usually added to this figure. If values are calculated to one decimal place, e.g. 7.6 and 5.8, the range is the difference between the extreme scores plus 0.1, while 0.01 is added if values are calculated to two decimal places, e.g. 7.64 and 5.83.

The range is very simple to work out. However, while it can give a rough idea of the dispersion of a set of scores, it is not a very precise measure. For example, where there is an extreme score (as in activity 13 c), the range can give a distorted picture of the data. Similarly, if we take these two sets of scores as an example:

10 10 11 11 11 19 and 10 18 18 18 19 19

the range in each case would be the same, while the distribution of scores is very different, each with an extreme score at opposite ends of the distribution.

The **standard deviation** (SD) is a more sophisticated measure of dispersion, since it calculates the average distance from the mean of all the scores. It is a more precise measure of dispersion than the range, since the values of all the scores contribute towards the calculation. Because it is a more precise measure, it is particularly suitable when the data themselves are precise, i.e. at interval or ratio level, such as the time taken to react to a visual stimulus. Where the data are less precise, e.g. in the form of ratings on a rating scale, which are ordinal level data, the range is more likely to be used as a measure of dispersion.

Activity 15: calculating the standard deviation

1 Read through this worked example for the set of scores out of 20 in a Psychology test.

12 10 8 4 8 18

a Work out the mean by adding all the scores and dividing by the number of scores:

60 divided by 6 = 10

b Subtract each score from the mean:

–2 0 2 6 2 –8

c Square each of these numbers and add them:

4 + 0 + 4 + 36 + 4 + 64 = 112
(NB the – values in **b** are now +)

d Divide this number by the number of scores:

112 divided by 6 = 18.67. This is known as the **variance**.

e find the square root of this number: 4.32. This is the **standard deviation**.

2 Calculate the standard deviation for this set of scores:

10 15 7 22 14 18 12

Measures of central tendency and measures of dispersion are both ways of summarising large amounts of data. These measures are very useful in giving an easily accessible overview of the general trend of the data produced by a study, and for this reason they are often included in a table in the results section of a research report.

- **Descriptive statistics** offers ways of summarising data.
- The **mean**, the **median** and the **mode** are three **measures of central tendency**, i.e. they offer a way of representing a set of scores with one statistic.
- The **range** and the **standard deviation** are **measures of dispersion**, which give information about the spread of scores.

Graphical representation

Psychologists carrying out research often present their data graphically. This way of summarising results has the advantage of presenting the data very clearly, in such a way that the overall findings are immediately accessible to the reader of a research report. Four of the most frequently used types of graphical representation are histograms, frequency polygons, bar charts and scattergraphs. We will look at each of these in turn, and consider when they are an appropriate way of presenting data, the underlying principles of their use and how they are interpreted.

Histograms

A histogram is used when representing interval- or ratio-level data. It divides data into categories, each represented as a bar. The bars are of equal width, and are drawn touching each other. Since histograms can only be used with continuous data, i.e. where there are no gaps between scores for the categories, categories which do not contain scores must also be shown, as in the first category in activity 16 (see opposite). The categories are shown on the x-axis, with the mid-point of each category being identified, and the frequency with which each category occurs is shown on the y-axis.

Let us take as an example the results of a memory test, where participants have been asked to learn a set of 30 words and then write down as many as they can remember.

Activity 16: interpreting a histogram

Look at this histogram and answer the questions below:

Histogram showing the number of words recalled on a memory test

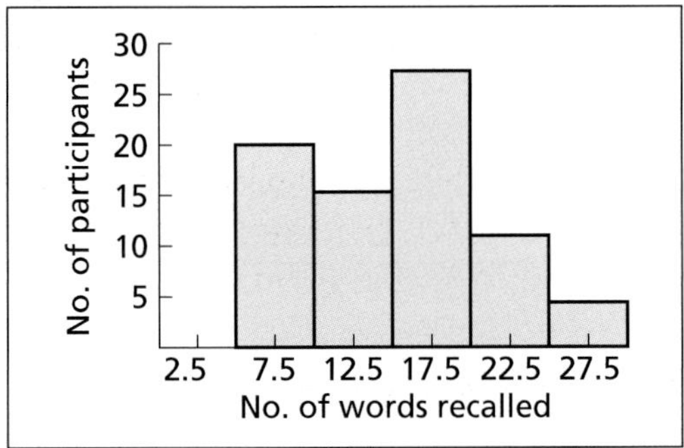

1 How wide is the range of scores within each category?
2 What is the range of scores making up the category on the extreme right?
3 How many participants had scores in the largest category?

When you have finished, see the notes on page 87.

Frequency polygons

A frequency polygon is an alternative to a histogram. Instead of using bars, the mid-points at the top of each bar are joined. It is a useful technique to show the results of two or more conditions at once. To take the data from activity 16 as an example, these scores could be data from a condition in an experiment in which participants were asked to use rehearsal as an aid to recall. Data from another condition, where participants were asked to use story linkage, could be shown on the same frequency polygon, so that comparison of the results of the two conditions could be made (figure 3).

Bar charts

Bar charts look similar to histograms, in that they consist of bars of equal width, but there are important differences. They are used with ordinal or nominal data, and so can be used with non-continuous frequencies on the *x*-axis. They are often used to show the means for different conditions in an experiment. They are usually drawn so that one bar does not touch the next, so that they do not seem to suggest that the data are continuous. Two examples of bar charts are shown in figure 4. The first shows means for the two conditions of a

Figure 3: frequency polygon showing the number of words recalled on a memory test

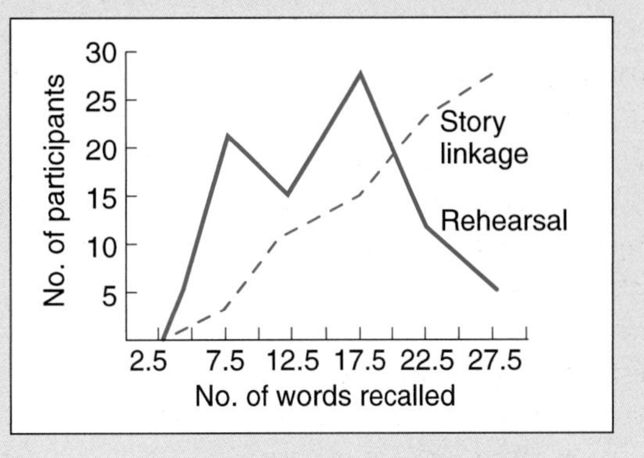

Figure 4: examples of bar charts

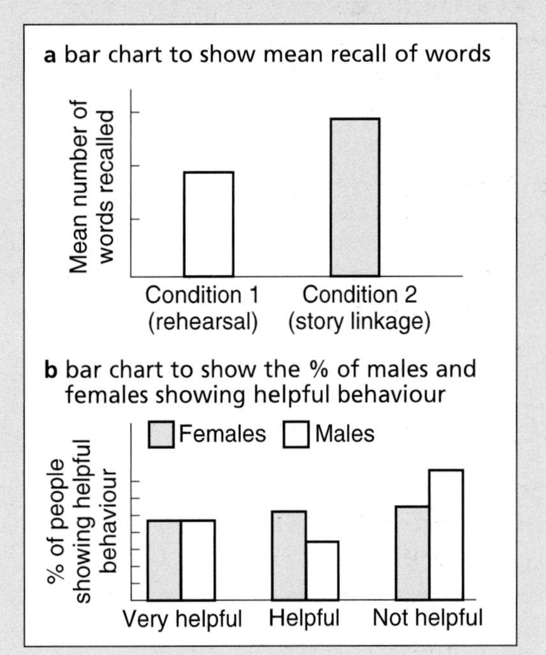

memory experiment, comparing the effectiveness of rehearsal and story linkage on recall of words. The second compares the helpfulness of males and females in terms of opening doors for someone carrying heavy shopping.

Activity 17: interpreting a bar chart

Look at this bar chart and answer the questions below:

Bar chart to show the number of aggressive acts observed in children at play

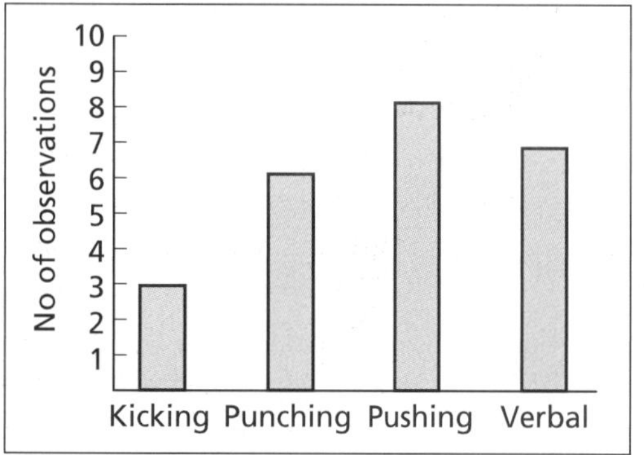

1 Which behaviour was observed most frequently?
2 Which behaviour was observed least frequently?
3 How many acts of verbal aggression were observed?

When you have finished, see the notes on page 87.

Scattergraphs

Scattergraphs (or scattergrams) are used to show sets of data where a correlational technique has been used. Each of the two variables being correlated is represented on one axis. The crossing point of the two scores for each individual being tested is marked on the scattergraph.

In practice, a perfect positive or a perfect negative relationship is extremely rare, particularly as the number of observations increases, so a scattergraph can be used to assess the direction and strength of any relationship between the two variables being correlated. It can be helpful to draw a line of best fit on a scattergraph to help show whether the relationship between the two variables is generally a positive or a negative one, and to show the strength of that relationship.

Figure 5: scattergraphs

a a perfect positive correlation

b a perfect negative correlation

c no relationship between the two variables

d a curvilinear relationship (see earlier section on correlation)

To work out where a line of best fit should go, the average value of each variable is worked out, and the resulting point – the **pivot point** – is marked on the scattergraph. A straight line is then drawn through this point in such a way that each point is as close to the line as possible, and with the same number of points above and below the line:

Figure 6: scattergraph with line of best fit

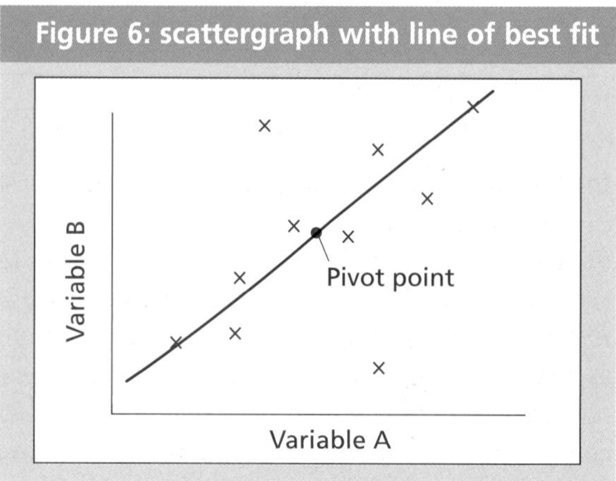

In figure 6, since the line of best fit is in the same direction as in figure 5a, the relationship between the variables being correlated is a positive one. As most of the points are reasonably close to the line, the correlation is fairly strong. There are two points which are quite a distance from the line of best fit;

these are called **outliers**, and mean that the strength of the correlation is reduced.

Activity 18: drawing and interpreting a scattergraph

Here are data from a correlational study to investigate a possible relationship between IQ (scores on an intelligence test) and points scores at A-level (where A=10, B=8, C=6, D=4, E=2):

participant	IQ scores	A-level scores
1	125	20
2	110	14
3	127	24
4	135	18
5	118	22
6	142	20
7	122	16
8	112	10
9	128	18
10	108	10

Use these data to draw a scattergraph, and draw on a line of best fit.

a Does your scattergraph show a positive or a negative relationship?

b Are there any outliers?

c How strong is the relationship between IQ and performance at A-level?

When you have finished, see the notes on page 87.

- **Graphical representation** provides a clear way of displaying data.
- **Histograms** take the form of bars, and are used with continuous data, of at least interval level.
- **Frequency polygons** are an alternative to histograms, and are useful for showing two or more sets of data at once.
- **Bar charts** can be used with non-continuous data at ordinal or nominal level. They can also be used to show the **means** for different conditions in an experiment.
- **Scattergraphs** are used to display correlational data. They give an indication of the direction and strength of the relationship between two variables.

2.7 Ethics in psychological research

Carrying out psychological research is not just a matter of operationalising the variables in which you are interested, choosing an appropriate design, controlling possible confounding variables and handling the data which have been collected. It is also extremely important that researchers make sure that they take full account of the ethical guidelines laid down by professional bodies such as the British Psychological Society. These point out the kinds of issues which researchers need to bear in mind when planning and carrying out research.

Because of the subject matter of psychology, research is carried out on people (or in some cases animals), and this raises special concerns in terms of the way those who take part in psychological research are treated. Ethical issues arise for psychologists more than for other scientists mainly because they study living organisms. Human beings and animals are sentient beings; they can feel pain and fear. The humans involved are also thinking beings, and may experience an experimental situation as threatening, embarrassing, stressful or humiliating. It is generally considered unacceptable for a person to induce feelings of self-doubt or inadequacy in another person, so researchers need to think carefully whether what they are planning to do could affect participants in this way.

Until fairly recently, people taking part in psychological research were known as 'subjects', and you may find this term used in older textbooks. However, the term 'participants' is now widely used, and recommended by the British Psychological Society. This change in terminology emphasises the fact that people freely give their time and effort when they offer to take part in a psychological study, and so deserve respect and concern for their well-being.

'Unethical' refers to procedures which are not only morally wrong but which are also professionally unacceptable. One famous study which has been widely criticised on ethical grounds was carried out by Milgram (1963).

It is unacceptable to induce feelings of self-doubt and inadequacy

Volunteers from the general public were told that they were taking part in a study into the effect of punishment on learning. They were instructed to give electric shocks to another participant every time he failed to remember a word-pair in a memory test, and to increase the amount of shock with each wrong answer. The learner was in fact a confederate of the experimenter and no shocks were given. This was actually a study of obedience, which aimed to see to what extent ordinary people would give painful shocks to someone when instructed by an authority figure – a scientist in a white coat – to do so. Surprisingly, two-thirds of those tested were prepared to give extreme shocks, even though the shock machine indicated that this was dangerous.

Milgram's work has been widely criticised on ethical grounds, and it is perhaps the study most psychologists think of first when the topic of ethics in research involving human participants is raised. Critics claim that not only were participants deceived as to the nature of the study; they were also subjected to considerable stress. There are still differences of opinion about the ethical justifications of this research, with some psychologists seing it as highly unethical and some seeing it as work of the highest moral quality, in that it provided nformation about obedience which could not have been gained in any other way. It is perhaps worth noting that the American Psychological Society investigated the ethics of Milgram's research shortly after it appeared, and concluded that it was morally acceptable, while in 1965 the American Association for the Advancement of Science awarded him a prize for his outstanding contribution to psychological research.

One undoubted result of Milgram's study, and the debate on ethics which arose from it, was an increased focus on ethical issues in psychological research. To help researchers consider these issues, professional bodies such as the British Psychological Society (BPS) in Great Britain and the American Psychological Association (APA) in the USA produce regularly updated guidelines. Both these sets of guidelines stress that the aims of psychological research should be a better understanding of people and the promotion of human welfare, which require an atmosphere of free enquiry. At the same time, research needs to be carried out responsibly, and with concern for the welfare of people who take part in it.

We will be looking in this section at the Ethical Principles for Conducting Research with Human Participants (1993), produced by the BPS. The BPS has a register of chartered psychologists who work professionally in research or applied fields. People can be struck off the register if they fail to maintain professional standards, and it is hoped that this system will create an accredited body of professional psychologists in whom the general public can have confidence.

We will look in a little more detail at some of the issues considered by these guidelines.

Consent

In order to give consent to take part in a study, participants need to be given full information beforehand on which to base their decision. There is some evidence that sufficient information is not always routinely provided. Epstein and Lasagna (1969), for instance, found that only a third of

Figure 7: summary of BPS Ethical Principles for Conducting Research with Human Participants (1993)

1. **introduction:** in good psychological research, there should be mutual confidence and respect between participants and researchers. Guidelines are necessary to help to establish whether research is acceptable.
2. **general:** researchers have a duty to consider the ethical implications of their research before it is carried out. They should eliminate possible threats to the physical and psychological well-being of participants. When researchers do not have sufficient knowledge of possible implications of their research for people varying in age, gender or social background, they should consult people with relevant characteristics.
3. **consent:** whenever possible, participants should be given full information about an investigation so that they can make an informed decision about whether or not to take part. Especial care should be taken with research involving children or others who may be unable to give full informed consent. Participants should not be pressurised into taking part in research when the researcher is in a position of influence or authority over them, or by financial reward.
4. **deception:** deception should be avoided wherever possible, and particularly if participants are likely to feel troubled when debriefed.
5. **debriefing:** when participants are aware of having taken part in a study, at the end of their participation the researcher should offer full information. They should discuss any aspects of the research which may have had negative consequences for the participant.
6. **withdrawal from the investigation:** participants should be told at the outset that they have the right to withdraw from the study and have their data destroyed, even when the study has been completed, and whether or not they have been paid to take part.
7. **confidentiality:** information gathered about participants during research should be kept confidential, and if published should not be identifiable.
8. **protection of participants:** participants should be protected from any physical or psychological harm greater than that experienced in everyday life. Where personal information is collected, participants should be protected from stress and assured that personal questions need not be answered.
9. **observational research:** unless consent is given for behaviour to be observed, observation only of behaviour which could normally be observed by strangers is acceptable. Researchers should be sensitive to cultural values, and to intruding on the privacy of people being observed, even if they are in a public place.
10. **giving advice:** if the researcher becomes aware of physical or psychological problems of which the participant is apparently unaware, these problems should be raised with the participant. An appropriate source of professional advice should be recommended.
11. **colleagues:** a researcher who is aware of a colleague carrying out research not following these principles should encourage the colleague to consider the ethical issues arising from their research.

people volunteering to take part in a study had any real understanding of what was involved. However, this study was carried out some time ago, and with ethics emerging in recent years as a very real issue in psychological research, it may be that researchers are now more aware of the importance of giving full information.

In some circumstances, it can be difficult to obtain consent based on a full understanding of the implications of taking part in a study. The study of children poses problems here, since they may not be able to understand the situation. It is generally agreed that if children are too young to understand the research aims, or below the legal age of consent, their parents must be asked for consent in their place. Informed consent can also be a problem for some adults; for example, people with a mental disorder or people with learning difficulties.

There may be further problems when there is an existing relationship between potential participants and the researcher, particularly when the researcher is in a position of authority over participants. For example, many studies are carried out by university lecturers in Psychology, using their students as participants. In this case, steps must be taken to ensure that consent is freely given, with no inducements offered for taking part, such as participation being counted towards course grades, nor any suggestion that there might be negative consequences in deciding not to take part.

Within the university system of the United States, Psychology undergraduates have to take part as participants in research, and participation counts towards their final grades. The choice is not whether to take part or not, but only which research to participate in. They are paid for participation. However, students are aware that this is a course requirement, and it could be argued that participation may provide the students both with insights into psychological procedures and a sensitivity towards their participants when they carry out research themselves.

Deception

Menges (1973) found that 80% of a sample of 1000 experiments involved giving participants incomplete information about the study. They were given full information about the dependent variable in only 25% of the studies, and complete information about the independent variable in only 3%. In other words, deception appeared to be widespread in psychological research. Again, however, it is worth noting the date when this research was carried out; it is possible that deception is now no longer as widespread as Menges suggested.

Deception is linked to informed consent: if participants have been deceived about the nature of the study, it is not possible for them to make an informed decision as to whether or not they are willing to take part. Deception is also likely to have wider repercussions, in that participants who have been deceived are likely to be angry, and disillusioned about the way psychology studies are carried out, and so psychology may be brought into disrepute. For these reasons, the use of deception should be considered very carefully, and only used when it is essential to the study.

It has been argued that some forms of deception are worse than others. For example, if you turned up to take part in a psychology study which you thought was investigating memory, and were then told that the study was actually researching the type of person who replied to advertisements requesting volunteers, it is unlikely that you would be unduly distressed. On the other hand, deception such as that suffered by Milgram's participants, where there may be damage to people's self-image and self-esteem, is clearly potentially more serious.

One way of approaching the question of whether deception is acceptable is to consult people, similar to those to be tested, before carrying out the study. They should be given full information about the aims and procedures of the proposed study, together with the nature of the deception involved and why it is considered necessary. If they say they would have agreed to take part given this information, then there is some support for the use of deception.

Kelman (1967) has suggested that one way to overcome the problem of deception is to ask people to role-play. In some experiments, this may be a valuable strategy. At the same time, there are clearly limitations to the kind of research where this might be useful, and there will in any case inevitably be some doubt about the extent to which role-play accurately represents participants' normal behaviour.

Debriefing

Debriefing can be linked to the idea of protecting participants from harm (guideline 8). Participants are given full information about the study in which they have taken part (if this has not taken place beforehand) and are reassured about their own performance. In many cases, this is not problematical.

However, many people who have had no previous experience of taking part in psychology experiments – and these are ideal participants, since they are less likely than, for example, Psychology students, to be influenced by previous knowledge of psychology – are concerned that in some way judgements will be made either about their ability or their mental health. Careful and thorough debriefing does therefore need to be given serious consideration.

It is perhaps worth noting that debriefing can provide additional benefits for both researcher and participant. During debriefing, participants can often provide additional information about their performance which may be useful to the researcher in understanding the phenomenon being investigated. For the participant, the understanding gained during debriefing can be an educational experience shared with the researcher.

Right to withdraw

This guideline has links with the need for informed consent. Informed consent may be given at the outset of the study, but participants have the right to withdraw their consent and decide at any point that they no longer wish to take part. This right should be made clear to them, and that it applies even if (as in the case of Milgram's participants) they have accepted payment for participation. They should also know that they have the right to withdraw any data they have provided, and to have it destroyed, even when the study is completed.

In some circumstances, the right to withdraw needs to be given particular consideration. For example, in the earlier example of Psychology lecturers using their students as participants, it is particularly important that the right to withdraw at any time without negative consequences is emphasised.

Confidentiality

The importance of confidentiality is highlighted in the BPS guidelines, unless participants have agreed in advance to waive this right. Confidentiality is a legal right under the Data Protection Act, but a further argument for its importance comes from Coolican (1990), who points out that potential participants in psychology studies would soon become very hard to find if they were not assured of confidentiality!

It is standard practice in most psychology studies to assign participants a number. If their results are to be singled out for discussion in a research report, they can then be referred to by this number, and so not be identified. In some areas of research, the case study method is used, where one person or a small group of people with some unusual psychological characteristic are studied in some detail. In this case, participants are usually identified only by their initials, or by a pseudonym, as in the case of Genie (box B).

However, there may be exceptions to the practice of maintaining confidentiality, when psychologists feel they have a wider ethical duty. If we take as a hypothetical example research involving participant observation of gang behaviour, during which a researcher became aware that a crime was being planned, the researcher might consider that his ethical responsibility should be to society as a whole, and that he should therefore report the planned crime. Similarly, on a more personal level, if a researcher became aware that a participant was planning to commit suicide, he might not feel bound to respect the participant's confidentiality, if he considered this not to be in the person's best interests.

Protection from harm

There is seldom any risk of physical harm to participants in psychology experiments. Some experiments have used electric shocks or loud noise, or have deprived participants of food or sleep, or have induced nausea. However, if this is the case, participants are warned beforehand so that they can decide whether or not they wish to take part.

When it comes to psychological harm, Aronson (1988) proposed that researchers should ensure that participants leave the experimental situation in a frame of mind that is at least as sound as when they entered it. In most studies, this is not problematic if participants are given as much information as possible beforehand and fully debriefed at the conclusion of the study, and reassured that their performance is in no way out of the ordinary.

A well-accepted principle of psychological research is that if a researcher is unsure about a study and its effects on participants, they should seek advice from a colleague. This should preferably be someone who has carried out similar research before, and who is not likely to be affected by the outcome of the research, and will therefore be unbiased in the advice they give. Milgram, whose studies were mentioned earlier, followed this principle, and consulted 14 Psychology students and 40 psychiatrists before he carried out his first experiment. These people suggested that participants were very unlikely to obey the orders they were given. As we now know, their predictions were very inaccurate. However, following this basic principle can help to ensure that any possibility of harm to participants is minimised.

In some studies – again, notably those of Milgram – protection from harm is a contentious issue. It is clear that participants did not leave Milgram's studies in the same frame of mind as when they entered it, since the vast majority of them had gained an awareness of their willingness to inflict harm on an innocent human being when ordered to do so. But does the psychologist have a responsibility to protect people against self-knowledge, however unwelcome?

A cost–benefit analysis might be useful here, weighing up the costs of the immediate distress of the participants in Milgram's study against the benefits both to them personally (84% were glad to have taken part, and 75% said they had learned something useful) and more generally, in increasing our understanding of human psychological functioning in this area.

Observational studies

In many observational studies, people are unaware that their behaviour is being observed. This usually means that they have not consented to take part in the study and are not debriefed afterwards. In some cases a situation may be set up by the researcher, such as someone pretending they need help because their car has broken down, so deception may also be involved. This kind of study involves what is called **involuntary participation**, and may involve **invasion of privacy**.

It could be argued that if normally occurring behaviour in a public place is observed, consent is implicitly given. If the study you are carrying out involves observing whether men or women are more likely to hold a door open for someone passing through the door after them, the ethical considerations are fairly minimal. But if you are observing rather more sensitive behaviour – perhaps the way mothers interact with their children, or public courtship behaviour – you need to be aware of possible ethical objections. A study illustrating this problem was carried out by Humphreys (1970) who investigated the behaviour of consenting homosexuals, himself acting as a 'lookout' at a public convenience. Those being studied were completely unaware that they were being studied and that their car registration numbers were recorded in order to obtain more background information later on.

Giving advice

There is one problem that is encountered by psychologists far more frequently than by other scientists. People sometimes take the opportunity of talking to a psychology researcher about educational or mental health problems, mistaking the researcher for a clinical psychologist or a counsellor. In this case, the researcher is advised to recommend an appropriate source of professional help, and explain the misunderstanding to the person involved.

The BPS guidelines go even further than this, suggesting that advice should be offered if the researcher becomes aware that the participant may have a problem, even when the participant apparently does not realise it and has not asked for advice.

The morality of carrying out research: psychology and the ethical imperative

One further aspect of ethics in psychological research needs to be mentioned. As Brehm (1956) has pointed out: 'We must not overlook the other side of the ethical issue: the ethical imperative to gain more understanding of important areas of human behaviour'. This idea is echoed by Aronson (1988), who pointed out that psychologists have an 'ethical responsibility to society as a whole'. The BPS guidelines suggest that increasing our understanding of people's behaviour improves people's lives, and 'enhances human dignity'. In other words, if we are to understand people's behaviour and improve the quality of their lives, we must carry out research. But it must be carried out with an awareness of the rights of the participants involved.

All the ethical considerations discussed here are relevant to many pieces of research. One overall question, however, applies to *every* piece of psychology research: 'Do the ends justify the means?'. In other words, will the knowledge gained from the research outweigh any possible costs to the participants?

Aronson (1988) has suggested that psychologists may face an ethical dilemma when there is a conflict between their responsibility towards research participants and to society as a whole. For example, it could be argued that Milgram's research into obedience has highlighted aspects of important social issues with potential benefit to society, and this benefit may be considered to outweigh the cost to participants.

- **S** Psychology research can raise serious ethical issues. Various professional bodies have produced **ethical guidelines**.

- Psychology research should avoid causing physical or psychological **harm** to participants.
- Participants should give **informed consent** to taking part in a study, and should be made aware that they can **withdraw** at any time. Special care must be taken with participants who cannot give informed consent. Researchers need to be aware of possible problems in invading the **privacy** of others.
- **Deception** is sometimes unavoidable, but **debriefing** can help to minimise its effects.
- A **cost–benefit analysis** should be made before embarking on research.
- Psychologists also have an ethical responsibility to carry out research to increase knowledge about human behaviour and so potentially improve the quality of our lives.

Notes on activities

1 **a** IV = age. DV = whether or not they give way at the junction.

b IV = time of day. DV = number of soft toys produced.

c IV = instructions. DV = number of words correctly remembered.

2 There are any number of possibilities. Here are a few suggestions:

a **possible subject variables:** the gender of drivers; how pressed for time they were.

possible situation variables: how far away from the junction each driver was; the speed at which they were travelling.

b **possible subject variables:** different kinds of workers could be employed on each shift, e.g. younger workers on the early shift and older workers on the evening shift.

possible situation variables: only one period might cover a loo break; different toys, one more complicated than the other, could be produced by the different shifts.

c **possible subject variables:** some participants might find it easier to form mental images than others; those with better memories might by chance be allocated to one group.

possible situation variables: if the groups were tested in different places, there might be more distractions in one place than the other.

3 **a** a fairly strong positive correlation, say 0.8. The correlation would not be perfect because there are some tall people with relatively small feet and some short people with big feet.

b since both tests are to do with words, some positive correlation would be expected; this would probably not be particularly strong – say 0.4 – since some people who are good at English might well have little interest in French.

c a fairly strong negative correlation, say –0.8, might be expected, since there is good evidence for a relationship between stress and poor health; again, there would be exceptions, since some people seem to thrive on moderate amounts of stress.

d there doesn't seem any reason why there should be a relationship between these variables; perhaps people who spend a lot of time developing skills on video games might lead a more sedentary lifestyle and so be more likely to be overweight, so there might be a very small positive correlation, say 0.1.

4 Closed-ended questions provide data which are easier to analyse. For example, the percentage of participants choosing each response would be very easy to work out. However, it is possible that none of the answers corresponds with how the person answering the question would ideally like to respond. In the example here, the person could be taking A-level Psychology because it was the only option available which would fit in with their timetable for other subjects, and for which there were still places available. Open-ended questions may lead to more detailed information being given, but it is likely to be more difficult to analyse.

5 You may have thought it was pretty obvious what the questions were testing; you probably realised here that 'no' answers to questions 1 and 4, and 'yes' answers to questions 2 and 3, would contribute to a high score for extroversion. This awareness could possibly affect the way you answered the questions, i.e. you could respond to the **demand characteristics** of the procedure. Your answers could also be influenced by **social desirability**; people could answer so as to put themselves in a good light. It is of course rather unfair to form a judgement on the basis of a few questions; in reality, these items would be embedded in a much longer questionnaire, and one covering neuroticism as well as extroversion.

The range of possible answers could be seen as constraining; sometimes people find it hard to limit themselves to Y/N answers (even with ?). Another problem here is that the questions are a little vague and don't relate to a defined context, e.g. what kind of novel situation is meant in question 4? This could perhaps affect how you would want to answer the question. Eysenck has shown, however, that people do respond consistently over time to this kind of question.

More generally, you may have thought that answering this kind of question requires you not only to be prepared to answer the questions honestly (which may be problematic, particularly if something important – like being offered a job – depends on the outcome) but also to have enough insight to be able to do so.

6 Open-ended questionnaires, unstructured interviews, case studies, participant observation and to some extent clinical interviews are all likely to produce qualitative data.

7 a IV = interest. People could be asked to use a scale of 1 (very boring) to 10 (extremely interesting) to rate for interest potential topics on which they might be tested. The operational definition of interest would be the interest ratings.

DV = memory. People could be given questionnaires on passages they were asked to memorise. The operational definition of memory would be the questionnaire scores.

b IV = gender, i.e. whether children were boys or girls.

DV = aggression. Both boys and girls could be observed at play. A list of aggressive behaviours could be drawn up (e.g. pushing, name-calling etc.). The number of times these behaviours were shown during the observation period would be the operational definition of aggression.

c IV = neuroticism. This could be operationalised as the N scores on Eysenck's EPI. People scoring above a certain point on the scale would be classed as 'neurotic' and those below a certain point as 'non-neurotic'.

DV = the extent to which participants suffer from phobias. A questionnaire could be used to establish which phobias people suffer from and the extent to which they fear phobic objects and situations. The operational definition would be the scores on the phobia questionnaire.

8 a two-tailed. One-tailed = people who eat fish will score higher on an intelligence test than those who do not eat fish.

b two-tailed. One-tailed = there will be a positive relationship between extroversion and a preference for loud music.

c one-tailed. Two-tailed = there will be a difference in the number of words remembered in a foreign language when the information is presented in picture form and as words alone.

9 Some suggestions here are that the sample should include: both sexes; mature students as well as students studying for A-levels immediately after finishing their GCSEs at school; students in both their first year and second year of study; those taking different combinations of A-levels, e.g. science, languages and so on.

10 This kind of sample is very easily biased. You might, for example, tend to approach people you are friendly with, and they might differ in important respects from the parent population, i.e. the population from which they are drawn. For example, in activity 9 these could be students following similar A-level courses, leaving out those studying other courses.

11 **a** stratified sample. It may not be representative because only gender and choice of academic subjects are taken into account, which may overlook other important characteristics. It could be, for example, that those tested all smoke and drink, so people who do not use these kinds of substances are not represented.

b cluster sample. It may not be representative because the schools chosen may be atypical in some way, for example being part of a multi-ethnic community, excluding from the sample those with no experience of other cultures.

c self-selecting sample. It may not be representative because people who volunteer to take part in studies may be a particular type of person.

d opportunity sample. It may not be representative because the students may prefer to ask others from their year group whom they know well.

e random. It may not be representative because it could happen, for example, that the sample comprises the more intelligent females and the less intelligent males from the population.

12 **Independent measures:** order effects are eliminated; demand characteristics are reduced; fewer materials are required.

Repeated measures: individual differences are reduced, though not eliminated.

Drawbacks: the main drawback of the matched pairs design is the time involved in matching up participants, or indeed in finding participants who can be matched in this way. Complete matching is not really possible, and it may be that participants have not been matched on a characteristic which turns out to be important. If one participant drops out of the study, the nature of the design means that two participants are lost.

13 **a** the mean, median and mode are all 11.

b nobody actually has 2.4 children. The mode, i.e. the number of children a family is most likely to have, might be a more realistic way of putting this information across.

c the mode could be used. This would be a bimodal distribution, with modes at 18 and 31. On the other hand, there are a lot of scores which have different values from these. The mean could be used, but would give a rather distorted picture, since the score of 64 is extreme, well out of line with the other scores. The median would probably give the most accurate picture.

14 **mean:** advantages **b** (yes) and **c** (yes); disadvantages **a** (no) and **d** (yes).

median: advantages **d** (no) and **b** (yes); disadvantages **a** (only with an odd number of scores) and **c** (no).

mode: advantages **a** (yes) and **d** (no); disadvantages **b** (no) and **c** (no).

15 4.63.

16 **1** five; **2** 26–30; **3** 27.

17 **1** kicking; **2** pushing; **3** seven.

18 The scattergraph should look like this:

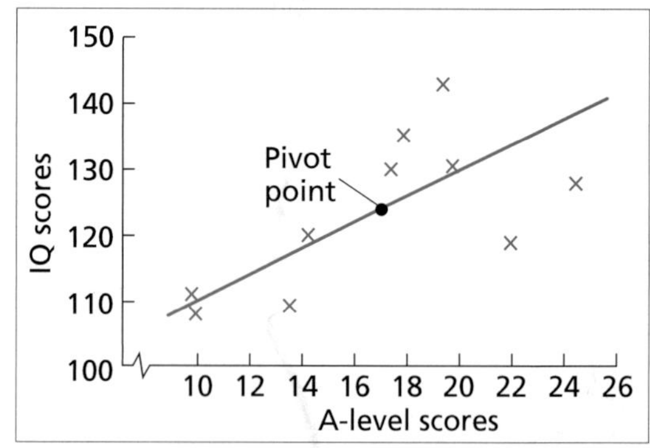

1 The line of best fit indicates a positive correlation.

2 Most of the points lie fairly close to the line of best fit, though there are some outliers.

3 This indicates a reasonable but not particularly strong positive correlation between IQ and A-level points scores.

Psychology of gender

3.1 Concepts in gender research

To start this discussion of the psychology of gender, we need first of all to define our terms. Many psychologists draw a distinction between sex and gender. **Sex** refers to the biological aspects of being male or female; anatomy, physiology, hormones, brain biochemistry, and so on. **Gender** refers to social and cultural aspects, including attitudes and behaviour.

While in many areas of psychological functioning no differences have been found between males and females, some general differences have been established. In terms of cognitive functioning, Maccoby and Jacklin (1974) found that females tend to do better than males on tests of verbal ability, while males tend to do better than females on tests of visuospatial ability. Males are also on average more aggressive than females, especially where physical aggression is involved, although according to Eagly and Steffen (1986) this difference is much less marked when aggression involves psychological rather than physical harm. At the same time, even where such differences have been found, there is a considerable overlap on almost any psychological variable which has been measured. For example, many females are more aggressive than many males.

Gender identity refers to the sense of oneself as male or female. As we will see later, it is not until they are about six years old that children develop a full sense of themselves as being permanently male or permanently female. **Gender roles** are beliefs, attitudes, values and behaviour which a particular society sees as appropriate for males or for females. These roles are a part of what is acquired through the process of **socialisation** during childhood, which, through interaction with parents and others, will equip the individual with the understanding and skills to function effectively within the society in which they are growing up. Much of the socialisation process – for example, knowledge of the language and culture, and an understanding of moral rules – will be very similar irrespective of the sex of the child. By definition, however, an understanding of gender and its implications will differ depending on whether the child is a boy or a girl.

Many theories, for example that of Kohlberg, see the formation of **gender stereotypes** as an important factor in the acquisition of relevant gender roles. Stereotypes have been defined as 'widely shared assumptions about the personalities, attitudes and behaviour of people based on group membership, for example ethnicity, nationality, sex, race and class' (Hogg and Vaughan 1995). All members of that category or social group are perceived as sharing the same characteristics, and any individual belonging to that category is assumed to have these characteristics. Gender stereotypes therefore provide a somewhat generalised understanding of the characteristics and behaviour of males and females.

Activity 1: gender stereotyping

Run a small-scale study to investigate gender stereotyping. Give your participants the following list of characteristics, and ask them to indicate for each one whether they think it is more typical of a man or a woman :

1 emotional	**5** rational	**9** hard-headed
2 resourceful	**6** cautious	**10** fussy
3 witty	**7** affectionate	**11** warm
4 forgiving	**8** cruel	**12** confident

Box A: Rubin *et al.* (1974)

Procedure: Parents were asked to describe their newborn infants. Male and female

infants were matched on size, weight and muscle tone, to eliminate individual differences as a possible confounding variable.
Results: Sons were more likely to be described as strong, active and well-co-ordinated. Daughters were more likely to be described as beautiful, little, delicate and weak.
Conclusion: From birth, parents have different expectations of children, based on their sex.

Activity 1 includes sample items from the 300 descriptions used in a study by Williams and Best (1990). They found that numbers 1, 4, 6, 7, 10 and 11 are commonly associated with females, and the others with males. It is perhaps worth noting, however, that the design of the study did not allow for participants to consider characteristics as being neither typically male nor typically female. You should also bear in mind that while stereotypes are often thought of as negative, it is also possible to have positive stereotypes; for example, some of the stereotypical associations in activity 1 are positive, e.g. warm and confident.

We apply stereotypes based on gender very early on:

Children themselves also develop gender stereotypes, and we will be returning to this in the context of theories about the nature of gender development.

Children's understanding of their gender and its implications is important in that it forms part of their sense of identity. A basic understanding of whether they are a boy or a girl is often developed by the age of two. Gender distinctions are often made in talking to children, for example referring to them as a 'good boy' or 'clever girl'. Moreover, in some cultures, this focus is supported by marking gender differences – for example, by clothing, hair style or adornment. In Juxtlahuaca in Mexico, the ears of little girls are pierced in the first weeks of life, and all females wear earrings. Children's basic understanding of gender continues to develop, as we shall see, throughout childhood, and gender remains an important part of the self-concept.

Much research into gender has focused on diferences between males and females. Masculinity and femininity have formed part of many personality tests; an item is considered to show masculinity and femininity if most men respond to a test statement in one way and women in another. For example, we might expect most men to agree with the statement: 'I prefer watching football to shopping for clothes', and most women to disagree with it. This research tends to assume that a person can be either masculine or feminine, but not both. However, there is no reason why a person could not enjoy both activities, or neither. It is therefore possible that a person could be highly masculine (i.e. having well-developed masculine characteristics) and at the same time highly feminine. Bem (1974) uses the term **androgyny** (from the Greek 'andros', man and 'gyne', woman) to refer to this.

Activity 2: how androgynous are you?

Indicate how accurately each of the following characteristics describes you on this scale: *1* (never/almost never true); 2 (usually not true); 3 (sometimes but not often true); *4* (occasionally true); 5 (often true); 6 (usually true); 7 (always/almost always true).

1 self-reliant
2 helpful
3 cheerful
4 moody
5 independent
6 conscientious
7 conventional
8 affectionate
9 assertive
10 ambitious
11 having a strong personality
12 loyal
13 unpredictable
14 forceful
15 reliable
16 sympathetic
17 jealous
18 having leadership ability
19 sensitive to needs of others
20 truthful
21 understanding
22 secretive
23 compassionate
24 sincere
25 eager to soothe hurt feelings
26 conceited
27 dominant
28 warm
29 solemn
30 willing to take a stand
31 tender
32 friendly
33 aggressive
34 gullible
35 efficient
36 acting as leader
37 adaptable
38 individualistic
39 competitive
40 gentle

When you have finished, see the notes on scoring and interpretation on page 104.

There is quite a lot of research supporting the idea that androgyny brings with it psychological and social advantages. For example, Davison (2000) found that among older women (who are often at the receiving end of both sexism and ageism in our society), those who scored high for androgyny also reported higher levels of subjective well-being than less androgynous women. In a rather different area, Gana *et al.* (2001) found that highly androgynous husbands showed greater participation in household tasks than those who were less androgynous.

Bem herself claimed that the benefits of androgyny come about as the result of integrating masculine and feminine characteristics. However, it has also been argued (e.g. by Schneider 1988) that the advantage which androgynous individuals have arises simply from them having more good characteristics. There is some evidence for this:

Box B: Spence and Helmreich (1979)

Procedure: Participants were divided into those who were: high on masculinity; high on femininity; androgynous (high on both); and undifferentiated (low on both). The levels of self-esteem of participants were also measured.

Results: Highly androgynous participants had the highest self-esteem, followed by those high on masculinity, then those high on femininity. The undifferentiated group had the lowest self-esteem.

Conclusion: A combination of good traits, both masculine and feminine, is linked to high self-esteem.

One question that arises in the context of gender research is the extent to which gender differences are due to innate, biological factors (**nature**), and how much they depend on the different experiences – personal, social and cultural – of girls and boys (**nurture**). We will be looking later in the chapter at the biological and biosocial approaches to gender development, generally in line with a nature approach, and then at various psychological accounts – social learning theory and cognitive–developmental theory – which give rather more weight to nurture factors. Psychodynamic theory is not at either extreme, focusing as it does on the interaction of biological sex and environmental experience.

We cannot assume that psychological differences between men and women are entirely innate, i.e. based on the sex into which an individual is born. Richardson *et al.* (1979) found that women can be as aggressive as men in circumstances where aggression is socially approved, which suggests that social factors have a part to play in gender differences of this kind. We will be looking at this in more detail when we come to look at theories of gender development.

A further area of interest is the extent to which gender roles and gender stereotypes are universal or show **cultural diversity**. The Williams and Best (1990) study on which activity 1 is based was carried out in 30 countries all over the world. They found considerable agreement in gender-stereotyping using this kind of material.

Women can be as aggressive as men in circumstances where aggression is socially approved.

Similarly, Costa *et al.* (2001) collected personality data from 26 cultures, and found universal gender differences broadly in line with gender stereotypes. However, they also point out that gender differences are small compared with individual variation within genders.

- Psychologists draw a distinction between **sex** (the biological aspects of being male or female) and **gender** (social and cultural factors).
- Our **gender identity** is our sense of ourselves as male or female. **Gender roles** are beliefs, attitudes, values and behaviour which are seen as socially appropriate for males or for females. **Gender stereotypes** are beliefs about typically male or female characteristics. They start to be developed in early childhood.
- **Androgyny** represents the idea that an individual can have both stereotypically male and stereotypically female characteristics.
- A major issue in gender research is the extent to which gender development is seen as the result of innate physical characteristics (**nature**) or is influenced by personal, social and cultural factors (**nurture**). **Cross-cultural research** looks at the extent to which gender roles and gender stereotypes are universal across cultures.

3.2 Methods in gender research

There are a great many ways of investigating any topic in psychology, and a range of different methods has been used in gender research, depending on the nature of the issue. The **experimental method** is widely used in psychological research, including research into gender. You will remember from chapter 2 that this involves manipulating an independent variable, and an element of random selection and/or allocation of participants to conditions. An example of a study using this method is shown in box C:

Box C: Condry and Condry (1976)

Procedure: Adults were shown a videotape of a nine-month-old child. Some were introduced to the child as a boy ('David') and some as a girl ('Dana'). The child was shown responding to various stimuli, such as a jack-in-the-box, and participants were asked to describe the emotions the child showed.

Results: Although the child's emotional response to the jack-in-the-box was unclear, the emotion tended to be labelled as anger by people who believed the child was a boy, and fear by those who believed it was a girl.

Conclusion: The labelling of the child's emotional response was influenced by the child's presumed sex.

While experimental methods have been used to some extent in research into gender, other methods have also been found to be useful. They include case studies, content analysis and observational methods. It is perhaps worth noting that since much research into gender involves comparing males and females, a lot of research is **quasi-experimental**, since sex is the independent variable.

As we saw in chapter 2, case studies, which investigate in detail one person or a small group of people, are often the most appropriate method to use when something unusual is being researched. One example is the study of Mr Blackwell, a rare case of hermaphroditism, a condition in which a person is physiologically both male and female. This study was able to shed some light on the relative influence of nature and nurture on gender identity:

Box D: Goldwyn (1979)

Goldwyn described the case of Mr Blackwell, a hermaphrodite. Hermaphroditism is a very rare condition – Mr Blackwell was only the 303rd recorded case – in which a proportion of the person's cells are the female type (XX) and the rest are the male type (XY). It is thought that this comes about by the egg being fertilised both by a sperm carrying an X chromosome and by one carrying a Y chromosome.

Half his body was male and the other half female. He had functioning sexual characteristics of both a male and a female, with an active testicle on one side and an active ovary on the other. He had both a vagina and a penis. At 14 he developed breasts, and began to ovulate and menstruate. Further tests revealed that his brain biochemistry was female in the way that his sex hormones were regulated.

He had been brought up as a boy. He was quite certain he was a male, and his female parts were surgically removed. He went on to function as a male. His upbringing as a male seems to have been a major influence on gender development.

There are two further examples of the use of this method in gender research in activity 3, the Batista family study and Money's study of an accidental penectomy during circumcision. The development of some members of the Batista family is unusual, in that they have female anatomy as children, but go on to develop male sexual characteristics at puberty. Money's study also investigates a (thankfully) rare case. Because of their very unusual nature, the case study approach was appropriate in both cases, as a way of throwing some light on the nature of gender development.

Another method which has been found useful is **content analysis**, which analyses existing material. For example, it has been suggested that the media may be one source of gender stereotypes, and children's books or TV programmes can be analysed in terms of how frequently characters show behaviour which is gender stereotyped. One example of this kind of study looked at gender stereotypes in the media:

Box E: Craig (1992)

Procedure: A sample of prime time TV advertisements was examined. A comparison was made of how males and females were portrayed in advertisements for over-the-counter drugs and non-drug commercials.
Results: Women were significantly more likely than men to appear as characters in drug commercials. This was not the case for other commercials. In drug commercials, women were frequently portrayed as experts on home medical care, often as mothers caring for sick children.
Conclusion: In drug advertisements, advertisers portray women in terms of gender stereotypes, as nurturers and caregivers.

You can carry out a similar piece of research of your own in activity 4, looking at the way children are portrayed in children's TV programmes, to investigate whether or not the media promote or influence gender-typed behaviour. One strength of this approach is that in looking at already existing material, it has high ecological validity. However, it is clearly limited in the kinds of areas it can investigate.

Observational methods can also be used, and can be very useful when very young chilren are to be studied. Asking young children about their concept of gender may be problematical. For example, Kohlberg's studies – which we shall look at later, when we discuss his cognitive–developmental theory – asked children about their understanding of gender. One of the criticisms made of his work is that the complexity of the questions he used may have meant that the children who were interviewed did not fully understand what was required of them. Moreover, children may also have problems in expressing themselves. Since young children are usually very eager to please, it may also be the case that they may tell researchers what they believe they want to hear, rather than being entirely honest.

To avoid such problems, researchers may decide to observe children's behaviour – for example, who they choose to play with, or what toys they prefer. This can provide valuable information, particularly if the children are not aware that they are being observed. Box F describes an example of a study taking this approach:

Box F: O'Brien and Huston (1985)

Procedure: Children aged beween one and three were given sets of play materials. Adults had rated these toys in advance as 'male', 'female' or 'neutral'. The toys which boys and girls chose to play with was observed.
Results: Even the youngest boys tended to choose 'male' toys, and there was little change in this respect after the age of 20 months. Girls' tendency to chose 'female' toys emerged rather later than boys' preferences. In both sexes, a pattern of sex-typed play was clearly established well before the age of three.
Conclusion: A preference for gender-appropriate toys emerges very early in a child's life. Since it emerges so early, it is likely that behaviour precedes conscious awareness and understanding of these choices.

Even the youngest boys tended to choose 'male' toys ...

Given the age of the children in this study, an observational approach obviously made data collection easier. However, such studies can be open to observer bias, and an element of interpretation of the data is often necessary.

Recently, there has been a lot of interest in gender similarities and differences across different **cultures**. Two studies which investigated gender stereotypes in terms of beliefs about male and female characteristics across cultures – those by Williams and Best (1990) and Costa *et al.* (2001) – were mentioned in the previous section. Studies into gender stereotypes in the media, such as the one by Craig (see box E), have also been carried out cross-culturally. For example, Furnham *et al.* (2000) found gender stereotyping in TV advertisements both in France and in Denmark, although Danish advertisements were in general rather less gender stereotypic in their portrayal of women than those in France. Furnham and Mak (1999) reviewed 14 studies, comparing gender stereotyping across cultures, which had looked at cultures as diverse as Australia, Hong Kong, Mexico, and Italy. They found that sex-role stereotyping was universal.

The underlying rationale for cross-cultural research has been that if there are similar findings across cultures, then these characteristics must be genetically determined (a nature viewpoint). On the other hand, if there are differences between cultures, then environmental factors are seen to be important (a nurture viewpoint). One way of explaining the similarity of the cross-cultural findings of sex-role stereotyping could therefore be that gender stereotypes reflect real differences between males and females, which could be innate and genetically determined. On the other hand, it could also be that women's status and the roles they are expected to fill are similar across many of the cultures studied.

However, not all cross-cultural studies have identified similarities between cultures. As in the Furnham *et al.* study comparing gender stereotypes in France and Denmark, differences between cultures have also been found. Hofstede (1984) has suggested that countries themselves can be characterised in gender terms, and describes as 'masculine' those cultures which use the biological existence of the two sexes to define very different social roles for men and for women. Milner and Collins (2000) found that variation between cultures on this characteristic could be linked to sex-role portrayal in the media, with 'masculine' cultures featuring fewer depictions of male–female relationships than cultures which were not so easily described in this way.

While a lot of gender research has used adult participants – for example, the Rubin study in box A and the Condry and Condry study in box C – much research into gender, particularly that carried out by psychologists interested in the development of gender identity, has used children as participants. While an awareness of **ethical issues** is important in all psychological research, particular care needs to be taken when children are being studied. In the BPS ethical guidelines in chapter 2 (figure 7), guideline 3 raises the issue of young children being unable to give full informed consent to take part in a study. Guideline 8, which relates to the protection of participants, is also particularly relevant to children. It is clearly the duty of the researcher to consider very carefully how a study is to be run, so that child participants are in no way badly affected by taking part in a study.

- Methods used in gender research include **experiments**, **case studies**, **content analysis** and **observational studies**. The method chosen will depend on the nature of what is to be investigated.
- **Cross-cultural research** makes comparisons between cultures. While many studies have found similarities, some have identified cultural differences.
- As with any topic in psychology, gender research needs to take **ethics** into account, particularly when children are to be studied.

3.3 Explaining gender

Biological and biosocial approaches

Before we consider the biological approach to gender development, we need to look briefly at biological sex differences. Sex can be defined in terms of three kinds of physical differences between males and females. Firstly, it refers to whether the egg was fertilised by a sperm carrying an X or a Y **chromosome**. It can further be defined in terms of **gonads**, i.e. testes in males and ovaries in females. Finally, there are **hormonal** differences, with males producing androgens (the most important of which is testosterone), and females producing oestrogen and progesterone. While both males and females can produce all the hormones, males produce very much more of the male hormones than females, and vice versa.

Both males and females begin as an egg bearing an X chromosome. If the egg is fertilised by a sperm carrying another X chromosome, the embryo will develop as a girl, and the two gonads will become ovaries. The embryo has both male and female interior anatomy, but the male elements spontaneously disintegrate, while the female ones thicken and grow into a womb. At the same time, the exterior anatomy, which has the same beginning for both sexes, develops into female genitalia, and the result is a girl. As we shall see, even without ovaries, development follows the female route; the natural route of the human is the female one.

To become a male means interfering with that natural route. If the sperm carries a Y chromosome, the gonads develop into testes. They pump out a hormone which actively absorbs the female parts which would otherwise begin to grow, and then produce the major male hormone, testosterone. This stops the male parts degenerating. It thickens the spermatic cord, and switches the genitalia away from the female route. The result is a male.

At puberty, under the influence of hypothalamic and pituitary hormones, the male or female gonads release hormones – testosterone in the male and oestrogen and progesterone in the female – which stimulate the development of secondary sexual characteristics such as the development of breasts and pubic hair.

Normal females inherit two X chromosomes, one from each parent, designated XX. Normal males inherit an X chromosome from the mother and a Y chromosome from the father. Two X chromosomes are needed for the complete development of both internal and external female characteristics, and the Y chromosome needs to be present for male development. A gene on the Y chromosome called TDF (**testis-determining factor**) is responsible for testis formation and male development.

However, some people do not have the normal XX or XY pattern. We have already looked at hermaphroditism in the case study of Mr Blackwell (box D), some of whose cells were XX and some XY. While this condition is very rare, there are also more common syndromes which show variations in the normal XX or XY pattern.

For example, in boys with **Klinefelter's syndrome** there is an extra X chromosome, so the pattern is XXY. This is caused by a complex fault in the cell division of one of the parents' sex cells, either the ovum or the sperm, which go to form the new baby. There is also a mosaic form of Klinefelter's syndrome, where an individual has some cells with the XXY pattern, and others the normal XY pattern. Men with Klinefelter's syndrome have small testes and a small penis, and they are infertile. There is no growth of body hair at puberty, and a feminine type of breast development often takes place. Testosterone therapy, started at around the age of 11 or 12, can help to bring about the development of more normal sexual characteristics, which can help to reduce the psychological problems which are common at adolescence.

Girls with **Turner's syndrome** have only 45 chromosomes instead of the normal 46, the missing chromosome being lost during cell division. As this is one of the X chromosomes, Turner's syndrome girls are designated XO. As with Klinefelter's syndrome, a mosaic form of this syndrome is also possible, with some cells having the full complement of sex chromosomes. The most obvious physical problem in this syndrome is short stature, with girls typically not becoming taller than 4′8″ (about 1.2 m). The ovaries fail to develop, so girls with true Turner's syndrome cannot conceive, though some with the mosaic form have done so. However, since the uterus is normal, in-vitro fertilisation using donor ova is possible. At puberty, breasts do not develop, pubic hair does not appear, and menstruation does not occur. These aspects of the disorder can be treated by giving oestrogen, from the age of about 12 or 13 until the natural age for menopause.

A biological account of gender differences argues that where there is a normal XX or XY pattern, innate genetic and hormonal differences between males and females are responsible for their different psychological characteristics. For example, inherent differences in musculature, testosterone levels and so on would mean that males are pre-programmed to be aggressive, while the different physiological make-up of females suits them for a nurturant role.

Usually there is little doubt about whether an individual is biologically male or female, so it is difficult to distinguish between the effects of being biologically male (**nature**), and the effects of being treated as male by others (**nurture**). Occasionally, however, the situation is not so clear-cut:

Activity 3: the Batista family

Read through these case studies:

(1) the Batista family – Imperato-McGinley *et al.* (1974)

Some members of the Batista family, living in the Dominican Republic, do not follow the normal course of sexual development. Where both parents carry a mutant gene from a common ancestor, some of the children are born as girls. They have normal female genitalia and body shape, and are raised as girls.

However, at the age of about 10 their vagina heals over, and they develop testicles and a penis. They all adapt their gender identity well to their new sex, take men's jobs and marry women, and are treated as men by others.

The Batista boys are genetically male. The fertilising sperm carries a Y chromosome, and enough testosterone is produced during development to preserve the male elements of their interior anatomy. However, they do not develop male genitalia at this stage due to lack of a chemical called dihydrotestosterone. At puberty, testosterone production forces up the level of dihydrotestosterone, leading to the development of male external genitalia.

(2) Accidental penectomy – Money (1974)

One of a pair of male MZ twins accidentally had his penis removed during circumcision. It was decided to raise him as a female. His male sex organs were removed, an artificial vagina constructed, and he was given female hormones. 'She' was always treated as a girl.

According to Money, who had recommended gender reassignment, as a four/five-year-old 'she' preferred to wear dresses, and was neater and tidier than 'her' twin, but showed some tomboyish behaviour, e.g. a liking for rough-and-tumble play. When 'she' reached her teens, a follow-up study (Diamond, 1982) found 'her' to be generally unhappy, with few friends. 'She' was confused about 'her' gender, and looked rather masculine. 'She' was later reassigned as a male.

a What evidence do these cases give for a biological view of gender development?

b On the basis of these studies, how could factors in the social environment be said to play a part in gender development?

When you have finished, see the notes on page 104.

Studies of individuals with **testicular feminising syndrome** suggests that gender isn't necessarily tied to chromosomes, gonads and hormone production. In this syndrome, the egg is fertilised by a sperm carrying the Y chromosome, the gonads become testes and the female parts are absorbed. However, body cells are insensitive to testosterone, so development does not continue along the male route. At birth, the individual has normal-looking female external genitalia, but has only a very short

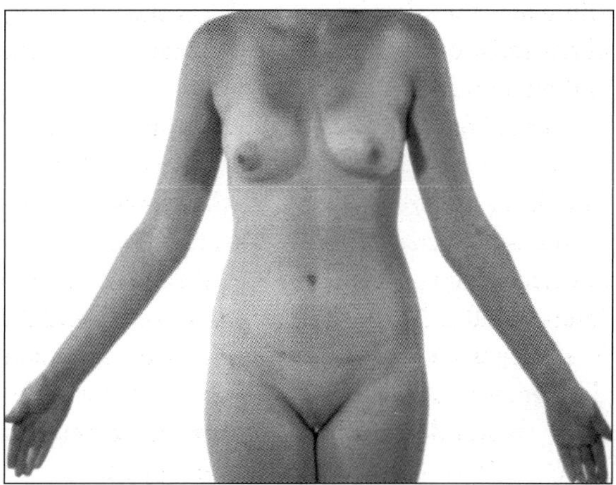

A case of testicular feminising syndrome

vagina. At puberty, breasts develop, but there is no menstruation, since the person does not have a womb. Such a person is biologically male. However, they look female, are raised as females and consider themselves female.

The case study of the hermaphrodite Mr. Blackwell mentioned earlier (Goldwyn 1979) also underlines the strength of nurture, since his upbringing as a boy influenced his gender identity as a male, overriding his female brain biochemistry. Furthermore, the surgeon who carried out the operation on Mr Blackwell also treated 25 other cases of hermaphroditism. All the people treated were in no doubt about their gender, which was always in line with the way they had been raised, either as a male or as a female. It therefore seems that biological factors alone do not account for gender development.

These findings can best be accounted for by a **biosocial approach**. This approach, while stressing the importance of biological factors, at the same time claims that it is the interaction of biological and social factors which is important. The social aspect here focuses on the idea that different characteristics of babies influence how other people treat them. One of these characteristics is the baby's sex:

Box G: Smith and Lloyd (1978)

Procedure: Mothers were asked to play with a young baby that they didn't know. A baby was dressed in pink or blue clothing and was introduced to the mother using a boy's or a girl's name. The same baby was presented to different participants as a boy or a girl. The ways in which the mothers interacted with the babies were analysed.
Results: Mothers tended to stimulate a 'boy' more than a 'girl', for example by bouncing or jiggling 'him'. The toys offered to the baby were also sex-typed, with a 'boy' being more likely to be offered a hammer, and a 'girl' given a soft toy.
Conclusion: The sex of a baby influences the ways in which parents interact with them.

Money and Ehrhardt (1972) argued that gender identity is influenced by this kind of labelling. Being categorised as a boy or a girl on the evidence of biological differences influences how we are treated, and this further social element plays a part in developing gender identity. They argued that before the age of about two or three, it is possible to change the sex of rearing without any psychological harm being done. After this sensitive period, that is no longer possible.

There is some support for this idea:

Box H: Money and Ehrhardt (1972)

Procedure: Ten individuals with testicular feminising syndrome were studied. They had all been categorised as girls at birth on the basis of their external genitalia, and raised as females.
Results: While they tended to be more tomboyish than other girls, they nonetheless showed a strong preference for the female role.
Conclusion: The interaction of biological and social factors is important in explaining gender development.

In the light of the other evidence we have looked at in this section, the relative contribution of nature and nurture remains unclear, but most psychologists agree that both are important.

The other approaches we will be looking at are less interested in the influence of physiology, and more interested in the role of psychological factors in gender development.

- The **biological** approach explains gender development in terms of physiological differences between males and females. One difference between males and females is **chromosomal**, with males being XY and females XX. However, there are cases where this distinction is not clear cut. Another difference relates to the **gonads**, i.e. testes in males and ovaries in females. There are also **hormonal** differences.
- The **biosocial** approach emphasises the interaction of biological and social factors, and suggests some flexibility in the development of gender identity.
- While biological sex differences are important, they are not the only factor in the development of gender identity.

The social learning approach

Social learning theory is based on the principles of operant conditioning, discussed in chapter 1, in that it suggests that much of our behaviour (including social behaviour) is learned, and is likely to be repeated if it is positively reinforced. Bandura, one of the foremost proponents of this theory, claims that we learn through observing the behaviour of others, and seeing the results of their behaviour. This is called **observational learning**. Social behaviour is learned through **modelling**. Bandura suggested that there were three main sources of models : the family, the subculture (the people we mix with outside the immediate family), and the mass media.

Social learning theory: sources of models

Modelling is rather more than just imitation, since Bandura sees the psychological effects of modelling as being much broader than just copying what we see; it is general rules and principles which are learned. This theory therefore also introduces cognitive factors to behavioural theory, such as attending to relevant features of the modelled behaviour, and remembering its critical features so that they can be accurately reproduced. He and his co-workers have shown this effect in a series of studies. One is described in box I:

Box I: Bandura *et al.* (1963)

Procedure: Children observed an adult behaving aggressively towards a large, inflatable Bobo doll. The adult attacked the doll in unusual ways (e.g. hitting it with a hammer, and saying things like 'Pow ... boom ... boom'). The children were then left in the playroom and their behaviour was observed. A control group of children also played in the playroom with the same toys, but did not observe the adult model attacking the doll.

Results: The behaviour of the experimental group was very similar to that of the adult model. The control group did not display similar behaviour.

Conclusion: Children imitated the behaviour of the adult model they had observed.

In a later study (Bandura, 1965), he demonstrated a further feature of SLT: **vicarious conditioning**. Children learn through observing in others the outcomes of particular behaviours. In this study, one group of children went straight into the playroom after they had observed the adult model.

A second group saw the adult being rewarded for aggressive behaviour before they were let into the playroom, while a third group saw the adult punished. There was little difference in the number of imitated aggressive behaviours shown by the first two groups, but the third group showed significantly fewer imitated behaviours.

This seems to suggest that seeing a model punished leads to less learning. However, Bandura then offered rewards to the children who had seen the adult punished if they could reproduce the behaviour they had observed. The number of imitated aggressive behaviours shown by this group then rose to the level of the other two groups. Bandura concluded from this that modelling is sufficient for behaviour to be *learned*, but for those whose behaviour is inhibited by watching others punished, reinforcement is necessary for the behaviour to be *performed*.

In relation to gender, social learning theory is concerned with gender-appropriate behaviour, and in particular with socialisation processes. The family is the most immediate source of gender models. However, as we saw earlier, the media – e.g. children's TV and books – also provide models. There is also evidence that the gender stereotypes portrayed by the media affect children's concept of gender. For example, Leary *et al.* (1982) found that children who frequently watched TV were more likely to hold gender stereotypes, and to conform to culturally appropriate gender roles.

Activity 4: investigating TV stereotypes

Are girls and boys portrayed differently in the media? Watch a range of TV programmes intended for children, and where children are the main actors. Before you start, prepare a checklist of behaviours which relate to stereotypical male and stereotypical female characteristics. Here are some to start you off:

aggression (kicking, punching, shouting)
nurturing (hugging, comforting, sympathising)
leadership (planning, giving orders)

You will probably be able to think of several you can add.

Prepare two copies of the checklist, one for boys and one for girls. As you watch the programmes, put a tick on the relevant checklist against each kind of behaviour as it occurs .

Are some behaviours shown more frequently by boys than girls, and vice versa?

In practice, features of operant conditioning, in which parents' responses reinforce gender-related behaviour, and features of SLT, where behaviours could come about by modelling and vicarious conditioning, are likely to occur together. The child notes both the consequences of his or her own behaviour, and also the behaviour of the model, and its consequences.

A social learning account of gender would suggest that parents and others respond very differently to girls and boys, and so reinforce gender-typed behaviour. While some studies have failed to find differences, a lot of research supports this idea, for example the Smith and Lloyd study in box G.

With older children, Sears *et al.* (1957) found that parents expect and even encourage aggression in boys. A survey of children's bedrooms, by Pomerlau *et al.* (1990), found that boys' rooms were more likely to contain vehicles and action-orientated toys, while girls' rooms were more likely to contain dolls, and to be decorated in a floral style.

Block and Dworkin (1974) also found differences beween parents, in that fathers were more likely to use sex-typed language to describe their children. They were more concerned with the cognitive development of their sons, and the development of social skills in their daughters. Langlois and Downs (1980) found that fathers were particularly hostile to gender-inappropriate behaviour in their sons.

One study, which looked in detail at parental attitudes and behaviour is described in box J:

Box J: Fagot (1978)

Procedure: A sample of 24 families was studied, each family with a child just under two. Parents were extensively observed interacting with their children, with the child's behaviours classified under 46 headings. Parents also

completed questionnaires, rating the 46 kinds of behaviour for appropriateness for boys and girls.
Results: Behaviours which occurred significantly more often in boys included play with bricks and transportation toys, and manipulating objects. Play with dolls and soft toys, dressing up, dancing and asking for help occurred significantly more often in girls. The questionnaire responses showed that parents considered playing with dolls, dressing up and dancing as more appropriate for girls,

Parents considered dressing up and playing with dolls as more appropriate for girls ...

... and rough-and-tumble play and aggressive behaviour as more appropriate for boys.

and rough-and-tumble play and aggressive behaviour as more appropriate for boys. However, parental responses to behaviour did not always match the questionnaire responses. There was no difference in their reactions to boys and girls playing rough-and-tumble games. Girls asked for help three times as often as boys, but parents did not rate this behaviour as more appropriate for girls.
Conclusion: There is some indication that parental reactions to a child's behaviour influence that behaviour, and that children's behaviour influences parental reactions. However, the relationships between parental attitudes, a child's behaviour and parental reactions is not clear-cut.

Social learning theory, then, helps us to understand children's gender development. The relationship between parental attitudes, children's behaviour, and parental reactions to children's behaviour can perhaps be best understood in terms of the mutual influences of a transactional model.

However, this approach may not sufficiently take into account the child's cognitions, i.e. his or her *understanding* of gender role, and the influence this understanding can have on development. With this in mind, Bandura (1986) has adapted traditional social learning theory to put more emphasis on cognitive factors. This is called **social cognitive theory**. The child's own judgements of how they feel when engaged in gender-appropriate and gender-inappropriate play are seen to play an important part in gender development:

Box K: Bussey and Bandura (1992)

Procedure: Children aged three and four were asked to say whether they would feel 'real great' or 'real awful' when playing with a range of toys. They thought they were making these judgements anonymously.
Results: By the age of four, boys felt 'great' about playing with trucks and robots, but

'awful' about playing with dolls and kitchen sets. The opposite was true of girls.
Conclusion: Children learn early to feel uncomfortable with gender-inappropriate behaviour. Since the reactions were given anonymously, they could be considered to be the result of the child's self-evaluation, rather than factors such as the demand characteristics of the situation.

There are also other criticisms to be made of the social learning theory approach. In assessing the impact of parents' response to their children, Schaffer (1996) claims that the amount of reinforcement given to children relating to gender is actually quite limited, but even those children who are treated in a unisex way by their families develop gender stereotypes. He goes on to point out that there is a problem in establishing a cause and effect relationship between parental behaviour and children's gender-typed behaviour. The fact that parents treat boys and girls differently does not necessarily mean that any behavioural differences in the children are the result of such treatment; it is possible that behavioural differences bring about these differences in treatment. There is some evidence to support this idea:

Box L: Snow *et al.* (1983)

Procedure: Fathers were observed interacting with their one-year-old sons and daughters in the presence of various potentially disaster-producing objects, such as a jug of water and a vase of flowers. The children's spontaneous attempts to touch the tempting objects were counted, together with the number of physical and verbal interventions made by the fathers. The same father–child pairs were also observed in a play situation with harmless toys. The amount of encouragement to play given to boys and to girls was observed, together with the number of spontaneous attempts to play with the toys made by boys and by girls.

Results: In the first situation, the fathers of boys intervened much more frequently than the fathers of girls. However, the boys made significantly more attempts than the girls to touch the tempting objects. In the second stuation, girls' fathers made more attempts to encourage their children to play than boys' fathers; boys made more spontaneous attempts to play with the toys than girls.
Conclusion: Parents' treatment of their children may be a response to sex-specific characteristics of girls and boys.

- Bandura developed social learning theory. Children learn by **observational learning**, **modelling** and **reinforcement**. The child's environment therefore influences gender development.
- Research suggests that from a very early age, parents respond differently to sons and daughters.
- The interaction of parents' attitudes, children's behaviour and parents' reactions to this behaviour may be more complex than social learning theory suggests.
- Bandura has developed **social cognitive** theory, which builds on social learning theory, putting more emphasis on cognitive factors.
- There have been some **criticisms** of social learning theory, particularly in terms of problems in establishing cause and effect relationships.

Kohlberg's cognitive–developmental theory

The cognitive–developmental approach sees children as actively developing their understanding of gender. This understanding moves through stages, as a result of interaction with the physical and social environment.

Activity 5: exploring children's understanding of gender

If you have access to young children, ask them the following questions. Ideally, one of the children you investigate should be two–three years old, and one about five or six:

a Are you a boy or a girl?
b When you're 10, will you be a boy or a girl?
c When you grow up, will you be a man or a woman?
d If you have children of your own when you grow up, will you be a mummy or a daddy?
e If you wanted to, could you be a daddy/mummy?
f If you put on a boy's/girl's clothes, would you be a boy/girl?

These kinds of questions have been used by many researchers into children's understanding of gender. On the basis of their findings, Kohlberg (1966) suggested that a child's understanding of gender has three stages. Children do not have to be taught the constructs in these stages; they emerge spotaneously. In the first stage, children acquire **gender identity**, i.e. an awareness of being male or female. He found that children can answer question a correctly by the age of about two. However, children do not yet have the more sophisticated knowledge required by the other questions. By the age of four or five, **gender stability** – the understanding that gender is permanent – has developed. It is not until the age of six or seven that **gender constancy** is achieved. This involves recognising that gender remains the same in spite of superficial changes, e.g. in clothes, or the kinds of toys that the child prefers to play with.

Martin and Little (1990) found evidence that understanding of gender does develop in the sequence Kohlberg suggested, and Munroe *et al.* (1984) established that this sequence applies across cultures.

However, a major weakness in Kohlberg's theory is that he seems to be claiming that it is only when children have achieved gender constancy that they will behave consistently in a sex-typed way. As we have seen (for example, the Fagot study in box J and the Bussey and Bandura study in box K), children show clear signs of sex-typed behaviour long before the age when gender constancy is established.

The use of the kinds of questions in activity 5 has been criticised, since they may be difficult for very small children to understand. Question d, for example, is grammatically complex. Given this kind of problem, it is possible that even if stages such as those sugested by Kohlberg apply, children's understanding may develop more quickly than research has shown.

One way of simplifying the task for young children has been to use drawings and photographs. Emmerlich *et al.* (1977) found that children were less likely to show gender constancy when drawings were used. They typically do better with photographs (e.g. Bem, 1989), but do best when asked questions about themselves. It is possible that children understand gender constancy as applied to themselves before they learn to extend it to other people, and it is also possible that drawings and photographs confuse the issue. It is, after all, perfectly possible to change drawings permanently.

Research has also investigated young children's understanding of gender role:

Box M: Kuhn *et al.* (1978)

Procedure: Children aged two-and-a-half to three-and-a-half were shown paper dolls called Michael and Lisa. They were asked whether Michael or Lisa would be likely to make statements such as: 'I like to help mummy', 'I like to fight' and 'I need some help'.

Results: Boys and girls shared some beliefs about gender roles, e.g. that girls like to help mummy, talk a lot and ask for help, and that boys like to play with cars, help daddy and say 'I can hit you'.

Boys also have beliefs about girls, which girls don't share (e.g. that girls cry and are not very clever). Similarly, girls have beliefs about boys, which boys don't share (e.g. that boys fight and are unkind).

Boys and girls also have beliefs about positive aspects of themselves not shared by the opposite sex. For example, girls (but not boys) believe that girls look pretty and never fight. Boys (but not girls) believe that boys like to work hard and are loud.

Conclusion: Gender-role stereotypes are held by very young children. There is an affective aspect to these cognitions, since the stereotypes tend to value their own sex and devalue the opposite sex.

Cognitive–developmental theory implies that there should be little gender-appropriate behaviour before gender constancy is achieved, and the findings of Kuhn *et al.*, as well as those of similar studies, suggest that this is not the case. Nonetheless, it is reasonable to see cognitions as contributing to gender development.

A theory which brings together social learning theory and cognitions is **gender schema theory** (Bem 1981). Like social learning theory, it proposes that gender role is learned. From a cognitive point of view, it suggests that children develop schemas (or concepts) which help them to understand, organise and make sense of information. Gender is the basis of a very powerful schema, which can affect the way in which children interpret gender-related information. These ideas have been supported by research:

Box N: Martin and Halverson (1983)

Procedure: Children aged five and six were shown pictures of children carrying out activities which were either gender-consistent (boys playing with trucks) or gender-inconsistent (girls sawing wood). They were asked to recall the pictures a week later.
Results: During recall, participants tended to change the sex of the children in gender-inconsistent pictures.
Conclusion: Memory is distorted to fit in with existing gender schemas.

Gender-consistent and gender-consistent behaviour

Since it brings together elements of social learning and cognitions, gender schema theory may have something to offer in terms of explaining how children's understanding of gender, and its relationship to their own gender roles, develops.

- **Cognitive–developmental theory** sees gender development as passing through a series of stages. Kohlberg suggested that children follow the sequence of **gender identity**, **gender stability** and **gender constancy**. While Kohlberg's methods have been criticised, research has offered some support to these ideas.
- **Gender-role stereotypes** are present in very young children.
- **Gender schema theory** combines social factors and cognitions. A gender schema is developed, within which gender-related information is interpreted.

Freud's psychodynamic theory

The major psychodynamic theory to attempt to explain gender development is that of Freud. Freud believed that 'anatomy is destiny'. For him, genital differences determine the psychological characteristics of males and females. It is not the physiological differences as such which determine gender development, though. Rather, children develop an understanding of gender when they recognise the *significance* of the differences.

The key to gender development is the Oedipus conflict experienced by boys at around the age of five to six. The equivalent process – the Electra conflict – is experienced by girls at the same age. The conflict is resolved when children identify with the parent of the same sex. They aspire to the behaviours and characteristics of this parent, and as a result adopt the culturally approved models of masculinity and femininity. These developmental processes are described in chapter 1, in the section on the psychodynamic perspective in psychology. You should look back now to this material to remind yourself of the details of these ideas.

However, as in other areas of development, Freud's account of gender development has been criticised. Many theorists have questioned whether the Oedipus conflict, which underpins Freud's ideas on gender development, actually takes place. For example, a study of Trobriand islanders carried out by Malinowski (1929) found no evidence that young boys had experienced the Oedipus conflict.

Activity 6: problems with Freud's account of gender development

The Oedipus conflict apart, can you think of aspects of Freud's theory which don't fit in with research findings in this area? You may find it helpful to look back through the discussion of other theories in this section. Can you identify any other problems?

When you have finished, see the notes on page 104.

Freud himself recognised that his account of gender development in girls was not entirely satisfactory, and other theorists working within the psychodynamic tradition (e.g. Chodorow, 1978) have given a fuller account. They stress the importance of early relationships, particularly with the mother, since she is usually the main caregiver. These relationships provide a pattern for how to relate to other people. As they grow older, girls continue to follow the pattern provided by the mother, and come to understand femininity and closeness in relationships as being inextricably linked. On the other hand, boys need to establish their masculinity by breaking away from this pattern. For them, masculinity comes to be defined as a lack of closeness in relationships.

However, this approach still focuses on relationships within the family. Freud's theory was developed when the nuclear family – father, mother and children – was the norm. Variations in family make-up are now extremely common, but appropriate gender development still takes place:

Box O: Green (1978)

Procedure: Gender role in 37 children between the ages of three and 20 was studied. They were being brought up either by lesbians or parents who had undergone sex reassignment (transsexuals). The younger children were tested by asking them about the kinds of games they preferred, what kinds of clothes

they liked to wear and what they wanted to be when they grew up. Older participants were asked about their sexual behaviour, desires and fantasies.
Results: With the possible exception of one participant, all those studied had developed heterosexual preferences and conformed to cultural gender roles. For example, the younger children expressed a preference for playing with others of the same gender. Little boys wanted to be firemen and engineers when they grew up, and girls wanted to be nurses and housewives.
Conclusion: Appropriate gender development still takes place when there is no same-sex parent in the family, or when the family varies in some other way from a nuclear family.

The psychodynamic model can also be criticised for its emphasis on the family. While the family is undoubtedly an influence, at the same time it makes sense to assume that the models children use extend beyond the immediate family, as social learning theory suggests.

- Freud links gender development to the resolution of the **Oedipus** and **Electra conflicts**. Anxiety is overcome by **identification** with the same-sex parent.
- This explanation has been widely criticised. Firstly, the existence of the Oedipus conflict has been questioned. Gender development also starts much earlier than the theory suggests. Finally, it may put too much emphasis on the influence of the family.

Notes on activities

2 This is a modified form of the Bem Sex Role Inventory. The full form uses 20 stereotypically feminine characteristics, 20 stereotypically masculine characteristics, and 20 filler items. For your masculinity score, add your ratings for these items: 5; 9; 11; 14; 18; 27; 30; 33; 36; 39. For your femininity score, add your ratings for these items: 2; 19; 21; 23; 24; 25; 28; 31; 32; 40. The other items are distractor items which don't count towards any score. In each case, 10–30 = relatively low; 31–39 = average; 50–70=fairly strong. For your androgyny score, add together your masculinity and femininity scores, and multiply by 2. Below 130 = low; 130–189 = average; 190–280 = high.

3 The ease with which the Batista boys adopt a male gender role suggests that biological factors are indeed important. They had been treated as girls in the early years of their lives, but this did not seem to interfere with their conceptions of themselves as male when the biological changes of puberty occurred.

In the early years, the case of the twin who was treated as a girl seemed to show that nurture – which included treating the twin as a girl and giving 'her' female hormones – could outweigh nature. 'Her' behaviour corresponded to the female gender role. In adolescence, however, the gender confusion the twin experienced seems to indicate nature reasserting itself.

6 Freud's theory claims that children become gender-typed at around the age of five to six. A lot of the research we have looked at, eg the Bussey & Bandura study (box K) and the Kuhn *et al.* study (box M), suggests that this may happen a lot earlier than Freud believed. Children as young as two or three have started to grasp the idea of gender, and relate it to behaviour.

Freud's theory suggests that gender identity develops all at once at around the age of five. As we have seen, there is evidence to support Kohlberg's claim that it is a gradual process, with children pasing through identifiable stages before a full concept of gender and its implications is achieved.

The process of identification with the same-sex parent is, according to the theory, less strong for girls than boys. There is no evidence, though, that girls have greater problems in gender development than boys.

Attitudes

4.1 The structure FUNCTION OF AT

What are attitudes?

Attitudes can be described in terms of three components: cognitive, affective and behavioural (sometimes called conative). The **cognitive** component of an attitude includes the knowledge, ideas and beliefs connected to a specific opinion. The **affective** component is to do with emotions and values; whether you like or dislike someone or something. The **behavioural** component is to do with how you act towards people or things about which you have an attitude; this includes verbal behaviour. These three components are usually linked:

Activity 1: identifying the three components of attitudes

Copy and complete the following table:

components		
cognitive	affective	behavioural
		Shihan avoids air travel.
	Helen feels sorry for people living on the street.	
Jack believes the Labour Party will improve social services.		

As you filled in the table, did any problems about the connections between these three components occur to you ?
When you have finished, see the notes on page 130.

There is some evidence that the cognitive and affective components of attitudes do not always coincide with behaviour:

Box A: LaPiere (1934)

Procedure: LaPiere travelled round America with a Chinese couple, expecting to meet discrimination as a result of anti-Chinese feeling. They visited 67 hotels and 184 restaurants. Six months after their return, all the establishments they had visited were sent a letter, asking whether they would accept Chinese guests.

Results: They were only refused at one of the establishments they visited, and were generally treated very politely. Of the 128 establishments which responded to the letter, however, 91% said they were not willing to accept Chinese guests.

Conclusion: Cognitive and affective components of attitudes are not necessarily expressed in behaviour.

The slightly more complex relationship between beliefs (cognitive), values (affective) and behaviour which these findings suggest can be shown diagramatically (see figure 1).

This analysis can be used to define an attitude in terms of beliefs and values. This attitude then determines whether you are *likely* to act in a particular way or not, indicated by 'intentions' on the diagram. An appropriate working definition of 'attitude' might then be: 'a learned predisposition to respond in a consistently favourable or unfavourable manner with respect to a given object' (Newcomb 1950). This suggests that attitudes are learned through experience, that they make it more probable that we will act in a particular way, and that our behaviour is consistent. We shall be looking at this aspect in a little more detail later on. The favourable/unfavourable part of the definition reflects the affective component of an attitude. It is also worth bearing in mind, however, that some psychologists define attitudes purely in terms of the affective component, e.g. 'attitudes are likes and dislikes' (Bem 1970).

- Attitudes are often thought of as having three components: **cognitive**, **affective** and **behavioural**, which usually (but not always) coincide.
- Some psychologists believe that attitudes should only be defined by beliefs and values, since attitudes do not necessarily correspond to behaviour. Others focus only on the **affective** component.

The function of attitudes

The functional approach to attitudes looks at what function attitudes serve for the individual. A particular attitude may be held by an individual for any of a number of reasons. Katz (1960) made four suggestions, later taken up in a slightly different form by other attitude theorists. They are now generally labelled adaptive, knowledge, self-expressive, and ego-defensive.

The **adaptive** function is to do with relationships with others. If we show socially acceptable attitudes, other people reward us with approval and social acceptance. Attitudes, then, are to do with being part of a social group. People seek out others who share their attitudes, and develop similar attitudes to those they like.

The **knowledge** function refers to our need for a world which is consistent and relatively stable. This allows us to predict what is likely to happen, and so gives us a sense of control. Attitudes help us to organise and structure our experience.

Figure 1: structural analysis of attitudes

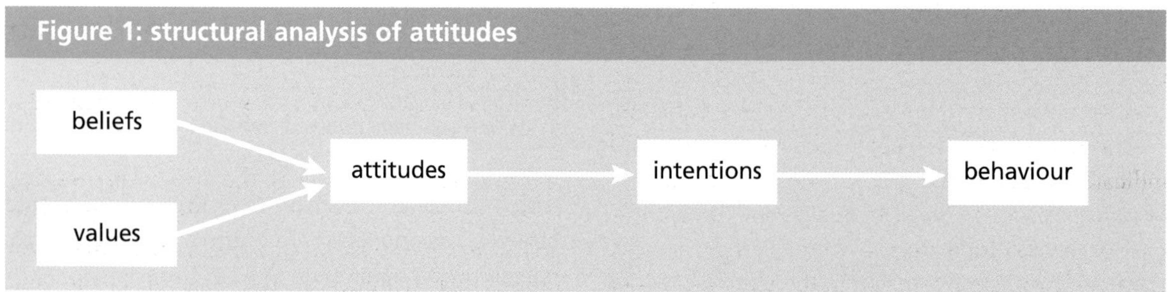

The **self-expressive** function relates to our self-concept. The psychodynamic theorist Erik Erikson believed that a sense of identity is crucial for psychological well-being. Our attitudes are part of our identity, and help us to be aware through self-expression of our feelings, beliefs and values.

Attitudes can also have a protective function. Positive attitudes to ourselves, for example, have an **ego-defensive** role in helping us to preserve our self-image. We can also cope with threats to our self-esteem by projecting our own conflicts on to other people, expressed in our attitudes towards them. As you will have gathered from the mention of ego-defences and projection, this function of attitudes is related to Freud's theory, discussed in chapter 1. As we will see later in this chapter, this can be a way of explaining prejudice.

Knowing the function an attitude serves is important in attitude change. If a person's attitude serves the knowledge function, for example, you are more likely to be successful in changing this attitude by giving them new information. This approach is unlikely to work, however, if the attitude serves an ego-defensive function.

S Attitudes may serve any of four functions for the individual: **adaptive**, **knowledge**, **self-expressive** and **ego-defensive**. To bring about attitude change, it is important to know what the function of that attitude is for the person holding it.

4.2 Measuring attitudes

Perhaps the most straightforward way of finding out about someone's attitudes would be to ask them. However, as we have seen, attitudes are in part to do with self-image and social acceptance. In order to preserve a positive self-image, people's responses may be affected by **social desirability**. They may well not tell you about their true attitudes, but answer in a way that they feel is socially acceptable.

Another problem is that while this method will indicate whether the person has a positive or negative attitude to an issue or a person, it can only give a general indication of the strength of that attitude. If you are interested in the effectiveness of attempts to change attitude, it would be useful to have a more precise measure of the strength of an attitude before and after these attempts are made.

With such problems in mind, several structured ways of measuring attitudes have been developed. However, all of them have limitations. In particular, the different measures focus on different components of attitudes – cognitive, affective and behavioural – and, as we have seen, these different components do not necessarily coincide.

Indirect measures

To avoid the problem of social desirability, various indirect measures of attitudes have been used. Either people are unaware of what is being measured (which has the ethical problem of invasion of privacy) or they are unable consciously to affect what is being measured.

Physiological techniques include measuring pupil dilation, heart rate and GSR (the galvanic skin response, which indicates arousal). Hess (1965) has shown a relationship between pupil size and positive attitudes; pupils dilate when we feel positively about someone or something, and constrict when we have negative feelings. This measure only gives us limited information, though, and is not accepted by all psychologists. The other measures only indicate that a person holds a strong attitude, but not whether it is postive or negative, so they too are very limited.

It is also possible to measure behaviour:

Activity 2: behavioural measures of attitude

Suggest ways in which you might use behaviour to assess attitudes to:

a religion

b classical music

Can you think of any problems with this kind of measurement?

When you have finished, see the notes on page 131.

A final indirect method is the use of **projective tests**. These involve asking people to respond to ambiguous material, in the belief that they will project their attitudes on to it. Samples of the kind of material that might be used to assess attitudes to authority are shown in figure 2. The person being tested would be asked to fill in the bubble in answer to what the authority figure has said:

Figure 2: using projective tests to measure attitudes

As with other indirect methods, this only gives us general information and does not offer a very precise measurement of attitude strength, since it is qualitative rather than quantitative. A person's response to this test needs to be interpreted by the tester, so there is the possibility of **experimenter bias**. At the same time, the person is unlikely to guess what it is that is being measured, and so this method may be useful when investigating attitudes on very sensitive topics.

Direct measures

Several kinds of rating scale have been developed to measure attitudes drectly. The most widely used is the **Likert scale**. Likert (1932) developed the principle of measuring attitudes by asking people to respond to a series of statements about a topic, in terms of the extent to which they agree with them, and so tapping into the cognitive and affective components of attitudes. We have already looked briefly at the Likert scale in the discussion in chapter 2 on methods in psychology. A series of statements is prepared, relevant to the particular attitude to be measured, with half the statements being favourable and half unfavourable. Statements are presented in random order and participants rate each statement on a five-point (sometimes seven-point) scale, to which numerical values are attached. Examples of the sorts of items which might be used to measure attitudes to vegetarianism, together with the scoring system, are shown in figure 3:

Figure 3: sample of a Likert scale to measure attitudes

1 People would be much healthier if they adopted a vegetarian diet.

strongly agree	agree somewhat	undecided	disagree somewhat	strongly disagree
5	4	3	2	1

2 Something would be lacking in my diet if I gave up meat and fish.

strongly agree	agree somewhat	undecided	disagree somewhat	strongly disagree
5	4	3	2	1

You will see that in figure 3 a high score shows a favourable attitude to vegetarianism, and a low score an unfavourable attitude. A person's attitude is the sum of their scores from all the items. The numbers would not appear on the questionnaire completed by participants; they are only there to show you how the system works.

Activity 3: using a Likert scale

Try out this way of measuring attitudes. Think of an interesting topic to investigate, and prepare some suitable statements. About 30 statements would be ideal. Don't forget to use an equal number of favourable and unfavourable items, and list them in your questionnaire in random order.

You could re-administer the questionnaire to the same participants a few weeks later to see whether your scale is reliable, i.e. gives consistent results. A scattergram (see chapter 2) of the two scores of each participant will help to show this.

Was this an easy test to administer? Did your participants find it straightforward to complete? Do you feel you know more about their attitudes to the topic than you did before you started? Make a list of what you consider to be the good points of this technique, and any limitations.

When you have finished, see the notes on page 131.

When the Likert scale is used properly, an **item analysis** is carried out. Before the main study, a different sample of people from those to be tested is asked to respond to statements which are being considered for inclusion in the final draft of the questionnaire. When these questionnaires have been scored, items are identified on which people with a high overall score have tended to score high and those with a low overall score have tended to score low. In this way, items which discriminate between high and low scorers are identified, and are retained for the final draft.

One of the strengths of the Likert scale is the item analysis. It may be that items which do not obviously relate to what is being tested actually discriminate rather well between high and low scorers. For example, if we were testing attitudes to immigration, we might find that people with a negative attitude tend to agree with a statement such as: 'We all have a strong need to feel rooted in our community'. If this kind of item discriminated well, it might then predict fairly accurately negative attitudes to immigration, without it being obvious what is being tested, and so avoid the problem of demand characteristics.

One major criticism which has been made of Likert scales is how the midpoint – 'undecided' – should be interpreted. Does 'undecided' mean that respondents have no opinion either way or that they are torn between feelings in both directions? Partly as a result of this ambiguity, overall scores which fall near the centre of the distribution (for example, close to 50 out of a possible score of 100) are also somewhat ambiguous. This kind of score could be the result of a lot of 'undecided' answers. Alternatively, it could be the result of a lot of 'strongly agree' and 'strongly disagree' answers cancelling each other out. In this case, the scale would seem to be measuring two different attitudes.

Another direct method of measuring attitudes is the **semantic differential** technique, developed by Osgood *et al.* (1957). This taps into the affective component of an attitude. It uses a seven-point rating scale, which respondents tick to indicate how they feel about what is being measured. Ratings are made for each of a pair of at least nine bipolar adjectives, i.e. with opposite meanings. The scale provides information on three dimensions: **evaluation** (i.e. whether our feelings are positive or negative), **potency** (powerful or weak) and **activity** (active or passive). Here is a partial example of how attitudes to euthanasia might be tested.

Activity 4: the semantic differential technique

EUTHANASIA

good	... ...	bad
strong	... ...	weak
ugly	... ...	beautiful
cruel	... ...	kind
active	... ...	passive
clean	... ...	dirty

Match up each pair of adjectives to one of the dimensions given above.

When you have finished, see the notes on page 131.

Like the Likert scale, the information from the semantic differential can be expressed in numerical form, so it is possible to analyse statistically the data obtained. What is being measured is perhaps slightly less obvious than with the Likert scale. Position response bias, i.e. the tendency to use a particular point on the scale, may be even more of a problem here than with the Likert scale, since the points of the scale are not labelled, and again there is the problem of interpreting the midpoint of the scale.

- **Indirect methods** of measuring attitudes avoid the problem of social desirability. They include **physiological** and **behavioural** measures, and **projective** tests. While all have their uses, they all have their limitations.
- **Rating scales** are **direct** methods. Two examples are the **Likert scale** and the **semantic differential**, both of which have the advantage of providing **quantitative data**, though the scoring method is rather crude. The Likert scale may lead the respondent to give socially desirable answers.

4.3 Attitudes and behaviour

As we saw in LaPiere's study in box A, the cognitive and affective components of attitudes do not necessarily coincide with behaviour. In this section we will try to establish under what circumstances there is likely to be a mismatch and when there is not. Let us start by looking again at LaPiere's findings:

Activity 5: inconsistency in LaPiere's findings

Can you think of any possible reasons to explain the discrepancy between the way in which LaPiere and the Chinese couple were treated on their journey and the negative responses to the letter?

When you have finished, see the notes on page 131.

Wicker (1969) published a review of the studies carried out to examine the relationship between attitudes and behaviour. He came to the conclusion that it was much more likely that they would be unrelated, or only slightly related, than closely related. He suggested that the relationship might be weak because we need to take account of a range of other factors, both personal and situational.

Let us look first at **personal factors**. Some people are less consistent in their behaviour than others. They are more likely to respond to what they see as the demands of a particular social situation than in ways consistent with their beliefs. People may also have competing motives and other attitudes which affect their behaviour. The LaPiere study is a nice example of this, where possibly the hotelkeepers and restaurant owners did not want the Chinese couple, but did want their money.

There is a whole range of **situational factors** which are likely to affect behaviour.

Activity 6: situational factors and attitudes

Read through the following situations, and give reasons in each case why these people behave in a way inconsistent with their attitudes:

1. Sarah is out with her friends and they want to go to McDonald's. She doesn't think much of fast food, but goes along anyway, and has a Big Mac.
2. Jared meets a member of the Conservative party canvassing on his doorstep. He is a Liberal Democrat supporter, but talks politely to the canvasser.
3. Steve is very keen to find out the previous day's football results. He doesn't like the tabloid press, but only the *Mail* and the *Express* are left in the shop. He buys a copy of the *Express*.
4. James thinks all Essex girls are stupid. He meets a girl from Romford at a club. They get on really well, and arrange to meet again.
5. Ned believes that people with learning difficulties should be helped to play a full part in the community. He finds out that there are plans for a house in his street to be used by a group of people with learning difficulties, and signs a petition protesting about this.

When you have finished, see the notes on page 131.

There are lots of reasons, then, why attitudes and behaviour may differ. In addition, as we have already seen, the methods used to measure attitudes are imprecise and are fraught with methodological problems, so inaccurate attitude measurement may also in part account for the discrepancy found between attitudes and behaviour. On the other hand, is it possible to identify circumstances when attitudes and behaviour are likely to be the same?

Ajzen and Fishbein (1977) argue that attitudes can predict behaviour if the attitude being measured relates very specifically to the behaviour being observed. One problem with LaPiere's research, for example, is that general attitudes to the Chinese were being measured in the letters he sent out, but the behaviour being assessed was specific, i.e. serving a well-dressed, professional Chinese couple accompanied by a white American. Research has suggested that this may indeed help to explain why differences are often found between measured attitudes and behaviour:

Box B: Davidson and Jaccard (1979)

Procedure: Married women's use of oral contraceptives in the two years following the start of the study was correlated with **a** attitudes to birth control, **b** attitudes towards oral contraceptives, and **c** attitudes towards oral contraceptive use over the next two years.
Results: The correlation coefficients were respectively 0.08, 0.32 and 0.57. The better the match between the attitude being measured and the behaviour being observed, the higher the correlation.
Conclusion: The more closely related the attitude being measured is to behaviour, the better able attitudes are to predict behaviour.

Another factor which may be important is the time between measuring an attitude and observing a behaviour. Schwartz (1978) gave Israeli students questionnaires on socially responsible behaviours. They were later asked specifically whether they would help to tutor a blind child. Those contacted after three months were far more likely to help than those contacted after six months.

Several studies have also shown that if an attitude is based on **direct experience**, it is more likely to correspond to behaviour. Direct experience means that we have more information about the people, objects or ideas towards which we hold an attitude.

- Many early studies found that there was little correlation between attitudes and behaviour. This discrepancy may be because of **personal** or **situational** factors.
- Attitudes are a better predictor of behaviour if the attitude being measured relates specifically to the behaviour being observed.
- The link between attitudes and behaviour is likely to be stronger when there is only a short time between measuring an attitude and observing behaviour, and when the attitude rests on direct **experience**.

4.4 Attitude change

Several theories have been put forward to explain attitude change. We will look here at cognitive dissonance, persuasive communication and dual-process models.

Cognitive dissonance

Attitudes may change because of factors within the person. An important factor here is the principle of **cognitive consistency**, the focus of Festinger's (1957) theory of **cognitive dissonance**. This theory starts from the idea that we seek consistency in our beliefs and attitudes in any situation where two cognitions are inconsistent. Festinger claims that when this happens we experience dissonance, defined as 'a negative drive state which occurs whenever an individual holds two cognitions ... which are psychologically inconsistent'. As the experience of dissonance is unpleasant, we are motivated to reduce or eliminate it, and achieve consonance.

Dissonance can be reduced in one of three ways. We can change one or more of the beliefs, opinions or behaviours involved in the dissonance; we can acquire new information which will reduce the dissonance; or we can reduce the importance of the cognitions which are in a dissonant relationship.

Activity 7: reducing dissonance

Martin smokes cigarettes. He knows that cigarettes cause cancer.

Make a list, using headings related to these three ways, of how he could reduce the dissonance brought about by this inconsistency.

When you have finished, see the notes on page 131.

This theory has been widely researched in a number of situations to develop the basic idea in more detail, and identify factors which may be important in attitude change. This research can be divided into three main areas: **decision-making**, **forced-compliance behaviour**, and **effort**. We will look at the main findings to have emerged from each.

Decision-making

Activity 8: decision-making and dissonance

Imagine you are going on holiday. Think of two different places you would like to go. Make a list of what each has to offer (e.g. maybe you've not been there before, or it's cheap) and the drawbacks (e.g. maybe you can't speak the language, or it's a long flight time). Use your lists to decide what your choice is going to be.

Now imagine you have booked and paid for the holiday. Why are you now likely to experience dissonance? (Remember, there were some good points about the holiday you rejected.) How could this dissonance be reduced?

When you have finished, see the notes on page 132.

The strategy of focusing on the good aspects of a choice once it has been made, and downplaying the positive aspects of what has been rejected, has been shown in a study by Brehm:

Box C: Brehm (1956)

Procedure: Women were asked to rate a series of household appliances, and then were asked to make a choice between the two they had found most attractive. They were given what they had chosen, and then asked to rate again both of their top choices.

Results: After the choice had been made, the chosen item was rated as more attractive and the other as less attractive.

Conclusion: The dissonance experienced after a choice has been made between two attractive alternatives is reduced by focusing on the positive aspects of what has been chosen and downgrading the merits of what has been rejected.

Further support for this idea comes from a survey carried out by Ehrlich *et al.* (1957), who found that people prefer to read advertisements for the car they have bought than for other makes they considered but rejected.

Forced-compliance behaviour

When someone is forced to do something they really don't want to do, dissonance is created between their cognition (I didn't want to do this) and their behaviour (I did it). The behaviour can't be changed, since it is already in the past, so dissonance will need to be reduced by re-evaluating their attitude to what they have done. This prediction has been tested experimentally:

Box D: Festinger and Carlsmith (1959)

Procedure: Participants were given the extremely boring task of turning pegs in a peg-board for an hour. They were then asked to tell the next participant that the task was really good fun to do, and were paid either $1 or $20 to do so. After they had carried this out, they were asked to rate how interesting they had found the peg-board task.

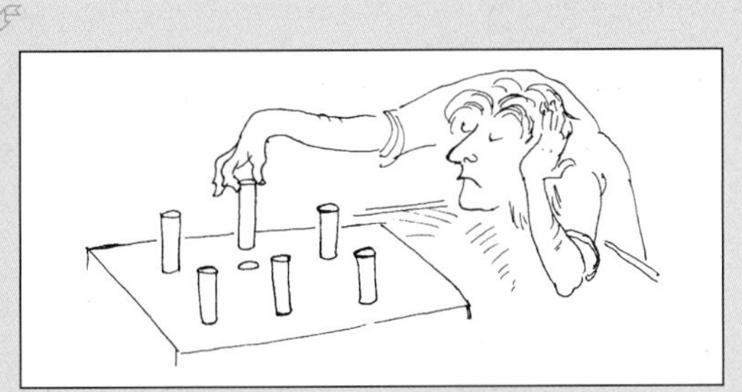

Results: Participants who had been paid $1 rated the peg-board task as more interesting than those who had been paid $20.

Conclusion: For participants paid $20, the reward justified the lie they had told the next participant. Little dissonance was therefore experienced, so they did not need to reduce it by changing their cognition about the interest level of the task when asked to rate it. For participants paid $1, the money was too little to justify the deception. Participants therefore experienced dissonance between what they had said to the next participant and their experience of carrying out the task. This was reduced by modifying their view of how interesting the task was, expressed in their more positive ratings.

Of course, we need to assume that people like to think of themselves as basically decent and honest; if lying is not seen as a problem, then no dissonance will be experienced. We must also assume that this attitude towards themselves has some importance to the person, or again there is likely to be little dissonance. This relates to to Aronson's (1968) proposal that cognitive dissonance theory should be narrowed down: dissonance should be defined in terms of inconsistency between a person's self-concept and a cognition about their behaviour.

Activity 9: applying dissonance theory

See if you can use the information on forced-compliance behaviour to work out the results of an experiment carried out by Aronson and Carlsmith (1963).

Children were told not to play with an attractive toy. One group as given a mild threat and the other a severe threat. The children did as they had been told. According to the theory, which group would then like the toy less? Why?

When you have finished, see the notes on page 133.

Is this kind of dissonance and attitude change inevitable? In fact, it only happens when we feel we have some kind of choice. If we really have no choice, there is no dissonance, and so no attitude change. The degree of personal commitment to the behaviour is also important. In the Festinger and Carlsmith study (box D), participants were forced to lie to the waiting participants face to face. However, in a situation when participants were forced to lie in an anonymous essay, and so personal commitment was less, dissonance was not found.

Effort

If we put effort into a task which we have chosen to carry out, and the task turns out badly, we experience dissonance. To reduce this dissonance, we are motivated to try to think that the task turned out well. A classic dissonance experiment demonstrates the basic idea here:

Box E: Aronson and Mills (1959)

Procedure: Female students volunteered to take part in a discussion on the psychology of sex. In the 'mild embarrassment' condition, participants read aloud to a male experimenter a list of sex-related words like 'virgin' and 'prostitute'. In the 'severe embarrassment' condition, they had to read aloud obscene words and a very explicit sexual passage. In the control condition, they went straight into the main study. In all conditions they then heard a very boring discussion about sex in lower animals. They were asked to rate how interesting they had found the discussion, and how interesting they had found the people involved in it.

Results: Participants in the 'severe embarrassment' condition gave the most positive ratings.

Conclusion: If a voluntary experience which has cost a lot of effort turns out badly, dissonance is reduced by redefining the experience as interesting. This justifies the effort made.

This kind of outcome has been called the **suffering-leads-to-liking effect**. You can probably think of similar examples from your own experience.

The suffering-leads-to-liking effect

'When prophecy fails'

All the studies on cognitive dissonance we have looked at so far have been experimental investigations. We will look finally at a study of a genuine series of events which Festinger investigated.

Activity 10: when prophecy fails

Read this account of an event reported by Festinger *et al.* (1956) in their book *When Prophecy Fails*, and answer the questions which follow. You may need to look back through previous parts of this section on cognitive dissonance:

A suburban housewife, Mrs Marian Keech, claimed to have received messages by automatic writing, sent by superior beings from the planet Clarion. They told her that the whole of the area from the Arctic Circle to the Gulf of Mexico would be submerged in a huge flood. She was told this would happen on 21 December. The story was printed in the local paper in September.

Mrs Keech soon attracted a following of believers. Many of these believers gave up their jobs and gave away their possessions. One of them, Dr Armstrong, spread the word among a group of his students, known as the Seekers.

On 20 December Mrs Keech received a message that a space ship would come at midnight to take her and the other believers to a place of safety. The group gathered at Mrs Keech's house to wait, though most of the students (the Seekers) were at home with their families for the Christmas vacation.

Midnight came and went, and the spaceship failed to arrive. Everyone was very quiet, until at 4.45 am Mrs Keech announced that she had received another message. The group had been such a power for good that God had saved the world from destruction.

The next day, the group were very keen to give interviews, although they had refused to talk to the press since September. All the members of the

Waiting for the Clarion spaceship on 20 December at midnight

group who had waited with Mrs Keech were eager to make converts to their cause. The Seekers who had been at home with their families, however, gave up their beliefs.

Which two aspects of this situation are in dissonance here?

Why is it significant that people gave up their jobs and gave away their possessions?

What were the possible ways to reduce dissonance when the spaceship failed to arrive?

Why do you think those of Mrs Keech's group who waited with her for the arrival of the space ship were eager to make converts after the event, while the Seekers at home with their families were not?

When you have finished, see the notes on page 133.

Evaluation of cognitive dissonance theory

There has been a great deal of research into cognitive dissonance, providing some interesting and sometimes unexpected findings. It is a theory with very broad applications, showing that we aim for consonance, and may not use very rational methods to achieve it. It has the advantage of being testable and falsifiable. Even though it has sometimes been falsified, the theory still seems to have intuitive appeal.

However, there are some problems. The idea that dissonance creates tension has been supported to some extent by physiological measures such as the GSR, but we can't be sure that this tension was caused by dissonance. It might equally well be caused, for example, by anxiety about the possible outcome of a decision.

There is also some ambiguity about the term 'dissonance' itself. Is it a perception (as 'cognitive' suggests), or a feeling, or a feeling about a perception? Aronson's revision of the idea of dissonance as inconsistency between a person's self-concept and a cognition about their behaviour makes it seem likely that dissonance is really nothing more than guilt.

Perhaps even more importantly, there is no independent measure of dissonance; it has only been assumed to occur. Let us take as an example the Festinger and Carlsmith study (box D). The evidence for greater dissonance in those being given \$1 is that they rated the peg-board task as more interesting. But the fact that they rated the task as more interesting is evidence of greater dissonance. As you can see, the argument here is essentially circular.

There are also individual differences in whether or not people act as this theory predicts. Highly anxious people are more likely to do so. Many people seem able to cope with considerable dissonance and not experience the tensions the theory predicts.

It is also possible to account for the findings of research into dissonance in other ways. In **self-perception theory** (1965, 1967), Bem suggests that we often have little direct access to our emotional states, and so make attributions about our own behaviour in the same way that we make attributions about the causes of the behaviour of others. To use one of Bem's examples, 'since I eat brown bread, I must like brown bread'.

We can illustrate this by going back once more to the \$1/\$20 study (box D). The larger incentive of \$20 would account for participants lying, so there would be no need for them to assume that their behaviour was a reflection of their real attitude to the peg-board task. On the other hand, \$1 is not really much of an incentive, so participants would think that the only way of explaining why they said the task was fun was because this was what they really thought.

Impression management theory puts forward yet another way of explaining the results of studies of cognitive dissonance studies. Tedeschi *et al.* (1971) suggest that our behaviour is aimed at making us appear consistent, rather than arising from any need to *be* consistent. The participants in the \$1/\$20 experiment could have been pretending that they thought the task was interesting, so that it would not look as if they had let themselves be bribed.

- Festinger claims that we experience **cognitive dissonance** when we have two conflicting attitudes. This can be reduced by changing one or both attitudes, seeking additional information or reducing the importance of the dissonant cognitions.
- The theory has been investigated by looking at **decision-making**, **forced-compliance** behaviour and **effort**.

❺ The theory has been widely researched and has broad applications. However, it has been criticised for using concepts which can't be measured, and defining dissonance in a circular way. **Self-perception theory** and **impression management theory** have provided alternative explanations for much of the evidence used to support cognitive dissonance theory.

Persuasive communication

Attitudes may also be changed as the result of persuasive communication, a deliberate attempt to change someone's attitude. Three elements have been investigated: the characteristics of the **source** of information, i.e. the person attempting to change an attitude, the **structure of the message**, and the characteristics of the **recipient** at whom the message is aimed. We will now look at each in turn. However, bear in mind that although these elements are treated separately, this can be rather an artificial distinction, since these different factors may interact.

Source factors

One important characteristic of the source is how credible it is seen to be. In general, the more knowledgeable or expert the source is seen to be, the more likely it is that it will be effective in bringing about attitude change:

Box F: Kelman and Hovland (1953)

Procedure: Participants heard a talk on juvenile delinquency, suggesting that young delinquents should be treated leniently. They believed the talk to be given either by a juvenile court judge (high credibility), a drug dealer (low credibility) or a randomly chosen member of the public (neutral credibility). The effect of the talk on participants' attitudes was measured.

Results: Participants were more likely to be influenced by the 'judge', and least likely to be influenced by the 'drug dealer'.

Conclusion: The greater the credibility of the communicator, the greater the effect the communication has. A source seen to be arguing for their own interests (the drug dealer) has low credibility.

However, this study also showed a **sleeper effect**, i.e. an effect which only emerges later. The differences associated with different sources had disappeared after four weeks. People were more likely to remember the content of the message than its source, so the importance of the credibility of the source may only be important in the short term.

The importance of the belief that the source is arguing for or against their own interests has also been investigated in a further study:

Box G: Walster *et al.* (1966)

Procedure: Adolescents read newspaper articles, some of which argued that the courts should have more power, and others that they should have less. Half the participants believed the articles to have been written by a man serving a jail sentence, and half thought the source was a public prosecutor. The effect of the articles on their attitude towards the power of courts was measured.

Results: The greatest attitude change was found in those who read the article by a criminal arguing for greater power for the courts, or one by a prosecutor arguing for less power for the courts. The sources in these conditions were also rated as more trustworthy.

Conclusion: Sources who are seen to be giving a message against their own interests are seen as more trustworthy. They are likely to have a greater effect than when seen to be acting in self-interest.

People are less likely to be influenced when they believe a source is deliberately setting out to change their attitudes. Walster and Festinger (1962) set up a situation where the message was 'overheard', and

the effect of this message was compared with the effect of a message which participants knew was directly aimed at them. Participants were more affected by the 'overheard' message. However, this was only true if the topic was of particular relevance to them. For example, married male participants were more likely to be influenced by an 'overheard' message that husbands should spend more time at home with ther wives, while for single participants there was no difference between the two conditions. This is a nice example of the interaction of elements noted earlier, in this case source and recipient.

The perceived attractiveness of the source can also be important. Unsurprisingly, someone who is witty and charming is likely to have more effect than someone who is not. The effect of the attractiveness of the source is an example of the **halo effect**, where someone who is attractive is seen to to have other positive characteristics – for example, to be wise and knowledgeable. A part of this attractiveness relates to non-verbal communication, and in particular personal space. Someone who invades our personal space is seen as less attractive, and is therefore less likely to be effective in changing attitudes. On this principle, Abelson and Zimbardo (1970) advised political canvassers to maintain a distance of 4–5 feet.

- Research has focused on the source of a communication, features of the **message** and **recipient** factors.
- The perceived **credibility** of the **source** of information is important to attitude change. This effect may be only short-term. Sources who argue against their own interests are seen as more trustworthy.
- People are less influenced when they think that a **deliberate** attempt is being made to change their attitude.
- An attractive source is more influential.

Message factors

Non-verbal communication is also an important factor in the message. For example, face-to-face communication is likely to be more effective than attempts by the mass media, since the source is able to use non-verbal feedback from the audience – facial expression, body posture, and so on – to modify the message or how it is being put across.

The confidence with which the message is presented is important:

Box H: Maslow *et al.* (1971)

Procedure: Participants were asked to read legal documents arguing for the innocence of an accused person. Half the participants read documents using a confident tone, with phrases such as 'obviously' and 'I believe'. The others read more tentative versions, with phrases such as 'I'm not certain' and 'I don't know'. They were asked to assess the guilt or innocence of the accused person.

Results: Those who read the 'confident' version were more likely to think the accused not guilty.

Conclusion: If a message is put across confidently, it is more effective.

Expressing an opinion with which you do not necessarily agree is also influential in bringing about attitude change:

Box I: Eiser and Ross (1977)

Procedure: Participants were asked to write essays on capital punishment. Some were asked to include words associated with arguments against capital punishment, e.g. 'callous' and 'barbaric', while the others were to include words associated with a positive attitude to capital punishment, e.g. 'over-sentimental' and 'starry-eyed'. The participants' shift in attitude after writing the essays was measured.
Results: Participants' attitudes towards capital punishment changed in line with the opinions they had been asked to express.
Conclusion: Expressing an opinion is likely to bring about a shift in the opinion held to bring it closer to what has been expressed.

This finding can be related to **cognitive consistency**, the idea that we aim for consistency in our beliefs, attitudes and behaviour, and so reduce dissonance.

There is some question about whether it is better to make the message explicit, so that there is no doubt about the conclusion to be drawn, or whether a message is more effective if it is implicit, and recipients are left to interpret the message for themselves. Heller (1956) found that participants were more likely to remember advertising slogans they had been shown when these were incomplete and they had to fill in the missing parts themselves. Some brands of cigarette have turned the compulsory health warnings on packets of cigarettes to their advantage; the health warning in advertisements is enough to identify the kind of product being advertised, so the name of the specific product does not need to be included, and can be indicated in other ways. One advertisement for Silk Cut cigarettes, for example, showed a piece of purple silk with a slash in it, using colour and a graphic representation of the name to identify the product. An implicit message may be more effective.

The role of emotion in attitude change, particularly fear, has also been investigated:

Box J: Janis and Feshbach (1953)

Procedure: Participants were given a presentation with colour slides about caring for teeth and the effects of tooth decay. One group (high-fear) heard 71 references to the unpleasant effects of not looking after your teeth, including toothache, painful dental treatment, and possible secondary diseases such as blindness and cancer. The moderate-fear group heard 49 references and the low fear group 17. A control group heard a talk about the eye. Attitudes to dental health were measured a week later.
Results: The high fear group were the most worried about their teeth, but this condition was the least effective in changing behaviour.
Conclusion: Extreme fear may help to focus attention on a message, but is less effective in changing behaviour.

The high fear group was most worred about their teeth

Similar results have been found (Janis and Terwillinger 1962) with a message concerning smoking and lung cancer. Recent pamphlets on stopping smoking from the Health Education Council, for example, have focused on practical advice on how to stop smoking rather than emphasising the dangers of not doing so.

However, it has also been found that if a frightening message is accompanied by information about how the dangers described can be avoided, then fear may be very effective in changing behaviour. There are also individual differences, though, in how effective fear is. The Janis and Feshbach study found that highly anxious participants were less influenced by a high-fear message than participants with low anxiety but more influenced by a low-fear message.

McGuire (1969) sugests that very low fear arousal may be ineffective because the message is not attended to, while messages using high fear arousal may trigger off defence mechanisms such as denial ('this couldn't happen to me') or repression (the message is pushed into the unconscious).

A further area of interest is whether a message presenting both sides of an argument or only one side is more effective:

Box K: Hovland *et al.* (1949)

Procedure: During the Second World War, soldiers were given articles to read suggesting that it would take at least two years to end the war with Japan. One group was given a one-sided message, while for the other group both sides of the argument were covered.
Results: There was no overall difference between the two groups in terms of attitude change. Those who were less educated, however, were more influenced by the one-sided argument, while the better educated were more influenced if the argument was two-sided. Education level apart, participants whose initial attitude was similar to the article were more influenced by the one-sided presentation, and the two-sided presentation was more effective for participants who already knew quite a lot about what was being discussed.
Conclusion: Education, existing attitude, and prior knowledge all influence whether a one- or two-sided presentation is more effective in changing attitudes.

The order in which arguments for and against a topic should be given has also been investigated. Several studies have found a **primacy effect**, when the first argument heard has the most effect. McGuire (1957), for example, tried to persuade his participants to take an educational course. His efforts were more effective if the positive aspects of taking the course were given first, and more negative aspects afterwards. It is possible that more attention is paid to what comes first, or that once one side of the argument has been heard, a decision is reached which is then hard to shift.

Other research has found evidence for a **recency effect**, when the last argument heard has the most effect. This is likely to happen when people know very little about a topic, or are not very interested in it. Miller and Campbell (1959) also investigated primacy and recency effects in a simulated courtroom study. They found that the timing of the presentation of the two sides of the argument is important. If there is an interval between hearing the arguments and coming to a decision, a primacy effect is likely, while if there is a delay between argument and counterargument, and then a decision is made immediately, there is likely to be a recency effect.

- The **confidence** with which a message is put across and the **language** used both play a part in the effectiveness of the message. An implicit message may be more effective than one where the conclusions to be drawn are explicit.
- High levels of **fear** are ineffective in changing behaviour unless recipients are given information about how to avoid the dangers described. There are **individual differences** in how effective fear is.
- Level of **education**, **existing attitude** and prior **knowledge** determine whether a one- or two-sided argument is more effective. With a two-sided argument, there may be a **primacy** or a **recency effect**.

Characteristics of the recipient

Some of the research already covered has shown that characteristics of the recipient – such as their previous knowledge of a topic, their existing attitude to it, their level of interest in the topic and their level of education – are important in attitude change. Different kinds of people may respond to the same message in different ways:

Activity 11: recipient characteristics

Look back through the previous two sections. List which characteristics of the recipient have been found by research to influence whether a message is effective in changing attitudes. You may also find the section headed 'The function of attitudes' useful. Check your list with the discussion which follows.

The studies of Walster and Festinger and Walster *et al.* (box G) show that whether the attempt to influence attitudes is seen as deliberate, and whether it is seen to be for or against the interests of the source, both influence the effectiveness of the message. This suggests that cognitions are important, i.e. how the recipient perceives the situation. While the overall situation may contain cues, as in these studies, there may be room for different interpretations.

Similarly, the attractiveness of the source is relevant. There are general characteristics which lead us to find people attractive, but again, there is room for individual variation.

The Janis and Feshbach study (box J) suggests that personality characteristics, in this case anxiety levels, are important. McGuire (1968) goes beyond this to suggest that persuasibility may be a personality characteristic, so that some people are much easier to influence than others.

In general, though, there is little evidence for this kind of consistency; characteristics of the situation seem to be more important. Janis and Mann (1965) found that the style of delivery of the message played an important role in attitude change. Participants who role-played cancer patients were more likely to change both their attitudes and their smoking behaviour than a control group who had heard tape-recorded information.

You will remember from the section headed 'The structure and function of attitudes' that attitudes serve different functions for different people. If an attitude serves the knowledge function for an individual, it may be open to change if additional information is given. Attitude change is less likely where the function of the attitude is, for example, ego-defensive.

Early studies suggested that there may be gender differences, with women being easier to influence than men. However, these differences are more likely to have come about as a result of the topics chosen in this research. Levels of self-esteem may also be a factor. Males with high self-esteem are more difficult to influence than those with low self-esteem. Women with moderate self-esteem appear to be the easiest to influence.

Some people are much easier to influence than others

- Characteristics of the **recipient** influence the effectiveness of a message.
- **Cognitions** may be important. **Personality differences** are likely to be less important than **situational factors**.
- **Prior knowledge**, **education level**, **level of interest** and **initial attitude** have been shown to affect persuasibility.
- There is some doubt whether gender is a factor, though it may be related to persuasibility through levels of self-esteem.

Dual-process models

The **elaboration likelihood model (ELM)**, proposed by Petty and Cacioppo (1981) suggests that there are two ways of processing information.

Central processing involves focusing on *arguments*, i.e. thinking carefully about information, weighing up facts and using logical reasoning. However, where recipients are unwilling or unable to spend the time and make the effort to carry out this kind of extensive processing, **peripheral processing** may be used. This involves only shallow processing of information, and focuses on *cues*, with attention given to features which are less relevant to the message being put across – for example, the attractiveness or expertise of the source. Over a period of time, an individual is likely to use both central and peripheral processing – although, as we shall see, there is some evidence that we have a preference for one mode over the other.

'Elaboration likelihood' refers to the probability of a person critically evaluating the arguments put forward in a communication. The extent to which they will do so depends on both motivation and ability. Motivation is important because of the amount of time and effort involved, while ability is determined by such factors as previous knowledge about the content of the message.

While both kinds of processing can lead to attitude change, the factors which influence this change in each case vary. For example, a person is more likely to be motivated to think carefully about something and use central processing if the message has personal relevance. When it has little personal relevance, the motivation to think about the message is low, and peripheral processing is used:

Box L: Petty *et al.* (1981)

Procedure: Student participants received a persuasive communication, contrary to their previously expressed opinion, in support of a major change to the university exam system. Three aspects of the communication were manipulated: whether the speaker was an expert or not; whether strong or weak arguments were used; and whether the topic was of high relevance to the recipient (the new exam system was to be brought in the following year) or low relevance (the change would be in 10 years' time, and so would not affect them).

Results: When the topic was of high personal relevance, agreement with the communication was predicted by the strength of the arguments. Where personal relevance was low, agreement was predicted by the expertise of the speaker.

Conclusion: High personal relevance leads to use of the central route, and low personal relevance to the peripheral route.

A further factor is mood. Bless *et al.* (1990) found that people in a bad mood were more affected by the quality of an argument presented, which suggests that they were using central processing. Those in a good mood were more likely to use peripheral processing.

There are also individual differences in terms of which is the generally preferred route. Cacioppo and Petty (1982) developed the Need for Cognition scale (NFC), as a measure of the extent to which people enjoy thinking. They predicted that those scoring high on this scale would be more likely to use central processing than low scorers. This prediction has been generally supported by research. For example, Bakker (1999) presented messages about safe sex to a sample of 119 adolescents. For high-NFC participants, a written message was more effective in bringing about attitude change than the message in cartoon form, while the opposite was true for low-NFC participants.

A further dual-process model, the **heuristic–systematic model (HSM)** proposed by Chaiken (1980), is in many respects similar to the ELM. It too suggests that there are two kinds of processing. Like central processing, **systematic processing** is active, conscious and cognitively demanding, and is only likely to happen when a person is highly motivated. **Heuristic processing** is similar to peripheral processing. A heuristic is a short cut taken in processing information, using non-content cues. For example, if in the past a person has learned to trust people they like, they will apply a 'liking-agreement' heuristic, such as 'people I like usually have correct opinions'.

There are differences in the effectiveness of these two kinds of processing:

Box M: Chaiken (1980)

Procedure: Participants were given a message including either two or six arguments in favour of a particular issue. In condition 1 (systematic processing), they were told they would later be interviewed about the issue. In condition 2 (heuristic processing), they were told they would be interviewed about a different topic. The two groups were compared for amount of attitude change, factors involved in that change and how stable the change was.
Results: Participants in condition 1 were more affected by six arguments than two. Their attitudes remained stable when tested again 10 days later. Participants in condition 2 were not affected by the number of arguments presented, but they were affected (unlike condition 1) by whether or not they had liked the speaker. Their attitude change was less stable.
Conclusion: Using systematic processing is likely to provide more lasting attitude change than using heuristic processing.

Dual-process theories do not discount the possibility that both kinds of processing can occur a the same time. For example, where close attention to the arguments of a message does not lead to a clear-cut conclusion, we may then use heuristic cues. This idea was supported by the findings of a study by Chaiken and Maheswaran (1994). They found that when the arguments in a message were ambiguous, the credibility of the source (a peripheral cue) influenced attitudes, even when the task was of high personal relevance.

Much of the time, we make use of peripheral/heuristic processing. We are motivated to make sense of our world, but we act as 'cognitive misers', simplifying this task as much as possible to avoid cognitive effort. We therefore think only enough to meet the minimum demands of the situation. Advertising takes advantage of this tendency by using the peripheral route, giving us short, simple and straightforward messages which do not require much processing. For example, one successful electoral campaign run for the Conservative Party showed a long queue of people stretching into the distance, with the slogan 'Labour isn't working' – a simple but very effective message.

- **Dual-process theories** of attitude change propose that here are two ways of processing information, **central/peripheral** in **ELM**, and **systematic/heuristic** in **HSM**. The choice of route depends on **motivation** and **ability**, and can be affected by **mood**. Both can bring about attitude change.
- Although we are capable of using both routes, there are **individual differences** in which is preferred.
- There is a general tendency to use peripheral/heuristic processing, a tendency exploited with success in **advertising**.

4.5 Prejudice and discrimination

Baron and Byrne (1991) defined prejudice as 'an attitude (usually negative) toward the members of some group, based solely on their membership in that group'. A study of history suggests that prejudice, together with the violent mistreatment of some people by others which arises from it, has always been widespread, and is likely to remain so. Examples come only too readily to mind – the apartheid regime in South Africa, Nazi genocide in the Second World War, killings of Catholics by Protestants and Protestants by Catholics in Northern Ireland, and the 'ethnic cleansing' by Serbian forces of Albanians in Kosovo.

Since prejudice is an attitude, in common with other attitudes it has three components: **cognitive** (our beliefs about a particular group: our stereotypes), **affective** (how we feel about them: hostility) and **behavioural** (how we act towards them). The behavioural part of prejudice is **discrimination**, which Secord and Backman (1964) defined as 'the inequitable treatment of individuals considered to belong to a particular social group'.

Activity 12: expressing prejudice

Think of examples of how extreme hostile attitudes have been expressed in the past. Think also about how prejudice is expressed in society today; looking through current newspapers may help you with this. Make a list of as many different examples as you can. If you are working in a group, pool your ideas.

Keep your notes to compare with Allport's stages described in figure 4.

Allport (1954) distinguished five different levels of the behavioural component of prejudice:

Figure 4: Allport's five stages of the expression of prejudice

1. *antilocution:* expressing hostility verbally, e.g. making derogatory and insulting remarks about the target group, and telling jokes about them.
2. *avoidance:* making efforts to avoid any kind of contact, physical or social.
3. *discrimination:* excluding the target group from housing, civil rights and employment opportunities.
4. *physical attack:* violence against members of the target group, or their property.
5. *extermination:* extreme violence against an entire group, up to and including genocide.

You should be able to match the items on the list you made in activity 12 against Allport's five stages. Examples of all five stages are (unfortunately) not hard to think of.

While cognitive, affective and behavioural elements of prejudice usually occur together, this is not always the case; as we saw in the LaPiere study (box A). In this example, prejudiced beliefs and feelings were not expressed in behaviour. It makes more sense to think of these aspects as *predisposing* someone to act in a prejudiced way; whether they do so or not is affected by situational factors.

- **Prejudice** is an attitude towards people based on their group membership. It therefore has **cognitive**, **affective** and **behavioural** components. The behavioural component is **discrimination**.
- Allport distinguished five **stages** of the expression of prejudice, ranging from antilocution to extermination.

Attitudes and stereotyping

Hogg and Vaughan (1995) define stereotypes as 'widely shared assumptions about the personalities, attitudes and behaviour of people based on group membership, for example ethnicity, nationality, sex, race and class'. All members of that category or social group are perceived as sharing the same characteristics, and any individual belonging to that category is assumed to have these characteristics.

The use of stereotypes is a major way in which we simplify our social world, since they reduce the amount of processing we need to carry out when we meet a new person. Asch (1952) pointed out that in a lot of situations, our behaviour is indeed determined by group membership. Active Christians tend to go to church, for example. Stereotyping can therefore be seen as a useful short cut method (a heuristic) for understanding the social world.

It is perhaps worth noting that much of the research into stereotypes has been carried out in the USA, where political ideology demands that everyone who lives in the USA is 'American first', whatever their cultural or ethnic origins. Stereotypes, with their focus on difference, present a challenge to this political ideal, and are therefore seen negatively.

Tajfel (1969) has argued that within a European tradition cultural diversity is seen in a more positive way, so stereotyping can be seen as straightforward cognitive processing. It is purely an example of categorisation, which involves picking up on similarities within groups, and exaggerating differences between groups, in order to help us understand our social world.

LeVine and Campbell (1972) suggest that many stereotypes are rooted in social and cultural facts. The stereotype of Jews as being mercenary and grasping, for example, could be explained by their history of persecution. With many ways of earning a living closed to them, trading was one of the few remaining options. Similarly, before slavery was abolished in the USA, it was illegal to educate slaves, so the stereotype of blacks as being less intelligent should not really be surprising.

However, the oversimplification stereotyping involves is likely to lead to overgeneralisation about group characteristics, and so cause us to make faulty judgements. Campbell (1967) points to the serious problems stereotypes can cause. They overestimate the differences between groups and underestimate the differences within groups. They distort reality, and are usually negative. They are seldom questioned and can therefore be used to justify hostility and discrimination.

Once stereotypes are formed, they are very resistant to change. Two processes which help to maintain them are **selective remembering** (we remember information which supports the stereotypes we hold) and **negative memory bias** (we tend to remember information which is critical of groups against whom we are prejudiced).

Stereotypes can also be maintained by a **self-fulfilling prophecy**. The classic example to illustrate what this means is the fall of the Last National Bank in the USA. The bank was sound, but it was rumoured to be about to collapse. As a result of the rumours, people rushed to draw out their money, causing the bank to collapse. In other words, an initially false definition of a situation brought about a behaviour which made the originally false idea come true. The same principle can be applied interpersonally.

Activity 13: stereotypes and the self-fulfilling prophecy

A teacher believes that black children are unintelligent. How might the self-fulfilling prophecy support her stereotype?

When you have finished, see the notes on page 132.

Stereotypes can be formed on the basis of something as simple as first names. Harari and McDavid (1973), for example, found that teachers graded essays supposedly written by students with attractive names on average a letter grade higher than those written by students with unattractive names.

However, much of the research into stereotyping and its relation to prejudice has focused on ethnicity, investigating stereotypes held about people from other cultures, and in particular those of a different race.

An early method of investigating ethnic stereotypes is shown in box N:

Box N: Katz and Braly (1933)

Procedure: American university students were given a list of nationalities and ethnic groups (white Americans, African Americans, Germans, Irish and so on), and a list of 84 personality traits. They were asked to pick out five or six traits which they thought were typical of each group.

Results: There was considerable agreement in the traits selected. White Americans, for example, were seen as industrious, progressive, ambitious, materialistic and intelligent, whereas African Americans were seen as superstitious, lazy, happy-go-lucky, ignorant and musical. There was a greater tendency to agree about derogatory traits. Participants were quite ready to rate ethnic groups with whom they had had no personal contact.

Conclusion: Ethnic stereotypes are widespread, and shared by members of a particular social group.

In criticism of this study, it should be noted that participants were not given the option of stating that traits are not typical of ethnic groups. When this research was replicated by Gilbert (1951), using students from the same institution, participants were less ready to make this kind of generalisation. In a similar study by Karlins *et al.* (1969), participants again showed ethnic stereotyping, but were more likely to use positive terms. This variation over time indicates that stereotyping is a social and cultural phenomenon, affected by social change and the ethos of the time. However, it should be noted that this kind of study, which relies entirely on verbal reports, is extremely low in ecological validity. The limited information that participants are given is also likely to create demand characteristics.

Activity 14: ethnic stereotypes

You might like to replicate these studies in a modified form. Focus on just a few ethnic groups, e.g. French, Germans, Japanese and Irish, and ask participants to write down five or six words which they think best describe a typical member of each group.

How willing were your participants to carry out this task? Was there any similarity in the descriptions they used? Were they more likely to use positive or derogatory terms? Compare your findings with those of the three studies described above.

- **Stereotypes** are judgements made about people on the basis of their **group membership**.
- Stereotyping helps us to simplify our social world. It may be seen negatively because of the cultural traditions in the USA within which much research in this area has been rooted. At the same time, stereotypes can be dangerous, in that they can be used to justify discrimination.
- There may be **historical** and **cultural** reasons which explain particular stereotypes. Stereotypes may contain some truth, which serves to maintain them. They are also maintained by **selective remembering** and **negative memory bias**.
- **Ethnic stereotyping**, on which much research has focused, is widespread, but the readiness with which people are prepared to stereotype others has been shown to vary across the decades. This suggests a cultural basis for stereotyping.

The formation of prejudiced attitudes

There are three broad approaches to explaining why prejudiced attitudes are formed. The **individual** approach looks for causes within the individual, e.g. personality characteristics. This approach is also interested in differences between people. The **interpersonal** approach focuses on processes occurring within social groups, for example shared beliefs, stereotypes within a culture and conformity to social and cultural norms. The **intergroup** approach looks at relationships between different groups of people, e.g. intergroup competition.

Splitting up the various theories in this way provides a manageable framework within which we can look at prejudice. At the same time, it is likely that the three different approaches complement rather than contradict each other; they all have something to contribute to our understanding of prejudice.

Individual explanations of prejudice

There are two possible ways of explaining prejudice based on the individual. One way focuses on individual differences, and investigates whether prejudice is associated with a particular personality type. The second assumes that individuals are basically the same, and looks at the processes which can lead to prejudice in any of us. However, both kinds of explanation are examples of **externalisation**: the individual deals with personal problems and conflicts by projecting them on to others.

Adorno *et al.* (1950) developed the theory of the **authoritarian personality**, which proposed a connection between a particular kind of personality and prejudice. Adorno produced scales to measure personality, the most famous of which is the F-scale (F standing for 'fascist'). This takes the form of statements, assessed by a Likert scale (see chapter 2), in which the respondent indicates the extent to which they agree or disagree with each statement. Some sample items are shown in figure 5:

Figure 5: sample statements from the F-scale

The most important thing to teach children is obedience to their parents.

Homosexuals are hardly better than criminals, and ought to be severely punished.

Any good leader should be strict with people under him in order to gain respect.

When a person has a problem or worry, it is best for him not to think about it, but to keep busy with more cheerful things.

People can be divided into two distinct classes, the strong and the weak.

Some day it will probably be shown that astrology can explain a lot of things.

The F-scale measures characteristics such as conventionality, submission to those in authority, aggression to those over whom you are in authority, toughness, destructiveness and superstition. The scale was successful in identifying people who were likely to be prejudiced, since prejudiced people would be likely to have these characteristics and so to agree with all these statements. Adorno referred to a high scorer on these scales as an **authoritarian personality**.

As you will have seen, none of the items relates directly to attitudes towards ethnic minorities, but they aim to tap into the general personality characteristics which Adorno *et al.* believed were linked to prejudiced attitudes.

Adorno *et al.* explained the development of the authoritarian personality within the framework of Freud's theories (see chapter 1). They believed that the causes lay in childhood experience. On the basis of interview data they had collected, they claimed that people who scored high on the F-scale had often experienced a harsh upbringing, where they were punished for any misdemeanour and were seldom shown affection.

Freudian **defence mechanisms**, in particular **displacement** and **projection,** also form part of the picture. Consciously, people with an authoritarian personality thought highly of their parents, but often showed unconscious hostility towards them. Adorno *et al.* believed that this unconscious hostility was displaced on to minority groups. The authoritarian personality also projects his or her own unacceptable sexual and aggressive impulses on to these groups, and so sees them as threatening.

There is supporting evidence that some people are more likely to be prejudiced than others. One example is shown in box O:

Box O: Hartley (1946)

Procedure: Participants were asked their opinions about mythical but plausible-sounding ethnic groups (Wallonians, Danerians and Pirenians); for example, how they would feel if a member of this group came to live next door to them, or wished to marry their daughter.

Results: While some participants refused to answer, many expressed extreme prejudice against these groups. These people were also very prejudiced against Jews and black people.
Conclusion: This prejudice could not have developed through experience, since the groups did not exist. The roots of prejudice must therefore lie within the person.

Even when a group does not exist people can still be prejudiced against them

However, the theory has been criticised both on methodological and conceptual grounds.

Activity 15: methodology and the F-scale

Look back at the sample statements from the F-scale shown in figure 5. Can you identify a possible source of bias?
When you have finished, see the notes on page 132.

A further methodological problem is that the people carrying out the interviews knew the F scores of the people they were interviewing, so there is a possibility of **experimenter bias** when they came to analyse the results. Adorno *et al.* have also been criticised for their limited sample.

A conceptual problem has been raised by Hyman and Sheatsley (1954). They suggested that we do not need to use personality to explain prejudice; levels of education, linked to socioeconomic status, are a more plausible explanation. They found that the percentage of people agreeing with questions from the F-scale decreases as educational levels increase. However, correlation does not necessarily imply causation. It may be, for example, that a low level of intellectual ability underpins both high scores on the F-scale and low socioeconomic status.

A further problem is that a theory which focuses on the individual cannot account for prejudice which is widespread in a particular community at a particular time; for example, anti-semitism in Nazi Germany. It also cannot explain rapid changes in levels of prejudice. Again taking Nazi Germany as an example, anti-semitism rose rapidly over a period of about 10 years. It does not seem credible that a whole generation of Germans changed their child-rearing patterns over so short a time.

A final criticism is that this theory associates prejudice with extreme right-wing ideology. In his book *The Open and Closed Mind*, Rokeach (1960) suggested that authoritarianism is associated with the extreme left as well as the extreme right. People at both extremes are likely to have 'closed minds', i.e. to be rigid thinkers, intolerant of those different from themselves. He referred to this as **dogmatism**, and developed a questionnaire to measure it. As he had predicted, dogmatism was found among people at both extremes of the political spectrum.

The **frustration–aggression hypothesis** of Dollard *et al.* (1939) provides another explanation of prejudice at the level of the individual. It is not interested in individual differences, though, but rather in the processes which can lead to prejudice in people in general.

This hypothesis states that frustration always leads to aggression, and aggression is always caused by frustration. Frustration is used here to refer to goal-directed activity being prevented from achieving the goal at which it is directed. The connection with prejudice is based on Freud's ego defence mechanism of **displacement** (see chapter 1), where aggressive impulses which cannot be expressed directly are displaced on to someone or something else. For example, if someone is frustrated by being unemployed they might blame the government. There is no direct way of expressing their aggression against the government, so a **scapegoat** is found on whom the aggressive feelings can be displaced. When an individual is frustrated, they will express their aggression as prejudice against a group to which they do not belong.

This idea has been tested experimentally:

Box P: Weatherley (1961)

Procedure: Participants were two groups of students, high- and low-scorers on an anti-semitism questionnaire. Half of each group were insulted, in order to create frustration, while filling in another questionnaire. All participants were later asked to write stories about some pictures of men, two of whom were given Jewish names.

Results: Those who scored high for anti-semitism responded more aggressively to the 'Jewish name' pictures than those who scored low. There was no difference between high and low scorers who had been insulted in the amount of aggression directed at the other pictures

Conclusion: When frustrated, highly anti-semitic people target their aggression specifically at Jews.

However, there are problems in interpreting this study in terms of the frustration–aggression hypothesis. Insulting someone is likely to make them angry, but does not frustrate them in the sense of preventing them from achieving their goal. The study therefore fits better with the modification to the frustration–aggression hypothesis put forward by Berkowitz (1969), who suggested that the link between frustration and aggression is mediated by anger. What is important about frustration is that it is psychologically painful, which may lead us to show aggression in the form of prejudice against a target group.

The choice of scapegoat is not random. In England in the 1930s and 1940s, Jews were the main scapegoat, followed by West Indians during the next two decades, and later by Asians, in particular Pakistanis. The fact that these particular groups were picked out at these periods, rather than prejudice being more widely targeted at other minority groups, suggests that groups chosen as scapegoats are in some way socially approved. This in turn suggests that in order to explain prejudice, we need to look beyond the individual and focus on their social group, and this approach is explored in the next section.

- Theories of prejudice focus on **individual**, **interpersonal** or **intergroup** levels.
- Adorno *et al.* suggested that prejudice is linked with the characteristics of the **authoritarian personality**. This personality type is associated with extreme right-wing ideology. It has its roots in childhood experience.
- While there is some support for the theory, methodological and conceptual criticisms can be made.
- Rokeach linked this type of personality with extreme political ideology of both left and right. He describes it as **dogmatism**.
- The **frustration–aggression hypothesis** suggests that we displace aggression on to minority groups when we are frustrated. They become **scapegoats**.

The interpersonal approach to prejudice

Ideas about prejudice which look at processes within groups of people focus on stereotyping, discussed earlier, and conformity to **social** and **cultural norms**.

Social norms – behaviour considered appropriate within a social group – are one possible influence on prejudice and discrimination. People may have prejudiced beliefs and feelings and act in a prejudiced way because they are conforming to what is regarded as normal in the social groups to which they belong:

Box Q: Minard (1952)

Procedure: The behaviour of black and white miners in a town in the southern United States was observed, both above and below ground.
Results: Below ground, where the social norm was friendly behaviour towards work colleagues, 80% of the white miners were friendly towards the black miners. Above ground, where the social norm was prejudiced behaviour by whites to blacks, this dropped to 20%.
Conclusion: The white miners were conforming to different norms above and below ground. Whether or not prejudice is shown depends on the social context within which behaviour takes place.

Pettigrew (1959) also investigated the role of conformity in prejudice. He investigated the idea that people who tended to be more conformist would also be more prejudiced, and found this to be true of white South African students. Similarly, he accounted for the higher levels of prejudice against black people in the southern United States than in the north in terms of the greater social acceptability of this kind of prejudice in the south.

A study by Rogers and Frantz (1962) found that immigrants to Rhodesia (now Zimbabwe) became more prejudiced the longer they had been in the country. They gradually conformed more to the prevailing cultural norm of prejudice against the black population.

Conformity to social norms, then, may offer an explanation for prejudice in some cases. At the same time, norms change over time, so this can only go some way towards explaining prejudice.

❺ People may be prejudiced because they are conforming to **social** and **cultural norms**.

The intergroup approach to prejudice

At the intergroup level, prejudice has been explained in terms of **intergroup conflict**. One theory using this idea is **relative deprivation theory**: when people feel that they are deprived in relation to other groups, they become prejudiced against the groups with whom they are comparing themselves.

In support of this idea, Vanneman and Pettigrew (1972) found that white people who were most prejudiced against black people also believed that white people were badly off compared to black people. They were actually better off, but the idea of relative deprivation depends on a subjective evaluation of a situation, rather than a realistic assessment.

Activity 16: relative deprivation theory

What criticism could be made about the conclusion drawn in the Vanneman and Pettigrew study, that relative deprivation leads to prejudice? Can you think of an alternative interpretation of the findings?

When you have finished, see the notes on page 132.

Another approach is **realistic conflict theory**, proposed by Sherif (1966). He carried out a series of experiments investigating aggression in boys at a summer camp. A sample study is described in box R:

Box R: Sherif (1966)

Procedure: The participants in this study were 11- and 12-year-old boys at an American summer camp. In the first stage of the study, the boys mixed with each other and took part in sports and outdoor activities. During this period, friendships were formed.
The boys were then divided into two groups, with friends being split up. Each group again took part in the normal range of camp activities, but only within their own group. There was no contact with the other group. Each group shared a dormitory and took their meals together. Very soon, friendships were formed, and a strong sense of group identity had developed. A leadership structure

emerged, and each group gave themselves names, the Eagles and the Red Devils. In the next stage, competitions in various activities were arranged between the two groups.
Results: A lot of intergroup hostility was shown, e.g. name calling, raids on each other's dormitories and graffiti.
Conclusion: Competition between groups can result in aggressive behaviour.

On the basis of this research, Sherif suggested that intergroup conflict comes about as the result of a conflict of interest. He claimed that this is enough to create hostility and discrimination. There is a lot of evidence that when people compete for scarce resources, there is a rise in intergroup hostility. For example, many studies have shown that in times of high unemployment there are high levels of racism among white people who believe that black people have taken away their jobs.

However, Tyerman and Spencer (1983) have challenged Sherif's conclusions. In a similar study of a summer camp, they found that competition did not lead to the hostility Sherif described. This could have been because the boys all knew each other well, and the cohesiveness of the whole group was encouraged by the leader.

We need finally to look at historical explanations of prejudice, based on relationships between groups. Racial prejudice against some minority ethnic groups in Britain may have its roots in colonialism. For example, when India was a British colony, white men ran its tea plantations while the labour was supplied by the native Indians. The two groups thus had very different roles, and the prevailing British view of the inhabitants of the colonies was that they were inferior to white Britons. Prejudice in Britain today against people from former British colonies may be, in part at least, a hangover from this attitude. A similar argument applies to prejudice against black people in America, in the historical context of slavery.

Finally, the role of the mass media in encouraging prejudice against particular groups of people should not be forgotten. For example, Nazi propaganda films depicted Jews as vermin, thus laying the foundation for the genocide which was to follow. Similarly, the Serbian assault on Kosovo followed years of intensive anti-Albanian propaganda.

- Prejudice has been explained in terms of **intergroup conflict**. Two theories taking this approach are **relative deprivation theory** and **realistic conflict theory**.
- There may be **historical** reasons for hostile inter-group relationships.
- **Media propaganda** can play a role in encouraging prejudice.

Notes on activities

1 The cognitive part of Shihan's attitude to air travel is likely to be a belief that air travel is dangerous, and planes often crash. She feels frightened at the thought of going on a plane – the affective component. Helen may believe that people living on the street are there because they have been unlucky, and that there is nothing they can do to improve matters. She may express her attitude by buying the *Big Issue*, or giving money to people asking for spare change. Assuming he believes that improving social services is a good thing, Jack is likely to have positive feelings about the Labour Party and Labour politicians. He might vote for the party in elections, or become a party member.

While you probably found it straightforward to work backwards from Shihan's behaviour to the other components of her attitude to air travel, you may have queried whether the cognitive and affective components of Helen's and Jack's attitudes would always be shown in their behaviour. Jack may well have positive beliefs about the Labour Party, and value their political aims, for example, but not join the party and perhaps not even bother to vote.

2 Attitudes to religion might be measured by how frequently people attend a church or other place of worship. Attitudes to classical music could be measured by how often people go to concerts or buy CDs of classical music. One problem, as we have seen, is that attitudes and behaviour don't necessarily coincide. It could be, for example, that the person whose attitude to classical music you are measuring lives in a village and has little opportunity to go to concerts, and can't afford to buy many CDs.

3 The Likert method is relatively easy to construct and administer. It provides quantitative data, so that it would be possible to measure attitude change over time, for example, or as the result of giving people information.

It does have the problem of demand characteristics, as it may be fairly obvious what a questionnaire of this kind is testing, and this could lead to people giving socially desirable answers. The scoring method is rather crude; it is possible that people with similar scores have actually responded quite differently to the different items. People may also interpret the statements in slightly different ways. Some people may also prefer always to use the extremes of the scale, while others group their responses round the middle point, though this doesn't necessarily show that their attitudes are any less strongly held. This is called **position response bias**, and means that it may be difficult to make accurate comparisons between people. Finally, of course, it is only as good a measure of an attitude as the statements which have been provided!

4 Active–passive relates to the activity dimension, and strong–weak to the potency dimension. For reasons which are not quite so clear as for the other dimensions, Osgood also relates cruel–kind to potency. The other three items relate to the evaluative dimension. In practice, this last dimension is considered the most important, as it measures the strength of a person's attitude to what is being measured.

5 It is possible that the presence of LaPiere himself could have made the Chinese couple more acceptable, and more difficult to refuse, when looking for accommodation or getting served in a restaurant. He did, however, try to avoid his presence becoming a factor by letting his friends enter hotels and restaurants ahead of him, while he concerned himself with the car or luggage. It would also not be in the financial interests of hotel keepers to turn away custom. It should also be noted that LaPiere's Chinese friends were well dressed, with good-quality luggage and very polite; these factors may have affected how they were treated in a face-to-face situation.

6 The most likely explanation of Sarah's behaviour is normative influence. We often behave in ways which are inconsistent with our attitudes when we are in a group of people who share a different attitude, and we want to feel part of the group. Jared is responding to the social norm of politeness. Steve has a conflict to resolve between his attitude to tabloid newspapers, and his wish to read about the football. His eagerness to find out the football results is stronger than his attitude towards the tabloid press. James' behaviour is an example of the importance of specificity. His attitude towards Essex girls is a stereotype, but when he meets this specific Essex girl, she does not conform to his stereotype. Ned has conflicting attitudes. While he has a positive attitude towards people with learning difficulties, he has an attitude about what his own living environment should be like which is in conflict with this.

7 Martin could either change his smoking behaviour, or approach this from another angle by modifying his cognition about the link between smoking and cancer. He could change his smoking behaviour by stopping smoking, or by smoking low-tar cigarettes. The alternative approach could include making light of the evidence for this link; the evidence in humans is only correlational. He could associate with other smokers, on the principle 'If Kate smokes, then it can't be that dangerous'. He could convince himself that he really enjoys smoking, so it is worth the risk. Finally, he could make a virtue out of being unconcerned about the dangers of smoking.

It should be clear from this range of possibilities that Festinger sees people not as rational (since some of Martin's options are not very sensible) but as rationalisers. They try to appear rational, both to others and to themselves. The fact that many people carry on smoking in full knowledge of the dangers also suggests that there are individual differences in the level of dissonance which can be tolerated.

8 Once the decision has been made by paying for the holiday, you are likely to experience dissonance because this kind of decision is never a straightforward one between good and bad, which would give us perfect consonance between information and decision. You have rejected a choice with some positive aspects, and made a choice with some negative aspects. In effect you have made a trade-off which you hope will work out, but you can't be sure.

This dissonance can be reduced by focusing on the positive aspects of the choice you made, and the negative aspects of the holiday you turned down. An example of this is shown in the study carried out by Ehrlich *et al.* (below box C).

9 The children given the mild threat would experience more dissonance, because it would be harder for them to justify doing as they had been told. To reduce this dissonance, their liking for the toy would be reduced.

10 The two aspects of this situation which were in dissonance were the group's belief that the flood would happen and that the spaceship would arrive, and the fact that neither of these two events materialised. Giving up their jobs and giving away their possessions were acts of public commitment, mentioned in the section on forced-choice behaviour. This would make it less likely that they would give up their beliefs.

You will remember that one possible way of reducing dissonance is to change one of the elements in the dissonant relationship. The non-arrival of the flood and spaceship could not be changed, and, given the degree of public commitment, it would have been difficult for the believers to give up their beliefs. This would also mean that reducing the importance of the dissonant cognitions would not be likely. The final option is to acquire new information to increase consonance, and this is what happened with the final message.

Festinger explains the eagerness of Mrs Keech and her group to make converts in terms of social support. As a group, the believers strengthened and maintained their belief system. The Seekers were isolated, and without this support system lost their belief.

13 She might spend less time with the black children in her class, preferring to concentrate on children she thinks are more likely to benefit from her help. She might also set the black children less challenging tasks, which do not stretch them. The black children might then fail to make good progress, and so confirm her initial belief.

15 You may have noticed that all the statements are structured in such a way that they score positively for authoritarianism; there are no statements with which an authoritarian personality might disagree. This is true for all the items on the scale. The trouble with this is that a person filling in the questionnaire might develop a response set, ie once they had agreed with the first few statements, they would mechanically agree with the others without reading the items carefully. In this case, the questionnaire might not be measuring authoritarianism, but acquiescence.

16 This is a correlational study, so can only establish an association between variables, not the cause and effect relationship that a sense of relative deprivation leads to prejudice against a group seen as better off. It is equally possible that prejudice against blacks leads white people to search for a justification for their prejudice, achieved by rationalising it in terms of adopting a belief that blacks are better off than they are.

Social influence

5.1 Conformity

Conformity refers to behaviour change in the direction of the behaviour of others as a result of group pressure. This pressure doesn't necessarily need to be expressed, and may even just be in the mind of the person who experiences it; for example, Mary may feel that she should study languages at university because this is what her two older sisters have done. Sometimes, there is more explicit pressure; for example, if the rest of the family suggest that this is what Mary might like to do.

Research into conformity goes back a long way. Allport (1924) asked participants to judge the pleasantness of smells, and found that if people made this judgement in groups, individual judgements tended to be in general agreement with the average judgement for the group as a whole. Similarly, when Jenness (1932) asked participants to judge the number of beans in a bottle, and then revise their estimates after discussion in a group, the second estimate tended to move towards the average group judgement. Another study, shown in box A, demonstrated conformity using a visual illusion called the **autokinetic effect**: when there is a point of light in an otherwise darkened room, it seems to move about:

Box A: Sherif (1935)

Procedure: Participants were asked individually to estimate how far and in what direction the point of light moved. Average scores were worked out for each participant over a series of trials. They were then divided into groups, each group containing participants with very different averages calculated from the individual trials. Participants were then asked to make individual judgements while in their groups.

Results: After a few trials, individual judgements tended to move towards agreement within the group. The effect was still evident when the tests were repeated later, with participants tested individually.

Conclusion: When making judgements in a group, there is a tendency for individual judgements to drift towards group consensus, i.e. to conform to the average for the group.

It is worth noting that Sherif's study did not *ask* participants to arrive at a group estimate. It is a nice example of conformity where there is no direct and explicit pressure to change behaviour; influence comes about through the individual's perception of the situation.

This study has not been without its critics, however. Asch, who went on to carry out his own series of studies on conformity (see box B), pointed out that Sherif's study had put participants into a situation of uncertainty, i.e. where a correct answer was not apparent: since the light does not actually move at all, but only seems to move, there is no right or wrong answer.

He argued that for a real understanding of conformity, we need to look at what happens in an *un*ambiguous situation. In other words, there should be one clearly correct solution to the task, and we should look at whether participants move from a position held with certainty to conform to obviously wrong answers given by others.

Box B: Asch (1951)

Procedure: All participants were given the simple task of matching a standard line with one of three comparison lines (see figure 1). They were tested in groups of seven, of whom six were confederates of Asch. They were asked for their decisions in order, going round a table, with the genuine participant sitting last but one. On some trials, the confederates were asked to give the (same) wrong answer.

Results: Participants conformed to the group's incorrect judgements in about 32% of trials on average. This can be compared to a control group, with no confederate participants, where judgements were virtually 100% correct.

Conclusion: In a group situation, there is a tendency to conform to the judgements of others, even where this judgement is clearly incorrect.

Figure 1: the Asch task

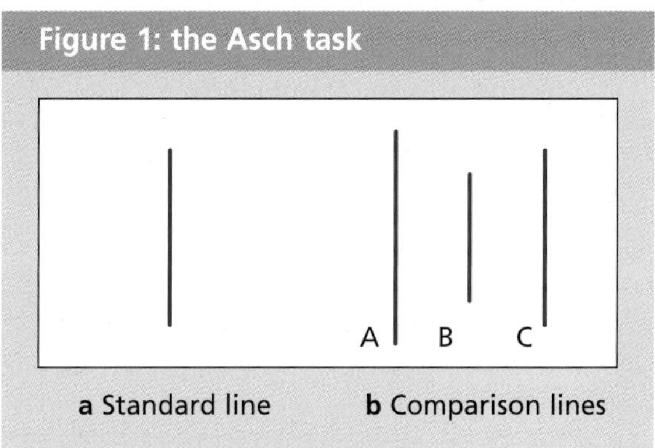

a Standard line **b** Comparison lines

Asch found that about a quarter of his participants *never* conformed to the group's wrong judgement, leaving three-quarters who *did* conform at least once. Some participants conformed on only a few trials where incorrect judgements were made, and only about 1 in 20 conformed each time. We will be returning to the question of individual differences in susceptibility to social influence later in the chapter.

Participants who conformed to the majority gave a variety of reasons for conforming.

Activity 1: explaining Asch's findings

Imagine you had taken part in this study, and conformed at least occasionally to the incorrect judgements of the group. How might you explain what you did?

When you have finished, see the notes on page 155.

Asch followed up his original study with some variations, to look in more detail at some of the possible variables which could affect conformity.

Activity 2: other conformity research by Asch

Here are some of the questions Asch investigated in later studies. What do you think his findings were? Try to give reasons for your answers:

a How would more/fewer confederates affect conformity?
b What would be the effect of having one of the six confederates giving the *right* answer?
c What would happen if someone agreed with the genuine participant (as in question 2) to start with, but then gave the majority answer in later trials?
d What would happen if the task were more difficult, i.e. the lines closer in length?
e How would a majority of naive participants react to only *one* confederate in the group giving a wrong answer?
f Would the effect be the same if the genuine participant could give his answer in private?

When you have finished, see the notes on page 155.

Another question is whether other people need to be physically present for conformity to occur, or if the belief that others are carrying out the same task is all that is necessary. To investigate this question, Crutchfield set up an experimental situation where participants worked in booths on their own, so were not directly exposed to other participants. They were asked to indicate agreement or disagreement by means of switches which would turn on lights. They were aware of the judgments of other people from a display of lights, and believed that their own responses were similarly available to other participants (see box C).

The information they were given about other judgements was, of course, actually manipulated by the experimenter.

Crutchfield's results were in broad agreement with those of Asch, and extended Asch's work by

Box C: Crutchfield (1954)

Procedure: More than 600 participants were tested, including American college students and military personnel. They were tested for conformity on a range of tasks, including clearly incorrect factual statements and personal opinions, e.g:

a agreement with statements such as: 60–70% of Americans are over 65 years old; Americans sleep 4–5 hours a night, on average
b an Asch-type task
c agreement that a star had a larger surface area than a circle (in fact it was a third smaller)

d agreement with the statement 'I doubt that I would make an effective leader.'
e agreement with the statement 'Free speech being a privilege rather than a right, it is proper for a society to suspend free speech when it feels itself threatened'. Participants might have been expected not to agree with this opinion, given that free speech is enshrined as a right in the American constitution.

Results: The degree of conformity varied with the nature of the task. There was 46% conformity to **c**, for example, and only 30% conformity to **b**. Thirty-seven per cent agreed with **d**, none of whom did so when asked on their own. Substantial numbers of participants agreed with the 'facts' given in **a**, and the opinion given in **e**.

Conclusion: There was conformity both to incorrect facts and to opinions. The extent to which conformity was shown depended on the nature of the task.

demonstrating conformity not only in factual judgements, but also beliefs. Like Asch, Crutchfield found that some participants never conformed to an incorrect judgement made by the majority, some always conformed and most conformed some of the time.

- Early studies into conformity used situations in which the answer was uncertain. The classic study by Asch, using a task where there was a clearly correct answer, found a high rate of conformity. Variations on this study isolated particular factors such as group size which affect conformity.
- Some conforming participants in Asch's study showed **public conformity**, but no **private change**. Others changed their judgement as a result of social influence.
- Crutchfield's study extended conformity research to opinions.

Cultural differences in conformity

You will have noticed that many of the studies referred to were carried out some time ago, and mostly used American students as research participants, i.e. they provided a snapshot of a particular culture at a particular time. But can these findings be generalised to other populations, and more recent times?

Larsen (1974) replicated Asch's original experiment with American college students, to investigate whether cultural changes in the preceding 20 years would affect conformity rates. Participants still conformed, but at a lower rate than the 32% of the Asch study. Perhaps at that time the US had become a less conformist culture? A further replication in 1979, however, found a rise in conformity.

There may be some variation as culture is modified with the passing of time, but what about **cross-cultural** differences? Using Asch's technique, there have been findings similar to those of Asch in Brazil, Hong Kong and the Lebanon. A higher conformity rate, however, was found among the Bantu in Zimbabwe (Whittaker and Meade, 1967). Every culture needs a degree of conformity, to simplify social life by giving it order and predictability. How this need is translated into practice, though, would be expected to vary across cultures, since what are regarded as important **social norms** – i.e. what is considered to be appropriate behaviour within a particular social group – will vary from culture to culture.

- The conformity rate has been found to alter across time within a **culture**, though overall trends are far from clear. There is also variation between cultures. These differences are related to **social norms**.

Why do people conform?

We will be looking in his section at four explanations of why people conform. **Normative influence** refers to the social influence of others which may lead a person to conform to social norms. **Informational influence** may bring about change as the result of information gained from other people. We may also be influenced by **social roles**, behaving in ways which are thought to be appropriate to a person in a particular kind of situation, and which we think others expect, for example as a caring mother. Finally, we may conform to people we like or admire, because we want to be like them. This is known as **identification**.

Let us start by looking again at the Asch study. Those of Asch's participants who conformed to judgements which were clearly incorrect fell into two groups. A distinction was made between those who changed their behaviour, but not their opinion (public conformity), and those who changed both their behaviour and their opinion (private change).

Kelman (1958) picked up on this distinction, referring to **compliance** (i.e. public conformity) and **internalisation** (i.e. private change). These two different kinds of conformity have been related to two different kinds of influence: what Deutsch and Gerard (1955) have called normative influence and informational influence (see figure 2).

Figure 2: public conformity and private change

Asch's terms	Kelman's terms	what happens	influence
public conformity	compliance	behaviour changes opinion doesn't	normative
private change	internalisation	behaviour changes opinion changes	informational

Asch's study highlights the effect of normative influence, but it may also be that some participants asked themselves: 'Can it be possible that what I think is the right answer is not actually correct here?' This is suggested by the increased conformity found with variation (d) in activity 2.

Let us look first at **normative influence**. As you will remember from the last section, social norms relate to behaviour which is considered appropriate within a particular social group. There are norms, for example, about queuing at supermarket checkouts and apologising when you accidentally step on someone's toes.

Activity 3: identifying and understanding norms

What are the social norms when you are:

a at a Psychology lecture?

b in a restaurant?

What kinds of behaviour would go against these norms?

Why are there unwritten social conventions and how do we know what they are?

What are the consequences when we do not observe these conventions?

When you have finished, see the notes on page 155.

The observation of social norms helps to explain the conformity people show in some of the studies we have looked at. People very readily identify themselves as part of a group; Tajfel *et al.* (1971) found that people quickly identified themselves as members of a group artificially created by the experimenter even when group membership was decided by something as arbitrary as the toss of a coin. Asch's participants said they felt it was important to maintain group harmony, and that disagreement would damage this. The importance of acceptance and approval emerges clearly in the phrases which they used when Asch asked them after the study why they had conformed to the majority answer; many said they didn't want to 'create a bad impression', 'be different' or 'look stupid'.

This kind of concern has also been verified by physiological measures. Bogdonoff *et al.* (1961) looked at autonomic arousal in participants in a study similar to Asch's. (Autonomic arousal is related to anxiety and stress and is covered in more detail in chapter 1. Blood pressure and heart rate are examples of some of the ways in which it can be measured.) A high level of arousal was found when the participant was faced with an incorrect majority judgement. This dropped if the participant conformed, but remained high if they disagreed with the judgement.

Informational social influence is another factor, which stems from the desire to be right:

Activity 4: decision making and social influence

Imagine you are taking up a new sport, e.g. skiing or tennis, and are planning to buy some equipment. You have heard of a few brand names, but don't know much about the different makes available. How would you go about choosing what to buy?

When you have finished, see the notes on page 155.

Activity 5: summarising conformity theory

To link these studies and ideas, complete the blanks in these sentences, picking a word or phrase from those given underneath.

One form of conformity is ...., where there is public acceptance of a group decision, but private disagreement. It depends heavily on .... influence, and is motivated by .... It is more likely in .... situations, such as the study by ....

The other form of conformity is ...., where there is both public and private acceptance. It depends more heavily on .... influence, and is motivated by .... It is more likely in .... situations, such as the study by ....

internalisation normative compliance
the need for approval/acceptance Asch
informational the need to be right
unambiguous Sherif ambiguous

When you have finished, see the notes on page 156.

But is the distinction between the two processes as clear-cut as activity 5 suggests? It has been suggested that both normative influence and informational influence may be factors at the same time:

Box D: Insko *et al.* (1983)

Procedure: Participants worked in groups of six. They were shown a colour slide, and had to decide which of two other slides had the more similar colour. A control condition tested participants alone, to establish the most frequent answers. Four confederates answered before the genuine participant, disagreeing with these answers. There were two independent variables:

a public vs. private answers
b determined vs. undetermined

'Determined' referred to trials where the experimenter claimed to have apparatus which could check the accuracy of the judgements made. In the 'undetermined' trials, it was claimed that there was no possibility of making this check, and that the degree of similarity between the colours was simply a matter of opinion.

Results: Conformity was more frequent in the 'public' than the 'private' condition. It was also greater in the 'determined' than the 'undetermined' condition. There was greater conformity, both 'public' and 'private', in the 'determined' condition.

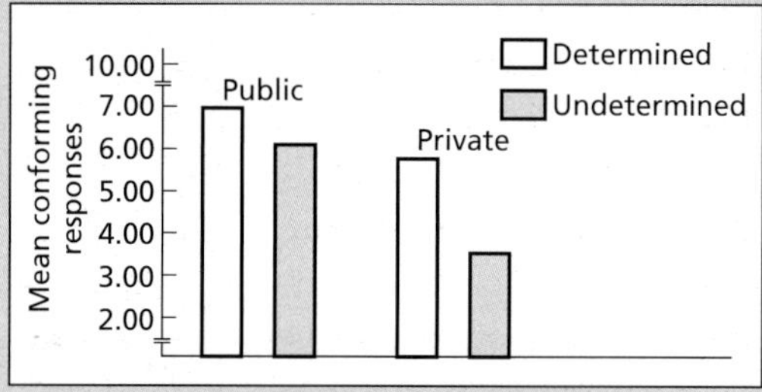

Mean conformity data from Insko *et al.* (1983)

Conclusion: The 'public' vs. 'private' comparison showed normative influence. The 'determined' vs. 'undetermined' comparison showed informational influence. The final finding suggests that informational influence can add to normative influence, so the two can work together to increase conformity.

Another important reason why people conform is to do with **social roles**. A role is a set of behaviours which are thought to be appropriate to a person in a particular kind of situation. The role of 'student', for example, implies dressing casually and having a wild social life, as well as studying and writing essays. We all play roles in social situations and our in-role behaviour is shaped by our beliefs about the demands of the situation and the expectations of other people.

A major study in this area, carried out by Zimbardo *et al.* (1973), was interested in how people adapted their behaviour to fit the roles which they had been asked to take on:

Box E: Zimbardo et al. (1973)

Procedure: Student volunteers were asked to role-play prisoners and guards in a simulated prison situation. They were chosen to participate on the basis of tests for emotional stability and physical health, as well as having clean legal records. They were then randomly assigned to be prisoners or guards. For the prison, the basement of Stanford University was converted to be as authentic as possible. 'Prisoners' were arrested, charged, finger-printed, strip-searched and deloused. They were then issued a uniform. 'Guards' were also issued uniforms, together with whistles, handcuffs and dark glasses, to make eye-contact with 'prisoners' impossible.

Results: Both prisoners and guards acted in character to an extreme degree. Guards became increasingly more aggressive, and seemed to enjoy the control they had over the prisoners. They went far beyond the minimum requirements for fulfilling their role, e.g. making prisoners clean out toilets with their bare hands. Prisoners became passive, and showed extreme stress reactions, such as uncontrolled crying and depression. Some prisoners, wanting to withdraw from the study, asked to 'be paroled'. One developed a serious rash when his 'parole' was rejected. It had been intended to run the study for two weeks; it had to be stopped after six days because of the extreme reactions of the prisoners.

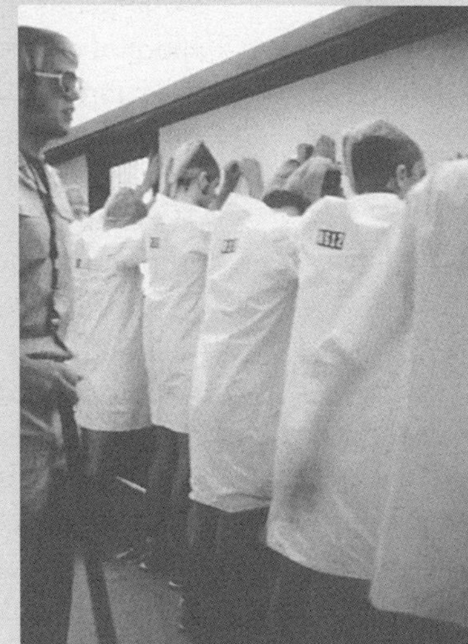

Zimbardo's volunteers

Conclusion: People easily respond to roles assigned to them, particularly where the environment supports these roles. The behaviour people demonstrate 'in role' may be very different from their normal behaviour.

Activity 6: Zimbardo's prison simulation experiment

Read through the prison simulation experiment in box E, and answer these questions:

1 Why do you think potential participants were screened before being accepted?
2 Why were they not allowed to choose which role to take?
3 Both prisoners and guards assumed their roles very rapidly, and showed extreme behaviour. How could you explain this?
4 Participants were paid for taking part in this study. How might this have affected their behaviour?
5 What are the implications of Zimbardo's findings for the prison system?

Compare your ideas with the discussion which follows.

The first two questions relate to Zimbardo's attempts to make his study as unbiased as possible, and so avoid methodological criticisms. Screening the participants ensured that the participants were 'ordinary' people. They had had no direct experience of the law which might have distorted their role-play. They were not unstable, and so were not likely to behave in pathological ways, but could be taken to be representative of people in general. They were also not likely to be badly affected in what was expected to be something of a stressful experience (though not as stressful as it in fact turned out to be).

The behaviour shown cannot be accounted for in terms of existing personality differences, or differences in relevant experiences, then, but can be taken to show how ordinary people are affected by roles allocated to them, and the environment in which they find themselves. If participants had been allowed to choose their roles, it is possible that this might have biased the results; for example, with aggressive people choosing to be guards. (In fact, all the participants had stated a preference for being a prisoner.)

The relative ease and thoroughness with which roles were adopted perhaps has something to do with the media. The prisoners–guards scenario is, after all, a standard one on TV, and the behaviour of both prisoners and guards in Zimbardo's study reflects rather stereotypical pictures of how in general prisoners and guards might be expected to behave. Other role models involving power and subordination are also very widespread in people's lives, e.g. parent–child; teacher–pupil; boss–employee. We can call on our experience of this kind of relationship when it is required in a particular situation.

The fact that participants were paid quite well for taking part may have encouraged them to throw themselves wholeheartedly into their roles. It may also have made it harder for them to withdraw from the study. It is possible, then, that payment may have biased the study in some way.

Zimbardo's study was heavily criticised on ethical grounds, particularly since the participants were clearly distressed by their experience. However, Zimbardo claimed that the study had provided a lot of information which could not have been established any other way. The feedback from the students themselves is interesting; for example, many of the guards mentioned the pleasure they had experienced from their control over others. It is not just 'monsters' or disturbed individuals who have these feelings, but ordinary well-balanced people, if the environment is right.

Perhaps even more importantly, though, Zimbardo's study was instrumental in bringing about changes to the prison system in America, in particular providing support for the notion that an institution itself can have a substantial effect on behaviour.

A final factor in conformity is the power of **reference groups** – people we like or admire, who we conform to because we want to be like them. Relating to role models in this way is known as **identification**. This term was originally used by Freud, and refers to the resolution of a boy's Oedipus conflict; this is described in chapter 1, in the subsection headed 'Psychosexual development'. Taking a behavioural approach, Bandura adopted the term and incorporated it into social learning theory, which you will find described in chapter 3, section 3, in the subsection called 'The social learning approach'.

- In explaining conformity, a distinction can be drawn between **compliance** (public conformity, but no private change) and **internalisation** (public and private change).
- Compliance can be linked to **normative influence**, where people are motivated to observe social norms in order to have the acceptance and approval of others. This kind of conformity is more likely in **unambiguous** situations.
- Internalisation is linked to **informational influence**, where people are motivated by the desire to be correct. It is most likely in **ambiguous** situations.
- The distinction is not necessarily very sharp: both kinds of influence may simultaneously underlie conforming behaviour.
- **Social norms**, the often unwritten rules which allow social groups to function, help to explain social influence.
- Zimbardo's prison simulation study showed how roles and the environment can affect behaviour in situations involving power and subordination.
- **Reference groups** – people we adopt as role models – may also be associated with conformity. This is known as **identification**.

Minority influence

A limitation of most conformity research is that its design only allows a one-way influence; individual participants can either conform to the majority or not. Other research has looked at the possibility of

Fact or majority opinion

influence in the other direction. To what extent can a minority affect the judgement of a majority? There are many examples in history where a single person has changed majority opinion. For example, Galileo's belief that the earth moved round the sun contradicted opinion at the time, but is now accepted.

An early research study by Moscovici *et al.* in the area of minority influence is described in box F below.

Moscovici proposed that different factors are at work in majority influence and minority influence. He distinguished between compliance (when a majority influences a minority) and conversion (when a minority influences a majority).

In **compliance**, change is to do with the power of greater numbers and factors connected with social norms; people respond to normative influence. There is public agreement with the majority, but private agreement may not last long when a person is no longer in the presence of people holding the majority opinion.

In **conversion**, however, Moscovici believed that an undecided person may pay attention to the viewpoint of a minority because they are interested in the reasons for this different viewpoint. A majority may therefore respond to informational influence, and there is likely to be lasting change in the opinion held, i.e. **internalisation** in Kelman's terms.

This suggests that minority influence should be linked to the **behavioural style** of the influencing minority. Moscovici has suggested that a minority is more likely to bring about conformity by a majority if the minority point of view is put across confidently and consistently.

Research has demonstrated the role of confidence in minority influence. Lee and Ofshe (1981), for example, confirmed the effectiveness of a confident non-verbal behavioural style, while Nemeth and Wachtler (1973) found that minorities who appear certain about their position achieve more conformity than those who seem less confident. However, while confidence is important, this should not be allowed to tip over into dogmatism if minority influence is to be effective. Mugny (1984) found that opinion statements putting forward minority viewpoints were far less effective in bringing about change when they were written in slogan-like terms than when they were expressed in more moderate language. It seems that flexibility on the part of the minority, defined as a willingness to make concessions to others to reduce conflict, while at the same time remaining consistent, is more effective than dogmatism.

The study by Moscovici *et al.* in box F demonstrates the importance of consistency. In a variation

Box F: Moscovici *et al.* (1969)

Procedure: Participants were tested in groups of six. Two were confederates of the experimenter. Each participant was asked to judge the colour of 36 slides, all of which were blue. The confederates consistently judged them to be green. Participants were also asked to name the colour of the after-image. (This is the colour which is perceived when you have been staring at a colour, and then look at a white surface; the complementary colour is seen.)

Results: A third of all genuine participants judged a slide to be green at least once. They also tended to label the after-image red/purple. Controls who had not taken part in the judgement task used yellow/orange labels.

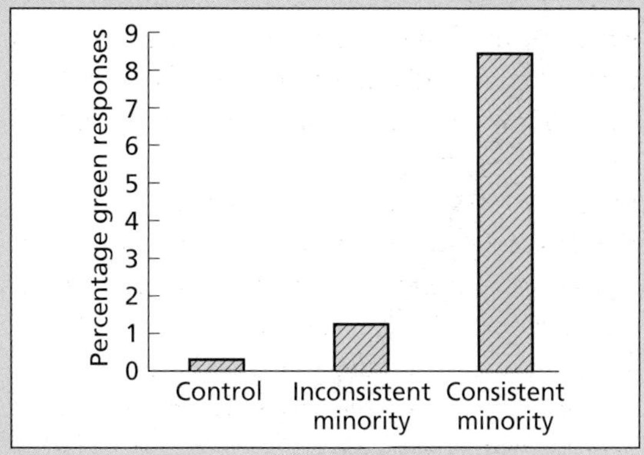

Conclusion: A minority can influence a majority if they are consistent in their judgements. The label given to after-image colours suggests that change was genuine and lasted beyond the presentation of the original stimulus.

of the basic study, Moscovici *et al.* (1969) found that an inconsistent minority had little effect on the judgements of the majority.

Other factors may also be important:

Box G: Moscovici and Nemeth (1974)

Procedure: Groups of five people (four participants and one confederate of the experimenter) were asked to take jury-type decisions. The confederate took a minority view. In one condition, he chose to sit in either position A, B or C at the table (see figure 3), while in the other he was assigned to one of these seats.

Results: There was little minority influence when the confederate was assigned to a seat. When he chose where to sit, he was highly influential when he sat in position C, but not when he chose seats A or B.

Conclusion: Minority influence is more likely when a person holding a minority opinion is seen to act autonomously and when he is the focus of attention.

Figure 3: seating in the Moscovici and Nemeth (1974) study

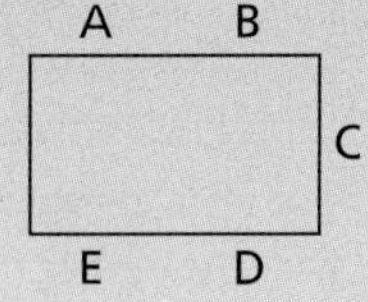

The status and power of the individual is also relevant. If someone putting forward a minority viewpoint is perceived by others as having high status or as being able to exert power over others, these characteristics can help to bring about change in a majority viewpoint. However, Wiggins *et al.* (1967) found that these characteristics are of little use if the person hinders the group from reaching its goal.

Other factors also work against minority influence. If the minority is seen as having something to gain from the opinion they are putting forward, their perceived self-interest is likely to make them less effective in bringing about change in the majority. The same is true if two or more people are in the minority and cannot agree among themselves.

Group size may also be a relevant factor in whether a minority can influence a majority:

Activity 7: conformity and group size

Imagine yourself as one of a group of 12 people, who need to come to a unanimous decision. You are in a minority of one. Then imagine the same situation with a smaller group, say six. In which group would you be more likely to conform to the majority? Why?

When you have finished, see the notes on page 156.

This question is relevant to jury size. The Supreme Court in the USA has shown some interest in reducing the size of juries. This would cut costs, and could well lead to greater efficiency in terms of the time taken to reach a verdict. At the same time, a jury decision will affect people's lives, so every effort must be made to find the size of group which will make the best quality decisions.

In the film *Twelve Angry Men*, made in 1957, a murder case jury, about to vote 'guilty', was persuaded to change its verdict by one doubting member. The behaviour shown by the one man wanting to bring in a 'not guilty' verdict was very much in line with Moscovici's suggestions for conversion: he was consistent, he argued his case and discussed the objections of the other jury

Henry Fonda acts persuasively in 'Twelve Angry Men'

members, rather than just dogmatically repeating his view. This is of course fiction, but nonetheless provides a nice example of how a minority can influence majority opinion.

In a jury of 12, one member who does not agree with the others is under considerable social pressure to conform, whereas fewer people will mean less pressure. The Supreme Court was influenced by Asch's work. They came to the conclusion that a jury of six would be efficient in terms of cost and time, and would also have the advantage of being less likely to be under pressure to conform (though it is worth noting that Asch's studies did not find that a group of six was under less pressure to conform than a group of twelve!). This could well ensure a more just verdict.

- ❺ A distinction can be made between **compliance**, where a majority can affect the judgement of a minority, and **conversion**, where a minority can affect the judgement of the majority.
- ❺ **Conversion** is best achieved if a minority view is put confidently and consistently not dogmatically.
- ❺ This research could be relevant to considerations of effective **jury size**.

Evaluation of conformity research

Much of the research into conformity has been criticised on methodological grounds. As you read through the previous section, you may have had doubts about the **ecological validity** of studies such as those of Asch and Sherif. Can we really find out much about a social phenomenon like conformity within the confines of a laboratory situation? While this approach does have the advantage of controlled conditions, in which exact measurements can be made and compared (e.g. the estimates of the distance the light appeared to move in Sherif's study in box A), it also has a number of disadvantages.

If we take the Asch study as an example, we are often put into situations where we can conform or not, but we are seldom faced with a task as artificial as line-matching. There would seem to be room to test the basic ideas suggested by this kind of research in a more naturalistic way. Crutchfield's technique could arguably be seen as being even less realistic than the Asch studies.

There is also the question of **demand characteristics**. Even when participants are not aware of the true nature of an experiment, they are aware of taking part in a psychological experiment of some sort. This knowledge may lead them to think about what the study may be investigating and so to behave in ways which do not necessarily correspond to the way they would act naturally.

Another problem is the sharp distinction made between 'fact' and 'opinion' in accounting for different findings. There are of course judgements which fall neatly into one or other category. The Asch study (box B), for example, is concerned with a fact: one line of the three comparison lines was the same length as the standard line. Some of the judgements in the Crutchfield study (box C), on the other hand, looked at what were clearly matters of opinion.

However, there seems also to be a grey area between fact and belief, which could be explored in more depth. There is quite a lot of knowledge which we might define as 'fact', but which is in truth culturally determined. Beliefs which are widely held within a particular culture are often considered to be 'fact', but are majority beliefs and facts the same thing? Before Galileo, for instance, it was an accepted 'fact' that the sun moved round the earth. Similarly, the distinction between normative and informational influence is not clear-cut, as the Insko study (box D) suggests.

You may also have had ethical concerns. As we saw earlier, Bogdonoff *et al.* (1961) showed that participants experienced the situations they were put in as stressful.

You may have come away from these studies with the impression that conformity is somehow wrong or ridiculous; this emerges quite clearly in Asch's work, and is a judgement he himself explicitly made. It is not the job of psychological research to provide answers about social desirability, and it is in any case open to question whether conformity is necessarily undesirable.

As pointed out earlier, conformity serves a very positive and necessary function in helping social interaction to run smoothly. Normative influence helps us to make the compromises necessary in social life to fit into social situations. If a friend were to take you to an event at the local Conservative Club, for example, you might wear a suit and keep your radical green views to yourself. Informational influence helps us to learn appropriate behaviour in times of uncertainty; for example, learning how to taste wine involves a lot of acceptance of others' definitions of what makes a wine 'good', when to the beginner it may not taste very pleasant at all. However, most conformity research has tended to focus on demonstrating conformity, rather than broadening its scope to consider in detail the functions it might serve in different situations.

At the same time, these studies do give us a good basis for understanding conformity. This research has implications for group situations: we can't expect disagreement and therefore discussion to arise naturally in groups, and at the same time, we can't assume that agreement shows consent.

- ❺ Conformity research has attracted a certain amount of criticism. Its **ecological validity** is often poor, and there are also **ethical concerns**.
- ❺ It may also rest on questionable **assumptions**, e.g. drawing a sharp distinction between fact and belief, and normative and informational influence. It tends to be **descriptive** rather than providing functional explanations.
- ❺ Research has given us some understanding of conformity, which may be applicable in practical situations.

5.2 Obedience

Milgram's research

After the Second World War, German war criminals who had been involved in the Holocaust – the wholesale killing of Jews, together with other 'undesirables' such as gypsies, homosexuals and the mentally ill – were put on trial for war crimes. These trials continued for a number of years and roused considerable public interest.

Those on trial did not appear to be monsters. On the contrary: Hannah Arendt, writing about the trial of Adolf Eichmann, was struck by just how ordinary he seemed, using the phrase 'the banality of evil'. Yet at the same time, he had been very directly involved

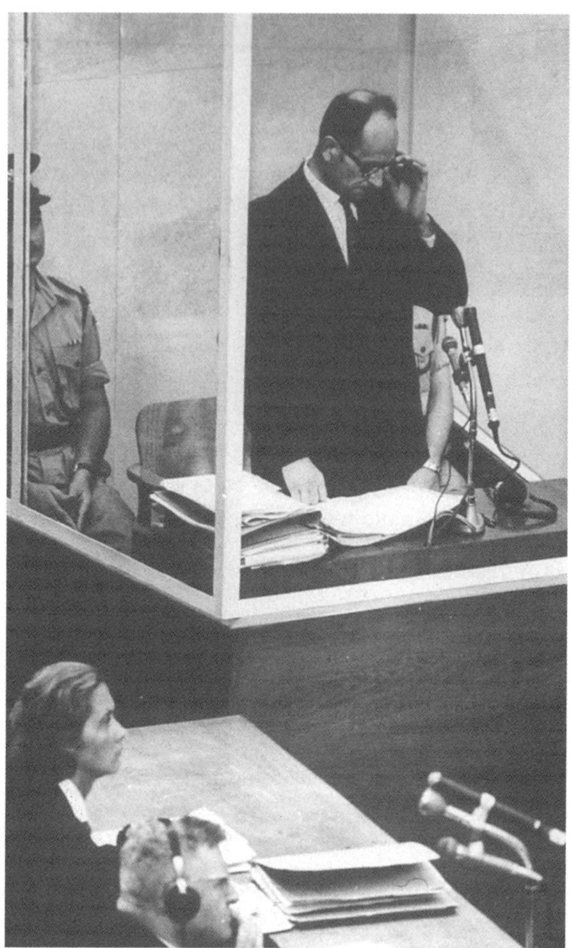

Adolf Eichmann in the dock

in the concentration camp programme. His defence against the charges brought against him, like that of many other war criminals, was that he was 'only obeying orders'.

Milgram was intrigued by the apparent contradiction between the ordinariness of the men involved and the terrible deeds they had carried out. He was interested in how the idea of obeying orders fitted into the picture, and in the extent to which ordinary people would obey orders to harm an innocent fellow human being. He brought these factors together in a series of studies. The basic study is described in box H (page 146).

Milgram later ran a number of variations of the basic study, to find out more about the particular factors which might influence obedience. Some of these, together with the results, are listed in box I.

Box H: Milgram (1963))

Procedure: Male volunteers, aged 20–50, were recruited through a newspaper advertisement to take part in a 'scientific study of memory and learning'. Each worked in pairs with Mr Wallace, apparently another participant, who was in fact a confederate of Milgram and an accountant in his late fifties. His part in the study had been planned in advance and was scripted.

The study was run at Yale University Psychology Department by a young man in a white lab coat. He told the participant and Mr Wallace that the study was investigating the effects of punishment on learning. The two men drew lots to decide who was to be the teacher and who the learner in the experiment, though this was rigged so that Mr Wallace was always the learner. In view of the teacher, Mr Wallace was strapped into a chair and attached to electrodes, linked to a shock generator. At this point, Mr Wallace said he had a heart condition, but was assured that though the shocks were painful, there would be no permanent damage. The teacher's job was to administer a shock every time the learner made a mistake in learning a list of paired associates.

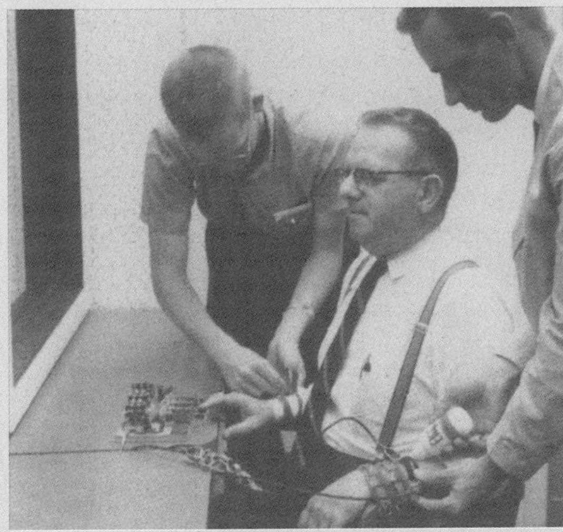

Milgram's (1963) apparatus and Mr Wallace being connected up to it

The teacher was then taken to another room containing the shock generator. This had a 30-point scale showing an increasing level of shocks from '15 volts–mild shock' up to '450 volts–XXX'. The size of shock was to be increased every time an error was made. The teacher was given a 45 volt shock in case he had any doubts that the shock apparatus was real. No further shocks were given, though the teacher was unaware of this.

Results: All the participants gave increasing shocks in the early part of the experiment. No one stopped below '300 volts–intense shock'. Some participants were unwilling to continue, but did so when told by the experimenter: 'Please continue' or 'The experiment requires that you continue'. These instructions (which Milgram called 'prods') were followed despite Mr Wallace banging on the wall, refusing to continue to take part in the experiment, and asking for the shocks to stop. Many teachers continued to give increased shocks even when, at 315 volts, Mr Wallace let out a violent scream, and when at 330 volts there was complete silence from the next room – the teacher had been told that no response counted as a wrong response. In all, two-thirds of the men (65%) continued to increase the shocks up to the maximum level of 450 volts.

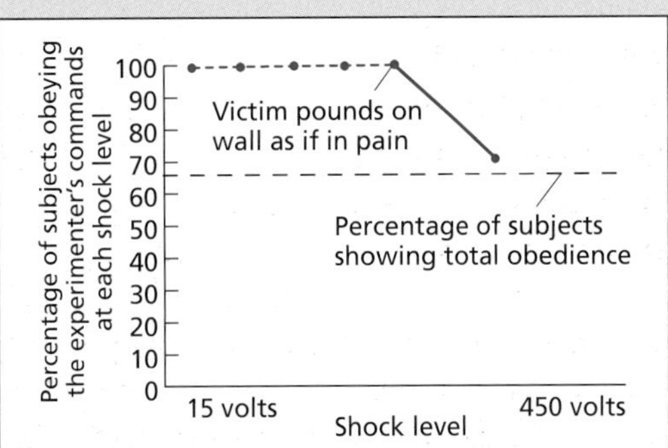

Conclusion: Ordinary people are likely to follow orders given by an authority figure, even to the extent of killing an innocent human being.

Box I: variations on Milgram's experiment

disobedient models: When the 'teacher' was in the presence of two other participants (actually confederates of the experimenter) who refused to administer shocks, the level of obedience fell from 65% to 10%.

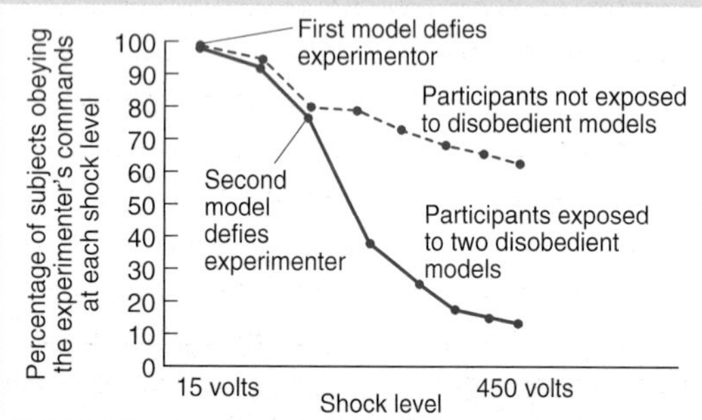

encouragement: The participant was not instructed to increase the shock each time an error was made. The average shock given remained around 50 volts across the series of trials. When two confederates urged the participant to increase the shock level, the average strength of the shock given after 20 trials was more than 150 volts.

location: The study was carried out in a run-down office, rather than at Yale University.

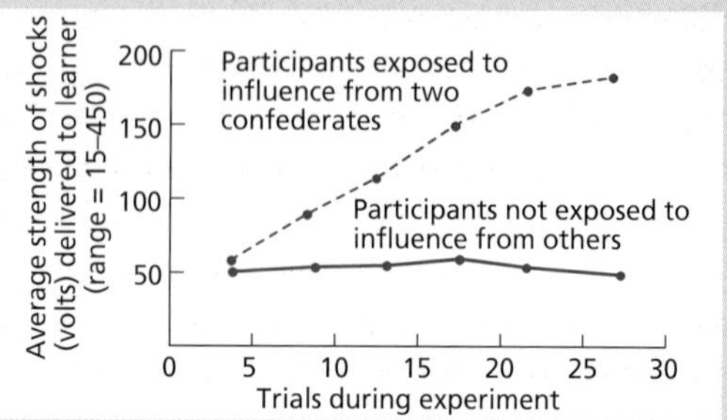

Just under 50% of participants continued to increase the shocks to the maximum 450 volts.

proximity of the learner: When the learner was in the same room as the teacher, the obedience level dropped to 40%. It dropped still further to 30% when the teacher had to force the learner's hand on to the shock plate.

proximity of the experimenter: When the experimenter left the room and gave instructions over the phone, the obedience level dropped to around 20%.

two teachers: A teacher was paired with another (confederate) teacher who administered the shocks. The genuine participant had only to read out the words. The obedience level was 92.5%.

Activity 8: explaining Milgram

Use the information in box H and box I to identify:

a the factors which influenced obedience in this series of experiments

b the relative strength of each.

Can you explain exactly how each factor might have influenced behaviour?

Compare your ideas with the discussion which follows.

The degree of personal **responsibility** which participants experienced is obviously of major importance here. In the original study, it was easy for participants to hand over responsibility to the experimenter, since he was giving them instructions and reminding them of their role when they protested (i.e. 'prods'). Participants were also assured by the experimenter that he was responsible for the welfare of the learners. There was therefore plenty of reason for the participants not to accept personal responsibility. When a person considers himself to be carrying out the orders of another, he is in what Milgram terms the **agentic state**, as opposed to the **autonomous state**, in which a person accepts responsibility for their own behaviour.

In the 'two teachers' variation, the high level of obedience can perhaps be explained in terms of the situation allowing the participant to shift responsibility from themselves to the person actually administering the shocks. In the 'disobedient models' variation, the refusal of the models to follow instructions is likely to have demonstrated to the participant that it was possible to take responsibility and act accordingly. This may be one reason why there was such a dramatic drop in obedience in this situation. Taking personal responsibility would also have been an important factor in holding down the hand of the 'victim', though the effect here was much smaller. We will be coming back to the question of responsibility later in this chapter, when we discuss reasons why some participants did *not* obey the experimenter.

The marked drop in obedience when the experimenter was in the next room (from 65% to 20%) also underlines the importance of the physical **presence of the experimenter**. Together with the effect of a disobedient model, this is one of the most important factors.

A related factor is the **authority of the experimenter**. Given the mention of a 'scientific study' in the advertisement, the experimenter's white coat and the prestigious setting of Yale University, the experimenter would be seen as a legitimate authority figure. When in one variation the experimenter was 'called away' and a stand-in (introduced as a research participant) suggested the stepwise increase in shocks as his own idea, obedience was greatly reduced, again suggesting the importance of authority.

The impressiveness of **location** does not seem to have played a major part here, though, since obedience only dropped by 15% when the location was changed.

Another factor is the **gradual** change in the behaviour required from the participant. A 15-volt shock is extremely mild, and willingness to deliver it paves the way for the next shock, also pretty mild, and so on.

Peer influence clearly played a major role, since the encouragement of others was enough to produce a major increase in disobedience. The fact that 35% of participants ceased to be obedient before the end of the experiment suggests that some of the remaining 65% who did obey may well have had qualms about their behaviour; in fact, many participants showed clear signs of conflict and distress, stuttering, twitching and verbally abusing the experimenter. In a few cases, participants had seizures. In this case, a disobedient model would be enough to tip the balance towards disobedience. It is possible that the behaviour of disobedient models reminded participants of a possible alternative response: some participants made remarks at the end of the basic study, where they were not exposed to disobedient models, such as 'I didn't realise I could'. At the same time, participants tended to increase shocks when encouraged by others to do so; social influence can work both ways.

The effect of the presence of the learner in the same room as the teacher, and in particular of the teacher having to hold the learner's hand on the shock plate, is perhaps surprising. Obedience dropped in both these conditions, but was still at quite a startling level. Being brought face to face with the consequences of your actions does not seem to have as much influence as you might suppose.

Activity 9: the ethics of Milgram's study

Milgram's work has been widely criticised on ethical grounds. What are the ethical objections to this study? You may find it helpful to look at the British Psychological Society guidelines, shown in chapter 2 in the section on ethics, for carrying out research with human participants.

How justified are these objections? How, if at all, could they be overcome?

Compare your ideas with the discussion which follows.

Ethical factors in Milgram's research

There are three main considerations here: **deception**, right of **withdrawal** from the experiment at any time and the **stress** or loss of self-esteem which may have been experienced by participants as a result of taking part.

The participants were deceived about the nature of the experiment, so they were unable to give their **informed consent** to participate in it. They were also not informed that they could withdraw from the experiment at any time. On the contrary, they were explicitly instructed to continue, and clearly felt under some pressure to do so. One way of avoiding this kind of criticism would be to give participants full information about the experiment, and to ask them to role-play their usual behaviour, but in this case role-play would be unlikely to be a true representation of normal behaviour. Alternatively, naturally occurring behaviour could be observed, but such an approach does not lend itself easily to this particular topic.

One way of mitigating this kind of ethical problem, where participants cannot be given full information about the nature of the study, is the use of **debriefing**. This involves giving participants as much information as possible about the study after it has taken place. They are told about the aims of the investigation, and any deception that was necessary. They are also encouraged to ask questions, and the use to be made of the findings is discussed. They are reassured that the way they behaved was perfectly natural in the circumstances, and not in any way unusual or shameful. Given the nature of Milgram's study, though, this last aspect of debriefing might be both inappropriate and ineffective.

A further study looked at the value of debriefing in this kind of study:

Box J: Ring *et al.* (1970)

Procedure: Milgram's experiment was replicated, using female students as participants. One group was thanked after the experiment, but not debriefed. A second group was thanked and debriefed, and reassured that their behaviour was quite normal. A third group was debriefed, but not reassured about their behaviour. They were told they should have defied the experimenter.
Results: Both group 1 (who thought they had really hurt the learner) and group 3 (who were not reassured about their behaviour) were very upset about the experiment, compared to group 2. However, only group 1 regretted having taken part in the experiment.
Conclusion: Careful debriefing, which includes both information and reassurance, can go a long way towards overcoming ethical problems.
NB: *All* participants received a complete debriefing at the end of the study.

Perhaps even more serious is the **stress** caused by participation in Milgram's experiment – at least one participant suffered convulsions – and the loss of self-esteem which many participants experienced as a result of taking part in this study. Baumrind (1964) argued that adequate measures had not been taken to protect participants from psychological harm.

In replying to this kind of criticism, Milgram argued that the study was not intended to cause stress for the participants, and that Baumrind was confusing the outcome (i.e. stress experienced by participants) with what was expected to happen. He pointed out that before carrying out the study, he had asked many people, including psychiatrists, what they expected the outcome to be. There was general agreement that perhaps only one person in a hundred would obey throughout the experiment, and that most would stop at 150 volts. Milgram also carried out a follow-up study (Milgram, 1964) when he surveyed those who had taken part. He reported that 84% were glad to have taken part in the experiment, 75% said they had learned something useful and only 1.3% were sorry or very sorry to have taken part. Milgram argued that the ethics of a study are best judged by those who have taken part, rather than in absolute terms.

However, many if not all of the participants must have experienced some **loss of self-esteem**, knowing that they had been prepared to hurt another human being, and had been unable to resist obeying an authority figure. This must have been all the more hurtful, since the experimenter had no real authority; although the participants were paid for taking part in Milgram's study, they were paid before the study started, so there was no real incentive to continue.

In answer to those who point to the loss of self-esteem suffered by those who took part in the experiment, it has been argued that it is not the duty of psychologists to hide from people truths about their own nature, however much they may not wish to know those truths.

This leads on to the question of the extent to which stress was *caused* to the participants by taking part in this study. It could be argued that it was the way the participants *responded* to the situation which led them to experience stress. As Milgram points out, the whole point of the study is that participants had a choice, and that most chose obedience.

A further justification of this study is that the ends had justified the means: the study had gathered valuable information about human behaviour which could not really have been established in any other way. Perhaps more than any other experiment, Milgram's study highlights the capacity of ordinary people for homicidal – even genocidal – behaviour. This carries clear implications for international courts, but it also changes our perceptions of ourselves. By knowing about this study, we are ourselves less likely to obey in similar situations.

With these kinds of considerations in mind, Elms (1972) wrote that he considered Milgram's experiment to be one of the most significant ever carried out in modern psychology, and one of the most moral, both in its attempts to understand important phenomena and its concern for the welfare of its participants.

- Milgram was interested in the defence offered by war criminals that they were 'only obeying orders'. He carried out a series of studies to investigate obedience.
- In his original study, 65% of his participants were prepared to give what they thought were lethal electric shocks to someone they believed to be a fellow-participant in a learning experiment.
- Variations of the study looked at various factors in more detail. There was, for example, a drop in obedience when the participant was exposed to disobedient models. The authority of the experimenter, cues to reduce the sense of personal responsibility and the gradual increase in the strength of shocks given all seem to be important factors.
- Milgram's study has been criticised on **ethical** grounds: participants were deceived and subjected to stress and loss of self-esteem. However, Milgram found that very few participants regretted taking part in the study. The stress experienced can be seen in terms of the participants' choice of behaviour. Valuable information has been gained with important implications.

There has also been considerable criticism of the methodology of Milgram's studies. One suggestion (Orne and Holland, 1968) was that participants did not actually believe that they were giving genuine electric shocks to the learners. Far from the participants being deceived, they suggest, it was Milgram himself who was deceived into thinking that his participants accepted the experimental situation at face value!

Activity 10: Milgram's methodology

Imagine you were a participant in Milgram's study. What aspects of the experimental situation might have struck you as rather odd and would perhaps have made you suspect you were being deceived? When you have finished, see the notes on page 156.

One way to clear up the question of whether Milgram's participants behaved as they did because they did not believe that the 'victim' was genuine was to set up a study in which participants also serve as their own victims:

Box K: Kudirka (1965)

Procedure: Participants were instructed to eat 36 quinine-soaked biscuits.

Results: Grimaces, moans and occasional gagging showed that this was clearly unpleasant. Nonetheless, virtually all the participants ate the biscuits.

Conclusion: Suggestions that participants are obedient because they don't accept the experimental situation as real are not supported. There are still high levels of obedience when the reality of the situation is quite unambiguous.

A second question mark hangs over the **ecological validity** of the study: can the findings of an artificial laboratory study be related to real-world situations?

It has been argued that there were some crucial differences between Milgram's studies and obedience in Nazi Germany. Firstly, the experiments were presented to participants in a positive way, i.e. as aiming to increase knowledge about human learning, while many Germans recognised the aims of the Nazis as immoral. Secondly, there were no penalties for disobeying Milgram's orders, whereas it would have been very dangerous to have disobeyed orders in Nazi Germany. Finally, Milgram's participants were told explicitly that the shocks they would give would cause no permanent damage, while people like Eichmann knew they were sending other people to their deaths.

These differences may not be so very clear-cut, however. The Nazi programme was presented to the German people in a very positive way, in terms of racial purification and the creation of a Nazi homeland. Most of Milgram's participants, on the other hand, recognised what they were doing to be wrong – as we have seen, many became very upset in the course of the experiment and protested at what they were being asked to do – but they nonetheless continued to give the shocks. Similarly, although participants were told that the shocks would do no permanent damage, it is hard to see what other interpretation could be put on the pleas from the victim for the experiment to stop, followed by a scream and then silence. Indeed, when they were reunited with Mr Wallace after the experiment, many 'teachers' stated that they thought they had killed him.

In one very important way, Milgram's study mirrored the experience of the Nazis who were 'only obeying orders'. In both cases, people were put into a situation unlike any they had ever experienced and instructed to carry out an extremely distasteful task. In real life, people being given orders to harm or kill others is not an everyday situation. For example, during the Kosovo conflict newspapers carried reports of groups of Kosovan men being machine-gunned to death and then set on fire, and of refugees being herded on to a bridge to be bombed, so that they would appear to be victims of NATO aggression. Presumably the people who obeyed these orders were not in a normal, everyday situation. It could be that it is the strangeness of the situation which makes obedience more likely. It could therefore be argued that as Milgram's participants were in an unusual situation, his studies had *higher* ecological validity.

This leads to the question of whether people show the same level of obedience in a more everyday situation. This can only really be tested by carrying out a naturalistic study, in such a way that the participants are not aware of being studied:

Box L: Hofling *et al.* (1966)

Procedure: A man claiming to be a doctor rang a hospital on 22 separate occasions. Each time, he asked a nurse to give medicine to a patient. This would require the nurse to break three hospital rules:

- **a** they were not allowed to accept instructions over the phone.
- **b** the dose was double the maximum limit stated on the box.
- **c** the medicine itself was unauthorised, i.e. not on the ward stocklist.

On each occasion, the nurse's behaviour was monitored.

Results: In reply to questionnaires, most nurses said they would not obey such an order. In reality, 21 of the 22 nurses followed the orders they were given.

Conclusion: There is some support for obedience to authority in less extreme situations than that tested by Milgram: a very high proportion of people follow unjustified orders if told to do so by an authority figure.

When they were debriefed, some of the nurses said that this kind of situation often arose. They followed instructions because otherwise the doctors would be annoyed. This doesn't really explain away what they did, however, but rather says something about the relationships between authority figures and their subordinates which may lead to orders being obeyed.

Stimulated by Milgram's original experiments, a more recent set of 19 studies, the Utrecht studies of obedience, was carried out by Meeus and Raaijmakers in the 1980s. In these studies, participants were asked to inflict what Meeus and Raaijmakers termed 'administrative violence' on people who they thought were their fellow-participants. This involved making negative remarks about their performance on tests, and denigrating remarks about their personality. Two sample studies are described in box M:

Box M: Meeus and Raaijmakers (1986)

Procedure: In a bogus personnel selection procedure, 39 participants aged 18–55 were instructed to make job applicants nervous, and to disturb them while taking a test as part of the application procedure. In consequence, applicants failed the test and remained unemployed. Forty-one participants aged 18–55 took part in variations of this basic study, when the experimenter was out of the room and when another participant was present who refused to obey the orders given by the experimenter.
Results: In the basic experiment, more than 90% of participants – a much higher percentage than in Milgram's experiment – complied with the orders they had been given, even though they considered them unfair and did not enjoy carrying out the task. In the variations of the study, obedience was much lower than in the equivalent variations of the basic Milgram study.
Conclusion: Participants show willingness to obey orders to inflict psychologic harm on others when instructed to do so. As in Milgram's studies, however, obedience is reduced in the absence of an authority figure, or in the presence of a disobedient peer.

On the basis of observing participants' behaviour, analysis of questionnaire responses and debriefing, Meeus and Raaijmakers concluded that participants had found the task stressful but had attempted to hide the stress they were experiencing and act as though nothing were wrong, behaving as an 'official'. They therefore explained their findings in terms of attitudes to social institutions, and distant relationships with fellow citizens.

- ❺ Milgram's studies have been criticised on methodological as well as ethical grounds.
- ❺ The studies may have given rise to **demand characteristics**, and their **ecological validity** has been questioned. Later studies have gone some way towards refuting these criticisms. It may be unwise to assume, however, that the findings of laboratory studies can be directly extrapolated to behaviour in Nazi concentration camps.

Gender, culture and victim characteristics

Activity 11: gender, culture and obedience

Would you expect gender and/or culture to be a factor in obedience in this kind of study? Give reasons for your answer.

When you have finished, see the notes on page 156.

The participants in Milgram's original study were all men, but the effect of gender has been explored in similar studies. The Ring *et al.* study (box J) found no difference between levels of obedience in men and women, and a later study by Milgram (1965), using a relatively small sample of 40 females, had similar findings. Another study focusing on gender produced even more startling results:

Box N: Sheridan and King (1972)

Procedure: Male and female participants were asked to give a puppy genuine electric shocks of increasing strength. Participants could see the puppy yelping, howling and struggling to free itself in response to the shocks.
Results: High levels of obedience were found in both men and women. Every female participant gave the puppy the maximum shock.
Conclusion: Women are just as likely as men to obey orders involving the infliction of pain.

You probably feel that this is a very distasteful study, but it does address the issue of gender very directly. It is perhaps also worth noting here that many women were among the concentration camp personnel involved in the Nazi programme of killing Jews and members of other 'undesirable' groups.

To investigate possible cultural differences, several researchers have replicated Milgram's study at different times and in different countries. For example, Mantell (1971), using a German sample, found an obedience level of 85%, while Kilham and Mann (1974), using an Australian sample, found somewhat lower rates of obedience than the 65% recorded by Milgram.

It is difficult to draw any very definite conclusions from these findings, though, since the behaviour of some participants in these later studies may well have been affected by knowledge of Milgram's original work. Another problem in making comparisons is that the studies were not exact replications of Milgram's work. In any case, even relatively small differences in the make-up of the sample – age, educational level, and so on – make direct comparisons unreliable. At the same time, the possibility that there are cultural differences in obedience cannot be excluded.

Let us look finally in this section at a study investigating the characteristics of the *victim*:

Box O: Farina *et al.* (1966)

Procedure: Milgram's basic procedure was followed. The teacher was introduced to the learner before the experiment began, on the pretext that getting to know someone helps communication. The learner then talked about himself and his past in either a negative way (unhappy childhood, history of illness, parents divorced and so on) or positively.

Results: More intense shocks were given to the learners who had talked about themselves negatively. Teachers also showed through questionnaire answers that they were less interested in getting to know the 'negative' learners than the 'positive' ones.

Conclusion: The results support what has been called the 'just world hypothesis': people who suffer do so because in some way they deserve to suffer. The 'negative' learner identifies himself as a loser in a world where people get what they deserve. He is therefore a legitimate target.

You may have found the results of this study a little surprising. There is quite a widespread belief that people are sympathetic to the underdog, but in practice this doesn't seem to be the case. It is perhaps worth noting that the Nazis went to a great deal of trouble to put across the idea of Jews as underdogs, and this may perhaps have had a part to play in the readiness of the camp guards to kill them.

- Most studies have found no **gender** difference in obedience levels.
- There are **cultural differences** in obedience levels, but precise comparison is difficult.
- Characteristics of the **victim** may also be relevant. The widespread belief that we show sympathy for the underdog seems to be false.

5.3 Individual differences in response to social influence

Up till now we have been considering social influence in general terms. Another approach has been to look at individual differences between people in terms of the extent to which they are affected by such influence. This may offer some insight into the reasons why some people are more likely than others to conform or to obey orders given by an authority figure.

In all the conformity studies discussed earlier in the chapter, you will remember that there were individual differences in conformity, with some people being much more likely to conform than others. This kind of pattern has been found in other research, looking at conformity both on judgements of facts, as in the Asch studies (box B), and on opinions, included in the Crutchfield study (box C).

Several researchers have looked at individual differences in conformity and obedience, including Crutchfield (1955) and Elms and Milgram (1966), and links with various characteristics have been found. For example, higher levels of obedience have been found among prejudiced and intolerant people, those achieving lower educational levels, and scientists and engineers (compared to doctors and teachers). Sub-cultural differences have also been found, with the military and Catholics (compared to Jews and Protestants) being more likely to conform. But the correlations are often rather weak, so any one factor of this kind is unlikely to play a large part in determining susceptibility to social influence.

One important theory, however, which links conformity and obedience to personality is Adorno's work on the **authoritarian personality**. This is described in detail in chapter 4, in the section 'Individual explanations of prejudice'. One characteristic typical of the authoritarian personality is a tendency to conform. A relationship has also been shown between high scores on the F-scale and obedience in studies like that of Milgrim (box H). There is some evidence that a tendency to conform is related to upbringing. Frenkel-Brunswik (1942) found that someone with an authoritarian personality was likely to have been strictly disciplined as a child, and punished for disobedience.

From Adorno's work, it emerges that the authoritarian personality has a greater need than most for approval and acceptance. You will remember that **normative influence** is related to these needs, and is one factor in conformity; conformity is a way of satisfying these needs. Support for this comes from Stang (1973), who found that people with high self-esteem (and therefore less in need of the approval and acceptance of others) were less likely to conform than those with low self-esteem.

- ❺ There is some support for the idea that personality plays a part in conformity.
- ❺ One of the characteristics of the **authoritarian personality** identified by Adorno is conformity.
- ❺ This kind of personality has a high need for the approval and acceptance of others. It is related to a harsh, disciplinarian upbringing.

5.4 Independent behaviour

Why people conform to the behaviour of others or obey orders are interesting questions, but equally interesting is why others do not. After all, 13 of the 50 participants in Asch's experiments (box B) did not conform with the majority, and 35% of the participants in Milgram's experiment resisted the order to continue giving shocks, at least to the extent of refusing to give the most extreme shocks.

Asch interviewed his participants after his experiment, and found that those who had not conformed fell into one of three groups. For one group, the essential factor was that they were **confident** that their judgement was correct. This can be related to the findings of Perrin and Spencer (1981), who replicated Asch's study. Very few of their participants conformed. In order to avoid using participants who knew about the Asch series of studies, they used medical and engineering students. Both these groups deal with physical phenomena, where accurate observation and measurement are crucial. Given the nature of the task, their knowledge and skills could have made them more sure of the judgement they were asked to make. This study also confirms the findings of Wiesenthal *et al.* (1976), that people who see themselves as competent at a particular task are much less likely to conform to a majority.

A second group maintained their independence by **withdrawal**, mentally withdrawing from the group, avoiding eye contact with the others, and so on. A third group experienced tension in the situation, but chose to **focus** on the requirements of the task.

Another factor in independent behaviour is **past experience**. Convincing evidence for this idea comes from one of Milgram's studies, and in particular from two participants who would not follow the experimenter's instructions.

One of them, Gretchen Brandt, refused to obey when the voltage was raised to 210V. It emerged that she had grown up in Nazi Germany. When she was asked to explain why she had not obeyed the order to give shocks, she replied: 'Perhaps we have seen too much pain'. The other, Jan Rensaleer, had lived in Holland during the Second World War. He also had direct experience of the potentially terrible consequences of unquestioning obedience. To return to a previous point made in the discussion of Milgram's studies, unlike some of the other participants, both accepted responsibility for their own behaviour, rather than giving control to the experimenter.

Here we are looking at people affected by unusual and extreme experiences. What about people without this kind of experience? A study set up to investigate independent behaviour is described in box P:

Box P: Gamson *et al.* (1982)

Procedure: Participants were told the study was to investigate community standards, and was being carried out by a human relations company. In groups of nine, they were asked to fill in questionnaires on a wide range of topics. This was to establish the extent of anti-authority attitudes for each participant. They were also asked to sign an agreement to be videotaped, which stated that the tape would remain the property of the company. They were then asked to discuss the case of a petrol station manager, who was living with someone he wasn't married to. They were told that the company had fired him on moral grounds, and he was suing for breach of contract. The co-ordinator asked three of the participants to argue as if they were offended at the manager's conduct. Their discussion was videotaped. This was repeated for three more members of the group. They were then asked to repeat these views individually in front of the camera, and sign an agreement that the videos could be used as evidence in a court case.

Results: Out of 33 groups, only one followed the procedure all the way through. There was a high correlation between anti-authority attitudes and disobedience, but there was also disobedience in groups where anti-authority attitudes were low. In some groups, some of the participants signed the affidavit, but in many groups, disobedience became the group norm.

Conclusion: There is considerable readiness to disobey when people feel they are being manipulated. Although disobedience is linked to anti-authority attitudes, this is not enough to explain disobedience.

Activity 12: comparing Milgram and Gamson *et al.*

Look back to Milgram's study (box H). Compare this with the Gamson *et al.* study in box P. What factors could have influenced people to be more ready to disobey in the Gamson *et al.* study?

When you have finished, see the notes on page 156.

- **Personality**, **competence** and **experience** may all influence non-conformity and disobedience.
- Disobedience is more likely when people are aware that they are being manipulated.

Notes on activities are on page 155.

Notes on activities

1 A variety of reasons were given. Some participants claimed that they thought a mistake had been made; they did not want to upset the experiment, which might create a bad impression; they did not want to seem different from everyone else; they did not want to look stupid. All these reasons show **public conformity**, i.e. changing the answer they would have given if asked on their own, but no **private change** – their actual judgement of the lines was not affected.

Some participants, however, seemed to believe that the incorrect decision of the majority was actually correct; they showed private change as well as public conformity. They suggested reasons why their own judgements might have been wrong; perhaps they were suffering from eye strain, or the position of their chair did not allow them to see properly.

2 **a** Asch found that the conformity effect emerges with only three confederates; increasing the size of the group beyond this does not increase the size of the effect. There was a less marked effect when there were only two confederates. What seems to be crucial here is not the size of the group, but the fact that there is complete agreement among group members.

b The reverse is also true: if the judgements made are no longer unanimous, and there is one confederate who gives the correct answer, the rate of conformity drops to about 5%. Allen and Levine (1971) found this to be true even when the non-conforming confederate wore glasses with pebble lenses; his judgements might not be very reliable! Curiously, this also seems to happen if one confederate gives a different *wrong* answer from the other confederates. However, this only seems to apply to physical judgements, like Asch's lines task; if a social or political judgement is involved, another answer diverging from both the majority and the participant results in the participant conforming to the majority decision (Allen and Levine 1968). This may be because we expect there to be a variety of opinions on social questions, but we expect consensus on physical judgements.

c When the dissenter from the group changes to agreement with the majority, the conformity effect reappears, with the same strength as in the original situation.

d Making the task more difficult tends to increase conformity; presumably participants then have less confidence in the correctness of their judgments.

e If only one person in the group gives a wrong answer, the rest of the group tend to be sarcastic and make fun of him. It seems that the participants in the original study who were afraid of being ridiculed were justified!

f This perhaps helps to explain why, when Asch allowed the genuine participant to write down his answer, while still being aware of the answers of the confederates, conformity dropped to just over 12% – he would no longer be vulnerable to this kind of reaction.

3 In a lecture, you listen to the information you are given and make notes. You are quiet; any talking is done in a whisper. It would be inappropriate to stand up and start singing a rugby song, or to take all your clothes off. Similarly in a restaurant, you order food, eat it with the cutlery provided and pay before you leave. You wouldn't take your own food and ask the waiter to cook it for you, or sit with your elbows in the soup.

Social conventions help to ensure that social interaction with others runs smoothly. Because these conventions are unwritten, many of them are acquired as part of the socialisation process. What is (and is not) appropriate behaviour is picked up by observing the behaviour of others. The consequence of not observing social conventions is loss of the acceptance and approval of others.

4 You would probably ask the advice of people you know who are already involved in the sport, and could well end up buying the same make of equipment as they did. This kind of conformity doesn't have anything to do with needing their approval. The fact they have more information than you is what is crucial in your decision to conform, so this is known as **informational influence**. It has a role in particular in situations where there is some degree of uncertainty, i.e. lack of information.

5 In the first paragraph, you should have linked **compliance**, **normative**, the **need for approval/acceptance**, unambiguous and **Asch**, leaving the other terms for the second paragraph.

7 You probably decided that you would be more likely to conform in a group of 12. Convincing 11 people that you are right is much more of an uphill struggle than convincing five!

10 Firstly, this was presented as a study on the effects of punishment on learning, but participants were not doing anything which the experimenter could not have done just as well for himself. It must also have seemed very odd when the experimenter showed no reaction when the learner pounded on the wall and demanded that the experiment should be stopped. There were possibly other subtle clues which could have been picked up: it is very difficult, for example, to treat a confederate in exactly the same way as a complete stranger. These factors could well have led to participants trying to guess the *real* purpose of the study, i.e. to respond to **demand characteristics**.They may have come to realise that they themselves were actually the ones being studied.

In reply to this, Milgram claimed that a follow-up survey showed that 80% of participants had no such doubts. Additionally, many participants showed clear and unambiguous stress responses, such as trembling, stuttering and sweating.

11 Gender might be expected to make a difference. In our society and many others, a woman's role has traditionally been that of carer, protecting others from harm rather than inflicting it. Social behaviour reflects the varying cultural norms and values of different societies. It therefore seems probable that obedience, like other social behaviours, will vary from culture to culture.

12 The Gamson *et al.* study was carried out nearly 20 years after Milgram's. During this time, there were many social changes, one of which could have been that it had become more acceptable to question authority, a change to which knowledge of Milgram's studies could itself have contributed. Milgram's study received widespread publicity. One of the participants in the Gamson *et al.* study even referred to Milgram's work as a reason for not conforming!

Perhaps also the participants were less intimidated by a company representative than a researcher from a prestigious university.

In addition, people were working in groups. You will remember from our discussion of Milgram's study that obedience was reduced to 10% when the participant was exposed to disobedient models.

Finally, the participants in this later study can have been in no doubt that they were being cynically manipulated, whereas in the Milgram study they might have believed that what they were doing was of some academic value.

Social cognition

6.1 Social perception and impression formation

Just as we try to make sense of the physical world around us, so we also try to make sense of our social world. We do not just passively observe other people, but actively use the information available to us to seek to understand and draw conclusions about them and why they behave as they do. This allows us to make predictions about what is likely to happen in social situations, and so gives us some feeling of control over what is going on around us. Social cognition looks at the mechanisms we use in taking in information about our social world, the processes involved in acquiring information about other people, and the use we make of this information. We will look first at 'schema theory', which has provided a useful framework for the first of these issues.

Schema theory

A **schema** can be defined as a cognitive structure, which represents a person's knowledge in a particular area. For example, you have a schema about what is involved in studying Psychology – what happens in lessons, where to find sources of information, the kind of work you are expected to do out of the classroom, and so on. Having this schema means that you can draw on your previous experiences of studying Psychology, and so cut down on the amount of information to be processed.

Having schemas means that we will approach something new with certain expectations. A schema will determine what aspects of a situation we attend to, and which parts of the available information we take in, and so on. Schemas have many advantages: they help us to make sense of something new by focusing only on particular aspects, which in turn reduces the time and effort it takes us to process new information, and interpret and evaluate it. However, though, schemas also have disadvantages: by focusing on particular aspects of a situation, we may overlook something which is crucial, and thus draw inappropriate conclusions.

Baron and Byrne (1984) draw attention to three types of schema commonly used in social interaction: self schemas, person schemas and role schemas. Activity 1 will give you an idea of what these involve:

Activity 1: exploring social schemas

a Write down a short list of things which describe you as a person. These should include what you think it is that makes you a unique individual, different from everybody else.

b Now do the same for a member of your family and a close friend. Again, you will need to focus on ways in which they are different from each other, but also ways in which they may be alike.

c Finally, list briefly the characteristics of a doctor and a DJ, again focusing on similarities and differences.

In carrying out this activity, you were using (i) your self schema, (ii) your person schema and (iii) your role schema. We also have schemas for groups of people who share a particular characteristic, e.g. women or Americans or estate agents. These are called **stereotypes**, and are discussed in detail in chapter 4. You may have drawn on stereotypes – for example, that doctors are caring, and that DJs are outgoing – in your response to activity 1c.

Schemas explain how information is represented in memory. However, because we have such a vast amount of information, we need to use short cuts to apply it efficiently to our social world. One way we do this is by the use of **heuristics**, defined as: 'problem-solving strategies which involve taking the most probable or likely option ... (they) provide a way of reducing a complex task to a manageable set of tasks' (Stratton and Hayes 1993). Some important types of heuristic used in social cognition are representativeness, availability, and anchoring.

Representativeness involves deciding whether a particular person or event falls into a particular category simply on the basis of how representative they are of members of that category. If Afzal is labelled 'Dr', works in a hospital and talks about 'patients', there is a match between this person and your 'doctor' schema, and you are likely to conclude that Afzal is a medical doctor. Since these characteristics are representative of doctors, you are probably right (but not necessarily – Afzal could be an administrator with a PhD in History).

The representativeness heuristic can override statistical probability. Let us take, for example, a short, bespectacled, serious student Emily, who enjoys writing poetry, and is working towards a degree in either Psychology or Chinese Studies. Given the number of students taking Psychology and Chinese Studies, Emily is about a hundred times more likely to be studying Psychology. Because she fits the stereotype of what students of Chinese studies are like, however, people may quite often judge that she is more likely to be taking Chinese Studies.

Availability refers to judging the likelihood of an event on the basis of the number of instances which come to mind, i.e. are available. If you have a lot of friends who are studying A-level Psychology, for example, you may conclude (rightly, as it happens!) that Psychology is a very popular A-level subject.

When we have insufficient information to draw firm conclusions, we may use **anchoring**, i.e. making use of related information as an 'anchor' to help us in our judgements. If you were asked how likely it was that a fellow-student would choose to go clubbing on Saturday nights, for example, and you didn't know her very well, you might base your judgement on yourself, and how likely it is that you would choose to spend Saturday nights in this way.

These kinds of heuristics simplify information-processing – they allow us to act as 'cognitive misers' – and most of the time work very well. Sometimes, though, because we are using only partial information, we may jump to inappropriate conclusions. You can probably think of examples in your own experience where initial conclusions you have drawn have turned out to be wrong.

We also simplify the way we process information by the use of **categories**. Putting people into categories – for example, by gender, race, age or profession – helps us to simplify our social world. Categories are associated with **prototypes**, typical examples of what we expect a member of a particular category to be like, as we did in activity 1c.

Activity 2: exploring prototypes

List the characteristics you associate with:
a a rugby player **b** a politician **c** a mother
When you have finished, see the notes on page 177.

While categorisation has the advantage of simplifying the processing of social information, at the same time this kind of generalisation is maintained by cognitive distortion. Some common forms of biases and errors which categorisation can lead to are the confirmatory bias and the false consensus bias.

The **confirmatory bias** refers to the tendency to focus on information which confirms our categories. We are likely to pay more attention to the local rugby team celebrating loudly in the bar after a match, for example – which is in line with our 'rugby player' category – than the team member helping an old lady across the road, which falls outside it.

We may also use what we know about ourselves in forming judgements about others. The **false consensus bias** suggests that we tend to assume that other people are much like us, and may therefore interpret what they say and do in terms of our own attitudes and behaviours. For example, Gilovich (1990) found that people asked to estimate the proportion of others who agree with their opinions about drugs and abortion consistently overestimate the degree of agreement.

- We try to make sense of social experience. **Schemas** help us to simplify this process. In a social context, we use **self**, **person** and **role** schemas. **Stereotypes** are schemas about groups of people.
- **Heuristics** are ways of simplifying the processes we use to make judgements. The include **representativeness**, **availability** and **anchoring**. While they are often useful, they can mislead us into drawing inappropriate conclusions.
- We make use of **categories** in forming social judgements. While this is a simple way of making sense of our social world, it can also lead to distortion; the **confirmatory bias** and the **false consensus bias** are two examples.

Central and peripheral traits

One aspect of the way people come to understand their social world is the kinds of information on which they tend to focus when drawing conclusions about other people. One factors which has been found to be important is the use of central and peripheral traits, i.e. which kinds of characteristics are seen to be important (central) and which less important (peripheral). These different kinds of information are influential in shaping our general impression of people:

Box A: Asch (1946)

Procedure: One group of participants was given a list of adjectives describing a fictitious person:

intelligent; skilful; industrious; warm; determined; practical; cautious

A second group had the same list, except that *warm* was replaced by *cold*. For further groups, *warm* was` replaced by *polite* or *blunt*. All participants were then given another list of traits (*generous, reliable, serious* and so on) and asked to indicate which of these would also describe the target person.

Results: There was considerable variation in the adjectives chosen by the *warm* and *cold* groups. No such differences were found between the *polite* and *blunt* groups.

Conclusion: *warm* and *cold* are considered to be central traits, which influence general impressions of people. Traits seen as being more peripheral, such as *polite* and *blunt*, do not have this effect.

Activity 3: problems with Asch's experiment

Can you think of any reasons why we might need to be cautious in drawing general conclusions from Asch's study?
When you have finished, see the notes on page 177.

The study in box B investigates a similar idea in a more naturalistic setting:

Box B: Kelley (1950)

Procedure: Students were informed that their class would be taken by a substitute teacher, whom they didn't know. They were told something about him. For one group, this description included *rather warm*, and for another group *rather cold*; otherwise the biographical details were identical. After the class, the students were asked to assess the teacher on 15 rating scales, e.g. *good-natured – irritable*, and also to write a description of him.

Results: The *rather warm* group responded significantly more favourably on both measures. They also took more part in class discussion than the *rather cold* group.

Conclusion: The characteristic of warmth is central to how we perceive others, and affects how we interact with them.

The overall picture may not be as simple, however, as this implies. It has been suggested that how traits are perceived depends on the context in which they are presented. For example, Zebrowitz (1990) notes that 'proud' can be interpreted as 'confident' when presented with positive traits, but as 'conceited' when presented with negative traits.

The primacy–recency effect

The primacy–recency effect looks at the effect on the impression we have of people of the order in which we are given information. If people are asked to learn a list of words, they typically remember those at the start and at the end better than those in the middle. The better recall for the first few words is called the **primacy effect**, and for those at the end, the **recency effect**. There is some evidence of similar effects in social cognition, and we have already considered this in chapter 4, in the subsection headed 'Persuasive communication'.

Early impressions are likely to have a strong influence

Our early impressions of someone we meet are likely to have a strong influence on how we think of them. You can investigate for yourself the possibility that the order in which information about people is presented affects the impression we form of them.

Activity 4: investigating the primacy–recency effect

Read through these two descriptions about the experiences of a school student in America:

1 Jim left the house to get some stationery. He walked out into the sun-filled street with two of his friends, basking in the sun as he walked. Jim entered the stationery store which was full of people. Jim talked with an acquaintance while he waited for the clerk to catch his eye.* On his way out, he stopped to chat to a school friend who was just coming into the store. Leaving the store, he walked towards school. On his way out he met the girl to whom he had been introduced the night before. They talked for a short while and then Jim left for school.

2 After school Jim left the classroom alone. Leaving the school, he started on his long walk home. The street was brilliantly filled with sunshine. Jim walked down the street on the shady side. Coming down the street towards him, he saw the pretty girl whom he had met on the previous evening. Jim crossed the street and entered a candy store.* The store was crowded with students and he noticed a few familiar faces. Jim waited quietly until the counterman caught his eye and then gave his order. Taking his drink, he sat down at a side table. When he had finished his drink he went home.

You will probably agree that the first story describes extroverted behaviour and the second introverted behaviour. (Extroversion and introversion are explained in chapter 2, activity 5).

To investigate the relative importance of primacy and recency, read some participants (group 1) the first half of story 1, up to the asterisk (*), followed by the second part of story 2, and other participants (group 2) the first half of story 2 followed by the second part of story 1. When they have heard the story, ask each participant to rate how extrovert they think Jim is. You could use a scale of 1 (extremely introverted) to 10 (extremely extroverted).

Is there any difference in the ratings of the two groups of participants? If there is a primacy effect, group 1 should rate Jim as more extroverted than group 2, and vice versa if there is a recency effect. You could make up stories of your own if you prefer, but remember to include enough detail of extroverted/introverted behaviour to make evaluation possible.

This activity replicates a study by Luchins (1957). You may have found, as Luchins did, that there was a primacy effect; people's social judgements are more influenced by the information which they first receive than by what comes later.

Again, with this study, as with Asch's cold/warm study, there is the problem of **ecological validity**; participants are asked to respond to hypothetical people. A similar investigation using real people in a real situation is decribed in box C:

Box C: Jones *et al.* (1968)

Procedure: Participants watched a student (a stooge of the experimenter) attempting to solve a set of 30 problems. In one condition, he was more successful with the early problems, and in the other with the later ones. In both conditions, 15 problems were correctly solved. Afterwards participants were asked to rate the student's intelligence.

Results: Participants who had seen the student successfully solve the earlier problems rated him as more intelligent than those who had seen him be more successful with later ones.

Conclusion: Social judgements show a primacy effect.

This effect may also have real world implications, e.g. for jury verdicts in criminal trials. Pennington (1982) asked participants to read an account of a rape trial, varying the order in which the information was presented. He found guilty verdicts were more likely when the strongest prosecution evidence was given first.

A possible explanation for the primacy effect, put forward by Luchins, is that people tend to pay more attention to earlier information, and tend to ignore what comes later. They may make judgements on the basis of the initial information they receive, which they are then unwilling to revise. Asch has suggested that later information may be interpreted in the light of what we already know, to achieve consistency with the impression we have already formed.

While the primacy effect has been confirmed in many studies, it has been found experimentally to be affected by the instructions participants are given. Hendrick and Constantini (1970), for example, found that the effect disappears if participants are reminded to take account of *all* the information they are given. The primacy effect is also more evident when initial information is negative rather than positive, and there is more likelihood of a recency effect when we know the people concerned than if they are strangers.

- **Central traits** are personal characteristics which strongly influence the judgements we make of others. **Peripheral traits** have less effect.
- There is a **primacy effect** in social judgements, where information we get first is more likely to shape our judgements than later information.

Cultural differences in social perception

Quite a lot of research has shown that there are differences between cultures in terms of how we perceive others. For example, Argyle *et al.* (1978) found that Japanese participants tended to explain the behaviour of others in terms of situational factors, while English participants used dispositional explanations, related to personal characteristics, such as personality and abilities. This tendency to use dispositional rather than contextual explanations is known as the **fundamental attribution error** – although it is perhaps better thought of as a bias rather than an error – and we shall return to it later in this chapter. A study by Korten (1974), while showing some similarities between cultures, had similar findings:

> **Box D: Korten (1974)**
>
> **Procedure:** Thirty-nine Ethiopian students and 47 American students were asked to describe fellow students.
> **Results:** While both groups talked about the interests and activities of other students, Ethiopians focused more on interpersonal interactions and beliefs, while Americans focused on personality, ability and knowledge.
> **Conclusion:** While there are some cross-cultural similarities in interpersonal perception, there are also differences between people of different cultures in their perception of others.

In a study of children's perceptions of the causes of youth crime Pfeffer *et al.* (1996), found that British 12- and 14-year-olds tended to use personal explanations (e.g. 'for fun' or 'because I am bored'), while Nigerian children of the same age tended to use situational explanations (e.g. 'I have no home training' or 'I am poor'). In a similar study with adults, Hamilton and Sanders (1983) compared explanations of wrong-doing in response to various scenarios. They found that Japanese adults tended to place more emphasis on the role and social context of the people involved in the story, while Americans tended to focus on individual responsibility.

Japanese adults tended to place more emphasis on the social context, and Americans on individual responsibility

It seems likely that these cultural differences are related to the distinction made by Hsu (1971) between individualist and collectivist cultures. In **individualist** cultures, the emphasis is on the goals and needs of the individual, and the importance of personal choice. Priority is given to personal achievement and self-reliance. This is thc typical pattern of Western cultures, of which the USA is a good example. In **collectivist** cultures, however, the emphasis is on the goals and needs of the social group, and the duties of the individual towards the group to which they belong. Priority is given to the welfare and the unity of the group. This is more typical of non-Western cultures, of which Japan is a good example.

Miller (1984) argues that the Western focus on the individual leads us to assume that enduring traits underpin behaviour across different situations, while the non-Western focus on the social group leads to an emphasis on the interdependence of the person and the social context. She suggested that these cultural differences develop with age:

Box E: Miller (1984)

Procedure: Participants were 8-, 11- and 15-year-old Hindu children in India, and middle-class Hindu adults in India, together with a similar sample of non-Hindu North Americans. They were asked to talk about deviant and prosocial behaviour (e.g. helping others) and asked to explain why people behaved in these ways.

Results: Non-Hindu American participants used more trait descriptors with increasing age, but Hindu Indians did not. Hindus used more contextual descriptions with increasing age, while the reverse was true of American non-Hindus.

Conclusion: Children learn to make the type of attributions appropriate to their culture.

If we assume that people become more socially skilled with age, perceiving people in terms of disposition must be adaptive in an American context, whereas perceiving people in a more contextual way is adaptive in some non-Western cultures. In the USA and other cultures relatively unconstrained by social roles, people's behaviour will vary significantly with their traits, so using descriptive categories is useful. In cultures where people are relatively more constrained by social roles, the use of contextual factors may be more relevant. In support of this, Argyle *et al.* (1978) found that, in England, extroverted behaviour shows more variability between people than between situations, while the opposite is true in Japan.

In making sense of the findings in this area, we should bear in mind the **target effect**, i.e. the effect due to the people about whom judgements are being made. Research in this area tends to ask people to make judgements about others from their own culture. It could be that explanations in terms of social and situational factors are more appropriate in predicting the behaviour of people from collectivist, non-Western backgrounds, whereas traits are more appropriate for predicting the behaviour of people from individualist Western cultures. In other words, it may be that the differences in attributional style do not so much reflect differences lying within the person making the attributions as the differences in the target.

While the individualist–collectivist distinction is useful in helping to explain some cross-cultural differences, more specific cultural values, beliefs and traditions also affect interpersonal perception. For example, Kimmel (1988) points out that perceptions of elderly people vary across cultures, which reflects in part cultural differences in the valuation of ageing. He contrasts the United States, where negative attitudes to the elderly are common, with Japan, where older people and what they have to offer are valued.

Another example is the perception of marital relationships. Stander *et al.* (2001) found differences between couples from China and from the USA in attributions of responsiblity and blame

in marriage breakdown. Similarly, Delgado *et al.* (1997) found that British participants, responding to scenarios involving a husband battering his wife, considered the husbands to be more responsible and guilty than did Spanish participants. When jealousy was the motive for the assault, Spanish participants were much more likely than British participants to see the assault as uncontrollable.

- Cultures vary in their tendency to explain others' behaviour in terms of either **dispositional** or **situational** factors. This difference may be related to the distinction between **individualist** and **collectivist** cultures.
- Cultural differences develop with age, and are **adaptive** in terms of being relevant to the kind of culture within which they develop.
- **Specific cultural values** also influence interpersonal perception.

6.2 Self-perception

What do we mean by 'self'?

As with many other terms in psychology, we have an intuitive feel for what the concept of 'self' means to us, but it is not easy to put this into words. Some aspects of the self remain constant over the years, while some are less long-lasting. There may be differences between what we think we are and what we would like to be. What we think we are may also differ from the way others perceive us and the way we think they perceive us.

One basic term we need here is the **self-concept**, which refers to a general awareness of self. This can be broken down into three components: **self-image** is how we see ourselves, **self-esteem** is the value we put on ourselves, and **ideal self** is how we would like to be.

Activity 5: who am I?

This activity aims to help you explore your sense of self. Before you read the next section, try to write down 20 answers to the question: 'Who am I?' Start each answer with: 'I am ...'.

What you have just completed is the **twenty-statements test (TST)** devised by Kuhn and McPartland (1954). They found that people's responses tended to fall into two main categories. The first category is linked to **roles**. This includes family relationships (e.g. 'I am a daughter'), work (e.g. 'I am a nurse'), religious identity (e.g. 'I am a Methodist') and activities (e.g. 'I am a keen golfer'). The second category covers **personality traits** (e.g. 'I am a moody person'). It is of course possible for one statement to include both categories (e.g. 'I am a hard-working student'). It is likely that most of your answers could be put into these categories.

The TST can be related to a distinction made by William James (1890), one of the first psychologists to write about the self-concept. He drew a distinction between the 'I' and the 'me', now often referred to as the **existential self** and the **categorical self** (Lewis 1990).

The 'me' (or categorical self) is the self-as-object. It refers to those aspects of the self which can be known when we stand back and observe ourselves: our physical characteristics, values and attitudes, roles, social identity and behaviour. It is the self-concept which you were describing in the TST.

The 'I' (or existential self) is the self-as-subject. It refers to our capacity for conscious awareness, the active process of our experience as an individual, our sense of our uniqueness and of continuity in our identity. James also referred to what he called **reflexiveness** as part of the 'I', by which he meant our awareness of our own awareness.

The distinction between the 'I' and the 'me' brings together our sense of being unique and distinct from other people, and so our individuality (the 'I'); and our awareness of how we relate to others, and so are shaped as individuals by social influences (the 'me').

Many psychologists have been interested in the nature of the self, and we will look now at what C. H. Cooley, a writer on psychological and sociological issues, had to contribute.

Cooley's looking-glass self

Cooley (1902) saw the self, including both the 'I' and the 'me', as an essentially social construction, and believed that every aspect of a person's self develops as a result of their interaction with others. Our understanding of our own identity represents a reflection of how we are seen by others; we judge ourselves as we imagine others see and judge us. The 'I' and the 'me' are part of a dual perspective, since at the same time we are the 'I' doing the viewing and the object 'me' being viewed. We build up our sense of self as a result of the way that other people respond to us, and how we believe they see us, which Cooley referred to as the **internalised other**. To describe this idea, Cooley used the term the **looking-glass self**:

> 'As we see our face, figure, and dress in the glass, and are interested in them because they are ours, and pleased or otherwise with them…, so in imagination we perceive in another's mind some thought of our appearance, manners, aims, deeds, character, friends, and so on, and are variously affected by it.'

Cooley went so far as to propose that there could be no barrier between the individual and society: 'a separate individual is an abstraction unknown to experience', and 'there is no sense of "I" without its correlative sense of "you", or "he" or "they"'. Society and individuals cannot be regarded as separable, but are aspects of the same thing.

Three principal elements make up the looking-glass self:

Figure 1: the elements of the looking-glass self

1 We imagine how we appear to other people.
2 We imagine their judgement of that appearance.
3 As a result, we experience a positive or a negative feeling.

In the first of these elements, we consider how we present ourselves to others, e.g. am I tall? clever? witty? We then consider whether they see us as we see ourselves, or see something else, and can then use these interpretations of others' reactions to develop our sense of self. If we sense that other people agree with our self-perception, our self-concept is strengthened, and the behaviour which we are considering is likely to continue. However, if we sense that other's perception of us is different from our own, our self-concept is weakened, and we are likely to change our behaviour. Failure to meet the expectations of others and of ourselves can lead to a sense of inferiority.

Failure to meet the expectations of ourselves and others can lead to a sense of inferiority

Cooley provided an example to illustrate these rather abstract ideas, and the multiple perspectives present in any encounter:

Box F: Cooley (1902)

Imagine that Alice (who has a new hat) meets Angela (who has a new dress). We then have:

a The real Alice
b Alice's idea of herself, e.g. 'I look well in this hat'.
c Alice's idea of Angela's idea of her, e.g. 'Angela thinks I look well in this hat'.

d Alice's idea of what Angela thinks she (Alice) thinks of herself, e.g. 'Angela thinks I am proud of my looks in this hat'.

e Angela's idea of what Alice thinks of herself, eg 'Alice thinks she is stunning in that hat'.

There will be similar perspectives relating to Angela.

Cooley laid particular stress on the development of the self-concept during early childhood, believing that the influence of others is stronger at this time than later in life. Young children are particularly concerned about how other people react to them, particularly what Sullivan (1947) called **significant others**. This refers to people whose opinion the child values, e.g. parents or brothers and sisters. When the child starts school, significant others will broaden to include the peer group and teachers. As the sources of information widen, different significant others will become relevant to different aspects of the self-image. Feedback from the teacher is important, for example, as far as academic ability is concerned, but peers are likely to be more important in determining how popular the child feels.

Rosenberg (1979) asked children how much they cared about what different sorts of people thought of them. He found that younger children relied heavily on adults' evaluations, with older children being more influenced by the opinion of their peers, and adolescents more concerned about what their best friend thought of them.

However, although the early years are important, Cooley believed that a person's self is capable of change throughout life. A famous story told by Guthrie (1938) illustrates how the reactions of others can change an adult's self-image. A group of male students decided to play a trick on a dull and unattractive female student, by pretending that she was the most attractive girl in the college, drawing lots for a turn to take her out, and so on. After a while, the male students no longer had to pretend that the girl was attractive. Their reactions to her had changed her self-image; seeing herself as attractive and popular influenced the way in which she interacted with others – perhaps she became more confident and fun-loving? – and so made her attractive to them.

Feil (2001) carried out a study which attempted to test Cooley's ideas:

Box G: Feil (2001)

Procedure: Participants were 70 female Psychology students who did not know each other. They were asked to interact in pairs, and then completed ratings, e.g. of extroversion, emotional stability and likeability, in terms of how they perceived themselves, and how they imagined the people with whom they had interacted to perceive them.
Results: Participants showed considerable insight into how they were perceived by others in relation to their self-concept.
Conclusion: People are sensitive to others' perception of them.

However, while the findings of this study are in line with what Cooley proposed, it examined only one aspect of Cooley's theory: that we are aware of and can accurately assess the feedback we receive from others. While this is an important part of the theory, it is difficult to see how other aspects, e.g. the multiple perspectives Cooley suggested, could be tested in a systematic way.

- Theorists interested in the self-concept have made a distinction between the **I (self-as-subject)** and the **me (self-as-object)**.
- This distinction has influenced Cooley's concept of the **looking-glass self**. Cooley saw the self as a **social construction**, with society and the self as inseparable.
- The influence of others is strongest during childhood, but the self can change throughout life.
- There is some support for these ideas, but the complex and abstract nature of the theory makes it difficult to test.

Self-perception and self-esteem

Self-esteem refers to the extent to which we value ourselves. Many aspects of the self-concept have values attached to them, i.e. we regard them positively or negatively. Look back at your answers to activity 5. It is likely that you have positive or negative feelings about at least some of the aspects of self you described. This can be true even of physical characteristics. A man who is very tall, for example, could see this as positive, perhaps as an indication of manliness. A very tall woman could see this aspect of the self negatively, perhaps as a source of social embarrassment. Since we make value judgements about many aspects of the self, self-esteem can be seen as an important part of the self-concept.

James (1890) related self-esteem to success and pretensions. By 'pretensions' he meant the value we put on various aspects of the self. If you do badly in a Chemistry exam, for example, but Chemistry is something which has little value for you, your lack of success will not lower your self-esteem. But if being good at Chemistry is something which is important to you, your self-esteem will suffer as a result of doing badly in the exam. Self-esteem, then, depends on internal, psychological factors.

Activity 6: self-perception, self-esteem and pretensions

Go back to your responses to the TST in activity 5. Which of these characteristics are important to your self-esteem? Do they include aspects about which you feel negatively but which do not lower your self-esteem? If so, are these characteristics which you feel to be relatively unimportant, as James suggested? Can you identify any other personal characteristics not covered by your TST responses which increase or lower your self esteem? Is their effect on your self-esteem related to how important you rate them?

Self-esteem is also affected by comparisons with others. In interviews with adolescents, Rosenberg (1965) found that those with the highest self-esteem were those who, in comparing themselves with others, had done better at school and had been leaders in social groups such as clubs.

Harter (1982) suggested that we need to look at self-esteem not as a single concept, but as multi-dimensional. She identified five areas or **domains** of the self-concept, shown in figure 2, which could each individually contribute towards a child's general level of self-esteem:

Figure 2: Harter's self-concept domains

intellectual achievement: how capable the child feels in relation to schoolwork
athletic competence: how competent the child feels in physical skills, competence at sport and in games
interpersonal relationships: how well-accepted by others the child feels
behaviour: the extent to which a child feels s/he behaves appropriately
appearance: how happy the child is with the way s/he looks

To investigate self-perception and self-esteem, Harter developed a **self-perception profile** for children. This presents children with pairs of linked statements. They are asked to tick one of four boxes to rate how much they think each statement is true of them. Some examples of the statements Harter used are given in figure 3.

The ticked boxes give scores. Points are therefore given for statements giving a positive self-image. Statements related to each of Harter's five domains are included, so it is possible to build up a profile of the different areas of the child's self-image and level of self-esteem. She found that children often produce ratings which differ across the different domains.

Harter asked a group of children to say how important each of the five domains were to them. She found a strong correlation between performance in an area which the child considered to be important and their level of self-esteem. This relationship between success in a particular area and the value placed on that area confirms James's definition of self-esteem, which we looked at earlier.

Much of the research on self-esteem has focused on childhood. For example, a study carried out by Harter (1990) has shown that overall levels of self-

Figure 3: items from Harter's self-perception profile for children

Children are asked to tick boxes about themselves and 'other kids'. The boxes are empty but have been filled here with the scores given for the various responses.

Really true for me	*Sort of true for me*				*Sort of true for me*	*Really true for me*
1	2	Some kids have trouble figuring out the answers in school	BUT	Other kids almost always can figure out the answers	3	4
4	3	Some kids do very very well at all kinds of sports	BUT	Others don't feel that they are very good when it comes to sports	2	1
4	3	Some kids are popular with others their age	BUT	Other kids are not very popular	2	1
1	2	Some kids usually get into trouble because of the things they do	BUT	Other kids usually don't do things that get them into trouble	3	4
1	2	Some kids wish their physical appearance was different	BUT	Other kids like their physical appearance the way it is	3	4

esteem vary during childhood. There is a sharp dip between the ages of about 11 and 13, followed by a steady rise. While self-esteem is not fixed, it does seem to be a fairly stable personality characteristic after the age of about seven or eight. However, there has also been research looking at factors which contribute to self-esteem, or lower it, in adolescents and adults, and we will look now at some of those which have been identified.

One important area of research concerns **body image** (box H). Garfinkel and Garner (1982) claim that dancers and models account for 7% of cases of anorexia, so there is a case, as Bettle *et al.* point out, for the use of strategies aimed at enhancing self-esteem in dancers, as a way of helping them avoid developing an eating disorder.

Body image and self-esteem are also linked in further studies. For example, Kim and Kim (2001) found that over three-quarters of their sample of 303 female Korean adolescents, aged 15–19, wished they were thinner even though only 2.6% were overweight. Their perception of having a weight problem was a significant predictor of low self-esteem. Again, the participants belong to a group – adolescent females – who are more likely than any other to develop an eating disorder, so

Box H: Bettle *et al.* (2001)

Procedure: ninety ballet school students (aged 11–17) and 156 controls (aged 13–17) completed a series of questionnaires designed to assess body image and self-esteem.
Results: Female ballet students had a less favourable body image and lower self-esteem than controls.
Conclusion: Taking part in an activity where body size and shape is important is associated with poorer body image and lower self-esteem.

intervention to increase self-esteem among this group could be helpful.

Other physical characteristics, such as **motor co-ordination**, are also linked to self-esteem:

Box I: Skinner and Piek (2001)

Procedure: Fifty-eight children (aged 8–10) and 51 adolescents (aged 12–14), all with developmental coordination disorder (DCD), completed questionnaires to assess their perceived competence and self-esteem.
Results: Overall, DCD participants perceived themselves as less competent than controls, and reported lower self-esteem. The difference was more marked for adolescents than for younger children.
Conclusion: Poor motor co-ordination is linked to poor self-esteem. This link increases as children get older.

Another major area of interest has been a possible link between perceived **academic competence** and self-esteem:

Box J: Alves-Martins *et al.* (2002)

Procedure: Academically successful and unsuccessful secondary school students, aged 13–19, completed a scale of attitudes towards school, and a questionnaire to assess self-esteem.
Results: Students with low levels of self-esteem had increasingly less favourable attitudes towards school. For the younger children, there were significant differences between the levels of self-esteem of successful and unsuccessful participants, though not for the older participants.
Conclusion: One strategy to protect self-esteem threatened by a negative self-evaluation of school competence may be to develop negative attitudes towards school.

This study can be seen as an example of the link James proposed between success and pretensions. Students who feel negatively about school, have no pretensions to succeed academically, and so their self-esteem is protected when they do not do so.

However, low self-esteem has also been found to be related to high academic achievement. Sonnak and Towell (2001) investigated the **imposter phenomenon**, identified by Clance (1985), defined as an intense feeling of intellectual inauthenticity experienced by many high-achieving individuals. They found that low levels of self-esteem were a significant predictor of imposter fears.

There is also a strong relationship between **childhood abuse** and poor self-esteem. In a study of adults, Talbott (2001) found that those who had been neglected or abused had lower self-esteem than controls.

We will look finally at the relationship between perception of **past selves** and current self-esteem. Wilson (2001) investigated a possible link between current self-esteem, perceptions of self in the past, and psychological distance of the past self, i.e. the extent to which past selves are seen as belonging to current identity or distinct from it. She found that participants who reported unfavourable former selves had higher self-esteem if the former self was psychologically distant than if it were experienced as close. Conversely, self-esteem was higher for participants who reported favourable former selves if the former self was psychologically close.

- **Self-esteem** is the value we place on ourselves. It is a relatively stable personality characteristic from the age of about seven or eight.
- Negative self-perceptions are more likely to damage self-esteem if they are in areas which are important to us. Self-esteem is affected by **comparisons** with others. It can be divided into different domains.
- Physical aspects of the self, e.g. **body image** and **motor coordination**, are related to self-esteem, together with **academic achievement**, a history of **abuse**, and our perception of our **past self**.

6.3 Theories of attribution

An attribution is the process of giving reasons for why things happen. Heider (1944) laid the foundations of attribution theory. He proposed that people have a strong need to make sense of their social world, and that we do this by developing ideas and theories about what is going on around us. Some of these ideas relate to the *causes* underlying events and behaviour, and it is with this aspect of social cognition that attribution theory is concerned. The strength of this tendency to identify causes behind what we observe was shown in an early study:

Box K: Heider and Simmel (1944)

Procedure: Participants were shown an animated cartoon of three geometric shapes (a large triangle, a small triangle and a circle) moving around, and in and out of, a square. They were asked to describe what they saw.

Results: Participants often talked about the shapes as if they had human intentions. Many people saw the two triangles as men fighting over a woman (the circle). The large triangle was seen as an aggressive bully, the small triangle as a defiant hero, and the circle as shy.

Conclusion: There is a strong tendency to link behaviour with personality and intentions, even when the behaviour being observed is that of inanimate objects.

According to Heider, one major way in which we explain a person's behaviour is by seeing the causes either as lying within the person (a **dispositional attribution**), or within the situation they find themselves in (a **situational attribution**). For example, if Mary gets a good pass in her Business Studies exam, a dispositional attribution could be that she has done so well because she is very clever or worked very hard. A situational attribution could be that the exam was very easy, or that she was well taught.

We will be looking at some ideas in the general area of attribution theory in the following sections. As you read through this section, it may help to bear in mind that these ideas are not really in conflict with one another, but rather offer us different insights into the attribution process.

Correspondent inference model

According to Jones and Davis (1965), the first thing we do in establishing causes is to decide whether an action is deliberate or not. If we believe an action to be deliberate, we then look for a personal characteristic which could have been responsible for the action. This matching of a behaviour with a personal characteristic to which it corresponds is what Jones and Davis referred to as a **correspondent inference**. For example, if Jane assists an elderly lady with her heavy shopping, the behaviour can be labelled 'helpful' and Jane's disposition can be labelled 'kind'.

In this theory, developed originally by Heider, there are three important concepts. The first is that we prefer to find **stable causes** for behaviour. It is only stable causes which can fulfil the need to be able to predict what is likely to happen in a given situation. Secondly, we need to be able to judge whether or not an action is **intentional** in order to be able to interpret it. The final distinction is between dispositional and situational attributions, mentioned above.

For example, Jack throws a ball which hits Robert. If we decide that Jack did this on purpose, we would try to explain his action in dispositional terms, e.g. that Jack is an aggressive person. This would be a stable cause because aggression is seen as an enduring aspect of Jack's character. If we interpreted his action as accidental, on the other hand, we would be more likely to make a situational attribution, e.g. that the ball flew out of his hand when he stumbled.

Jones and Davis suggested that we have a tendency to assume that actions are deliberate, and to make dispositional rather than situational attributions. Once we have decided that an action is deliberate, we can then attempt to make the correspondent inference about the aspect of the person's disposition underlying that action. Correspondent inference theory can only be applied where the actor is seen as having a choice of action, since the correspondent inference process rests on the judgement that the action is deliberate.

However, there is some evidence that the tendency to make dispositional rather than situational attributions does not always hold true and may be related to experience:

Box L: Guimond and Palmer (1990)

Procedure: Students taking social science, commerce and engineering courses were asked to give explanations of poverty and unemployment at the beginning and again at the end of their first year of study.

Results: There were no differences between student groups in the explanations offered at the beginning of the year. At the end of the year, social science students were more likely than the other groups to give explanations related to the sociopolitical system.

Conclusion: Background information can affect whether a dispositional or a situational attribution is made.

Jones and Davis identified three major factors which influence whether or not a dispositional attribution is made. One is the **principle of non-common effects**. For example, Anne has to choose between three resorts for her skiing holiday. All three resorts offer similarly priced holidays and all have a good snow record. Only one, however, is known for its lively après ski, i.e. a factor which the three resorts do not have in common. If this is the resort Anne chooses, we are likely to make a dispositional attribution about her choice of holiday, and conclude that she has decided to go to that particular resort because for her après ski is an important part of the holiday.

Personalism refers to the extent to which an action affects us personally. We are more likely to see behaviour as intentional, and to make a dispositional attribution, if the effects of an action have personal consequences for ourselves. For example, if a driver knocks down a close friend or relative of ours, we are more likely to condemn them as 'negligent' than if they had knocked down a stranger.

Finally, **hedonic relevance** relates to the extent to which we experience the effects of an action as pleasant or unpleasant. Actions are more likely to be judged as intentional, and dispositional attributions made, if the effects of the outcome are either pleasant or unpleasant rather than neutral. For example, a driver whose failure to apply his handbrake has no serious consequences is less likely to have a personal attribution made about his behaviour than a driver whose car runs into a school playground, injuring children.

- **Attribution theory** is about how we explain the causes of behaviour. Attributions can be **dispositional** or **situational**.
- **Correspondent inference theory** claims that we prefer to make dispositional attributions. We need to decide whether a behaviour is **intentional** before we can make sense of it, and we prefer to make **stable** attributions. 'Correspondent inference' refers to the process of matching a behaviour to a stable personal characteristic.

Covariation model

Kelley's model (1967; 1973) again focuses on whether we see the causes of someone's behaviour as internal (dispositional) or external (situational). He has suggested that we look for three kinds of information: consensus, distinctiveness and consistency.

To illustrate what Kelley meant by these terms, let us take the hypothetical situation of Jane getting a low mark for a Psychology assignment. **Consensus** refers to the extent to which other people behave in a similar way. If most of the other students in the class also get low marks, then consensus will be high. If Jane is the only one, then consensus is low.

Distinctiveness relates to whether Jane behaves in a similar way in comparable situations. If she gets low marks for assignments for her other subjects, then distinctiveness is low; there is nothing distinctive about Psychology. Distinctiveness is high if she gets high marks in her other subjects.

Consistency relates to how stable Jane's behaviour is over time. If she usually gets low marks for Psychology assignments, then consistency is high, but if this is unusual, then consistency is low.

Kelley suggested that it is the pattern produced by these three kinds of causal information which determines what kind of attribution we make.

Activity 7: making attributions

Read through these scenarios and decide for each how you might explain the behaviour described. Make a note in each case of whether your attributions are dispositional or situational, and whether each shows high or low consensus, distinctiveness and consistency:

Heather always buys organic potatoes. Her friends don't buy organic fruit and vegetables. Heather usually buys organic fruit and vegetables.

Marie goes to a local meeting to discuss the possibility of a bypass round her village. Many of her friends have gone to the meeting. Marie does not usually become involved in local issues.

When you have finished, see the notes on page 177.

Kelley believed that the combination of low consensus, low distinctiveness and high consistency

Kelley's covariation model

will lead to a dispositional attribution, and that any other combination will lead to a situational attribution. To return to the example of Jane's low mark for her Psychology essay: if other students have not got a low mark for their assignment (low consensus) and she usually gets low marks in other subjects (low distinctiveness) and she usually gets low marks for Psychology asignments (high consistency), then a dispositional attribution will be made – for example, that she is a lazy student. However, with a different pattern – if for example, everyone got a poor mark for this asignment (high consensus) and she usually gets good marks in other subjects (high distinctiveness) and she usually gets good marks for Psychology assignments (low consistency), then a situational attribution will be made – for example, that the assignment was marked too harshly.

There has been some support from research into Kelley's ideas. One example is shown in box M:

Box M: McArthur (1972)

Procedure: Participants were given a series of one-sentence descriptions of actions, opinions and feelings, e.g. Sue is afraid of the dog; George translates the sentence incorrectly; John laughs at the comedian. With each sentence, information was supplied showing high or low consensus, distinctiveness and consistency, similar to the information given in activity 7. Participants were asked to make causal attributions.

Results: Participants were likely to make dispositional attributions when there was low consensus, low distinctiveness and high consistency. Other combinations were likely to produce situational attributions.

Conclusion: Information on consensus, distinctiveness and consistency is important in determining causal attribution. The patterns that Kelley suggested allow us to predict whether a dispositional or a situational attribution will be made.

Activity 8: investigating Kelley's covariation theory

Try a replication of the McArthur study described in box M. You can use his descriptions and/or make up some of your own. You will need to look back to the definitions of consensus, distinctiveness and consistency in order to provide the additional information to go with each description. Make sure that you use a range of different combinations of high and low for each kind of information.

Your findings were probably similar to what Kelley suggested. However, there are a few problems with his theory. One problem is that people do not seem to use all three sources of information equally. Major (1980) found that participants tend to focus mostly on consistency, and much less so on distinctiveness and consensus, with consensus in particular having a very weak effect. For example, if Jane usually gets low marks for Psychology assignments, she is likely to be seen as a lazy student, no matter how well she does in other subjects or how many other students have done badly on this particular assignment. Other studies have shown similar findings. This could be another aspect to explore in activity 8.

People may also use other kinds of information when making attributions. Garland *et al.* (1975) found that people prefer to use information about personality and the context in which a behaviour is taking place, if such information is available.

A further problem is that the theory implies that a lot of mental effort is involved in using all the relevant information in making causal attributions. As we will see, people tend to make as little effort as possible in making sense of their social world – they act as 'cognitive misers' – and so use relatively little information to reach conclusions. It is also possible that in real situations, people do not act as logically as the theory suggests.

Causal schemata model

In response to some of these criticisms, and to try to explain attributions in situations where we do not have information about consensus, distinctiveness and consistency, Kelley (1972) developed another model.

In situations where we have little information he suggested that we use **causal schemata**, which he defined as 'general conceptions a person has about how certain kinds of causes interact to produce a specific kind of effect'.

One kind of schema is that of **multiple sufficient causes**. For example, there could be a whole range of reasons why someone might choose to go to an evening class in German. They could be planning to go to Germany on holiday, or some knowledge of German might be useful to them for their job, or they might go to the class to keep a friend company, or they may have just moved into the area and are hoping to make new friends. Any one of these causes would be sufficient to account for their behaviour.

A further schema, showing our tendency to situational rather than dispositional attribution, is the **discounting principle**. Sometimes we have reason to believe that one explanation is more likely than the others. We are then likely to accept this reason and discount the other possibilities. For example, an actress advertising a brand of shampoo could be doing so because she believes it is a really good product, or as a favour for a friend in the company which makes the shampoo, or because she is very well paid to do so. Any one of these causes is sufficient to account for what she is doing. If it seems to us that the last is the most likely, we assume that money explains her behaviour and discount the other possible reasons.

Similarly, when behaviour is 'in role', we are likely to make a situational rather than a personal attribution, and vice versa. For example, a doorman who holds a door open does so because it is his job; a passing stranger does so because he is considerate.

A second kind of schema is that of **multiple necessary causes**. Some behaviour can only be explained by a combination of causes. For example, to explain why someone won a marathon we would need to consider them to have been very fit, to have undergone a period of training, to have worn appropriate shoes, to have been highly motivated, and so on. One of these reasons alone would not be enough to explain their success.

- **Kelley's covariation theory** focuses on **consensus**, **distinctiveness** and **consistency**. The pattern of this information determines whether we make a dispositional or situational attribution.
- Sometimes people do not use all this information or choose to use other kinds of information.
- Kelley suggested we use **causal schemata** when we have insufficient information on consensus, distinctiveness and consistency.
- One type of causal schema is that of **multiple sufficient causes**, where several ways of explaining behaviour are possible. If one way seems much more likely than the rest, the **discounting principle** comes into play.
- A second type is **multiple necessary causes**, where several reasons are required to explain behaviour.

6.4 Attributional biases

It has already been suggested that people do not necessarily draw conclusions as logically and rationally as Kelley proposed. Because we take short cuts, such as focusing on some sources of information and ignoring others, perceptions and judgements of our own and other people's behaviour get distorted; errors and biases are liable to creep in.

The fundamental attribution error

Ross (1977) defined the fundamental attribution error (FAE) as 'the tendency to underestimate the importance of situational determinants and overestimate the degree to which actions and outcomes reflect the actors' dispositions'. In other words, we are more likely to make a dispositional attribution, even though a situational explanation may be equally possible. For example, we are more likely to believe that someone drops a cup because they are clumsy than because the cup was wet.

This again fits in with the idea that we behave as 'cognitive misers'. Individual behaviour is conspicuous, and so is simpler to focus on than the

The fundamental attribution error (FAE)

context of a situation. We don't feel the need to take possible situational influences into account unless there is no adequate personal explanation. The FAE has been demonstrated experimentally:

Box N: Ross *et al.* (1977)

Procedure: Participants were randomly allocated to be questioners or contestants in a general knowledge quiz. The questioners made up their own questions, and additional participants watched the quiz. Afterwards questioners, contestants and observers were asked to rate the general knowledge of questioners and contestants.
Results: Both observers and contestants (but not questioners) assessed the questioners as being more knowledgeable.
Conclusion: The observers and contestants overestimated dispositional factors in making their ratings. They ignored the situational factor of questioners being able to draw on their particular areas of expertise in setting the questions.

Similarly, Bierbrauer (1979) found that participants watching a film of Milgram's experiments on obedience (these are described in chapter 5 in the section on obedience) were more likely to use dispositional attributions to explain the behaviour of the 'teachers' (e.g. 'they were cruel') than situational attributions (e.g. 'they were intimidated by the experimenter'). There is some evidence, then, to support the idea of the FAE.

It has also been found that once a dispositional attribution has been made, it is quite difficult to change:

Box O: Ross *et al.* (1974)

Procedure: Female students were told they had done either well or badly on a problem-solving task. They were then told that the scores they had been given were false, and the feedback they had been given on their performance was not necessarily true. They were then asked to rate their ability at the task, to estimate how well they had done, and to say how well they thought they might do if they were to carry out the task again.
Results: Those who were initially told they had done well gave themselves higher ratings and made more positive estimates than those who had been told they had done badly.
Conclusion: Participants made dispositional attributions (i.e. in terms of their ability) on the basis of the initial feedback they received. Even though they knew the feedback had been false, the attributions they had made affected their self-ratings.

Activity 9: does the FAE always occur?

Look back through the last section on causal schemata. Can you find an example when the FAE was less likely to occur?
When you have finished, see the notes on page 177.

Fiske and Taylor (1991) have suggested that the idea of the FAE is something of an over-simplification. They also suggested that the FAE should not be thought of as an error, but rather as a bias. That term may be more appropriate, since this kind of judgement represents a distortion rather than something which is necessarily wrong.

It is also possible that the FAE may be related to culture. Miller (1984) found that Indian children were more likely to make situational attributions than North American children, though this study has been criticised on methodological grounds.

The actor–observer effect

Activity 10: explaining choices

Write down brief reasons why you have chosen to study Psychology.
Write down also brief reasons why a friend has chosen one of his or her subjects.
When you have finished, see the notes on page 177.

There is a tendency to see our own behaviour as a response to a particular situation, and so quite variable in different situations. At the same time, we tend to explain the behaviour of others in terms of personal characteristics and intentions. This pattern is known as the actor–observer effect (AOE).

How might this be explained? The actor has more direct information about the event and his own previous behaviour than the observer. An observer may be at some distance from the event, so might not be aware of a situational cause. In addition, the focus of attention is different for actor and observer. The actor focuses outwards on the situation, while the observer focuses on the actor. A study by Storms (1973) illustrates the relevance of this point:

Box P: Storms (1973)

Procedure: Two participants took part in a short conversation. Questionnaires were used to assess participants' attributions about their behaviour in the conversation. In one condition, participants saw a video of the conversation they had taken part in before completing the questionnaire.
Results: Participants who had seen themselves on video made more dispositional attributions than those who had not.

Conclusion: When actors become observers, they are more likely to make dispositional attributions. This confirms the attentional explanation of the AOE.

Self-serving bias

Activity 11: reasons for success and failure

Think back to an exam or test in which you did well, and one in which you did badly. Why did you do well in one and not so well in the other?
When you have finished, see the notes on page 177.

According to the self-serving bias, we tend to make dispositional attributions to account for our success. This tendency has been called the **self-enhancing bias**. We tend to make situational attributions to explain our failure. This is known as the **self-protecting bias**. This kind of effect is perhaps best explained in terms of **self-esteem**. Self-esteem is increased if we take credit for good performance, and is protected if we do not take responsibility when things go wrong.

These kinds of effect were shown by Johnson *et al.* (1964). They found that teachers accounted for poor performance by their pupils as being the fault of the pupils, while they saw themselves as responsible when pupils' performance improved.

This kind of bias can also work at the group level. For example, if you are a member of a successful football team you are likely to see success as the result of skill, hard training and so on, while failure could be seen to be due to unexpected injury or a biased referee.

Abramson *et al.* (1978) found that depressed people are an exception to this bias. They tend to explain success in terms of external factors such as luck and chance, and failure in terms of their own shortcomings. There is also some evidence that women are more likely to show this reversed pattern than men.

An offshoot of the self-serving bias is what Berglas and Jones (1978) have called **self-handicapping**.

Imagine that you are waiting with your friends to go into an exam room. You are rather worried about the exam, and think it quite likely that you will not do very well.

In this kind of situation, people often provide reasons to account for possible failure before it happens. If they then do badly, creditable reasons which do not damage their self-esteem are already in place.

As an example of self-handicapping, Berglas and Jones (1978) have suggested that alcoholics may drink too much in order to provide themselves with an external attribution for failure; poor performance can be put down to alcohol, rather than to any lack of ability.

- The attribution process shows **errors** and **biases**. The **FAE** refers to our tendency to prefer dispositional attributions to situational ones. Once made, this error is difficult to reverse. The FAE is not always made. It may be culture-specific.
- The **AOE** refers to the tendency of people to explain their own behaviour using situational attributions, and the behaviour of others using dispositional attributions.
- Explanations for our own success or failure often show the **self-serving bias**. We are likely to make dispositional attributions for success and situational attributions for failure. This bias helps to maintain **self-esteem**.
- We are engaged in **self-handicapping** when we provide acceptable reasons in advance of possible failure.

Notes on activities

2 You might here have thought of the prototypical rugby player as, for example, gregarious, outgoing and perhaps a little insensitive; a politician as untrustworthy; and a mother as warm, kind and caring.

3 You have probably raised the question of its ecological validity. Asch's participants were not responding to a real person in a real situation.

7 You probably concluded that Heather buys organic potatoes because she believes that organic produce is a healthy option, or because she is worried about possible chemical contamination in non-organic produce. This is a dispositional attribution, and Heather's behaviour shows low consensus, low distinctiveness and high consistency. Marie is likely to have gone to the meeting because the issue of the bypass is a particular concern for her. This is a situational attribution, and Marie's behaviour shows high consensus, high distinctiveness and low consistency.

9 The example of the celebrity advertising shampoo is one case where a situational attribution (getting paid) is likely to be preferred over an equally plausible dispositional attribution (the celebrity thinks the shampoo is an excellent product). The example of a doorman holding open the door is another.

10 When Nisbett *et al.* (1973) asked students to carry out this task, they found that the students tended to make dispositional attributions when asked to give reasons for a friend's choices (e.g. in terms of personality), while using situational attributions to account for their own (e.g. in terms of what the course had to offer). A similar pattern of attributions was made in giving reasons for their own and a friend's choice of girlfriend or boyfriend.

11 You are likely to have made dispositional attributions for your success; for example, you worked hard or were good at that particular subject. You are also likely to have made situational attributions to explain your failure; perhaps the subject wasn't interesting, or the teaching was poor.

07

Social psychology of sport

7.1 Social facilitation

People may perform better at a task when there are other people present. This phenomenon is known as **social facilitation**. Conversely, people may show **social inhibition**, and perform less well when there is an audience. Research in this area has looked at **audience effects** (the effects of the mere presence of others who are not taking any part in the task a person is carrying out), and **coaction effects** (the effects on task performance when other people present are independently carrying out the same task) and **competition effects**.

Studies of social facilitation have a long history in psychology, starting with an observation by Triplett (1898) that cyclists rode faster when racing with others than when racing alone. He tested this experimentally by asking children to wind fishing reels, either on their own or in pairs, and found that they completed the task faster in pairs. Triplett suggested that the physical stimulation of the presence of other people might be the reason for this effect. An example of an early study of audience effects is shown in box A:

Box A: Travis (1925)

Procedure: Twenty people were trained to carry out a hand–eye coordination task until their performance reached a set standard. This involved tracking a light as it moved around a circular track. They then carried out 10 trials of the task in front of an audience. This performance was compared with their performance on the best 10 trials carried out alone.
Results: Eighteen participants performed better with an audience. Sixteen of them achieved their best score under these conditions.
Conclusion: Carrying out a task in front of an audience can facilitate performance.

Other studies into the effect of mere presence, however, produced rather conflicting results. Pessin (1933), for example, found that participants needed fewer trials to learn a list of nonsense syllables (e.g.

VOK, LUB or ZIF) when they were alone than when they were in front of an audience. However, when they were later asked to recall the syllables, their performance was better with an audience than alone. Similarly Schmitt *et al.* (1986) found that the presence of someone else improved performance when participants were asked to type their name into a computer, but inhibited performance when they were asked to type their name in backwards, inserting ascending numbers between each letter.

Zajonc's drive theory of social facilitation

Zajonc (1965) explained these results in terms of task difficulty. He suggested that the physical presence of an audience creates **arousal**. He saw arousal as an innate response, which is adaptive in that it prepares a person to respond to any unexpected action carried out by someone else. The **Yerkes–Dodson law** (see figure 1) states that a certain amount of arousal leads to improved task performance, while too much arousal has a negative effect on performance. Furthermore, the more complex the task is, the lower the optimum level of arousal.

Figure 1: The Yerkes–Dodson law

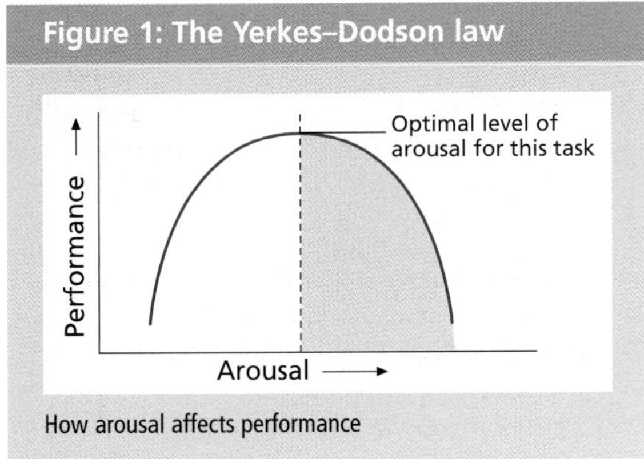

How arousal affects performance

According to Zajonc, arousal makes it more likely that what he called a **dominant response** would be produced. A dominant response is the most likely response to be given in a stimulus situation. In simple tasks, where an appropriate response is well learned, such as the performance of the cyclists observed by Triplett, the correct response is dominant, so performance is facilitated. In more complex tasks, where the appropriate response is not well learned, such as reasoning or learning tasks, wrong answers are more likely to be dominant, and therefore the presence of an audience inhibits performance.

In complex tasks the presence of an audience may inhibit performance

Figure 2: Zajonc's drive theory

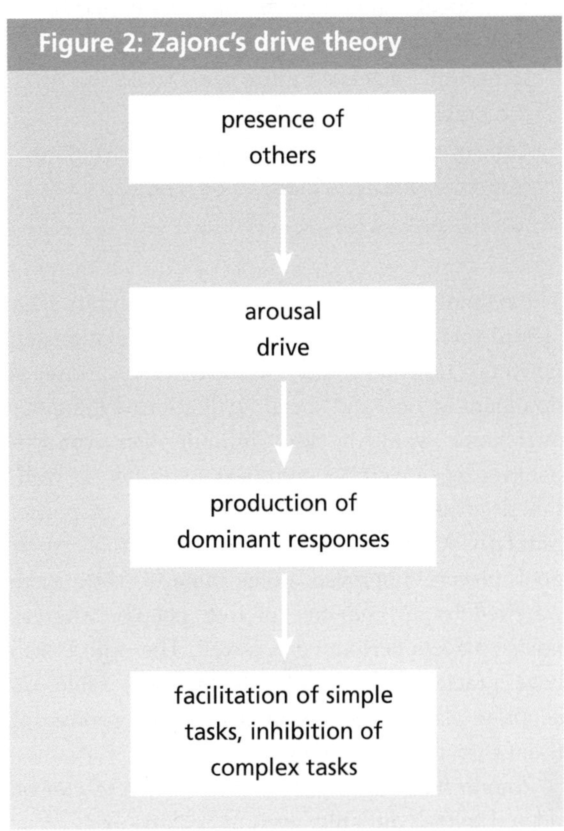

The idea of dominant responses and their relationship to the presence of others has been supported experimentally:

Box B: Zajonc and Sales (1966)

Procedure: Participants were presented with a series of verbal stimuli, supposedly Turkish words, but actually nonsense words. They saw some of these words several times, so that they would become dominant over the words presented less often. Participants were then shown these words using a tachistoscope, a piece of apparatus which allows visual stimuli to be shown for very brief periods of time so that the viewer cannot be confident of recognition. They were asked to identify the word they had been shown, either with or without an audience. On some trials they were in fact shown only a blank screen.
Results: On the 'blank screen' trials, participants tended to 'identify' the words they had seen most often (the dominant response). They were more likely to do this in the presence of an audience.
Conclusion: In conditions of arousal, dominant responses are more likely to be made.

The name-typing study carried out by Schmitt *et al.* (1986) mentioned earlier supports the relationship between task difficulty, whether a response is dominant or not, and social facilitation. Typing our own name would be less difficult than typing it backwards, inserting numbers, and as a well-practised skill would be the dominant response. Similarly, Michaels *et al.* (1982) found that expert pool players improved their game if they were watched by an audience of four people, whereas novice players performed less well. The experts will have practised their skills at the pool table, so accurate play will be a more dominant response for them than for the novices.

Zajonc has shown that audience effects can be related to task difficulty even in cockroaches:

Box C: Zajonc *et al.* (1969)

Procedure: Cockroaches were put in a maze with a bright light at the start to get them to run away from it. On some trials, the maze was straight, while on others it was made more complex by the addition of a right-hand turn. On some trials, the mazes were run in pairs, and on some they were run alone. On some they were run with no audience, and on some with an audience of four other cockroaches in plexiglas boxes.
Results: Cockroaches ran faster on the easy maze in pairs or with an audience. They were faster on the more complex maze alone and without an audience.
Conclusion: The effect on task performance of coactors or an audience depends on the complexity of a task.

Activity 1: mere presence and task complexity

Test the relationship between task complexity and social facilitation or inhibition for yourself.

simple task: Prepare a set of 24 small plain cards. On each card stick a small circle or square of coloured paper; these should be of four colours, with each colour being used on six cards. The task will be to sort the shuffled cards into four piles by the colour of the shapes.

complex task: Prepare another set of 24 cards. On each one write a fairly common word. The task is to sort the cards into alphabetical order. The task should not be too simple. For example, all the words could begin with 'c', some should have the same first two letters (e.g. chalk; cheese), and some should have the same first three letters (e.g. chief, child, chimney).

You should ask all your participants to carry out both tasks. Some should carry out the simple task with others present and the complex task alone, while others should carry out the simple task alone and the complex task with others present.

You will need to note how long it takes each participant to carry out each task. Complete the following table to compare the mean performance of people who carried out the simple task with and without an audience, and the performance of both groups on the complex task.

average time taken to carry out the task

simple task		*complex task*	
audience	*alone*	*audience*	*alone*

Were your results in line with Zajonc's ideas?

However, Zajonc's explanation of the conflicting findings of research into social facilitation has been extended by other theorists. A study by Dashiell (1935) found that there is a coaction effect even when people are simply *told* that other people are carrying out the same task in another room. Other people do not have to be physically present to create arousal, since the belief that others are carrying out the same task is sufficient to produce a coaction effect.

- **Social facilitation** refers to improved task performance in the presence of others (**audience effects**) or when there are others present who are independently carrying out the same task (**coaction effects**). **Social inhibition** refers to impaired performance in these circumstances.
- Whether facilitation or inhibition takes place is related to **task difficulty**.
- **Zajonc** proposed that social facilitation and inhibition were related to **arousal** in the presence of an audience, and **task difficulty**. Arousal facilitates the **dominant response**. In an easy or well-learned task, this response is likely to be correct, but not in a difficult task, and so results in social inhibition.

Alternative theories

Another explanation for social facilitation effects on task performance has been proposed by Baron (1986). This is known as the **distraction–conflict model**. Baron suggests that the physical presence of other people is distracting – for example, because of noises or gestures, or because the person asked to carry out the task may think about others approving or disapproving of his performance.

The physical presence of others is distracting

This leads to **response conflict**, i.e. conflict between attending to the task in hand and attending to the audience. This in turn leads to an overall negative effect on task performance, whether or not the task is simple or difficult. However, response conflict also increases arousal and motivation to do well at the task, and so makes us work harder to overcome the distraction. As in Zajonc's theory, increased arousal makes a dominant response more likely, so on simple tasks, this will facilitate task performance, but performance of more difficult tasks will suffer, since the positive effects of increased motivation cannot compensate for the negative effects of distraction.

It has also been suggested that social facilitation effects are due simply to increased competitiveness.

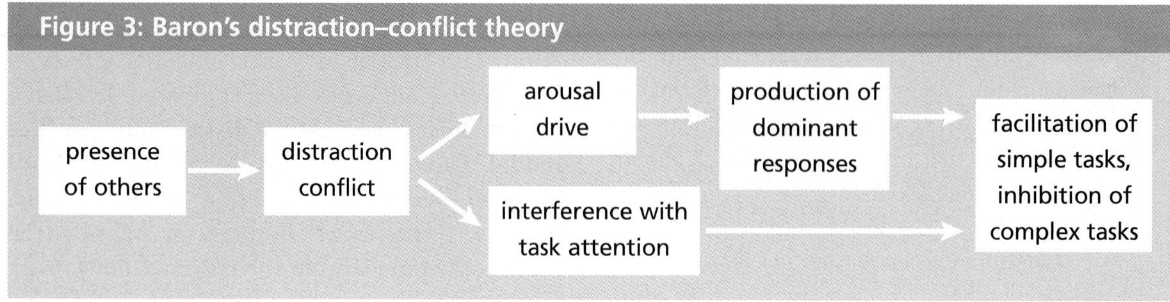

In coaction studies, for example, even though people are merely working alongside others at the same task, task performance could be facilitated by competition. The idea that coaction effects can be explained purely in terms of competitiveness, however, has been challenged in a study by Allport (1924). He asked participants to carry out a variety of tasks – crossing out the vowels in a newspaper article, multiplication, and identifying logical flaws in arguments – in which they were instructed not to compete. Since there was still a coaction effect, Allport argued that competition is not a necessary element. However, even if people are instructed not to compete, this doesn't mean that they will necessarily follow these instructions.

Cottrell (1968) also included a cognitive element in his theory of social facilitation. He accepted the link with arousal which Zajonc suggested, but believed this response in the presence of others was learned rather than innate. He suggested that we are aroused in the presence of others because we have learned to associate their presence with evaluation of our performance on a task. Since this evaluation can be negative as well as positive, an audience creates **evaluation apprehension**, i.e. concern that others will judge us. This idea was supported by Cottrell *et al.* (1968), who repeated the 'Turkish word' study (box B), but with the audience blindfolded, so that they were in no position to judge the participant's performance. The effect of the presence of other people on task performance disappeared.

An audience creates concern that others will judge us

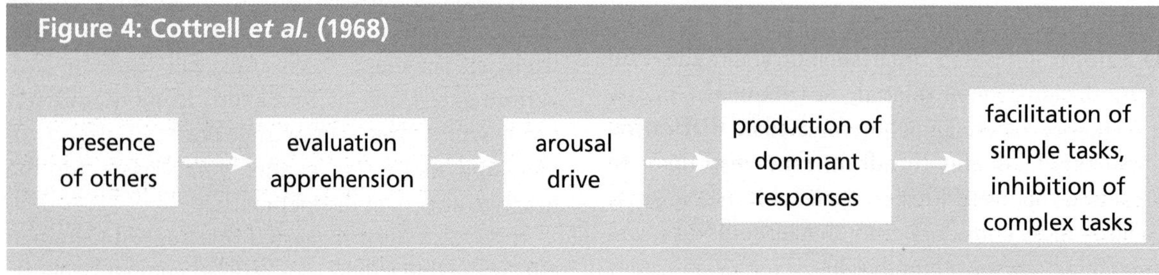

There is other research supporting Cottrell's ideas:

Box D: Henchy and Glass (1968)

Procedure: Participants' performance on tasks was assessed in one of four conditions. The task was carried out:

- **a** alone
- **b** in the presence of two others, introduced as experts
- **c** in the presence of two non-experts
- **d** alone but filmed for later evaluation by experts.

Results: Easy tasks were facilitated in conditions **b** and **d**, but not in conditions **a** and **c**. Performance in conditions **a** and **c** was similar.

Conclusion: For the presence of others to facilitate task performance, there must be some concern about being evaluated.

Self-presentation theory, put forward by Bond (1982), explains the effects of an audience in terms of how we present ourselves to other people. This theory suggests that social facilitation effects come about because we want to make a good impression on other people. If we are asked to carry out a simple task, we can concentrate on the task, knowing that we are doing it well. With difficult tasks, however, we need to concentrate on the task, while at the same time we are aware that any errors or inappropriate strategies will be obvious to people watching us. This can lead to embarrassment or anxiety, which in turn may make it more difficult to concentrate on the task.

However, there are some problems with explanations which include a cognitive element. As we saw earlier (Zajonc, box C), there is an audience effect when cockroaches are tested. The same is true of ants. Chen (1937) found that ants excavated three times as much soil if they were in the presence of other ants. It is not likely that cockroaches and ants are concerned with the impression they are making on other cockroaches and ants, and experience evaluation apprehension, so it seems that a cognitive level of explanation is not always necessary. This lends support to theories which do not involve cognition.

It has also been shown that with human participants, evaluation apprehension is not necessary for there to be a social facilitation effect. Schmitt *et al.* (1986) asked students to carry out a complex task in the presence of someone wearing a blindfold and headphones, and who therefore could not evaluate a participant's performance. In contrast to the Cottrell *et al.* findingsin the 'Turkish words' study, performance was nonetheless inhibited.

Activity 2: which theory?

Read through these explanations for social facilitation, and decide which of these theories each relates to. *Note:* each statement can refer to more than one theory.

1. Zajonc (drive theory)
2. Baron (distraction–conflict model)
3. Cottrell (evaluation apprehension)
4. Bond (self-presentation theory)

- **a** Social facilitation is related to arousal.
- **b** We are affected by the judgements we think other people may make of us.
- **c** The distraction caused by the presence of others has an overall negative effect on performance.
- **d** The presence of others creates anxiety which impedes performance of a difficult task.
- **e** Increased arousal makes a dominant response more likely.
- **f** Our judgements as to how well we are able to carry out a task are an important factor in explaining social facilitation and inhibition.

When you have finished, see the notes on page 192.

It is worth noting that these theories are not necessarily contradictory. They are in agreement that the presence of other people leads to arousal; the area of disagreement here is why this should be so. It is possible that all the factors which different theories consider to be important could affect task performance, depending on the nature of the task and the circumstances in which it is carried out.

- The **distraction–conflict model** suggests that the presence of others distracts us, but the arousal it creates also increases motivation. On simple (but not difficult) tasks, increased **motivation** compensates for distraction in making a correct **dominant response** more likely.
- Cottrell includes a **cognitive** element, in which arousal is linked to **evaluation apprehension**.
- **Self-presentation theory** relates audience effects to a desire to make a good **impression** on others.
- There are **problems with cognitive theories**, since cockroaches and ants also demonstrate audience effects. However, all these theories may have something to offer.

7.2 Home ground advantage

Psychological research has had practical applications in many areas, of which sport psychology is a major example. However, in the area of social facilitation, Landers *et al.* (1978) have noted that although some laboratory studies have supported Zajonc's ideas, these findings have not been generalised to sport settings, so their practical value is limited. Indeed, some research in this area has contradicted the idea that the presence of an audience facilitates performance of a well-practised task. For example, Paulus and Cornelius (1974) found that gymnasts tended to perform less well in the presence of an audience.

An audience facilitates performance of a well-practised sport

It is also the case that Zajonc talks about 'mere presence' as bringing about social facilitation or inhibition, and the audience at sports events is typically much less passive than this term implies. Although the presence of an audience is likely to affect sports performance, the situation is not strictly comparable with the kinds of conditions explored in the laboratory.

However, one practical issue involving audiences and sport performance which has been studied is the home advantage, when sport performance is better at home than away. The existence of a home advantage has been established for a wide range of sports. One of the most extensive pieces of research is described in box E:

Box E: Schwartz and Barsky (1977)

Procedure: Statistical information was gathered on 1880 major league baseball games, 1092 professional and collegiate football games, 542 National Hockey League games and 1485 college basketball games. The percentage of games won at home and away was calculated.

Results: The home team won 53% of the time in baseball, 60% in football, and 64% in basketball and ice hockey.

Conclusion: In all the sports studied, there was a clear home advantage. Indoor sports benefited slightly more from this advantage than outdoor sports.

Similarly, Snyder and Purley (1985) found that the home team in the Mid-American Conference won 66% of the basketball games played during the 1982–83 season.

Schwartz and Barsky looked only at team sports. There has been comparatively little research in this area in individal sports, but there is some evidence that the home advantage also applies:

Box F: McAndrew (1993)

Procedure: The performance of 4172 high school wrestlers in dual meets, i.e. matches between two teams, was analysed.
Results: Wrestlers competing at home won significantly more of their matches, compared with visitors.
Conclusion: The home advantage also operates at an individual level.

Gayton and Langevin (1992) also investigated wrestling, with similar results. A significant home advantage was found, with 61% of home matches being won.

Leonard (1989) analysed performance in the Olympics, including both individual and team events, and found that the host country won a greater number of bronze, silver and gold medals than in the previous or following Olympics.

The extent of the home advantage varies with the level at which the sport is played. For example, McCutcheon (1984) found that the home advantage was stronger for professional and college sports teams than for high school teams.

How does performance differ at home and away?

As part of their study described in box E, Schwartz and Barsky (1977) analysed the nature of play at home and away games to try to establish differences which might account for the home advantage. They found that there was more offensive play (e.g. hits, goals and shots) at home matches, but defensive play (e.g. errors, saves and fouls) did not differ between home and away games. A greater amount of offensive play is therefore associated with improved home performance.

This idea was extended in a detailed analysis of the performance of basketball players at home and away:

Box G: Varca (1980)

Procedure: Differences in play by basketball teams at home and away were analysed.

Results: There were no differences between home and away teams in terms of field goal percentages, free-throw percentages or turnovers. However, home teams showed more what Varca termed 'functionally aggressive behaviour', including the skills of rebounding, steals and blocked shots. Visiting teams showed more what he called 'dysfunctional aggressive behaviour', committing more fouls than home teams.
Conclusion: Differences in the frequency of different kinds of play are associated with the home team advantage in basketball.

Cox (1994) points out that the use of the word 'aggressive' here is perhaps somewhat misleading, since the functional aggressive behaviours Varca describes are not aggressive in the sense that they are intended to harm. He suggests that 'assertive' might be a better way of describing the kinds of play which are likely to lead to success. However, he goes on to say that personal fouls are an excellent example of dysfunctional aggressive behaviour.

What factors influence the performance of home players?

Activity 3: explaining the home advantage

Before you read this section, think about possible ways of explaining the improved performance which leads to home advantage. Which factors might be important in enhancing the performance of the team or individual at home? Are there also reasons why visiting players might perform *less* well?
Compare your ideas with the discussion which follows.

Varca interpreted his findings in terms of the increased **arousal** of the home team brought about by a supportive audience. As we saw in figure 1, arousal (up to a certain point) improves performance, and so would enhance the performance of the home team in the productive kinds of play Varca describes as 'functionally aggressive behaviour'.

The presence of the crowd also increases the arousal level of visiting teams. However, in this case arousal led to more unproductive kinds of play, in the form of personal fouls. Varca explained this in terms of the **frustration–aggression hypothesis**, proposed by Dollard *et al.* (1939). This hypothesis states that frustration always leads to aggression, and aggression is always caused by frustration. In the case of team sports, the unsupportive behaviour of the crowd towards visiting teams (such as whistling at players who commit personal fouls) would increase frustration and so lead to dysfunctional aggressive play. However, this may be better explained by the **frustration–anger hypothesis** proposed by Berkowitz (1969). Whistling at visiting players would not frustrate them in the sense of preventing them achieving their goals, but might well anger them, and this anger could lead to aggression.

The unsupportive behaviour of the crowd towards visiting teams leads to dysfunctional aggressive play

Further support for the idea that the home advantage is the result of functionally aggressive behaviour of the home team, and dysfunctional aggression of the visiting team, comes from a study of ice hockey:

Box H: McGuire *et al.* (1992)

Procedure: Data were collected from a season of ice hockey games (1987–88). Thirteen different kinds of aggressive behaviour were identified, and levels of aggression of home and visiting teams were compared.

Results: Home teams were more aggressive in games which they won, and visiting teams in games which they lost.

Conclusion: Levels of aggression are related to success in ice hockey matches. Aggression is productive for the home team, but not for the visiting team.

McGuire *et al.* went on to suggest that aggression from home players energises the home crowd, and the expression of support this leads to in turn energises home players.

It may not be just the fact of playing in front of a supportive home crowd which gives the home team an advantage. Mizruchi (1985), in a 10-year study of professional basketball, identified further factors. He found that the home advantage was stronger for teams with a strong tradition, and who played in a distinctive city centre arena. Simlarly, Agnew and Carron (1994) found that in ice hockey, crowd density was significantly related to home advantage.

These explanations of the home advantage focus on the positive effect of a supportive home crowd. This view appears to be widely accepted by sports writers and commentators. Certainly the presence of a crowd does have a part to play, as Courneya and Carron (1990) found that for softball teams the home advantage disappeared when there was no crowd present. However, it is also possible that the negative effects of travel to away matches could contribute to an away *dis*advantage as opposed to a home advantage. For example, visiting players may be unfamiliar with the venue and with local playing conditions. They may be more tired than those playing at home; in the Olympics, for example, most competitors will have travelled a long way, perhaps crossing time zones, and they may be jetlagged:

Box I: Pace and Carron (1992)

Procedure: Travel-related variables in visiting team performance in the National Hockey League were investigated. These included the number of time zones crossed, direction of travel, distance travelled, preparation/ adjustment time, time of season and the number of previous games played on the tour.
Results: Poor performance by visitors was related to the number of time zones crossed and increased preparation time. Success was more likely in later games in the tour. Success was not related to the other factors investigated.
Conclusion: There is only a small relationship between travel-related factors and the performance of visiting teams.

Visitors may be more tired than those playing at home

Other research looking at the possible influence of travel factors has had similar results. For example, Courneya and Carron (1991) also found very little relationship between travel factors and success or failure in baseball games.

Another suggestion has been that referees may make decisions which are biased towards the home team. Harville and Smith (1994) investigated the effect of crowd behaviour on referee decisions, and found that referees tended to make decisions biased towards the home team when they were being harassed by the crowd. This idea has also been supported by a study into tennis and golf carried out by Nevill *et al.* (1997). They found very little evidence of any home advantage in international grand-slam tennis and major golf tournaments. They suggested that this may be the result of the scoring systems in tennis and golf being relatively objective, unlike the subjective decisions made by referees in team games such as soccer.

Finally, in some circumstances there may be a home *disadvantage*:

Box J: Baumeister (1984)

Procedure: Data from World Series baseball games and professional basketball games were studied, and in particular the outcomes of the final decisive games played in a series.
Results: Home teams tended to do less well in these final games than earlier in the series.
Conclusion: In some circumstances, playing in front of a home crowd can be a disadvantage. It may be that the opportunity to win a championship in front of a home crowd increases self-consciousness and so disrupts skilled performance.

Activity 4: the generalisability of home advantage

You have probably noticed that most of the research discussed in this section is American, and investigated sports such as baseball which are more widely popular in the USA than elsewhere. Use the Internet to find sport statistics relating to other sports, such as Premier league football and cricket, to see whether the findings in this area can be generalised more widely.

There is evidence of a home advantage in many **team sports**, and for some **individual sports**. The advantage is stronger at higher levels.

- Teams at home show more **functional aggressive** play, while visiting teams show more **dysfunctional aggressive** play.
- The home advantage has been explained in terms of **arousal** when playing before a home crowd, but other factors such as **crowd density** may also be important.
- It has also been suggested that the difference in performance at home and away could in part be due to **away disadvantage**, though the effects of such factors as **travel** are small. A home advantage has not been found to be as strong in sports with a relatively objective scoring system, suggesting the influence of bias in **refereeing decisions**.

7.3 Team cohesion

What is team cohesion?

Carron (1982) defines cohesion as 'a dynamic process which is reflected in the tendency for a group to stick together and remain united in the pursuit of its goals and objectives'. This is an appropriate definition for sport teams, although perhaps something of a general statement. To provide a clearer framework for research in this area, Carron has developed a model which differentiates between **task cohesion**, i.e. commitment to team goals and performance objectives, and **social cohesion**, which covers friendship, affiliation and socioemotional support.

The model also identifies four kinds of factors which contribute to team cohesion: environmental, personal, leadership and team factors. **Environmental factors** refer to regulations within a sport and local rules, such as when local teams will hold practices. **Personal factors** are the characteristics of the team members. **Leadership factors** relate to such aspects as coaching behaviour. All these three kinds of factors contribute to **team factors**, the characteristics and relationships of the group, group norms and the stability of the group. In a study of female golfers, Widmeyer and Williams (1991) found that personal factors were the most important predictor of team cohesion, followed by team factors, leadership factors and environmental factors.

The model also differentiates between group and individual outcomes of cohesion. **Group outcomes** include the stability and the performance of the team, while **individual outcomes** include member satisfaction and individual performance. In practice, most research has focused on group outcomes, and specifically whether or not teams are successful but, more recently, individual outcomes have also been of interest to sport psychologists.

The framework Carron suggests is shown in figure 5.

Activity 5: applying Carron's conceptual system

Decide whether each of the following is an environmental (E), personal (P), leadership (L) or team (T) factor:

a We respect the ability of our coach.
b We are all keen for the team to improve its peformance.
c We have been together as a team for quite a long time.
d The facilities our team uses are excellent.
e I feel I have an important part to play within the team.
f Our captain has good organisational skills.
g We all get on really well together as a group.
h The timing of practices is arranged to fit in with team members' other commitments.

When you have finished, see the notes on page 192.

The measurement of team cohesion

In sport, it is widely assumed that a group of individuals working together will be more effective than the same individuals working independently, i.e. that cohesion will lead to improved performance. To achieve cohesion, it may be necessary for individual members to make personal sacrifices for the good of the team. Cox (1994) gives the example

Figure 5: Carron's conceptual system for cohesiveness in sport teams

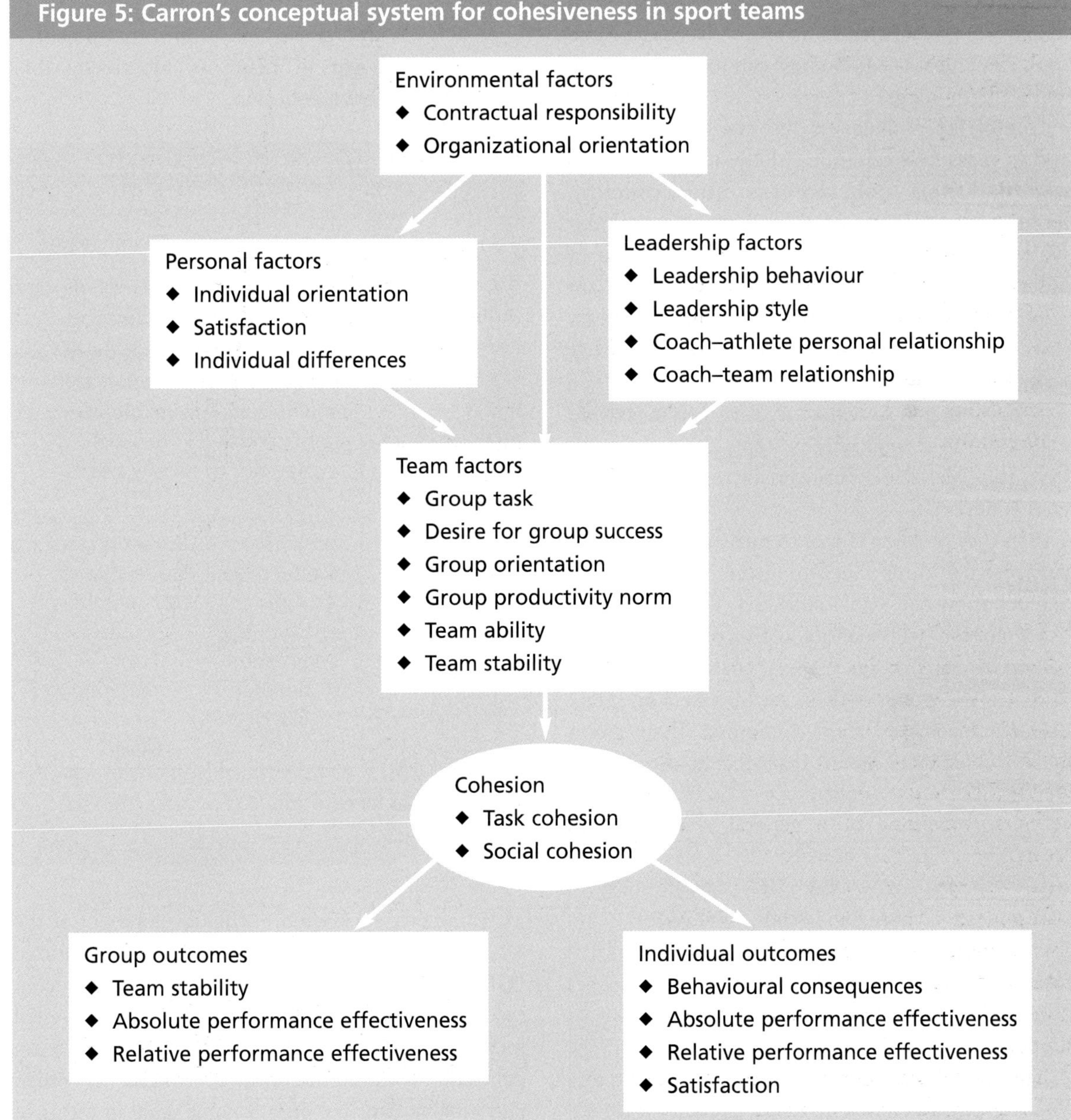

of a basketball team, where many players may be capable of making high scores, but in the interests of team success, the coach may require that some of them take a less high-profile, non-scoring role. Acceptance of this role is necessary if the team is to be successful. It also seems logical that teams will do better if its members like each other.

However, research evidence on the relationship between team cohesion and success has had mixed findings. Some studies have found a positive relationship between these two factors, e.g. Martens and Petersen (1971) for basketball teams, Arnold and Straub (1972) for baseball teams, Ball and Carron (1976) for ice hockey teams and Bird (1977) for volleyball teams.

However, other research has found no relationship between team cohesion and success, e.g. Melnick and Chemers (1974 for basketball).

Some research has even found a negative relationship, (e.g. Fiedler 1954 for basketball and Lenk 1969 for rowing). So how can we explain these conflicting findings?

One of the problems is the way in which early studies measured cohesion. Many of these studies used the **sport cohesiveness questionnaire**, developed by Martens *et al.* (1972). This includes two kinds of items. The first are direct ratings of closeness or attraction to the group. The second are ratings of interpersonal attraction and friendship. Most of the findings showing a positive relationship between team cohesion and success involved the first kind of items, while negative findings were related to the second kind of items. In some ways, then, this was not a very satisfactory measure of team cohesion.

A further problem is that in measuring cohesion, early research often failed to differentiate between task cohesion and social cohesion. Groups high in task cohesion will identify with group goals and experience satisfaction if these goals are attained. However, for groups high in social cohesion, social interaction may be more important than group goals, so it may mean that the team is less successful.

Social interaction may be more important than group goals

Because of the problems with this kind of approach, Widmeyer *et al.* (1985) developed a framework, shown in figure 6, identifying four dimensions of team cohesion:

Figure 6: the four dimensions of team cohesion (Widmeyer *et al.* 1985)

		Athlete's perception of team	
		group integration	*individual attraction*
Group orientation	*social*	bonding to the team as a whole to satisfy social needs (GI-S)	attraction to the team and team members to satisfy social needs (ATG-S)
	task	bonding to the team as a whole to satisfy task-completion needs (GI-T)	attraction to the team and team members to satisfy task-completion needs (ATG-T)

GI = group integration, ATG = attraction to the group.

This framework resulted in the development of the 18-item **group environment questionnaire (GEQ)**, which has been widely used in more recent research. This allows a more sensitive and detailed measurement of different features of team cohesion. It is in the form of statements which participants can rate on a 9-point scale in terms of agreement with each statement. A sample item is shown in figure 7:

Figure 7: sample GI-T item from the GEQ

Our team is united in trying to reach its goal for performance

1 2 3 4 5 6 7 8 9

strongly disagree strongly agree

Activity 6: identifying the four elements of team cohesion

Read through these statements, and decide whether each relates to

GI-S GI-T ATG-S ATG-T

a All the team members are very keen to improve our performance.
b I enjoy working with others towards a shared goal.
c I enjoy socialising with some of the other members of the team.
d I am keen to work with other team members to improve performance.
e All the team members enjoy spending time together.
f Many team members have become good friends through playing together.
g We are all determined to work together well as a team.
h Part of what makes it rewarding to be part of the team is spending time with the others in the clubroom after a practice.

When you have finished, see the notes on page 192.

Widmeyer and Williams (1991) found that all four dimensions of the GEQ are good indicators of different aspects of team cohesion. It therefore allows any specific area in which cohesion is weak to be identified and interventions to strengthen it to be put in place.

- Carron's model of team cohesion differentiates between **task cohesion** and **social cohesion**. It identifies four kinds of factors which contribute to team cohesion: **environmental**, **personal**, **leadership** and **team factors**. It also distinguishes between **group** and **individual outcomes**.
- Early research into team cohesion had conflicting findings as a result of **measurement problems**. The GEQ, which measures different aspects of cohesion, is now widely used.

Team cohesion and success

There is a lot of evidence that success is linked to team cohesion, and specifically task cohesion. Social cohesion does not seem to be so important. For example, in 1978 there were well-publicised personal problems between players in the New York Yankees baseball team. However, they worked together well as a team, and won the World Series in that year. Lenk (1969) gave a similar example relating to rowers.

A lot of the research evidence we have looked at is correlational, i.e. teams which are successful also tend to be cohesive. It is clear that a team must have high task cohesion in order to be successful. However, could it also be that being successful creates cohesion? There is some evidence that this is the case:

Box K: Slater and Sewell (1994)

Procedure: The cohesiveness of 60 participants, three male and three female teams of hockey players, was measured early in the season, midway through it, and at the end of the season. The aim was to establish whether early cohesion was associated with later success, and whether early success was associated with later cohesion.
Results: The stronger relationship was between early cohesion and later success, but there was also a relationship between early success and later cohesion.
Conclusion: The influence of success and cohesion is mutual; cohesion leads to success, but success also leads to cohesion.

Although task cohesion is essential for success, it does not follow that it will necessarily lead to success. There are many factors which influence success – ablity of the players, quality of coaching, and so on. So how does cohesion contribute to team success? Zander (1971) suggests that cohesion increases motivation and commitment to team goals. However, he goes on to point out that if there is too much emphasis on team goals to the exclusion of recognition and encouragement of individual contributions, performance may suffer.

The contribution team cohesion makes to success will also depend on group norms. Schachter *et al.* (1951) found that highly cohesive teams enjoy more success than those which are less cohesive, but only if achieving better performance is a group norm. For teams playing at a high level, this is likely to be the case. This can be the case even where the norms require individual sacrifice for the good of the team. However, for more informal recreational groups, enjoying taking part in sport may be equally as important as success, so there will be less emphasis on the task cohesion which contributes to success.

The size of the group is also influential, with Widmeyer *et al.* (1990) suggesting that team cohesion decreases as team or group size increases. Other studies support this idea:

Box L: Carron and Spink (1995)

Procedure: The relationship between group size and cohesion in exercise groups was investigated, using the GEQ. One-hundred and thiry-four members of small and large exercise classes were tested in the eighth week of group development, when the groups were well established.
Results: Participants in smaller groups considered that task and social cohesion were higher in their groups than those in larger groups.
Conclusion: The size of the group is related to members' perception of cohesion.

Team cohesion also appears to be more important in some sports than others. Most of the research reporting a positive relationship between team cohesion and success relate to **interactive sports**, where a high degree of interaction and cooperation between team members is necessary, e.g. basketball and volleyball. With **coactive sports**, where performance is relatively independent, such as bowling and archery, the link is far less strong.

The relationship between team cohesion and success is a dynamic one. For example, Brawley *et al.* (1993) found that the group properties of teams changed as a result of group development. There is still research to be done to establish how cohesion develops and changes, both over time and in different situations. For example, Ruder and Gill (1982) investigated the effects on team cohesion of winning and losing, and found that success increases cohesion, while failure decreases it. This kind of study could be extended to look at the effects of winning and losing over a longer time scale. Other factors which influence team cohesion also need more extensive research, such as the effect of changes in team composition due to injury, and different coaching styles.

- Social cohesion is less important for success than **task cohesion**. The importance of cohesion for success is related to **group norms**. It is more important in **interactive sports** than **coactive sports**. It is related to **group size**.
- There is a **two-way relationship** between cohesion and success. While a cohesive team is likely to be more successful than one which is not cohesive, success can also increase cohesion.
- Cohesion should not be emphasised at the expense of individual recognition.

Notes on activities

2 **a** 1; 2; 3; 4. **b** 2; 3; 4. **c** 2. **d** 3; 4. **e** 1; 2. **f** 3; 4.

5 **a** L; **b** T; **c** T; **d** E; **e** P; **f** L; **g** P; **h** E

6 **a** GI-T; **b** ATG-T; **c** ATG-S; **d** ATG-T; **e** GI-S; **f** ATG-S; **g** GI-T; **h** GI-S

08

Perception and attention

8.1 What is perception?

At first sight, perception does not seem problematical; we become aware of information which reaches the sense organs – eyes, ears, tongue and so on. It seems to be such a simple and automatic process that we take it for granted. However, we need to make a distinction between sensation and perception. Detecting sensory information through the sense organs is called **sensation**, while **perception** involves making sense of that information by interpreting and organising it. Roth (1986) defined perception as: 'the means by which information acquired from the environment via the sense organs is transformed into experiences of objects, events, sounds, tastes, etc.'.

To illustrate this distinction, try activity 1:

Activity 1: what do you see?

When you have finished, see the notes on page 227.

While perception relates to all the senses, we will be focusing in this chapter on visual perception. This is the dominant sense in human beings, and far more is known about it than about the other senses.

Sensation refers to information reaching the sense organs. **Perception** refers to interpreting and organising this information, and thus making sense of the external world.

8.2 Constancy

We recognise objects despite variation in retinal information. For instance, we may perceive a cup from the side or from the top, close to us or further away, in bright or dim light. All these factors lead to variation in the image which reaches the retina, but the cup is still recognised as the same object. The ability to do this is known as **constancy**.

Constancy is necessary if we are to cope effectively with the environment. If our perception of objects did not have this kind of stability, our perception of the environment would be extremely confused. Constancy shows how the brain uses memory, knowledge and expectation in interpreting environmental stimuli.

We see objects as having more or less constant brightness even though this changes with the level of illumination. This is **brightness constancy**. If illumination is constant, white things reflect more light than black things. For example, white paper reflects 90% of light falling on it, whereas black paper reflects only 10%. However, snow in deep shadow still looks white, for example, and coal in bright sunlight still looks black, even though the intensity of light reaching the retina is much stronger in the case of the coal than the snow. Perceived brightness depends on **relative luminance**, i.e. how much light an object reflects relative to its surroundings. Coal viewed in bright sunlight reflects less light than its surroundings and so still appears black. You can try this for yourself:

Activity 2: brightness constancy

You will need a piece of black paper on which a strong light is shone. Look at this through a narrow tube, so that you can only see the paper. You should find that the paper no longer looks black but greyish, since it will reflect quite a lot of light, and you cannot see its surroundings for comparison.

Shape constancy refers to the ability to perceive an object as remaining the same shape, as in the cup

Figure 1: shape constancy

example in figure 1, in spite of changes in the angle at which we see it. This is explained by the knowledge and expectations we have about the object at which we are looking. We have considerable experience of cups, and so are able to compensate when we view one from an unusual angle. Shape constancy is also helped when an object is seen in a place where it is expected to be. If this is not the case, we may have slightly more difficulty in compensating for distortion and recognising the object.

When we watch a person moving away from us, the image they form on the retina gets smaller. We don't perceive the person as actually getting smaller, though, but as someone of constant size getting further away. This is **size constancy**, and comes about because the perceptual system takes into account how far away the person is whom we are watching, using distance cues.

One distance cue is **linear perspective**. Lines appear to converge as they get further away, e.g. railway lines stretching into the distance, which influences the perceived distance of an object. Relative brightness and colour cues also give us information about distance. Objects closer to us reflect more light to the eyes, and so appear brighter, and the colour of objects close to us is perceived as more intense.

Figure 2: depth cues

linear perspective

colour intensity

Activity 3: size constancy

Look at the picture of these two men and note their relative size:

Now turn to the picture on the next page.

In the first picture, the bareheaded man is perceived as being the same size as the man in the hat although his image on the retina is smaller. The smaller picture of the man from the next page is probably much smaller than you would have expected. To maintain size constancy, the brain adjusts the image of objects which are further away; this is called **constancy scaling.** The picture of the two men on the next page shows the degree of adjustment the perceptual system is able to make.

A study using operant conditioning (see chapter 1) suggests that size constancy may be innate:

Box A: Bower (1966)

Procedure: Two-month-old babies were conditioned to turn their heads in response to a 30 cm cube at a distance of 1 metre. The reinforcement used was an adult popping up in front of the baby in a game of peek-a-boo. The apparatus used is shown in figure 3. Babies were then tested on the original presentation and three different ones:

(a) 30 cm cube at 3 metres
(b) 90 cm cube at 1 metre
(c) 90 cm cube at 3 metres

The number of conditioned responses in each condition was noted.

Results: The original presentation produced a total of 98 conditioned responses, condition (a) produced 58 responses, (b) produced 54 and (c) 22.

Conclusion: The babies showed some degree of size constancy.

Figure 3: Bower's apparatus

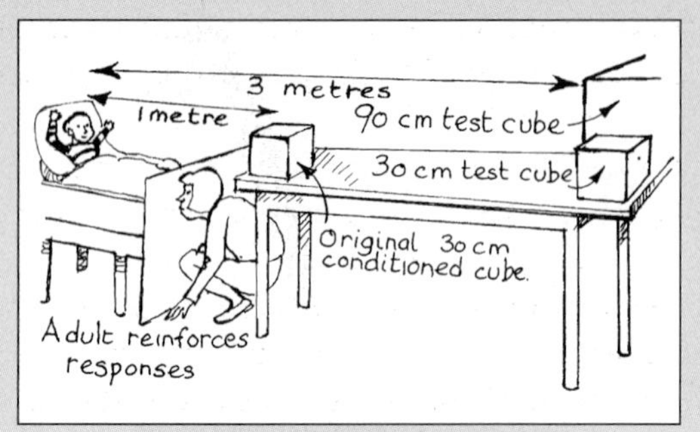

Activity 4: evaluating Bower's study

1 Which condition – (a), (b) or (c) – produced the same retinal image as the original presentation?
2 In which condition would a conditioned response show size constancy?
3 Which comparison is the critical one for testing size constancy?
4 On the basis of these comparisons, do you think that size constancy is innate or learned?

When you have finished, see the notes on page 227.

Shape constancy may also be innate. Bower (1966) conditioned two-month-old infants to respond to a rectangle, and found that they still showed a CR when the rectangle was turned slightly to produce a trapezoidal retinal image.

We also have colour constancy, the tendency for an object to be perceived to be the same colour when viewed in different light conditions. We seem to be able to compensate for darkness, or even for coloured light shining on an object, and still make fairly accurate judgements about its colour. For example, colours still appear to be much the same when you are wearing green-tinted sunglasses.

The colour we perceive is influenced by the colour of the **surroundings**, and our **knowledge** of an object's colour; we often know what colour particular objects are likely to be. Land (1964) carried out a study which provides a good demonstration of colour constancy:

Box B: Land (1964)

Procedure: This study used a large display of around 100 pieces of matt coloured paper, which Land called a 'colour Mondrian', from the painter whose work consisted of large blocks of colour. Participants were asked to identify the colours of squares of different coloured papers, e.g. white and red. The amounts of red, green and blue light coming from each were measured. Using red, green and blue filters, the illumination of the red square was then adjusted so that the same amount of red, green and blue light came from the red paper as from the previously-tested white paper. Participants were again asked to identify the colour of the paper.
Results: Participants continued to report the red paper as 'red'.
Conclusion: The participants showed colour constancy.

Land's research showed that the colour of the surroundings is an important cue. If coloured light is shining on to an area, the colour of an object in that area will be perceived fairly accurately, i.e. colour constancy will be shown.

If, however, the coloured light is restricted to just that object, colour constancy breaks down.

- **Brightness constancy** compensates for the degree of illumination with which objects are seen.
- We recognise objects in spite of changes in the angle from which they are seen. The adjustment which makes this possible is **shape constancy**.
- We also have **size constancy**, compensating for changes in the size of the retinal image, achieved through the use of distance cues.
- **Colour constancy** is the tendency to see an object as being the same colour under different lighting conditions.

8.3 Visual illusions

We experience an illusion when what we perceive does not correspond to the physical characteristics of what we are looking at.

Gregory (1983) divides visual illusions into four categories: distortions, ambiguous figures, paradoxical figures and fictions.

Distortions are geometrical illusions, when we mistakenly perceive a stimulus with which we are presented. Some examples are shown in figure 4:

Figure 4: distortions (geometrical illusions)

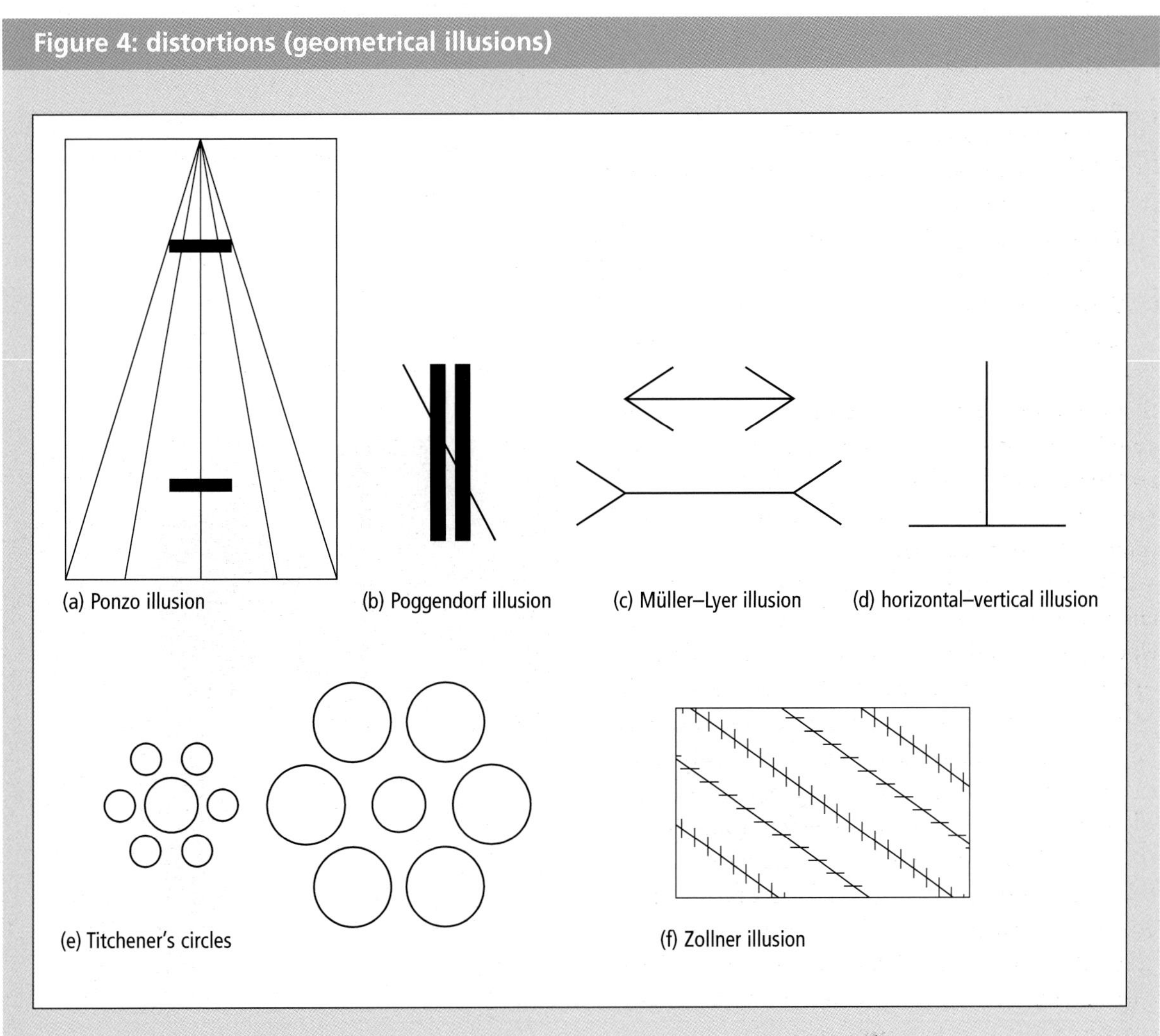

Activity 5: exploring distortions

Look at the illusions in figure 4, then answer these questions:

a Which of the two horizontal lines appears longer?

b Does the diagonal line seem continuous or discontinuous?

c Which of the two horizontal lines appears longer?

d Which of the two lines appears longer?

e Which of the central circles seems larger?

f Do the long diagonal lines appear to be parallel?

What can these illusions tell us about the nature of perception?

When you have finished, see the notes on page 227.

Figure 5 shows some examples of **ambiguous** (or **reversible**) figures:

In all these examples, the information can be interpreted in two ways. In the Necker cube, the face marked with crosses can be seen as either the front face or the back face. Boring's old woman–young woman can be seen as an old woman with a hooked nose and a pointed chin, or as a young woman with her head turned away. The third example can be seen as either a duck or a rabbit, and the final one as either a Native American or an Eskimo.

Both ways of perceiving these figures are equally valid in terms of the visual information provided. The visual system therefore has no way of deciding which is the 'correct' view, and so what is perceived tends to switch spontaneously from one possibility to the other.

Figure 5: ambiguous (reversible) figures

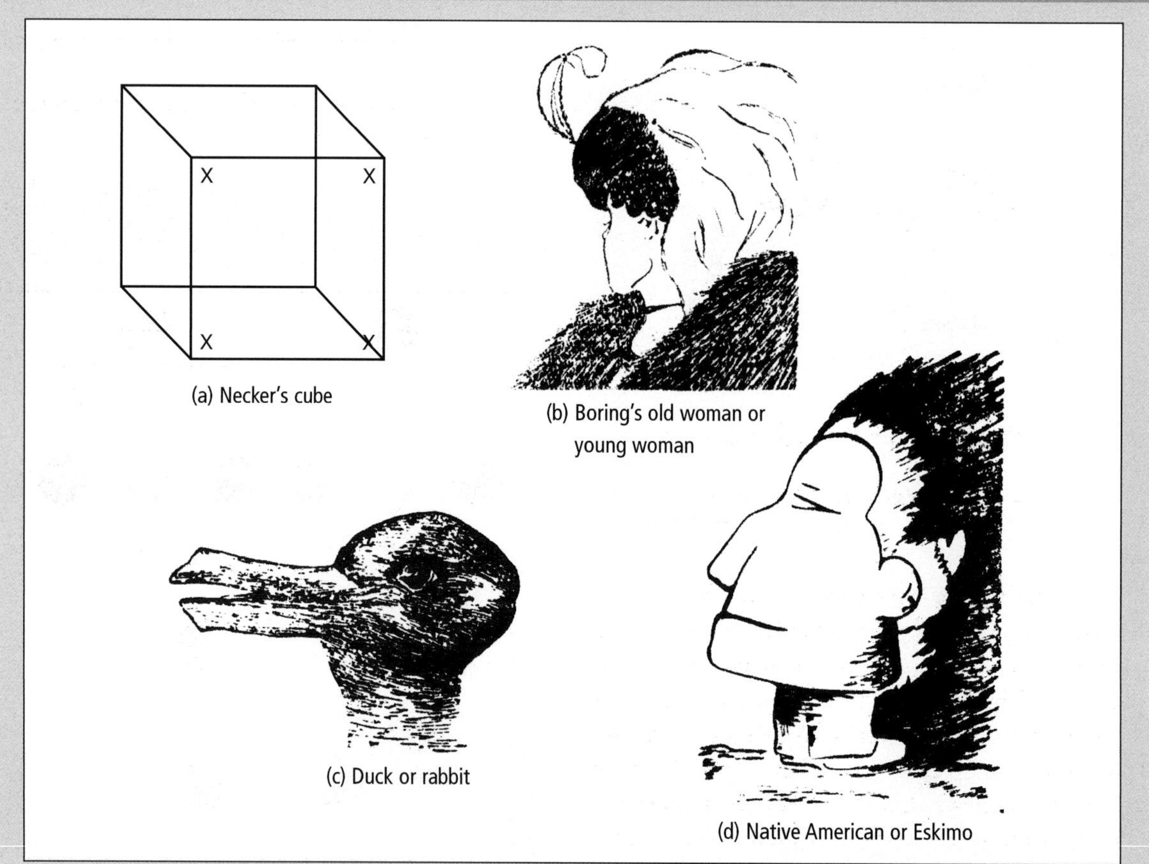

(a) Necker's cube

(b) Boring's old woman or young woman

(c) Duck or rabbit

(d) Native American or Eskimo

Paradoxical figures are figures which could not actually exist:

Figure 6: paradoxical figures

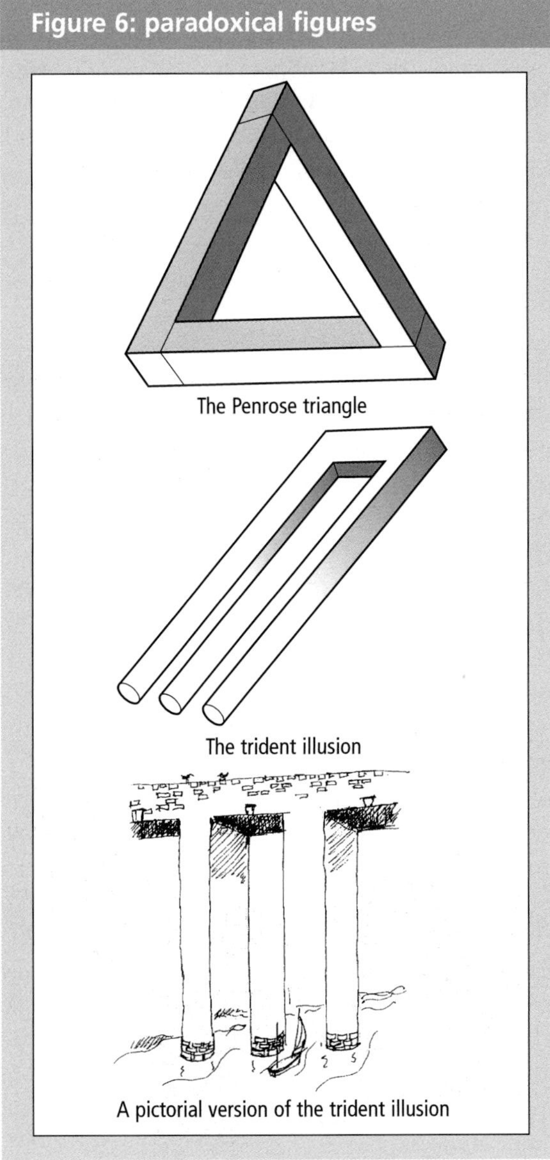

If you focus on the dark grey face of the Penrose triangle, there is no third front face to fit with it, and this is also true if you focus on the white or the light grey faces. The trident illusion has two prongs at one end but three at the other. In each case, we find it impossible to focus on the whole figure because we are automatically translating a two-dimensional picture into three dimensions, which in these cases is impossible.

This idea has been used in the work of Escher (see figure 7), whose elaborate pictures depict scenes which are three-dimensionally impossible:

Figure 7: impossible picture by M. Escher

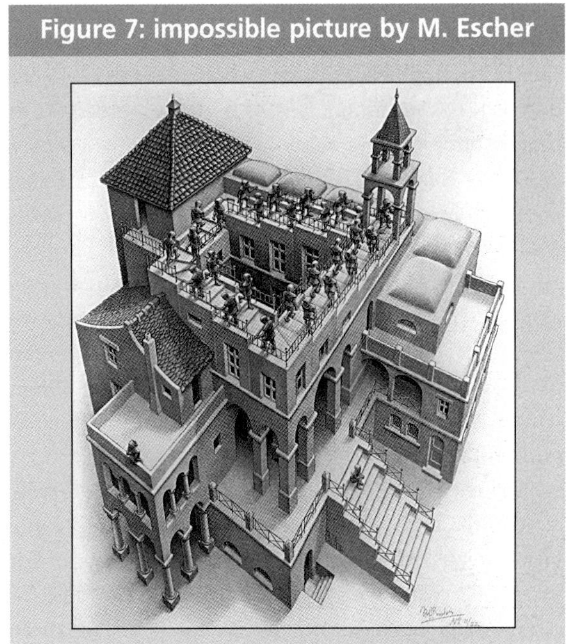

Fictions are illusions in which we see something that isn't actually there:

Figure 8: fictions – Kanizska's triangles and square

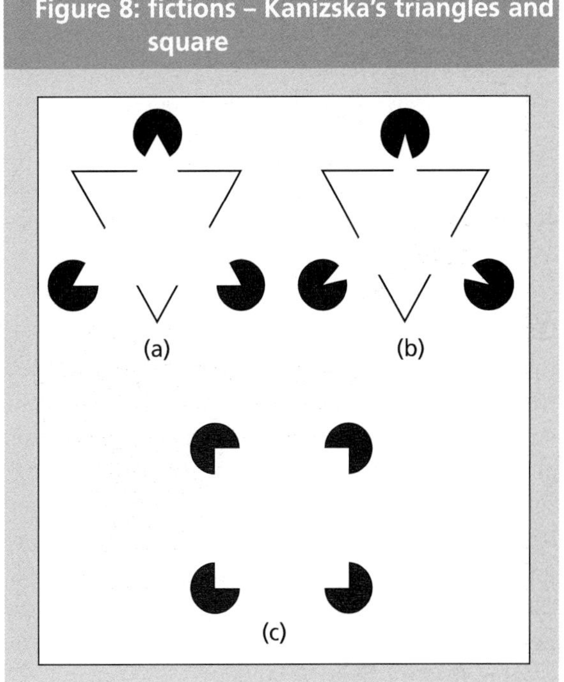

In (a), you should see a white triangle, in (b) a white triangle with curved sides, and in (c) a white square. These kinds of illusion relate to our use of contours to identify shapes. In these figures, the perceptual system uses **subjective contours** rather than physical ones, which Kanizsa (1976) defined as the boundaries of a shape perceived in the absence of physical contours.

In the Kanizsa triangles, there are some physical contours where the white triangle and the discs overlap. However, these would probably not be enough to lead us to perceive a complete figure, and they certainly don't account for the curves we see in (b). The white square we see in (c) can perhaps be related to interposition,when an object which blocks the full view of another object is perceived to be in front of it.

All these illusions are, of course, extremely artificial compared to real-life perceptions. However, they do relate to real-life illusions. For example, two-dimensional pictures make use of perspective cues so that they are seen in three dimensions. Illusions may still therefore help us to understand how perception works, and we shall be returning to them in the next section.

❻ **Visual illusions** fall into four categories: **distortions**, **ambiguous figures**, **paradoxical figures** and **fictions**. They give some insight into the way the perceptual system works.

8.4 Bottom-up and top-down theories of perception

One major distinction in theories of perception is the relative importance given to bottom-up and top-down processing. Some psychologists emphasise the importance in explaining perception of starting with the analysis of sensory inputs, i.e. sensory data. This information is then transmitted to higher levels of analysis, so that sensory information builds up to a mental representation. This is known as **bottom-up** processing, or **data-driven** processing, since perception is driven by sensory data.

Other theorists in contrast claim that sensory information is not enough to explain perception, since it is fragmentary and may be ambiguous. They emphasise the importance of stored knowledge in processing sensory information. This is called **top-down** (or **context-driven** or **schema-driven**) processing, since knowledge and expectations work downwards to influence how we interpret sensory inputs.

Bottom-up theories

(i) Feature detection theories

Feature detection theories suggest that the perception of objects is built up from the detection of their elementary features, so adopt a bottom-up approach. Perhaps the best known model is Selfridge's (1959) **pandemonium model.** This proposes that we have detector cells (called **demons** in Selfridge's theory) which are sensitive to particular elements of visual input. The detection of an element contributes to the final identification of the object. Lindsey and Norman (1972) have applied this model to letter recognition, shown in figure 9.

The response of the demons to elements of the retinal image is shown here by the lines leading from one column of demons to the next. This can be thought of as a shriek (hence 'pandemonium'). The strength of the shriek relates to the weighting given to each figure. If the feature is definitely present, the demon will shout loudly (indicated by a heavy black arrow), while if the evidence is not so strong, it will shout less loudly (shown by a thin arrow), and if the feature is not present it will not shout at all.

There is some evidence to support this general idea. It relates well to what we know about neural processes in the visual system, which is organised as a hierarchy. Each layer of cells responds to the firing of lower levels of cells.

Supporting evidence also comes from a classic study described in box C.

Feature detection theory is also supported by **visual search** studies, originally carried out in a series of experiments by Neisser (1963). In a visual

Figure 9: Selfridge's (1959) pandemonium model

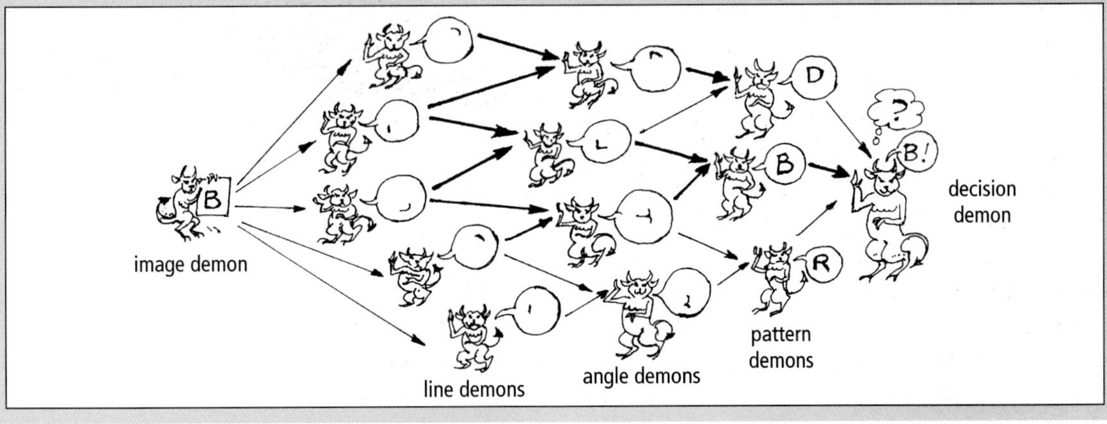

Box C: Hubel and Wiesel (1959)

Procedure: A microelectrode was implanted in a single cell of the visual cortex of an anaesthetised cat. The background electrical activity of the cell was recorded to form a baseline against which any change could be measured. A screen was placed in front of the cat on to which a pinpoint of light could be projected. The cat's head was fixed so that there was a one-to-one correspondence between the screen and the cat's retina. Changes in the firing rate of the cell when the light was moved around the screen were measured using an oscilloscope.

Results: Each cell in the visual cortex fired in response to light stimulation on some areas of the retina, while firing was inhibited in other areas. Complex patterns of light stimulation were necessary to increase or decrease firing activity. The receptive fields were often a slit-like shape.

Conclusion: Cortical cells respond to bars of light falling on specific parts of the retina. The patterns of light which excite or inhibit these **feature detection cells** provide information corresponding to edges between slit-shaped areas of light and dark. This would help to indicate boundaries of objects in the environment and so facilitate object recognition.

search task, participants are asked to scan a display and pick out target items from among background items. Try the method for yourself:

Activity 6: visual search

You will need to find a participant to carry out this activity. Ask your participant to scan through each of these sets of letters in turn, starting from the top and working down. In each set, they should tap the table when they have found the letter G. Use a stopwatch to time how long it takes for each set. It is a good idea to cover the sets of letters. Expose the one to be scanned as you instruct your participant to start, and at the same time start your stopwatch.

CUPOJR	VATILM	BROPPD	XVTELZ
OCQSQJ	YZMXYT	QDOCSQ	XHZKYL
CDOQRC	XKHNXY	DUPQOB	FEAYXZ
BUOPRS	FELKNH	DROBRP	VNEAWX
CUPOJR	VATILM	BROPPD	XVTELZ
OCQSQJ	YZMXYT	QDOCSQ	XHZKYL
BRUGUP	VXNMTA	PORDOC	VTGYXN
BUPOCP	NIYXML	BSROPU	XILKET
CDOQRC	XKHNXY	DUPQOB	FEAYXZ
BOUSRQ	VEAGIK	RSGUPR	FTELIH
CUPOJR	VATILM	BROPPD	XVTELZ
BUOPRS	FELKNH	DROBRP	VNEAWX

Add together the search times for the first and third sets, and for the second and fourth sets. Which were faster, and why?

The G was in the seventh row of the first and fourth sets of letters, and in the tenth row of the second and third sets, to make a fair comparison between sets 1 and 3 and sets 2 and 4 possible.

Neisser (1963) found that when participants were asked to find target letters from a display of letters, this was easier when the distractor items were different in shape from the target letters than when they were similar. It is likely that your participants identified the G faster in sets 2 and 4. The difference here is in the shape of the background letters. G is a curved letter, and the background letters (known as **distractor items**) for sets 1 and 3 are other curved letters, whereas the background letters of sets 2 and 4 are all angular.

In this task, presumably every non-target letter must be compared with a representation of the target stored in the memory, before it can be rejected. If non-target items are fully recognised, there is no reason why the nature of the distractor items should make a difference to search time. The relative speed of picking out the G from the angular background letters suggests that analysis is only partial. Features of each non-target item are analysed, but analysis only needs to be sufficient to establish that the item is not a target.

Gibson's theory of direct perception

Gibson (1986) believed that we receive enough sensory information to allow us to perceive the environment in a direct way. There is no need for any kind of processing, since the information we receive – about size, shape, distance, movement and so on – is sufficiently detailed to enable us to interact directly with the environment.

For Gibson, sensation *is* perception. There are no intermediate stages between light falling on the retina and the response of the perceiver. No interpretation needs to take place, no hypotheses need to be formed. With its emphasis on the richness of sensory data, this theory is in tune with bottom-up theories of perception, though it is not strictly speaking a bottom-up theory, since it claims that no processing is necessary for perception to take place.

Gibson pointed out that vision is not static, but the result of people moving around in a visual environment. Because of this movement, there are continuous changes in what Gibson calls the **ambient optic array** – all the transmitted and reflected light rays from the environment – and these changes give us new information.

Gibson called his theory an **ecological approach**, since it emphasises the direct contact between the perceiver and meaningful aspects of the environment. Gibson sees perception as a necessarily adaptive process: if animals are to survive, they need to be able to respond both to relatively unchanging aspects of their environment, such as sources of water, and to aspects which change, such as the presence and location of other animals.

Gibson developed his theory as a result of his experience in training pilots. During the Second World War, he was asked to provide training films for pilots, and in particular to focus on the problems experienced by pilots during take-off and landing. These two manoeuvres require skill and concentration, and Gibson became interested in researching just what information pilots had available to them at these times; he called this information **optic flow patterns**:

Figure 10: the optic flow patterns as a pilot approaches the landing strip

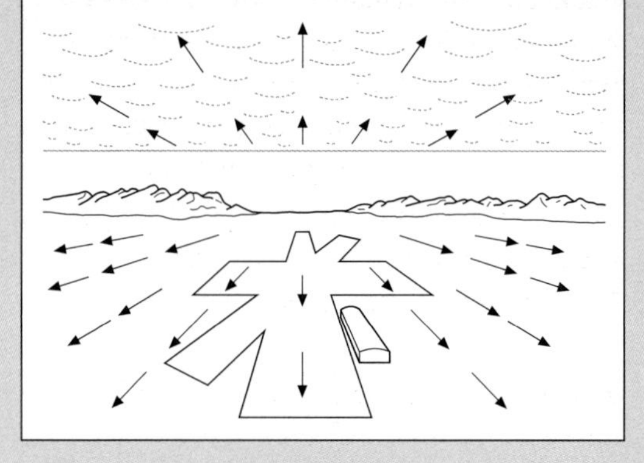

Gibson pointed out just how much information was available. The point to which the pilot is moving is invariant, i.e. static within the display, but all around that point is a moving display giving a great deal of unambiguous information about speed, direction and altitude.

He extended the idea, that all this information is received and responded to directly, to the concept of **affordances**. Affordances refers to the function of perceived aspects of the environment, i.e. the possible uses an object affords, such as for shelter or for use as a tool. For example, a chair is perceived as something to sit on.

The main strength of Gibson's model is that it stresses an **ecological approach**; it relates to the perceptual experience of people and animals in real-life situations. He is right to point out that we spend a lot of our time in motion, producing moment-by-moment changes in the optic array, which increase the richness of sensory data available to us. This approach is in stark contrast to the impoverished visual information available in the artificial setting of many traditional laboratory experiments.

There are, however, some problems with these ideas. Firstly, the theory cannot explain illusions, which we discussed earlier. Gibson's argument is that illusions come about as the result of deliberately ambiguous information in artificial situations, and therefore cannot tell us anything very useful about real-life perception. He has a point here, but some illusions do hold true in real life:

Activity 7: the vertical–horizontal illusion

Look back to figure 4(d) for this illusion. To reproduce this illusion in a real-life setting, you will need a cup, a saucer and two similar teaspoons. Put one spoon in the saucer next to the cup, and the other upright in the cup.

Which spoon looks longer? You should find that the spoon in the cup (vertical) looks longer than the one on the saucer (horizontal).

The theory also has difficulties in explaining the influence of **perceptual set**, a bias or readiness to interpret visual stimuli in a particular way, which we shall be looking at in the next subsection in the context of Gregory's theory. Nor can it explain cultural differences in perception, which we shall be looking at later in this chapter.

The links made between humans and other animals may also not be entirely appropriate in this instance. Animals appear to be preprogrammed to attend and respond to particular aspects of their environment which are relevant to navigation. A lot of human behaviour, on the other hand, is governed by higher-order processes, such as remembering and planning, between stimulus and response.

When we come to the idea of affordances, the parallel between humans and other animals seems particularly weak. Clearly we need to draw on culturally-relevant knowledge to understand that a pencil affords drawing or a washing machine affords cleaning clothes.

Gibson's theory seems to be better at explaining some aspects of perception than others. This can be related to the distinction referred to by Fodor and Pylyshyn (1981) between 'seeing' and 'seeing as'. They illustrate this with the example of a man lost at sea who sees the Pole Star. If he sees it as just another star ('seeing'), then he will be just as lost as ever, whereas if he sees it as the Pole Star ('seeing as'), it is a potential navigational aid which could help him to find his way. Gibson's theory is better at explaining 'seeing', while having little to say about 'seeing as'.

- Gibson claimed that there is a vast amount of information in the **ambient optic array** as a person or animal moves round their environment. This means that perception does not need to depend on processing but is direct.
- **Affordances**, i.e. the function of objects in the environment, are also perceived directly, though this may be more true for animals than humans.
- The main strength of the theory is Gibson's **ecological approach**, but the theory is better at explaining 'seeing' than 'seeing as'. It has difficulty in explaining **visual illusions**, **perceptual set** and **cross-cultural differences** in perception.

Top-down theories

Gregory's constructivist theory

Gregory's (1973) constructivist theory is a good example of a top-down theory. He claimed that we construct our perceptions 'from floating, fragmentary scraps of data signalled to the senses and drawn from the brain memory banks, themselves constructions from the snippets of the past'.

Gregory's theory of visual perception is a **constructivist** model because it claims that we actively construct our perception of reality, drawing on our past knowledge and experience. What we perceive goes beyond the often incomplete sensory information received through the sense organs. We may also need to select which aspects of the visual input we attend to. Gregory suggested that we form a **perceptual hypothesis**, i.e. make a 'best bet' about what we see, and then check this hypothesis against the available data.

Some visual illusions are one source of support for these ideas. We attempt to make sense of visual illusions in the same way that we normally make sense of our visual environment, but in the case of illusions these attempts are misleading. Illusions are examples of inappropriate perceptual hypotheses which are not confirmed by the data.

Look back now to the distortions shown in figure 4. The Ponzo illusion can be explained in terms of our past experience of using depth cues provided by perspective. A similar explanation can be offered for the Müller–Lyer illusion, where the arrow heads pointing inwards suggest that the horizontal line is close to us, while the arrow heads pointing outwards suggest that the horizontal line is further away; we use size constancy scaling to make automatic adjustments to the perceived length of the horizontals.

The Zollner illusion and Titchener's circles both show the effect of context on what we perceive. Our perceptions of the diagonals in the Zollner illusion and the central circles in Titchener's circles are influenced by the context provided by the other parts of the presentation.

The figures in figure 5 provide ambiguous information. Our interpretation therefore switches between the alternatives, probably influenced by where our attention is focused.

We have similar problems interpreting the **paradoxical figures** shown in figure 6. There should be no difficulty in taking in the sensory data these figures provide, but we have trouble seeing the whole stimulus in each case because we automatically try to interpret the two-dimensional stimulus as a three-dimensional representation, which in these cases is not possible.

Finally, in the fictions shown in figure 8, the subjective contours of the white triangles and square go beyond the available information. The triangles and the square are perceived because there is enough evidence for us to assume that they exist. We do not simply take in information; we go beyond it to draw conclusions.

A further source of support for Gregory's ideas comes from constancy phenomena, already noted above in the discussion of the Müller–Lyer illusion. What we perceive does not necessarily correspond to the retinal image, since the brain makes automatic adjustments to our perception of colour, size, shape and brightness in line with our knowledge of the physical world and our past experience of it.

There is also support from cross-cultural studies, which show that the inference of a third dimension in two-dimensional picture needs to be learned and is therefore the result of experience. We shall be returning to this later in this chapter.

The idea of **perceptual set** mentioned above also supports Gregory's ideas. For example, a study by Bruner and Minturn (1955) found that participants were more likely to perceive the fourth item in this sequence:

E C D B A

as a B and in this sequence:

16 15 14 B 12

as 13, although they are identical. What was perceived was affected by expectation and context.

While there are good sources of evidence for Gregory's ideas, there are also possible problems. To return to the Müller–Lyer illusion, Gregory's explanation in terms of misplaced size constancy has been challenged by other research. Delboeuf (1892) used variants of the illusion:

Figure 11: variants of Müller–Lyer

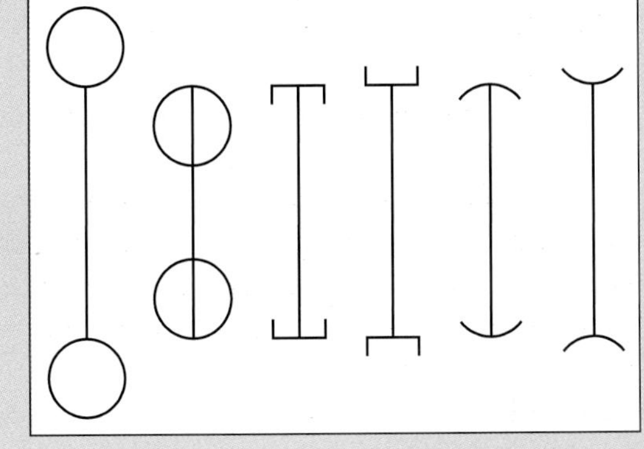

In spite of changing the arrows to the dumb-bells, brackets and curves shown in figure 11, the illusion was still effective. It would be hard to explain this effect in terms of misapplying depth cues. Another variant was used by Morgan (1969):

Figure 12: Morgan's variant of the Müller–Lyer

The dot here is in the middle of the horizontal line, but appears to be closer to the right-hand end. This implies that the arrow is seen as sloping away from us, which seems no more likely than that it is sloping towards us.

A more general problem is that knowledge may not lead us to modify our perceptions. For example, even when we know that the two horizontal lines of the Müller–Lyer are the same length the illusion still remains – we are not able to change our perceptual hypothesis in the light of additional information, as Gregory suggested. Simply knowing that a perception is inaccurate cannot remove the illusion. Clearly 'visual knowledge' needs to be incorporated at an unconscious level.

This inflexibility is shown even more startlingly in the Ames room illusion (figure 13). The figure on the right is seen as very much larger than the figure on the left. This effect is achieved by using a distorted room, shown schematically in figure 13. We know that the perceived difference in size of the people is a virtual impossibility, but the illusion is none the less effective.

A further criticism is that visual illusions are static and two-dimensional, and are therefore very far removed from the richness of detailed information which usually reaches the visual system in real-life situations. It may therefore be unwise to generalise too freely from this source of information.

Activity 8: Gregory and Gibson

Read through these statements. For each one, decide whether it applies to Gregory's constructivist theory, Gibson's theory of direct perception or both:

a The environment provides us with a vast amount of unambiguous information.

b Illusions are a good way of helping us to understand perceptual processes.

c Perception is an active process.

d Top-down processes are important in perception.

e The environment provides the necessary information for making sense of visual stimuli.

f Visual perception is made possible by light reflected by surfaces and objects.

g Basing conclusions on illusions lacks ecological validity.

h Memory and experience are important in making sense of visual stimuli.

i A physiological system is necessary for perception.

When you have finished, see the notes on page 227.

❺ Gregory's **constructivist** theory of perception takes a **top-down** approach. We form **perceptual hypotheses** which are then checked against the sensory data.

- Visual **illusions** can be seen as inappropriate perceptual hypotheses. They lend support to Gregory's ideas. His theory is also supported by **cross-cultural** findings that depth perception needs to be learned, and by the phenomenon of **perceptual set**.
- Some variants of illusions have questioned Gregory's interpretations. His theory cannot provide satisfactory answers to some perceptual phenomena.

Figure 13: the Ames room

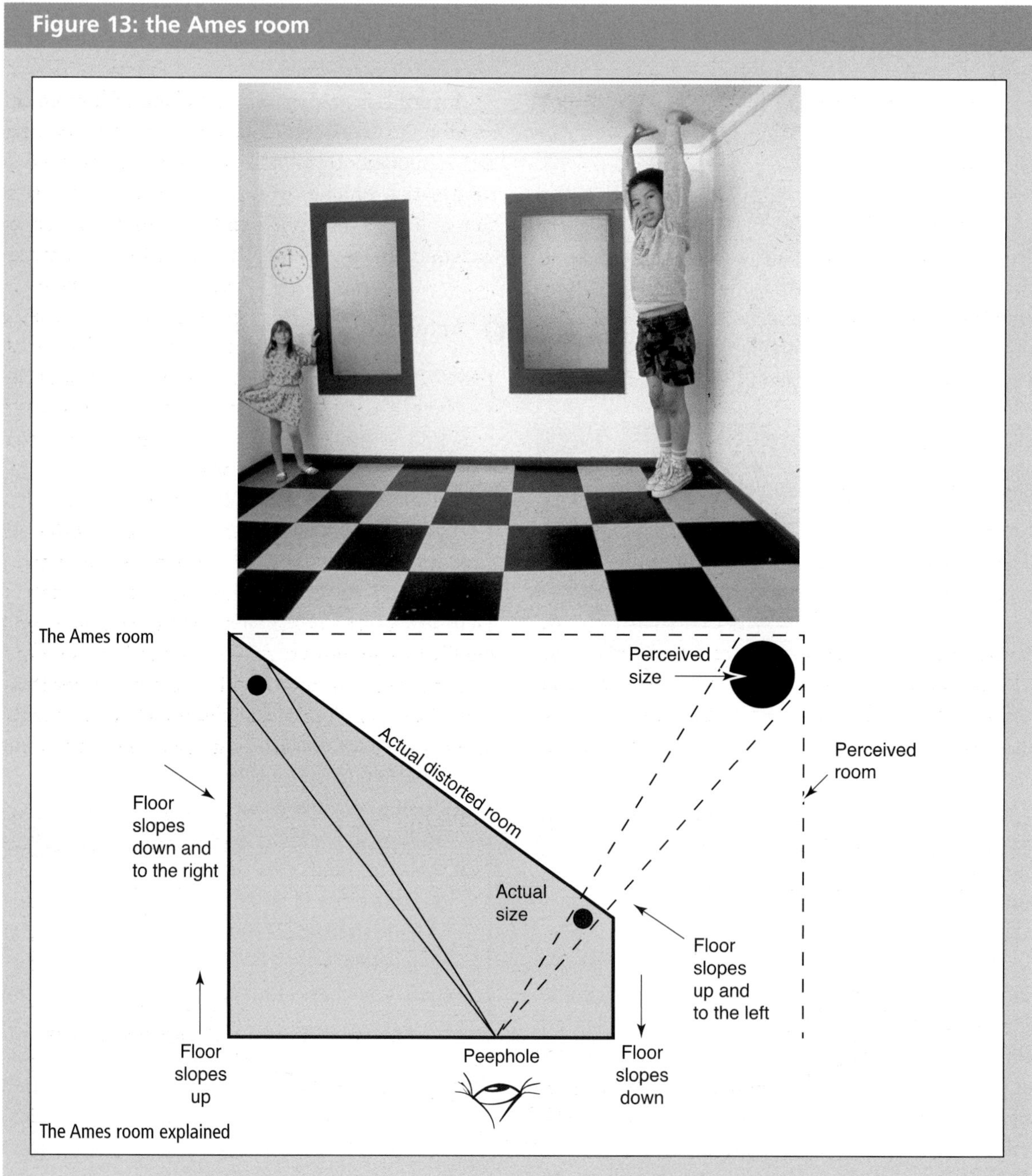

Theories combining bottom-up and top-down approaches

Neisser's cyclic model of perception

We have looked at Selfridge's pandemonium model of perception as an example of a model which focuses on bottom-up processing, and the emphasis in Gibson's theory of direct perception on the richness of sensory data available to the perceiver is also very much in line with this viewpoint. We have also looked at Gregory's constructivist model which takes a much more top-down approach. One example of an attempt to combine the best of both approaches is Neisser's (1976) cyclic model (figure 14).

In Neisser's theory, top-down and bottom-up processes are used in a continuing cycle during perception. He assumes that perception starts with **schemas**, i.e. ideas and expectations of what we expect to see in a particular context. Schemas influence the way we explore our perceptual environment as we seek to confirm our expectations. We sample the information available in the environment in a preliminary analysis of the sensory cues, and on this basis we form a **perceptual model**, i.e. a mental representation of a likely object or event.

The perceptual model is then used to initiate an active search of the sensory cues in the environment. If sensory cues are found to confirm the perceptual model, there is an **elaborative effect**, i.e. details are added to the model. If not, the perceptual model will need to be revised, i.e. there is a **corrective effect**. Perception therefore involves a continuous process of checking and rechecking sensory data in line with modifications to the perceptual model we have formed.

Neisser calls his model an **analysis-by-synthesis** theory, since perception involves extracting information about aspects of the environment (analysis) and generating a perceptual model (synthesis), as a cyclical process.

A major strength of Neisser's theory is that it attempts to show that the interaction of bottom-up and top-down processing is important in perceiving the environment; we have already seen that both have a part to play. It has a lot in common with Gregory's idea of perceptual hypotheses, though in Neisser's model, the hypotheses we form are much more general than those suggested by Gregory. Both models also see perception as an active process. Another positive point about Neisser's model is that it makes a link with attention, in that the process of checking sensory data is directed towards aspects of the environment which are relevant to the perceptual model we have formed.

However, there are some limitations to this theory. For one thing – as with the theories of Gregory and Gibson – it is descriptive rather than explanatory, since it does not explain the actual processes of perception – directing, sampling and modifying – in terms of neural activity. It is therefore best thought of as a general framework, rather than a precisely stated and testable model. The amount of processing which may be involved also raises the

Figure 14: Neisser's cyclic theory (1976)

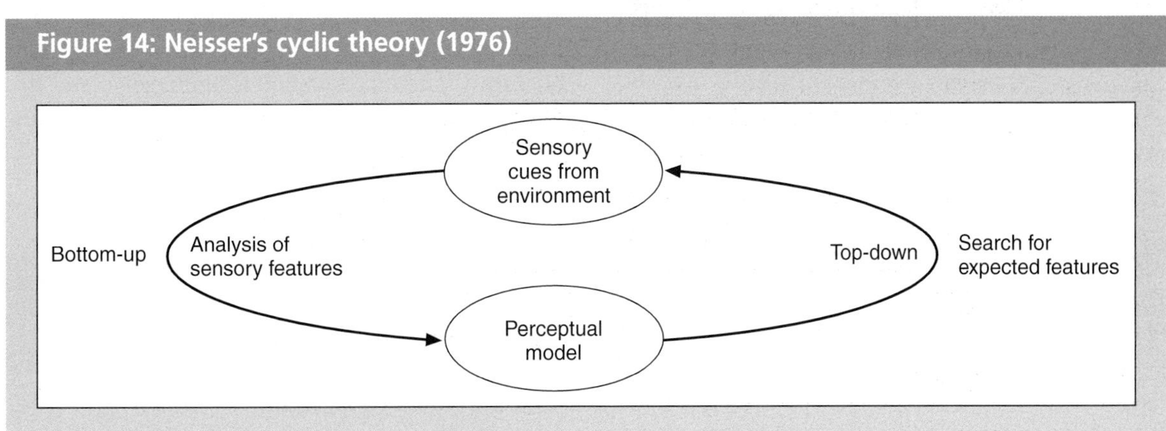

question of where exactly in the cycle perception can be said to have taken place. Does this happen when an initial hypothesis is formed, or not until the perception is fully confirmed? Finally, there are problems when it comes to trying to test this theory in a natural environment; given the cyclical nature of perception, it is difficult to see how this could be done.

- In Neisser's **cyclic model**, we generate a **perceptual model** based on expectations. The model is then checked against **sensory data** and revised if necessary, in a continuing process.
- One strength of the model is that it combines **top-down** and **bottom-up** processing in an interactive model. It has been criticised, however, for being **vague**, and **descriptive** rather than explanatory.

Marr's computational theory

Marr's computational theory also combines top-down and bottom-up processing in its account of perception. Marr developed his ideas about perception as the result of attempting to program a computer with the ability to perceive. Computer programs must have exact specifications to work, and attempts to specify the exact processes involved in visual perception have shown what an extraordinarily complicated ability it is.

Marr (1982) proposed that any explanation of perception needs to work on three levels. The **hardware** level specifies the biological processes involved in perception, i.e. neurological structures. The **algorithmic** level specifies the rules and processes involved in perception. The **computational** level is concerned with the functions of perception. It aims to analyse what the perceptual system is doing, what information it needs, and why. It is this level with which Marr is chiefly concerned.

A key aspect of Marr's theory is **representation**. The theory is concerned in particular with how the visual system can acquire a reliable representation of objects in the real world from the information contained in the retinal image. Visual representation is seen as the result of information being processed through a system, which consists of a sequence of four independent sub-systems or modules. The first stage has as its input the pattern of light rays on the retina (or a screen) and each of the later stages has as its input the output from the previous stage :

Figure 15: stages in Marr's computational theory

1. **grey level description:** the intensity of light at each point in the picture or retinal image is analysed.
2. **primal sketch:** the analysis of stage 1 leads to detection of edges and lines, which leads to outline shapes of objects.
3. **2.5D sketch:** stage 2 allows a picture to be built up from what is visible in the sketch, but this is viewpoint-dependent, i.e. descriptions depend upon the viewpoint of the observer (or computer). This stage includes information about orientation and depth.
4. **object recognition:** the 3D identity of the object is recognised by matching the 2.5D sketch with prototypes in memory. At this point allowance can be made for unseen parts, e.g. where one object partly obscures another, and angle of presentation. This representation is viewpoint-independent.

The first three stages focus on the sensory data, and so reflect a bottom-up approach, whereas the final stage draws on memory, and so is the top-down part of the processing system. This final part is only necessary when information is ambiguous, and this idea goes some way towards incorporating constructivist ideas into a bottom-up approach.

Clinical evidence supports Marr's ideas :

Box D: Warrington and Taylor (1978)

Procedure: Brain-damaged patients with problems with object recognition. were shown photographs of objects taken from a

conventional viewpoint (e.g. a flat-iron seen from above) and at an unusual angle (e.g. showing the base and part of the handle). They were also shown pairs of photographs of objects, with conventional and unusual views, and asked whether both showed the same object.
Results: Patients were poor at identifying objects shown at an unusual angle. They were also poor at identifying pairs of pictures as being of the same object, thus showing difficulty in identifying objects from an unusual angle even when the paired picture suggested what it might be.
Conclusion: Patients could identify objects from a conventional angle, i.e. using information provided by the 2.5D sketch, but could not achieve the full recognition of the final 3D stage.

The ideas are also suported by the development of computer programs which analyse information in this way. Of course, just because computers can do it this way, it does not necessarily follow that the same form of processing is used by humans. However, Marr's theory is also useful because it combines top-down and bottom-up approaches, and is specific in that it divides perception into stages or modules, and specifies for each one the input and output representation, together with the processes which transform input into output.

- **Marr's computational model** is concerned with the representation of objects. Information is processed through a sequence of four stages or **modules**: **grey level description**, **primal sketch**, **2.5D sketch** and **object recognition**.
- The first three stages work on **bottom-up** principles, while the final stage involves **top-down** processing.
- There is some clinical evidence to support Marr's ideas. The stages can be modelled by computer, and the theory provides specific accounts at all four stages.
- Humans may not process information in the same way as computers.

8.5 Factors in perception

Expectation, motivation and emotion

We have already had a brief look at the role of expectation in perception. Expectation has a role to play in **constancy**. For example, we have expectations about the shape of a cup, triggering shape constancy which allows us to compensate for the angle at which it is viewed. **Top-down** theories also emphasise the role of expectation in perception. We draw on existing knowledge which provides the expectations which allow us to form hypotheses, and so interpret sensory inputs. The concept of **perceptual set** also recognises the influence of expectation on perception. The study by Bruner and Minturn (1955) in which B was seen as B in a sequence of letters but as 13 in a series of numbers provides an example of the effect of expectation on perception.

Previous knowledge can also influence our perception of colour:

Box E: Bruner and Postman (1949)

Procedure: Participants were shown playing cards in which the colours were reversed, i.e. black hearts and diamonds and red clubs and spades, and asked to identify the colours. The cards were presented using a tachistoscope, which exposes visual material for very brief but accurately measured periods of time.
Results: With extremely brief exposure, cards were reported to be their normal colours, e.g. hearts were perceived as red. With slightly longer exposure, hearts or diamonds were often reported to be purple or brown.
Conclusion: Existing knowledge leads to expectations which influence perception. When hearts or diamonds were seen as purple or brown, the reported colour blended the colour participants were expecting and the colour of the stimulus material.

Prior knowledge can also create an expectation which influences our ability to detect motion. Sekuler (1995) found that participants were much quicker to perceive a moving target if they were given information about the direction in which it would move.

The effect of motivation and emotion in perception can also be related to perceptual set. Set can work in two ways. In **perceptual sensitisation**, things which are relevant to us, and which we are therefore motivated to perceive, are perceived as larger, brighter or more attractive. In **perceptual defence**, things which are unpleasant or threatening, and therefore are associated with negative emotions, are harder to perceive at a conscious level.

We will look first of all at perceptual sensitisation and the effect of motivation on set:

Box F: Gilchrist and Nesberg (1952)

Procedure: Participants were deprived of food and water for periods of up to eight hours. They were then shown pictures of objects related to food and drink and were asked to estimate their brightness. They could then eat and drink as much as they wanted, and were tested again.
Results: The perceived brightness of the pictures increased as the length of deprivation increased. After eating and drinking, perceived brightness decreased.
Conclusion: Perceptual judgements are affected by current motivation.

A further classic study in the area of perceptual sensitisation looked at the effect of the value of objects on set :

Box G: Bruner and Goodman (1947)

Procedure: Children were asked to turn a knob to control a patch of light on a screen. They were asked to adjust the patch of light so that it was the same size as coins of various denominations. The responses of children from poor and wealthy families were compared.
Results: All the children tended to overestimate the size of the coins, but children from poor families made larger overestimations.
Conclusion: The coins were seen as more valuable by the children from poor families, leading to perception of them as larger.

Studies of the effect of emotion on perception have tended to focus on perceptual defence, a term first used by McGinnies :

Box H: McGinnies (1949)

Procedure: Words were shown to participants using a tachistoscope, an apparatus which presents visual material for very brief, measured fractions of a second. The length of exposure was increased until participants could identify the words. Some of the words were neutral words such as 'table', 'chair' and 'apple', while others were taboo words, matched for length, such as 'bitch'. 'whore' and 'penis'. The GSR, which measures the electrical resistance of the skin, and is correlated with emotional arousal, was also taken.
Results: Longer exposures were needed for the taboo words to be identified. There was also a higher GSR to the taboo words.
Conclusion: Perception can be influenced by emotional responses.

However, given the time at which this study was carried out, it is possible that the taboo words were less familiar than the neutral words. Postman *et al.* (1953) matched taboo words for relative frequency with neutral words. His findings did not support the idea of perceptual defence. It also seems extremely likely that participants would be embarrassed by saying the taboo words. They might not believe that they were being shown such words in an academic study, and might want to be absolutely sure that they had identified them correctly before committing themselves to a response.

To avoid the problems associated with this method of investigating perceptual defence, Worthington (1969) took a different approach:

Box I: Worthington (1969)

Procedure: One hundred and sixty participants were shown two spots of light and asked to judge which was brighter. In fact they were both equally bright, but a word was embedded in each which was too dim to be perceived consciously. The words had previously been rated for their emotional content.

Results: The spots of light with words with high emotional content were consistently perceived as dimmer than those with low emotional content.

Conclusion: Emotional content, even at a subliminal level, influences perception.

- The role of **expectation** on perception is demonstrated by **constancy**, **top-down** theories of perception and the effect of **perceptual set**. Previous knowledge creates expectations which influence perception.
- The effect of **motivation** on perception has been demonstrated using a **perceptual sensitisation** paradigm, while the effect of **emotion** has been demonstrated using **perceptual defence**.

Culture

There is a lot of evidence that the ways in which we perceive the world are influenced by cultural factors. Several studies have used visual illusions to examine cultural differences in perception. Probably the earliest study in this area was carried out by Rivers (1901), who compared English adults and children with adult and child Murray Islanders. The Murray Islanders were less susceptible to the Müller–Lyer illusion and more susceptible to the horizontal–vertical illusion (see figure 4).

Allport and Pettigrew (1957) used a rotating trapezoid:

Figure 16: the rotating trapezoid

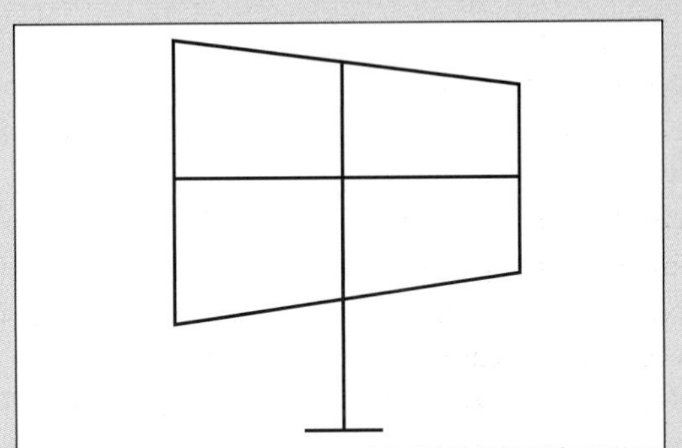

When this revolves, Western observers tend to perceive it as a rectangle swinging backwards and forwards.

They believed that this illusion depends on our perceiving the display as a window, and that therefore people from cultures which do not have this kind of window would be less likely to experience the illusion. Tests on rural Zulus supported this idea.

Segall *et al.* (1963) carried out a similar study testing people from a range of cultures:

Box J: Segall *et al.* (1963)

Procedure: The horizontal–vertical illusion (see figure 4) was tested on members of three African cultures: the Batoro and Bayankole who live in open country, and the Bete who live in dense jungle. Filipinos, South Africans of European descent and Americans from the mid-western state of Illinois were also tested.

Results: The Batoro and Bayankole were the most susceptible, and the Bete the least susceptible.

Conclusion: The open country where the Batoro and Bayankole live makes it possible to see for long distances. Vertical objects are therefore important indicators of distance and an important part of visual experience, so people from these cultures are more susceptible to the horizontal–vertical illusion. The opposite is true of the Bete who live in dense jungle.

Based on these findings, Segall *et al.* (1963) put forward the **carpentered world hypothesis**. People in Western societies live in a world of straight lines in which most retinal images of lines meeting at an angle can be realistically interpreted, using shape constancy, as right angles. For example, in the Müller–Lyer illusion, it would make sense to interpret the figure with fins extending out from the vertical as the corner of a room, with the fins defining the walls coming towards us.

Segall claimed that we interpret two-dimensional drawings in three-dimensional terms; we add the extra dimension of depth which is not actually there. You might find it useful to look back at this point to Gregory's constructivist theory of perception, which says something similar.

Some studies have supported Segall's hypothesis. Annis and Frost (1973) found that Cree Indians living in a non-carpentered environment were good at making judgements about whether two lines were parallel, irrespective of the angle at which the lines were shown. Crees living in a carpentered environment were good at judging horizontal and vertical lines, but less good when the lines were at other angles. However, the results of a study by Jahoda (1966) which tested Ghanaians and one by Gregor and McPherson (1965) with Australian aborigines were not in line with what this hypothesis would predict.

Illusions have not been the only method of investigating cross-cultural differences in perception. An interesting insight relating to real-world experience was given by Turnbull (1961). He took a pygmy, whose home was in dense rainforest, to a plain where a huge herd of buffalo was grazing. The pygmy said he had never seen such insects before. As they rode towards the buffalo, the pygmy believed their increasing size was due to magic. His lack of depth perception and size constancy, at least over large distances, supports the idea that these aspects of visual perception are influenced by experience. However, this kind of evidence is only anecdotal.

Studies have also used pictorial material:

Activity 9: interpreting drawings (pictures adapted from Hudson, 1960)

In each of these pictures, at which animal is the man aiming his spear: the antelope or the elephant? Which animal is nearer to the man? Which cues in the pictures give you this information?

When you have finished, see the notes on page 227.

People from several African cultures were shown these pictures, and believed that in (a) the man was aiming his spear at the elephant. They did not perceive depth in this picture, in other words see the picture as a two-dimensional representation of a three-dimensional scene, as Westerners do.

However, the methodology of this kind of study is open to criticism. Deregowski (1972) found that the Me'en of Ethiopia were better at recognising pictorial representations when they were made on cloth (with which they were familiar) rather than unfamiliar paper, and when there were no distractions such as borders.

A further problem is the relative lack of depth cues in Hudson's material. If you look back to the section on depth perception, you will find that there are quite a number of potential sources of information about depth other than those used by Hudson. Serpell (1976) described a study by Kingsley *et al.* in which texture gradients were added to Hudson's pictures. This made it more likely that the Zambian children who were tested would give three-dimensional answers about pictorial material.

Serpell went on to suggest that cultural differences in perception might instead be stylistic preferences. Deregowski (1972) found that several African cultures preferred the 'split elephant' to the top view perspective (see figure 22), though one person was not keen on the split elephant, which seemed to him to be jumping around dangerously.

Figure 17: Deregowski (1972)

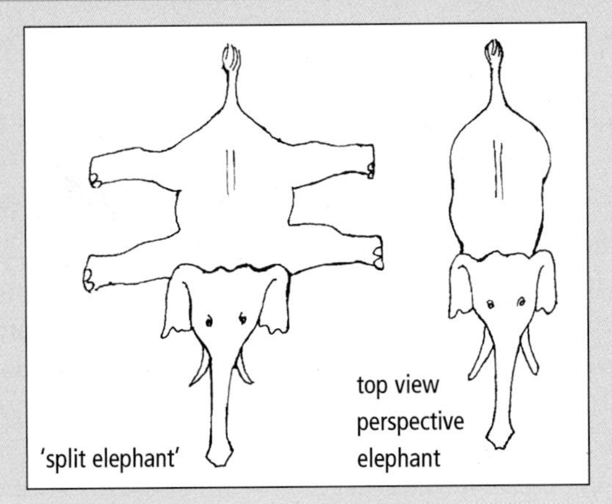

There are other conventions in pictorial representation which we take for granted, but which could be very confusing to someone who does not share our understanding of these conventions.

Activity 10: interpreting pictures

Have a look at picture (a). What information is the artist giving us about the character in the way he has been drawn? How would you interpret picture (b)?

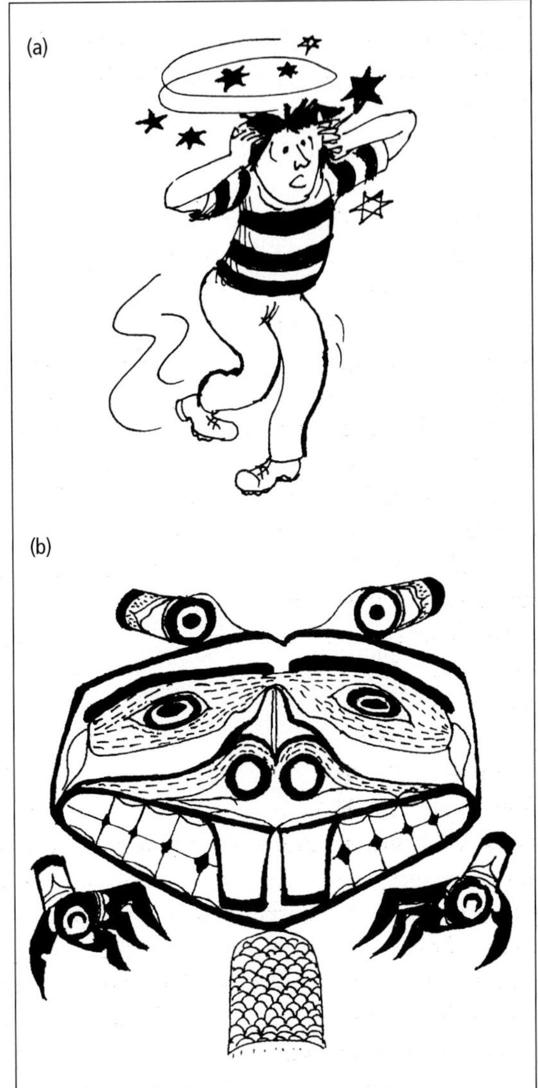

Compare your ideas with the discussion which follows.

Duncan *et al.* (1973) tested rural African children on items like (a). Conventions such as the stars in this picture showing that the person has been stunned, and the curved lines indicating a staggering movement, were not understood by African children. In the same way, a Western observer would not understand that in ancient Egyptian art, a figure with feet apart depicts a live person, while one with feet together signifies that the person is dead.

This idea of conventions which may confuse research into perception should be even more clear from (b). This is an example of Native American art, showing a beaver. The significant parts of what is being drawn have been picked out to describe them graphically for the observer. Without some background knowledge it is impossible for the Western observer to understand clearly what is represented.

- There are differences between cultures in their susceptibility to **visual illusions**. One explanation is the **carpentered world hypothesis,** though research evidence is ambiguous.
- There is anecdotal evidence of the influence of culture on perception.
- Other studies using **pictures** have found cultural differences in **depth perception.** The use of pictures can be criticised since **interpretation** of the findings is necessary, which may be influenced by **cultural bias**.

8.6 What is attention?

While you are looking at the words on this page, you are still probably aware at some level of other people around you, the colour of the walls in the room, the view outside the window, and so on. At the same time you are probably aware of sounds – perhaps someone near you talking or the sound of pages being turned over. You could be aware of the chair you are sitting on and the feel of the pen you are holding. In other words, there are lots of elements in your environment of which you are partially aware, and on which you could choose to concentrate.

Selective attention refers to our ability to select one element to attend to among all the things going on around us, and ignore everything else. It is also called **focused attention**, because it is concerned with our ability to focus on a particular sensory input. In this case, you are focusing your attention on what you are reading (I hope!) and largely shutting out a lot of the other things that are going on around you.

Attention theorists are also interested in our ability to attend to more than one thing at a time, or **divided attention**. It is possible that while you are reading this, you are also listening to music on a Walkman, and so paying attention to two things at once. Another example would be a skilled car driver, who would have no trouble in carrying on a conversation with a passenger, or eating a sandwich, at the same time as driving.

At first glance, neither selective nor divided attention seems problematical, but nonetheless they both raise questions which are of interest to psychologists.

Theorists concerned with focused attention ask such questions as:

- how do we select what we attend to?
- how much awareness do we have of the other sensory information we have chosen to ignore?
- to what extent do we consciously *choose* what we attend to?

Researchers investigating divided attention look at such questions as:

- how many different things can we attend to at once?
- what are the constraints on this ability?

In order to answer the kinds of questions posed by attention theorists, we need a theoretical framework which allows us to develop and link ideas about attention. One way of considering these questions has been to see the brain as an information-processing system, using the analogy of a computer. In the same way as information is fed into a computer, information reaches our senses from the environment: these are **input processes**. Just as a computer works on the information it has been given, the brain will then select, manipulate and store information (**storage processes**). Finally, appropriate responses are produced (**output processes**). This is shown in figure 18 opposite.

We can relate this model to the driving analogy. We receive a wide range of information from the environment as we are driving, and from this we select the information we need in order to drive

Figure 18: the information-processing model

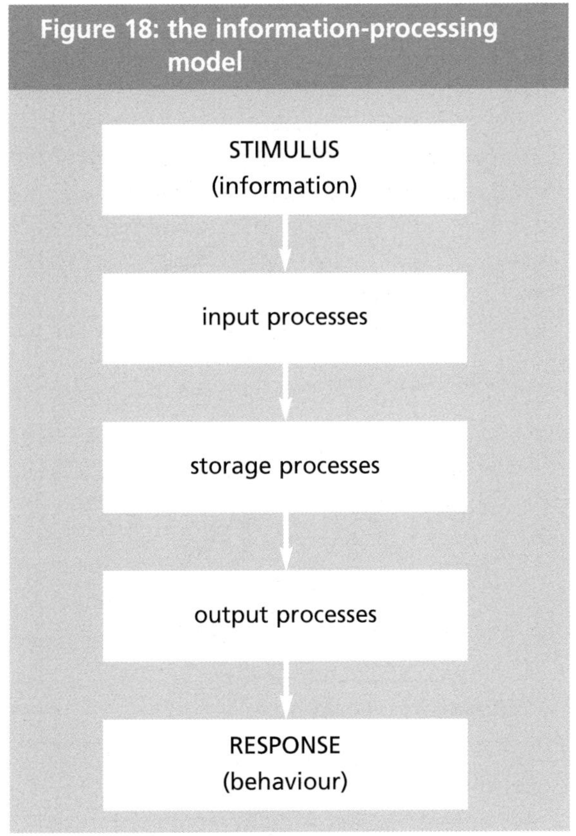

safely. This information is compared with what we have in our memory, e.g. what a red light means, thinking about where we are going and how our driving needs to be adapted for the conditions. This information is then fed along the system so that it can be processed and translated into appropriate behaviour, e.g. changing gear and steering. So this model talks about information being processed by the brain through a series of stages.

Different sensory inputs can be thought of as different **communication channels**, and we have to choose which will have our attention. It may help to compare this with deciding which television channel to watch; when you switch to a particular channel, you are setting up a flow of information through the transmission system. In the same way, we have to select from our immediate environment what to attend to and process, and what to ignore. The idea of **stages** of processing allows us to look at each part of the process individually and in detail, to see how each contributes to the overall picture.

Another important idea here is that of **attentional capacity**. In the same way that only one television programme can be watched at a time, so the information that can be processed by our systems is limited: we can only deal with a certain amount of information at once, and this fact has been central to the information-processing model of attention.

- Attention theorists are concerned with two aspects of attention: selective or **focused** attention (the ability to focus on one particular stimulus), and **divided** attention (the ability to divide attention across two or more activities).
- An **information-processing model**, using the analogy of the brain as a computer, provides a framework within which questions of attention can be explored.
- This model emphasises the idea of a **one-way flow** of information along a communication channel, through various stages of processing. The capacity to handle information is limited.

8.7 Models of selective attention

There are several theories of selective attention, based on the information-processing model. The theories vary in two main ways. Firstly, where in the system does the selection of items for attention take place? Secondly, to what extent does non-attended information continue to flow through the system?

Broadbent's filter theory

One of the earliest theories of selective attention was developed by Broadbent (1958). His interest arose out of his work with air traffic controllers. In their job, they are faced with a vast amount of information from pilots, and selecting what is important is obviously vital if air disasters are to be avoided. Broadbent wanted to find out precisely what processes were involved in their ability to do this.

Given the complex nature of their job, it would not have been practical to have carried out research by looking at their performance in real-life situations. For example, it wouldn't have been very

The work of air traffic controllers is very complex.

ethical to manipulate the conditions under which they were working – the result might have been fatal! Broadbent therefore carried out experiments in a laboratory, where he could isolate and manipulate various aspects of selective attention. Obviously this approach may not have high **ecological validity**, but at the same time it does permit very precise data to be collected. Broadbent reasoned that by overloading the attentional system, and analysing the errors people made on the tasks he devised, it would be possible to find out about the precise processes involved.

He developed a procedure called **dichotic listening** ('dichotic' means 'two ears') in which the two ears receive different messages simultaneously. A typical experiment uses the **split-span procedure**, and an example is described in box K:

Box K: Broadbent (1958)

Procedure: Participants were required to listen through headphones to a set of three numbers coming to the right ear, while at the same time, a different set of three numbers reached the left ear. They were then required to report all six numbers either (a) ear-by-ear or (b) pair-by-pair.

Results: Participants found it very much harder to report pair-by-pair than ear-by-ear, and made more errors in this condition.

(a) reporting ear-by-ear

(b) reporting pair-by-pair

Conclusion: Switching physical channels decreases efficiency in tasks requiring focused attention.

Before we discuss Broadbent's results, you may like to try dichotic listening yourself. Broadbent used fairly sophisticated apparatus, but activity 11 gives a simplified version:

Activity 11: dichotic listening

You will need to work in a group of three, two of you saying the numbers and the third being a 'dichotic listener' and reporting back, either ear-by-ear or pair-by-pair. Take it in turns to be the listener.

Prepare sets of six numbers. Each set should contain six different single-figure numbers in no particular order. Ten sets is about right, so that the listener can have five trials reporting ear-by-ear and five reporting pair-by-pair.

The two speakers will need to speak their sets of numbers simultaneously, so a bit of practice will be necessary before you start. You might find that nodding your head as you speak helps you to keep time with each other.

When you are ready, each of the speakers should position themselves reasonably close to one ear of the listener. Before each trial, remind the listener whether they are to report ear-by-ear or pair-by-pair, and write down what is reported.

You will find it easier to draw up a table before you start, which can be filled in as you go along, e.g:

Numbers	Ears/Pairs	Response
259 176	ears	259176
462 983	pairs	

and so on ...

When all the trials have been completed, make a rough analysis of which condition, ear-by-ear or pair-by-pair, was more difficult. How many numbers were not reported, or were wrong, or in the wrong order? Ask your participant for an introspective report too.

Though there are usually quite wide differences in people's ability to carry out this task (a point we shall be coming back to later), it is likely that you found it quite difficult. Probably, though, you had similar results to Broadbent and found the ear-by-ear condition relatively easier than pair-by-pair.

How can we explain Broadbent's results? When recalling pair-by-pair, it is necessary to switch from one ear to the other and back again, making at least three switches to group the numbers in pairs. In the ear-by-ear condition, only one switch is necessary, so an explanation of the differences between the conditions is likely to have something to do with the frequency of switching that is necessary to carry out the task. To see why this should make a difference, we need to look at Broadbent's theory. He suggested the model in figure 19, where the arrows represent information passing through the system.

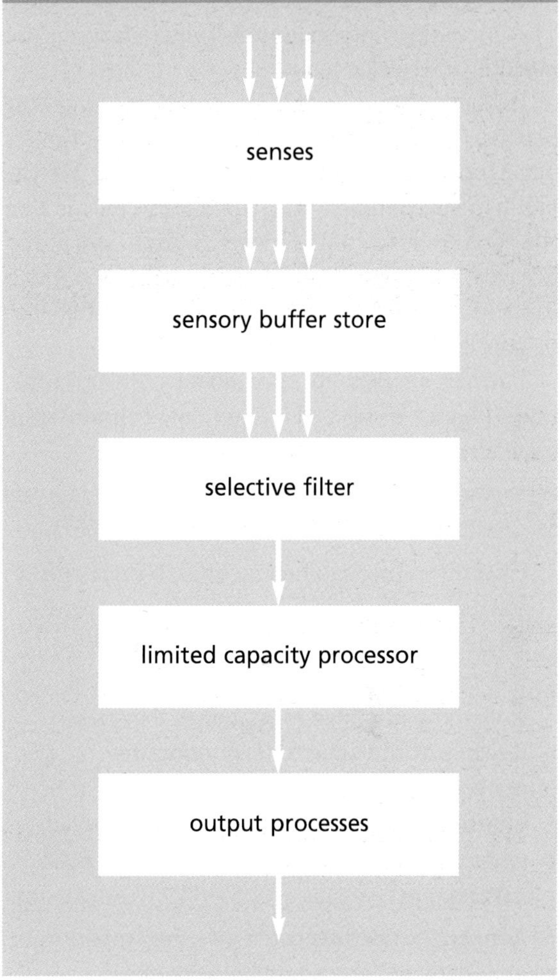

In the dichotic listening experiment, Broadbent assumed that the ears were acting as separate communication channels, and so gave two sources of auditory input. This sensory information is passed to the **sensory buffer store**. This is a memory store which only lasts a very short time, where incoming information is held until it can be processed. He suggested that the processing system could only deal with one channel at a time, which is why his is a **single-channel theory** of attention. There is a **selective filter** operating which selects the channel we will attend to. He also suggested that the channel was chosen only on the basis of **physical characteristics**: for example, acoustic features, such as whether the sound was loud or soft, high-pitched or low; or the actual physical channel through which it was

Figure 19: Broadbent's model of selective attention

senses

sensory buffer store

selective filter

limited capacity processor

output processes

received, depending on the direction it was coming from. In the dichotic listening experiment, the key factor is the ear to which each input is coming. The incoming information is only analysed for meaning *after* selection.

In the dichotic listening experiment, switching between channels takes up time, and more time is taken up with the extra switches needed for the pair-by-pair condition. This time lapse means that the material in the sensory buffer store has decayed, and so is no longer available, which explains why people tend to do less well on the pair-by-pair condition.

Further support for Broadbent's theory came from research using a technique called **shadowing**, originally developed by Cherry:

Box L: Cherry (1953)

Procedure: Through headphones, participants were played two different passages of prose simultaneously, one to each ear. Their task was to repeat aloud one of the passages (called the **attended message**) as they heard it, while at the same time ignoring the material being played into the other ear (the **unattended message**). They were then asked what they had noticed about the *unattended* message.

Results: Participants could give information about the physical characteristics of the unattended message (e.g. whether the voice was high or low, or whether the message changed from speech to a tone), but were unable to say anything about what the passage had been about.

Conclusion: These findings support Broadbent's ideas. Input channels are distinguished by physical characteristics. Meaning plays no part in selection.

However, there are problems with Broadbent's model. The first problem is how we define a channel. On the face of it, the idea of the ears acting as two separate channels seems plausible. In real life, though, we seldom have two entirely separate sets of information coming to each ear individually. For example, if you are listening to a piece of music played by an orchestra, you can pick out different instruments, even though this information is going to both ears, but it doesn't seem sensible to think of all the different instruments as separate channels.

Secondly, how does the selective filter operate? Broadbent claims that selection is on the basis of physical characteristics, and that meaning is not a factor. His dichotic listening experiments used information whose channels couldn't be selected on the basis of meaning (since both channels carried numbers) so there doesn't seem a very sound basis for this claim. Gray and Wedderburn (1960) decided to test whether meaning could be used as a basis for message selection:

Box M: Gray and Wedderburn (1960)

Procedure: The procedure was basically the same as that followed by Broadbent (1958). The only difference was that instead of two sets of numbers, each ear received a mixture of words and numbers, e.g.:

Participants were asked to report ear-by-ear or category-by-category, i.e. grouping the numbers together and the words together.

Results: Participants found it as easy to report category-by-category as ear-by-ear. Dividing the stimulus material into meaningful categories made switching less of a problem than in Broadbent's experiment.
Conclusion: Meaning must be analysed *before* selection.

- Broadbent used a technique called **dichotic listening**.
- His **filter model** suggests that there is a filter which lets only one channel of information through to the limited capacity processor. This filter operates on the basis of physical characteristics. Meaning is only analysed *after* selection.
- Broadbent's definition of a channel is problematical. His technique eliminates any possible effect of meaning.
- Evidence from Gray and Wedderburn suggests that meaning must be analysed *before* selection.

Treisman's attenuation theory

Treisman followed Cherry's shadowing technique for further studies into the basis of selection, using a variety of materials. In a series of experiments (examples are given in box N) she found considerable support for the conclusion drawn by the Gray and Wedderburn study (box M), i.e. that meaning is a factor in the selection process. It seems that the studies of Broadbent and of Cherry do not give us the complete picture.

Box N: Treisman (1960; 1964)

(a) Bilingual participants were asked to carry out a shadowing task. The attended message was in English, and the unattended message was a French version of the English. If the French version followed the English version after a slight lapse in time, most participants were aware that the messages had the same meaning.

(b) Participants were asked to shadow a string of words similar to English sentences (e.g. I saw the girl song was wishing ...) which was presented to one ear. A similar word string to the other ear was to be ignored. There were intrusions from the unattended channel when the words from that channel would make sense in the context of the attended channel.

Conclusion: Even though participants were focusing attention on one input, the meaning of the other input was unconsciously monitored. The meanings of messages are recognised before selection takes place.

Activity 12: cocktail party effect

Imagine you are at a party and are having a very interesting conversation with someone you have just met. Suddenly your attention switches to something that is said on the other side of the room. What might have been said to make your attention switch in this way?

When you have finished, see the notes on page 227.

The **cocktail party effect** was first described by Cherry (1953). It has also been shown experimentally; Moray (1959) found that participants recognised their own name on the unattended channel of a shadowing task. The phenomenon can only really be explained if we accept that we are monitoring much more of the information around us than we are consciously aware of, and that we have some knowledge of the meaning of this information. It is the nature of the information which causes us to switch attention when there is something of particular relevance to us.

These findings led Treisman to suggest a modified version of Broadbent's theory of selective attention (see figure 20 overleaf):

The cocktail party effect

Treisman's model partly follows Broadbent's. She agrees with him that there is a selective filter where one channel is selected on the basis of its physical features. However, she suggests that other channels are not blocked off entirely, but instead are **attenuated**. This means that the information those channels carry is only passed on in a weakened form. Imagine the various input channels as radios, broadcasting different programmes. In the attenuation process, one of them is turned right up and all the rest are turned down so they are just a low background murmur. In figure 3, the selected channel is represented by the heavier arrow going from the selective filter to the next stage in the system, while the attenuated channels are shown by the arrows with thinner lines.

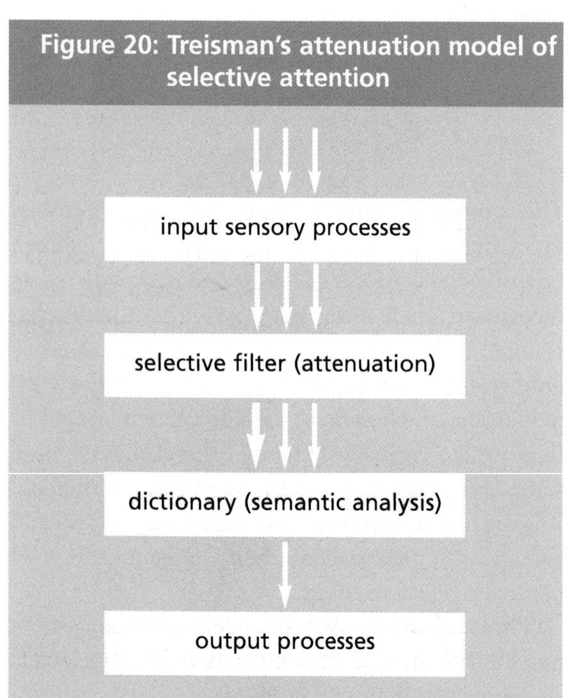

There is then a further selection process, where material is selected through **semantic analysis**, i.e. on the basis of its meaning. This stage of selection consists of a mental **dictionary**, listing words and their meanings. Each item is known as a **dictionary unit**, each of which has a specific **threshold**. The threshold is the intensity a word needs to have to trigger that particular dictionary unit. For some words, such as our own name, this threshold is very low. This means that even if this information is carried on an attenuated channel, the words will be very easily triggered. We can relate this to the party example, where you catch the sound of your own name across the room (on an attenuated channel), not in the conversation you are actually having (the selected channel).

Our own name is always important to us, and so will have a permanently low threshold. Thresholds can also change according to the situation. For example, if you are hungry then words associated with food will temporarily have a low threshold until you have had something to eat. They will then have a higher threshold (unless, of course, food is something which is always of major interest to you!).

Activity 13: thresholds and dictionary units

a Which of these words have a permanently low threshold for most people?
For which particular kinds of people might the other words have a permanently low threshold?

kennel *help* *Olympics* *fire* *mummy*

b For each of these situations, give examples of words whose threshold may be temporarily lowered:

taking your driving test *going on holiday*

When you have finished, see the notes on page 227.

It is at the dictionary stage, then, that the final selection is made. If there is nothing on attenuated channels with a particularly low threshold, then the already selected channel will be attended to and information on the other channels lost. But the originally selected channel can be overridden if an attenuated channel contains something with a permanently or temporarily lowered threshold. In this case, attention will switch (as in the cocktail party example) to this attenuated channel.

Activity 14: Broadbent and Treisman

For each of these statements, indicate whether they refer to Broadbent's theory, Treisman's theory, or both:

a All input channels are initially processed simultaneously.

b One channel is selected on the basis of physical characteristics.

c Information from the other channels is blocked.

d Information from the other channels is passed on in a weakened form.

e A response can include items from an unattended channel.

When you have finished, see the notes on page 227.

On the face of it, Treisman's model can account for phenomena, like the cocktail party effect, which Broadbent's theory doesn't really cover, but how satisfactory is it?

There are two ways in which it has been criticised. Firstly, the concept of attenuation is tricky. It seems clear what the *function* of attenuation is, i.e. to reduce the amount of information being processed through the system and facilitate the selection process. But how does it actually operate? In what sense is the information content of the attenuated channels reduced?

There is also a problem in the notion of a selection process based on the *meaning* of the various inputs. The findings of Gray and Wedderburn (box M) and the cocktail party effect as well as Treisman (box N), suggest that unattended channels are processed for meaning. But processing for meaning must be a complex process, and Treisman's model does not really explain very clearly what the semantic mechanisms are which allow switching between an attended and an unattended channel.

- Treisman used the technique of **shadowing**. Her **attenuation theory** of selective attention suggests that the selective filter does not block unattended information; it attenuates it.
- We can (and do) switch to another channel when material on that channel has a low **threshold** for us.

- Like Broadbent's filter theory, attenuation theory claims that we are only able to attend to one channel at a time.
- The theory has been criticised for failing to explain how attenuation works. It also fails to explain clearly the semantic mechanisms involved in switching.

The Deutsch and Deutsch pertinence model

The theories of Broadbent and Treisman are both **bottleneck theories**. This means that only some of the information available to us can pass all the way through the attentional system, with the rest blocked along the way. They agree that the bottleneck occurs at the recognition stage, and so some selection must take place before this is reached. Other theorists have suggested that *all* incoming stimuli are processed for meaning. This processing is virtually automatic, and so makes few demands on the system. Only after this initial analysis is one input selected for further processing. The bottleneck in the system comes nearer to the response stage.

This framework was first proposed by Deutsch and Deutsch (1963) and later revised by Norman (1968). It is illustrated in figure 21 below.

Deutsch and Deutsch suggested that all incoming stimuli are recognised and processed by being matched against information in long-term memory. The recognition process is not a bottleneck, as Broadbent and Treisman proposed, but nonetheless acts as a filter. The filter weighs up the relative importance of the stimuli, and only what is most pertinent, i.e. relevant, in a particular context is selected for further processing and is consciously attended to. For this reason, this model of attention is sometimes known as the **pertinence model**. Other stimuli will only be attended to if they become more relevant.

Activity 15: pertinence

In each of these scenarios, what event might cause unattended stimuli to become pertinent, and so reach conscious awareness?

1 Sarah is watching her favourite soap opera, and is engrossed in a particularly interesting twist in the story. There is the steady sound of cars passing the house. She is looking forward to going out that evening with a friend, who is coming to pick her up in his car. He is already a little late.

2 Malik is playing football with his brother in the garden. He is concentrating on not letting his brother shoot goals past him. Their father is

Figure 21: late selection models of attention

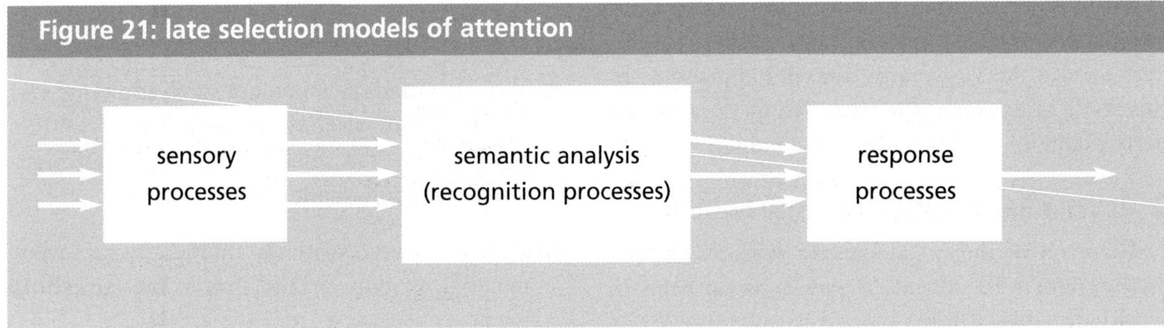

cooking lunch on the barbecue. It is already well past Malik's normal lunchtime.

When you have finished, see the notes on page 227.

The pertinence theory suggests that in a dichotic listening experiment, the fact that participants are unaware of unattended material doesn't mean that this material has not been recognised. Rather, it means that it has not reached consciousness.

However, if we want to test this distinction between recognition and consciousness, relating it to an observable response, we come up against a problem. Participants would respond in exactly the same way to material that had been recognised, and then forgotten before they became conscious of it, as they would to material which had not been recognised at all. This is illustrated by the first Treisman study described in box N. Participants realised that the two stories were the same, but only if they were very close together in time. This suggests that the information in the unattended message was recognised, but quickly forgotten. However, this problem was overcome in an ingenious way (box O).

The fact that Corteen and Wood found that a GSR was produced by city names not included in the original list strongly suggests that the unattended material was processed quite deeply, to a level in which the semantic category of an item was recognised.

Box O: Corteen and Wood (1972)

Procedure: A mild electric shock was given to participants, paired with a series of city names. This resulted in a conditioned GSR (galvanic skin response – sweating detectable by an electrode placed on the skin) to the city names. Participants then carried out a shadowing task.
Results: A GSR was produced whenever one of the city names occurred on the unattended channel. A similar response was shown to other city names on which participants had not been trained. They were not consciously aware that they had heard any city names.
Conclusion: Unattended information is unconsciously processed for meaning.

Von Wright *et al.* (1975) carried out a similar study. They found a GSR on only a few of the trials. It seems that thorough processing of unattended information only happens some of the time, challenging the Deutsch and Deutsch view that all input must be analysed before selection. A further challenge comes from another study:

Box P: Treisman and Riley (1969)

Procedure: Participants carried out a shadowing task. They were also asked to identify target words which could appear in either the attended or unattended channel. They were instructed to stop shadowing and to tap as soon as they heard a target word in either message.
Results: Many more target words were detected in the shadowed message than the unattended message.
Conclusion: The unattended message was not fully analysed for meaning.

There is some evidence, then, that Treisman's ideas about attenuation may be more accurate than the full semantic analysis required by late selection theories.

The Deutsch and Deutsch theory has also been criticised for proposing a rather rigid processing system. A more flexible model has been suggested by Johnston and Heinz (1978). They suggested that selection may be possible at various stages of processing. They made two assumptions. Firstly, the more stages of processing that take place before selection, the greater the demands on processing capacity. Secondly, in order to minimise these demands, selection takes place as early as possible, depending on the specific demands of the situation.

There is some support for the flexibility they suggested (box Q).

The original debate about selective attention assumed that information passes through the attentional system, and that at some point there is a bottleneck, where selection takes place. The issue was at what point in the system this bottleneck occurs. Early selection theories placed the bottleneck at the recognition stage, whereas late selection theories suggested that the bottleneck occurs nearer to the response stage.

The argument now seems to have shifted somewhat, to the nature of recognition. Broadbent's original theory suggested that recognition was an all-or-nothing process, but Treisman's theory and more particularly late selection theories suggest that recognition is not that simple; there may be degrees of recognition. The Johnston and Heinz model goes further, to suggest that the degree of recognition will depend on the demands of the task.

Box Q: Johnston and Wilson (1980)

Procedure: Using a dichotic listening technique, participants were asked to identify target words belonging to a particular semantic category, e.g. clothing. 'Socks' would be a sample target word. Each target word was ambiguous, having at least two meanings. The presentation of each target word was accompanied by a non-target word. This would either bias appropriately (e.g. 'smelly'), bias towards the inappropriate meaning (e.g. 'punches') or was a neutral word (e.g. 'Tuesday'). On some trials, participants were told the ear in which they would hear the target words. On some trials they were not given this information.

Results: When participants did not know which ear targets would arrive at, appropriate non-target words improved target detection, and inappropriate ones impaired it. These effects were lost when participants knew in which ear they would hear the target words.

Conclusion: Non-target words were processed for meaning only when participants did not know in which ear they would hear the target words. Whether or not semantic processing of unattended material takes place depends on whether it is necessary to the task.

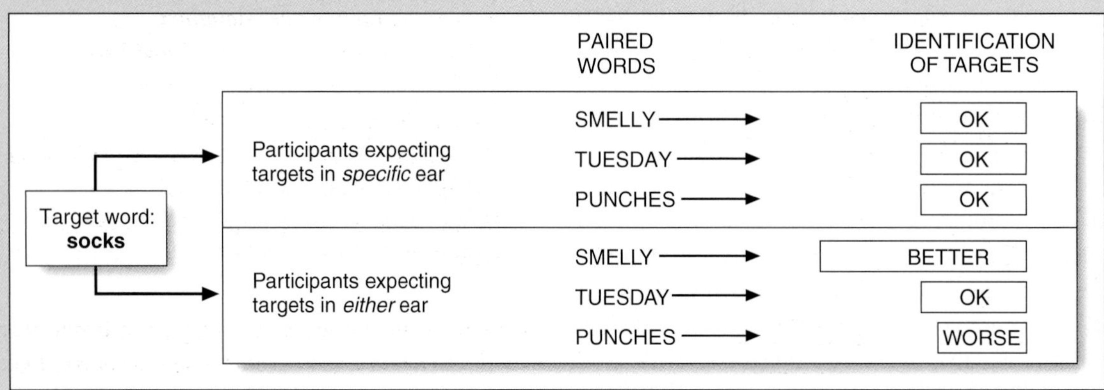

- The Deutsch and Deutsch/Norman **pertinence model** suggests that all incoming information is processed for meaning, and that the bottleneck is at the response stage. As with the Broadbent and Treisman models, only one channel can be attended to at a time.
- Attention switches when unattended information becomes more pertinent.
- Research evidence does not entirely support this model. It has also been criticised for being too rigid. Johnston and Heinz have proposed a more flexible model, in which processing depends on the requirements of the task.
- The nature of recognition is problematical. There may be different degrees of recognition.

Kahneman's capacity theory

It seems clear that some tasks require more attention – more **mental effort** – than others. If a task does not require our complete attention, it is possible to attend to something else at the same time. There are also limits to the number of things which we can attend to at once, however little of our attention each takes up. You would probably find it extremely difficult, if not impossible, to read a book, hum a tune, tap your foot and sew on a button, all at the same time, even if all these tasks are routine and well-practised.

This seems to suggest that there is a pool of attentional resources which, although limited, can be flexibly allocated to tasks. Kahneman's model (1973) includes a **central processor** which governs **resource allocation**. The model assumes that we have considerable control over how resources are allocated.

There are limits to the number of things we can attend to at once.

Another important factor is **arousal**. Arousal determines how much processing capacity we have, which in turn influences allocation. For example, if you are half asleep you might find that a simple task like getting out of a car takes all your concentration; you have less attentional capacity than if you are fully alert, so there is no spare capacity to be given to another task.

Finally, the central processor allocates resources in response to external factors. Kahneman differentiates between **enduring dispositions**, i.e. aspects of the environment which are always of interest to a person, and **momentary intentions**, i.e. those aspects which are only of current interest.

Activity 16: momentary intentions and enduring dispositions

In each of these scenarios, imagine that the person is in a TV shop where the sets are tuned to different channels. Pick out from the list at the bottom which programme s/he is likely to attend to, relating to (a) momentary intentions and (b) enduring dispositions:

Peter is a keen runner, running several miles a day. This evening he and his girlfriend are on their way to see a film.

Tonya has got her driving test this afternoon, and is really worried she won't pass. She needs to have her licence so that she can get to the drama course she is about to start.

a report on the London Marathon
a drama workshop *the Grand Prix*
a report from the Cannes film festival
a trailer for a new crime series
the weather forecast *a cookery programme*
an athletics meeting in Gateshead

When you have finished, see the notes on page 227.

How relevant a stimulus is to a person is one factor in whether it is attended to. Generally, current goals are most important in deciding resource allocation.

However, there are also other factors. Enduring dispositions include factors to do with survival, which would explain why attention switches very rapidly when someone shouts 'Fire!' The intensity of a stimulus, and its novelty, can also be important in overriding attention to the current goal.

All these elements come together in Kahneman's model.

Figure 22: Kahneman's capacity model of attention

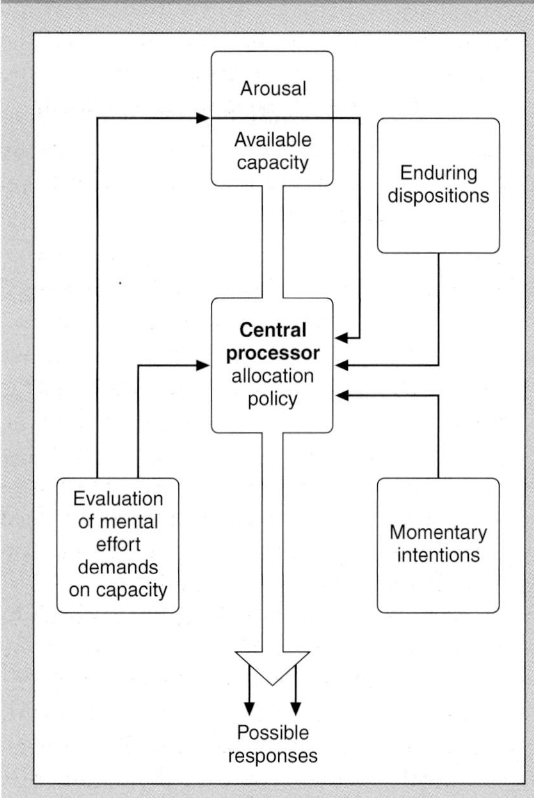

This model is much more flexible than those proposed by earlier theorists such as Broadbent, and takes account of the wide range of factors which research has shown to be important. What it still has in common with earlier models, though, is the idea of attention as a process.

Neisser, however, has suggested that we may need to think of attention as a skill. He illustrated his idea with the example of two participants in a study he carried out with colleagues (Spelke *et al.* 1976). After considerable training over a period of weeks, they could write and understand dictated words, while being able *at the same time* to read a different text, and understand that as well.

The idea of attention as a skill is relevant to simultaneous translating. This involves hearing a message in one language and, as it is heard, producing a spoken translation in another language. Training for this work involves first of all shadowing a heard message in the translator's native language. This gets the translator used to dealing with combining 'language-in' with 'language-out'. They can then move on to the more difficult task of translating the 'language-in', and speaking the translated version as 'language-out'.

The idea of attention as a skill would also help us to understand individual differences in attention:

Activity 17: attention as a skill

Can you think of examples of jobs where people would develop the skill of attending selectively to a particular stimulus, while at the same time monitoring unattended information?

When you have finished, see the notes on page 227.

- **Kahneman's capacity theory** brings together much of the information we have about attention.
- Attention is flexibly allocated by a **central processor** between one or more tasks. Overall capacity is related to **arousal**. Allocation decisions are influenced by **enduring dispositions** and **momentary intentions**.
- **Neisser** has suggested that attention should be regarded as a **skill** rather than a process. There is some support for this idea.

Notes on activities

1 Most people see a spiral, radiating from a central point. However, if you try to trace the spiral with your finger, you will find that it is not a spiral at all but a series of circles. Your sense organs – in this case your eyes – have provided accurate information about the figure, but what you see is rather different. When you perceive the spiral, you are interpreting the information which reaches your eyes. There is a discrepancy here between sensation and perception.

4 The retinal image was the same in conditions (a) and (c). The much larger number of conditioned responses to condition (a) suggests that babies were responding to the actual size of the cube, not the size of the retinal image. Since the babies were so young, the results give some support to the view that size constancy is innate.

5 **a** the line nearer the top of the diagram; **b** discontinuous; **c** the bottom line; **d** the vertical line; **e** the circle on the left; **f** no. These illusions demonstrate the effect of context on perception, e.g. in e. and f. Illusions a. and c. suggest that we may impose the conventions of 3D representation on 2D drawings, automatically and inappropriately responding to depth cues.

8 Gregory: **b d h** *Gibson*: **a e g** both: **c f i**

9 The hunter in (a) is aiming at the antelope, even though the tip of the spear is pointing at the elephant. We know this using the depth cues of relative size and interposition.

12 Something that almost always catches our attention is someone saying our own name: we seem to be very keen to know if anyone is talking about us. Attention-switching can also happen with other topics which we find interesting. For example, if you're a Spurs fan, the words 'Tottenham' or 'White Hart Lane', or the name of one of the players, are all likely to catch your attention.

13 Because they relate to possibly dangerous situations, 'fire' and 'help' are likely to have a permanently low threshold for everyone. 'Kennel' would be likely to be picked up by someone interested in dogs, perhaps a dog breeder, and 'Olympics' by a sports enthusiast. Mothers often automatically respond to 'mummy' from other people's children long after their own have left home. And of course Egyptologists might too!

If you are taking your driving test, words like 'driving instructor', 'Highway Code' and 'pass' have a temporarily lowered threshold. Once the test is over and done with, they will soon lose their significance and be no more likely to be picked up on an attenuated channel than thousands of other words. Similarly, if you are going on holiday, the threshold for words like 'airport', 'passport' or the name of the place you are visiting is likely to be lowered temporarily.

14 Statements **a** and **b** refer to both theories, while **c** refers only to Broadbent's model, and **d** and **e** only to Treisman's model.

15 Sarah is unconsciously aware of the traffic outside. She might find her attention switching if she hears a car pulling up in front of the house. Malik is hungry, and is aware at an unconscious level that his father is cooking. It is likely that his attention will switch from saving goals when the smell of cooked food drifts towards him. What Sarah and Malik are unconsciously aware of – the sound of a car stopping and the smell of food – have become pertinent, i.e. more relevant than what they are consciously attending to.

16 Based on enduring dispositions, Peter is likely to attend to the London Marathon report, or the athletics meeting, while for Tonya the drama workshop is likely to be more relevant. Momentary intentions could make Peter switch his attention to the report from the Cannes film festival, particularly if the film he is planning to see is mentioned. The words 'drive', 'car' and so on could be enough to make Tonya's attention switch to the Grand Prix.

17 There are several possibilities here. For example, you may have suggested that this would be a useful skill for primary school teachers, or mothers with several very young children. It could be that because their attentional skills have developed through practice, these people would be quite competent at dichotic listening tasks.

09

Remembering and forgetting

9.1 The nature of memory

There are three main processes in memory. **Registration** is the process by which your sense organs detect information and enter that information in the memory system; **storage** is the process by which information is kept in the memory; and **retrieval** is the process by which information in memory can be recovered.

Sometimes in psychology a model of a particular process is used, a way of thinking about a process that helps us picture it better. This provides a framework within which research can take place. We will be looking in the next sections at four models which aim to throw some light on how memory works.

The multi-store model

This model, developed by Atkinson and Shiffrin (1968, 1971) is also often called the **two-process model** because of the importance attached to the two stores of **short-term memory (STM)** and **long-term memory (LTM)**. You may also find it referred to as the **modal model**; 'modal' here means 'most frequently occurring', as this model shares a number of common features with other similar models. Finally, it is sometimes called the **structural model**.

This model describes memory in terms of information flowing through a system. Information is detected by the sense organs, and enters the **sensory memory (SM)**, and can be kept there if

Figure 1: Atkinson and Shiffrin's model of memory (1968 and 1971)

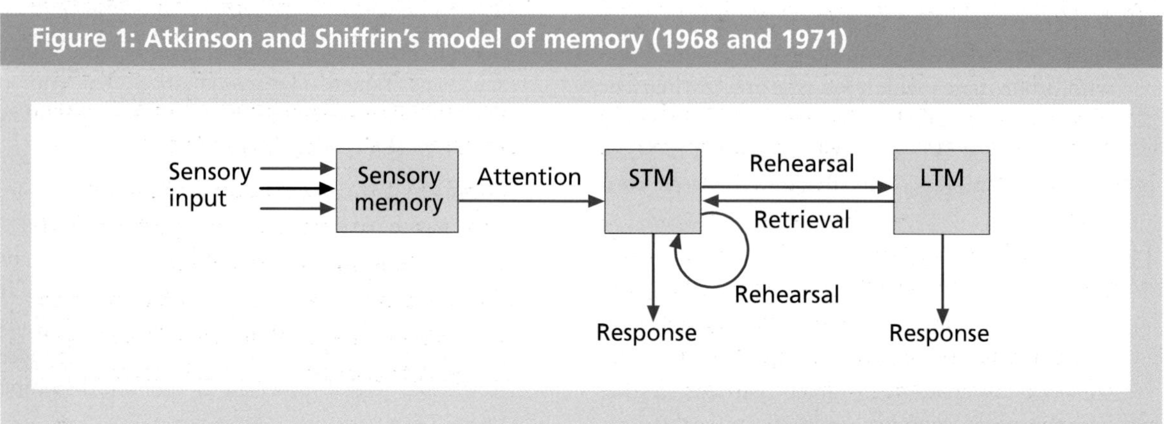

rehearsed. If we attend to this information, it enters the **STM**. Information from the STM is transferred to the **LTM** only if that information is rehearsed. If **rehearsal** does not occur, then the information is forgotten.

There are different types of rehearsal. Craik and Watkins (1973) distinguished between **maintenance rehearsal**, (for example, a word is repeated out loud a number of times) and **elaborative rehearsal**, in which information is processed in terms of its meaning. They suggested that maintenance rehearsal may be enough to keep information in STM, while elaborative rehearsal is necessary to transfer it from STM to LTM.

The three memory stores can be compared in terms of how much information they can hold, how long they can hold that information, and how information is encoded:

Figure 2: comparing SM, STM and LTM

	SM	STM	LTM
Capacity	small	7±2 items	unlimited
Duration	0.25–2 seconds	up to 30 seconds	indefinite period of time
Encoding	modality-specific	mainly acoustic	semantic/ visual/acoustic

Sensory memory

SM is what happens after information has reached the sense organs, and it travels to the brain for interpretation. This lingering of information in the nervous system (very briefly) gives the brain time to interpret it. There are two types of sensory storage: **iconic storage**, the store associated with visual information, and **echoic storage**, associated with heard, or auditory, information. You can probably imagine iconic storage if you remember what happens when someone takes your photograph with a flash – you often see an after-image of the flash for a brief moment, and this is iconic storage. Box A explores the nature of SM:

Box A: Sperling (1960)

Procedure 1: Replicating many previous studies, Sperling asked participants to look at an array of letters. He used a device called a tachistoscope, a machine which can display letters or numbers on a screen for very short and accurately controlled periods of time. In one trial, the participants were shown three rows of four letters (such as that shown below) for 50 milliseconds. They were then asked to recall as many letters as they could from the whole display.

sample display:

G	B	T	F
S	R	D	W
E	N	Z	X

Results: Participants could recall on average about 4.5 of the 12 items.

Procedure 2: Sperling then introduced his own idea, a partial report condition in which the participant was asked to recall only part of the display. A tone was played just after the display – if the tone was a high-pitched tone they should recall the top row of the display, a low-pitched tone indicated the bottom row, and a medium-pitched tone indicated the middle row.

Results: When the participants were cued to recall one row of the display immediately after the display was switched off, their average recall was 3.3 letters. As the tone was increasingly delayed, the average number of letters recalled decreased as the after-image faded.

Conclusion: Since the proportion of items remembered was greater in the partial report condition than for the total display, participants must have been reading the letters from an after-image – their iconic stores. Iconic storage lasts approximately half a second.

A study by Averbach and Coriell (1961) has provided a more sensitive measure of the capacity of SM, with information about how material is lost from this store:

Box B: Averbach and Coriell (1961)

Procedure 1: Participants were shown two rows, each of eight letters chosen at random, for 50 milliseconds. A small mark then appeared just above one of the letter positions. Participants were asked to state which letter had been in the position of the marker.
Results: Letter identification was 75% accurate.
Conclusion: Twelve letters can be held in SM, i.e. 75% of the 16 letters shown.

Procedure 2: Using a tachistoscope, participants were shown a letter, followed after a short time interval by another letter. They were asked to identify the first letter.
Results: If the time interval between the presentation of the two letters was less than 100 milliseconds, **superimposition** occurred (e.g. F followed by L was reported as E). If the time interval was longer than 100 milliseconds, backward visual masking **(displacement)** occurred (e.g. F followed by L was reported as L).
Conclusion: The iconic store forgets by displacement; the second letter displaces the first. For this to occur, there must be at least 100 milliseconds between the original stimulus and the displacing stimulus.

Treisman (1964) found that echoic memory has similar characteristics. Participants were asked to shadow (i.e. repeat out loud) the contents of a message presented to one ear, while ignoring the message presented to the other. When the non-attended message preceded the shadowed message, the two messages were only perceived to be the same when they were within two seconds of each other. This suggests that unattended auditory information remains in the echoic store for a similar period of time as visual information remains in the iconic store.

Short-term memory (STM)

In figure 2, the capacity of STM is given as 7±2 items. This idea was put forward by Miller (1956), as a result of having reviewed many already-existing studies of STM: '7±2' means 'seven plus-or-minus two', so Miller was suggesting that STM can store between five and nine pieces of information. STM can store only a limited number of items because it has only a certain number of 'slots' in which items can be stored. But Miller didn't specify the amount of information that could be held in each slot – indeed, his idea was that we can increase that amount by **chunking** the material; for example, by grouping letters together into words or into abbreviations that have meaning for us.

Activity 1: chunking

Write the letters listed below on a large piece of paper, and test participants to see how many of the letters they can recall in a free recall task (they should try to remember as many as they can, in any order):

M S C G C S E P H D B S C A S

Now group the letters so that they form the chunks below, and write them on a second large piece of paper. Test a different set of participants to see how many of the letters they can recall.

MSC GCSE PHD BSC AS

Work out which list was recalled more accurately.

You probably found that the second condition allowed people to recall significantly more letters than the first. In terms of Miller's idea, the first set of letters (15 items) would be too many for the 7±2 slots of STM to hold. But if we group the letters so that they form the chunks MSC, GCSE, PHD, BSC and AS, they give six 'chunks' of information (at least to English-speaking people who know something about the English education system) which is within the range of STM.

A further task to investigate STM which you could try on your participants is what is known as the **Brown–Peterson technique**. Peterson and Peterson (1959) asked their participants to remember **trigrams** – groups of three consonants like KMG or PNS. But to prevent the participants from rehearsing the trigrams, they were asked to count backwards aloud in threes, from a number such as 176. This prevented rehearsal, and they found that information was rapidly forgotten; they concluded that, without rehearsal, material in STM is forgotten within 6–12 seconds. Although Atkinson and Shiffrin believe it lasts rather longer (see figure 2), these findings give a general indication of the **duration** of STM, and show that **rehearsal** is necessary to enable information to be transferred to LTM.

Activity 2 investigates how material is encoded in STM:

Activity 2: encoding in STM

You will need to find participants to help you carry out this activity.

Draw each of the letters listed below on to a separate piece of white card, in large clear lettering. Put the letters into two piles – list 1 and list 2.

List 1:	B	V	T	C	D	G	E	P
List 2:	M	R	W	L	Z	Y	Q	A

Tell participants that they will be shown a series of eight letters and that they should write down as many as they can, in the order in which they were presented. Now show each letter of list 1 briefly to your participants. Next, repeat the procedure with list 2.

To make it a better test, you should present half your participants with list 1 followed by list 2, and the other half with list 2 followed by list 1. This technique is known as **counterbalancing**, and eliminates **order effects**, such as practice, fatigue or boredom.

Work out which list was remembered most accurately. What is the difference between the two lists?

You will have noticed that the letters in list 1 all sound like each other – they are acoustically similar. You may have found that your participants were far more likely to make errors when recalling the letters that were acoustically similar than when recalling different sounding letters, so made more mistakes when they tried to recall list 1 than with list 2. Bear in mind that this happened even though the letters were presented visually – you didn't read the letters out loud and in doing so show that list 1 letters all sounded similar. The results of this study imply that information stored in STM is stored in an **acoustic code**. Other studies support this idea:

Box C: Conrad (1964)

Procedure: Participants were shown sequences of 6 letters, chosen from B C F M N P S T V X. They were asked to write them down as they appeared, but presentation was too fast for participants to keep up, so the information had to be held in STM. The errors made were analysed.

Results: The errors were generally acoustic confusion errors, where the original letters were replaced by ones with a similar sound, e.g. S for X or M for N.

Conclusion: Coding in STM is acoustic, even when material is presented visually.

Long-term memory (LTM)

According to the multi-store model, LTM can hold unlimited amounts of information for an indefinite period of time. Together with **visual** and **acoustic** coding, this store uses mainly **semantic coding**, i.e. is based on the meaning of information:

Box D: Baddeley (1966)

Procedure: Participants were presented with a short list of words which were semantically similar (e.g. neat/clean/tidy/smart). They were also given a list of words that were acoustically similar (e.g. heat/sweet/greet/sheet). Recall was tested immediately, and again after a period of time had elapsed.

Results: When testing immediate recall, there was acoustic confusion between acoustically similar words, while those with similar meanings were easily remembered. When participants were tested again later, however, the words with similar meanings caused problems.

Conclusion: The confusion on semantically similar lists after a period of time is evidence that LTM mainly uses a semantic code. The confusion on lists that sounded similar is evidence that encoding in STM is acoustic.

- Atkinson and Shiffrin's **multi-store model** described information flowing through a memory system composed of **sensory memory (SM)**, **short-term memory (STM)** and **long-term memory (LTM)**.
- **SM** has very limited capacity, and is **modality-based**. Information is held only very briefly in the sense organs through which it is received.
- **STM** uses an **acoustic code** and has a capacity of 7±2 items. It lasts between 6 and 12 seconds, but can be extended by **rehearsal**.
- **LTM** has unlimited capacity and can potentially last indefinitely. It mainly uses a **semantic code**, but information can also be encoded visually or acoustically.

Evidence for the multi-store model of memory

Evidence for this model comes from a number of sources, one of which you can find out for yourself in activity 3.

Activity 3: a free recall task

Read out the following instructions to your participants: 'I am going to read you a list of words. When I have finished, I would like you to write down as many of the words as you can remember, in any order.'.

Now read out the following list of words, with a gap of a second or two in between each word. Read them in the same order for each participant.

1. scissors	2. file	3. grass	4. lion
5. computer	6. carpet	7. room	8. knife
9. book	10. dish	11. idea	12. sand
13. card	14. cushion	15. parrot	16. fire
17. milk	18. house	19. pencil	20. wall

Give your participants 2 or 3 minutes to write down as many of the words as they can remember. To analyse your results, write down the 20 words in the order in which you read them out. Now go through your participants' recall lists, and count up how many people recalled each word. Your results table should look something like this:

word	position of word in list	number of people who recalled that word
scissors	1	3
file	2	2
grass	3	3
lion	4	0

When you have finished the table, plot a graph like the one below:

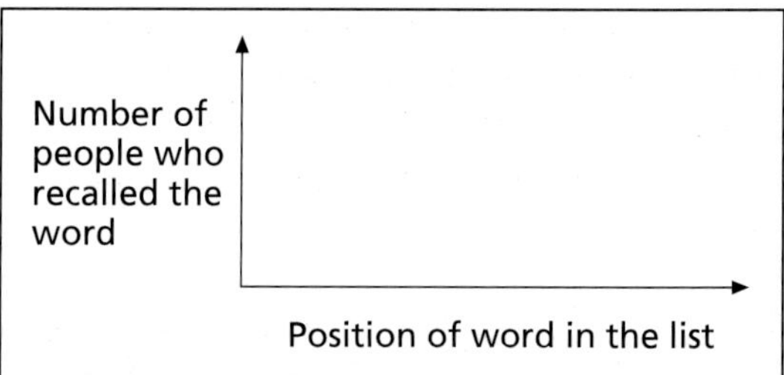

Was the position of the word in the list related to the number of people who recalled it?

You may have found no particular pattern in your graph, especially if you only tested a few participants. On the other hand, you may have a curve that looks like the one in figure 3 opposite.

As far back as 1885, Ebbinghaus carried out similar experiments using nonsense syllables, e.g. LIF and DAK and found that, typically, words near the beginning and end of the list were better recalled than those in the middle. The effect whereby the first few words are well recalled is known as the **primacy effect** (P on the graph) and the effect whereby the last few words are well recalled is known as the **recency effect** (R on the graph).

Figure 3: serial position curve

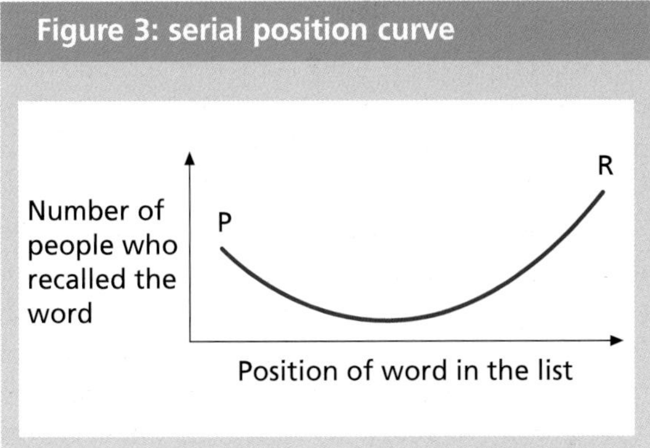

Activity 4: interpreting the serial position curve

What does the serial position curve show? How does it support the two-process model?

When you have finished, see the notes on page 248.

Evidence that the recency effect is due to retrieval from STM is given by Glanzer and Cunitz (1966) who found that the recency effect occurs only if the last items on the list are recalled immediately; if recall is delayed, the effect disappears.

Clinical evidence also supports the two-process model:

Box E: Milner (1996)

Scoville and Milner described the now classic case study of HM, a man who had drastic brain surgery to cure his epilepsy. One consequence of this procedure was that he suffered from **anterograde amnesia** – he could recall events that happened before the operation, such as details of friends he knew before the surgery, but very little of what occurred afterwards. He re-read newspapers unaware that he had just read them, and only knew what time it was for about 15 seconds after he looked at the clock. All the people he met after the surgery had to be 're-met' each time they visited him, as he couldn't remember who they were.

The case of HM supports the two-process model, because it supports the idea that the brain uses different mechanisms for holding information for a short time, and for holding it relatively permanently. HM could remember a lot from before the surgery, so presumably his existing LTM was unaffected by the operation, but he did not seem able to transfer new information from his STM into his LTM.

One other piece of evidence for the two-process model is that different types of encoding are used in STM and LTM, as previously discussed (see box D). The fact that short-term encoding is so different from long-term encoding supports the idea that there are two distinct stores.

Criticisms of the multi-store model of memory

Atkinson and Shiffrin's model has made a valuable contribution to memory research, distinguishing clearly between the *structures* and the *processes* of memory. However, the model is no longer accepted as entirely plausible.

One problem is that it implies that, to reach LTM, information needs to flow through STM. Shallice and Warrington (1970) carried out a case study of KF, who suffered brain damage as the result of a motorcycle accident. His STM was seriously impaired, but his LTM was relatively intact, including memory for information *after* his accident. This suggests that information does not have to flow through the STM in order to reach LTM.

Another problem is that the multi-store model takes no account of the *nature* of information to be recalled, concentrating only on the *quantity* of information. It treats all information as the same, whereas we know intuitively that the nature of what we are trying to remember is very important in whether or not it is remembered. For example, some people find it very easy to remember football scores, but have great difficulty in remembering relatives' birthdays.

The importance of the nature of the information to be recalled is shown by the phenomenon of **flashbulb memory**, a term coined by Brown and Kulik (1977). This is where people have a particularly strong, vivid and often detailed memory of where they were and exactly what they were doing when a specific major event occurred. For example, you may know people who remember in great detail where they were on VE day at the end of the Second World War when the Germans surrendered unconditionally (1945) or when the American president John F Kennedy was shot (1963) or when Mrs Thatcher resigned as Prime Minister (1990) or when they heard that Diana, Princess of Wales had died (1997), or when they heard of the destruction of the World Trade Centre (2001).

We can have flashbulb memories of personal events as well as public events – for example, events related to an accident or injury. According to Brown and Kulik, the most important factors in triggering a flashbulb memory are that the event is surprising, is seen to be important, and is associated with a high level of emotional arousal. Flash bulb memories seem to go straight into LTM, without the rehearsal which the multi-store model suggests is necessary.

The two-process model can also be criticised for its lack of detail about the nature of LTM; it does not go beyond defining capacity, the coding involved and duration of storage.

Finally, a major problem with the model is that there is evidence that neither STM nor LTM is a unitary store. Each may more usefully be seen as being made up of different subsystems, an idea we will be looking at in more detail in later sections of this chapter.

- The **primacy** and **recency effects**, the case of **HM**, and the fact that different **codes** are used in **STM** and **LTM** are all evidence for the multi-store model.
- This model has been criticised for being too simplistic in its assumption that memory flows in one direction through the different stores. It does not take into account the nature of the material to be remembered.
- There is evidence that neither the **STM** nor the **LTM** is a unitary store.

Working memory (WM)

The working memory model of Baddeley and Hitch (1974) deals only with STM and recently-activated parts of LTM. Working memory concentrates on systems by which information is processed in STM, and emphasises the idea of an **active processor**. In the multi-store model the stages of the model are passive stores through which information flows, in strong contrast to this idea of memory as an active process.

Working memory consists of a **central executive** which controls three **slave systems**. The central executive is used when you are dealing with difficult mental tasks such as problem-solving. Information can be briefly held within a slave system while new information is being processed. In doing a complicated addition sum, for example, the number to be carried forward from one column of figures can be held while the next column is added up. The central executive also acts as an attention system, deciding which information entering from the sense organs should be attended to, and directing the work of the slave systems.

Figure 4: working memory (Baddeley and Hitch, 1974)

Central executive

Articulatory loop (inner voice)

Visuo-spatial scratch pad (inner eye)

MEMO

Primary acoustic store (inner ear)

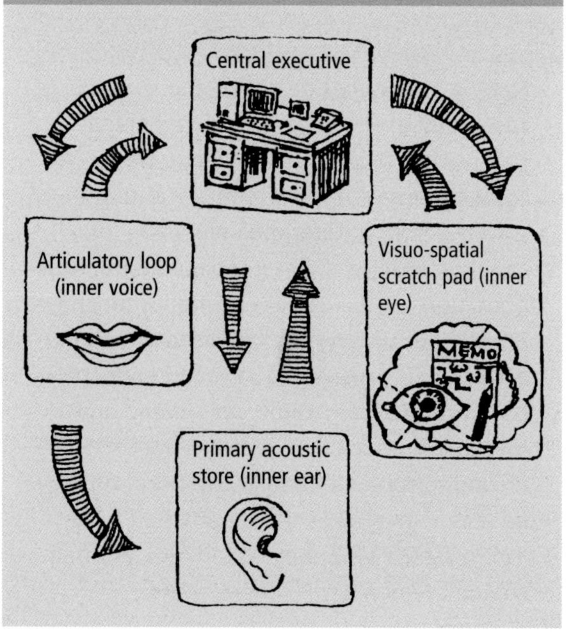

The central executive is the most important part of the system as it controls all the other systems. It is very flexible: it can process information from any of the senses, and can even store information for a short period of time. The three slave systems are the **visuo-spatial scratch pad**, the **articulatory loop** and the **primary acoustic store**.

The **visuo-spatial scratch pad**, also known as the **inner eye**, uses a visual code and deals with visual and spatial information, such as the layout of the inside a house.

The **articulatory loop** is known as the **inner voice**. It is a **verbal rehearsal loop** which holds words in an articulatory code. It is like an inner voice because you 'hear' in your head the telephone number you are attempting to remember; for example, while you search for a pen and notepad. The capacity of the articulatory loop was discovered when Baddeley *et al.* (1975) showed that people involved in a recall task could immediately recall as many words as they could read out in two seconds, but no more. The articulatory loop therefore works rather like a continuous cassette loop: the amount of information it can hold is determined only by how long it takes that information to be spoken out loud, and not by the number of items, as Miller suggested.

You may have unwittingly come across evidence for the articulatory loop. Perhaps you have been having a conversation with somebody and asked 'What did you say?' when you thought you hadn't heard them correctly. But in the time it took you to ask the question, you realised that you did know what it was they said. This is your articulatory loop in action; like a cassette loop, the information was played back to you, and you heard what was said.

You can also try out for yourself how the articulatory loop works. If you repeatedly say a phrase out loud, you are occupying your articulatory loop so that it can't be used to hold other information in working memory at the same time. The idea of repeating a phrase at the same time as learning a list of words, or reading a book, is called **concurrent verbalisation**. If the task being carried out is hampered by the concurrent verbalisation task, then you can assume that the task normally utilises the articulatory loop.

Activity 5: a concurrent verbalisation task

Pick a textbook that you sometimes use in your studies, but that you find fairly difficult. Read a page of text silently, simultaneously saying the phrase 'cognitive psychology' out loud. When you finish reading the page, see how much of the text you can remember.

You may well have found that you could not remember much of the text you had read, because your articulatory loop was being used to repeat the phrase 'cognitive psychology'. This is called **articulatory suppression**. The reason it was suggested that you pick a fairly difficult textbook was because concurrent verbalisation has more effect if the material is quite difficult to understand.

Activity 6 looks at the ways information is coded using the visuo-spatial scratch pad and the articulatory loop:

Activity 6: encoding in working memory

You will need to draw carefully the display grid below on a large piece of paper. You also need to draw a number of blank grids, exactly the same as the first one but without the letters in. Then you will need to draw two patterned grids similar to the one shown below, each with a slightly different pattern of squares coloured in.

Display grid

M			K		
		Z			
			A		G
F		R			

Patterned grid

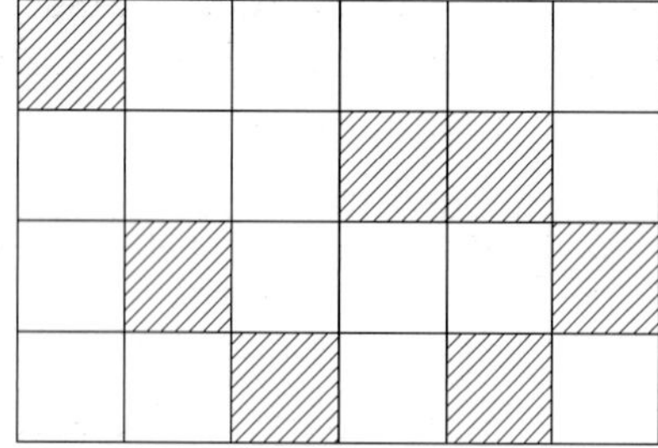

Half your participants will be performing a verbal task in between seeing the display and recalling it; the other half will perform a visual task.

Tell your participants that they will be shown a grid with seven letters on it. They should try to remember the letters and where each one was in the grid. If they remember a letter but not where it went, they should put it anywhere. If they remember there was a letter in a particular square, but cannot remember what it was, they should put any letter in the square.

Show half your participants the display for five seconds. Then ask them to count backwards aloud from 100 and time this counting for 10 seconds. (This is the **verbal task**). Finally, ask them to fill in one of the blank grids you prepared earlier, to see how much of the display they can recall.

Repeat this procedure with the rest of your participants, but instead of the verbal task, ask them to look at two of the patterned grids you prepared earlier, and tick which parts of the two grids match (time them doing this for 10 seconds) – this is the **visual task**.

Score your participants' answers separately in two ways. For each condition each participant should have a score out of 7 for number of letters recalled correctly, and a score out of 7 for the number of positions recalled correctly.

Before reading the next paragraph, see if you can predict which score will be affected in each case.

Activity 6 is similar to an experiment carried out by Den Heyer and Barrett (1971). You probably found that your participants' recall of the letters was more disrupted by the verbal task, and their recall of the letters' positions in the grid was more disrupted by the visual task. Den Heyer and Barrett suggested that the experiment gives evidence that the letters themselves were encoded acoustically (because the verbal task prevented their recall) and that the position of the letters was encoded visually using the visuo-spatial scratchpad (because the visual task prevented their recall).

Very little is known about the **primary acoustic store**, or **inner ear**, which was added to the original model in 1982; it is thought to receive auditory information directly from the ears or via the articulatory loop, and to store it in an acoustic code. It was added to the original model when it was found that information which is presented acoustically is not affected by articulatory suppression. This can be contrasted with the silent reading you used in activity 5.

Evaluation of working memory

Although working memory is one of the more recent models of memory, it is limited in that it considers only STM and recently-activated LTM. However, it is a strength of the model that it points out just how closely connected these two aspects of memory are.

There is also a problem with the central executive part of the model, the most important part of the whole system. Baddeley (1996) suggests that it has four components: it can co-ordinate performance on two different tasks, allocate attention, switch retrieval strategies, and provide processing capacity available to be used by any of the slave systems. He goes on to say that it has yet to be established whether it is more appropriate to see the central executive part as a unified system with multiple functions, or as a set of independent though interacting control processes.

None the less, it seems to make more sense to see STM as a group of processing mechanisms rather than as a single store in which information is held. In terms of encoding, the working memory model gives more emphasis to the use of visual encoding in STM, compared to the multi-store model which sees coding as primarily acoustic.

Its main advantage is the way it portrays memory as an **active process**, and not merely a series of passive stores. Cognitive psychologists also find it useful to see attention and memory as part of the same system, since we tend to use the two processes together, and the central executive part of the model is in part an attentional system.

Another strength of the working memory model is that it ties in neatly with PET scan studies of brain activity during different memory tasks. PET stands for positron emission tomography, and this type of scan displays a three-dimensional representation of the brain's structures and provides images which show brain activity in different areas while carrying out different tasks. Activity in different areas corresponds with the four systems the model proposes:

Figure 5: brain localisation and working memory (from Carter, 1998)

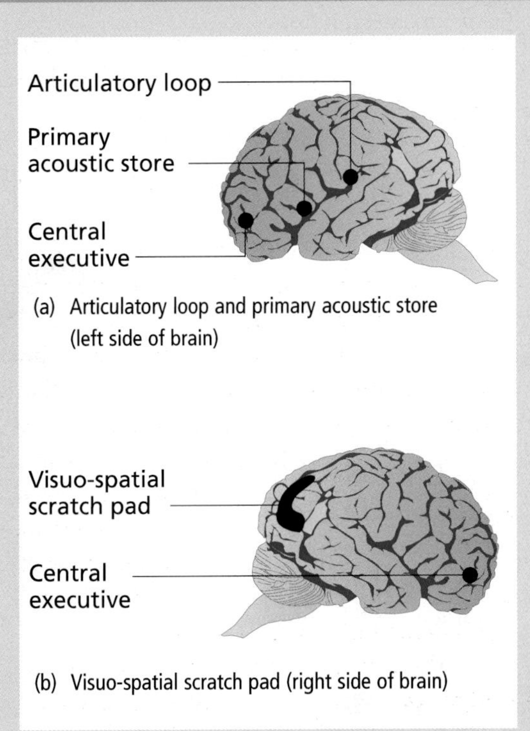

(a) Articulatory loop and primary acoustic store (left side of brain)

(b) Visuo-spatial scratch pad (right side of brain)

Working memory has practical applications – for example, in teaching children to read. If children with normal intelligence are having difficulties learning to read, and they also have trouble in recognising rhyme, it suggests a problem with their articulatory loop. When we understand the systems better, we will be able to help such children and put our theoretical knowledge to good use.

- The **working memory** model of Baddeley and Hitch is a model of short-term memory.
- This memory system is seen as an active processor, consisting of a **central executive** in control of three slave systems – **the visuo-spatial scratchpad**, the **articulatory loop** and the **primary acoustic store**.
- **Concurrent verbalisation** tasks provide evidence that the articulatory loop is involved in processing information.
- The model places more emphasis on **visual** aspects of STM.
- The idea of different subsystems is supported by evidence from **PET scans**.
- **Applications** of the working memory model include helping children learn to read.

Levels of processing (LOP)

The LOP model was put forward by Craik and Lockhart (1972), partly as a result of the criticisms levelled at the multi-store model. Instead of concentrating on the stores involved, i.e. STM and LTM, this model concentrates on the *processes* involved in memory. The basic idea is that memory is really just what happens as a result of processing information. What is important is what you do with the information to be remembered.

Craik and Lockhart suggested that storage of information varies along a continuous dimension depending on the depth to which it has been encoded. They defined 'depth' in terms of the meaningfulness extracted from material. Information which has been processed deeply, i.e. more extensively, will be better stored, and so is more likely to be recalled, information which has been processed in a more shallow way, i.e. more superficially, is more likely to be forgotten.

Although depth is a continuous dimension, this idea has generally been tested using three levels:

Figure 6: possible levels in Craik and Lockhart's levels of processing model (1972)

structural level	What does the word *look* like? e.g. capitals or lower case letters?	shallow
phonological level	What does the word *sound* like? e.g. does it rhyme with 'cat'?	↓
semantic level	What does the word *mean* ? e.g. is it a type of food?	deep

The LOP model has been tested by research:

Box F: Craik and Tulving (1975)

Procedure: Participants were shown a series of words, on each of which they were asked a question. The questions required either **a** structural, **b** phonological or **c** semantic processing, (see figure 6).
They were then given an unexpected recall task in which they were asked to pick out the words they had been shown from others they had not seen.
Results: Participants were significantly better at recognising words they had processed semantically.
Conclusion: The effectiveness of recall is related to the level at which material has been processed, with deeper processing producing better recall.

Elias and Perfetti (1973) also tested the levels of processing model. They asked participants to work through a list of words, performing different types of processing on each word (such as thinking of a word that rhymed with each word on the list, or a word with a similar meaning). On an unexpected recall test, they recalled significantly more words which had been semantically processed, giving evidence for the levels of processing model.

Activity 7: testing the levels of processing model

Make up a set of 18 cards. For each set, each of these words should be written on a separate card:

celery carrot plumber lawyer ferret bear spinach broccoli secretary painter hamster hyena potato parsnip doctor printer tiger rabbit

Write two vegetables, two professions and two animals in fairly small lower case letters (but so they can still be read easily), two of each group in fairly large lower case letters and the remaining six words in capital letters:

celery | plumber | FERRET

For the first set (condition 1), prepare instructions asking participants to sort the cards into three groups of words which are related in meaning. For the second set (condition 2), ask them to sort the cards into three groups by the style of writing in which they are written. They should do this as quickly as possible.
Participants should not be told that this is a memory test; tell them you will explain what the study is about after they have carried out the task. When each participant has carried out the sorting task, remove the cards and ask them to write down as many words as they can remember in any order. You will need to test different participants in each condition. In which condition did people tend to recall more words correctly?

According to levels of processing theory, you are likely to have found that the people you tested recalled more words if they were asked to sort them by meaning than by writing style.

The distinction Craik and Watkins (1973) made between maintenance rehearsal and elaborative rehearsal, which we mentioned earlier, is relevant here. You will remember that in **maintenance**

rehearsal, a word or number is repeated again and again, and this is enough to keep it in STM. For example, if a friend reads out their telephone number to you, you might well repeat that number out loud again and again while you find pen and paper to write it down. This is **phonological** processing, and in the levels of processing model it is relatively shallow.

Elaborative rehearsal, on the other hand, is where you elaborate the material to be remembered in terms of its meaning. For example, you might remember the phone number 2954, by thinking: 'Uncle Jim is 29 and he lives at number 54'. This elaborative rehearsal which is necessary to retain information in the LTM involves deeper **semantic** processing.

These ideas about rehearsal have implications for revision and study skills. For effective recall, it would make sense to use elaborative rehearsal – i.e. to process the information by its meaning, as deeply as possible.

Activity 8: improving revision techniques

List specific ways in which you could make your revision as effective as possible, using the ideas of processing outlined above.

When you have finished, see the notes on page 248.

Evaluation of the levels of processing model

Craik and Lockhart's model of memory has contributed to research in this area of psychology because it concentrates on the *processes* of memory. It emphasises that how likely you are to retrieve a particular item from your memory successfully depends on how you process that piece of information, and not on how hard you try to rehearse it. However, the model is criticised for being descriptive rather than explanatory, in its failure to explain *why* deeper processing leads to better recall – an opinion which Craik and Lockhart themselves counter by claiming that their idea was not intended to be a theory of memory, but rather a 'conceptual framework for memory research'.

One of the main problems of this approach is that it is very difficult to measure how deeply a piece of information has been processed. It is a circular argument to say that something you remember well is something that you have processed deeply; but the only way to tell whether it has been processed at a deep level is by seeing if you can recall it!

It is also a problem that the levels of processing model makes no distinction between STM and LTM, and you have already read about the evidence which suggests that there are two quite distinct memory stores.

One further problem is that the improved recall of some words could be due to **processing effort** rather than depth of processing:

Box G: Tyler *et al.* (1979)

Procedure: Participants were given two sets of anagrams to solve. Some of the anagrams were easy (e.g. FAMIYL); others were difficult (e.g. YMALFI). Participants were later given an unexpected recall test.

Results: Significantly more of the difficult anagram words were remembered than the easy ones.

Conclusion: Recall of the words depended on the effort that was put into processing them, and not the depth of processing since all words were processed at the same depth (i.e. semantically).

You can probably see that the participants would also have spent more *time* processing the more difficult anagrams, and this is another potential **confounding variable**. It is impossible to establish which variable is having an effect (processing effort, *or* length of time spent processing, *or* depth of processing) if the variables cannot be separated.

There may also be factors other than depth of processing which influence how well something is remembered:

Box H: Craik and Tulving (1975)

Procedure: Participants in a standard recognition test were shown a word and a sentence containing a blank. They were asked whether the word would fit into the

sentence. On some trials, the sentence was complex (e.g. 'the great bird swooped down and carried off the struggling ...') and in some trials less so (e.g. 'she cooked the ...).
Results: Using cued recall, participants recalled twice as many words accompanying complex sentences.
Conclusion: As both kinds of trial required semantic processing, increased recall for the words accompanying more complex sentences can be explained by greater *elaboration* of processing, i.e. the amount of processing of a particular kind.

Flashbulb memory, mentioned earlier, suggests that distinctiveness, too, is a factor in whether or not information is recalled.

There is also evidence that semantic processing does not always lead to improved recall:

Box I: Morris *et al.* (1977)

Procedure: Participants were presented with words and asked to answer questions involving either meaning or rhyme. Recall was tested either by a standard recognition test (see box H) or by a rhyming recognition test, in which they were asked to pick out words which rhymed with the stimulus words.
Results: On the standard recognition test, recall was better for words which had been processed semantically than for those where questions about rhyme had been asked. On the rhyming recognition test, however, the opposite was true.
Conclusion: Semantic processing does not always lead to superior recall compared with phonological processing. Recall may depend on the relevance of the kind of processing to the memory test.

- Craik and Lockhart's levels of processing model suggested that information is processed at one of three levels – at the **structural** level, the **phonological** level, or the **semantic** level.
- The deeper the information is processed, the better it is recalled.
- Its main strength is that it focuses on how information is processed rather than on separate memory stores.
- The levels of processing model has been criticised on the grounds that it is difficult to measure how deeply information has been processed.
- **Processing effort** and the **time** taken to process information, may also be responsible for improved recall with semantically processed information.
- **Elaboration** and **distinctiveness** are also factors in recall. On some tasks, semantic processing may not be the most effective technique.

Types of long-term memory

One of the criticisms of the multi-store model is that it has very little to say about the nature of LTM. This area has been elaborated by other theorists.

Just as STM is now considered to consist of more than one system, it has been suggested that LTM may also not be a unitary system. Tulving (1972) suggested there are two systems within LTM, **semantic memory** and **episodic memory**. Semantic memory consists of facts such as the capital of Chile, and that the word 'flamingo' refers to a large bird. Episodic memories are those which form a sort of autobiography of a person; they are memories personal to you, such as places you have visited, and public events like earthquakes or assassinations. Episodic and semantic memory are closely related. General knowledge about holidays, for example (semantic memory), can be related to personal holiday experiences in episodic memory. Cohen and Squire (1980) grouped the two systems together as **declarative memory**.

However, there is some evidence that they should be considered as separate (though strongly interdependent) systems. Butterworth (in Radford 2002) described the case of Dr S, a neurologist, who fell while skiing. When the people he was skiing with caught up with him, he was surprised to find that his wife looked extremely old, and he failed to recognise some of his younger colleagues. This was explained by the loss of episodic memory he appeared to be suffering as a result of his fall, in which the previous 25 years were a blank. However, when he was taken to the local hospital, he asked for a brain scan (which he would have learned about in the missing 25-year period), and made a correct diagnosis of transient global amnesia when he saw the scan. His semantic memory therefore seemed to be intact.

Less anecdotally, Tulving (1989) reported that when participants were asked to think about personal events (episodic memory) or information about a particular topic (semantic memory), different parts of the brain were active. With episodic memory, there was increased activity in the frontal cortex, while with semantic memory, regions towards the back of the cortex were active.

Cohen and Squire (1980) went on to draw a distinction between declarative memory and procedural memory, which includes information of which we are not usually aware, e.g. complex skills such as remembering how to swim. A slightly different example of procedural memory is your knowledge of how to combine words appropriately when speaking or writing your native language. The complex grammatical rules which you apply automatically are often very difficult, if not impossible, to describe to someone else.

Activity 9: procedural memory

You will need a volunteer and a pair of lace-up shoes or trainers for this activity. Put the shoes or trainers on your feet, but don't lace them up. Ask your participant to give you verbal instructions that explain how to lace up the shoes. They must not use their hands at all.

Your participant probably found it very difficult (if not impossible) to explain effectively how to lace your shoes up using words.This is because procedural memory is stored not using a verbal code but a **motor code**. This also explains why children are taught to tie their laces by being shown the process, and not by saying 'Take one end of the lace in your left hand …' and so on. You can imagine how difficult it would be to learn to ride a bicycle from a book, or to learn to swim without being in the water. Motor codes seem to be particularly resistant to forgetting – you may not play tennis for years after learning how to, but you could probably play either task without too much difficulty.

One useful way of distinguishing between semantic, episodic and procedural memory is to describe the first two as 'knowing that' and the last as 'knowing how'. These distinctions in LTM are supported by clinical evidence. In the example of

Types of LTM – Cohen and Squire (1980)

Dr S, episodic memory was temporarily damaged, while semantic memory was intact. Procedural memory was also intact, since he skied to the bottom of the mountain on his way to hospital. The case of HM (box E) provides further evidence. Although there were problems with declarative memory, HM's procedural memory was undamaged. Blakemore (1988) describes a further case study:

Box J: Blakemore (1988)

Clive Wearing suffered brain damage as the result of a brain infection. Like HM (see box E) he found it impossible to transfer information from STM to LTM. Unlike HM, however, his existing LTM was also affected.

His **episodic memory** was affected, in that he could remember general features of his past life, such as where he had been to school, and highlights such as singing for the Pope, but these memories lacked detail.

His **semantic memory** was similarly affected. He had written a book about the composer Lassus, for example, but again had only limited knowledge about him after his illness.

In contrast, his **procedural memory** was relatively intact. He could still carry out activities learned before the illness, e.g. reading music and playing the organ. Like HM, he was also able to learn new skills, though (also like HM) he needed to be reminded what new skills he was able to do, because of the impossibility of transferring material from STM to episodic LTM.

This approach to memory is of course limited, in that it only looks at LTM. However, its main strength is that it gives us far more information about LTM than the multi-store model.

- Tulving divided LTM into semantic memory (remembering information) and **episodic memory** (remembering past experiences). Together they make up **declarative memory**.
- A further distinction is between declarative and **procedural memory** (remembering skills). Procedural memory is very robust.
- Though the episodic and semantic systems are linked, there is some evidence that they are different systems. The distinction between episodic, semantic and procedural memory is supported by clinical evidence.
- This approach gives us far more information about LTM than the **multi-store model**.

9.2 Reasons for forgetting

To understand the nature of forgetting, it is important to make a distinction between availability and accessibility. **Availability** is whether the information you are trying to recall is still actually stored; **accessibility** is whether or not it can be retrieved at will. Obviously, information that is not available (because it wasn't stored in the first place or is no longer stored) will not be accessible.

Many years ago, psychologists such as Freud believed that memories were permanent, and forgetting was merely a failure to retrieve information successfully. Evidence for this idea came from Penfield (1969). He stimulated the surface of the brain of epileptic patients on whom he was operating, to try to identify which area of the brain was involved in producing their attacks:

Figure 7: Penfield (1969)

Locations where stimulation elicitated snatches of memory during Penfield's investigations

He found that this procedure led to some people recalling long-forgotten memories with great clarity. It follows that failure to retrieve information should be because memories are inaccessible.

However, not everybody agrees that memories are available but not necessarily accessible. In particular, only a small percentage of Penfield's stimulation triggered vivid memories, and it has been suggested that many of the 'memories' were merely fantasies (rather like dreams) resulting from the stimulation. If this is the case, then forgetting must be due to unavailability – the memory is no longer stored.

We will discuss here some of the theories which have been put forward to explain forgetting, some of which relate to lack of accessibility and others to lack of availability. The theories we will be looking at also differ in whether they seek to explain forgetting from STM or LTM or both.

Displacement

Displacement seeks to explain forgetting in STM, and suggests that it is due to lack of availability. It refers to the limited number of slots in STM, suggested by Miller to be 7±2. When more items are introduced into STM than there are slots, some of the existing information must be knocked out of its slot, or displaced. As you put a new piece of information into STM, the displaced piece of information is lost. This suggests that if information is to be retained, it must be processed into LTM. There is some evidence to support this idea:

Box K: Shallice (1967)

Procedure: A serial probe task was used in which participants were presented with 16 digits, at the rate of either 1 per second or 4 per second. One of the digits (the 'probe') was then repeated, and participants were asked which digit had followed it.

Results: Recall was much better when only a few digits followed the probe. Recall was also better in the more rapid presentation condition.

Conclusion: The finding that recall was better when there were only a few digits after the probe supports the idea of displacement. However, the effect of differences in presentation speed cannot be explained in this way, and are more easily explained by trace decay (see the next section).

The **primacy–recency effect** can also be explained in terms of displacement. The first items in a list are remembered because they have been processed into LTM; the most recent items are still in STM; but those in the middle have been displaced by following items.

Trace decay

This theory relates to both STM and LTM, and also relates to lack of availability. Peterson and Peterson (1959) suggested that forgetting in STM is due to trace decay. Learning something creates a memory trace or **engram**, which gradually fades. Evidence comes from the **Brown–Peterson** technique, described earlier, in which participants are asked to recall trigrams, but after presentation are asked to count backwards in threes. Using this technique, Peterson and Peterson found that the counting task brought about forgetting, and suggested that this was because it prevents the rehearsal which is necessary to replenish the trace before it decays completely. However, forgetting in this case could also be accounted for in terms of displacement, since it could be argued that the numbers counted backwards are put into STM and so displace the trigrams.

The findings of Shallice (1967), described in box K, that more rapid presentation led to less forgetting, also supports the idea of trace decay, though displacement was also important here.

Some information may be lost from LTM as a result of trace decay, in that if we do not revisit memories they will fade over time. However, Penfield's findings, discussed earlier, suggest that at least some information in LTM is forgotten not because it is unavailable, but because it is inaccessible.

It has also been found that some memories, at least, do not necessarily decay, even if they have not been replenished from time to time. This seems to be particularly true of procedural memory. If you have learned how to ride a bicycle, for example, you will have little difficulty in riding again, even if you have not ridden for years.

The same seems to be true of memory for faces:

Box L: Bahrick *et al.* (1975)

Procedure: Several years after their graduation from high school, participants were shown five picures from year books. One picture of the five was of a person with whom they had graduated.
Results: The participants were accurate in identifying 90% of their classmates. Even those participants who had graduated more than 40 years previously could identify 75% of their classmates corectly.
Conclusion: Memory for faces shows little evidence of trace decay.

- A distinction can be made between forgetting due to lack of **availability** or lack of **accessibility**.
- **Displacement** explains forgetting in **STM** as lack of **availability**, when new information pushes out existing information. There is some evidence that displacement may contribute to forgetting, but other factors also seem to be involved.
- **Trace decay** explains forgetting in both **STM** and **LTM** as lack of **availability**. The **engram** created by a memory fades over **time** unless it is replenished. Research supports the contribution of trace decay to forgetting in STM. However, in LTM, **procedural memory** and memory for **faces** show little decay.

Interference

The idea behind this theory is that memories may be interfered with either by what we have learned before, or by what we may learn in the future, and it can be applied to both STM and LTM. **Similarity** is the main factor in forgetting. Forgetting increases with time because of interference from similar competing memories which have been acquired over time.

If you have ever sunburnt your left arm and put your watch on your right wrist for a few days, you are likely to glance at the wrong wrist on the first few occasions you try to tell the time. This is **proactive interference (PI)** – wearing your watch on the left wrist (old knowledge) has interfered wth the new knowledge that your watch is actually on your right arm.

When the sunburn cools off, you return your watch to the original left wrist. Now you have learned to look at your right wrist, and this new learning will interfere with the old knowledge of where to look for the time. This is **retroactive interference (RI)**.

Figure 8: proactive and retroactive interference

PI: learn A: learn B: interference from A affects recall of B

RI: learn A: learn B: interference from B affects recall of A

This theory is basically associationist. In the example of the watch, the stimulus of wondering 'What time is it?' is associated with the response of looking at your wrist. Interference comes from the very similar responses of looking at your right or left wrist.

In support of interference theory, McGeoch and McDonald (1931) found that for participants learning a word list, forgetting was greatest when a subsequent interference task was similar to what had been learned originally. There was little effect on recall from interference when the subsequent task involved unrelated material, but more when it involved antonyms, words with the opposite meaning from those on the original list. Most forgetting occurred when the interference task involved synonyms of the original list.

Activity 10: investigating interference

This study involves learning lists of paired associates:

List A	List 2
kettle–miserable	rainbow–excited
nightingale–depressed	island–frightened
sheet–gloomy	envelope–silly
penguin–unhappy	ticket–hopeful
armchair–mournful	staircase–talkative
trousers–heartbroken	chair–friendly
cinema–melancholy	pineapple–tired
pencil–sorrowful	gerbil–helpful

Explain to each participant that they will be shown eight pairs of words. They will have 15 seconds to learn the pairs. They will then be shown the first items of each pair (in random order) and they should provide the second item of each pair. Carry out this procedure with list A, and note down how many trials were necessary before all the pairs were correctly completed. Repeat this procedure with list B. Some participants should start with list A followed by list B, while others should learn them in reverse order, to avoid order effects.

You should find that participants take more trials to remember list A, since the second items all have similar meanings, which should cause interference.

One problem with this theory, though, is that it may not apply very widely to everyday forgetting. There are some examples – such as problems in adjusting when driving a car with the lights and indicators on the opposite sides of the steering column from what you are used to – but as Baddeley has pointed out, PI in particular has been very hard to establish outside the laboratory.

There is some disagreement as to whether interference should be thought of as lack of accessibility or lack of availability. There is some evidence that it is due to lack of accessibility:

Box M: Tulving (1966)

Procedure: Participants were given a list of words to remember. Recall was tested on three separate trials.

Results: Participants recalled similar numbers of words on all three trials. What the specific words were, however, varied from trial to trial. Only about half the words were remembered on all three trials.

Conclusion: Recalling words on later trials which had not been recalled on the first trial suggests that the initial lack of recall could not have been due to lack of availability. It is likely that different retrieval cues were used on each trial.

- **Interference** applies to both STM and LTM, and is likely to be due to lack of **accessibility**.
- In **proactive interference**, existing memories interfere with new ones, while in **retroactive interference**, new memories interfere with existing ones. Interference is more likely when the memories are **similar**.
- There is some support for this theory, but it does not apply widely to everyday forgetting.

Retrieval failure

Retrieval failure relates to forgetting in LTM, and suggests that forgetting is due to lack of accessibility.

One theory arising from this idea is **cue-dependent forgetting**, a term used by Tulving (1974). It refers to two related phenomena: **context-dependent** forgetting and **state-dependent** forgetting. Tulving suggested that information about the physical surroundings (external context) and about the physical or psychological state of the learner (internal context) is stored at the same time as information is learned. Reinstating the context makes recall easier by providing retrieval cues which trigger memory for relevant information, while retrieval failure occurs when appropriate cues are not present. You may have experienced the effect of context on memory if you have ever visited a place where you once lived. Often such a visit helps people recall lots of experiences about the time they spent there which they did not realise were stored in their memory.

An early study by Abernathy (1940) found that people had better recall for nonsense syllables when they were in the same context in which they had originally learned them. An unusual study showing the effect of context is described in box N:

Box N: Godden and Baddeley (1975)

Procedure: Diver participants learned a list of words either on land or underwater. Later, both groups were tested for their recall either on land or underwater.

Results: The divers who learned the words underwater recalled more accurately when tested underwater. The divers who learned the words on land recalled them more accurately when tested on land.

Conclusion: Recall of information is better in the same context in which it was learned.

It is not always possible to make practical use of this finding; for example, it is unlikely that you will be able to sit your AS exams in the rooms in which you learned the material. However, what may help is *imagining* the environment in which you learnt the information. Zechmeister and Nyberg (1982) showed that this can help recreate the conditions in which you learned the information.

Memory can also be enhanced by recall in the same physical state in which material was learned:

Box O: Miles and Hardman (1998)

Procedure: Participants learned lists of words either while at rest or exercising on bicycles. Recall was tested in either the same state as learning, or in the alternative state.

Results: Words learned during exercise were best recalled during exercise, Those learned at rest were best recalled in the same state.

Conclusion: Physical state provides cues which can assist recall.

Williams and Markar (1991) provide a further striking example. They reported the case of a student who withdrew money from his bank account two weeks before being admitted to hospital for mania. He gave some of the money to a church and hid the rest. When his mood stabilised, he could not remember where he had hidden the money. However, he found it when he had another manic episode some months later.

Recall is also improved when people are in the same emotional state as during learning:

Box P: Bower *et al.* (1978)

Procedure: Participants were hypnotised, and imagined a happy or unhappy mood whilst learning information.

Results: Those participants who recalled in the same mood as that created during learning recalled better than those who recalled in a different mood.

Conclusion: Participants' recall was affected by the internal context in which they learned the information.

While this theory seems able to explain some forgetting, we cannot assume that all information in LTM is potentially recoverable if appropriate cues are present. However, this theory has an important practical application in the **cognitive interview**, discussed in chapter 11, the police technique used to question eyewitnesses of a crime.

A further theory which suggests that forgetting is the result of retrieval failure is the theory of **repression**. Freud suggested that we forget because there is great anxiety associated with certain memories, and the psychological pain of recall would be too great to cope with. When this is the case, we may use the unconscious defence mechanism of repression to push such memories out of consciousness. The memories continue to exist, but in the unconscious mind. For example, memories of being abused as a child may be too disturbing for a person to cope with, and may be outside conscious recall.

Freud's theories do not readily lend themselves to experimental investigation, but there have been attempts to test this theory experimentally:

Box Q: Levinger and Clark (1961)

Procedure: Participants were asked to give immediate free associations to negatively charged words (e.g. *quarrel, anger, fear*) and neutral words (e.g. *window, cow, tree*). They were then given the cue words again and asked to recall the associations they had made.

Results: Particpants took longer to provide associations to negatively charged words, and also showed a higher GSR to them. The associations made to negatively charged words were less well remembered than those to neutral words.

Conclusion: The relative inaccessibility of negatively charged words and the higher GSR provide a link between emotion and forgetting, so lending some support to Freud's idea of repression.

However, Parkin *et al.* (1982) found that although highly arousing words are poorly remembered on an immediate test, this effect reverses on a later test, when they are better remembered than neutral words. This can be explained in terms of arousal. High levels of arousal at the time of the immediate test would impair recall, which would improve later when arousal had decreased. However, it cannot be explained by repression; if information is repressed, it should continue to be repressed.

Psychoanalytic therapy also offers some support for the idea of repression. Part of the therapy involves bringing repressed memories into consciousness. Memories retrieved during therapy are known as **recovered memories**. However, such memories are recovered, often long after the event, and so may not always be reliable. This has given rise to the concept of **false memory syndrome**, discussed in more detail in chapter 11. People sometimes 'recall' traumatic childhood abuse, usually with the help of their therapist, which their families claim could not have happened.

Loftus (1994) described the case of a woman who 'remembered' during therapy having been involved in a satanic cult, having sex with animals, and watching an eight-year-old friend being murdered. When she left therapy, she realised that these memories were fantasies brought about during therapy. However, memories accessed during therapy may indeed be recovered memories despite the obvious problems in deciding what is true about events many years in the past. In addition, you will remember that research into flashbulb memory found that people have clear memories of events which they found traumatic, and remember in some detail the circumstances in which they became aware of these events. This suggests that high emotional distinctiveness of an event leads to a better ability to recall it, in contrast to Freud's suggestion that if an experience is traumatic, it will be repressed.

- **Cue-dependent forgetting** applies to LTM. It suggests that we find it more difficult to recall material when we are in a different **context** or **state** than when the material was learned. The lack of cues provided by the context or state leads to forgetting.
- The theory has been successfully applied in the **cognitive interview technique**.
- However, some memories may no longer be **accessible**, even with cues present.
- Freud suggested that we may fail to retrieve painful information from LTM as a result of **repression**. Attempts to test this theory experimentally have not been very satisfactory.
- The evidence offered by **recovered memories** during therapy may be unreliable. This has gven rise to the concept of **false memory syndrome**. **Flashbulb memory** also challenges the idea of repression.

Lack of consolidation

When we take in new information, a certain amount of time is necessary for changes to the nervous system to take place – the consolidation process – so that it is properly recorded. During this period information is moved from STM to the more permanent LTM. Lack of consolidation has been demonstrated experimentally:

Box R: Norrie and Henry (1978)

Procedure: Participants practised climbing a free-standing ladder for 20 one-minute trials separated by one-minute periods of practice on a different skill called the pursuit rotor task, which involves tracking a light moving along a circular track. They were tested on ladder-climbing a week later. A control group underwent the same procedure, but the periods on the pursuit rotor task were replaced by rest periods.
Results: For the controls, there was no deficit in the ladder-climbing skill. The experimental group showed a memory deficit when tested.
Conclusion: The pursuit rotor task interfered with consolidation of the ladder-climbing skill, so that the gain in skill was not processed into LTM.

There is evidence that the consolidation process is impaired if there is damage to the **hippocampus**. You will remember the case study of HM (box E) whose hippocampus was destroyed during surgery for epilepsy; although his STM functioned well, he was unable to process information into LTM.

Vanderploeg *et al.* (2001) found that **traumatic brain injury (TBI)** can lead to loss of consolidation. TBI patients showed no deficits in encoding or retrieval in comparison with matched controls, but their pattern of memory deficit supported the idea that the consolidation process was impaired. Blake *et al.* (2000) found similar consolidation problems in patients with epilepsy. Quig (1996) also explained the memory impairments of people with Alzheimer's disease as a problem with the consolidation process.

Ageing can also impair our ability to consolidate information. Giambra and Arenberg (1993) tested the memories of participants aged between 17 and 74 for sentences over periods ranging from 10 minutes to 7 hours. They interpreted the significant deficits in older participants over shorter periods as lack of consolidation.

- Forgetting can occur through **lack of consolidation** when information cannot be processed from STM into LTM.
- Forgetting can occur if consolidation is prevented. Lack of consoldation can also affect people with **brain damage**, and as the result of **ageing**.

Notes on activities

4 The shape of the curve implies that the first few words on the list are recalled well because they have been stored in LTM, whereas the last few words are recalled from STM. The first few words go into LTM because time has elapsed and they have been processed semantically, whereas the last few words have not had time to be transferred into LTM so are still in STM. The shape of the graph therefore gives evidence for the fact that we have two distinct stores in memory, as Atkinson and Shiffrin suggested.

8 You could have come up with any number of ideas that involve the deep, semantic processing of information – for example, drawing up spidergrams to summarise your notes, asking yourself questions about a topic, or trying to explain a particular idea to a lay person. It is obviously important to understand the material if you are to process it semantically and you can improve your understanding by 'teaching' the topic to a fellow student (taking it in turns), or presenting part of a topic to the class. You may find that your teachers try these techniques in an attempt to persuade you to process your notes more deeply. This is also why this book contains a large number of activities designed to help you process deeply the material it presents.

10

Language and thinking

10.1 What is language?

Rather generally language is used every day in rather general terms to mean social interaction which communicates a message. Used in this way, we can say that animals have language. For example, as we shall see, bees communicate the distance and direction of a food source when they return to the hive, and chimpanzees and gorillas have a range of calls and gestures which carry meaning to others in the group. We also talk about 'body language'; for example, we interpret dilated pupils in someone we are talking to as signifying interest in us or what we are saying, and arms crossed tightly over the chest as a defensive gesture. However, it is clear that human language goes beyond this rather general definition.

One important feature of human language is that it uses words as **symbols**. The symbols a language uses are arbitrary. There is no reason, for instance, why the sound 'curtain' rather than 'splot' should mean a piece of cloth in front of a window, or why 'Vorhang' should carry the same meaning in German. We are capable of combining these symbols in an infinite variety of patterns which make sense to others who share our language. We can refer to past events and plans for future ones. We can use language to think about abstract ideas, like beauty or the nature of love, and to consider hypothetical circumstances ('What would happen if ...?'). Human language has two main functions: **external** (to communicate with others) and **internal** (to represent our thoughts). The everyday use of the word 'language' concentrates only on its external function.

Linguists study the structure of language. They look at four main aspects: syntax, the lexicon, semantics and phonology.

Syntax refers to the grammar of the language; how words can be put together to make structurally acceptable sentences. 'The dog barked at the postman' is a grammatical utterance, so is syntactically acceptable. 'The dog barking at the postman' is not a grammatical sentence in standard English. Word order is another aspect of syntax, which explains why 'The postman the barked dog at' is not a grammatical sentence.

The **lexicon** is the vocabulary of a language, so 'curtain' is part of the English lexicon, whereas 'splot' (as far as I know) is not. **Semantics** brings together syntax and the lexicon, since it refers to putting words together to make sentences that are both grammatical and meaningful. So 'The dog barked at the postman' is semantically acceptable, while 'The dog slept at the postman' is not, although there is nothing wrong with it as a sentence as far as syntax and the lexicon are concerned.

Activity 1: syntax, the lexicon and semantics

Say whether each of these sentences is correct in terms of:

- **a** English syntax
- **b** the English lexicon and
- **c** English semantics:

The cat sat quietly on the mat.

The cat laughed at the mat helpfully.

The plink sat feltfully on the flong.

When you have finished, see the notes on page 283.

Phonology is the study of the sounds of a language. When children develop language, phonics are learned first, followed by lexical items. Finally, syntax is acquired.

A final aspect of language with which social psychologists are particularly concerned is **pragmatics**. This relates language to the social context in which it is used. For example, when we communicate with others we take into account what the person we are communicating with already knows. If we say 'The postman came today', the person we are communicating with can assume that he delivered a letter or a package, although this has not been stated explicitly. In addition, we adjust what we say, and how we say it, depending on the situation and who we are communicating with. For example, there would probably be marked differences in how you explain why you want a particular job to the person interviewing you for the job, and to your best friend.

- Language is used loosely to refer to meaningful communication. Human language, with its use of **symbols**, stands alone in its ability to be detached from the immediate environment and to let us think abstractly and hypothetically.
- Linguists are concerned with four aspects of language: **syntax** (grammar), the **lexicon** (word meanings) **semantics** (the production of meaningful utterances) and **phonology** (the sounds of a language).
- Social psychologists are particularly interested in **pragmatics**. This relates utterances to the particular social context in which they occur.

Animal communication

Communication takes place when a **message** is passed from a **signaller** to a **receiver**. Like humans, animals use a range of ways of communicating. Some of their methods have parallels with human communication, but they also use other means of communication which are far less important in humans.

Visual communication is quite common. For example, the display of the peacock signals courtship to a female. Many animals have ways of making themselves seem as large as possible when facing an aggressor, e.g. the pilomotor response in domestic cats, where their fur stands on end. Colour may also be used. Lack (1943) found that territorial aggression in robins was triggered by seeing the red breast of an intruder.

Olfactory communication (i.e. using smell) is also common. For example, scent plays a role in the mutual recognition of a mother goat and her kid. As another example, many animals, including cats, mark their territory using scent markers. A further kind of olfactory communication is provided by **pheromones**, chemicals which affect the hormone system of the receiver. They are widely used by animals, and are often linked to sexual communication. For example, Melrose *et al.* (1971) found that sows exposed to a particular pheromone immediately assumed the position for mating. Some moths can detect pheromones released by a potential mate at a distance of several miles.

Touch is also used to communicate. One example of **tactile communication** is used by the male of one species of spider, in which the male is eaten by the female. He strokes the female to indicate that he wishes to mate, so that she becomes receptive and won't eat him. Lawick-Goodall (1974) noted that the contact chimpanzees make while they are grooming each other can have the effect of calming animals who have been fighting.

A lot of animal communication uses **sound**:

Activity 2: auditory communication

What kinds of advantages might sound offer as a communication medium? You might find it useful to compare sound with the other forms of communication described in this section, picking up on any drawbacks they might have which would not apply to sound.

When you have finished, see the notes on page 284.

- Communication takes place when a **message** is passed from **signaller** to **receiver**.
- Animals use various forms of communication: **visual**, **olfactory** (including **pheromones**), **tactile** and **auditory**. Auditory communication has many advantages and is widespread.

Many signals given by animals are relatively **stereotyped**. It is possible that each action on the part of the signaller may trigger appropriate behaviour in the receiver, and vice versa. There is some support for this idea:

Similar kinds of signalling rituals often take place in **conflict** situations. When red stags compete with each other for females, the two animals start the contest by roaring at each other. If the defender of a group of females can roar faster, the intruder usually retreats. This part of the contest sends the signal: 'I am in good physical shape'. If the challenger matches the defender in roaring, or outroars him, the next stage involves a parallel walk. Presumably this stage allows the two animals to assess each other's strength at close quarters, and withdraw or continue with the contest on the basis of what they have seen; many fights end at this point. The final stage involves interlocking antlers and pushing. If

Box A: Tinbergen (1951)

Procedure: The courtship and mating display of sticklebacks was observed.

Results: The behaviour of both male and female follows a stereotypical pattern. The male does a zig-zag dance in front of the female. This induces her to deposit her unfertilised eggs in his nest. This in turn results in him chasing her from the nest, entering it himself and fertilising the eggs. If at any point this pattern is not followed, the interaction is broken off.

Conclusion: Both male and female act in response to the behaviour of their partner.

the contest has got as far as this final stage, there is a good chance that both animals will be injured. The earlier stages provide opportunities to bring the conflict to a close, avoiding the costs of loss of life or serious injury.

Many species also show **appeasement gestures**. These are gestures which express vulnerability and 'switch off' aggression in an attacker. For example, in one species of jackdaw the nape of the neck is a very vulnerable area, and clearly marked off from the rest of the body by its plumage. When this part of the body is offered to an attacker, aggression stops instantly. These kinds of signals serve a similar purpose as the roaring and parallel walk in stags: serious harm is usually avoided.

All the signals described so far are **honest signals**; they provide accurate information to the receiver. Sometimes, however, **deceptive signals** may be sent. An individual, in order to win a fight, may signal a willingness to fight in the hope that the prospective opponent will back off. This is a risky strategy, because the bluff may be called, and a fight may lead to injury or even death; however, if it works, it does so at very low cost. For example, lower tones in the call of male cricket frogs are associated with larger frogs. Wagner (1992) found that males may lower the tone of their call to give the impression that they are larger (and therefore stronger) than they actually are.

Dishonest signalling is also common in **predator–prey** situations. For example, hoverflies mimic wasps, signalling to predators that they are dangerous, and so avoiding attack.

- Many animals show **stereotypical** ritualised behaviour in **courtship** and **conflict** situations.
- These kinds of behaviour may have developed to contribute to evolutionary **fitness** in terms of survival and successful mating.
- In some situations, particularly in **conflict** or **predator–prey** situations, **deceptive signals** are sent. These can be successful low-cost strategies, but also carry some risk.

Red stags in each of the three stages of conflict: roaring, parallel walk, interlocking antlers

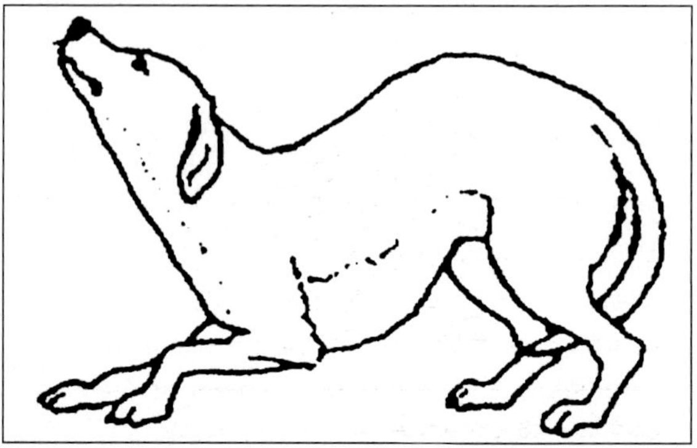

Appeasement response of submissive dog

We have discussed briefly the different kinds of signals that animals give and receive. We will now look a little more closely at systems used by two different kinds of species: bees and non-human primates.

Communication in bees

One of the tasks of worker bees is to locate sources of food, and bring it back to the hive. When they find a rich source, they need the help of other bees. Worker bees perform a **bee dance** to communicate to other workers the distance and direction of food sources. This dance was first observed and written about by von Frisch (1950).

The worker bee performs the dance on the vertical surface of a comb. If the food source is relatively close, within 50–100 m of the hive, this will be a round dance. The bee stays on the spot, and turns once to the left, once to the right, and so on for half a minute or so (see figure 1a).

When the source of food is further away, the bee performs a waggle dance. This involves running a short distance while waggling the abdomen, then turning a full circle to the left back to the starting point. This is repeated to the right, then left again, and so on. In repeating this routine, a figure-of-eight pattern is created (see figure 1b).

If the food source is close by, there is no real need to communicate the direction in which other bees will need to fly in order to locate it. If it is further away, this is clearly essential information, so how do the bees use the dance to communicate how far away a food source is? On the basis of his observations of 3885 dances, von Frisch found that the closer the source was to the hive, the more turns were included in the dance.

The way that direction is communicated is even more intriguing. The waggle part of the dance is always at a constant angle. The size of this angle from the vertical corresponds exactly to the angle between the sun and the source of food:

Figure 1: bee dances

a the round dance

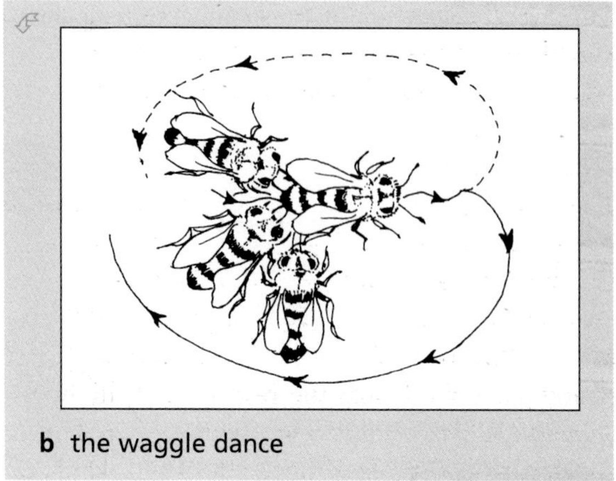

b the waggle dance

Figure 2: the relationship between the angle of the dance and the direction of the food source

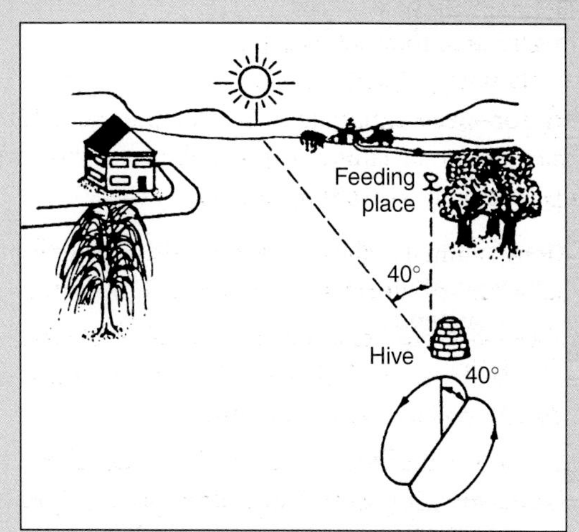

The angle between the orientation of the dance and the vertical is the same as that between the sun and the food source, as measured at the entrance to the hive.

However, bees do not just respond automatically to the dance of a fellow worker:

Box B: Dyer (cited in Gould 1984)

Procedure: Worker bees were trained to collect food from a boat in the middle of a lake (the lake station), and later from a boat moored at a similar distance on the opposite side of the lake from the hive (the shore station). The response of other workers to the bee dance made by the worker when returning from these journeys was observed.

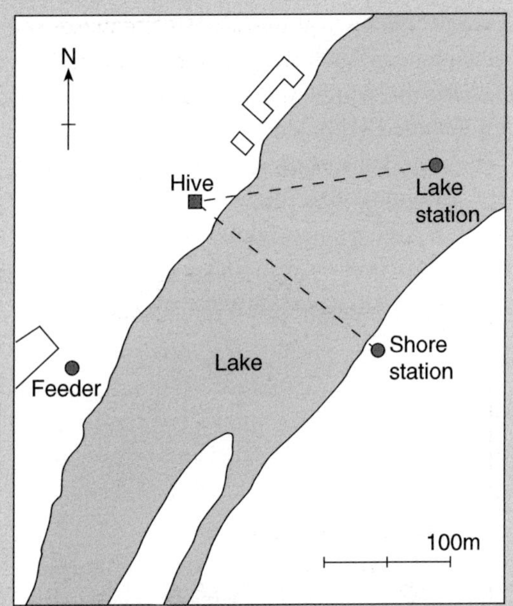

Results: The workers did not respond to the dance indicating food at the lake station, but they did when the shore station was indicated.

Conclusion: Bees have a cognitive map of their immediate surroundings. When the information given in the dance does not correspond to the information this map provides – there are hardly likely to be flowers in the middle of a lake – bees do not act on it.

There are still some aspects of the dance that we don't fully understand. It is thought that the liveliness of the dance indicates how rich the food source is. Bees also make small sounds during the waggle part of the dance, and bees ignore dancers who do not make these sounds, so it seems likely that sound forms part of the total message.

- **Bees** communicate the distance and direction of food sources in a **dance**. The **number of turns** in the dance indicates the **distance**. The **angle** of the dance shows the **direction**.
- This information is only acted on when it corresponds to the bees' **cognitive maps**.

Communication in non-human primates

Like humans, chimpanzees communicate emotions by facial expressions. A relaxed animal has what is known as a **play-face**, the mouth slightly open and the teeth covered by the lips. When it is frightened it shows a **fear-grin**, with the lips pulled back exposing the teeth. A nervous chimpanzee shows a **closed grin**, when the jaws are closed but the teeth exposed.

Chimpanzees also communicate using **eye-contact**. They avoid eye-contact if threatened, but stare if they are threatening another animal. As with many other animals, this threat display is accompanied by a threatening posture, with the animal pulling itself up to its full height with fur erect.

They also make a range of noises. The threat display is accompanied by a series of hoots, ending in a screech. A milder form is the **pant-hoot**, a series of hooting noises with breathing sounds in between. This pant-hoot is also used as a social signal; groups of animals make this noise as a sign of excitement. Lawick-Goodall (1974) suggested that it is also a way of locating the rest of the group, since each animal has its own variation of the pant-hoot. Grunts are used to show contentment, e.g. during grooming, or in greeting.

One study looked at whether chimpanzees could communicate to each other about absent or hidden objects:

Box C: Menzel and Halperin (1975)

Procedure: A group of young chimps was studied. One was taken out of the cage and out of sight of the others, and shown where some food was hidden. It was taken back to the cage, and the whole group released. A similar procedure was followed when a snake was hidden.

Results: Usually the chimp led the others to the food. Sometimes, however, other members of the group would run ahead, apparently looking in possible hiding places. When a snake had been hidden, one of the other chimps would pick up a stick, and poke carefully around. This behaviour was only shown when the leader was let out with the others, and in groups which had lived together for some time.

Conclusion: Chimpanzees are capable of communicating information about something not physically present. This information is limited, since they did not communicate exactly where the food or snake was hidden.

It seems, then, that communication between chimps is limited. However, it could also be argued that in the wild this kind of communication would have very little place; for example, a chimp finding food would only need to let out a series of pant-hoots to alert the others, since they would be likely to be nearby. It seems probable, that communication is mainly used for social purposes among chimps.

A study of social communication in vervet monkeys has investigated further the abilities of primates (box D).

Seyfarth and Cheney also observed that young monkeys would sometimes make these calls inappropriately, such as giving the 'leopard' call in response to a warthog. However, the mistakes they made were always systematic; the 'leopard' call was only ever given if a ground-based animal was sighted and never in response to a bird. This seems to suggest that young monkeys have some understanding of categories.

If a young monkey gave an alarm call, adults would repeat it if it were appropriate, but would otherwise ignore it. This suggests that there is an element of **observational learning** in giving appropriate alarms.

Box D: Seyfarth and Cheney (1980)

Procedure: Vervet monkeys are vulnerable to three types of predator: eagles, leopards and snakes. These monkeys have three types of alarm call, one for each type of predator. Tape-recordings were made of these calls, which were then played back to the monkey group.

Results: Different behaviours were shown in response to each of the calls. When they heard the 'eagle' call, the monkeys would look up into the sky and hide. They climbed trees in response to the 'leopard' call, and would search the ground carefully if they heard the 'snake' call.
Conclusion: Vervet monkey calls give precise information about predators.

- Chimpanzees communicate using **facial expression**, **eye-contact** and **posture.** They also make a range of noises which serve social purposes.
- They are able to communicate information, but only in a very limited way.
- Vervet monkeys give calls to alert others to predators. There are different calls for different kinds of predator. **Observational learning** may be involved in developing accurate use of these calls.

Do animals have language?

As we have seen, animals communicate with each other in a range of ways. But can any of these communication systems be classed as a language? This of course depends on how 'language' is defined. Many definitions include the idea that language ability is specific to humans, e.g. 'the institution whereby humans communicate and interact with each other by means of habitually used oral–auditory arbitrary symbols' (Hall, 1964). This question has been of particular interest to researchers aiming to test Chomsky's assertion that humans have a species-specific **language acquisition device (LAD)** which, if it exists in the way Chomsky claims, would by definition mean that animals could not be said to have language. However, other theorists have looked more closely at the specific characteristics by which language may be defined.

Aitchison (1983) focused on four criteria which she believed were important in classifying communication as language:

Figure 3: Aitchison's four language criteria

semanticity: the use of symbols to refer to objects or actions.
displacement: the ability to convey information about something not physically present, or removed in time.
structure dependence: this refers to the patterned nature of language, e.g. the relevance of word order. 'The man bites the dog' conveys a different meaning from 'The dog bites the man', although the same items are used in each case.
productivity: The ability to use language creatively; to produce and understand novel utterances.

Aitchison claimed that these features are unique to human language, but to what extent can any of them be applied to the communication systems of other animals?

Activity 3: is animal communication language?

Look back through the sections on bees, and non-human primates. Do the communications of any of these animals meet any of Aitchison's criteria?

Draw out a table listing the two kinds of animals and Aitchison's four features:

	semanticity	displacement	structure dependence	productivity
bees				
primates				

Note in each cell whether the criterion applies, and if it does, give evidence to support your conclusions

When you have finished, see the notes on page 284.

The main problem in studying natural animal communication to assess whether or not animals can be said to have language is that it has been impossible to translate what messages are being communicated. However, from the research we have looked at, there is no evidence that the natural communication of animals fulfils all the criteria for language.

- Aitchison identified **semanticity**, **displacement**, **structure dependence** and **productivity** as being crucial aspects of language.
- Some forms of natural animal communication show some of these features, but there is no evidence to support the idea that animals have language.

10.2 Language and thought

How are language and thought related? This may seem to have a fairly straightforward answer: we have thoughts which we can then express in language. But this is an area where there is considerable disagreement.

Thought is possible without language. For example, babies attempt to solve problems, and so show reasoning, before they have developed language. You have probably also experienced the 'tip of the tongue' phenomenon, where you are aware of an idea, but have temporarily forgotten the word you need to express it.

So thought and language need to be seen as separate. Several theorists have put forward ideas about the nature of the relationship between them, and we will look now at some of their ideas.

Whorf: the linguistic relativity hypothesis

Two theorists, Sapir and Whorf, independently suggested that people around the world do not think about the world in the same way. Rather, the language that people speak determines the way they see the world and think about it. This theory has come to be known as the Sapir–Whorf hypothesis, or **linguistic relativity hypothesis**. In other words, thought is *relative*, and depends on the way concepts are expressed in a particular language.

Whorf gave many examples to support this idea. Perhaps the most famous is that the Inuit (Eskimo) people have very many more words for snow than, say, English speakers – falling snow, snow on the ground, slushy snow and so on. He argued that the Inuit people therefore perceive and think about snow very differently from English people. What evidence is there that the way people see and think about different categories of objects is affected by the way they are labelled? Carmichael *et al.* (1932) set out to test the proposition that the labelling of shapes would affect the way they were learned:

Box E: Carmichael *et al.* (1932)

Procedure: Participants were shown simple line drawings which could be interpreted in various ways. They were later asked to reproduce them. One group was shown the drawings with one set of labels. Another group was shown them with a different set of labels. A control group saw the drawings with no labels.
Results: Participants produced very different drawings depending on which set of labels they had seen. Here are some examples:
Conclusion: Verbal labelling can affect memorising and recall.

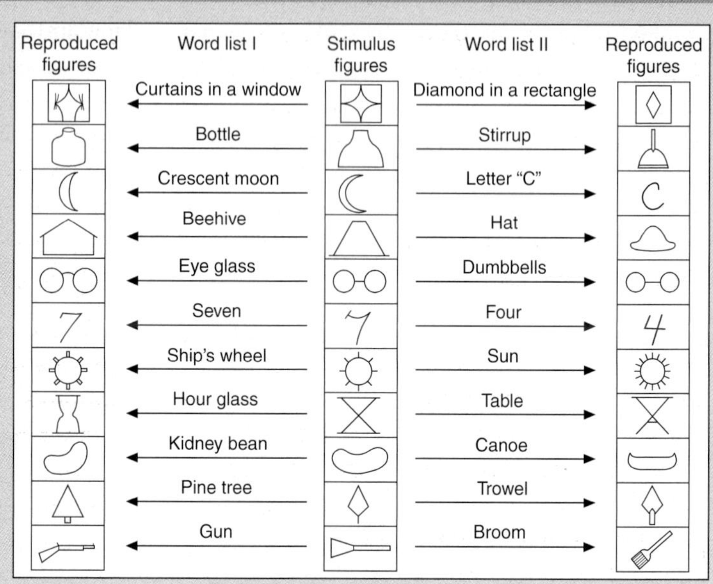

However, there are several points which argue against Whorf's claim that our whole world view is determined by the language we speak. First of all, it is relatively easy to translate into English the kinds of snow which the Inuit language distinguishes. We may not have a one-word label for 'snow which is good for building', but we can express the idea in a phrase. This suggests that there must be some universal, shared knowledge of the physical world. Wherever you live and whatever language you speak, the sky is blue, rain falls more or less frequently, some things are heavy and difficult to move, and so on.

In addition, perhaps differences in culture shape language in the first place. For the Inuit people, snow is an important part of the environment. They need to draw attention to differences, and the words they have invented reflect this need. It could be, then, that the nature of the environment determines the *labels* used in a particular language, rather than language constraining the way in which the environment is perceived. It is perhaps also worth noting that expert skiers have a wide variety of terms for different types of snow such as 'powder', which lends support to this idea.

Some of the most important studies in this area have been concerned with colour labels. There is a wide range of colour labels in different languages. Berlin and Kay (1969) studied 98 languages and found that they all use terms from among the 11 basic (or focal) categories shown in figure 4:

Figure 4: focal colour categories

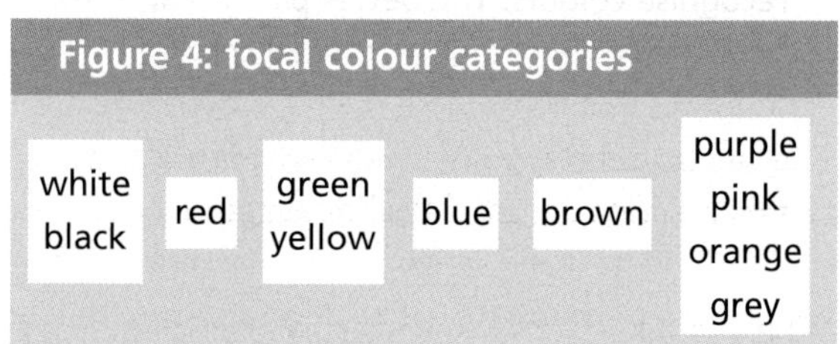

There is a reason why the 11 focal colours have been set out in this way. Many languages use fewer than 11 colours. For example, the Jale language has only two colour terms, and Ibibio only four. But these terms are not chosen randomly from the 11 possibilities. If a language has one of these colour terms, then it must also have terms for all the colours to the *left* of it in the diagram. So the Jale language distinguishes between black and white, while the Ibibio language makes this distinction but also has terms for red and green/yellow.

The universal order in which colours are encoded in different languages suggests that there are universal (natural) categories in colour naming, which in itself challenges the linguistic relativity hypothesis. However, Whorf's belief would also suggest that speakers of languages with few colour terms, like Jale or Ibibio, should be unable to make colour discriminations in the same way that speakers of, say, English can. This has been explored in the research in box F:

Box F: Rosch (1973)

Procedure: A colour memory test was given to American participants, and to Dani speakers, whose language distinguishes only between bright and dark. They were presented with a range of colour samples, including both focal colours (i.e. 'good' examples of the 11 colours shown in figure 4) and non-focal colours. After a 30-second delay, they were asked to pick out the colours they had been shown from a large array of colours.
Results: Both groups recognised the focal colours better than the non-focal colours.
Conclusion: The lack of colour names in a language does not affect the ability to recognise colours. The better performance of both groups in recognising focal colours suggests that there is a universal response to basic colour categories, even when relevant terms are not used in the language.

What we have been discussing so far is the 'strong' form of the linguistic relativity hypothesis: language *determines* thought. As we have seen, this idea has very little support. However, the 'weak' form – that language *influences* thought – is more persuasive. Carroll and Casagrande (1958) investigated this by comparing English and Navaho speakers. Unlike English, the Navaho language has different words for 'give', depending on the nature of the object – for example, whether the object to be given is flat and flexible like cloth, or long and rigid, like a stick. They were interested to see if this difference affected the way in which objects were categorised:

Box G: Carroll and Casagrande (1958)

Procedure: Native American children, all living on the same reservation in Arizona, were tested. Children who were predominantly Navaho speakers and children who were predominantly English-speaking were presented with groups of three objects, e.g:

(a) yellow stick	blue rope	yellow rope
(b) blue cube	white cube	blue pyramid

They were asked to decide which two objects of the three presented 'went best' together.
Results: The Navaho speakers tended to group by form, e.g. in (a) putting the ropes together, and in (b) putting the cubes together, while the English speakers tended to group by colour, e.g. in (a) putting the two yellow items together and in (b) putting the two blue items together.
Conclusion: The different words for 'give' in the Navaho language led the Navaho speakers to favour form or shape over colour when carrying out the task.

However, Carroll and Casagrande carried out the same task with white middle-class children living in a suburb of Boston. Their responses were more similar to the Navaho-dominant children, with a tendency to group by form and shape rather than by colour. Carroll and Casagrande suggested that this finding could be explained by the influence of toys which focus attention on form, such as where shapes have to be fitted into holes. They therefore suggested that while language may influence thought, other characteristics of the environment will modify this influence.

- Whorf proposed the **linguistic relativity hypothesis**. In its strong form, this states that language determines thought. The weak form is that language influences thought.
- Research into different languages, particularly on colour naming, does not support the strong version of the hypothesis, though there is more general acceptance of the idea that language influences thought.

Piaget's theory

Piaget was interested in the nature of cognitive development. He believed that children go through four distinct stages between birth and about 11, each of which is characterised by a different way of thinking, until they are capable of the thought of an intelligent adult. He proposed that children are intrinsically motivated to act on the environment, and it is the result of a child's actions on the environment, together with maturation, which drives the development of thought. In contrast to Whorf, Piaget believed that thought precedes language, and that language merely reflects thought.

Piaget pointed out that thinking can occur without language. For example, Piaget claimed that thought is taking place, even when a young child who has not yet developed language observes what someone else is doing, and later imitates it.

The stages described by Piaget represent a decrease in what he called **egocentrism**, which is characteristic of the first two stages. By this he meant the inability to detach oneself from one's immediate perceptions. In the first **sensori-motor stage** (birth to about 18 months or two years), thinking is driven by the child's actions on the environment and the sensory feedback this provides. However, children are tied in to their own viewpoint. According to Piaget, they are so deeply egocentric that if they cannot see or touch something, for them it ceases to exist.

Towards the end of this stage they develop what he called the **general symbolic function**. This is the ability to form a mental represention (i.e. to imagine) things which are not physically present, and so is a move away from the deep egocentrism of the first stage, and into the second or **preoperational stage**, lasting from the age of about 18 months or two years up to about seven. One example of the general symbolic function is the drawings and paintings children start to produce at this time. Piaget saw language as a further example; the development of children's thinking allows them to refer to people, objects and events beyond the immediate situation. Language is therefore the result of the development of children's general ability to think.

The role of language in Piaget's theory means that language cannot promote more advanced thinking; this can only come about as the result of maturation and the child's experience of interacting with the physical world. This has been demonstrated using a **conservation task**, one of the tasks Piaget used in testing children. In one version, the conservation of liquid quantity, children are shown the display in figure 5(a) and are asked whether both glasses have the same amount of liquid in or whether one has more. If the child agrees that both have the same amount, the contents of one glass are poured into another, differently-shaped glass (see figure 5(b)). They are then asked the same question about the transformed display (figure 5(c)). Piaget found that before the age of about seven, children were likely to say that the taller glass has more in it ('because it's higher') or that the original glass has more in it ('because it's wider'). They focus on one perceptual aspect of the situation, e.g. the height of the liquid, and do not understand that nothing has been taken away during the transformation, nor that the height of the liquid in the new container is compensated for by its width.

Figure. 5: conservation of liquid quantity

(a)

A

B

(b)

A

A2

B

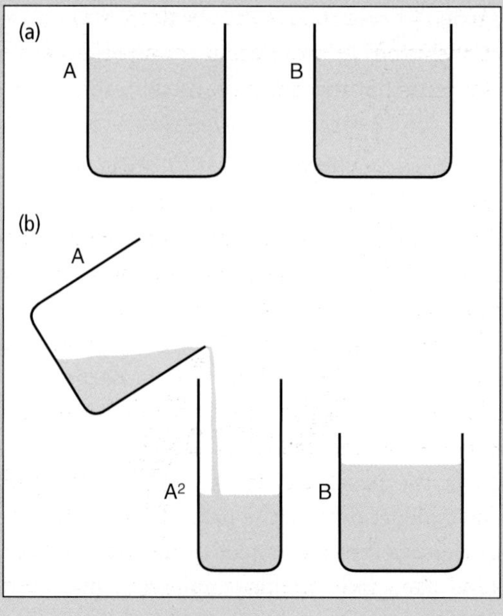

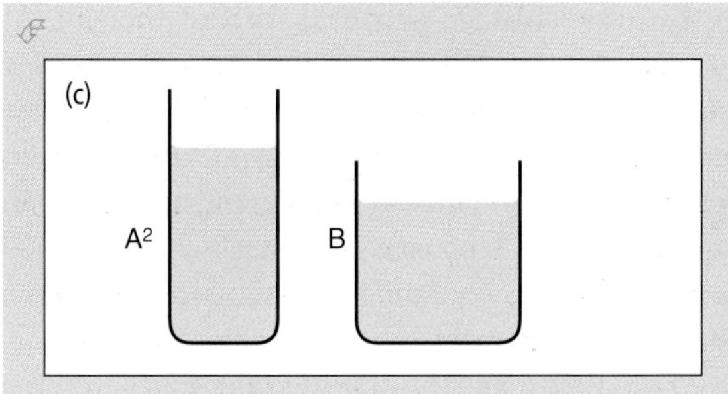

Piaget's belief that the use of appropriate language cannot promote the child's thinking in this task has been investigated:

Box H: Sinclair-de-Zwart (1969)

Procedure: Children in the preoperational stage were tested on the conservation of liquid task. Most were unable to conserve. These children did not use comparative terms like 'larger', and tended to overgeneralise words like 'big' to mean 'tall', 'long', and 'many'. The researcher taught the non-conserving children language relevant to the conservation task, and then tested them again.
Results: After language tuition, only about 10% of these children could conserve.
Conclusion: Appropriate language skills are of little use in promoting thinking.

There is some support, then, for Piaget's view that thinking develops as the result of maturation and a child's actions on the environment, with language having little part to play in development. However, Donaldson (1978) has argued that children's understanding and use of language may indeed influence their thinking. She points out that children may be interpreting what is said to them in the conservation task in terms of the whole social context within which the exchange is taking place, rather than focusing precisely on the words themselves. If you are asked a question and answer it, and then someone asks you the same question again, it is usually because you got it wrong the first time. Children may therefore believe that in the conservation task they are being asked about the change (figure 5(b)). It is their understanding of social and conversational conventions, i.e. of pragmatics, which leads to their apparent inability to conserve. The use of the conservation task in its original Piagetian form may therefore not be a suitable way of investigating the relationship between language and thinking.

There is some support for this argument:

Box I: Light *et al.* (1979)

Procedure: A group of 80 six-year-old children was tested. In condition 1, half were given a standard Piagetian task. Two identical beakers were filled with pasta shells. When the child agreed that there was the same amount in each beaker, the contents of one were poured into a wider beaker, and the children were asked if the beakers had the same amount or if one had more. In condition 2, the task was modified. The children were told that the pasta shells were to be used in a competitive game. When they had agreed that there was the same amount in each beaker, the experimenter 'noticed' that one of the beakers was chipped. He found an alternative (larger) beaker and poured the shells in, and then asked if the beakers had the same amount or if one had more.
Results: In condition 1, only 5% of the children conserved. In condition 2, 70% of the chldren conserved.
Conclusion: The emphasis on 'fair shares' in the context of a game and the practical reason for replacing the chipped beaker changed children's understanding of the task so that most could conserve.

Piaget drew a distinction between egocentric speech and social speech. **Egocentric speech** is the first to appear, and takes the form of repetition or monologue, where children talk to themselves. He believed that this is later displaced to a large extent by **social speech**, when the child understands that language can be used to communicate with other people. Neither of these forms of speech has a function in the development of children's thinking; rather, language is a way of allowing concepts to be expressed. However, the distinction between egocentric and social speech is also made by Vygotsky, whose rather different ideas we will be looking at next.

- Piaget proposed that thinking develops as the result of **maturation**, and the child's experience of the physical world and their **actions** on it. Language does not influence the development of thought, but allows concepts which have already been developed to be expressed.
- The idea that language can not promote thought has been tested using a **conservation task**. However, problems with this method mean that it may not give a true picture of the relationship between language and thought.
- Piaget distinguished between early **egocentric speech** and the later **social speech** which largely replaces it.

Vygotsky's theory

The Russian psychologist Vygotsky shared Piaget's view that children's thinking is fundamentally different from that of adults, and that they pass through stages before they are able to think as an adult. Like Piaget, he also believed that children were active in their own development. However, he emphasised the social context of children's development, and believed that cognitive development is a fundamentally social process. Children develop within a cultural context, and their cognitive development reflects the demands of their culture. They need to acquire what he called **cultural tools** – of which language is an important example – if they are to function adequately within their culture.

Vygotsky considered thought and language to have quite separate and independent roots. Very young children can think without language – for example, when they are manipulating objects in play. Vygotsky described the infant's first attempts to communicate – for example, emotional cries – as having a purely social function, and suggested that in this way language occurred without thought. At around the age of two, language and thinking gradually start to merge, when children are able to use words as symbols for thought. As a result, language can influence thinking, and thinking can be expressed in language. The stages he described focus on the changing relationship between language and thought.

In the first stage, the **social stage** (birth to three years), language is used to express simple thoughts and feelings, and to control the behaviour of other people, eg asking for food. The **egocentric stage** (three to seven years) comes next. Language now starts to be used to direct and control the child's own behaviour, but it is still external speech, ie spoken aloud. It is only in the final **inner stage** (seven onwards) that the child uses inner speech, when language and thought fuse together into a tool which can then be used to shape and direct thinking. At this point, language has two functions: internal language which monitors and directs thinking, and external language through which thoughts can be communicated to others.

Vygotsky's ideas have been explored in a series of studies by Diaz and Padilla (1985). They found that inner speech has important functions in cognitive areas such as planning, abstract thinking and problem solving, so lending some support to the relationship between language and thought which Vygotsky proposed.

Activity 4: comparing Vygotsky and Piaget

Decide whether each of these statements applies to Piaget's theory, Vygotsky's theory or both theories:

1. Children's thinking goes through a series of stages before they are able to think as an adult.
2. Language is important in promoting thought.
3. Language reflects the development of thought.
4. At first language and thinking are independent of each other.
5. Language can occur without thought.
6. There is an important turning point in children's thinking at around the age of seven.

7 Thinking develops through maturation and action.
8 An important function of language is to communicate thoughts to others.
9 Egocentric speech is largely replaced by social speech as children mature.
10 Inner speech continues to play an important role in monitoring and directing the thinking of adults.

When you have finished, see the notes on page 284.

- Vygotsky believed that **social interaction** was fundamental to the development of thinking. Language is an important **cultural tool** acquired during development.
- Language and thinking are initially separate, but merge at around the age of two.
- At around seven, language has an internal function, directing and monitoring thinking. It also has the external function of communicating thoughts to others.

10.3 Ways of thinking

The term 'thinking' covers a wide range of mental activities. In this section, we will look at some of the various ways in which thinking takes place.

Insight

Often when we are attempting to solve a problem, we are aware of trying different approaches in order to reach a solution. However, sometimes a solution suddenly comes to mind, in what can be described as an 'aha!' experience. In other words, we have an insight into the nature of the problem which allows us to restructure the way we are thinking and solve it. This kind of insight was demonstrated early on in a classic study of chimpanzees:

Box J: Koehler (1925)

Procedure: Bananas were suspended out of reach from the ceiling of a chimpanzee's cage. Several boxes of different sizes were scattered around the cage.

Results: The chimp initially jumped up and down, trying in vain to reach the bananas. It then stayed relatively quiet for a time. After a while it jumped up, piled the boxes up, and climbed up to reach the bananas.

Conclusion: The chimp showed insight in solving the problem. It formed a mental representation of the complete problem which allowed it to reach a solution.

Koehler carried out experiments with several chimpanzees, covering a range of problems. For example, one involved using a short stick to reach a longer stick outside the cage. This could then in turn be used to retrieve a banana. He found the same kind of pattern of behaviour as that shown in box J.

While Koehler's findings are not in doubt, his proposal that the chimpanzees showed insight has been challenged. Windholz and Lamal (2002), for example, suggest that the behaviour of Koehler's chimpanzees can be explained not as insight but as the end result of a process of trial-and-error. The solution to the problem was the end result of trying out at random a series of inappropriate behaviours until by chance a correct solution was found.

However, Koehler's research into insight has been followed up in investigations into insight in people:

Box K: Maier (1931)

Procedure: Participants were put in a room in which two strings were suspended from the ceiling. Their task was to tie the strings together. However, when taking hold of one string, the other was too far away to reach. A number of other objects, e.g. poles and pliers, were also in the room.

Results: Participants often found no immediate solution to the problem. However, many of them then produced the pendulum solution, tying the pliers to one of the strings, setting it swinging, taking hold of the other string, and catching the string with the pliers attached as it swung near enough to reach.

Conclusion: When a problem has no immediately obvious solution, people can show insight in finding a way in which it can be solved.

Maier also allowed some participants to get to a point where the were unable to find a solution, then 'accidentally' brushed against one string, making it swing. In many cases, participants then produced the pendulum solution, even though many of them were apparently unaware of noticing what he had done. The hint was enough to allow participants to restructure the problem and so reach a solution.

Ohlsson (1992) has developed **insight theory** as a framework for explaining both the difficulty in reaching a solution, and how one may be reached through insight. The theory starts from the idea that insight may occur in a situation when a person is unable to solve a problem, but is in fact capable of doing so. An impasse – a state of mind in which the thinker does not know what to do next – is reached when the thinker has constructed an inappropriate representation of the problem, and so is unable to apply their knowledge to reach a solution. The basic principles of the theory are shown in figure 6:

Figure 6: Ohlsson's Insight Theory

1 Ways of solving problems are stored in memory.
2 An impasse is reached when the current way in which the problem is represented does not activate the appropriate memory.
3 Reinterpeting or restructuring the problem may trigger an appropriate memory.
4 Reinterpretation or restructuring can come about through elaboration (i.e. adding new information), constraint relaxation (changing some of the characteristics which prevent the goal being reached) or re-encoding (recategorising or ignoring some information).
5 This may lead to insight in which an appropriate memory is triggered.

In the Maier study (box K), the hint provided by making the rope swing is an example of elaboration, while classifying the pliers as a weight rather than a tool is an example of re-encoding.

Activity 5: investigating insight theory

Try these problems with a participant:

a Provide six matches, and ask your participant to create four equilateral congruent triangles. The length of each side of each triangle must be equal to the length of the matches.

b Draw this pattern of dots on a piece of paper. Ask your participant to draw four straight lines to connect all these dots, without taking their pencil off the paper.

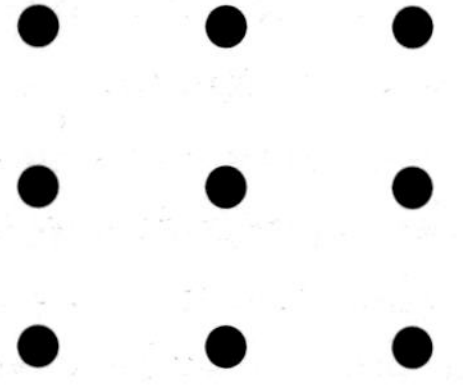

If the participant can not see the solution to either of these problems, try elaboration and constraint relaxation. For problem a, say that the matches do not have to be flat on the table. For problem b, say that the lines to be drawn do not have to stay within the area of the paper covered by the dots. This should allow your participant to restructure the problem as Ohlsson suggests, and reach a solution.

When you have finished, see the notes on page 284.

Schooler *et al.* (1993) carried out a study in which participants were interrupted when trying to solve a problem and asked to verbalise the strategies they were using. Their performance on the task was compared with a control group, who were interrupted by being asked to carry out an unrelated activity. They found that verbalisation interfered with reaching a solution, and concluded that the processes critical to achieving insight solutions are non-verbal.

But is insight always necessary to solve a problem whose solution is not immediately obvious? Hayes and Broadbent (1988) suggested that problem-solving can proceed through insight or through trial and error, depending on the nature of the task. This idea was tested by Svendsen (1991) on a computer task, in which some participants were to respond using commands, and some using direct manipulation of the elements of the problem. They found that in the 'command' condition, participants showed insight, while performance in the 'direct manipulation' condition was best described in terms of trial-and-error.

- Insight is suddenly realising how to reach the solution to a problem. There is some disagreement whether insight is shown by **animals**, but it has been demonstrated experimentally in **humans**.
- When we reach an impasse in solving a problem, **elaboration**, **constraint relaxation** and **re-encoding** allow restructuring which may lead to insight into how it may be solved.
- Both insight and **trial and error** are useful in problem-solving.

Cognitive styles

There are wide individual differences in the way people prefer and indeed are able to think. One important distinction is between **convergent thinking** (the ability to narrow down possibilities to one correct answer) and **divergent thinking** (the ability to generate a broad range of possible answers to a problem). Traditional intelligence tests require the person taking the test to reach the one correct solution to each test item, and so measure convergent thinking. One of the criticisms made of these tests is that they are therefore sampling only a small proportion of the thinking ability of those tested.

In a move away from this focus on convergent thinking, Guilford (1967) developed his **structure of the intellect model**, basing his ideas on a theory of how intellectual tasks can be classified. He proposed that a mental task has three aspects: **content** (the type of mental representation, or what is being thought about); operations (the type of thinking or approach used to deal with the task); and products (the type of outcome or answer required). Guilford identified five different possible contents, five operations and six products. Multipying these together gives a total of 150 different cognitive abilities, each of which represents a different combination of content, operation and product. He suggested that each could be measured separately using a special task. One of the abilities he identified was divergent thinking, and the task he developed to test it is called the **Unusual Uses Test**. People are asked to think of as many unusual (but feasible) uses for everyday objects as they can. Try this out yourself:

Activity 6: divergent thinking

In two minutes, write down as many uses as you can think of for a brick.

If you are working in a group, compare what you have written with other people's ideas.

Uses for a brick: No. 82

You may have found that you came up with half a dozen ideas – for example, propping open a door, or building shelves. Some people manage to come up with a whole range of less obvious ideas: demonstrating Archimedes' principles, blocking up a rabbit hole, as part of an abstract sculpture, as a paperweight, taking part in a smash-and-grab raid, and so on.

Guilford suggested that this type of thinking is associated with three abilities:

Figure 7: abilities associated with divergent thinking

- **a** Fluency: the ability to generate large numbers of possible solutions to problems.
- **b** Flexibility: the ability to shift easily from one kind of problem-solving strategy to another.
- **c** Originality: the ability to see different or unique solutions to a problem.

Since Guilford put forward his original theory, many other tests of divergent thinking have been developed, and have been widely used in research, including Torrance's Tests of Creative Thinking and Leontiev's Pictorgraphs.

There is some evidence that convergent and divergent thinking should be seen as separate abilities. In general, correlations between intelligence test scores and scores on tests of divergent thinking are weak. Wallach and Kogan (1965), for example, report a correlation of only 0.1. Moreover, Razoumnikova (2000) reported differences in EEG patterns, i.e. brain activity, when participants were engaged in tasks using convergent and divergent thinking.

Some theorists have proposed that divergent thinking is the equivalent of creativity. 'Creativity' is difficult to define, but there is some consensus among psychologists that it involves new combinations or unusual associations of ideas, and that these ideas should have some theoretical or social value, or make an emotional impact on other people. However, some theorists have defined it more narrowly in terms of high scores on tests of divergent thinking, using the terms 'divergent thinking' and 'creativity' virtually interchangeably, and referring to tests of divergent thinking as 'creativity tests'.

However, Brophy (1996) argues that while the ability to think divergently is a necessary part of creativity, it is not in itself sufficient to define it. He has pointed out that problems which can be solved creatively vary widely in their complexity, in the knowledge required to solve them, and the relative amounts of divergent and convergent thinking which are necessary. While divergent thinking is likely to produce a lot of ideas, evaluation of these ideas (which involves convergent thinking) is also a necessary part of the creative process.

There is also some evidence that creativity may not be a general ability, but may vary across domains. Han (2000), for example, tested children's creative performance in language, art and mathematics, and found that creativity is somewhat, though not entirely, domain-specific. Those children who performed well in one area did not necessarily perform equally well in the others.

There has been considerable research into the characteristics of creative people. In an early study, Mackinnon (1962) carried out a study of architects to determine the personality characteristics of highly creative people. The characteristics he identified as being associated with those who were more creative included being open and receptive to new experiences, intuitive, flexible, and sensitive to the feelings of others.

McClelland (1962) reviewed several studies concerning the personality characteristics of creative physical scientists. He found that creativity was associated with being male, rather unsociable, hard-working to the extent of seeming rather obsessive, and showing a strong interest in analysis, e.g. of the structure of things, very early in life. Of course, this is correlational evidence, so it cannot be claimed that these characteristics bring about creativity. At the same time, they were very marked in the sample he analysed.

There are, of course, many different kinds of creativity. These two studies looked only at architects and physical scientists, and given the findings by Han (2000) that creativity is to an extent domain-specific, it could well be that different characteristics are associated with creativity in different fields.

Age may also be a relevant factor:

Box L: Haslett (1998)

Procedure: 50 younger participants (median age 20) and 50 older participants (median age 73) were given tasks involving both divergent thinking (generating ideas) and convergent thinking (evaluating these ideas).
Results: The younger group generated more answers and were better at distinguishing between adequate and inadequate answers.
Conclusion: Age is a factor in creativity when both divergent and convergent thinking are necessary.

However, there are also conflicting findings. Reese *et al.* (2001), in a test of divergent thinking, found that middle-aged participants (aged 40–50) scored higher on fluency, flexibility and originality than either younger participants (aged 17–22) or older participants (aged 60–70 and 75+). It may be that the different outcomes of various studies are associated with the different kinds of tasks used by researchers.

Other studies have looked at the relationship of age and divergent thinking in much younger age groups:

Box M: Pastor-Sarro and Perez-Fernandez (2001)

Procedure: The capacity for divergent thinking in younger (mean age 15) and older (mean age 17) high school students in the context of education in physics was compared, using the Divergent Thinking in Physics Test.

Results: The younger students showed significantly more divergent thinking than the older students.

Conclusion: The capacity for divergent-thinking at high school is age-related.

Hudson (1966) argued that the education system encourages convergent thinking but discourages divergent thinking, and therefore also a necessary part of creativity. There is an argument therefore for a less narrow focus in education, so that the convergent skills which are fostered in the classroom are complemented by rather more emphasis on divergent thinking skills.

- A distinction can be made between **convergent thinking** (the ability to narrow down choices to one correct answer) and **divergent thinking** (the ability to think widely about a problem). **Intelligence tests** measure convergent thinking. Several tests of divergent thinking have been developed.
- There is very little relationship between people's ability to think convergently and divergently. Both are necessary for **creativity**.
- Divergent thinking may be **domain-specific**.
- Links have been made between the ability to think divergently, **personality characteristics** and **age**, though the overall picture is rather unclear.

Reasoning

Deductive reasoning

Deductive reasoning relates to making specific inferences from a general rule, and much of the research in this area has made use of syllogisms. A syllogism consists of two premises (i.e. statements) and one conclusion, e.g.:

Premises: Polly is a pig. All pigs can fly.
Conclusion: Polly can fly.

From the first two statements, the final statement is a legitimate conclusion. Note that it is not whether the statements are accurate which is in question here, but the logic of the third statement if the first two are accepted.

Activity 7: syllogisms

In example, read through the two premises and decide whether the conclusion is valid:

1 *Premises:* Mary likes all vegetables. Peas are vegetables.
Conclusion: Mary likes peas.

2 *Premises:* If it is the end of the lesson, the bell rings. The bell does not ring.
Conclusion: It is not the end of the lesson.

3 *Premises:* On Saturdays Jane goes shopping. Jane goes shopping.
Conclusion: It is Saturday.

4 *Premises:* When it is raining, Bobby puts on his wellingtons. It is not raining.
Conclusion: Bobby does not put on his wellingtons.

When you have finished, see the notes on page 284.

Errors in syllogistic reasoning tasks are extremely common, so we might draw the conclusion that people tend not to think logically. It is possible, though, that errors come about not because people do not think logically but because they misunderstand the problem. To go back to the first example of Polly the flying pig, errors in this case might come about because people focus on whether the conclusion is objectively true, rather than if it follows logically from the premises.

Braine *et al.* (1984), in their **natural deduction theory**, have suggested that most errors in deductive reasoning come about as a result of how we interpret the premises. In the third example in activity 7, for example, the statement 'On Saturdays Jane goes shopping' is interpreted to mean that Jane only goes shopping on a Saturday and not on any other day of the week. Braine *et al.* suggest that this kind of error occurs because we generally expect others to give us information we need to know. They tested this idea by giving people modified syllogisms:

Box N: Braine *et al.* (1984)

Procedure: People were given modified syllogisms with an additional premise to clarify the first, e.g.:

Premises: On Saturdays Jane goes shopping.
On Thursdays Jane goes shopping.
Jane goes shopping.
Conclusion: ?

Results: The participants were much more likely to state (correctly) that no valid conclusion could be drawn when given syllogisms modified in this way.

Conclusion: Errors on syllogisms are the result of misinterpreting the premises rather than a failure to reason logically.

Braine *et al.* go on to argue that people tend not to have trouble with the kind of syllogism in the first example in activity 7 because we have a mental rule which corresponds to the way it is phrased. However, this is not always true:

Box O: Byrne (1989)

Procedure: Participants were given syllogisms using the pattern of the first example in activity 7. They were presented in two forms:

a *Premise:* If Rachel has an essay to write, then she will study late in the library. Rachel has an essay to write.
Conclusion: ?

b *Premise:* If Rachel has an essay to write, then she will study late in the library. If the library stays open, then Rachel will study late in the library. Rachel has an essay to write.

Conclusion: ?

Results: Participants were much less likely to draw the valid conclusion that 'Rachel will study late in the library' when presented with form **b**.

Conclusion: The processes involved in deductive reasoning are likely to be more complex than natural deduction theory suggests.

There is further evidence that more complex factors than failures of comprehension determine deductive reasoning. Janis and Frick (1943), for example, pointed to the importance of **belief bias**. They found that people were likely to say that conclusions drawn in syllogisms were valid if they agreed with the conclusion, i.e. if it agreed with their personal beliefs, but to say that it was not valid if they disagreed with it.

Another task which has been used to investigate deductive reasoning is the **Wason selection task**:

Activity 8: the Wason selection task

Try this yourself, and collect responses from other people if possible:

There are four cards lying on a table. Each card has a letter on one side and a number on the other:

There is a rule which applies to these four cards: If there is an R on one side of the card, then there is a 2 on the other side of the card.

Which cards need to be turned over to find out whether the rule is being followed?

You probably found that most people – wrongly – pick either the R card or the R and 2 cards. The crucial thing here is whether any of the cards *fail* to obey the rule. The R needs to be turned over, because if there is anything other than a 2 on the other side, the rule has been broken. The second card which must be turned over is the 7, because if there is an R on the other side, again the rule has been broken. The 2 is irrelevant. If there is an R on the other side, all this will tell us is that the rule *might* be true. This perhaps becomes clearer if we rephrase the task as a syllogism:

Premises: If there is an R on one side of the card, then there is a 2 on the other side. The 7 card does not have a 2 on it.

Conclusion: The 7 card should not have an R on the other side.

Activity 9: why do people find Wason's task so difficult?

This task is usually solved correctly by only about one in 20 university students.

From your own experience with it, why do you think so many people get it wrong?

When you have finished, see the notes on page 284.

The possibility that it is the abstract nature of the task which causes problems has been tested by presenting the same problem in a more concrete form:

Box P: Wason and Shapiro (1971)

Procedure: Participants were shown four cards:

MANCHESTER | LEEDS

CAR | TRAIN

They were given the rule: 'Every time I go to Manchester I travel by car', and asked to select only those cards which needed to be turned over to find out whether the rule was correct or not.

Results: Sixty-two per cent correctly identified that the 'Manchester' and 'train' cards needed to be turned over, compared with 12% who were successful with the Wason selection task in its original form (see activity 8).
Conclusion: Participants are significantly more successful at deductive reasoning when it is presented in a more meaningful form.

However, this is not the end of the story. Griggs and Cox (1982) tested American students in Florida and found that they were no more successful at the Wason and Shapiro version of the Wason selection test than at the original version. This may be because they had no experience of Manchester and Leeds. However, when the task was adapted to relate to the laws of Florida on age and drinking alcohol – 'If a person is drinking beer, then the person must be over 19 years of age' – there was a 73% success rate.

This led Griggs and Cox to put forward a **memory cueing hypothesis**: people need specific prior experience to be successful on the Wason selection task. Expressing the task in concrete terms is not in itself enough. However, they carried out a later study which did not support this hypothesis:

Box Q: Griggs and Cox (1983)

Procedure: Participants were given a version of the Wason selection task. The rule to be tested was: 'If a purchase exceeds $30, then the receipt must be approved by the department manager'.
Results: There was a 70% success rate, even though participants had had no direct experience of checking sales receipts.
Conclusion: Direct experience is not essential for success at the Wason selection task.

It is possible to explain these findings in terms of participants drawing on similar (albeit not identical) past experiences. Another possibility, according to the idea of **pragmatic reasoning schemata**, proposed by Cheng and Holyoak (1985), is that when we are faced with the task described in box Q, we bring to the situation our general past experiences of needing permission. These experiences allow us to develop rules (i.e. pragmatic reasoning schemata) which we can apply to reasoning involving pemission.

- **Deductive reasoning** starts from general rules to draw specific inferences. Much research on deductive reasoning has used **syllogisms**.
- Problems with syllogisms can arise from problems with **negative statements**, misunderstanding the **nature of the problem**, failure to understand the meaning of the **premises** and **belief bias**.
- The **Wason selection task** often causes difficulties in deductive reasoning. The success rate is higher when the task is expressed in a more meaningful form.
- The **memory cueing hypothesis** suggests that we need to be able to relate the task to our own direct experience to carry it out successfully, but the idea of **pragmatic reasoning schemata** suggests that we learn more general rules which can be applied where relevant.

Inductive reasoning

Inductive reasoning uses information from specific cases to form a general rule. An example of inductive reasoning is concept formation. This relates to abstracting the essential elements of something which is perceived. It can then be categorised with other items with similar characteristics, given a relevant label and responded to appropriately. Bourne (1966) states that a concept exists 'whenever two or more distinguishable objects or events have been grouped or classified together, and set apart from other objects on the basis of some common feature or property characteristic of each'.

Traditionally, a concept has been thought to comprise a set of features which are all necessary if an object or event is to be categorised as being an example of a particular concept. A chair, for instance, must have a back and provide a seat for one person. In other words, categorisation is an all-or-nothing process.

Activity 13: the availability heuristic

Do you think that K is more common as the first letter of a word or as the third letter of a word? If you can, ask other people the same question. Compare your answer with the discussion which follows.

Tversky and Kahneman (1973) found that most people guessed that K appears more often as the first letter of a word than as the third letter, though in fact K is three times as likely to appear in third place. They suggested that people make this error because it is very much easier to think of words beginning with K than those which have K as their third letter. In other words, letters beginning with K are more available, and so lead to an incorrect judgement of probability.

The use of the availability heuristic could also go some way to explaining why people who play the lottery prefer a seemingly haphazard combination of numbers, since this kind of sequence is seen winning much more frequently than apparently well-ordered sequences.

A recent example of the application of this heuristic is the effect of the destruction of the World Trade Centre on 11 September 2001. As a result of the wide publicity this was given, people's perception of the increased probability that planes would be hijacked and destroyed led to the number of people travelling by air dropping sharply, with some airlines going out of business.

An example of how using the representativeness heuristic can lead to errors is shown in activity 14:

Activity 14: the representativeness heuristic

Find some willing participants and ask them this question:

Linda is a former student activist, single, very intelligent, and a philosophy graduate. On a scale of 1–10, where 1 is 'extremely unlikely' and 10 is 'certain', how probable is it that she is: **a** a bank cashier, **b** a feminist or **c** a feminist bank cashier?

Compare your findings with the discussion which follows.

This is one of the questions used in a study by Tversky and Kahneman (1983). They found that most of their participants said that it was much more probable that Linda was a feminist bank cashier than a bank cashier. Given their results, it is likely that you had similar answers. This answer clearly cannot be correct, since the category 'bank-cashiers' must include 'feminist bank cashiers', as well as those with rather different views. Tversky and Kahneman called this kind of error the **conjunctive fallacy**; 'conjunctive' here means putting together different pieces of information.

The representativeness heuristic can mean that people ignore important information and so make errors when judging probabilities:

Box V: Kahneman and Tversky (1973)

Procedure: Participants were told that the descriptions of people they were going to be given had been selected at random from a set of 100 descriptions. Half the participants were told that 70 of the people described were lawyers, and the other 30 engineers. The numbers and professions were reversed for the other participants. They were read a description which corresponded well to stereotypes of both lawyers and engineers, and then asked to indicate the probability of the description being either of an engineer or of a lawyer.

Results: Most participants decided that the probability of the description relating to a lawyer or an engineer was 0.5. Probability is expressed as a figure between 0 and 1, where 0 means that there is no possibility of an occurrence, and 1 means that the occurrence is certain. The judgement here was therefore that there was a 50/50 chance that the description related to either profession.

Conclusion: Probability judgements were influenced by the representativeness heuristic, since the description was equally applicable to both. Participants did not take into account the base-rate information, i.e. the relative numbers of lawyers and engineers they were told made up the sample.

The conclusion Kahneman and Tversky drew was supported by a further finding in this study. Some participants were told a description had been picked at random, but were not given the description. In this situation, when they could not use the representativeness heuristic, they correctly estimated the probability of the description relating to an engineer or a lawyer as 0.7 or 0.3, in line with the base-rate information they had been given.

So why do people make use of availability and representativeness heuristics when they so often lead to errors? One reason is that such heuristics can often be accurate. When errors are made, it is usually because other information has been ignored, rather than the heuristic being irrelevant. Another reason is that heuristics give us a simple way of approaching a range of problems. People act as **cognitive misers**, in that they try to minimise mental effort. Heuristics are one way in which this can be achieved.

However, even when heuristics are not involved, people often ignore relevant information in judging probability:

Box W: Kahneman and Tversky (1982)

Procedure: Participants were given the cab problem (see figure 9).
Results: Most participants incorrectly estimated the probability that the cab was Blue as 0.8, in line with the credibility of the witness, and taking no account of the base-rate information, i.e. the relatively larger number of Green than Blue cabs.
Conclusion: People may ignore relevant information when making judgements of probability.

Figure 9: the cab problem

A cab was involved in a hit-and-run accident. Two cab companies, the Green and the Blue, operate in the city. You know that:

a 85% of the cabs in the city are Green; 15% are Blue.

b a witness says the cab involved was Blue.

c when tested, the witness correctly identified the two colours 80% of the time.

How probable is it that the cab involved in the accident was Blue, as the witness reported, rather than Green?

According to a statistical theory known as Bayes' Theorem, the base-rate information must be taken into account if the calculation of the probability is to be accurate. In this case it is 0.41, with a 0.59 probability that the cab was Green. The cab was therefore more likely to be Green.

In a further study, Tversky and Kahneman (1980) found that people were much more likely to make appropriate use of base-rate information when they were presented with problems in which its importance was stressed.

However, the conclusions drawn from this general line of research have been criticised. Firstly, the results found in research of this kind have not always been consistent. Moreover, Bar-Hillel (1983) has claimed that variations in the wording and context of a task can have a marked effect on bias in judgements. Smyth *et al.* (1994) go on to point out that in real-life situations we rarely have the complete information provided in these studies, so Bayesian reasoning cannot be applied. The formal way of thinking about probability which it describes therefore has little relevance to the kinds of everyday judgements we need to make.

- The estimates of probability we make are often inaccurate. One reason for this is our use of **heuristics**.

- The **availablity heuristic** means that we focus on information more readily available to us. The **representativeness heuristic** means that we interpret information in ways which correspond to our existing knowledge of the topic about which we are being asked.
- People may also ignore important information in making a probability judgement, most notably **base-rate information**.
- It has been argued that the formal reasoning tested by studies in this area has little relevance to the kind of reasoning suitable for everyday situations.

10.4 Representation of knowledge

There has been considerable interest in how information is represented in long-term memory (LTM). Since LTM can hold very large amounts of information over a long period of time, it is clear that there must be some kind of organisation if material is to be easily accessed and recalled. We will look here at some of the ideas psychologists have put forward to explain the nature of this organisation.

Schemas and scripts

Bartlett (1932) argued that memory is affected by the store of relevant prior knowledge we have, and not just by what information is presented. He believed that memory is a **reconstruction** rather than straightforward reproduction of information, and can be distorted by our existing **schemas**. A schema is a way of summarising events which enables us to predict what is likely to happen in various situations. For example, you have a 'holiday' schema, constructed from past experience, which contains information about what is likely to happen when you go on holiday. This allows you to predict what a holiday is going to be like, and so cuts down on the information-processing necessary to make sense of what is happening. However, if you were asked to remember a particular holiday, it could well be that you reconstruct what happened in the light of your previous experience, and so what you remember could become distorted.

The kind of organisation Bartlett is suggesting relates to both semantic and episodic memory (see chapter 9). Here is the Native American story he used in his research:

Activity 15: Bartlett's War of the Ghosts (1932)

Read this story, which is the Native American story Bartlett used in his research:

One night two young men from Egulac went down to the river to hunt seals, and while they were there it became foggy and calm. Then they heard war-cries and they thought: 'Maybe this is a war-party'. They escaped to the shore and hid behind a log. Now canoes came up, and they heard the noise of paddles, and saw one canoe coming up to them. There were five men in the canoe, and they said: 'What do you think? We wish to take you along. We are going up the river to make war on the people.' One of the young men said: 'I have no arrows'. 'Arrows are in the canoe,' they said. 'I will not go along. I might be killed. My relatives do not know where I have gone. But you,' he said, turning to the other, 'may go with them.' So one of the young men went, but the other returned home. And the warriors went on up the river to a town on the other side of Kalama. The people came down to the water, and they began to fight, and many were killed. But presently the young man heard one of the warriors say: 'Quick, let us go home: that Indian has been hit.' Now he thought: 'Oh, they are ghosts.' He did not feel sick, but they said he had been shot. So the canoes went back to Egulac, and the young man went ashore to his house, and made a fire. And he told everybody and said: 'Behold I accompanied the ghosts, and we went to fight. Many of our fellows were killed, and many of those who attacked us were killed. They said I was hit, and I did not feel sick.' He told it all, and then he became quiet. When the sun rose he fell down. Something black came out of his mouth. His face became contorted. The people jumped up and cried. He was dead.

Now cover up the story and write down as much of it as you can remember.

Bartlett's studies showed that a number of changes occurred to the story as it was recalled by his participants. He found that typically people gave shorter, more simplified versions of the story. You may also have found that you reconstructed the story to fit in with your 'story' schema using words like 'because', since the cause-and-effect links we are used to in English stories are not made here. Sometimes new information is introduced to make the story more logical by our standards.

This type of reconstruction Bartlett termed **rationalisation**. Such distortions are used to make sense of unfamiliar things. But Bartlett's most important finding was that the central ideas of the story were not really changed at all. He suggested that people store a few main facts about the story and then **reconstruct** it from those facts. This act of reconstruction Bartlett referred to as **effort after meaning**.

The inaccuracy of reconstructive memory was discussed by Allport and Postman (1966) in their classic study of rumour. They found that the selection, retention and reporting of events involve several types of transformation of the material, all of which make it more meaningful in terms of personal interests, needs and experience. **Levelling** is the process by which certain details are omitted, while the opposite is **sharpening**, where details which are of particular relevance to the individual's interests and needs are foregrounded. Underlying these processes is **assimilation**: aspects of the story are levelled or sharpened to make them more consistent with what is seen as the main theme of the story. Items relevant to this theme may be imported and those which are irrelevant omitted. Apparent gaps may be filled and details changed to achieve consistency.

That memory uses schemas to organise information, and that this can lead to distortion, has been shown experimentally:

Box X: Brewer and Treyins (1981)

Procedure: Thirty participants were asked individually to wait in an office while the experimenter supposedly checked the laboratory to see if the previous participant had finished. After 35 seconds, he returned and asked them to go into another room where they were asked to recall everything in the waiting room.

Results: People tended to recall items consistent with an 'office schema'. Nearly everyone recalled the desk and chair, but only eight people recalled the skull, while just one recalled the picnic basket. However, nine people 'recalled' books, which had not been there.

Conclusion: Schemas can produce distorted recall, with items consistent with the schema being incorrectly recalled, and inconsistent items forgotten.

While schemas help us, in that they allow us to predict what is likely to happen in particular situations, they have the drawback of making us inflexible, and less likely to respond appropriately if a situation is out of the ordinary, as in the example of people being asked to recall 'The War of the Ghosts'; distortions crept in which served to fit the story into their schema of what constitutes a story.

Bartlett's research has since been criticised on a number of counts. For example, the instructions Bartlett gave to his participants were deliberately vague. He claimed he did not want to influence their remembering, but it could be argued that he did not explain explicitly enough that they should attempt to remember every detail of the story.

Other theorists have put forward similar ideas using slightly different terminology. For example, Schank and Abelson (1977) put forward a theory of **scripts**. Scripts are blank templates containing slots into which memories for individual events can be organised and stored. They thus provide a structure within which encoding can take place. In recall, when the script is accessed, it provide cues for retrieving information.

Activity 16: writing a script

Write a brief script to describe what 'Going to a club' involves. You might find it helpful to imagine you are explaining the event to a person from a culture which does not have this concept. Concentrate on including as many aspects as possible – getting ready, what goes on when you have arrived, what happens while you are there and getting home. If you are working in a group, compare your script with what other people have written. How much overlap is there?

If you share similar experiences with others in your group, your schemas will overlap, and so your scripts will have quite a lot in common. Research has investigated the idea of scripts:

Box Y: Bower *et al.* (1979)

Procedure: Participants were asked to write down the 20 most important events in each of a number of situations, e.g. visiting a restaurant.

Results: There was much agreement between participants. When listing the events involved in visiting a restaurant, for example, 73% of participants mentioned sitting down, reading the menu, ordering food, eating, and paying the bill. Many other similar events were listed by large numbers of participants.

Conclusion: There are a large number of events common to many people's knowledge of what constitutes visiting a restaurant. People's scripts save time by making predictions easier in situations they encounter regularly, meaning that behaviour needs less consideration, and attention is freed for processing more unexpected informations.

- A **schema** (or **script**) is a summary of what happens in a certain situation. Schemas simplify the processing of new information, and so are a way of organising information in LTM.
- Bartlett used schema theory to suggest that memory is **reconstruction**. The major determinant of human memory is **effort after meaning**.
- Schemas allow us to **predict** what is likely to happen in particular situations, but may **distort** what we remember when we come across something unexpected.

The hierarchical model of concept organisation

The hierarchical network model, proposed by Collins and Quillian (1969), suggested that information in semantic memory is organised into hierarchical networks. This is a logical (rather than a psychological) suggestion as to how information might be stored, since it can explain how we can access information in semantic memory very quickly and easily.

Figure 10: hierarchical network model (Collins and Quillian, 1969)

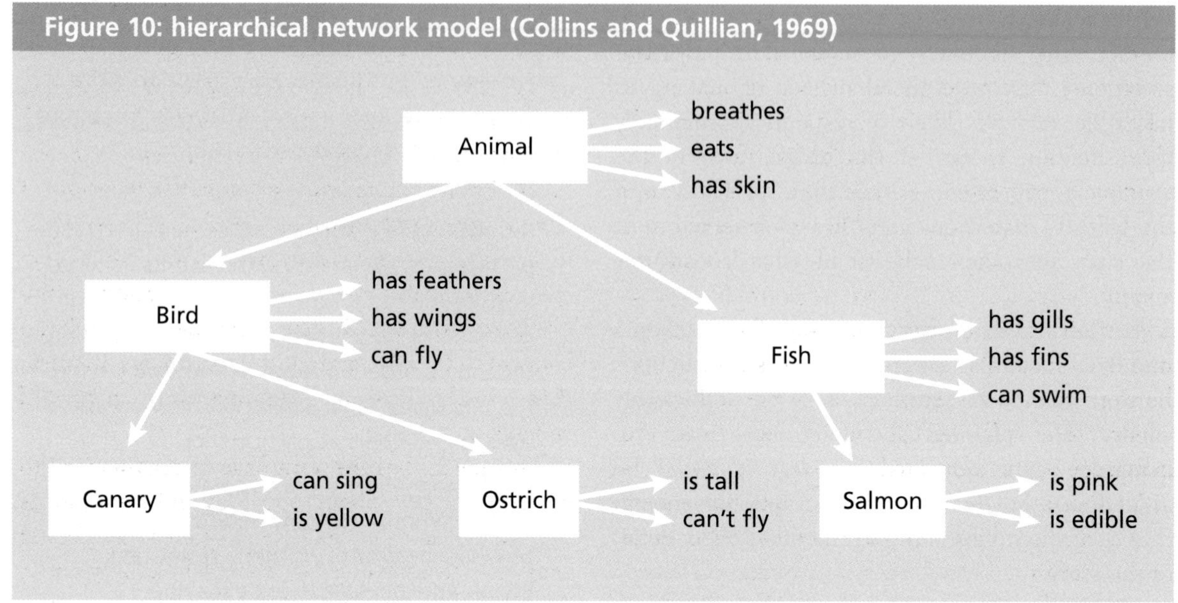

Collins and Quillian suggested that memory is organised into a hierarchy of levels, going from more general terms and ideas to more specific ones, as shown in figure 10. If this is the case, then it could be predicted that if a person is searching for information, the more levels a search has to pass through, the longer it should take to complete that search:

Box Z: Collins and Quillian (1969)

Procedure: Participants were shown a number of statements which linked concepts from the network. The experimenters timed how long it took participants to verify the statements. Some statements involved concepts from the same level of the hierarchy, e.g. 'An ostrich cannot fly'. Other statements, such as 'An ostrich has skin,' involved moving two levels – from 'An ostrich is a bird', through 'A bird is an animal', to 'Animals have skin'.

Results: The more levels a person had to pass through to test a statement, the longer it took for them to verify whether it was true or false.

Conclusion: Semantic memory is organised into a hierarchy as the hierarchical network model suggests.

Activity 17: testing the hierarchical network model

You can test the idea of the hierarchical network model yourself. You could use the information in figure 10, or make up your own hierarchy and levels, e.g. buildings rather than animals. Make a series of statements like the ones Collins and Quillian used, then test the idea that the more levels a person must pass through to test a statement, the longer it will take them to test that statement.

Compare response times to two sets of 10 statements. The statements in one set would need to link ideas on one level, while the other set would require movement between levels.

The hierarchical network model has the advantage of proposing an economical way of storing a huge amount of information. However, some experimental observations provide evidence that does not fit in with the model.

Rips *et al.* (1973) asked participants whether a number of statements were true or false. They found that participants could verify 'a bear is an animal' more quickly than 'a bear is a mammal', which is not what the model would predict; 'mammal' is only one level away from 'bear', whereas 'animal' is two levels away. However, this assumes that ordinary people use the same taxonomic stucture as zoologists. The non-scientist is perhaps more likely to make the connection 'bear–animal' than 'bear–mammal', since they are less likely to use the word 'mammal' very often. How hierarchies are constructed will necessarily depend on the knowledge of the individual.

Another problem is found with statements such as 'A robin is a bird', which can be verified more quickly than statements that involve atypical members of a category such as 'A penguin is a bird', despite the fact that the same number of levels must be passed through to test the statement. This is the **typicality effect**.

In response to criticisms of the hierarchical network model, Collins and Loftus (1975) suggested a revised **spreading activation model** (see figure 11). In this new version, concepts are interlinked. Closely related concepts have short links between them, and links that are often used become stronger (shown as thicker lines) than links that are rarely used. This can account for the typicality effect, as 'robin' and 'bird' are more closely linked than 'penguin' and 'bird'; we think of robins more often as birds than we think of penguins as birds This model also suggests that when one concept is activated, this activation spreads out to related concepts, so activating the word 'robin' would also activate the related concepts of 'red', 'bird' and 'Christmas'. In turn, these could lead on to apparently unrelated concepts.

This model has the advantage of relating well to what we know about the way information is represented in the brain as a pattern of neural activity. Activation of a concept can be thought of as corresponding to excitation of a neuron, with activation spreading to other neurons. Frequent activation could facilitate or inhibit particular links, making them easier or harder to excite. It is thought that long-term changes in synaptic connections account for long-term representation of information. This seems to relate quite well to the length and strength of connections in the spreading activation model.

Figure 11: spreading activation model (Collins and Loftus, 1975)

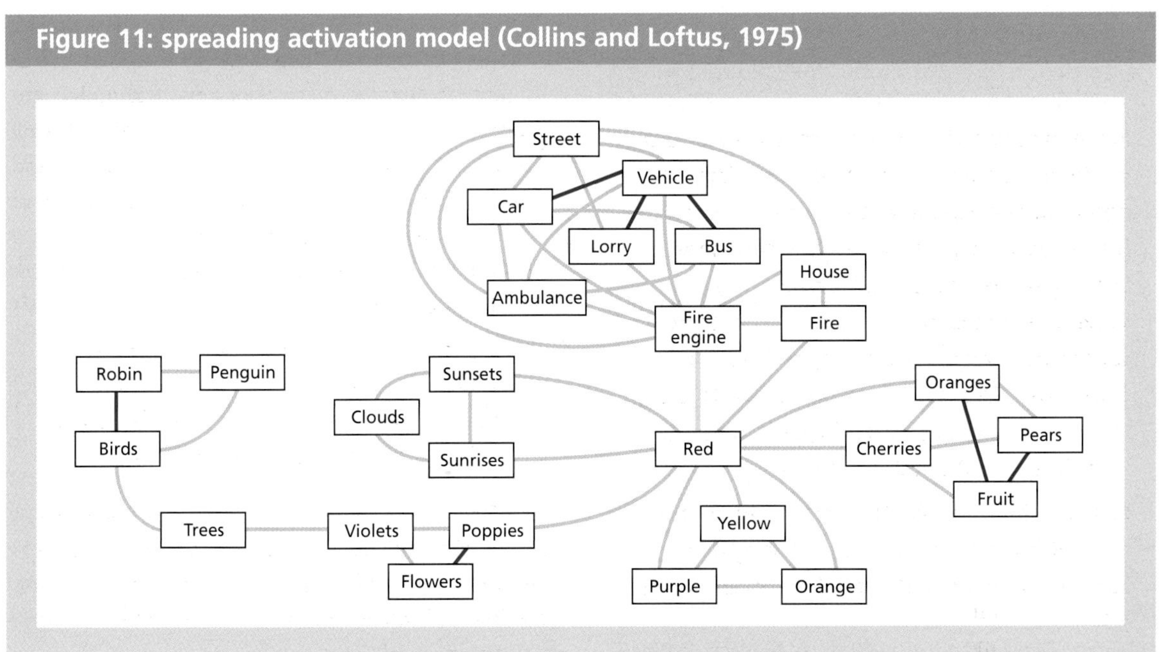

However, both these models assume organisation is semantic, and this is not always the case. Brown and McNeill (1966) conducted research into the **tip-of-the-tongue state (TOT state)**. You have probably come across a situation where you felt that a word that you knew well was 'on the tip of your tongue'. You knew the word was in your memory, and may even have been able to identify some of its features, e.g. the number of syllables or initial letter, but could temporarily not retrieve it from memory. Trying to explain such retrieval failures can be useful in terms of explaining the organisation of information in memory.

Box AA: Brown and McNeill (1966)

Procedure: Dictionary definitions of uncommon words were read to participants, who were asked to identify the word, e.g. 'a small boat used in the river and harbour traffic of China and Japan'. (The answer is 'sampan'.)

Results: Although participants were sometimes unable to identify the word defined, they could often recall features of the word, for example, its first letter, or how many syllables it contained, or its rhythm. Participants often found that related words resembling the target word came to mind whilst they searched their memory, but they did recognise these words as being incorrect. Related words were similar to the target either in meaning (e.g. 'junk' or 'barge') or in sound (e.g. 'sarong' or 'Siam').

Conclusion: The feeling of having the word on the tip of the tongue was due to the fact that participants could partially retrieve information about the word. Words can be organised by meaning, sound or alphabetically.

The organisation of material in **episodic memory** also seems not to use semantic organisation. If people are asked about particular events in their lives, and to 'think aloud' while they are trying to retrieve those memories, their responses typically follow this sort of pattern: 'I was living in London at the time ... we had a small flat in Belsize Park ... it was just after John had gone to Australia ....' This suggests the way in which this kind of material is organised is temporal and spatial, i.e. related to time and place.

- Collins and Quillian suggested that information in LTM is organised into **hierarchical networks**. The hierarchical network model cannot account for the **typicality effect**.
- The **spreading activation model** shows concepts connected by short or long, and strong or weak, links. It relates well to what we know about how information is represented in the brain.
- The **tip-of-the-tongue** state **(TOT state)** shows that information in LTM is organised alphabetically and by sound, as well as semantically.
- Organisation in **episodic memory** is **spatial** and **temporal**.

Imagery

It has also been suggested that imagery is a form of organisation in LTM. It relates to both semantic and episodic memory. Paivio (1969) suggested that the more easily a word evokes a mental image, the more easily it will be learned. This idea was supported by a study by Begg and Paivio (1969), which found that participants were better able to recall concrete words (those which readily trigger an image, e.g. horseshoe) than **concrete** words (e.g. justice). Paivio put forward the **dual-code hypothesis**, i.e. that different codes are used for words and pictures. Verbal material is held in a verbal store and non-verbal material in an imaginal store. According to Paivio, images are likely to trigger off corresponding words, while words are not so likely to trigger off images. Visual material can therefore be retrieved from either of the two scores, so there are two chances of remembering; this is why visual material is remembered better than verbal material.

This idea has been further supported:

Box BB: Frost (1972)

Procedure: Participants were shown a series of 16 drawings of common objects. They could be categorised semantically (i.e. animals, furniture, clothing and vehicles) or visually (with the long axis vertical, horizontal, tilted right and tilted left). Some participants were led to expect a recognition test, and some a free recall test. Both groups were actually given a free recall test.

Results: The responses of participants expecting a free recall test showed semantic clustering, i.e. items were recalled in meaningful groups, while those expecting a recognition test showed both semantic and visual clustering, i.e. items grouped in visual categories.

Conclusion: Participants expecting a recognition test had stored a visual image of the drawings in LTM, and used this information together with semantic information on the recall test.

However, Paivio's dual-code hypothesis has been criticised, notably by Pylyshyn (1973), who pointed out that storing detailed copies of everything we see would require an implausibly large amount of storage space. Anderson and Bower (1973) have suggested that rather than two codes, we should think of one code. They explain the superiority of recall for visual material in terms of visual input providing a richer memory trace.

There is no doubt that imagery aids recall, particularly when it is interactive:

Box CC: Bower (1970)

Procedure: Participants were given a paired associate learning task. This method uses unrelated words, presented in pairs. In the recall phase, participants are presented with the first word of the pair and are asked to supply the second. Group 1 was asked to form a short phrase linking the words, group 2 was asked to form images of the two words, separated in space, and group 3 was instructed to form an interactive image.

Results: Group 3 performed better than either group 1 or group 2. These two groups performed at a similar level.

Conclusion: Interactive imagery can enhance recall.

Bower's study presents some problems for the dual-coding hypothesis, since group 2 did no better than group 1. It seems that it is the interaction of images which is important. Moreover, Howe *et al.* (2000) found that for young children, interactive images are even more effective if they are are also bizarre.

- **Imagery** is another way of organising material in LTM. **Paivio** suggested in his **dual-code hypothesis** that there are two memory stores, verbal and imaginal. Images enhance recall because material can be retrieved from either store.
- This theory has been challenged, but imagery can aid recall, especially is it is **interactive** or **bizarre**.

Notes on activities

1 The first sentence is a well-formed English sentence on all three counts. The second sentence is syntactically correct and the words are all in the English lexicon, but semantically it is unacceptable, since it has no meaning. The final sentence also conforms to the rules of English grammar – it describes where and how the plink is sitting – but 'plink', 'feltfully' and 'flong' are not in the English lexicon, and so it is semantically not an English sentence.

2 Visual communication is limited because it usually requires light, and so cannot take place in the dark. The signaller and receiver need to be able to see each other, so they need to be relatively close, and with no obstacles to obscure the view. An olfactory communication will linger long after the message has been received, which may be dangerous for the signaller. Different messages require the production of different chemicals, and there is little possibility with olfactory messages of using patterning as a way of distinguishing one message from another. All of these drawbacks are overcome by auditory communication.

3 When assessing whether animal communication shows **semanticity**, there is always the problem that animals might just be showing an automatic response to a stimulus, rather than forming a mental representation of what is being referred to. However, the formation of categories by vervet monkeys (box D) could be interpreted as showing semanticity.

The bee dance clearly shows **displacement**, since it refers to a food source outside the hive. There is also displacement in the Menzel and Halperin study of chimpanzees (box D), although the communication in this respect is rather imprecise.

Neither bees nor non-human primates show **structure dependence**. This is not to say, of course, that their communication does not have this feature; all it means is that we do not have sufficient understanding of animal comunication to come to a conclusion.

There is no evidence of **productivity** in non-human primates, though again, just because we have no evidence of it doesn't mean that we can dismiss it as a possibility. To an extent, bees could be said to show productivity since they can communicate about a virtually unlimited number of spatial locations. On the other hand, the kind of information they can communicate is very limited.

This has been demonstrated in a further study by von Frisch and Lindauer (1954). They placed a hive at the bottom of a radio beacon and some sugar water at the top. The bees who were shown the sugar water performed the round dance, and the other bees flew around for several hours in all directions – except up. As von Frisch put it: 'The bees have no words for "up" in their language. There are no flowers in the clouds.' The bees were unable to pass on this extra essential piece of information.

4 Vygotsky: 2; 4; 5; 10. Piaget: 3; 9; 7. Both: 1; 6; 8.

7 In syllogisms such as these, most people accept as valid all the conclusions drawn. In fact, only the conclusions drawn in the first two examples follow on logically from the premises. In the third example, for instance, it is perfectly possible that Jane also goes shopping on other days as well as Saturday, and in the final example Bobby might like his wellingtons so much that he wears them whatever the weather. Syllogisms following the pattern of the second example can also cause problems. Evans (1989), for instance, found the error rate for this kind of syllogism to be rather more than 30%, possibly because we have some difficulty in coping with negatives.

9 As with syllogisms, one of the problems may be that the task involves negatives, which people tend to find harder to cope with than positives. You may also have thought that the task is very abstract, and so doesn't relate too well to the way we reason in everyday life.

12 Reporting verbally is rather a slow process, and is retrospective. It is very difficult, if not impossible, to report thought processes as they are happening. Describing thought processes out loud may affect how the task is carried out. It may, for example, encourage people to use particular strategies which are more easily described, or to take more time on the task. In addition, some of our thought processes happen at an unconscious level, so we don't have access to them. Storms and Nisbett (1970), for example, found that many people were unaware of the thought processes underlying their behaviour.

11

Cognition and law

11.1 Why cognitive psychology is important

Cognitive psychology is relevant to many areas of the law. For example, eye-witnesses of crimes may need to identify faces of possible criminals from mugshot albums, or recall and describe faces when making statements to the police. The police may need to match faces caught on surveillance cameras with other records they have of faces. Research into how we process faces can provide information to make these processes more efficient.

Eye-witness testimony covers a rather broader area than face recognition, since witnesses may be required to recall other details of what they have witnessed. Again, it is helpful to know how memory works; and, as we shall see, psychologists have used what they know about memory processes to work with the police in devising methods of interviewing witnesses which should lead to more information, and more accurate information, being produced by witnesses to a crime.

There are physical reasons why some people's memories are less efficient than others, which may also have implications in a legal context. We will be looking at some of these reasons – trauma, ECT, surgery, alcohol and ageing – later in the chapter.

An important controversy in memory research is the issue of recovered memories. There are many cases of people who have claimed to recover during therapy long-forgotten memories from much earlier in their lives, often of abuse they experienced as children. It has been suggested that these may not always be genuine memories, but examples of False Memory Syndrome. This issue has serious legal implications, particularly when people have taken those they accuse to court for the abuse committed against them.

11.2 Face recognition

Being able to recognise other people is of great significance in our lives. You can imagine how difficult life would be if you didn't recognise your mother, brother, best friend or partner. Human beings seem to have an amazing ability to recognise faces. Standing (1973) showed participants 10,000 faces over five days. When they were shown pairs of faces, one of which they had previously been shown, together with a new one, they were able to identify the face they had seen 98% of the time. This ability is also impressive when people are asked to identify faces which they have not seen for some time, as demonstrated by the study by Bahrick *et al.* (1975), and described in chapter 9, box L.

Psychologists have learned something about the processes of face recognition from people suffering from **prosopagnosia**. People with this disorder can't recognise the faces of people they know well – sometimes they cannot even recognise their own face in a mirror. They can, however, recognise friends and family from their voices, so the problem is not due to people having been forgotten.

There are two types of theory that try to explain this disorder. One suggests that it takes more precise discrimination to tell the difference between two faces than it does to tell the difference between a book and a pencil, for example, so failure to discriminate faces may lie in the lack of the ability to make this kind of fine distinction. The other type of theory suggests that there are specific processes that are needed if we are to recognise a face, and that these are lacking in prosopagnosics.

The idea that an inability to recognise faces is due to a lack of fine discrimination is not widely accepted. De Renzi (1986) worked with a prosopagnosic man who could make very good fine discrimination between different people's handwriting, for example, and between Italian coins, but could not recognise relatives' and friends' faces. Similarly, McNeil and Warrington (1991) reported the case of a farmer with prosopagnosia, who was nonetheless able to identify each of his 36 sheep without hesitation. It therefore does not seem likely that prosopagnosia is due to an inability to make fine discriminations.

The idea that there are processes specific to face recognition is more convincing. It is supported by the finding that there are regions of the **temporal lobes** of the cortex which deal specifically with face recognition. In extreme cases, damage to this area leads to prosopagnosia.

Information is also relayed to a subcortical area of the brain called the **limbic system**. It is here that emotional responses to familiar faces are generated. Where this pathway is damaged or underactive, the result may be **Capgras syndrome**. For Capgras patients, people they know look the same as usual, but something does not feel right emotionally when they see them. They may deal with this mismatch between appearance and feelings with the belief that those close to them have been replaced by imposters or even taken over by aliens. Blount (1986) refers to the case of a man who was so sure that his father had been abducted and replaced by a humanoid robot that he slit his father's throat to look for the wires which made him work.

Prosopagnosia and Capgras syndrome are extreme examples of what happens when the face recognition systems malfunction. But what does a theory of face recognition need to explain? When we fully recognise a face, we also recall other information about the person, including their name. For example, when we see a friend, we may remember that his name is Andy, that he works for an insurance company and that he enjoys windsurfing. Any theory of face recognition must therefore also include our ability to put a name to a face and to remember personal details. What happens when part of this process fails can help us to understand the normal processes which take place when we recognise a familiar face:

Box A: Young *et al.* (1985)

Procedure: A sample of 20 volunteers was asked to keep a diary of any errors they made in person recognition.

Results: 1008 incidents were recorded, four-fifths of which fell into four main categories. The number in each category is shown in brackets:

- **a** *failure to recognise a familiar person* (114). This typically happened when the appearance of the person had changed, for example if they had grown a beard or lost weight.
- **b** *misidentifying one person as another* (314). People thought they recognised a stranger; this was likely to happen in poor viewing conditions.
- **c** *recognising a person but not being able to place them or remember their name* (233). This was most likely to happen if the person was an acquaintance seen in an unfamiliar context, for example a familiar shop assistant seen in a restaurant.
- **d** *inability to remember someone's name* (190). Even though the name could not be recalled, some personal details were recalled, such as the person's job or where they were usually seen.

Conclusion: There are at least three separate systems involved in successful face recognition. Stored representations of familiar faces are held in a **face recognition** system. A **semantic** system includes general knowledge about people you know. The third system stores **names**.

Activity 1: systems in face recognition

For each type of error described in box A, identify which of the three systems contains a failure. What do these errors suggest about the order in which the different aspects of face recognition take place?

When you have finished, see the notes on page 310.

Hay and Young (1982) suggested that familiar faces are stored in the brain in neural circuits known as **face recognition units (FRUs)**. When we see a face, we scan our FRUs for a match, to decide whether or not the face is familiar. If a match is found, we can then access information about the person, such as their job and biographical information, which in turn may generate their name.

On the basis of this and other research into face recognition, Bruce and Young (1986) proposed the model of face recognition shown in figure 1:

Figure 1: Bruce and Young's model of face recognition (1986)

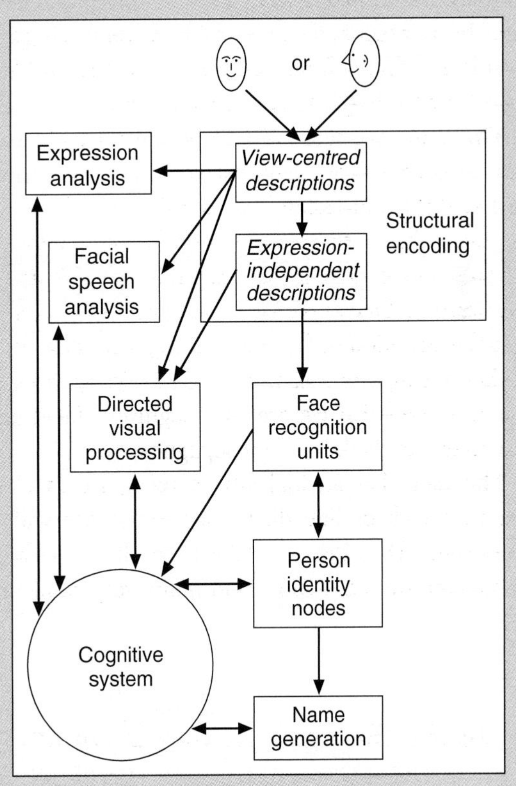

In figure 1, each box represents a separate processing mechanism or store, with arrows indicating the flow of information between them. Working down the right-hand side of the model, information is first encoded. This information is **expression-independent**, firstly because we recognise faces irrespective of their expression, and also because there is clinical evidence that faces and emotional expression are processed separately. Some patients with neurological damage can recognise faces but not emotions, while others can recognise emotions but not faces.

This structural encoding stimulates the **face recognition units (FRUs)**. The closer the correspondence between the face which is seen and information stored in a FRU, the stronger the activation will be. The FRUs are linked both to the cognitive system and to **person identity nodes (PINs)**. Face recognition makes available other information about the person from which identification can be made, such as their job or their hobbies. Information from the cognitive system to the PIN is included because we may often recognise someone using information other than their face, e.g. the sound of their voice or the way they walk. The PIN is the point at which recognising a person can be said to have taken place. After this, **name generation** can occur.

The directed visual processing unit is included because we can choose to focus on certain aspects of a face. For example, if we are meeting a friend in a crowded bar we may scan for someone with their style and colour of hair. The facial speech analysis unit is included because there is clinical evidence that lip reading is a separate ability from face recognition, as some patients with brain damage can read lips but not recognise faces, while others can recognise faces but not lipread.

Activity 2: errors in face recognition

Look back to the kinds of errors described in box A. How would the Bruce and Young model explain these kinds of errors?

When you have finished, see the notes on page 311.

Burton *et al.* (1990) have used the Bruce and Young model to develop a model (see figure 2) which can be simulated by a computer program:

Figure 2: interactive activation model of face recognition (Burton *et al.* 1990)

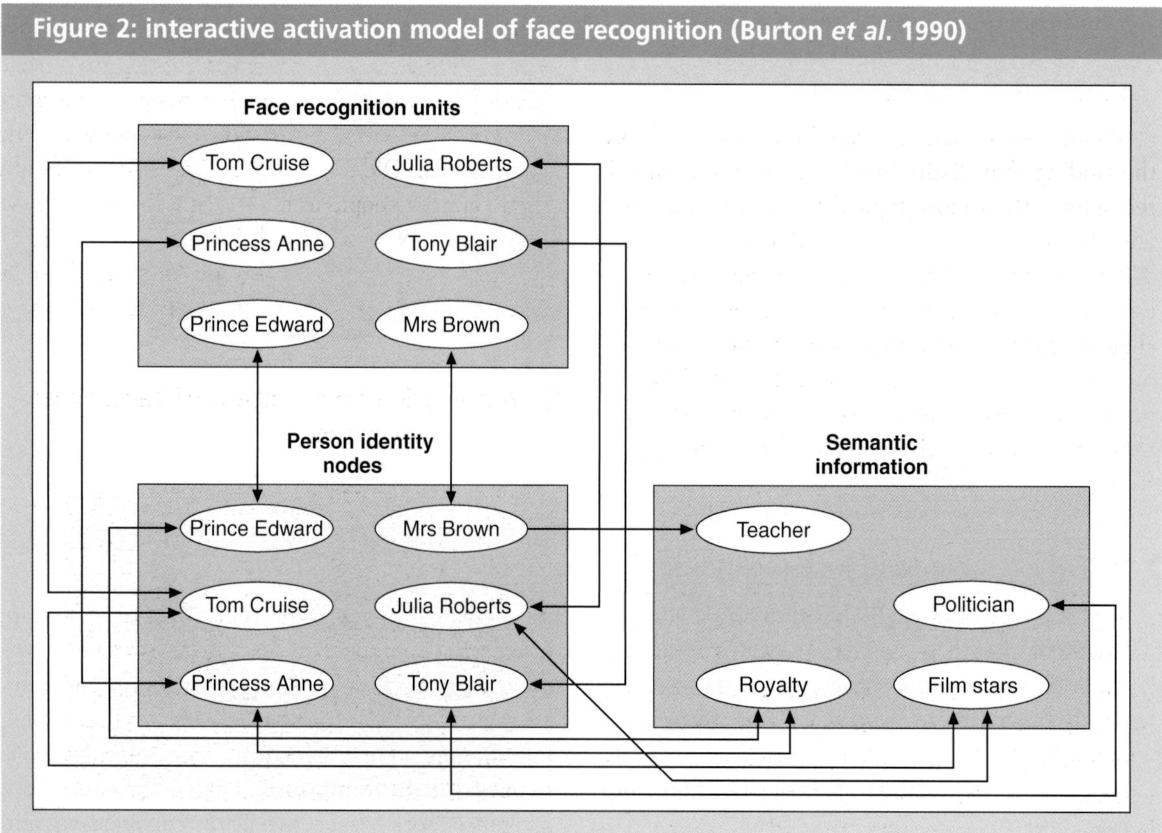

Like the Bruce and Young model, this model has three separate groups of interlinked units: one for FRUs, one for PINs, and one for semantic information. However, unlike the Bruce and Young model, semantic information is linked to PINs but not to FRUs. In this model, recognition occurs when activation in the relevant PIN reaches a given threshold. This excitation is then transmitted to other linked parts of the system.

The Burton *et al.* model has been very successful in simulating findings in face recognition research, such as the effects of **semantic priming**. Bruce and Valentine (1988) asked people to identify whether a face was familiar. They found that people recognised a familiar face more quickly if they had been primed by being previously shown another familiar associated face, rather than a familiar but unassociated face. For example, the Queen's face would be recognised more quickly as familiar after seeing Prince Philip's face, compared with seeing George Clooney's face. The Burton *et al.* model can simulate this priming effect by producing easier recognition when an associated face follows seeing a particular face than when the second face is unconnected with the first.

It can also simulate the **distinctiveness effect**, the finding that distinctive faces are more quickly recognised than more typical faces (e.g. Valentine and Ferrara, 1991). The model assumes that distinctive faces share fewer features than more typical faces, and this difference in the number of shared features was included in the computer model. When the model was run, the PINs for distinctive FRUs were more quickly and more strongly activated than those for more typical faces.

Unlike the Bruce and Young model, Burton *et al.* suggested that it is not necessary to assume that there is a separate name store. Burton and Bruce (1992) pointed out that unlike most semantic information about a person, their name is connected to only one PIN. For example, knowing that a particular person has a daughter is information which is likely also to apply to other known people, whereas someone's name is likely to be a unique link between the name and the PIN. When the computer model was run, it was found that names received the least activation of all the semantic information units, which could account for the difficulty people have in recalling them.

Ideas about face recognition are important in applied psychology, and are of particular relevance to the area of **eye-witness testimony** when people may be able to identify those suspected of carrying out a crime While people are usually extremely good at recognising faces, especially familiar faces, Shapiro and Penrod (1986) found that in eye-witness identification, people show inferior recall compared with traditional studies of face recognition. One reason for this may be that much of the research into face recognition has used photographs rather than actual faces as stimulus material and the same photos are often used for both the acquisition and recall stages of a study. Another reason may be that in eye-witness testimony, unlike in laboratory studies, the circumstances in which a face is first seen and when identification needs to be made may be quite different.

Other characteristics of face recognition also make identification problematic. Shepherd *et al.* (1974), for instance, found that people have more difficulty in recognising faces of people from another race. Older people also have more difficulty than younger people in recognising faces they have only seen once (Farramond, 1968).

Quite often an identification may need to be made from footage supplied by security cameras:

Activity 3: identification of faces from video

video picture

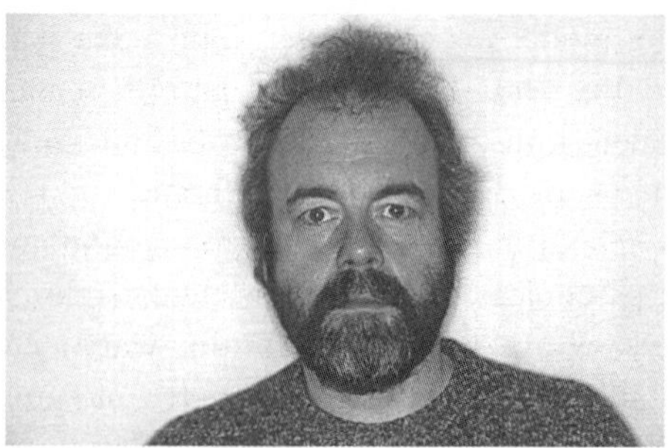
The man in the CCTV picture?

Are these pictures of the same man or of different people? How sure are you? Why is it difficult to make a judgment using this kind of material? Why might it be easier if the images were of someone you knew?
When you have finished, see the notes on page 311.

Psychologists have recently been liaising with the police to develop methods to help eye-witnesses identify criminals. If eye-witnesses are to help the police effectively in the identification of criminals, it is important to know what it is about a face which enables us to recognise it. The ways in which the police elicit information from eye-witnesses can then be tailored to the processes we use in face recognition. We will look now at what is known about the encoding of faces, and how this information has been used to elicit information about the appearance of criminals by eye-witnesses of crime.

- People are extremely good at recognising faces, even after a long period of time. Clinical conditions such as **prosopagnosia** and **Capgras syndrome** give us some information about the processes involved in face recognition.
- There are specific areas of the brain responsible for face recognition.
- The Bruce and Young model of face recognition proposes different modules in face recognition: **FRUs**, **PINs** and **name generation**.
- Burton *et al.* have developed this model using **computer simulation**. Their model can account for a range of findings in face recognition research. It also suggests that a separate name generation module is not necessary.
- Information about face recognition is important if **eye-witness identification** of criminals is to be accurate.

Feature analysis versus a holistic approach

An important area of debate has been whether we focus on the individual features which make up a face – eyes, nose, mouth, and so on – or whether we take a more holistic approach, focusing for example on the general shape of the face.

Activity 4: describing a face

Ask someone to describe the face of someone they know well, so that you would be able to pick them out of a group of people. Compare your findings with the discussion which follows.

You are likely to have found that the description lists separate features, such as 'blue eyes' or 'wide mouth'. Bruce and Young (1998) suggest that this may be because we have vocabulary referring to different features of the face or because these different features have different functions. However, it does not follow that the visual system processes information about faces in this way. It has been demonstrated experimentally that face processing does not analyse features:

Box B: Young *et al.* (1987)

Procedure: Faces were divided into upper and lower halves. Participants were shown the isolated top halves of faces, and the top half of faces as part of a composite, aligned with the bottom half of a different face. They were asked to identify the faces.
Results: Participants were quite good at identifying the isolated top halves of faces, but found it much more difficult to do so when it was part of a composite.
Conclusion: We do not recognise faces by analysing separate features, but take a more holistic approach.

There is other evidence that we take a holistic approach to face recognition:

Box C: Tanaka and Farah (1993)

Procedure: Participants were asked to learn the names, e.g. Larry, of a set of faces constructed from a pool of different features, so that each face had different features. They were then shown a pair of faces, one identical to the face they had learned, and one with one different feature, e.g. the nose, and asked the question: Which is Larry? They were also shown a pair of features, e.g. two noses, in isolation and asked: Which is Larry's nose?

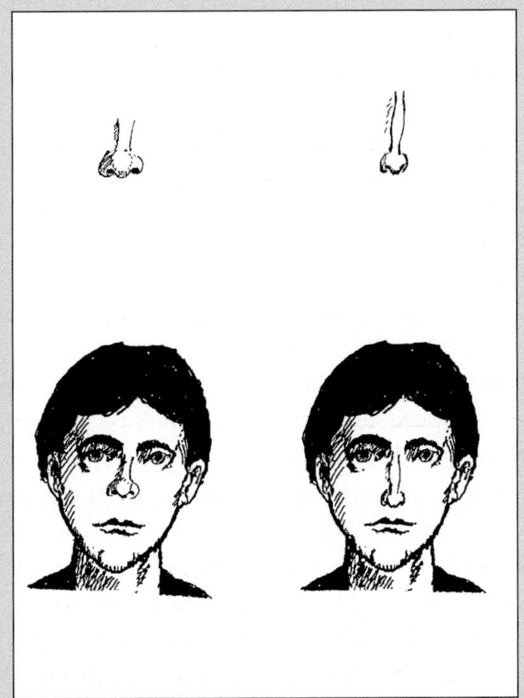

Results: The answers were much more accurate when features were shown in the context of the whole face than in isolation.
Conclusion: Face recognition is holistic rather than an analysis of different features.

There is some evidence that the processing involved may differ when we recognise familiar and unfamiliar faces. In line with the studies in box B and box C, Ellis *et al.* (1979) found that recognition of unfamiliar faces depends more on external features, such as the shape of the face and the hairline. However, for familiar faces, internal features are more important. Ellis *et al.* suggested that repeatedly meeting a person may lead us to focus more on specific features, which then become more prominent in our mental representations of familiar faces. According to Roberts and Bruce (1988), the area round the eyes is the most important, while the area round the nose is of least importance. However, in eye-witness testimony, witnesses are usually asked for information about unfamiliar faces.

One of the earliest aids used by police forces to help witness identification was the **PhotoFIT** system, developed by Penry (1971). This consisted of sets of photographed features – hair, eyes, nose, mouth and chin – from which the witness could select elements to build a representation of the face they had seen. This system could produce a general likeness, but was generally found to be poor in terms of creating a close likeness.

Box D: Ellis *et al.* (1978)

Procedure: Volunteer 'witnesses' were asked to reconstruct a face either by drawing it or by using PhotoFIT. This was done either from memory or in the presence of the target face. Participants were then asked to rate the accuracy of the faces produced.

Results: When the target face could be seen during the reconstruction, witnesses' drawings were rated as much better likenesses than those produced by PhotoFIT. When faces were reconstructed from memory, as would be the case for eye-witnesses of a crime, accuracy ratings dropped for both drawings and Photofit, with PhotoFIT being only marginally more accurate.

Conclusion: PhotoFIT is not a very effective way of reproducing faces from memory.

The obvious problem with the PhotoFIT system is that it is based on the analysis of individual features; and, as we have seen, this is not how we process faces, at least those which are unfamiliar to us. Sergent (1984) has shown that configural information, i.e. the way in which different facial features relate to each other, is important in the representation of faces in memory, and the PhotoFIT system is not flexible enough to allow these kinds of factors to be manipulated.

More recently, **E-FIT** (electronic facial identification technique) has been developed, using computer graphics. Again, faces are built from a library of features, selected on the basis of a verbal description by the witness. As well as giving a picture which is of similar quality to a photograph, this system has the advantage of being much more flexible in terms of the modifications which are possible, in that it allows very subtle adjustments to be made to the configuration of features making up the face, and so is better designed to fit in with the way we process information about faces.

Another way in which witnesses may be asked to identify criminals is by looking through albums of mugshots. This can be problematical, in that mugshot albums may be very large, and looking at a long series of faces may interfere with the mental representation of the target face. These problems have been addressed using a system called **FRAME** (facial retrieval and matching equipment), described by Shepherd (1986). This uses verbal descriptions of faces given by witnesses to retrieve possible matches from mugshots. The advantage of this system is that it uses the information which witnesses can give, and offers a solution to the problems arising from looking through a long series of mugshots, the vast majority of which bear no resemblance to the target face. The effectiveness of FRAME has been tested experimentally:

Box E: Ellis *et al.* (1989)

Procedure: Each participant saw a target face for 10 seconds, which they were later asked to identify. Using a database of 1000 male faces, a comparison was made between the effectiveness of the FRAME system and a mugshot album search.

Results: The FRAME system produced 69% correct matches, compared to only 44% for the album search. There was also a much higher percentage of false alarms when mugshot albums were used.

Conclusion: The use of verbal descriptions together with mugshot albums is more effective in leading to face recognition than the use of mugshot albums alone.

- There is evidence that we do not analyse separate **features** when recognising a face, but tend to take a more **holistic** approach. Feature anlysis is more important in recognising familiar than unfamiliar faces.
- The **PhotoFIT** system used by the police as an aid to eye-witnesses identifying criminals was not very effective, since it was based on putting together individual features.
- The **E-FIT** system is more flexible, and corresponds more closely to a holistic approach.
- The **FRAME** system uses the information which people offer about the faces of those seen committing a crime to select mugshots of possible suspects, and has been shown to be effective.

11.3 Eye-witness testimony (EWT)

As discussed in chapter 9, researchers such as Bartlett (1932) have suggested that memory is not a perfect representation of an event; it is a reconstruction, and as such can be inaccurate. In the eye-witness testimony in court, the accurate recall of events is important, in that it can mean someone's imprisonment or freedom.

Jurors seem to find eye-witness testimony extremely convincing. The Devlin Report (1976), which was concerned with eye-witness testimony, found that in more than 300 cases eye-witness identification was the *sole* evidence of guilt, yet the conviction rate was 74%.

Building on the idea of memory as reconstruction, a lot of research has been carried out, notably by Loftus and her associates, which has shown that people's accounts of events that they have witnessed can be very unreliable. An example of her research is shown in box F:

Box F: Loftus and Palmer (1974)

Procedure: Participants were shown a film of an accident between two cars, and then filled in a questionnaire about the accident. The important question involved the speed of the cars at the point of impact. The question was phrased differently for different groups of participants. Some were asked 'How fast were the two cars going when they hit each other?'; others were asked the same question but with *smashed, collided, bumped,* or *contacted* replacing the word 'hit'. A control group was not asked about the speed of the cars. One week later, the same people were all asked whether they had seen any broken glass in the film of the accident. (No broken glass had been shown.)

Results: The average speeds the participants gave are listed below:

verb used	speed given
hit	34 mph
smashed	41 mph
collided	39 mph
bumped	38 mph
contacted	32 mph

Of the participants who had heard the word *smashed*, 32% claimed to remember seeing broken glass, compared with 14% of those who had heard the word *hit* and 12% of the control group.

Conclusion: The speed at which the participants thought the cars were going was affected by the verb used in the question, so recall was distorted by the wording of the question. Information given after the event, in the form of the wording of the question, can interfere with an already existing memory.

Age can play a part in the accuracy of recall. Several studies (e.g. Dent, 1988) have shown that children typically give fewer details about an event they have witnessed than adults. Similarly, List (1986) found that older people may also recall less than younger people (see also box Y).

We will look in this section at other research into factors affecting the accuracy of eye-witness testimony in terms of the three processes involved in memory: **registration**, **storage** and **retrieval**.

Registration factors

Factors to do with the situation in which an event is witnessed can influence people's initial perception of an incident. One factor affecting the accuracy of recall is the level of stress experienced when witnessing a crime. This relationship can be shown by the Yerkes–Dodson law:

Figure 3: the Yerkes–Dodson law

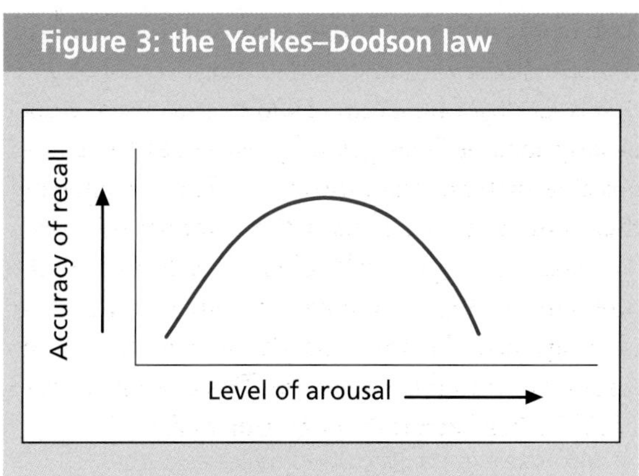

This law suggests that at very low levels of arousal, performance is poor. It improves with moderate levels of arousal, and then falls off again when arousal is high enough to be experienced as stress.

The effect of stress on memory has been supported by research:

Box G: Peters (1988)

Procedure: People going to a clinic to receive inoculations met a nurse who gave them the injection and another person (the researcher). They were exposed to each person for equal periods of time. They were later asked to identify the nurse and the researcher from a set of photographs.

Results: Participants were significantly better at identifying the researcher than the nurse.

Conclusion: The stress of having an injection, associated with the nurse who gave it, led to comparatively poor memory when asked to pick out her photograph.

So how do high levels of stress interfere with the registration process? This question has been addressed in a further study carried out by Loftus and her associates:

Box H: Loftus and Burns (1982)

Procedure: Participants were shown one of two versions of a simulated armed robbery on video. One version included a scene of a boy being shot in the face while the robbers were making their getaway.

Results: Recall of details of the event was much higher for participants who had seen the 'non-violent' version of the event. Those who had seen the 'violent' version had less accurate and less complete recall, not only for events immediately before the shooting, but also for events up to two minutes earlier.

Conclusion: The shock associated with the 'violent' event disrupted the processing of information into memory, and its consolidation.

However, in real-life situations, high levels of arousal may not impair the ability to register information:

Box I: Yuille and Cutshall (1986)

Procedure: Thirteen people who witnessed an armed robbery in Canada gave evidence to the police. They then agreed to take part in interviews with psychologists between four and five months after witnessing the robbery. During that later interview, participants were asked two misleading questions.

Results: Being asked two misleading questions did not affect the participants' recall four months after the event. There were few, if any, facts recalled by the participants that had been made up or reconstructed. There was no relationship between the levels of stress reported at the time of the crime and accuracy of recall.

Conclusion: In real-life situations, recall is not necessarily inaccurate, or susceptible to misleading questions. The level of stress experienced is not related to accuracy of recall.

This study shows that EWT of events occurring in a real-life situation is not necessarily as inaccurate as laboratory studies might lead us to expect. This is a good example of a study with high **ecological validity**: it was carried out on people who had witnessed a genuine armed robbery, and not merely watched a video of such an event, and therefore is more convincing as a piece of research.

However, one problem with this study is that those witnesses who experienced more stress were closer to what was going on. It is possible that the higher level of stress they experienced was counteracted by having better access to information, thus improving their recall of the event.

Expectations and **beliefs** can also influence the registration of information:

Box J: Buckhout (1974)

Procedure: Participants were shown a series of counter-stereotypical pictures, each for a very short time. One picture, for example, set in a subway, showed a scruffily dressed white man, holding a razor, threatening a well-dressed black man. It was assumed in this instance that many white people would have a stereotype of black people as having criminal tendencies.
Results: Approximately half the participants remembered the black man as holding the razor.
Conclusion: Memory can be distorted by the stereotypes we hold.

Another important factor is **exposure time**, i.e. the length of time for which a witness is exposed to an event. As long ago as 1885, a study by Ebbinghaus showed that the longer we are exposed to something, the better our memory of it is. However, people are often very poor at estimating exposure time:

Activity 5: overestimation of time

Why might this tendency to overestimate time be important in a legal context?
When you have finished, see the notes on page 311.

A further factor is what is known as **detail salience**. In an armed robbery, for instance, the presence of a gun may be a salient feature for witnesses. They may focus on the gun and so have their attention distracted from other important features of the situation, such as the characteristics of the robbers. This is known as **weapon focus**, and has been shown experimentally:

Box K: Loftus *et al.* (1987)

Procedure: Participants were shown a 30-second video of a simulated bank robbery and asked to estimate how long it had lasted.
Results: On average, the robbery was estimated to have lasted two and a half minutes. Very few participants correctly estimated the time, or underestimated it.
Conclusion: People tend to overestimate the length of time of an event which they have witnessed.

Box L: Loftus *et al.* (1987)

Procedure: Participants were shown one of two versions of a restaurant scene on video. In one version, a man pointed a gun at the cashier and she gave him money. In the other version, he gave her a cheque, and she gave him money. The eye movements of participants were monitored, and their recall for the event tested.
Results: Participants in the 'weapon' version fixated more on the gun than those seeing the 'non-weapon' version. Their recall for other details was also poorer, and they were less able to identify the man from a set of photographs.
Conclusion: A salient detail can focus attention, and so lead to poorer recall for other details of the event.

- Eye-witness testimony is given great weight by juries, but can often be unreliable.
- Memory for details of an event can be affected at the **registration** stage. Factors include **stress**, **expectations**, **detail salience** (in particular **weapon focus**) and the **violence** of the event.

Storage factors

Information is lost with the passage of time, which can be explained by the **trace decay** theory of forgetting, discussed in chapter 9. As with the influence of exposure time on memory, this too was demonstrated by Ebbinghaus (1885). It has also been shown in a naturalistic study of long-term forgetting:

Box M: Wagenaar and Groeneweg (1990)

Procedure: Seventy-eight survivors of Camp Erika (a Second World War Dutch concentration camp) were interviewed between 1984 and 1987 about their camp experiences. The information they gave was compared with earlier evidence they had given just after the end of the war.

Results: There was general agreement in the later interviews on basic information. All but three of 38 people who had been tortured by the camp commandant, for example, remembered his name. However, much of the detail had been lost. The names of guards, for instance, given at the earlier interviews, were largely forgotten.

Conclusion: While basic information may be well remembered over time, details tend to be lost.

The study by Loftus and Palmer, described in box F, has shown that memory can also be distorted once it has been stored; participants remembered seeing broken glass because of the effects of misleading information. It has also been shown that mentioning inaccurate details of an event to a witness after they have witnessed it can lead to these details being 'recalled' later; new information has been incorporated into what is remembered. For example, Loftus (1975) showed participants a film of a car accident. They were then asked questions about the accident. For one group one of the questions was: 'How fast was the white sports car going when it passed the Stop sign?'. For the other group one of the questions was: 'How fast was the white sports car going when it passed the barn?'. There was no barn in the film. A week later, participants were asked questions about the film, the final one being 'Did you see a barn?': 17.3% of the second group, compared with only 2.7% of the first group, claimed to have seen the barn.

Sometimes this effect is a compromise between what has been witnessed and the information provided in the question:

Box N: Loftus (1975)

Procedure: Participants were shown a three-minute video of a lecture being disrupted by eight demonstrators. They were later given a 20-item questionnaire. For some participants, this included the question: 'Was the leader of the 12 demonstrators a male?' For the others the question was: ' Was the leader of the four demonstrators a male?' A week later, they were asked how many demonstrators there had been.

Results: Those who had earlier been given the '12 demonstrators' question reported on average that there had been 8.9 demonstrators; those who had been given the 'four demonstrators' question reported on average that there had been 6.4 demonstrators.

Conclusion: Participants' memory had been distorted by the misleading information they had been given. Most participants compromised between the actual number of demonstrators they had seen and the misleading number.

However, this is less likely to happen when people are asked about something which is central to the event they have witnessed. Loftus (1979) found that 98% of people who had watched colour slides of a man stealing a red purse from a woman's bag correctly remembered it as red, even when it was implied that it was brown.

There are also individual differences in the extent to which people are susceptible to the influence of misleading information. Ceci *et al.* (1987) found that children were more likely to be misled than adults, and Loftus *et al.* (1991) found the same to be true of older people, particularly males.

It has been argued by McCloskey and Zaragoza (1985) that the influence of misleading information – the **misinformation effect** – has little to do with memory impairment, but more to do with two sources of bias in the testing procedure. The first of these they call **misinformation acceptance**. They suggest that one reason that participants can be misled is that they have failed to register relevant information when witnessing an event, and this is why they accept misleading information as being accurate.

The second source of bias is **demand characteristics**, i.e. features of the testing situation which may lead participants to (mis)interpret the task. In this case, participants might accept the misinformation as accurate because it was provided by the researcher, or because they wanted to 'do well' on the test.

- Storage factors can affect recall. Basic information is often retained, but detailed information is lost over time.
- Memory can be supplemented by later information. It can be distorted by misleading information, known as the **misinformation effect**. This can also lead to completely inaccurate information being given.
- This is less likely to happen about something central to the event witnessed. Children and older people are more susceptible to misinformation.
- The misinformation effect has been challenged in terms of whether it is the result of **memory impairment** or the effects of **bias** in the testing situation.

Retrieval factors

As we saw from the different estimates of speed in the Loftus and Palmer study in box F, the way in which questions are asked can significantly affect a person's testimony. Similarly, Loftus and Zanni (1975) showed participants a film of a car accident. They found that more participants recalled (incorrectly) seeing a broken headlight if they were asked 'Did you see *the* broken headlight?' than 'Did you see *a* broken headlight?'. The way in which questions are asked can therefore distort memory.

This has important implications for people like the police, who have to consider the phrasing of their questions very carefully. In recent years, psychologists have begun to evaluate police interview techniques, and have found that British police officers have little formal training in the interviewing of witnesses, and that they are often unaware of the shortcomings in their interview technique.

Officers typically aim to elicit descriptions of sex, height, age, dress, and so on. They ask for information which seems immediately useful, rather than information which may be useful later on. Standard police interviewing techniques may not be the best way to get the maximum amount of useful information from the witness.

It is widely believed that **hypnosis** may be a way of improving recall, but this is somewhat controversial. A comprehensive review of hypnosis research led Orne *et al.* (1984) to claim that testimony produced under hypnosis was not reliable, and that it should not be accepted unless it was confirmed by independent evidence. People who have been hypnotised are very susceptible to suggestions made by the interviewer and, for this reason alone, testimony produced under hypnosis needs to be treated with caution.

However, a technique called the **cognitive interview** has been developed as a way of trying to ensure that police interviews are carried out in such a way as to get maximum accurate recall from witnesses. This technique is now widely used by police forces in the UK and the USA.

Geiselman *et al.* (1984) developed a procedure called the **basic cognitive interview**, based on two principles of memory research: firstly, that there may be a number of retrieval paths to a memory, so a memory may be accessible if a different retrieval cue is used. Secondly, a memory trace is made up of several features, and the effectiveness of a retrieval cue depends on how much of it overlaps with the memory trace.

From these principles, a **memory retrieval procedure** was derived.

Figure 4: the basic cognitive interview

This technique involves:

- an eye-witness mentally reinstating the environmental and personal context of the crime. This includes reporting what was going on at the time, both in terms of the event witnessed and the witness's own thoughts and feelings

- the eye-witness being asked to report everything they can recall about the event, regardless of how unimportant it might seem
- encouraging an eye-witness to recount what happened in a variety of orders
- asking them to report from a variety of perspectives and points of view

Activity 6: linking the cognitive interview to memory research

Look back at section 9.2: Reasons for forgetting and section 10.4: Representation of knowledge. Can you make links between some of this material and the principles of the cognitive interview? When you have finished, see the notes on page 311.

When the basic cognitive interview was used, Fisher *et al.* (1987a) found it to be significantly superior to the standard police interview, in terms of the amount of information accurately recalled. Geiselman *et al.* (1986) found that this technique also seemed to strengthen the resistance of witnesses to misleading information.

The technique has now been refined further through an analysis of real, taped police interviews, which has the advantage of high ecological validity. On the basis of this research Fisher *et al.* (1987b) recommended additional techniques for interviewing eye-witnesses. This is known as the **enhanced cognitive interview** technique.

Figure 5: enhanced cognitive interview

This technique includes:

- minimising distractions
- getting the eye-witness to speak slowly
- tailoring language to suit the individual eye-witness
- reducing anxiety
- avoiding judgmental and personal comments

All these techniques are designed to help the witness to focus on the task and to reduce anxiety. Fisher *et al.* (1990) found that these techniques elicited 45% more correct statements than even the basic cognitive interview. A field test with detectives of the Police Department in Miami showed that detectives trained in the enhanced cognitive interview technique collected 63% more information than a control group of untrained detectives. Wilkinson (1988) found that such techniques could raise the EWT of children to adult level.

The cognitive interview seems to be a way that really can make a difference both to the amount of potentially useful information obtained from witnesses and to the accuracy of that information.

- **Hypnosis** as a way of improving recall is controversial.
- The **cognitive interview** has shown itself to be an effective way of increasing the completeness and accuracy of EWT.
- The **enhanced cognitive interview** can produce even more relevant information.

11.4 Amnesia

Amnesia is a clinical term referring to memory loss as the result of brain damage, although it is sometimes used more widely to refer to forgetting that has a psychological rather than a physiological basis. There are two basic types of amnesia, which are defined in terms of the nature of the memory loss. **Retrograde amnesia** is loss of memory for events in the period before the brain damage. It is a deficit in retrieval, since information from LTM which was already stored can no longer be accessed. **Anterograde amnesia** is the inability to remember events after brain damage has occurred. It is a deficit in storage, since new information cannot be put from STM into LTM. Whether a person with a memory deficit will suffer from retrograde amnesia, anterograde amnesia, or both, will depend on the nature of the damage suffered. We will look now at some of the causes of brain damage which can lead to amnesia.

Trauma

Following a blow to the head – for example, as the result of a car accident or a sports injury – people may suffer from concussion. As a result, a person may have retrograde amnesia and will probably not remember what happened immediately before the blow. Yarnell and Lynch (1973) investigated this phenomenon by asking footballers who had been concussed during play what strategy their team had been using immediately before the incident. The footballers could answer this question if asked straight away, but had forgotten if asked 20 minutes later. This suggests that concussion prevented the consolidation necessary for storage in LTM.

Concussion may develop into **postconcussional syndrome (PCS)**. This is associated with a cluster of symptoms. In the initial phase, these typically include headache and drowsiness. People may also experience dizziness, nausea, vomiting, and blurred vision. The middle phase is characterised by fatigue, anxiety and depression. In both phases there is memory loss, which Chan (2001) links to attentional deficit. McClelland (1996) reported that, while most patients experience symptoms for between six and 12 weeks, 70% have no further symptoms at six months. However, a significant minority, usually patients who are older and female, still have symptoms after a year.

According to Gasquoine (1997), the persistence of symptoms is not related to the severity of the brain injury, but rather to psychological factors. Patients who experience more emotional distress are more likely to have persistent symptoms, so the personal interpretation an individual makes of the trauma and its aftermath relates to the outcome for that patient.

There is some evidence that the degree of memory loss experienced is to some extent subjective. Chan (2001) looked at the base rate of symptoms similar to those experienced by PCS patients in a group of participants aged 18–50 without head injury. He found that nearly 60% reported memory problems, with no relationship between reported memory loss and performance on memory tests.

The degree of memory loss experienced by someone with PCS can be assessed using the **Self-Rating Scale of Memory Functions (SRSM)**. This has been used to establish factors which may be related to the degree of memory loss experienced:

Box O: Gfeller *et al.* (1996)

Procedure: A group of 42 patients, aged between 18 and 65, suffering from PCS as the result of car accidents, was asked to complete the SRSM. They also completed the Beck Depression Inventory and carried out a series of memory tests.
Results: All patients rated their memory as being significantly impaired compared with before the accident. The SRSM scores showed no pattern relating to age, education gender, and loss of consciousness. However, seriously depressed patients rated their memory as significantly more impaired than those who were not depressed. When depression had been taken into account, the SRSM scores correlated well with performance on the memory tests.
Conclusion: Memory loss in PCS is related to the severity of the depression experienced.

However, in contrast to Gfeller's findings, there is some evidence that the persistence of symptoms may be related to age:

Box P: Ogden and Wolfe (1998)

Procedure: Two groups of PCS patients, a young group (aged 16–26) and a middle-aged group (aged 40–56), were compared with two age-matched control groups on a range of tests including a verbal memory test.
Results: Overall, the middle-aged groups performed less well than the young groups, and the PCS groups did less well than the controls. However, head injury affected the

performance of the young group more than the middle-aged group.
Conclusion: There is a relationship between age and the persistence of memory problems in PCS patients.

Ogden and Wolfe suggested that their results could perhaps be explained by the middle-aged group taking more notice of medical advice to rest and return to work gradually to promote recovery. However, this is speculative, and since the results of different studies are somewhat contradictory, this would seem to be an area where more research would be useful.

As well as the physical trauma of head injury, amnesia has also been associated with psychological trauma. An example is Freud's theory of **repression**, discussed in chapter 9 and in section 11.4 of this chapter.

- People may suffer from **postconcussional syndrome (PCS)** after a head injury. One symptom is **retrograde amnesia**.
- The persistence of symptoms is linked to psychological factors, such as the **emotional response** to the injury and **depression**. There may also be a link with age.
- **Psychological trauma** has also been linked to amnesia.

Electroconvulsive therapy (ECT)

ECT is a treatment for depression, which involves passing an electrical current of between 70 and 130 volts through a patient's head for a fraction of a second. This induces a convulsion or **seizure**. The idea of using electricity to induce seizures was first proposed by Cerletti, an Italian doctor working in the field of epilepsy. He noticed that epilepsy and schizophrenia never occurred in the same person and thought that if he induced an epileptic fit in someone it might cure their schizophrenia.

ECT has had a very poor public reputation, partly as a result of serious problems with the procedure in the past. For example, physical injury was not uncommon during a convulsion, often leading to broken bones. Nowadays the procedure has been improved, and ECT is used for people whose severe depression has not been helped with drugs, though no longer for schizophrenia, where chemotherapy can be very effective.

Patients undergoing ECT are now anaesthetised and given a muscle relaxant to prevent physical injury during the seizure. Electrodes are attached to either side of the patient's head and the shock is administered. Because the patient has been given a muscle relaxant, the only sign of the seizure which has been induced is the twitching of the patient's toes. The current can also just be administered to one side of the brain (**unilateral ECT**), although bilateral ECT is more common, since doctors believe it to be more effective. Typically, the procedure is repeated three times a week for about a month. According to Sackeim (1988), between 60% and 70% of depressed patients improve with ECT, although the effects tend to disappear within the following year. Some patients regularly attend a clinic for **maintenance ECT** to keep their depression under control.

One ethical problem associated with the use of ECT as a therapy is that we do not understand how it works. The most likely explanation is that the shock produces biochemical changes in the brain, raising levels of the various neurotransmitters. These changes are stronger than those produced by drugs, so this may account for its effectiveness.

The side-effects of ECT cause some concern. These include temporary confusion and amnesia, although Benton (1981) found that this is reduced in unilateral ECT. Studies such as those by Sackeim (1988) and Malitz (1984) suggest that memory problems are minimal if very low electrical currents are used – just enough to induce the seizure. According to Friedberg (1977), it takes 5–10 minutes after ECT to remember who you are, where you are, and what day it is. In the first few weeks after a full course, there is some retrograde and to a lesser extent anterograde amnesia, but after that many patients are not aware of any further deficits.

However, many patients who have received ECT claim that the resulting memory loss is much more extensive than this suggests. Early studies report patients who forgot they had children (Tyler and

Lowenbach 1947), a woman who forgot how to cook familiar dishes (Brody 1944), and another who couldn't remember her own clothing, and wanted to know who had put these unfamiliar dresses in her wardrobe (Zubin 1948). Janis (1950) found that amnesia in ECT patients could involve childhood events dating back 20–40 years.

Friedberg quotes a 32-year-old woman five years after she had received 21 treatments of ECT:

Box Q: Friedberg (1976)

'One of the results of the whole thing is that I have no memory of what happened in the year to year and a half prior to my shock treatments. The doctor assured me that it was coing to come back and it never has. I don't remember a bloody thing. I couldn't even find my way around the town I lived in for three years. If I walked into a building I didn't even know where I was. I could barely find my way around my own house. I could sew and knit before, but afterward I could no more comprehend a pattern to sew than the man in the moon.'

There is general acceptance that memory for the period during which ECT was administered is impaired, but in spite of the anecdotal evidence which suggests there may be more extensive retrograde amnesia, the extent to which this is the case is controversial, since it is likely to be difficult to establish what the patient could recall before ECT. The extent of retrograde amnesia has been investigated experimentally:

Box R: Freeman *et al.* (1980)

Procedure: Participants who believed that they had suffered memory loss as the result of ECT treatment between 9 months and 30 years previously were compared with a matched control group who had not had ECT. They were assessed on a range of tests of cognitive functioning, and also completed scales to measure depression and to provide a self-assessment of memory difficulties.

Results: Of the ECT group, most claimed to have poor memory for the time when they received treatment. Some had retrograde amnesia for the events of several months before ECT. Some also claimed to have anterograde amnesia, with one participant, for example, being unable to remember a wedding six months after the course of ECT. Overall, the ECT group were more depressed that the controls. Compared to the controls, they scored significantly worse on memories of their own past and on the ability to put names to faces. These deficits corresponded well to the difficulties identified in their self-assessments.

Conclusion: The findings are compatible with the idea that ECT can cause serious memory loss. However, it is also possible that depression leads to poor memory.

There is further support for the role of depression in amnesia following ECT from Coleman *et al.* (1996). They found that ECT patients' self-ratings of memory function two weeks after treatment was similar to that of non-ECT controls, but that the severity of depressive symptoms was strongly associated with reported memory problems.

Whether amnesia following ECT can be largely attributed to depression, or whether it is the direct result of the treatment, there is no doubt that ECT does cause brain damage. Friedberg (1977) describes several studies into the effect of electric shocks to the brain, both on animals and on humans, which indicate that haemorrhages and nerve damage are common, while Meldrum *et al.* (1973) report damage to the hippocampus. Since this part of the brain plays an important part in memory, it is likely to be connected to the amnesia patients experience. For some patients, relief from crippling depression may outweigh the negative effects of memory loss, while for others this is too high a price to pay.

- ECT is a treatment for **depression** which involves giving patients **electric shocks** to the brain.
- **Memory loss** for the treatment period is usual, with some amnesia for the following few weeks.
- Some patients report enduring and extensive amnesia. This may be attributable to ECT or the result of depression.

Surgery

Surgery, particularly for epilepsy, can lead to amnesia. The most famous case is HM (see chapter 9, box E), a Canadian man who suffered from very severe epileptic seizures. The focal sites of these seizures were the temporal lobes, and since drug treatment had proved ineffectual, it was decided to remove parts of both these lobes to treat the condition. The surgery involved removal of most of the hippocampus, which we now know is extremely important for declarative memory, i.e. episodic and semantic memory. While surgery was successful in controlling his epilepsy, HM experienced severe and permanent anterograde amnesia after the operation:

Box S: the case of HM (Milner 1970)

Following the operation, HM suffered some **retrograde amnesia**. He was unable to recognise hospital staff whom he had known for some years, and was unable to find his way around the hospital. He was also unable to recall events from a few years before the operation, although he could remember events from the more distant past.

HM's STM is apparently unimpaired, though he is unable to process new information into LTM, and so shows **anterograde amnesia**. Some 40 years after the operation, he is constantly surprised when he looks in a mirror and sees an old man, because he continues to think of himself as he was before the operation.

HM's case is described as one of **pure amnesia,** since the retrograde amnesia he experienced was relatively slight, and his intelligence and personality were left relatively intact.

He is aware of his condition:

'Every day is alone in itself, whatever enjoyment I've had, and whatever sorrow I've had. Right now, I'm wondering. Have I done or said anything amiss? You see, at this moment everything looks clear to me, but what happened just before? That's what worries me. It's like waking from a dream; I just don't remember.'

Interestingly, the anterograde amnesia does not seem to have affected HM's **procedural memory**. Corkin (1968) found that HM was able to learn new skills, such as the pursuit rotor task (tracking a light moving along a circular track), and show an improvement with practice. However, he needed to be reminded on every occasion that this was something which he had learned to do, and given instructions on how to carry it out.

The effects of temporal lobectomy on amnesia have also been studied in other patients. Since the time when HM had his surgery, techniques have been refined, and there is interest in the differential effects on memory of right and left temporal lobe surgery:

Box T: Glosser *et al.* (1998)

Procedure: Memory deficits of patients undergoing unilateral temporal lobectomy (removal of part of the temporal lobe on one side only) to treat epilepsy were assessed before and after surgery.

Results: Compared with the pre-surgery baseline, memory for verbal material was more impaired for left temporal lobectomy patients, while memory for visuo-spatial material was more impaired for right temporal lobectomy patients.

Conclusion: The nature of memory loss after temporal lobectomy depends on whether the surgery is on the right or left temporal lobe.

Similarly, a study by Beardsworth and Zaidel (1994) of children and adolescents with epilepsy, who had undergone temporal lobe surgery, found that memory for faces was more impaired for those whose surgery was on the right temporal lobe.

Other brain surgery may also affect memory. Ogden (1986) investigated memory before and after surgery in three patients who suffered from hydrocephalus, a condition in which fluid fails to drain properly from the ventricles (fluid-filled spaces) in the brain, and who had been treated by the insertion of a ventricular shunt, an artificial drainage system. She found that in the patient whose condition was of recent onset, impaired memory function improved rapidly after surgery. In the two patients with a long period of hydrocephalus before surgery, however, memory impairments did not improve and had worsened after a year. Although Ogden studied only a very small sample, this suggests that the longer hydrocephalus remains untreated, the worse the prospects for improvement in memory.

The anaesthesia which accompanies any surgery can lead to amnesia in elderly patients. Berant *et al.* (1995) found retrograde amnesia in patients aged 60–84 years after elective surgery, compared with their pre-operative functioning.

- Surgery for **epilepsy** which involves the removal of one or both of the temporal lobes can result in amnesia. In HM it resulted in severe and permanent **anterograde amnesia**. Specific memory deficits with **unilateral temporal lobectomy** depend on which lobe is removed.
- **Other brain surgery** and **anaesthesia** can also result in amnesia.

Alcohol

Korsakoff syndrome occurs in people with a history of chronic alcohol use, and is a brain disorder caused by a deficiency in the B vitamin thiamine, which commonly accompanies habitual alcohol use. This syndrome may also be the result of malnutrition or other conditions which cause nutritional deficiencies. It usually affects people between 40 and 80 years old, and the onset is gradual. Without treatment, the syndrome causes death, and in any case the lifespan is likely to be shortened.

Symptoms include mental confusion, apathy, lack of muscle co-ordination, and sometimes agitation, together with amnesia. There is impaired STM, and anterograde amnesia, as patients are unable to put new information into LTM. They usually suffer from some retrograde amnesia as well. Patients typically show **confabulation**, i.e. they make up detailed and believable stories about experiences or situations to compensate for the amnesia. Memory loss is likely to be permanent.

As with the case of HM, procedural memory may be spared. Cermak *et al.* (1973) found that Korsakoff patients were able to learn the pursuit rotor task as well as controls. Cohen *et al.* (1985), using a different procedural task – the Tower of Hanoi puzzle – had similar findings.

Activity 7: Tower of Hanoi

Three discs are piled in size order on the first of three pegs:

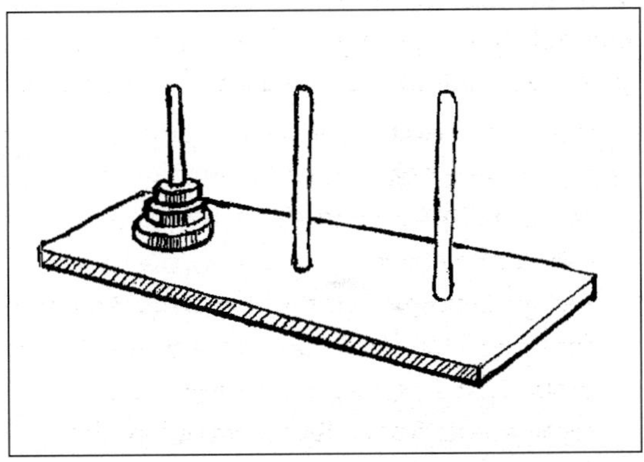

The task is to move them so that they are in the same order on the last peg. Only one disc can be moved at a time, and a larger disc can never be put on top of a smaller one. Can you do this in the minimum of seven moves?

When you have finished, see the notes on page 311.

Procedural memory, then, seems unaffected across very different kinds of task. However, **haptic memory** – memory for the sense of touch, for example what velvet feels like – is also impaired in Korsakoff patients. Strauss and Butler (1978) found that both verbal and haptic memory were impaired in STM tasks.

- **Korsakoff syndrome** is usually associated with a history of alcohol abuse.
- **STM** is impaired. Patients suffer from **anterograde amnesia** and there is usually some **retrograde amnesia**. Amnesia is likely to be permanent.
- **Procedural memory** across varied tasks is unaffected.

Ageing

There is a general belief that memory in elderly people becomes less reliable, and that there is a general decline in memory with age. This is clearly the case if a person develops dementia, of which Alzheimer's disease is the most common form. However, there is some evidence that this is more generally the case. In a longitudinal study carried out by Small *et al.* (1999), two groups of healthy adults, aged 60–69 and 70+, were assessed annually. The researchers found a relative decline with age, particularly in the acquisition and early retrieval of new information. More positively, retention of material for longer intervals did not show this decline, nor was there any decline in other cognitive abilities, such as abstract reasoning.

Elderly people have been found to have concerns about failing memory:

Box U: Reese *et al.* (1999)

Procedure: A sample of older adults responded to open-ended questions to provide information about their perceived memory problems, how they coped with these problems, and their more general concerns about failing memory.

Results: Some information, e.g. important dates such as birthdays and anniversaries, were in general well-remembered, while names were not. Most participants reported using memory aids to help them remember things. Fear of loss of independence as the result of memory problems emerged as an important concern.

Conclusion: There is some memory loss with age, but it is patchy rather than general. Elderly people use strategies to compensate for the problems they experience. However, they are concerned about the wider implications of memory loss.

Activity 8: memory problems in the elderly

If you know an older person, someone at least in their sixties, talk to them about their memory. Do they experience problems, and if so, with what kinds of memory tasks? You could ask about names and dates, as Reese *et al.* did in their study in box U, and also identify any other kinds of memory problems they have. What kinds of strategies do they use to try to compensate for the problems they experience?

You are likely to find that some kinds of memory tasks cause problems, while others do not. This variability has been confirmed:

Box V: Plude *et al.* (2001)

Procedure: The performance of 30 young adults (aged 16–27) and 30 older adults (60–87) was compared on three memory tasks: learning a word list, a name memory task, and an object-recognition task.

Results: Overall, the younger adults performed better on the word list and name memory tasks, but there was no difference between the groups in performance on the object-recognition task.
Conclusion: There is a drop in performance with age on some memory tasks.

Baeckman *et al.* (2001) found deficits in working memory and episodic memory with age. However, they report that semantic and procedural memory are less likely to be affected. While failing memory can be a problem, then, it is not the case that every aspect of memory declines with age.

Further studies have sought to establish not only the kind of material which is affected, but also which processing mechanisms are affected. In a review of the literature, Luszcz and Bryan (1999) concluded that there is strong evidence that speed of processing is an important factor in age-related memory loss, and that other mechanisms, in particular working memory, are also important. Differences in the functioning of working memory between younger and older people have been established by investigating brain function:

Box W: McEvoy *et al.* (2001)

Procedure: Changes in the functioning of working memory were investigated by recording the EEG of people carrying out simple and more complicated spatial tasks using working memory. Three age groups were compared, aged 18–25, 42–56 and 62–81.
Results: There were age differences in the patterns of EEG activity recorded. Younger adults appeared to use a strategy relying on parietal areas, while older adults used a strategy relying more on frontal areas. On complex working memory tasks, middle-aged and older adults showed a decrease in alpha power, associated with more neurons becoming active, in both parietal and frontal regions, while younger adults only showed this decrease in parietal regions.
Conclusion: Deficits with age in working memory are reflected in changes in EEG activity.

Despite this finding, there is some evidence that continued mental activity can limit the amount of memory impairment which takes place. Diamond (1993) reported that over 90% of people over 65 show very little memory deterioration; this is especially true of those who keep mentally active. Plude *et al.* (2001), in the study described in box V, also found that for older adults, years of education – which might be interpreted as being indicative of continued intellectual activity – correlated positively with performance on the word list and name memory tasks they used.

Continued mental activity also seems to be related to lifestyle:

Box X Holland and Rabbitt (1991)

Procedure: Memory for autobiographical events of two groups of elderly volunteers was compared, one group of 35 (aged 68–97) living in residential care, and another group of 16 (aged 70–85) living independent lives. The groups were matched for general intelligence.
Results: The residential group recalled and spontaneously rehearsed more memories from their early than from their more recent lives. The opposite was true for those leading independent lives.
Conclusion: Frequency of rehearsal indicates the use which people make of their memories, which in turn relates to lifestyle.

Memory impairment in elderly people has implications in the area of eye-witness testimony:

Box Y: Karpel *et al.* (2001)

Procedure: In a study of eye-witness testimony, young adults (aged 17–25) and older adults (aged 65–85) were shown a video of a robbery. The groups were then compared in terms of accuracy of recall and susceptibility to misleading information.

Results: The young adults were both more accurate and less susceptible to misleading information than the older adults.
Conclusion: Eye-witness testimony of elderly people may be less reliable than that of younger people.

However, the methodology of this study can be criticised:

Activity 9: evaluating video studies

What problems can you identify with the study described in box Y? Consider ecological validity, demand characteristics and differences between the two groups other than age.
When you have finished, see the notes on page 311.

- Elderly people show some memory deficits with increasing age. However, while some areas of memory (e.g. **names**) are affected, other areas (e.g. **procedural memory**) are not.
- Changes in memory functioning with age are related to differences in **brain functioning** between younger and older adults.
- Continued **mental activity** and **independent living** are related to fewer deficits.
- Older people's memory may be less reliable when they are questioned as **eyewitnesses** to a crime.

11.5 Recovered and false memories

A major issue concerning the reliability of memory is the controversy about recovered memory as against false memory. Many people have gone to therapists with psychological problems, the causes of which they cannot explain, and in the course of therapy claim to have become aware of repressed memories (i.e. recovered memories), often of childhood sexual abuse, which seem to make sense of the problems they are currently experiencing. Those they accuse of abusing them often deny that the abuse took place, and suggest that their accusers are suffering from **False Memory Syndrome (FMS)**, with these 'memories' having been implanted during therapy. There are support groups both for those who believe their recovered memories are accurate (e.g. Incest Survivors Anonymous) and for those who believe themselves to have been unjustly accused of abuse (e.g. the False Memory Syndrome Foundation). The issue is considered so important that in 2000 the American Psychological Association set up a Working Group on the Investigation of Memories of Childhood Abuse.

In many cases, it is clearly impossible to establish whether or not memories recovered during therapy are memories of real events. Such memories relate to the patient's childhood, often many years previously, so there may well not be any supporting evidence. At the same time, many abusers are unwilling to admit that the abuse took place.

Some psychotherapists believe that childhood sexual abuse is the specific cause of psychological problems later in life. They suggest that memory of the abuse is repressed shortly after it occurs so that it is no longer available to the conscious mind. For therapy to be effective, the abuse must be recalled, so that the person can come to terms with it, and so begin to cope with their problems.

This belief rests on psychodynamic ideas. Freud's concept of **repression** was discussed in chapter 9 in the section on retrieval failure, and the emphasis he placed on the importance of childhood for later development was discussed in chapter 1. Therapists who believe that childhood sexual abuse is central to adult psychological problems tend also to use methods in therapy which may be used in psychoanalysis, the therapy Freud developed – for example, **dream analysis** and **hypnosis**. Although Freud himself stopped using hypnosis early in his career in favour of free association, many therapists still continue to use it.

Some people think that memories recovered during therapy are confabulations, i.e. plausible but inaccurate accounts of events. This idea links to the constructivist view of memory proposed by Bartlett (1932). He described remembering as essentially a reconstructive process, in that we do not recall an exact copy of the original information but reconstruct detailed memories from the few basic ideas we have stored. Memory is therefore subject to distortion. There is some evidence for this viewpoint in section 11.2 on eye-witness testimony.

The recovered memories versus FMS controversy has legal implications, in that many people who have recovered memories in therapy have sued those who they claim have abused them, and those who have been accused of abuse have sued therapists, who they claim have created false memories leading to these accusations. The response of a jury to these kinds of cases has been investigated experimentally:

Box Z: Coleman *et al.* (2001)

Procedure: Mock jurors were asked to assess the recovered memory testimony of an alleged victim whom a therapist had treated using hypnosis. A further group of mock jurors was asked to assess the testimony of a therapist sued for allegedly influencing a client's recall of false memories.
Results: Jurors viewed the victim's testimony as accurate, and brought in verdicts favourable to them. However, they viewed therapists who used hypnosis as responsible for causing harm, and as likely to have created false memories.
Conclusion: In trials relating to recovered memories, jurors can be led to believe either in recovered memories or in false memories.

In this debate, two questions need to be considered. The first concerns repression, on which those kinds of therapy which it has been suggested may produce false memories are based. The second is how easy it is to create false memories.

We will look first at the concept of repression. The principles related to repression which underlie therapy are shown in figure 6.

Garry *et al.* (1994) asked students to complete questionnaires to establish their beliefs about how memory works. They found a widespread belief in the repression of traumatic events, and that these

Figure 6: therapeutic assumptions involving repression

- **a** People banish traumatic experiences from consciousness.
- **b** Special techniques can be used to recover these lost memories.
- **c** Memories can be reliably recovered.
- **d** These memories must be recovered to bring about a cure.

repressed memories were potentially recoverable. However, Loftus (1996) argued that there is no real basis for these beliefs. As we saw in chapter 9, the concept of repression is extremely difficult to test, and studies which have claimed to demonstrate it, such as that by Levinger and Clark (1961), described in box Q of chapter 9, are open to alternative interpretations. Indeed, the phenomenon of flashbulb memory, discussed in chapter 9, suggests that rather than being repressed into the unconscious, traumatic experiences are often remembered extremely vividly, which calls into question the reality of the concept of repression.

The techniques used to recover these memories include hypnosis and dream analysis, and while these techniques elicit new information, they may be problematical, in that it is often difficult to establish whether or not this information is accurate. Garry et al. (1999) reported that details of genuinely experienced traumatic events, where confirmation of the events was available, changed over time, so calling into question the reliability of recovered memories. Finally, there are many forms of therapy which do not use these kinds of technique but are nonetheless effective in helping people with psychological problems.

We will turn now to the question of how easy it is to create false memories:

Activity 10: creating false memories

Prepare a list of instructions for carrying out 14 actions relating to a few simple props, e.g. a pen, a spoon, a piece of paper, a cup, a scarf, a coin, and so on. For example:

- ◆ Put the spoon in the cup.
- ◆ Put the paper on your head.
- ◆ Toss the coin.

Ask a participant to carry out seven of the actions, and *imagine* carrying out the other seven. There should be no particular pattern in terms of whether the actions are actually to be carried out or just imagined, but be sure to keep a note of which were which.

A week later, give your participant a list of the actions, and ask them to indicate which they carried out and which they just imagined carrying out. For each action, ask them also to indicate how confident they are in their answers, on a scale of 0 (a guess) to 5 (absolutely certain).

Did your participant 'remember' carrying out any of the actions which they merely imagined? If so, how confident were they that this was the case?

In a similar study to this activity, Goff and Roediger (1998) found that participants were likely to claim that they had carried out actions that they had only imagined. However, this kind of study can be criticised on the grounds of poor ecological validity. After all, remembering that you have tossed a coin a week previously is rather different from remembering that you were abused as a child.

However, the possibility that **imagination** can create false memories is a key issue, since some therapists encourage imagination in the clients whom they believe to be victims of childhood sexual abuse. For example, in *The sexual healing journal*, Maltz (1991) advised readers to 'spend time imagining that you were sexually abused, without worrying about accuracy'. Similarly, in a survey of psychotherapists in the USA and Britain, Poole *et al.* (1995) found that more than 20% encouraged imagination as a memory technique for clients who could not remember being sexually abused.

The use of imagination in therapy in this way may well lead to recall of events which never happened:

Box AA: Garry *et al.* (1996)

Procedure: As a pre-test, participants were asked to complete the Life Events Inventory (LEI) to indicate how confident they were that a number of childhood events had or had not happened to them before they were 10. Two weeks later, they were given detailed scripts describing four childhood events from the LEI, e.g. 'broke a window with your hand' and 'had a lifeguard pull you out of the water', and were asked to imagine they were experiencing what was being described. In the final phase, they were again asked to complete the LEI.
Results: Participants who had been asked to imagine events became more confident that they had actually experienced the events described, even though in the pre-test they had said that these events were unlikely to have happened. A control group who had not taken part in the imagination part of the study did not show this change.
Conclusion: Imagining an event increases confidence that the event actually happened.

Garry *et al.* called this phenomenon the **imagination inflation effect (IIE)**, and it has since been replicated in a number of studies:

Box BB: Manning (2000)

Procedure: In a web-based experiment, 276 people first completed the LEI via the Internet. They later came into the laboratory and took part in a variety of imagination exercises related to LEI items. These included writing about the target events, and answering questions about the events which were designed to make what they were imagining more detailed – for example, who was involved? where did it happen? Finally, after one day, one week or two weeks, they completed the LEI again on the Internet.

Results: After one day, there was no difference in the confidence that the target events had actually been experienced between those who had taken part in the imagination exercises and controls who had not. However, those who completed the LEI a week later were significantly more confident that they had actually experienced these events than controls. There was a further increase in confidence for those who had completed the LEI two weeks later.

Conclusion: During the imagination phase, participants become familiar with the target events. If tested one day later, they ascribed this familiarity to having taken part in the imagination exercises. For those tested later, the familiarity they experienced was more likely to be ascribed to the events actually having happened.

While this kind of study has better ecological validity than that carried out by Goff and Roediger into memory for simple actions, there is none the less a problem: there is no proof as to whether the events occurred or not. It is perfectly possible that an imagination exercise might remind people of genuine childhood experiences. However, given the relatively large number of people tested in these studies who remembered events which they had previously claimed were unlikely to have happened, it does not seem probable that the researchers identified events which had actually happened to so many of them.

Dream analysis is very common practice in psychotherapy, and the possibility that it also may create false memories has been investigated:

Box CC: Mazzoni and Loftus (1998)

Procedure: A group of 46 participants reported on their childhood experiences in two sessions separated by between three and four weeks. In between these sessions, some participants had a simulated therapy session in which their dreams were interpreted to suggest that they had experienced a critical childhood event, e.g. being harassed by a bully, or lost in a public place, before the age of three. In the first session, they had reported that these events had not occurred.

Results: Compared with controls who did not undergo the dream interpretation part of the procedure, 'dream' participants were significantly more likely to increase their belief that the events described to them had actually occurred.

Conclusion: The use of dream analysis may lead people to 'remember' events which never happened.

There is quite strong evidence, then, that the use of imagination techniques and dream analysis can create false memories. So what are the overall aspects of the therapeutic situation which can lead to false memories? Key features appear to be the authoritativeness of the source making suggestions, plausibility and pressure to recall.

In a therapeutic situation, therapists are seen as **authoritative**, as experts with experience of psychological problems, their causes, and how best they may be cured. Any suggestions they make are therefore accepted within this framework. Mazzoni *et al.* (2001) found that suggestions which were made more **plausible** to participants were more readily accepted, even when they had initially seemed unlikely. Loftus (1997) suggested that the **pressure to recall** more and more can lead people to 'remember' events which never happened, citing a case in which people were convinced that they could remember events from the first year of life, when the memory system has not yet developed sufficiently for such memories to be laid down.

Another avenue which has been explored is whether there are certain kinds of people who are more likely than others to produce false memories.

Heaps and Nash (1999) found that people who have more lapses in memory and attention, and those who self-report a tendency to confuse fact and fiction, are more vulnerable. According to Horselenberg *et al.* (2000), there is also a link with greater imagery ability.

Another characteristic is **suggestibility**, indicated by susceptibility to hypnosis:

Box DD: Loftus (1997)

Procedure: The help of family members was enlisted to suggest to participants that they had experienced one of a variety of complex experiences, such as being lost in a shopping mall for a period of time, or spending a night in hospital. Characteristics of those who responded to these suggestions and those who did not were compared.
Results: People who were more easily hypnotised were more likely to believe that they had experienced these events.
Conclusion: Those who are more suggestible are more receptive to implanted false memories.

Since hypnosis is often used in therapy, the findings of this study suggest that this may be inappropriate if accurate memories of earlier experiences are to be produced in therapy, since those people in therapy who are easily hypnotised are also likely to be more receptive to implanted false memories.

However, although there is quite a lot of evidence that recovered memories may be inaccurate, this does not mean that memories of child abuse recalled by adults in therapy are necessarily false. Loftus (1996) suggests that even where such memories are not strictly true, they may be symbolically true, as a representation of the nature of an abusive relationship experienced as a child.

At the same time, the costs and benefits of this kind of therapy need to be assessed. Although some patients find such therapy helpful, it is difficult (if not impossible) to establish whether the memories recovered in therapy are genuine or the product of the therapeutic process, but the consequences can be devastating. Gudjonsson (1997) surveyed 282 members of the British False Memory Society, most of the questionnaires being completed by the parents of the person who claimed to have recovered memories of abuse. Most of the accusations appeared to have arisen in the context of therapy. Fifty-nine per cent of respondents reported discontinued contact with the family, in 14% of cases legal proceedings had been instigated, and in 29% of cases the accused person had needed psychiatric help because of the stress involved. Hyman and Loftus (1997) contend that memory recovery does not provide enough documented benefits to justify the risk of the creation of false memories.

- There is a debate as to whether it is possible in therapy to **recover memories** which have been repressed, or whether suggestions made by the therapist lead to **FMS**.
- Therapies which focus on recovering memories are based on the idea of **repression**, which is problematical. They are likely to use **imagination techniques** and **dream analysis**, both of which have been shown to create false memories in a laboratory situation.
- Characteristics of therapy which may lead to false memories include **authoritativeness**, **plausibility**, and **pressure to recall**.
- There are **individual differences** in people's susceptibility to suggestion.
- While recovered memories are not necessarily false, the **implications** for patients' families and patients themselves need to be weighed against generally accepting such memories as true.

Notes on activities

1 **a** and **b** show a failure in the face recognition system, **c** shows a failure in the semantic system, while **d** shows a failure in the name system. The errors in groups **a** and **b** suggest that face recognition comes first, while the errors in **c** and **d** suggest that the semantic system is activated before the name system.

2 **a** The change in someone's appearance would mean that there was not sufficient stimulation of a FRU for the face to be recognised.

b The similarity of the face which is seen and a familiar face is sufficient to activate wrongly a FRU.

c The relevant FRU has been activated, but the stimulation has not been strong enough to activate the cognitive system or the PIN and so retrieve more information about the person.

d There is a problem at the final stage between the PIN and the name generation system.

3 Burton *et al.* (1999) found that people had great difficulty in making this kind of identification. The video images are of poor quality, and there are differences in the lighting of the pictures and the angle at which the faces are seen. However, people do not find the task so difficult if the person is known to them, presumably because they are familiar with what a known person looks like from different angles, and there may be additional information from the way in which the body moves.

5 How long events lasted can be crucial in a criminal trial. When people overestimate the length of time they were exposed to an event, they create the impression that they had longer to look at something than they actually did, and this may falsely increase their credibility as witnesses.

6 Many of the ideas of the cognitive interview are based on cue-dependent forgetting (section 9.2). Talking about how the witness and other people present at the time might have felt is linked to state-dependent forgetting, so that reinstating the emotional state will provide cues which may trigger off additional information. Mentally reinstating the context may have a similar effect.

The spreading activation model (section 10.4) suggests that there is a complex interrelationship of links in memory, so asking a witness to recall information in different orders and from different perspectives increases the probability of a seemingly irrelevant piece of information triggering off something which may be useful. This is known as encouraging feature overlap.

7

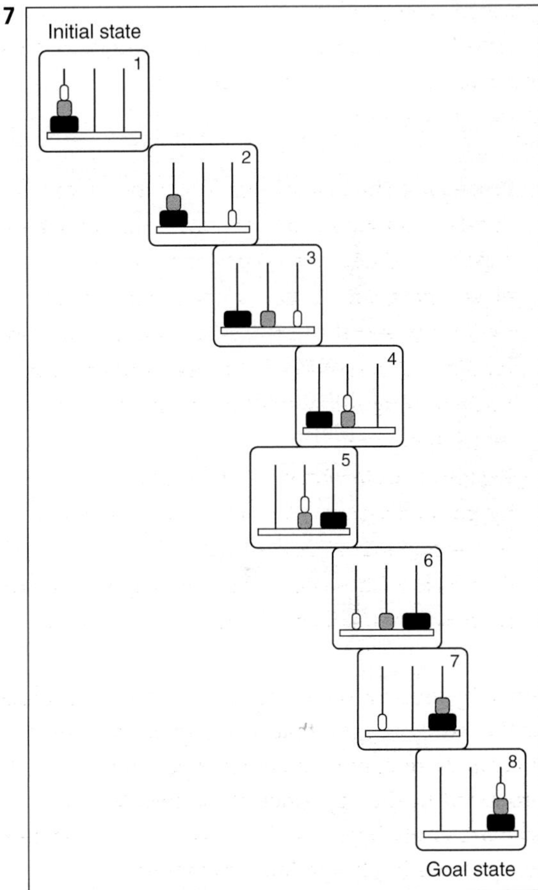

9 Watching a video is very different from being an eye-witness to a real crime. Since it is a filmed event, arousal is likely to be lower, and participants may well have guessed what was being tested. Since they knew they were being tested, they could have adapted their behaviour in line with what they perceived to be the aims of the study. It may well have been that there were differences between the two groups in their motivation to do well at this task, and the younger group may have spent more time watching filmed material than older participants.

12 Research issues

12.1 Planning research

In working through the previous chapters, you have read about a lot of varied psychological research. In planning your own research, there are several factors which you will need to bear in mind in order to make it as effective as possible.

The first consideration will be choice of topic. As you will write a report on your research, it makes sense to choose a topic in an area which you find interesting, and which links in with background theory and research, since the introduction to your report will need to show that your research hypothesis – what you expect to be the outcome of your research – is well grounded. At the same time, don't be too ambitious; it is highly unlikely that you will produce a ground-breaking study, nor are you expected to do so. For example, if you are carrying out experimental research, a comparison between an experimental and a control condition is fine; there is no need to complicate matters by making a three-way comparison. What is important is that you have produced a sound hypothesis to test, that you have planned how to test it in an appropriate way, and that in your report you communicate clearly where your idea came from, how you tested it, what your findings were and what you think they mean in terms of the hypothesis.

Once you have decided on a topic, a theory relevant to it needs to be identified, and a specific prediction that is implied by that theory (a hypothesis) needs to be made. If when tested this prediction is found to be correct, then there is support for the theory. The theory will be challenged if the prediction is found not to be correct. You will then need to decide which method you are going to use to test your hypothesis. In previous chapters, you have read many examples of psychological research, using a range of methods. Some studies have used the experimental (or quasi-experimental) method, though there are many examples of other non-experimental methods, such as correlational studies, observational methods, interviews and surveys. Psychologists carrying out research choose the method which is most appropriate for what they want to investigate. Whatever the topic under investigation, there is not just one way of collecting data, so when you carry out a research project of your own, you should give some thought as to which method would be most suitable. Before making this decision, you might find it useful to look through the account of the various methods in chapter 2 and remind yourself of the strengths and limitations of each.

Activity 1: which method?

For each of these methods of carrying out psychological research, what are its strengths? What are its limitations?

a laboratory experiments
b quasi-experiments
c field experiments
d naturalistic observation
e correlational analysis
f interviews and surveys

When you have finished, check your ideas with the material in chapter 2.

There are other issues in planning research, covered in chapter 2, which you might find useful. For example, if you are using the experimental method, you will need to consider the research design, the difference between the two conditions (the IV) and the way that you will be measuring the performance of your participants (the DV). In a correlational study, you will need to decide how to measure the variables to be correlated. You will also need to decide whether, on the basis of background theory and studies, the research hypothesis is one-tailed (directional) or two-tailed (non-directional). In practice, most research hypotheses are one-tailed. Hypotheses are discussed in chapter 2, section 2.3.

You will need to decide on the population from which your sample is to be drawn, and the sampling method to be used. Most student practicals use opportunity sampling as the most convenient method, though if your study takes the form of a naturalistic observation, you may be testing a self-selecting sample of people who happen to be where you are carrying out the observation.

Another consideration is how many participants to test. You will be analysing your data using a statistical test; all these tests require a minimum number of participants. However, these numbers are usually very low, and it is worth considering testing a few more participants than is necessary to meet the requirements of the test to try to reduce the relative importance of random variation in the results. At the same time, the disadvantage in testing large numbers of participants, which can be extremely time-consuming, needs to be balanced against possible gains.

One major factor you will need to bear in mind is ethics. The final section of chapter 2 outlines ethical guidelines for carrying out psychological research with human participants, and you should reread this carefully before making any final decisions about the study you plan to carry out. In particular, it is desirable that participants give informed consent to take part in your study, which means that the information given to them before they decide whether or not to take part should be as full as possible. If deception is necessary, you should offer a full debriefing. You also need to make sure that they know that they can decide at any time to take no further part in the study, and can have their data destroyed.

Finally, you will need to prepare any necessary materials. These may include standardised instructions, stimulus materials, questionnaires, rating scales and so on. It is always worth running a small pilot study, testing just two or three participants, to make sure that your instructions are clear, that your materials are appropriate, and that any timings (such as the time for which participants are exposed to stimuli) are neither too long nor too short.

It is unlikely that you will be short of ideas; it is probable that several possibilities have already occurred to you as you have worked your way through the topics in this book. The main thing is to keep notes of the planning process – in which books or articles or websites you have found the relevant background material relating to theory and research, the reasoning behind the various planning decisions you have made, and so on. Once you have carried out your research, these notes will make writing the report a lot easier.

12.2 Inferential statistics

The term 'inferential statistics' refers to carrying out statistical tests on data, which then allow inferences (or conclusions) about the data to be drawn. What the tests actually tell you is the probability of obtaining the results if the null hypothesis is in fact correct.

It is not possible to prove something true by observation alone. Take, for example, the assertion that 'All swans are white'. We could observe a great number of swans, and find that all of them are white. But however large a sample of white swans we observe, we cannot discount the possibility that we may at some point come across a black one. The best we can achieve, then, is a reasonable certainty that a research hypothesis which we have investigated is correct. It is for this reason that the word 'proved' is not used in relation to the research hypothesis when discussing the results of a study. Instead, the hypothesis is supported or not.

In psychological research, the 5% (0.05) level of probability is the conventionally accepted level at which a research hypothesis can be accepted. This means that we need to establish that the probability that our results could have come about by chance (and that the null hypothesis is actually correct) is 5% or less, and that we can therefore accept our results as supporting the research hypothesis with a 95% level of confidence, and reject the null hypothesis. If the results of a study reach the 5% significance level, they are said to be **significant** at this level.

The 5% level has been accepted in psychological research because it represents a reasonable compromise between making a **type 1** and a **type 2** error. If a researcher accepts that their research hypothesis is supported, whereas in fact the results have come about by chance, they are making a type 1 error. If on the other hand they wrongly infer that the research hypothesis has not been supported, they are making a type 2 error. The 5% level is stringent enough to allow a reasonable certainty in accepting the research hypothesis, while at the same time not being so stringent that genuine results are overlooked.

While statistical tests can tell us whether data reach the 5% criterion, they can also tell us whether a more stringent criterion, e.g. 1% (0.01), is reached. If so, we can then accept the research hypothesis with even greater confidence, i.e. 99%.

Standard tests are applied to psychological data to establish whether we can be sure, to the level of certainty which we have decided on, that results like those obtained could have occurred by chance alone. It is perhaps worth noting that if you are testing a one-tailed hypothesis, most of the tests cannot decide for you whether your results are in the direction predicted, or whether the difference is in the opposite direction. To establish this, you will need to look at the data before carrying out the test. For example, if you have predicted that scores in condition A will be higher than those in condition B, but the scores for condition A are in fact generally lower than those for condition B, the statistical test cannot lead you to reject the null hypothesis. It is also worth looking at your data before carrying out the test to consider how distinctively different the two sets are, and how likely it is that this has come about by chance.

12.3 Carrying out statistical tests

There are very many statistical tests available to psychologists; which one is suitable for analysing the data of a particular study will depend on several factors to do with the research design used in the study. Here we shall concentrate on what are called **non-parametric** tests. In contrast to parametric tests, which make various assumptions about the nature of the data collected, these tests have the advantage that they can be used with any level of quantitative data, and are quick and easy to use. Their main drawback is that they are somewhat insensitive, but this is usually not too much of a problem in student practicals. We will look at five tests which relate to different kinds of simple research design.

In order to decide which test is appropriate for a particular set of data, three questions need to be answered. The first question is whether the study is looking for a difference between conditions, or whether it is looking for a relationship or association. You will remember from chapter 2, that experiments look for a difference, while correlational designs look for a relationship. Observational studies could look for either.

The second question concerns the level of the

data. Chapter 2, section 2.6 describes the different levels of measurement which can be used. For parametric tests, the data need to be of at least interval level, while the non-parametric tests which we shall be looking at here can be applied whatever level of measurement is used. The critical distinction for these tests is between nominal (category) data, and data which are of at least ordinal level, i.e. in the form of scores which can be put in rank order.

If the study is looking for a difference between conditions, the final question to be asked is whether the design of the study uses repeated or independent measures. For the purposes of choosing a statistical test, a matched pairs design is treated in the same way as a repeated measures design. See chapter 2, section 2.5, if you have forgotten what these terms mean.

We will look here at five tests. How the answers to these questions relate to choice of test is shown in figure 1.

You may wonder how the chi square test can be used to establish either a relationship or a difference. It is in fact a test of association. For example, if you were investigating whether men or women are more likely to hold open a door for someone else passing through, the test would tell you whether there is an association between gender and this kind of helping behaviour. At the same time, it could tell you whether there is a difference between men and women in this respect.

Activity 2: choosing a statistical test

Read the following scenarios. For each one, decide

a whether the researchers are looking for a difference between performance in two conditions or a relationship/association between two variables

b what level of measurement is being used

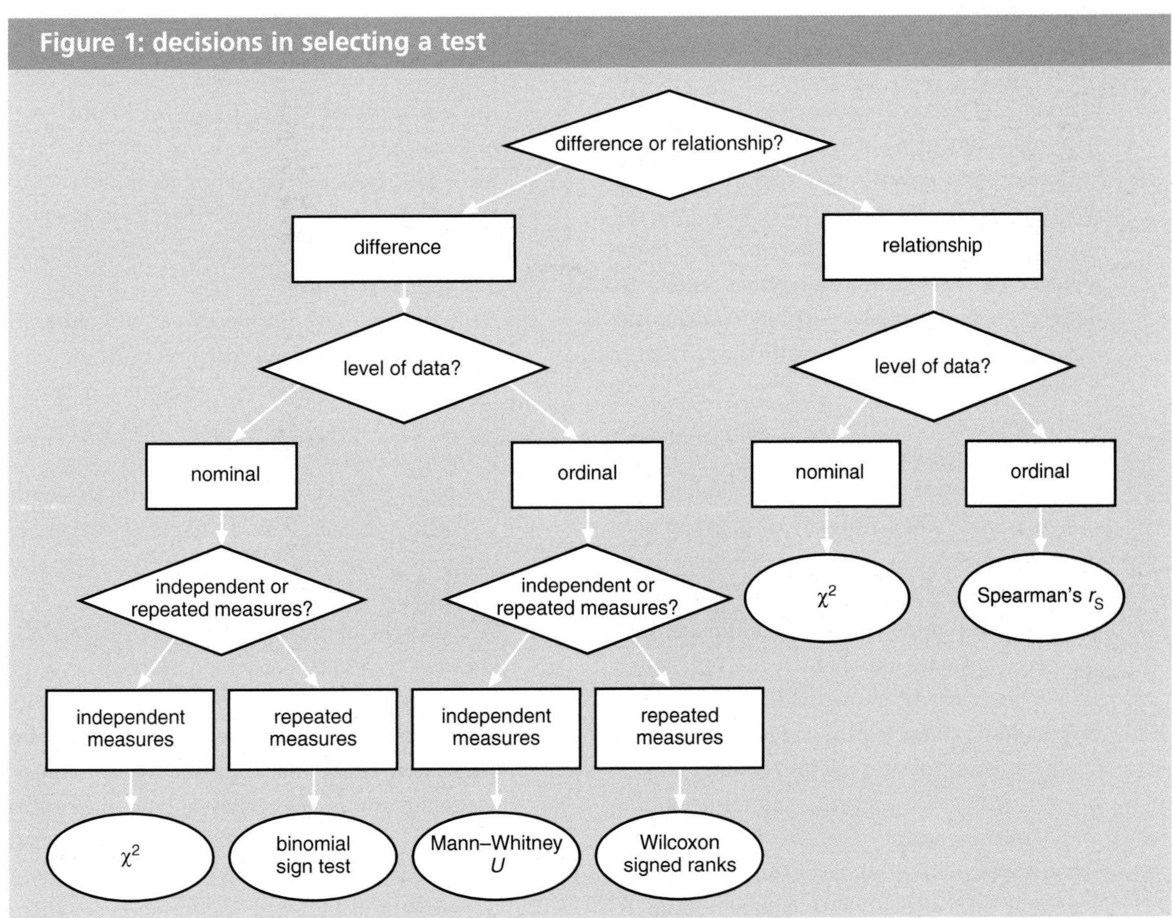

c if they are looking for a difference, whether they have used a repeated or independent measures design.

On the basis of your answers to these questions, decide which statistical test would be appropriate to analyse the data:

1 An A-level Psychology teacher is interested in whether there is a relationship between the amount of time students spend in paid employment and how well they do at A-level. She asks students how many hours they spend each week at work, and translates their predicted A-level grades into a points score (A=10, B=8 etc.).

2 Does the nature of the material to be learned affect how well it is remembered? Participants are asked to learn a list of 30 words, half of which are related to emotions (e.g. love, hate) and half of which are neutral words, matched for length and approximate frequency in the English language. They are asked to recall as many words as they can. Their scores for the two kinds of words are compared.

3 A primary school teacher is interested in the language skills of her pupils, and in particular whether there is a link between size of vocabulary and spelling ability. She gives them a vocabulary test, which requires them to match a series of words with their meanings, and compares their scores with those from a spelling test.

4 Researchers are interested in the effect on helping behaviour of watching altruistic behaviour on TV. One group of children is shown a video where friendly cartoon animals help old ladies across the road and help to carry their shopping, while another group is shown a Tom and Jerry cartoon. All the children are then exposed to situations where they could offer help. Observers decide whether each child is very helpful, quite helpful or not helpful, and compare the ratings for the two groups.

5 In a memory experiment, participants are asked to learn pairs of words. One group is asked to learn the words by repeating them over and over again, while another group is asked to create a visual image to link the words. They are then tested by being shown the first word of each pair, and asked to supply the second word. The number of words correctly remembered in each condition is compared.

6 Researchers are interested in whether information about party policy affects people's voting intentions. A sample of voters in Anytown is asked whether or not they are likely to vote for the Monster Raving Loony Party. They then attend a lecture on Monster Raving Loony Party policy, following which they are again asked whether they are likely to vote for this party. Researchers note how many people who had not originally intended to vote for the party changed their minds after attending the lecture.

7 Do children change their opinion of school subjects when they have spent some time at a particular school? Children entering Dotheboys Hall are asked to rate how interesting they find English, Maths and Science, using a scale of 1 (extremely boring) to 10 (absolutely great). They are asked to rate these subjects again when they have been at the school for a year, to assess whether there has been any change.

8 Gumrot plc have produced a new line in sweets called Dinosaur Droppings. They want to know whether there is a difference between the two possible packaging designs they have developed in terms of their appeal to girls and to boys. Sweets are displayed in both packaging designs. The numbers of each kind bought by girls and by boys are recorded and compared.

9 Researchers are interested in the truth of well-known sayings, in particular 'elephants never forget' and 'a memory like a sieve'. Participants are hypnotised and given a post-hypnotic suggestion either that they are an elephant or that they are a sieve. They are then asked to read and memorise a story. Recall for each group is compared, using a questionnaire on the content of the story.

10 Psychologists at Oxford Clinic for the Seriously Bewildered are interested in whether their therapy methods, which involve teaching clients A-level Psychology, can be shown to be effective. Staff are asked to rate a group of clients on the amount of bewildered behaviour they show, both before and after studying A-level Psychology.

When you have finished, see the notes on page 328.

We will now look in detail at how each of the five statistical tests in figure 1 is carried out. For each test, a formula is followed which allows you to work out what is called the **calculated** (or **observed**) **value** for the test you are using. This is then compared with the **critical value** in the relevant set of tables, included as appendices to this chapter, to indicate how likely it is that the results have come about by chance. The calculated value is first compared with the critical values at the 5% level; this is indicated on the table by $p < 0.05$, meaning that the probability of the results having come about by chance is less than 5%.

If the results are significant at this level, then the calculated value can be compared with critical values at more stringent levels. For example, $p = 0.01$ means that the probability that the results could have come about by chance is 1%, while $p = 0.005$ means that the probability that the results could have come about by chance is 0.5%. The smaller this probability, the greater the confidence with which the research hypothesis can be accepted.

It is also worth noting that, for some tests, the calculated value needs to be smaller than the critical value in the table in order to be accepted at this level, while for other tests, it needs to be larger. This is indicated in the worked examples and also at the top of each table.

Some of the tests we will be looking at – those which work on data which are of at least ordinal level – require the raw data (the actual scores which have been collected) to be ranked, i.e. put in order, in the same way that runners in a race can be put in the order in which they finish. This is done because non-parametric tests require that the ranks of the scores, rather than the scores themselves, are compared.

However, unlike the runners, in ranking for psychological tests the lowest score is ranked 1, the next lowest 2, and so on. If there is a tie of two equal scores, the next two positions are added and divided by two. Similarly, if there are three equal scores, the next three positions are added and divided by three.

Activity 3: ranking

Here is a sample set of scores which have been ranked:

scores	25	21	21	15	14	14	14	12	11
rank	9	7.5	7.5	6	4	4	4	2	1

Now rank these scores:

scores: 17 17 14 14 14 12 9 6 6

When you have finished, see the notes on page 328.

Mann–Whitney U test

We will relate this test to activity 7 in chapter 9. Each participant in two conditions is given a set of words written individually on cards to sort into three piles. In condition 1, they are asked to sort the words using meaningful categories, while in condition 2, they are asked to sort by the script in which the words are written. On the basis of the levels of processing theory (see chapter 9, section 9.1) the research hypothesis is that participants who have sorted by meaning (semantic processing) will remember more of the words in an unexpected recall test than those who sorted by script (structural processing).

The table of results, showing the number of words correctly recalled by each participant in each condition, is shown in figure 2. The Mann–Whitney *U* test requires that all the scores from both conditions are ranked together; these ranks are also shown in figure 2.

Figure 2: preparing data for the Mann–Whitney *U* test

participant	condition 1 (semantic)	rank	participant	condition 2 (structural)	rank
1	16	12	10	12	7
2	21	18	11	16	12
3	10	3.5	12	15	10
4	22	19	13	10	3.5
5	18	16.5	14	10	3.5
6	18	16.5	15	13	8
7	16	12	16	10	3.5
8	24	20	17	14	9
9	17	14.5	18	11	6
		$T_1 = 132$	19	9	1
			20	17	14.5

In this example, there are different numbers of participants in each condition; it is not necessary to have equal numbers for this test. The next step is to substitute numbers into the formula for the Mann–Whitney *U* test. The formula and workings are shown in figure 3.

Figure 3: calculations for the Mann–Whitney *U* test

For this test, the value of a statistic denoted by *U* is calculated using the formula:

$$U = n_1 n_2 + \frac{n_1(n_1 + 1)}{2} - T_1$$

n_1 is the number of participants in condition 1, n_2 is the number of participants in condition 2, and T_1 is the sum of the ranks in condition 1.
This gives $U = 99 + 45 - 132 = 12$
We then need to work out a further value called *U* prime (U') using the formula

$$U' = n_1 n_2 - U, \text{ so } U' = 99 - 12 = 87$$

The smaller values of *U*, in this case 12, is compared with the critical values in the tables. If we are to accept the research hypothesis, the calculated value of *U* needs to be equal to or less than the critical value.

Activity 4: assessing the results of the Mann–Whitney *U* test

1 Decide whether the research hypothesis was one-tailed or two-tailed. If it was one-tailed, check that the difference is in the direction predicted by the research hypothesis.
2 Turn to the tables for this test in appendix 1, page 335, selecting the 5% level(0.05).
3 Find the value of n_1 along the top of the table, and the value of n_2 down the left-hand side. Move down from n_1 and across from n_2; where they meet is the critical value.
4 Compare the critical value with the calculated value of 12. Can the research hypothesis be accepted at $p < 0.05$? If the calculated value is equal to or less than the critical value in the table, it indicates that the probability of the results having come about by chance is less than 5%. This is expressed as $p < 0.05$. Can it also be accepted at more stringent levels?

When you have finished, see the notes on page 328.

Wilcoxon signed ranks test

To illustrate this test, we will look at a variation of the Stroop effect. In the Stroop effect, people almost invariably take longer to identify the ink colour in which words are written if the words are colour words written in a conflicting colour (e.g. the word 'blue' written in red ink) than if they are words with no colour associations. As a variation on this, we will compare the time taken to identify ink colours in a set of words with a colour association, written in a conflicting colour (e.g. 'grass' written in red) and to identify the colours of a set of neutral words, matched for initial letter, length and relative frequency in the English language. The research hypothesis is that people will take longer to identify the ink colours of the colour-associated words than of the neutral words.

For this test, a statistic called T is calculated. To carry out this test, the two sets of scores are listed as shown in the table in figure 4, then the difference between each set of scores is calculated (the column headed 'd' for 'difference'). Any pairs of scores which are equal are discarded, and that participant's data are not included in the calculation. These differences are then ranked, ignoring whether they are minus or plus values (the column headed 'ranks of d'). For example, differences of +1, –5 and +6 would be ranked 1, 2 and 3 respectively.

Figure 4: calculation for the Wilcoxon signed ranks test

Time in seconds to complete colour identification task

participant	condition A (colour-associated words)	condition B (neutral words)	*d*	ranks of *d*	sign of *d*
1	24	16	+8	9	+
2	18	18	0	omit tie	
3	32	26	+6	7.5	+
4	21	23	–2	3	–
5	28	23	+5	5.5	+
6	41	35	+6	7.5	+
7	17	15	+2	3	+
8	18	20	+2	3	+
9	20	19	+1	1	+
10	22	17	+5	5.5	+

A column 'sign of d' is added to the table as shown. All the ranks corresponding to a minus sign are added and all the ranks corresponding to a plus sign are added. Whichever of these sums is smaller is the observed value of T. In this case, the only value in the 'rank of d' column to have a minus sign is the rank of 3 for participant 4, so this is clearly going to be smaller than the sum of all the plus ranks. Therefore, $T = 3$.

It is worth noting that if all the differences are in the same direction; for example, if all the signs in the final column are plus, then T would be equal to 0, i.e. the sum of the minus results, in this case.

To look up the value of T in the relevant table, you will also need to know the value of n, i.e. the number of participants. In this case, $n = 9$, since we are discarding the data of participant 2, who took the same time in each condition.

If the research hypothesis is to be accepted and the null hypothesis rejected, the calculated value of T needs to be equal to or less than the critical value.

Activity 5: assessing the results of the test

1 Decide whether the research hypothesis was one-tailed or two-tailed.
2 Turn to the table for this test in appendix 2, page 339, selecting the 5% level, i.e. the appropriate column headed 0.05.
3 Find the value of n, and compare the calculated value of 3 with the critical value in the table at 0.05. Can the research hypothesis be accepted, and the null hypothesis rejected, at this level? What about more stringent levels?

When you have finished, see the notes on page 328.

Spearman's coefficient r_S

In this test, a statistic usually denoted by r_S, but sometimes called rho, is calculated. We will relate this test to the data supplied in activity 18, chapter 2. The research hypothesis here is that there will be a positive correlation between students' IQ scores and A-level points scores. Ranking is again used, with each of the two sets of scores – IQ and A-level points – being ranked separately and the ranks compared. Since the research hypothesis predicts a positive correlation, it is expected that the rank for each score for each participant will be similar, i.e. that a participant with a high rank for one score will tend also to have a high rank for the other, and a participant with a low rank for one score will tend also to have a low rank for the other.

Once the two sets of ranks have been completed, the difference between the ranks for each participant is worked out (the column headed 'd') and then this difference is squared (the column headed 'd^2'). All the values in this last column are then added to give Σd^2. The sign Σ is the Greek letter sigma, and means 'sum', in this case finding the sum of the d^2 values.

Figure 5: working out Spearman's coefficient r_S

participant	IQ score	rank	A-level score	rank	d	d^2
1	125	6	20	7.5	–1.5	2.25
2	110	2	14	3	–1	1
3	127	7	24	10	–3	9
4	135	9	18	5.5	3.5	12.25
5	118	4	22	9	–5	25
6	142	10	20	7.5	2.5	6.25
7	122	5	16	4	1	1
8	112	3	10	1.5	1.5	2.25
9	128	8	18	5.5	2.5	6.25
10	108	1	10	1.5	–0.5	0.25

$\Sigma d^2 = 65.5$

Numerical values are then put into the formula:

$$r_S = 1 - \frac{6\Sigma d^2}{n(n^2 - 1)}$$ where n = the number of pairs of scores

$$r_S = 1 - \frac{6 \times 65.5}{10 \times 99}$$

$$r_S = 1 - \frac{393}{990} = 1 - 0.397 = +0.603$$

If the research hypothesis is to be accepted, the calculated value of r_S needs to be equal to or larger than the critical value in the table. In order to accept a research hypothesis predicting a negative correlation, the critical value is read as being a minus number, and the calculated value has to be between the critical value and –1.0.

Activity 6: using the table for Spearman's coefficient r_S

Using the table for this test in appendix 3, page 340, check to see whether the research hypothesis can be accepted at the 5% level. Do the results reach a more significant level than this? Why/why not? How would you interpret these results: do they show a very strong relationship between IQ and A-level scores? Quite a strong relationship? A weak relationship? (You may find it helpful to compare your assessment with the answers to activity 18, chapter 2.)

When you have finished, see the notes on page 328.

Chi square (χ^2)

For this test, a statistic called chi square (written as χ^2 and pronounced 'ky square') is calculated. We will return to the example given earlier of a study which investigates whether men or women are more likely to hold open a door for someone else passing through. The researchers position themselves outside a department store where they can observe door-opening behaviour without making themselves too conspicuous, and keep a tally of the numbers of men and women who hold the door open for someone else, and those who are in a position to do so but do not. The numbers in each of the four categories (men who helped; men who didn't help; women who helped; women who didn't help) are entered in a table with four cells, as shown in figure 6. Each person can therefore only be counted in one cell (a requirement for the chi square test); they are either male or female, and they either hold the door open or do not. The totals of the rows and columns also form part of the table. The data and workings are shown in figure 6.

Figure 6: working out χ^2

	men	women	total
held the door open	23	8	31
did not hold the door open	11	14	25
total	34	22	56

The numbers in the four main cells in the table are the **observed values.** The table also shows totals for the rows (31 and 25), totals for the columns (34 and 22) and the overall total number of observations (56).

The first step is to work out what are called the **expected frequencies** for each of the four cells, i.e. the frequencies we would expect if the null hypothesis were true. This is done for each cell by multiplying the marginal total of the relevant row by the marginal total of the relevant column, then dividing by the overall total. For cell 1 (men who held the door open), the expected value would be:

$31 \times 34 \div 56 = 18.82$

When all four expected frequencies have been calculated, they are put in the relevant cells:

23 18.82	8 12.18
11 15.18	14 9.82

To check that your calculations are accurate, the row and column sums for both the *E* and the *O* values should be worked out; they should be the same. For example, in column 1, 23 + 11 = 34 and 18.82 + 15.18 = 34.

For each cell, figures need to be substituted in the formula

$$\frac{(O - E)^2}{E}$$

where *O* = the observed value for that cell and *E* = the expected value.

For the first cell (top left), the calculation is

$$\frac{(23 - 18.2)^2}{18.2} = 0.93$$

For the second cell (top right), the result of this calculation is 1.43. The results for the third (bottom left) and the fourth (bottom right) cells are 1.15 and 1.78 respectively.

The formula for chi square is $\sum \frac{(O - E)^2}{E}$

so to find the value of χ^2, these four numbers must be added. In this case, the value is

$\chi^2 = 0.93 + 1.43 + 1.15 + 1.78 = 5.29.$

To reach significance, the calculated value of χ^2 needs to be equal to or larger than the critical value in the table.

Before we can look up this statistic in the table, we need to calculate the degrees of freedom (df). This is simply the number of rows minus 1, multiplied by the number of columns minus 1. In this example, there are two rows and two columns, so df = (2 – 1) x (2 – 1) = 1. It would be perfectly possible, however, to have more rows and/or columns; for example, people could be classified as 'very helpful', 'quite helpful' or 'not helpful', as in example 4 of activity 2.

Activity 7: using the table for chi square

Use appendix 4, page 341, to find out whether the results in figure 6 are significant, and if so, at what level. You will first need to decide whether the research hypothesis is one-tailed or two-tailed.

When you have finished, see the notes on page 328.

Binomial sign test

For this test, a statistic called S is calculated. As an example, we will look at a study which compares children's performance on a standard Piagetian conservation of liquid quantity task (see chapter 10, figure 5) and on a similar task which makes 'human sense', in which children are told that liquid needs to be poured out of the original container into another one because the original container is chipped, and so might hurt someone. The children carry out the standard task and the 'human sense' task on two separate occasions, and researchers expect that children who are unable to conserve on the standard task will be successful in carrying out the 'human sense' task.

A tick or a cross is put for each participant in each condition, according to whether they conserved successfully. For those who conserved in condition B but not in condition A, i.e. responded in line with the research hypothesis, a + sign is put in the final column. A – sign is given if they succeeded on task B but not on task A, i.e. the difference is in the opposite direction from that predicted. If they conserved on both tasks, or failed to conserve on both tasks, i.e. there was no difference between the two conditions, their data are not included in the calculation.

Figure 7: working out the binomial sign test

participant	condition A (standard task)	condition B ('human sense' task)	conserved in B but not in A
1	✗	✓	+
2	✗	✓	+
3	✗	✓	+
4	✗	✗	omit
5	✓	✗	–
6	✓	✓	omit
7	✗	✓	+
8	✗	✗	omit
9	✗	✓	+
10	✗	✓	+

The next step is to add up the number of + signs and the number of – signs in the final column. The smaller of the two numbers is the value of *S*. In this example, the data of participants 4, 6 and 8 would be discarded, since there was no difference in performance on the two conditions. Therefore $n = 7$; there are 6 + signs and 1 – sign, so $S = 1$.

In this example, we have looked only at the change in sign between conditions. However, this test can also be carried out when the data are in the form of scores. In this case, the final column will show a + sign when the difference between scores for the two conditions is positive, and a – sign when the difference is negative.

Activity 8: assessing the results of the sign test

Use the table in appendix 5, page 336, to assess whether the results of this test are significant, and if so at what level. You will need to decide whether the research hypothesis is one-tailed or two-tailed.

When you have finished, see the notes on page 328.

12.4 Writing research reports

Careful planning of a research project and appropriate analysis of the data are only part of research. It is also necessary to communicate clearly relevant information about the study in a report. There are conventions as to how this should be done which we will be looking at in this section. At the end of the chapter, in appendix 6 (page 337), there is a sample report written by a student, together with comments on its strengths and weaknesses. It is a study relating to the Craik and Lockhart levels of processing model of memory, which you read about in chapter 9, so you will be familiar with the material. You may find it useful to refer to the sample report as you read about how to write the various sections of a report.

Before starting to write the report, you will need to think of a suitable title. This should be concise, while at the same time giving a clear idea of the research question which you have investigated. It is a good idea to include in the title the IV and DV (or the two co-variables in the case of correlational research).

The report, with the exception of the research and null hypotheses, should be written in the past tense. It should not be longer than 1500 words, not counting any tables or appendices, so it is important to put the necessary information across succinctly. It is divided into sections, each with a different heading and serving a different function. The sections are: abstract; introduction; method; results; discussion; conclusion; references; and appendices. It helps to make the report easy to read if each section is given its appropriate heading. We will look at each section in turn in terms of what it should contain and how it should be structured.

Before we move on to the specific sections, there are a few general points to bear in mind in report writing. It is a convention that words such as 'I', 'we' and 'my' are not used. The report should be written in an impersonal style, so that instead of writing 'I read participants the instructions', you should write 'Participants were read the instructions'.

You should also aim to use a simple style throughout. Students are often tempted to use long words and write in long sentences, but this usually makes the report more difficult to read. You may find it helpful to ask someone else, who doesn't know anything about psychology, to read through your report when it is completed, and then consider rewriting any sections they find difficult to understand. You should write in sentences, and avoid lists.

Finally, make sure that there is a logical progression within each section; this can be a particular problem in the introduction and discussion sections. It pays to give particular attention to links between paragraphs, to ensure that there is a smooth transition from one idea to the next.

Abstract

The first part of a report is the abstract. This is a short summary of the report, including brief information about all the other major sections, i.e. introduction, method, results and discussion. It is therefore a good idea to write it after the other sections have been completed, even though it comes at the start of the report. In published research, the purpose of the abstract is to allow other people to have a clear and easily accessible overview of the study so that they can decide whether they would like to read about it in more detail.

The abstract should make brief reference to background theory or research, and should include the aims of the study, the research hypothesis and the expected findings. It should say how the idea was tested, who the participants were and how many were tested, and identify the test used to analyse the data. It should give the critical and calculated values from the statistical analysis, and say whether the results were significant, and if so, at what level. Finally, there should be some brief comment on any limitations of the research, and suggestions as to how the topic could be followed up in future research. It is also relevant to note any practical implications.

Introduction

The purpose of the introduction is to provide a rationale for the idea which you have chosen to test. Overall, it should not need to be longer than one and a half pages of typing. It helps to think of this section as being like a funnel, which starts from relevant but general information, and gradually becomes more specific, finishing with the research and null hypotheses. There needs to be a clear and explicit progression from the theory to the hypotheses you are testing.

It is likely that your study relates to a particular theory, so you will need to start with a theoretical outline. This should be quite brief, highlighting the main ideas, and mentioning the name of the theorist and the date of the theory.

From this, you will need to move on to research which supports the theory. You should be selective in what you choose to include; more is not necessarily better. Aim for between two and five studies, and use the ones which relate most closely to what you are going to be testing in your study, with the most relevant one coming last. This should lead to the aims of the study: what exactly are you trying to find out by carrying out the study?

You will then need to decide whether your research hypothesis is one-tailed or two-tailed, and justify your decision. This decision is based on the findings of the research studies you have described, but this link needs to be made explicit. You should end this section by stating the research hypothesis and the null hypothesis. It helps to set these out as separate paragraphs.

In many cases there are competing theories within the area which you have chosen to investigate. However, it is not necessary to look at more than one theory in the introduction. Alternative theories are best considered in the discussion, in the light of your findings. The exception to this is when you are testing a two-tailed hypothesis, where one theory predicts one outcome and another predicts the opposite. In this case, both theories, together with their supporting research, need to be covered in the introduction. This makes sense if you bear in mind that the aim of the introduction is to provide a clear rationale for the research hypothesis.

Method

This section of the report gives a detailed account of how the study was carried out. Think of it as being a bit like a recipe. It should be possible for someone reading this section to replicate your study exactly, so you need to include full details of how the study was carried out and samples of any materials used. The method uses four separate subheadings: design; participants; materials/apparatus; and procedure.

In the **design** section, you should state the method used – for example, that it was a laboratory experiment, or quasi-experiment, or a study using correlational analysis – and say why this design was chosen. If an experimental design is used, you should identify the experimental and control conditions. You should also say whether you used independent measures, repeated measures or matched pairs, and justify your choice. You should then identify the IV and the DV, or the two co-variables in the case of correlational analysis. If repeated measures are used, say whether counterbalancing or randomisation of conditions was used. If you are comparing two conditions, you need to state the basis on which participants were allocated to conditions.

Identify any controlled variables, i.e. factors which were kept the same in both conditions, such as the time for which participants were exposed to stimulus materials, or the conditions under which testing was carried out. Finally, you should state the significance level to be accepted, and say why this level was chosen. As noted above, the 5% level is the one conventionally used in psychological research, unless existing research is being challenged or there are safety implications in what is being tested.

In the **participants** section, you should identify the population from which your sample of participants was drawn. Say how many participants were tested overall, and how many were tested in each condition if you are carrying out an experimental or quasi-experimental design. You need to state the sampling method used, and say why your sample fits into this category. For example, you could say that an opportunity sample was tested, since people were tested on the basis of their availability and willingness to take part. It is usual to give the approximate age range of the participants, and the gender composition of the sample (though try to avoid ambiguous statements such as 'Participants were half male and half female'). There may be other information about participants which is relevant. For instance, in the example of the Stroop effect used above to show the working of the Wilcoxon signed ranks test, it would be relevant to say that no participants were colour blind.

The next subsection describes the **materials/apparatus** used. Apparatus could include a computer if you have presented stimulus materials using PowerPoint, or a stopwatch if you have timed participants' performance. You will also need to give details of any materials you have used such as tests, questionnaires or word lists. If you have prepared the materials especially for the study, you need to explain the basis on which this was done; for example, why the kinds of items used in a questionnaire were chosen, or the words in word lists selected.

You should include a sample of your materials in an appendix, and say here that you have done so. You should also include scoring systems for tests or questionnaires. You are likely to have several appendices by the time you finish the report, so number them in the order in which they are mentioned in the text, and refer to them using the relevant number. These references are usually made in brackets, e.g. '(for a sample word list, see appendix 1)'. You are also likely to have standardised instructions to include in this section. Even if instructions have been given verbally to participants, a written transcript needs to be included as an appendix, referred to in this subsection.

The final subsection of the method section is the **procedure**. This subsection describes exactly how the study was carried out, and you need to make sure that enough detail is given so that full replication would be possible, such as including the time allowed to carry out tasks. At the same time, you should avoid giving details such as the time of day, or a description of the room where the study was carried out, unless this is relevant to the study.

You need to note here any ethical problems (such as not giving participants full information about the study before they take part) and say how these were dealt with, or why they were not thought to be a problem. If there were no apparent ethical problems, you should say so. Don't forget to say that all participants were thanked and debriefed at the end of the study, or why debriefing was not thought to be necessary.

The method section overall should not need to be longer than a page of typing.

Results

The results section is very short. Its aim is to present the data in an easily accessible way, to give the results of a statistical analysis, to say whether the results are statistically significant, and if so, at what level. You don't need to say what the results mean in this section; this takes place in the discussion section.

You should start by presenting the data you have collected in summary form. This could take the form of a table of the means, medians or modes for different conditions (check back to chapter 2 to help you decide which measure of central tendency is appropriate). If your data are of at least ordinal level, you could also include here a measure of dispersion; for example, the ranges of the scores in different conditions.

Your summary could also take the form of a graphic representation of the data, such as a bar chart or frequency polygon (see chapter 2), and should directly reflect the hypothesis tested. Don't forget that any graphs should show *summary* data; for example, it is not acceptable to provide a bar chart showing each participant's individual score. If your study has used correlational analysis, probably the most suitable form of data presentation here is a scattergraph.

Don't forget to give any tables or graphs a title stating precisely what is shown, and to label axes on graphs, or bars on a bar chart. You should then write one or two sentences highlighting what the data seem to show.

The raw data (i.e. the individual scores of participants) should be put in a numbered appendix, and the reader should be referred to this material here. However, you do not need to include all the raw data, e.g. the detailed questionnaire responses for all participants. Remember that you should observe confidentiality about participants' data, so do not use participants' names but give each participant a number, as was done in the worked examples of tests earlier in the chapter.

The next step is to identify the statistical test used to analyse the data, and justify why this test has been chosen. For example, a Mann–Whitney test would be used if you were looking for a difference between conditions, if you used an independent measures design, and if your data were of at least ordinal level, i.e. in the form of scores which could be put in rank order.

You should state the calculated value which you have worked out using the test, e.g. the value of U for a Mann–Whitney test. Refer the reader to the calculations used to work out this statistic in an appendix. You should also give the critical value from the table. Don't forget to include the significance level of the critical value, e.g. $p < 0.05$, and whether the research hypothesis was one- or two-tailed. For a chi square you will also need to include the degrees of freedom (df).

As an example, your statement for a Mann–Whitney test should be something like: 'The critical value of U at $p < 0.05$, one-tailed, is 23', while for χ^2 it should be something like: 'The critical value of χ^2 at $p < 0.05$, one-tailed, df = 1, is 2.71'. If your results are more significant than $p < 0.05$, e.g. if they are significant at $p < 0.025$ or $p < 0.01$, use the most significant level for this statement.

You should then compare the calculated and critical values, and say whether your research hypothesis can be accepted, and whether the null hypothesis can be rejected or must be retained. For example, this statement could be: 'Since the calculated value of U at 25 is greater than the critical value of 23 at $p < 0.05$, the research hypothesis is not supported and the null hypothesis must be retained.'

Finally, write a sentence to relate the results of the test to your study. For example: 'There was no significant difference between the number of words recalled by participants instructed to use imagery to aid recall and by those to whom no particular strategy was suggested'.

Discussion

This section of the report is usually the longest, and perhaps the most difficult to write, but also attracts the most marks in an A-level report. It is here that you explain the results of your study, and consider the implications of your findings.

The first thing to do is to make links with the theory and studies outlined in the introduction. Do your results support the background theory? How do they compare with the research findings described in the introduction?

Whether or not your results were significant, you might find it helpful at this point to consider alternatives to the theory on which your study was based. Are there other theories which could also account for the results? If your results were not significant, is there another theory which might help to make sense of them? You could also describe related research whose findings are not in line with your results, and explain these differences.

Apart from theoretical issues, you will need to consider any methodological problems. If there were any uncontrolled factors which might have influenced the results of your study, you need to identify them and suggest what kinds of improvements would need to be made to eliminate them if the study were to be carried out again.

It is also possible that a different method might be a good idea in future research. For example, if you carried out a laboratory experiment, you may have thought that it had low ecological validity, and that therefore either a field experiment or a naturalistic observation or simply more suitable materials would be a useful way of testing your idea further. If this is the case, you need to outline briefly how this could be done.

The sample of people tested could also be considered. For example, if only a very small sample was tested, they are unlikely to be representative of the parent population. Even if the sample size was adequate, the sample might nonetheless be unrepresentative in other ways.

There are quite often practical implications of research findings, which also need to be discussed in this section. For example, if a memory experiment shows a particular method of learning material to be effective, then this could have implications within education, both in terms of ways in which information might be taught and in suggesting ways in which revision for exams might be carried out more efficiently. You should also note any limitations of these kinds of implications.

Finally, you need to consider the direction which future research in the area you have been investigating might usefully take. What kinds of questions remain unanswered? How might future researchers go about answering them?

Conclusion

This should be a very short section, just two or three sentences. It should include a short restatement of the findings of the study, say what conclusions can be drawn from them, and indicate briefly any theoretical or methodological problems.

References

In the introduction and discussion sections, you will have made reference to theories and research, in each case naming the relevant psychologist(s) and giving the date of the theory or research in brackets. In this section, you need to give full references for these names and dates, so that anyone reading your report could check your sources if they wished to do so. References need to be listed in alphabetical order.

There are standard ways of presenting references. If the reference is to a journal article, it should give the name(s) of the psychologist(s), the date of the article, its title, the name of the journal and its volume number (in italics or underlined), and the page numbers, e.g:

Allport, D.A., Antonis, B., and Reynolds, P. (1972). On the division of attention: A disproof of the single channel hypothesis. *Quarterly Journal of Experimental Psychology, 24*, 225–235.

If the reference is to a book, it should give the name(s) of the psychologist(s), the date of the book, the book title (in italics or underlined), the place of publication, and the publisher, e.g:

Gibson, J.J. (1966). *The senses considered as perceptual systems*. Boston: Houghton Mifflin.

Textbooks have a list of detailed references at the end, so usually you will be able to copy the reference from the book in which you found the theory or study. You may also have used information from a website. Some websites include references, but if not, you need to give full details of the URL.

It is a good idea at the planning stage of your research to make a note of the sources of the material you intend to use. This will make it very much easier to track down the references when you come to complete your report.

Appendices

You are likely to have several appendices which you have referred to in the method and results sections. Make sure that your appendices are numbered in the order in which they are referred to in the report, and that you use these numbers when referring to them in the main body of the report.

Notes on activities

2 **1** Spearman's r_s; **2** Wilcoxon signed ranks; **3** Spearman's r_s; **4** chi square; **5** Mann–Whitney U; **6** sign test; **7** Wilcoxon signed ranks; **8** chi square; **9** Mann–Whitney U; **10** Wilcoxon signed ranks.

3

scores	17	17	14	14	14	12	9	6	6
ranks	8.5	8.5	6	6	6	4	3	1.5	1.5

4 This is a one-tailed hypothesis, because it is directional; it was predicted that people who sorted semantically would remember more words than those who sorted structurally. The critical value of U at $p = 0.05$, one-tailed, where $n_1 = 9$ and $n_2 = 11$, is 27. Since the calculated value of 12 is smaller than this, the results are significant at this level and the research hypothesis can be accepted and the null hypothesis rejected ($p < 0.05$). It is also smaller than the critical value of 18 at $p = 0.01$, and the critical value of 16 at $p = 0.005$. It is therefore significant at the most stringent level available; there is a probability of only 0.005 (or 5 in 1000) that the differences between the two conditions could have come about by chance. The research hypothesis can therefore be accepted with 99.5% confidence.

5 The research hypothesis is one-tailed, since it predicts that people will take longer to identify the colours of the colour-associated words than the neutral words. The critical value for a one-tailed test at $p = 0.05$, where $n = 9$, is 8. Since the calculated value of 3 is smaller than 8, the results are significant at this level. Since the calculated value of 3 is equal to the critical value at $p = 0.01$, the results are also significant at this level, the most stringent level available for this test for a sample of this size. There is therefore a probability of only 0.01 (or 1 in 100) that the differences between the two conditions have come about by chance. The research hypothesis can be accepted with 99% confidence.

6 There is a fairly strong correlation between the two variables being measured, though it is a far from perfect correlation. The calculated value of r_S at 0.603 is larger than the critical value of 0.564 for a one-tailed hypothesis at $p = 0.05$, where $n = 10$. The results are therefore significant at this level ($p < 0.05$). The calculated value is not larger than the critical value at $p = 0.025$, so the results fail to reach this level of significance. However, as the 5% level is the conventional level used in psychological research, the research hypothesis can be accepted and the null hypothesis rejected.

7 The research hypothesis is two-tailed, since it is just suggested that there will be a difference in the helpfulness of men and of women; there is no indication as to whether men or women are likely to be more helpful. The critical value of χ^2 for a two-tailed hypothesis at $p = 0.05$ is 3.84. Since the calculated value of 5.29 is larger than this, the results are significant at this level ($p < 0.05$). However, the critical value of 5.41 at $p = 0.02$ is larger than the calculated value, so the results are not significant at this more stringent level.

8 The research hypothesis was one-tailed, since it was predicted that children who could not conserve on a standard Piagetian task would be able to do so on a task which made 'human sense'. Where $n = 7$, the critical value of S at $p = 0.05$, one-tailed, is 0. Since this is less than the calculated value, the research hypothesis cannot be supported, and the null hypothesis must be retained.

Appendix 1: Tables for Mann–Whitney *U* test

Critical values of U for a one-tailed test at 0.05; two-tailed test at 0.10 (Mann–Whitney)*

n_2 \ n_1	1	2	3	4	5	6	7	8	9	10	11	12	13	14	15	16	17	18	19	20
1	–	–	–	–	–	–	–	–	–	–	–	–	–	–	–	–	–	–	0	0
2	–	–	–	–	0	0	0	1	1	1	1	2	2	3	3	3	3	4	4	4
3	–	–	0	0	1	2	2	3	4	4	5	5	6	7	7	8	9	9	10	11
4	–	–	0	1	2	3	4	5	6	7	8	9	10	11	12	14	15	16	17	18
5	–	0	1	2	4	5	6	8	9	11	12	13	15	16	18	19	20	22	23	25
6	–	0	2	3	5	7	8	10	12	14	16	17	19	21	23	25	26	28	30	32
7	–	0	2	4	6	8	11	13	15	17	19	21	24	26	28	30	33	35	37	39
8	–	1	3	5	8	10	13	15	18	20	23	26	28	31	33	36	39	41	44	47
9	–	1	4	6	9	12	15	18	21	24	27	30	33	36	39	42	45	48	51	54
10	–	1	4	7	11	14	17	20	24	27	31	34	37	41	44	48	51	55	58	62
11	–	1	5	8	12	16	19	23	27	31	34	38	42	46	50	54	57	61	65	69
12	–	2	5	9	13	17	21	26	30	34	38	42	47	51	55	60	64	68	72	77
13	–	2	6	10	15	19	24	28	33	37	42	47	51	56	61	65	70	75	80	84
14	–	3	7	11	16	21	26	31	36	41	46	51	56	61	66	71	77	82	87	92
15	–	3	7	12	18	23	28	33	39	44	50	55	61	66	72	77	83	88	94	100
16	–	3	8	14	19	25	30	36	42	48	54	60	65	71	77	83	89	95	101	107
17	–	3	9	15	20	26	33	39	45	51	57	64	70	77	83	89	96	102	109	115
18	–	4	9	16	22	28	35	41	48	55	61	68	75	82	88	95	102	109	116	123
19	0	4	10	17	23	30	37	44	51	58	65	72	80	87	94	101	109	116	123	130
20	0	4	11	18	25	32	39	47	54	62	69	77	84	92	100	107	115	123	130	138

* Dashes in the body of the table indicate that no decision is possible at the stated level of significance.

For any n_1 and n_2 the observed value of U is significant at a given level of significance if it is *equal to* or *less than* the critical values shown.

SOURCE: Runyon R and Haber A, *Fundamentals of Behavioural Statistics* (3rd edn.), Reading, MA: McGraw-Hill,Inc (1976).

Critical values of U for a one-tailed test at 0.025; two-tailed test at 0.05 (Mann–Whitney)*

n_2 \ n_1	1	2	3	4	5	6	7	8	9	10	11	12	13	14	15	16	17	18	19	20
1	–	–	–	–	–	–	–	–	–	–	–	–	–	–	–	–	–	–	–	–
2	–	–	–	–	–	–	–	0	0	0	0	1	1	1	1	1	2	2	2	2
3	–	–	–	–	0	1	1	2	2	3	3	4	4	5	5	6	6	7	7	8
4	–	–	–	0	1	2	3	4	4	5	6	7	8	9	10	11	11	12	13	14
5	–	–	0	1	2	3	5	6	7	8	9	11	12	13	14	15	17	18	19	20
6	–	–	1	2	3	5	6	8	10	11	13	14	16	17	19	21	22	24	25	27
7	–	–	1	3	5	6	8	10	12	14	16	18	20	22	24	26	28	30	32	34
8	–	0	2	4	6	8	10	13	15	17	19	22	24	26	29	31	34	36	38	41
9	–	0	2	4	7	10	12	15	17	20	23	26	28	31	34	37	39	42	45	48
10	–	0	3	5	8	11	14	17	20	23	26	29	33	36	39	42	45	48	52	55
11	–	0	3	6	9	13	16	19	23	26	30	33	37	40	44	47	51	55	58	62
12	–	1	4	7	11	14	18	22	26	29	33	37	41	45	49	53	57	61	65	69
13	–	1	4	8	12	16	20	24	28	33	37	41	45	50	54	59	63	67	72	76
14	–	1	5	9	13	17	22	26	31	36	40	45	50	55	59	64	69	74	78	83
15	–	1	5	10	14	19	24	29	34	39	44	49	54	59	64	70	75	80	85	90
16	–	1	6	11	15	21	26	31	37	42	47	53	59	64	70	75	81	86	92	98
17	–	2	6	11	17	22	28	34	39	45	51	57	63	69	75	81	87	93	99	105
18	–	2	7	12	18	24	30	36	42	48	55	61	67	74	80	86	93	99	106	112
19	–	2	7	13	19	25	32	38	45	52	58	65	72	78	85	92	99	106	113	119
20	–	2	8	14	20	27	34	41	48	55	62	69	76	83	90	98	105	112	119	127

* Dashes in the body of the table indicate that no decision is possible at the stated level of significance.

For any n_1 and n_2 the observed value of U is significant at a given level of significance if it is *equal to* or *less than* the critical values shown.

SOURCE: Runyon R and Haber A, *Fundamentals of Behavioural Statistics* (3rd edn.), Reading, MA: McGraw-Hill,Inc (1976).

*Critical values of U for a one-tailed test at 0.01; two-tailed test at 0.02** (*Mann–Whitney*)

	n_1																			
n_2	1	2	3	4	5	6	7	8	9	10	11	12	13	14	15	16	17	18	19	20
1	–	–	–	–	–	–	–	–	–	–	–	–	–	–	–	–	–	–	–	–
2	–	–	–	–	–	–	–	–	–	–	–	–	0	0	0	0	0	0	1	1
3	–	–	–	–	–	–	0	0	1	1	1	2	2	2	3	3	4	4	4	5
4	–	–	–	–	0	1	1	2	3	3	4	5	5	6	7	7	8	9	9	10
5	–	–	–	0	1	2	3	4	5	6	7	8	9	10	11	12	13	14	15	16
6	–	–	–	1	2	3	4	6	7	8	9	11	12	13	15	16	18	19	20	22
7	–	–	0	1	3	4	6	7	9	11	12	14	16	17	19	21	23	24	26	28
8	–	–	0	2	4	6	7	9	11	13	15	17	20	22	24	26	28	30	32	34
9	–	–	1	3	5	7	9	11	14	16	18	21	23	26	28	31	33	36	38	40
10	–	–	1	3	6	8	11	13	16	19	22	24	27	30	33	36	38	41	44	47
11	–	–	1	4	7	9	12	15	18	22	25	28	31	34	37	41	44	47	50	53
12	–	–	2	5	8	11	14	17	21	24	28	31	35	38	42	46	49	53	56	60
13	–	0	2	5	9	12	16	20	23	27	31	35	39	43	47	51	55	59	63	67
14	–	0	2	6	10	13	17	22	26	30	34	38	43	47	51	56	60	65	69	73
15	–	0	3	7	11	15	19	24	28	33	37	42	47	51	56	61	66	70	75	80
16	–	0	3	7	12	16	21	26	31	36	41	46	51	56	61	66	71	76	82	87
17	–	0	4	8	13	18	23	28	33	38	44	49	55	60	66	71	77	82	88	93
18	–	0	4	9	14	19	24	30	36	41	47	53	59	65	70	76	82	88	94	100
19	–	1	4	9	15	20	26	32	38	44	50	56	63	69	75	82	88	94	101	107
20	–	1	5	10	16	22	28	34	40	47	53	60	67	73	80	87	93	100	107	114

* Dashes in the body of the table indicate that no decision is possible at the stated level of significance.

For any n_1 and n_2 the observed value of U is significant at a given level of significance if it is *equal to* or *less than* the critical values shown.

Source: Runyon R and Haber A, *Fundamentals of Behavioural Statistics* (3rd edn.), Reading, MA: McGraw-Hill,Inc (1976).

Critical values of U for a one-tailed test at 0.005; two-tailed test at 0.01 (Mann–Whitney)*

n_2 \ n_1	1	2	3	4	5	6	7	8	9	10	11	12	13	14	15	16	17	18	19	20
1	–	–	–	–	–	–	–	–	–	–	–	–	–	–	–	–	–	–	–	–
2	–	–	–	–	–	–	–	–	–	–	–	–	–	–	–	–	–	–	0	0
3	–	–	–	–	–	–	–	–	0	0	0	1	1	1	2	2	2	2	3	3
4	–	–	–	–	–	0	0	1	1	2	2	3	3	4	5	5	6	6	7	8
5	–	–	–	–	0	1	1	2	3	4	5	6	7	7	8	9	10	11	12	14
6	–	–	–	0	1	2	3	4	5	6	7	9	10	11	12	13	15	16	17	18
7	–	–	–	0	1	3	4	6	7	9	10	12	13	15	16	18	19	21	22	24
8	–	–	–	1	2	4	6	7	9	11	13	15	17	18	20	22	24	26	28	30
9	–	–	0	1	3	5	7	9	11	13	16	18	20	22	24	27	29	31	33	36
10	–	–	0	2	4	6	9	11	13	16	18	21	24	26	29	31	34	37	39	42
11	–	–	0	2	5	7	10	13	16	18	21	24	27	30	33	36	39	42	45	48
12	–	–	1	3	6	9	12	15	18	21	24	27	31	34	37	41	44	47	51	54
13	–	–	1	3	7	10	13	17	20	24	27	31	34	38	42	45	49	53	57	60
14	–	–	1	4	7	11	15	18	22	26	30	34	38	42	46	50	54	58	63	67
15	–	–	2	5	8	12	16	20	24	29	33	37	42	46	51	55	60	64	69	73
16	–	–	2	5	9	13	18	22	27	31	36	41	45	50	55	60	65	70	74	79
17	–	–	2	6	10	15	19	24	29	34	39	44	49	54	60	65	70	75	81	86
18	–	–	2	6	11	16	21	26	31	37	42	47	53	58	64	70	75	81	87	92
19	–	0	3	7	12	17	22	28	33	39	45	51	57	63	69	74	81	87	93	99
20	–	0	3	8	13	18	24	30	36	42	48	54	60	67	73	79	86	92	99	105

* Dashes in the body of the table indicate that no decision is possible at the stated level of significance.

For any n_1 and n_2 the observed value of U is significant at a given level of significance if it is *equal to* or *less than* the critical values shown.

SOURCE: Runyon R and Haber A, *Fundamentals of Behavioural Statistics* (3rd edn.), Reading, MA: McGraw-Hill,Inc (1976).

Appendix 2: Tables for Wilcoxon signed ranks test

Critical values of T in the Wilcoxon signed ranks test

	Level of significance for a two-tailed test			
	0.10	0.05	0.02	0.002
	Level of significance for a one-tailed test			
	0.05	0.025	0.01	0.001
n = 5	0	–	–	–
6	2	0	–	–
7	3	2	0	–
8	5	3	1	–
9	8	5	3	–
10	10	8	5	0
11	13	10	7	1
12	17	13	9	2
13	21	17	12	4
14	25	21	15	6
15	30	25	19	8
16	35	29	23	11
17	41	34	27	14
18	47	40	32	18
19	53	46	37	21
20	60	52	43	26
21	67	58	49	30
22	75	65	55	35
23	83	73	62	40
24	91	81	69	45
25	100	89	76	51
26	110	98	84	58
27	119	107	92	64
28	130	116	101	71
29	140	126	110	79
30	151	137	120	86
31	163	147	130	94
32	175	159	140	103
33	187	170	151	112

Calculated value of *T* must EQUAL or BE LESS THAN the table (critical) value for significance at the level shown.

SOURCE: Adapted from Meddis R, *Statistical Handbook for Non-Statisticians*, London: McGraw-Hill (1975).

Appendix 3: Tables for Spearman's coefficient r_S

Critical values of Spearman's coefficient r_S

	Level of significance for a two-tailed test			
	0.10	0.05	0.02	0.01
	Level of significance for a one-tailed test			
	0.05	0.025	0.01	0.005
n = 4	1.000	–	–	–
5	0.900	1.000	1.000	–
6	0.829	0.886	0.943	1.000
7	0.714	0.786	0.893	0.929
8	0.643	0.738	0.833	0.881
9	0.600	0.700	0.783	0.833
10	0.564	0.648	0.745	0.794
11	0.536	0.618	0.709	0.755
12	0.503	0.587	0.678	0.727
13	0.484	0.560	0.648	0.703
14	0.464	0.538	0.626	0.679
15	0.446	0.521	0.604	0.654
16	0.429	0.503	0.582	0.635
17	0.414	0.488	0.566	0.618
18	0.401	0.472	0.550	0.600
19	0.391	0.460	0.535	0.584
20	0.380	0.447	0.522	0.570
21	0.370	0.436	0.509	0.556
22	0.361	0.425	0.497	0.544
23	0.353	0.416	0.486	0.532
24	0.344	0.407	0.476	0.521
25	0.337	0.398	0.466	0.511
26	0.331	0.390	0.457	0.501
27	0.324	0.383	0.449	0.492
28	0.318	0.375	0.440	0.483
29	0.312	0.368	0.433	0.475
30	0.306	0.362	0.425	0.467

Calculated value of r_S must EQUAL or EXCEED the table (critical) value for significance at the level shown.

SOURCE: Zhar J H, Significance testing of the Spearman Rank Correlation Coefficient, *Journal of the American Statistical Association 67,* 578–80.

Appendix 4: Tables for chi square (χ^2)

Critical values of χ^2

	Level of significance for a two-tailed test					
	0.02	0.10	0.05	0.02	0.01	0.001
	Level of significance for a one-tailed test					
df	0.10	0.05	0.025	0.01	0.005	0.0005
1	1.64	2.71	3.84	5.41	6.63	10.83
2	3.22	4.60	5.99	7.82	9.21	13.82
3	4.64	6.25	7.82	9.84	11.34	16.27
4	5.99	7.78	9.49	11.67	13.28	18.47
5	7.29	9.24	11.07	13.39	15.09	20.52
6	8.56	10.64	12.59	15.03	16.81	22.46
7	9.80	12.02	14.07	16.62	18.48	24.32
8	11.03	13.36	15.51	18.17	20.09	26.12
9	12.24	14.68	16.92	19.68	21.67	27.88
10	13.44	15.99	18.31	21.16	23.21	29.59
11	14.63	17.28	19.68	22.62	24.72	31.26
12	15.81	18.55	21.03	24.05	26.22	32.91
13	16.98	19.81	22.36	25.47	27.69	34.53
14	18.15	21.06	23.68	26.87	29.14	36.12
15	19.31	22.31	25.00	28.26	30.58	37.70
16	20.46	23.54	26.30	29.63	32.00	39.25
17	21.62	24.77	27.59	31.00	33.41	40.79
18	22.76	25.99	28.87	32.35	34.81	42.31
19	23.90	27.20	30.14	33.69	36.19	43.82
20	25.04	28.41	31.41	35.02	37.57	45.31
21	26.17	29.62	32.67	36.34	38.93	46.80
22	27.30	30.81	33.92	37.66	40.29	48.27
23	28.43	32.01	35.17	38.97	41.64	49.73
24	29.55	33.20	36.42	40.27	42.98	51.18
25	30.68	34.38	37.65	41.57	44.31	52.62
26	31.80	35.56	38.88	42.86	45.64	54.05
27	32.91	36.74	40.11	44.14	46.96	55.48
28	34.03	37.92	41.34	45.42	48.28	56.89
29	35.14	39.09	42.56	49.69	49.59	58.30
30	36.25	40.26	43.77	47.96	50.89	59.70
32	38.47	42.59	46.19	50.49	53.49	62.49
34	40.68	44.90	48.60	53.00	56.06	65.25
36	42.88	47.21	51.00	55.49	58.62	67.99
38	45.08	49.51	53.38	57.97	61.16	70.70
40	47.27	51.81	55.76	60.44	63.69	73.40
44	51.64	56.37	60.48	65.34	68.71	78.75
48	55.99	60.91	65.17	70.20	73.68	84.04
52	60.33	65.42	69.83	75.02	78.62	89.27
56	64.66	69.92	74.47	79.82	83.51	94.46
60	68.97	74.40	79.08	84.58	88.38	99.61

Calculated value of χ^2 must EQUAL or EXCEED the table (critical) value for significance at the level shown.

Abridged from Fisher R A and Yates F, *Statistical Tables for Biological, Agricultural and Medical Research* (6th edn), Longman Group Ltd (1974).

Appendix 5: Tables for the binomial sign test

Critical values of S in the binominal sign test

	Level of significance for a two-tailed test				
	0.10	0.05	0.02	0.01	0.001
	Level of significance for a one-tailed test				
	0.05	0.025	0.01	0.005	0.0005
n = 5	0	–	–	–	–
6	0	0	–	–	–
7	0	0	0	–	–
8	1	0	0	0	–
9	1	1	0	0	–
10	1	1	0	0	0
11	2	1	1	0	0
12	2	2	1	1	0
13	3	2	1	1	0
14	3	2	2	1	0
15	3	3	2	2	1
16	4	3	2	2	1
17	4	4	3	2	1
18	5	4	3	3	1
19	5	4	4	3	2
20	5	5	4	3	2
25	7	7	6	5	4
30	10	9	8	7	5
35	12	11	10	9	7

Calculated value of *S* must EQUAL or BE LESS THAN the table (critical) value for significance at the level shown.

SOURCE: Clegg F, *Simple Statistics*, Cambridge University Press (1982).

Appendix 6: Sample research report

The effect of the type of processing on the amount of information recalled

Comment: A good title, linking the IV and the DV

Abstract

The Levels of Processing model of memory devised by Craik and Lockhart (1972) has three levels of processing information: structural, phonological and semantic. Semantic is the deepest level, phonological is more shallow and structural the shallowest. The model proposes that information processed at a deeper level will be remembered better than information processed at a more shallow level. This study aimed to test the idea that participants who used semantic processing would recall more words than those who used phonological processing.

An opportunity sample of twenty participants was asked to carry out a task matching pairs of words that rhymed (phonological condition) or had opposite meanings (semantic condition). The participants believed that they were being tested on the speed with which they matched up the pairs. Participants were given an unexpected recall test to see how many words they had remembered.

The Mann–Whitney U test was carried out to analyse the data. The calculated value of U was 44.5. This exceeded the critical value of 27 for a one-tailed hypothesis at $p = 0.05$, meaning the results were not significant, and the research hypothesis was not supported. This means that there was no significant difference in the number of words recalled at each level of processing.

The results may be due to theoretical flaws in the LOP model, in particular the idea that not only the level of processing but also the amount of time and effort spent on a problem may be a factor. There could also have been faults in the materials used to test participants. Some of the words were similar in meaning. This could have led to interference, or 'chunking', affecting recall.

Comment: A good, succinct summary of the background to the study, how it was carried out, what the results were, and how they might be interpreted. The student could have made brief reference to a study supporting the LOP model in the first paragraph, and the theoretical criticism in the final paragraph could have been a little clearer.

Introduction

In 1972, Craik and Lockhart attempted to move away from models of memory such as Atkinson and Shiffrin's multi-store model (1968) by proposing the Levels of Processing (LOP) model. This concentrates on the type of processing involved in memory, rather than suggesting that there are different STM and LTM stores. It suggests that remembering information is a by-product of processing, rather than processing being a means of organising information.

There are three levels of processing. The structural level is the most shallow. It involves analysing a word by physical characteristics, such as whether it is written in capital letters or not. A deeper stage is the phonological level. Here it is the sound of the word which is examined. The deepest level of processing involves analysing the word for meaning. It is known as the semantic level. Craik and Lockhart claimed that the deeper the level of processing, the more information would be retained.

Craik and Watkins (1973) differentiated between two types of rehearsal, which relate to different levels of the LOP model. Maintenance rehearsal is the repetition of information, relating to the phonological level of the LOP. Elaborative rehearsal relates to the semantic level of processing. It may involve composing a story or devising an image to link pieces of information.

Support for the LOP model comes from Craik and Tulving (1975). In this study, participants had to perform a variety of tasks on lists of words, which corresponded to different levels of processing. They were given an unexpected recognition test. Words which had been processed at a deeper level were remembered more than those processed at a shallower level.

In the Elias and Perfetti (1973) study, participants had to perform similar tasks to those in the Craik and Tulving study on a list of words. They were presented with an unexpected recall test, a technique called incidental learning. They found words from the deeper level of processing were more likely to be remembered.

The aim of this study was to test the LOP theory by comparing recall, using an unexpected recall test, when semantic and phonological processing is carried out. A one-tailed experimental hypothesis was devised. A one-tailed hypothesis was appropriate as the LOP model and the research supporting it predicted the direction of the results. Semantic processing would induce a higher level of recall than phonological processing.

The experimental hypothesis is:

Participants who carry out a task requiring semantic processing of words will recall more words in an unexpected recall test than participants who carry out a task requiring phonological processing.

The null hypothesis is:

There will be no difference in the amount of information recalled by participants who use different types of processing.

Comment: The underlying theory here is well explained. The research studies supporting the theory are well chosen, though the description of both could have given slightly more detail about the methods followed, i.e. the nature of the tasks to be carried out. The aims are clear, and the directional hypothesis is clearly justified. The hypotheses include the IV and the DV, and are well set out.

Method

Design

The experiment used an unrelated design, with independent measures. This ruled out the possibility of demand characteristics, and eliminated order effects.

There were two experimental groups. The task for condition 1 required phonological processing (matching pairs of rhyming words). The task for condition 2 required semantic processing (matching pairs of words with opposite meanings). The independent variable was the type of processing used in carrying out each task. The dependent variable was the number of words the participants could remember.

The study was carried out in a quiet room to minimise distractions from noise. All participants were tested on their own by the same experimenter.

The minimum level of statistical significance to be accepted was $p < 0.05$, because this is the conventional level in psychological research, unless there are safety implications, or existing research is being challenged.

Comment: The information here is in general clearly and succinctly put across. However, the use of an independent measures design does not rule out the possibility of demand characteristics, though it does help to reduce this possibility. Some indication could have been given as to what kinds of order effects might occur; in particular, an independent measures design was necessary here because the recall test needed to be unexpected. This would not have been possible if a repeated measures design had been used.

Participants

Twenty participants were tested. Ten participants were alternately allocated to each of the conditions. The participants were approximately 16–19 years of age, and included males and females. An opportunity sample was drawn on the basis of availability from a population of college students.

Comment: Again, brief but to the point. The student could have indicated how many males and how many females were tested, and if there were the same numbers of each in each condition. Given that the participants were asked to process words, it might have been worth mentioning that they were all native English speakers.

Materials

Each condition required a set of cards, with one word written on each card. A sample of the cards can be found in appendix 1. The words used were selected from a dictionary on the basis that they had fewer than eight letters, and were not more than two syllables long. The words also had to be frequently found in everyday language, so participants in the semantic condition could match them by meaning.

In the phonological condition (condition 1), the words were matched by sound, by checking that the end of the word had the same phonetic groups. In the semantic condition, the second word of the pair was found by reading the dictionary definition of a chosen word and finding a word with an approximately opposite definition.

Five confederates of the experimenter were provided with one word of the pairs and asked to supply the other word, to check the validity of the pairs. A full list of all the words can be found in appendix 2.

The experiment also used a stopwatch to time how long participants took to match the words (the task they believed they were being tested on), together with standardised instructions and a standardised debrief. These can be found in appendix 3.

Comment: The student doesn't state here how many word pairs were used in each condition. This information is available in appendix 2, but it should be included here too for ease of communication. Appendix 1 contained four sample cards, one pair from each condition. This is quite sufficient, since a complete list of words was included as appendix 2.

The criteria for selecting particular words are perhaps a little wide, but this is a problem picked up in the discussion. It was a good idea to check the validity of the pairs before carrying out the study.

The standardised instructions in appendix 3 set out clearly what the task was. A detailed standardised debrief is not really necessary; debriefing participants is part of a well-planned study, but apart from explaining the deception involved and why it was necessary, the experimenter could perhaps respond to the individual participant, in terms of how much they are interested in knowing about the study.

Procedure

The procedure for one participant is described below. It was followed for all the other participants. Each participant was tested alone.

A potential participant was approached and asked if they would like to take part in a psychology study. If they agreed, they were taken to a quiet room and the oral instructions were delivered. The participant was given the shuffled word cards and timed while they sorted them into matching pairs. In condition 1 (phonological) the words were sorted into pairs of rhyming words. In condition 2 (semantic) the cards were sorted into pairs with opposite meanings.

The participant was then asked to count out loud backwards from 200 down to zero in threes, at the rate of about one number a second, to prevent rehearsal from taking place. The cards were then collected in. When the participant had reached zero they were asked to recall as many words from the cards as possible in three minutes.

Finally, the participant was thanked and debriefed. This debriefing helped to combat the ethical problem of deceiving participants to prevent demand characteristics.

Comment: The student explains clearly and succinctly how the test was carried out. However, there seems no reason why an intervening task was used between sorting and recall. This kind of task is useful when participants are aware that they are taking part in a memory experiment, and the experimenter suspects that, as there is only a limited amount of information to be learned, there may be a ceiling effect, i.e. all participants are likely to get high scores. This would mean that the test would not discriminate between participants. As the recall test here was unexpected, this kind of problem is highly unlikely. However, if an intervening task were to be used, this should have been mentioned in the 'Design' section. Perhaps a little more could have been made of the ethical concerns, i.e. that the deception involved was fairly minimal and unlikely to have caused any serious problems.

Results

A summary of the data collected in the study can be seen in the table and bar chart below. The raw data can be found in appendix 4.

Table to show the mean number of words remembered in each condition

	Condition 1 (phonological)	Condition 2 (semantic)
mean number of words remembered	16	17.1

Bar chart showing the mean number of words remembered

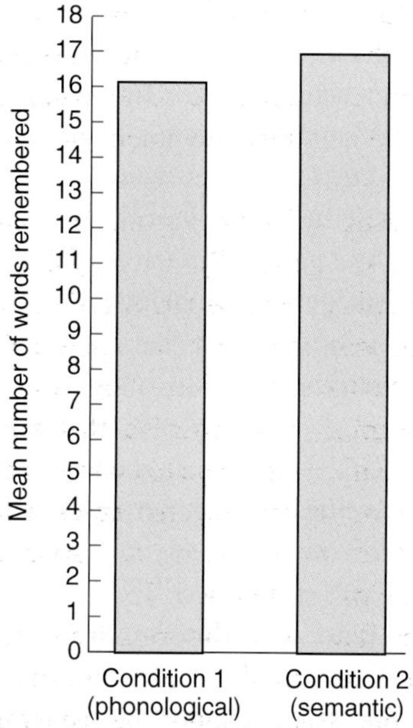

The table and bar chart show that the participants in condition 2 (semantic processing) recalled slightly more words on average than those in condition 1 (phonological processing), though the difference is very small.

A statistical test was carried out to see if this difference was significant. The experiment was a test of difference between the two conditions, and used an independent measures design. The data were determined to be of at least ordinal level, since the scores could be ranked. The Mann–Whitney *U* test was therefore used to analyse the data.

The calculated value of *U* was 44.5 (for calculations see appendix 5). The critical value of *U*, one-tailed at $p < 0.05$, is 27. Since the calculated value of *U* exceeds the critical value, the experimental hypothesis was not supported and the null hypothesis must be retained.

There was no significant difference in the number of words remembered between participants using phonological processing and those using semantic processing.

Comment: The table and bar chart are appropriate, and suitably titled and labelled. A frequency polygon showing the distribution of scores in each condition could also have been a good idea. The choice of means as a measure of central tendency was a good one, as the data were fairly precise. The standard deviation or range for each condition could also have been included. The use of the Mann–Whitney U test was fully justified. The results of the test were well set out.

Discussion

The difference between the two conditions was not statistically significant. The findings of this study therefore fail to support the principles of the LOP model. The results fail to replicate the findings of Craik and Tulving (1975) and Elias and Perfetti (1973), described in the introduction. It is possible that the results can be explained by limitations of the LOP model, or they may be the result of methodological flaws in carrying out the study.

Some criticisms have been made of the LOP model. Eysenck (1984) offered support to the model, as it presented memory, attention and perception as interdependent. However, he became frustrated at the lack of comment on how the information is stored and retrieved from memory. Baddeley (1978) also criticised the model for being over-simplified, and describing rather than explaining.

A specific criticism of the model is the difficulty in gauging which type of processing is being used and how much information is retained at each level. There is a circular logic in saying that more information is recalled because it has been processed deeply if the criterion for deep processing is that more information is remembered. The LOP is more of a concept than a portrayal of how memory works.

Another issue is that the model proposes that we do not automatically analyse a word in terms of meaning. It is hard to believe that a participant can look at a word and analyse it purely in terms of what it looks and sounds like, without being aware at some level of what the word means. Theories of attention suggest that automatic processing of all stimuli is unavoidable and without conscious effort. This is supported by the Stroop effect (Stroop 1935), where people take longer to identify the colour ink a word is written in if the word is a different colour word than if it is a word not connected with colour. Craik and Tulving used the term 'overspill coding' to describe the processing of a word at several levels of the model.

Sometimes it is desirable to process a word at more than one level. For example, when learning to speak a foreign language it is necessary to remember both what a word means and what it sounds like. Morris *et al.* (1977) discovered that rhyming words (processed at a shallower level) were remembered better than words processed at a semantic level, if they were eventually to be used in a task relating to sound. This contradicts the LOP model, and suggests the eventual use of information is significant to how it is processed.

Finally, it has been suggested that the different levels of processing correspond not to how information is encoded but the amount of time and effort required to process the information. Tyler *et al.* (1979) found that, despite both conditions using semantic processing, difficult anagrams were remembered better than anagrams which were easier to solve, because participants expended more time and energy on the harder task.

There were some methodological problems with this study. First, it has low ecological validity.

Another concern is the source material used as word cards. All the words were of varying length. Some of the pairings were obvious, using words which are frequently used together, such as 'hard' and 'soft'. The strong link between these words could lead to 'chunking', reducing the amount of information which needed to be stored. There were also similarities between some of the pairs in terms of meaning. For example, 'day' and 'night' and 'light' and 'dark' are closely related. This could either lead to chunking or cause interference.

An associated issue is the use of a mixture of concrete and abstract words. The semantic condition used some abstract words, whereas the phonological condition used mostly concrete words. This could have affected the results, as research (e.g. Richardson 1980) has found that imagery aids recall, and it is easier to form a mental image of a concrete word, e.g. 'cat' than an abstract word, e.g. 'justice'.

These concerns could be remedied by revising the word lists. They should contain only concrete words, with the words having the same length and frequency in the language. The pairs of words should not be extremely common, or semantically very similar.

Another issue is that participants may have found some words more personally meaningful than others, and so remember them better. Morris et al (1981) found that information which has a personal meaning is retained better than information which has no personal meaning. It is possible that participants' experiences could cause them to make semantic links between apparently unconnected words. This links to the concept of the spreading activation model of memory (Collins and Loftus 1975).

A major flaw was the relatively small and unrepresentative sample, which means that the results of the study cannot be generalised. To overcome this problem, a future study could use more participants from a wider age range.

However, the study could be modified for future research. The study focused only on retention in the short term. A modified form of the experiment could be implemented a week or two after the original study took place, to see if either form of processing produced better recall in the long term. The effect on recall of processing effort and time could also merit further investigation. Perhaps in one condition participants could be asked to pair obvious pairs of words, whilst the other group could be given more obscure words to pair, which would require more effort.

This is one theory which should be investigated further, as it has practical applications, for example in advising students on the most efficient way of revising. It suggests that strategies such as being tested are a more efficient form of revision than just reading through notes.

Comment: This discussion covered all the necessary areas: links made to the introduction, theoretical issues, methodological problems and how they might be overcome, practical applications and suggestions for future research. Good use was made of relevant theory and research, though in some cases (e.g. the Morris et al. study and the spreading activation model of Collins and Loftus) a little more detail would have been useful. It helps to think about writing for an intelligent and interested reader, but one who has no background knowledge of the theoretical area of the study.

The second and third paragraphs here raised rather general points about the LOP model, which do not help to explain the findings of this study. These kinds of points can legitimately be included in this section, but should perhaps come after the discussion of theoretical problems which might help to explain the results.

The fourth paragraph was well argued, and the argument supported by the Stroop effect. However, the concept of 'overspill coding' is not explained, so it doesn't really contribute much to the argument. Useful material in paragraphs 5 and 6, though a link with the findings of this study could have been explored. It is nice that the theoretical discussion is linked to the real world situation of language learning.

When the student comes to consider methodological problems, the point about ecological validity is sound, but needs a little more explanation in the context of this study. There were some very useful points about the shortcomings of the materials used, together with appropriate suggestions as to what improvements should be made. However, no suggestions were made about how the problem of personally meaningful words could be approached.

There were some sensible suggestions for future research, and a fairly brief mention of practical applications of this area of research, though this could perhaps have been developed in a little more detail.

References

Atkinson RC and Shiffrin RM (1968) Human memory: a proposed system and its control processes. In Spence KW and Spence JT (eds) *The Psychology of Learning and Motivation* (vol.2) London. Academic Press.

Baddeley AD (1978) The trouble with levels: a re-examination of Craik and Lockhart's framework for memory research. *Psychological Review, 85*(3), 139–152.

Collins AM and Loftus EF (1975) A spreading-activation theory of semantic processing. *Psychological Review,* 82, 407–428.

Craik F and Lockhart R (1972) Levels of processing. *Journal of Verbal Learning and Verbal Behaviour, 11,* 671–684.

Craik F and Tulving E (1975) Depth of processing and the retention of words in episodic memory. *Journal of Experimental Psychology: General, 104,* 268–294.

Craik F and Watkins M (1973) The role of rehearsal in short term memory. *Journal of Verbal Learning and Verbal Behaviour, 12,* 599–607.

Elias CF and Perfetti CA (1973) Encoding task and recognition memory: the importance of semantic coding. *Journal of Experimental Psychology, 99*(2), 151–157.

Eysenck MW (1984) *Handbook of Cognitive Psychology*. Hove: Lawrence Erlbaum Associates.

Morris CD, Bransford JD and Franks JJ (1977) Levels of processing versus transfer appropriate processing. *Journal of Verbal Learning and Verbal Behaviour, 16,* 519–533.

Morris PE et al. (1981) Football knowledge and the aequisition of new results. *British Journal of Psychology, 72,* 479–483.

Richardson JTE (1980) *Mental Imagery and Human Memory*. London: Macmillan.

Stroop JR (1935) Studies of interference in serial verbal reactions. *Journal of Experimental Psychology, 18,* 643–662.

Tyler SW, Hertel PT, McCallum MC and Ellis HC (1979) Cognitive effort and memory. *Journal of Experimental Psychology (Human Learning and Memory*), 5(6), 607–617.

INDEX